THE PROVINCES

OF THE

ROMAN EMPIRE

FROM CAESAR TO DIOCLETIAN

BY

THEODOR MOMMSEN

TRANSLATED

WITH THE AUTHOR'S SANCTION AND ADDITIONS

BY

WILLIAM P. DICKSON, D.D., LL.D.

PROFESSOR OF DIVINITY IN THE UNIVERSITY OF GLASGOW

VOL. I

BARNES
&NOBLE
BOOKS
NEW YORK

Originally published in 1885.
Published with corrections in 1909.

This edition published by Barnes & Noble, Inc.

1996 Barnes & Noble Books

ISBN 0-76070-145-8

Printed and bound in the United States of America.
M 9 8 7 6 5 4 3 2
BVG

PREFACE

A WISH has often been expressed to me that the History of Rome might be continued, and I have a desire to meet it, although it is difficult for me, after an interval of thirty years, to take up again the thread at the point where I had to let it drop. That the present portion does not attach itself immediately to the preceding, is a matter of little moment; the fifth volume would be just as much a fragment without the sixth as the sixth now is without the fifth. Besides, I am of opinion that, for the purposes of the cultured public, in whose minds this History is intended to promote an intelligent conception of Roman antiquity, other works may take the place of the Two Books, which are still wanting between this (the Eighth) and the earlier ones, more readily than a substitute can be found for that now issued. The struggle of the Republicans in opposition to the monarchy erected by Caesar, and the definitive establishment of the latter, are so well presented in the accounts handed down to us from antiquity that every delineation amounts essentially to a reproduction of their narrative. The distinctive character of the monarchical rule and the fluctuations of the monarchy, as well as the general relations of government influenced by the personality of the individual rulers, which the Seventh Book is destined to exhibit, have been at least subjected to frequent handling. Of what is here furnished—the history of the several provinces from the time of Caesar to that of Diocletian,—there is, if I am not mistaken, no comprehensive survey anywhere accessible to the public to which this work addresses itself; and it is owing, as it seems to me, to the want of such a survey that the judgment of that public as to the Roman imperial period is frequently incorrect and unfair. No doubt such a separation of these special histories from the general history of the empire, as is in my opinion a preliminary requisite to the right understanding of the history of the imperial period, cannot be carried out completely as regards various sections, especially for the period from Gallienus to Diocletian ; and in these cases the general picture, which still remains to be given, will have to supply what is wanting.

PREFATORY NOTE.

IN the fifth volume of his *Roman History*, issued in 1885, Mommsen described the Roman provinces as they were during the first three centuries of our era. It has been called, by one specially qualified to judge, Otto Hirschfeld, the best volume of the whole work. It is indeed a wonderful book. Here Mommsen summed up with supreme mastery a vast and multifarious mass of detail. Thousands of inscriptions yielded up their secrets; all scattered archaeological discoveries found recognition; the vast and dim areas of the provinces took definite shape and colour. Now at length it became easy to discern the true character of the Roman Empire. Our horizon broadened beyond the backstairs of the Palatine and the benches of the Curia to the wide lands north and east and south of the Mediterranean, and we began to realise the achievements of the Empire — its long and peaceable government of dominions extending into three continents, its gifts of civilisation, language, and citizenship to almost all its subjects, its creation of a stable and coherent order out of which rose the Europe of to-day. The old theory of an age of despotism and decay was overthrown. The believer in human nature could now feel confident that, whatever their limitations and defects, the men of the Empire wrought for the progress and happiness of the world.

The book was at once translated into English by, or

at least under the supervision of, the late Dr. W. P. Dickson, Professor of Divinity in the University of Glasgow. Twenty-five years before, the same translator had rendered the earlier volumes of the history into English, and rendered them to the satisfaction of all readers. The translation of the fifth volume was less happy. Its style was difficult, and its errors—at least in some chapters—were numerous and surprising. The ideal remedy for the evil would be a fresh version. But the ideal is seldom attainable in published literature, and good prose translations are particularly rare. When, therefore, the time came to reprint the book, it seemed best not to let it again appear as it was, but to attempt some revision, even though the existence of stereotyped plates confined that revision within very narrow limits. I have accordingly altered a large number of passages where Dr. Dickson's rendering was unintelligible or inaccurate, and I have tried to take account of the few changes which Mommsen himself introduced into the original German down to the fifth and last edition of 1904. In doing this I have had valuable help, which I desire to acknowledge, from Dr. George Macdonald. That I have left many defects, both by accident and by the exigencies of the stereotyped plates, is inevitable. But the alterations run into several hundreds, and at any rate "the government which prohibited voluntary fireworks" (freiwillige Feuerwehren), the "tribes who dwelt in hurdles" (Hürden), and the "crescents which gave the signal to run away" (Hörner), and some similar blots have vanished. As the translation is intended for English readers, I have added some notes on the chapter relating to Britain. It was far too large a task to do the same for other chapters. But a few references may be added here on two general questions. The results obtained by recent excavations on the Germano-Raetian Limes (Chapter IV., pp. 152 foll.) have been well summarised in E. Fabricius' *Die Besitznahme Badens durch die Römer* (Heidelberg, 1905), in an article by G. Lachenmaier in the *Württembergische Vierteljahreshefte für Landesgeschichte* for 1906, and in one by the late Professor Pelham in the *Transactions* of the Royal Historical Society, reprinted as Chapter IX. in his collected papers (Clarendon Press, 1909). The student should also consult the excellent *Berichte über die . . . römisch-germ. Forschung* for 1905-8, edited by Dr. H. Dragendorff (Frankfurt, 1905-9). The problem of the Hellenisation of Syria (Chapter X.) has been treated, with a solution unfavourable to the Hellenic element, by Theodor Nöldeke in the *Zeitschrift der deutschen morgenländischen Gesellschaft* for 1885 (xxxix. 332), and the two views have been compared by Mitteis in his *Reichsrecht und Volksrecht* (Leipzig, 1891, pp. 25 foll.).

F. HAVERFIELD.

CONTENTS

CONTENTS.

INTRODUCTION.

THE history of Rome under the Empire presents problems similar to those encountered in the history of the earlier Republic.

Such information as may be directly obtained from literary tradition is not merely without form and colour, but in fact for the most part without substance. The list of the Roman monarchs is just about as trustworthy and just about as instructive as that of the consuls of the republic. The great crises that convulsed the state may be discerned in outline ; but we are not much better informed as to the Germanic wars under the emperors Augustus and Marcus, than as to the wars with the Samnites. The republican store of anecdote is very much more decorous than its counterpart under the empire ; but the tales told of Fabricius and of the emperor Gaius are almost equally insipid and equally mendacious. The internal development of the commonwealth is perhaps exhibited in the traditional accounts more fully for the earlier republic than for the imperial period ; in the former case there is preserved a picture—however bedimmed and falsified—of the changes of political order that were brought at least to their ultimate issue in the open Forum of Rome ; in the latter case the arrangements are settled in the imperial cabinet, and come before the public, as a rule, merely in unimportant matters of form. We must take into account, moreover, the vast extension of the sphere of rule, and the shifting of the vital development from the centre to the circumference. The history of the city of Rome widens out into that of the country of Italy, and the latter into that of the Mediterranean world ; and of what we are most concerned to know, we learn the least. The Roman state of this epoch resembles a mighty tree, the main stem of which, in the course of its decay, is surrounded by vigorous offshoots pushing their way upwards. The Roman senate and the Roman rulers soon came to be drawn from any other region of the empire just as much as from Italy; the Quirites of this epoch, who have become the nominal heirs of the world-subduing legionaries, have nearly the same relation to the memories of the olden time as our Knights of St. John have to Rhodes and Malta; and they look upon their heritage as a right capable of being turned to profitable account—as an endowment provided for the benefit of the poor that shrink from work.

Any one who has recourse to the so-called authorities for the history of this period—even the better among them—finds difficulty in controlling his indignation at the telling of what deserved to be suppressed, and at the suppression of what there was need to tell. For this epoch was also one productive of great conceptions and far-reaching action. Seldom has the government of the world been conducted for so long a term in an orderly sequence; and the firm rules of administration, which Caesar and Augustus traced out for their successors, maintained their ground, on the whole, with remarkable steadfastness notwithstanding all those changes of dynasties and of dynasts, which assume more than due prominence in a tradition that looks merely to such things, and dwindles erelong into mere biographies of the emperors. The sharply-defined sections, which—under the current conception, misled by the superficial character of such a basis—are constituted by the change of rulers, pertain far more to the doings of the court than to the history of the empire. The carrying out of the Latin-Greek civilising process in the form of perfecting the constitution of the urban community, and the gradual bringing of the barbarian or at any rate alien elements into this circle, were tasks, which, from their very nature, required centuries of steady activity and calm self-development; and it constitutes the very grandeur of these centuries that the work once planned and initiated found this long period of time, and this prevalence of peace by land and sea, to facilitate its progress. Old age has not the power to develop new thoughts and display creative activity, nor has the government of the Roman empire done so ; but in its sphere, which those who belonged to it were not far wrong in regarding as the world, it fostered the peace and prosperity of the many nations united under its sway longer and more completely than any other leading power has ever succeeded in doing. It is in the agricultural towns of Africa, in the homes of the vine-dressers on the Moselle, in the flourishing townships of the Lycian mountains, and on the margin of the Syrian desert that the work of the imperial period is to be sought and to be found.   Even now there are various regions of the East, as of the West, as regards which the imperial period marks a climax of good government, very modest in itself, but never withal attained before or since ; and, if an angel of the Lord were to strike the balance whether the domain ruled by Severus Antoninus was governed with the greater intelligence and the greater humanity at that time or in the present day, whether civilisation and national prosperity generally have since that time advanced or retrograded, it is very doubtful whether the decision would prove in favour of the present.   But, if we find that this was the case, we ask of our surviving books for the most part in vain how it came to be so.   They no more give an answer to this question than the traditional accounts of the earlier republic explain the mighty phenomenon of the Rome, which, in the footsteps of Alexander, subdued and civilised the world.

The one void as little admits of being filled up as the other.   But it seemed worth our making the attempt for once to turn away our eyes from the pictures of the rulers with their bright or faded, and but too often falsified, colours, as well as from the task of linking into a semblance of chronological order fragments that do not fit each other ; and, instead of this, to collect and arrange such materials as tradition and the monuments furnish for a description of the Roman provincial government.   It seemed worth while to collate the accounts accidentally preserved by the one or by the other, to note traces of the process of growth embedded in its results, and to view the general institutions in their relation to the individual provinces, along with the conditions given for each by the nature of the soil and of the inhabitants, so as to work out by the imagination—which is the author of all history as of all poetry —if not a complete picture, at any rate a substitute for it.

In this attempt I have not sought to go beyond the epoch of Diocletian. A summary glance, at the utmost, into the new government which was then created may fitly form the keystone of this narrative ; to estimate it fully would require a separate narration and another frame for its setting—an independent historical work, carried out in the large spirit and with the comprehensive glance of Gibbon, but with a more accurate understanding of details. Italy and its islands have been excluded ; for the account of these cannot be dissociated from that of the general government of the empire. The external history, as it is called, of the imperial period is dealt with as an integral part of the provincial administration ; what we should call imperial wars were not carried on under the empire against those outside of its pale, although the conflicts called forth by the rounding off, or the defence, of the frontier sometimes assumed such proportions as to make them seem wars between two powers similar in kind, and the collapse of the Roman rule in the middle of the third century, which for some decades seemed as though it were to become its definitive end, grew out of the unhappy conduct of frontier-defence at several places simultaneously. Our narrative opens with the great work of pushing forward, and of regulating the frontier towards the north, which was partly carried out and partly failed under Augustus. At other points we bring together the events that occurred on each of the three chief arenas for frontier-defence—the Rhine, the Danube, the Euphrates. The remainder of the narrative is arranged according to provinces. Charms of detail, pictures of feeling, sketches of character, it has none to offer ; it is allowable for the artist, but not for the historian, to reproduce the features of Arminius. With self-denial this book has been written ; and with self-denial let it be read.

CHAPTER I.

THE NORTHERN FRONTIER OF ITALY.

THE Roman Republic extended its territory chiefly by means of the sea towards the west, south, and east : little was done towards extending it in the direction, in which Italy and the two peninsulas dependent upon it to the west and east are connected with the great mainland of Europe. The region which lay behind Macedonia was not subject to the Romans, nor yet even the northern slope of the Alps ; only the inland region behind the south coast of Gaul had been annexed by Caesar to the empire. Looking to the position occupied by the empire in general, this state of things could not be allowed to continue ; the fact that the inert and unstable rule of the aristocracy had been superseded could not but tell with preeminent effect in this sphere of action. Caesar had not charged the heirs of his dictatorial power with the extension of Roman territory on the north slope of the Alps and on the right bank of the Rhine so directly as with the conquest of Britain ; but in reality such an enlargement of the bounds suggested itself far more naturally, and was more necessary, than the subduing of the transmarine Celts, and we can readily understand why Augustus took in hand the former and omitted the latter. The task was divided into three great sections—the operations on the northern frontier of the Graeco-Macedonian peninsula, in the region of the middle and lower Danube, in Illyricum ; those on the northern frontier of Italy itself, in the region of the upper Danube, in Raetia and Noricum ; lastly, those on the right

bank of the Rhine, in Germany. Though conducted for
the most part independently, the military political measures in these regions had yet an inward connection ; and,
as they all had their origin from the free initiative of the
Roman government, they can only be understood in their
success or in their partial failure, when they are looked at
from a military and political point of view as a whole.
We shall, therefore, in our account of them, follow the
connection of place rather than the order of time ; the
structure, of which they are but parts, is better viewed in
its internal compactness than according to the succession
of the several buildings composing it.

Dalmatian
war.

The prelude to this great aggregate of action was
formed by the measures which Caesar the Younger, so
soon as he had his hands free in Italy and Spain, undertook on the upper coasts of the Adriatic and in the inland
region adjacent to them.   In the hundred and fifty years
that had elapsed since the founding of Aquileia, the
Roman merchant had doubtless from that centre possessed
himself more and more of the traffic ; yet the state,
directly as such, had made little progress.   Considerable
trading settlements had been formed at the chief ports of
the Dalmatian coast, and also, on the road leading from
Aquileia into the valley of the Save, at Nauportus (Upper
Laybach) ; Dalmatia, Bosnia, Istria, and Carniola were
deemed Roman territory, and the region along the coast
at least was actually subject ; but the founding of towns
in a legal sense still remained to be done, quite as much
as the subduing of the inhospitable interior.

Here, however, another element had to be taken into
account.   In the war between Caesar and Pompeius the
native Dalmatians had as decidedly taken part for the
latter as the Roman settlers there had taken the side of
Caesar ; even after the defeat of Pompeius at Pharsalus,
and after the Pompeian fleet had been driven from the
iv. 434. Illyrian waters (iv. 456), the natives continued their
resistance with energy and success.   The brave and able
Publius Vatinius, who had formerly taken a very effective part in these conflicts, was sent with a strong army to

Illyricum, apparently in the year before Caesar's death, and
that merely as the vanguard of the main army, with which
the Dictator himself intended to follow in order to overthrow the Dacians, who just then were putting forth their
rising power (iv. 305), and to regulate the state of affairs   iv. 291.
in the whole domain of the Danube.   The execution of
this plan was precluded by the daggers of the assassins.
It was fortunate that the Dacians did not on their part
penetrate into Macedonia ; Vatinius himself fought
against the Dalmatians unsuccessfully, and sustained
severe losses.   Thereafter, when the republicans took up
arms in the East, the Illyrian army joined that of Brutus,
and for a considerable time the Dalmatians remained free
from attack.   After the overthrow of the republicans,
Antonius, to whom, in the partition of the empire, Macedonia had fallen, caused the insubordinate Dardani in the
north-west and the Parthini on the coast (eastward from
Durazzo) to be put to rout in the year 715, when the   39.
celebrated orator Gaius Asinius Pollio gained triumphal
honours.   In Illyricum, which was under Caesar, nothing
could be done so long as the latter had to direct his whole
power to the Sicilian war against Sextus Pompeius ; but
after its successful termination Caesar personally threw
himself with vigour into this task.   The small tribes from
Doclea (Cernagora), as far as the Iapydes (near Fiume),
were in the first campaign (719) either brought back to   35.
subjection or now for the first time subdued.   It was not
a great war with pitched battles of note, but the mountain-
conflicts with the brave and desperate tribes, and the capture of the strongholds furnished in part with Roman
appliances of war, formed no easy task ; in none of his
wars did Caesar display to an equal extent his own energy
and personal valour.   After the toilsome subjugation of
the territory of the Iapydes, he marched in the very same
year along the valley of the Kulpa to the point where it
joins the Save ; the strong place Siscia (Sziszek) situated
at that point, the chief place of arms of the Pannonians,
against which the Romans had never hitherto advanced
with success, was now occupied and destined as a basis

for the war against the Dacians, which Caesar purposed next

34, 33. to undertake.   In the two following years (720, 721), the
Dalmatians, who had for a number of years been in arms
against the Romans, were forced to submit after the fall
of their fortress Promona (Promina, near Dernis, above
Sebenico).   Still more important than these military successes was the work of peace, which was carried on about
the same time, and which they were intended to secure.
It was doubtless in these years that the ports along the
Istrian and Dalmatian coast, so far as they lay within the
field of Caesar's rule, Tergeste (Trieste), Pola, Iader
(Zara), Salonae (near Spalato), Narona (at the mouth of
the Narenta), as well as Emona (Laybach), beyond the
Alps, on the route from Aquileia over the Julian Alps
to the Save, obtained, through Caesar's successor, some
of them town-walls, all of them town-rights.   The places
themselves had probably all been already long in existence
as Roman villages ; but it was at any rate of essential
importance that they were now inserted on a footing of
equal privilege among the Italian *municipia.*

Prepara-
tion for the
Dacian
war.   The Dacian war was intended to follow ; but the civil
war stepped in before it a second time.   It summoned the
ruler not to Illyricum, but to the East, and the heavings of the
great decisive struggle between Caesar and Antonius reached
even to the distant region of the Danube.   The people of
the Dacians, united and purified by king Burebista
iv. 291. (Boerebistas, iv. 305), now under king Cotiso, found itself
courted by the two antagonists—Caesar was even accused
of having sought the king's daughter in marriage, and
having offered to him in turn the hand of his five-year-old
daughter Julia.   It is easy to understand how the Dacian
should, in view of the invasion planned by the father and
ushered in by the son with the fortification of Siscia, have
attached himself to the side of Antonius ; and had he done
what people in Rome feared—had he, while Caesar was
fighting in the East, penetrated from the north into defenceless Italy ; or had Antonius, in accordance with the
proposal of the Dacians, sought the decision of the struggle
not in Epirus but in Macedonia, and drawn thither the

Dacian bands to help him, the fortunes of the war might perhaps have ended otherwise. But neither the one nor the other took place; moreover, at that very time the Dacian state, created by the vigorous hand of Burebista, again went to pieces; internal troubles, perhaps also the attacks from the north by the Germanic Bastarnae and by the Sarmatian tribes that subsequently environed Dacia on all sides, prevented the Dacians from interfering in the Roman civil war, in the decision of which their future also was at stake.

Immediately after that war was decided, Caesar set himself to regulate the state of things on the lower Danube. But, partly because the Dacians themselves were no longer so much to be dreaded as formerly, partly because Caesar now ruled no longer merely over Illyricum, but over the whole Graeco-Macedonian peninsula, the latter became the primary basis of the Roman operations. Let us picture to ourselves the peoples, and the relations of the ruling powers, which Augustus found there.

Macedonia had been for centuries a Roman province. As such, it did not reach beyond Stobi to the north and the Rhodope mountains to the east; but the range of Rome's power stretched far beyond the frontier proper of the country, although varying in compass and not fixed in point of form. Approximately the Romans seem to have been the leading power at that time as far as the Haemus (Balkan), while the region beyond the Balkan as far as the Danube had been possibly trodden by Roman troops, but was by no means dependent on Rome.[1] Beyond the Rhodope mountains the Thracian dynasts, who were neighbours to Macedonia, especially those of the Odrysians (ii. 309), to whom the greatest portion of the south coast and a part of the coast of the Black Sea were subject, had been brought by the expedition of Lucullus

Macedonian frontier.

ii. 290.

---

[1] Dio, li. 23, expressly says this as to the year 725 : τέως μὲν οὖν ταῦτ’ ἐποίουν (*i.e.* so long as the Bastarnae attacked only the Triballi — near Oescus in Lower Moesia, and the Dardani in Upper Moesia), οὐδὲν σφίσι πρᾶγμα πρὸς τοὺς 'Ρωμαίους ἦν· ἐπεὶ δὲ τόν τε Αἷμον ὑπερέβησαν καὶ τὴν Θρᾴκην τὴν Δενθελητῶν ἔνσπονδον αὐτοῖς οὖσαν κατέδραμον κ. τ. λ. The allies in Moesia, of whom Dio, xxxviii. 10 speaks, are the coast towns.

iv. 39. (iv. 41) under the Roman protectorate; while the inhabitants of the more inland territories, especially the Bessi on the upper Maritza, were perhaps called subjects, but were not so, and their incursions into the settled territory as well as retaliatory expeditions into theirs were of constant occurrence.
60. Thus, about the year 694, Augustus' own father,
43. Gaius Octavius, and in the year 711, during the preparations for the war against the triumvirs, Marcus Brutus had fought against them. Another Thracian tribe, the Dentheletae (in the district of Sofia), had, even in Cicero's time, on an incursion into Macedonia, threatened to besiege its capital Thessalonica. With the Dardani, the western neighbours of the Thracians, a branch of the Illyrian family, who inhabited southern Servia and the district of Prisrend, Curio, the predecessor in office of Lucullus, had fought successfully; and ten years later Cicero's colleague in the consulate, Gaius Antonius, unsuccessfully in the
62. year 692. Below the Dardanian territory, again, there were settled close to the Danube Thracian tribes, the once powerful but now reduced Triballi in the valley of the Oescus (in the region of Plewna), and farther on, along both banks of the Danube to its mouth, Dacians, or, as on the right bank of the river they were usually called by the old national name which was retained also by their Asiatic kinsmen, Mysians or Moesians, probably in Burebista's time a part of his kingdom, now once more split up into different principalities. But the most powerful people between the Balkan and the Danube at that time were the Bastarnae. We have already on several occasions met with this brave and numerous race, the eastmost branch of
ii. 290. the great Germanic family (ii. 308). Settled, strictly speaking, behind the Transdanubian Dacians beyond the mountains which separate Transylvania from Moldavia, at the mouths of the Danube and in the wide region from these to the Dniester, they were themselves outside of the Roman sphere; but from their ranks especially had both king Philip of Macedonia and king Mithridates of Pontus formed their armies, and in this way the Romans had often already fought with them. Now they had crossed the

Danube in great masses, and established themselves north of the Haemus ; in so far as the Dacian war, as planned by Cæsar the father and then by the son, had doubtless for its object to gain the right bank of the lower Danube, it was not less directed against them than against the Dacian Moesians on the right bank. The Greek coast towns in the barbarian land, Odessus (near Varna), Tomis, Istropolis, hard pressed by these movements of the nations surging around them, were here as everywhere from the outset clients of the Romans.

At the time of Caesar's dictatorship, when Burebista was at the height of his power, the Dacians had executed that fearful devastating raid along the coast as far down as Apollonia, the traces of which were not yet obliterated after a century and a half. It may probably have been this invasion that at first induced Caesar the elder to undertake the Dacian war ; and after that the son now ruled also over Macedonia, he could not but feel himself under obligation to interfere here at once and with energy. The defeat which Cicero's colleague, Antonius, had sustained near Istropolis at the hands of the Bastarnae may be taken as a proof that these Greeks needed once more the aid of the Romans.

In fact soon after the battle of Actium (725) Marcus Licinius Crassus, the grandson of him who had fallen at Carrhae, was sent by Caesar to Macedonia as governor, and charged now to carry out the campaign that had twice been hindered. The Bastarnae, who just then had invaded Thrace, submitted without resistance, when Crassus had them summoned to leave the Roman territory ; but their retreat was not sufficient for the Roman. He, on his part, crossed the Haemus,[1] at the confluence of the Cibrus (Tzibritza) with the Danube, defeated the enemy, whose king, Deldo, was left on the field of battle ; and, with the help of a Dacian prince adhering to the Romans, took prisoners all that had

29.
Subjugation of
Moesia by
Crassus.

---

[1] When Dio says (li. 23) : τὴν Σεγετικὴν καλουμένην προσεποιήσατο καὶ ἐς τὴν Μυσίδα ἐνέβαλε, the town spoken of, doubtless, can only be Serdica, the modern Sofia, on the upper Oescus, the key to the Moesian country.

escaped from the battle and sought shelter in a neighbouring stronghold.   Without offering further resistance the whole Moesian territory submitted to the conqueror of the Bastarnae.   These returned next year to avenge the defeat which they had suffered ; but they once more succumbed, and, with them, such of the Moesian tribes as had again taken up arms.   Thus these enemies were once for all expelled from the right bank of the Danube, and the latter was entirely subjected to the Roman rule.   At the same time the Thracians not hitherto subject were chastised, the national shrine of Dionysos was taken from the Bessi, and the administration of it was entrusted to the princes of the Odrysians, who generally from that time, under the protection of the Roman supreme power, exercised, or were assumed to exercise, supremacy over the Thracian tribes south of the Haemus.   The Greek towns, moreover, on the coast of the Black Sea were placed under its protection, and the rest of the conquered territory was assigned to various vassal-princes, on whom devolved accordingly, in the first instance, the protection of the frontier of the empire ;[1] Rome had no legions of her own

[1] After the campaign of Crassus the conquered land was probably organised in such a way that the coast went to the Thracian kingdom, as Zippel has shown (*Röm. Illyricum,* p. 243), and the western portion was, just like Thrace, assigned in fief to the native princes, in place of one of whom must have come the *praefectus civitatium Moesiae et Triballiae* (*C. I. L.* v. 1838), who was still acting under Tiberius.   The usual assumption that Moesia was at first combined with Illyricum, rests only on the circumstance that in the enumeration of the provinces apportioned in the year 727 between emperor and senate in Dio, liii. 12 it is not named, and so was contained in " Dalmatia."   But this enumeration does not extend at all to the vassal-states and the procuratorial provinces, and so far all is in due keeping with our assumption.   On the other hand, weighty arguments tell against the usual hypothesis.

Had Moesia been originally a part of the province of Illyricum, it would have retained this name ; for on the division of a province the name was usually retained, and only a defining epithet added.   But the appellation Illyricum, which Dio doubtless reproduces *l.c.*, was always in this connection restricted to the upper (Dalmatia) and the lower (Pannonia).   Moreover, if Moesia was a part of Illyricum, there was no room left for that Prefect of Moesia and Triballia, or in other words for his kingly predecessor.   Lastly, it is far from probable that in 727 a   27. command of such extent and importance should have been entrusted to a single senatorial governor.   On the other hand, everything admits of easy explanation, if small client - states arose in Moesia after the war of Crassus ; these were as such from the outset under the emperor, and, as the senate did not take part in their successive annexation and conversion into

left for these distant regions.   Macedonia thereby became an inland province, which had no further need of military administration.   The goal, which had been contemplated in those plans of Dacian warfare, was attained.

Certainly this goal was merely a provisional one. But before Augustus took in hand the definitive regulation of the northern frontier he applied himself to re-organise the provinces already belonging to the empire ; more than ten years elapsed over the arrangement of things in Spain, Gaul, Asia, and Syria.   How, when what was needful in these quarters was done, he set to work on his comprehensive task, we have now to tell.

Italy, which bore sway over three continents, was still, as we have said, by no means absolutely master in her own house.   The Alps, which sheltered her on the north, were in all their extent, from one end to the other, filled with small and but little civilised tribes of Illyrian, Raetian, or Celtic nationality, whose territories in part bordered closely on those of the great towns of the Transpadana— that of the Trumpilini (Val Trompia) on the town of Brixia ; that of the Camunni (Val Camonica above the Lago d'Iseo) on the town of Bergomum ; that of the Salassi (Val d'Aosta) on Eporedia (Ivrea)—and whose neighbourhood was by no means wont to be peaceful.   Often enough conquered and proclaimed at the Capitol as vanquished, these tribes, in spite of the laurels of the men of note that triumphed over them, were constantly plundering the farmers and the merchants of Upper Italy.   The mischief was not to be checked in earnest until the government resolved to cross the Alpine chain and bring its northern slope also under their power ; for beyond doubt numbers of these depredators were constantly streaming over the mountains to pillage the rich adjoining country.   In the direction

Subjugation of the Alps.

---

11.   a governorship, this might easily be unnoticed in the Annals.   It was completed in or before the year 743, seeing that the governor, L. Calpurnius Piso then waging war against the Thracians, to whom Dio (liv. 34) erroneously assigns the province of Pamphylia, can only have had as his province Pannonia or Moesia, and, as at that time Tiberius was acting as legate in Pannonia, there is left for him only Moesia.   In 6 A.D. there certainly appears an imperial governor of Moesia.

of Gaul also similar work had to be done; the tribes
in the upper valley of the Rhone (Valais and Vaud)
had indeed been subdued by Caesar, but are also named
among those that gave trouble to the generals of
his son. On the other side, the peaceful border-districts
of Gaul complained of the constant incursions of the
Raeti. The numerous expeditions arranged by Augustus
on account of these evils do not admit, or require, historical
recital ; they are not recorded in the triumphal Fasti and
do not fall under that head, but they gave to Italy for
the first time settled life in the north. We may mention
16. the subjugation of the already named Camunni in 738
by the governor of Illyria, and that of certain Ligurian
14. tribes in the region of Nice in 740, because they show
how, even about the middle of the Augustan age, these
insubordinate tribes pressed directly upon Italy. If the
emperor subsequently, in the collective report on his imperial administration, declared that violence had not been
wrongfully employed by him against any of these small
tribes, this must be understood to the effect that cessions of
territory and change of abode were demanded of them,
and they resisted the demand ; only the petty cantonal
union formed under king Cottius of Segusio (Susa) submitted without a struggle to the new arrangement.

Subjuga-
tion of the
Raeti.   The southern slopes and the valleys of the Alps
formed the arena of these conflicts. The establishment of
the Romans on the north slope of the mountains and in
15. the adjoining country to the northward followed in 739.
The two step-sons of Augustus reckoned as belonging to
the imperial house, Tiberius the subsequent emperor, and
his brother Drusus, were thereby introduced into the career
of generalship for which they were destined ; very secure and
very grateful were the laurels put before them in prospect.
Drusus penetrated from Italy up the valley of the Adige
into the Raetian mountains, and achieved here a first
victory; for the farther advance his brother, then governor
of Gaul, lent him a helping hand from Helvetia ; on the
lake of Constance itself the Roman triremes defeated the
boats of the Vindelici ; on the emperor's day, the 1st

August 739, in the vicinity of the sources of the Danube, 15.
was fought the last battle, whereby Raetia and the land
of the Vindelici—that is, the Tyrol, East Switzerland, and
Bavaria—became thenceforth constituent parts of the
Roman empire.   The emperor Augustus had gone in
person to Gaul to superintend the war and the organisation of the new province.   At the point where the Alps
abut on the Gulf of Genoa, on the height above Monaco,
a monument commanding a wide prospect of the Tyrrhene
Sea, and not even yet wholly effaced, was erected some
years later by grateful Italy to the emperor Augustus,
because under his government all the Alpine tribes from
the Upper to the Lower sea—the inscription enumerates
forty-six of them—had been brought under the power
of the Roman people.   It was no more than the simple
truth ; and this war was what war ought to be—the
guardian and the guarantee of peace.

A task more difficult doubtless than that of the war *Organisa-*
proper was the organisation of the new territory ; the more *tion of*
especially as considerations of internal policy exerted to *Raetia.*
some extent a very disturbing influence on it.   Since, as
things stood, the preponderance of military power might not
be located in Italy, the government had to take care that the
great military commands were removed as far as possible
from its immediate vicinity ; indeed one of the motives
that conduced to the occupation of Raetia itself was the
desire to remove the command, which probably up to this
time could not have been dispensed with in Upper Italy
itself, definitively away from that region, as was thereupon
actually done.   It might most naturally have been expected that there would be created on the north slope of the
Alps a great centre for the military posts indispensable in
the newly acquired territory ; but a course the very opposite
of this was followed.   Between Italy on the one hand, and
the great commands on the Rhine and Danube on the
other, there was drawn a girdle of small governorships,
which were not merely all filled up by the emperor, but
were also filled up throughout with men not belonging to
the senate.   Italy and the province of southern Gaul were

separated by the three small military districts of the
Maritime Alps (department of the Maritime Alps and the
province of Cuneo), the Cottian Alps with Segusio (Susa)
as its chief town, and probably the Graian Alps (East
Savoy).   Among these the second, administered by the
already named cantonal prince, Cottius, and his descendants for a time under the form of clientship,[1] was of most
importance, but they all possessed a certain military
power, and were primarily destined to maintain public
safety in the territory concerned, and above all on the important imperial highways traversing it.   The upper valley
of the Rhone again—that is, the Valais, and the newly
conquered Raetia—were placed under a commander of
higher standing not in rank, but doubtless in power ;
a corps, relatively speaking, considerable was here for
the time being indispensably requisite.   In order, however, to provide for its being diminished as far as possible,
Raetia was in great measure depopulated by the removal
of its inhabitants.   The circuit was closed by the similarly
organised province of Noricum, embracing the largest
part of what is now German Austria.   This wide and
fertile region had submitted without substantial resistance
to the Roman rule, probably in the form of a dependent
principality established in the first instance, but with its
prince erelong giving place to the imperial procurator, from
whom, for that matter, he did not essentially differ.   Some,
at all events, of the Rhenish and Danubian legions had
their fixed quarters in the immediate neighbourhood, on
the one hand of the Raetian frontier at Vindonissa, on the
other of the Norican frontier at Poetovio, obviously to keep
in check the adjoining province; but in that intermediate
region as little were there armies of the first rank with
legions under senatorial generals, as there were senatorial

---

[1] The official title of Cottius was
not king, like that of his father
Donnus, but "president of the cantonal union" (*praefectus civitatium*), as
he is named on the still standing arch
of Susa erected by him in honour of
9-8. Augustus in the year 745-6.   But the
position was beyond doubt held for
life, and, under reservation of the
superior's right to confirm it, also
hereditary ; so far therefore the union
was certainly a principality, as it is
usually so termed.

governors. The distrust towards the corporation governing the state alongside of the emperor finds very forcible expression in this arrangement.

Next to the protection of the peace of Italy the chief aim of this organisation was to secure its communications with the north, which were of not less urgent importance for traffic than in a military point of view. With special energy Augustus took up this task ; and he doubtless deserved that his name should still live at the present day in those of Aosta and Augsburg, perhaps also in that of the Julian Alps. The old coast-road, which Augustus partly renewed, partly constructed, from the Ligurian coast through Gaul and Spain to the Atlantic Ocean, can only have served purposes of traffic. The road also over the Cottian Alps, already opened up by Pompeius (iv. 28), was finished under Augustus by the already mentioned prince of Susa, and named after him ; in like manner a trading route, it connects Italy, by way of Turin and Susa, with the commercial capital of south Gaul, Arelate. But the military line proper—the direct connection between Italy and the camps on the Rhine—led through the valley of the Dora Baltea from Italy partly to Lyons the capital of Gaul, partly to the Rhine. While the republic had confined itself to bringing into its power the entrance of that valley by founding Eporedia (Ivrea), Augustus possessed himself of it entirely by not merely subjugating its inhabitants—the still restless Salassi, with whom he had already fought during the Dalmatian war—but extirpating them outright ; 36,000 of them, including 8000 fighting men, were sold under the hammer into slavery in the market-place of Eporedia, and the purchasers were bound not to grant freedom to any of them within twenty years. The camp itself, from which his general Varro Murena had achieved their final defeat in 729, became the fortress, which, occupied by 3000 settlers taken from the imperial guard, was to secure the communications—the town Augusta Praetoria, the modern Aosta, whose walls and gates then erected are still standing. It commanded subsequently two Alpine routes, as well that which led

Roads and colonies in the Alps.

iv. 27.

25.

over the Graian Alps or Little St. Bernard, along the
upper Isère and the Rhone to Lyons, as that which ran
over the Poenine Alps, the Great St. Bernard, to the valley
of the Rhone and to the Lake of Geneva, and thence into
the valleys of the Aar and the Rhine.   But it was for the
first of these roads that the town was designed, as it
originally had only gates leading east and west ; nor
could this be otherwise, for the fortress was built ten years
before the occupation of Raetia ; in those years, moreover,
the later organisation of the camps on the Rhine was not
yet in existence, and the direct connection between the
capitals of Italy and Gaul was altogether of the foremost
importance.   In the direction of the Danube we have
already mentioned the laying out of Emona on the upper
Save, on the old trade-road from Aquileia over the Julian
Alps into the Pannonian territory.   This road was at
the same time the chief artery for the military communication of Italy with the region of the Danube.   Lastly,
with the conquest of Raetia was connected the opening of
the route which led from the last Italian town Tridentum
(Trent), up the Adige valley, to the newly established
Augusta in the land of the Vindelici, the modern Augsburg, and onward to the upper Danube.   Subsequently,
when the son of the general who had first opened up
this region came to reign, this road received the name
of the Claudian highway.[1]   It furnished the means of
connection, indispensable from a military point of view,
between Raetia and Italy ; but in consequence of the
comparatively small importance of the Raetian army,

---

[1] We know this road only in the
shape which the emperor Claudius,
the son of the constructor, gave to it ;
originally, of course, it cannot have
been called *via Claudia*, but only
via Augusta, and we can hardly regard as its terminus in Italy Altinum,
in the neighbourhood of the modern
Venice, since, under Augustus, all the
imperial roads still led to Rome.
That the road ran through the upper
Adige valley is shown by the milestone
found at Meran (*C. I. L.* v. 8003) ; that
it led to the Danube, is attested ; the
connection of the making of this road
with the founding of Augusta Vindelicum, though this was at first only a
market-village (*forum*), is more than
probable (*C. I. L.* iii. p. 711); in
what way Augsburg and the Danube
were reached from Meran we do not
know.   Subsequently the road was
rectified, so as to leave the Adige at
Bautzen, and to lead up the Eisach
valley over the Brenner to Augsburg.

and doubtless also in consequence of the more difficult communication, it never had the same importance as the route of Aosta.

The Alpine passes and the north slope of the Alps were thus in secure possession of the Romans.   Beyond the Alps there stretched to the east of the Rhine the land of the Germans ; to the south of the Danube that of the Pannonians and the Moesians.   Here, too, soon after the occupation of Raetia, the offensive was taken, and nearly contemporaneously in both directions.   Let us look first at what occurred on the Danube.

The Danubian region, to all appearance up to 727 administered along with Upper Italy, became then, on the reorganisation of the empire, an independent administrative district, Illyricum, under a governor of its own.   It consisted of Dalmatia, with the country behind it, as far as the Drin—while the coast farther to the south had for long belonged to the province of Macedonia—and of the Roman possessions in the land of the Pannonians on the Save.   The region between the Haemus and the Danube as far as the Black Sea, which Crassus had shortly before brought into dependence on the empire, as well as Noricum and Raetia, stood in a relation of clientship to Rome, and so did not belong as such to this province, but withal were primarily dependent on the governor of Illyricum.   Thrace, north of the Haemus, still by no means pacified, fell, from a military point of view, to the same district.   It was a continued effect of the original organisation, and one which subsisted down to a late period, that the whole region of the Danube from Raetia to Moesia was comprehended as a customs-district under the name Illyricum in the wider sense.   Legions were stationed only in Illyricum proper, in the other districts there were probably no imperial troops at all, or at the utmost small detachments ; the chief command was held by the proconsul of the new province coming from the senate ; while the soldiers and officers were, as a matter of course, imperial.   It attests the serious character of the offensive beginning after the conquest of Raetia, that in the first instance the co-ruler

27.
Erection of Illyricum.

Agrippa took over the command in the region of the Danube, to whom the proconsul of Illyricum had to become *de iure* subordinate ; and then, when Agrippa's 12. sudden death in the spring of 742 broke down this combination, Illyricum in the following year passed into imperial administration, and the imperial generals obtained the chief commands in it.   Soon three military centres were here formed, which thereupon brought about the administrative division of the Danubian region into three parts.   The small principalities in the territory conquered by Crassus gave place to the province of Moesia, the governor of which henceforth, in what is now Servia and Bulgaria, guarded the frontier against the Dacians and Bastarnae.   In what had hitherto been the province of Illyricum, a part of the legionaries was posted on the Kerka and the Cettina, to keep in check the still troublesome Dalmatians.   The chief force was stationed in Pannonia, on what was then the boundary of the empire, the Save. This distribution of the legions and organisation of the provinces cannot be fixed with chronological precision ; probably the serious wars which were waged simultaneously against the Pannonians and the Thracians, of which we have immediately to speak, led in the first instance to the institution of the governorship of Moesia, and it was not till some time later that the Dalmatian legions and those on the Save obtained commanders-in-chief of their own.

First Pannonian war of Tiberius.   As the expeditions against the Pannonians and the Germans were, as it were, a repetition of the Raetian campaign on a more extended scale, so the leaders, who were put at their head with the title of imperial legates, were the same—once more the two princes of the imperial house, Tiberius, who, in the place of Agrippa, took up the command in Illyricum, and Drusus, who went to the Rhine, both now no longer inexperienced youths, but men in the prime of their years, and well fitted to take in hand severe work.

Immediate pretexts for the waging of war in the region of the Danube were not wanting.   Marauders from

Pannonia, and even from the peaceful Noricum, carried
pillage in the year 738 as far as Istria.   Two years there-   16.
after the Illyrian provincials took up arms against their
masters, and, although they returned to obedience without
offering opposition when Agrippa took over the command in the autumn of 741, yet immediately after his   13.
death the disturbances are alleged to have begun afresh.
We cannot say how far these Roman accounts correspond
to the truth ; certainly the pushing forward of the Roman
frontier, required by the general political situation, formed
the real motive and aim of the war.   As to the three
campaigns of Tiberius in Pannonia from 742 to 744 we   12, 10.
are very imperfectly informed.   Their result was stated
by the government as the establishment of the Danube as
the boundary for the province of Illyricum.   That this
river was thenceforth looked upon in its whole course as
the boundary of Roman territory, is doubtless correct ;
but a subjugation in the proper sense, or even an occupation, of the whole of this wide domain by no means took
place at that time.   The chief resistance to Tiberius was
offered by the tribes already at an earlier date declared
Roman, especially by the Dalmatians ; among those first
effectively subdued at that time, the most noted was that
of the Pannonian Breuci on the lower Save.   The Roman
armies, during these campaigns, probably did not cross
the Drave, and did not in any case transfer their standing
camp to the Danube.   The region between the Save and
Drave was at all events occupied, and the headquarters of
the Illyrian northern army were transferred from Siscia
on the Save to Poetovio (Pettau) on the middle Drave,
while in the Norican region recently occupied the Roman
garrisons reached as far as the Danube at Carnuntum
(Petronell, near Vienna), at that time the last Norican
town towards the east.   The wide and vast region between
the Drave and the Danube, which now forms western
Hungary, was to all appearance at that time not even
militarily occupied.   This was in keeping with the whole
plan of the offensive operations that were begun ; the
object sought was to be in touch with the Gallic army,

and for the new imperial frontier in the north-east the natural base was not Buda, but Vienna.

Thracian war of Piso.

Complementary in some measure to this Pannonian expedition of Tiberius was that which was simultaneously undertaken against the Thracians by Lucius Piso, perhaps the first governor that Moesia had of its own.   The two great neighbouring nations, the Illyrians and the Thracians, of whom we shall treat more fully in a subsequent chapter, stood alike at that time in need of subjugation. The tribes of inland Thrace showed themselves still more obstinate than the Illyrians, and far from sub-

16. ordinate to the kings set over them by Rome ; in 738 a Roman army had to advance thither and come to the help of the princes against the Bessi.   If we had more exact accounts of the conflicts waged in the one quarter

13, 11. as in the other in the years 741 to 743, the contemporary action of the Thracians and Illyrians would perhaps appear as concerted.   Certain it is that the mass of the Thracian tribes south of the Haemus and presumably also those settled in Moesia took part in this national war, and that the resistance of the Thracians was not less obstinate than that of the Illyrians.   It was for them at the same time a religious war ; the shrine of Dionysos,[1] taken from the Bessi and assigned to the Odrysian princes well disposed to Rome, was not forgotten ; a priest of this Dionysos stood at the head of the insurrection, and it was directed in the first instance against those Odrysian princes.   One of them was taken and put to death, the other was driven away ; the insurgents, in part armed and disciplined after the Roman model, were victors in the first engagement over Piso, and penetrated as far as Macedonia and into the Thracian Chersonese ; fears were entertained for Asia.

---

[1] The locality "in which the Bessi honour the god Dionysos," and which Crassus took from them and gave to the Odrysians (Dio, li. 25), is certainly the same *Liberi patris lucus*, in which Alexander sacrificed, and the father of Augustus, *cum per secreta Thraciae exercitum duceret*, asked the oracle respecting his son (Suetonius, *Aug.* 94), and which Herodotus already mentions (ii. 111 ; compare Euripides, *Hec.* 1267) as an oracular shrine placed under the protection of the Bessi. Certainly it is to be sought northwards of Rhodope ; it has not yet been discovered.

Ultimately, however, Roman discipline gained the superiority over these brave opponents ; in several campaigns Piso mastered the resistance, and the command of Moesia, instituted either already on this occasion or soon afterwards on "the Thracian shore," broke up the connection of the Daco-Thracian peoples, by separating the tribes on the left bank of the Danube and their kinsmen south of the Haemus from each other, and permanently secured the Roman rule in the region of the lower Danube.

The Germans still more than the Pannonians and the Thracians gave the Romans occasion to feel that the existing state of things could not permanently continue. The boundary of the empire since Caesar's time had been the Rhine from the lake of Constance to its mouth (iv. 258). It was not a demarcation of peoples, for already of old in the north-east of Gaul the Celts had on various occasions mingled with Germans, the Treveri and Nervii would at least gladly have been Germans (iv. 244), and on the middle Rhine Caesar himself had provided settlements for the remnant of the hosts of Ariovistus—Triboci (in Alsace) Nemetes (about Spires), Vangiones (about Worms). Those Germans on the left of the Rhine indeed adhered more firmly to the Roman rule than the Celtic cantons, and it was not they that opened the gates of Gaul to their countrymen on the right bank. But these, long accustomed to predatory raids over the river and by no means forgetting the half successful attempts on several occasions to settle there, came unbidden. The only Germanic tribe beyond the Rhine, which already in Caesar's time had separated from their countrymen and placed themselves under Roman protection, the Ubii, had to give way before the hatred of their exasperated kinsmen and to seek protection and new abodes on the Roman bank (716) ; Agrippa, although personally present in Gaul, had not been able, amidst the pressure of the Sicilian war then impending, to help them otherwise, and had crossed the Rhine merely to effect their transference. From this settlement of theirs our Cologne subsequently grew up. Not merely were the Romans trading on the

Attack of the Germans.

iv. 247.

iv. 233.

38.

right bank of the Rhine subjected to various injuries by
25. the Germans, so that even in 729 an advance over the
20. Rhine was executed, and Agrippa in 734 had to expel
from Gaul Germanic hordes that had come thither from
16. the Rhine ; but in 738 the further bank was affected by a
more general movement, which terminated in an invasion
on a great scale. The Sugambri on the Ruhr took the
lead, and with them their neighbours the Usipes on the
north in the valley of the Lippe, and the Tencteri on the
south ; they attacked the Roman traders sojourning
among them and nailed them to the cross, then crossed
the Rhine, pillaged the Gallic cantons far and wide, and,

Defeat of Lollius.

when the governor of Germany sent the legate Marcus
Lollius with the fifth legion against them, they first cut
off its cavalry and then put the legion itself to disgraceful
flight, on which occasion even its eagle fell into their
hands. After all this they returned unassailed to their
homes. This miscarriage of the Roman army, though
not of importance in itself, was not to be despised in
presence of the Germanic movement and even of the
troublesome feeling in Gaul ; Augustus himself went to
the province attacked, and this occurrence may possibly
have been the immediate occasion for the adoption of that
great movement of offence, which, beginning with the
15. Raetian war in 739, led on to the campaigns of Tiberius
in Illyricum and of Drusus in Germany.

38.   Nero Claudius Drusus, born in 716 by Livia in the

German war of Drusus.

house of her new husband, afterwards Augustus, and loved
and treated by the latter like a son—evil tongues said,
as his son—the very image of manly beauty and of winning
grace in converse, a brave soldier and an able general, a
pronounced panegyrist, moreover, of the old republican
system, and in every respect the most popular prince of the
imperial house, took up, on the return of Augustus to
13. Italy (741), the administration of Gaul and the chief
command against the Germans, whose subjugation was
now contemplated in earnest. We have no adequate
means of knowing either the strength of the army then
stationed on the Rhine, or how matters stood with the

Germans ; this much only is clear that the latter were not in a position suitably to meet the compact attack. The region of the Neckar formerly possessed by the Helvetii (iii. 182), then for long a debateable border-land between iii. 173. them and the Germans, lay desolate and dominated on the one side by the recently subdued district of the Vindelici, on the other side by the Germans friendly to Rome about Strassburg, Spires, and Worms. Farther northward, in the region of the upper Main, were settled the Marcomani, perhaps the most powerful of the Suebian tribes, but from of old at enmity with the Germans of the middle Rhine. Northward of the Main followed first in the Taunus the Chatti, farther down the Rhine the already named Tencteri, Sugambri, and Usipes ; behind them the powerful Cherusci on the Weser, besides a number of tribes of secondary rank. As it was these tribes on the middle Rhine, with the Sugambri at their head, that had carried out that attack on Roman Gaul, the retaliatory expedition of Drusus was directed mainly against them, and they too combined for joint resistance to Drusus and for the institution of a national army to be formed from the contingents of all these cantons. The Frisian tribes, however, on the coast of the North Sea did not join the movement, but persevered in their peculiar isolation.

It was the Germans who assumed the offensive. The Sugambri and their allies again seized all the Romans whom they could lay hold of on their bank, and nailed to the cross the centurions among them, twenty in number. The allied tribes resolved once more to invade Gaul, and even divided the spoil beforehand—the Sugambri were to obtain the people, the Cherusci the horses, the Suebian tribes the gold and silver. So they attempted in the beginning of 742 again to cross the Rhine, and hoped for 12. the support of the Germans on the left bank of the river, and even for an insurrection of the Gallic cantons just at that time excited by the unwonted matter of the census. But the young general took his measures well ; he nipped the movement in the Roman territory before it was well set agoing, drove back the invaders even as they were crossing the river, and then crossed the stream on his own part, in order to lay waste the territory of the Usipes and Sugambri. This was a repulse for the time ; the plan of the war proper, designed on a grander scale, started from the acquisition of the North Sea coast and of the mouths of the Ems and the Elbe. The numerous and valiant tribe of the Batavi in the delta of the Rhine was soon incorporated—to all appearance, at that time and by amicable concert—in the Roman empire; with its help a communication by water was established from the Rhine to the Zuyder See, and from the latter to the North Sea, which opened up for the Rhine-fleet a safer and shorter way to the mouths of the Ems and Elbe. The Frisians on the north coast followed the example of the Batavi and likewise submitted to the foreign rule. It was doubtless still more the moderate policy than the military preponderance of the Romans, which paved the way for them here ; these tribes remained almost wholly exempt from tribute, and were drawn upon for war-service in a way which did not alarm, but allured them. From this basis the expedition proceeded along the coast of the North Sea ; in the open sea the island of Burchanis (perhaps Borchum off East Friesland) was taken by assault ; on the Ems the fleet of boats of the Bructeri was vanquished by the Roman fleet ; Drusus reached as far as the Chauci at the mouth of the Weser. The fleet indeed on its return homewards encountered dangerous and unknown shallows, and, but for the Frisians affording a safe escort to the shipwrecked army, it would have been in a very critical position. Nevertheless, by this first campaign the coast from the mouth of the Rhine to that of the Weser had been gained for Rome.

11. After the coast was thus acquired, the subjugation of the interior began in the next year (743). It was materially facilitated by the dissensions among the Germans of the middle Rhine. For the attack on Gaul attempted in the previous year the Chatti had not furnished the promised contingent ; in natural, but still far from politic, anger the Sugambri had suddenly assailed the land of the Chatti with all their force, and so their own territory as

well as that of their next neighbours on the Rhine was occupied without difficulty by the Romans. The Chatti thereupon submitted to the enemies of their enemies without resistance ; nevertheless, they were directed to evacuate the bank of the Rhine and to occupy instead of it that district which the Sugambri had hitherto possessed. Not less did the powerful Cherusci farther inland on the middle Weser succumb. The Chauci settled on the lower stream were now assailed by land as they had been before by sea ; and thus the whole territory between the Rhine and Weser was taken possession of, at least at the places of decisive military importance. The return was, indeed, just as in the previous year, on the point of being almost fatal ; at Arbalo (site unknown) the Romans found themselves surrounded on all sides in a narrow defile by the Germans and deprived of their communications ; but the firm discipline of the legions, and the arrogant confidence of success withal on the part of the Germans, changed the threatened defeat into a brilliant victory.[1] In the next year (744) the Chatti revolted, indignant at the loss of their old beautiful home ; but now they for their part remained alone, and were, after an obstinate resistance, and not without considerable loss, subdued by the Romans (745). The Marcomani on the upper Main, who after the occupation of the territory of the Chatti were next exposed to the attack, gave way before it, and retired into the land of the Boii, the modern Bohemia, without interfering from this point, where they were removed beyond the immediate sphere of the Roman power, in the conflicts on the Rhine. In the whole region between the Rhine and Weser the war was at an end. Drusus was able in 745 to set foot on the right bank of the Weser in the canton of the Cherusci, and to advance thence to the Elbe, which he did not cross, and presumably was instructed not to do so. Several severe combats took place ; successful resistance was nowhere offered. But on the return-march, which led apparently up the Saale and

(marginal notes: 10. / 9. / 9. / Death of Drusus.)

---

[1] That the battle at Arbalo (Plin. *H.N.* xi. 17, 55) belongs to this year, is shown by Obsequens, 72, and so the narrative in Dio, liv. 33, applies to it.

thence to the Weser, a severe blow befell the Romans, not through the enemy but through an incalculable misfortune. The general fell with his horse and broke his thigh-bone ; after thirty days of suffering he expired in the distant land between the Saale and Weser,[1] which had never before been trodden by a Roman army, in the arms of his brother who had hastened thither from Rome, in the thirtieth year of his age and in the full consciousness of his vigour and of his successes, long and deeply lamented by his adherents and the whole people—perhaps to be pronounced fortunate, because the gods granted to him to depart from life young, and to escape the disillusions and embitterments which tell most painfully on those highest in station, while his brilliant and heroic figure continues still to live in the remembrance of the world.

Continuance of the war by Tiberius.

In the course of things, as a whole, the death of the able general made—as might be expected—no change. His brother Tiberius arrived early enough not merely to close his eyes, but also with his firm hand to bring the army back and to carry on the conquest of Germany. He commanded there during the two following years

8, 7. (746, 747), in the course of which there were no conflicts on a larger scale, but the Roman troops showed themselves far and wide between the Rhine and Elbe, and

---

[1] That the fall of Drusus took place in the region of the Saale we may be allowed to infer from Strabo, vii. 1, 3, p. 291, although he only says that he perished on the march between Salas and Rhine, and the identification of the Salas with the Saale rests solely on the resemblance of name. From the scene of the mishap he was then transported as far as the summer camp (Seneca, *Cons. ad Marciam* 3 : *ipsis illum hostibus aegrum cum veneratione et pace mutua prosequentibus nec optare quod expediebat audentibus*), and in that camp he died (Sueton., *Claud.* 1). This camp lay in the heart of the barbarian land (Valerius Max. v. 5, 3) and not very far from the battlefield of Varus (Tacitus, *Ann.* ii. 7, where the *vetus ara Druso sita* is certainly to be referred to the place

where he died) ; we may be allowed to seek it in the region of the Weser. The dead body was then conveyed to the winter-camp (Dio, lv. 2) and there burnt; this spot was regarded, according to Roman usage, also as the place of burial, although the depositing of the ashes took place in Rome, and to this is to be referred the *honorarius tumulus* with the annual obsequies (Sueton. *l. c.*). Probably we have to seek for this place at Vetera. When a later author (Eutropius, vii. 13) speaks of the *monumentum* of Drusus at Mentz, this is doubtless not the tomb, but the elsewhere mentioned Tropaeum (Florus, ii. 30 : *Marcomanorum spoliis et insignibus quendam editum tumulum in tropaei modum excoluit*).

when Tiberius made the demand that all the countries should formally acknowledge the Roman rule, and at the same time declared that he could only accept that acknowledgment from all the cantons simultaneously, they complied without exception ; last of all the Sugambri, for whom indeed there was no real peace. What progress in a military point of view had been made, is shown by the expedition, falling a little later, of Lucius Domitius Ahenobarbus. The latter was able, as governor of Illyricum, probably from Vindelicia as a basis, to assign to a restless horde of Hermunduri settlements in the land of the Marcomani itself ; and on this expedition he reached as far as, and beyond, the upper Elbe, without meeting with resistance.[1] The Marcomani in Bohemia were completely isolated, and the rest of Germany between the Rhine and Elbe was a Roman province—though still by no means reduced to tranquillity.

Of the military-political organisation of Germany, as at that time planned, we have but a very imperfect knowledge, because, on the one hand, there is an utter want of accurate information as to the arrangements made in earlier times to protect the Gallic eastern frontier, and, on the other hand, those made by the two brothers were in great part destroyed by the subsequent development of affairs. There was no attempt to move the Roman frontier-guard away from the Rhine ; to this matters might perhaps come, but they had not yet done so. Just as was the case in Illyricum at that time with the Danube, the Elbe was doubtless the political boundary of the empire, but the Rhine was the line of frontier-defence, and from the camps on the Rhine the connections in rear ran to the great towns of Gaul and to its ports.[2]

Camp on the left bank of the Rhine.

---

[1] What we learn from Dio, lv. 10, partly confirmed by Tacitus, *Ann.* iv. 44, cannot be apprehended otherwise. Noricum and Raetia must have been put under this governor as an exceptional measure, or the course of operations induced him to pass beyond the limit of his governorship. The assumption that he marched through Bohemia itself, which would involve still greater difficulties, is not required by the narrative.

[2] To a connection in rear of the camp on the Rhine with the port of Boulogne we might perhaps take the much disputed notice of Florus, ii. 30, to refer : *Bonnam* (or *Bormam*) *et Gessoriacum pontibus iunxit classibusque*

The great headquarters during these campaigns was what was afterwards named the "Old Camp," Castra vetera, (Birten near Xanten), the first considerable height below Bonn on the left bank of the Rhine, from a military point of view corresponding nearly to the modern Wesel on the right. This place, occupied perhaps since the beginning of the Roman rule on the Rhine, had been instituted by Augustus as a stronghold for curbing Germany ; and, if the fortress was at all times the basis for the Roman defensive on the left bank of the Rhine, it was not less well chosen for the invasion of the right, situated, as it was, opposite to the mouth of the Lippe which was navigable far up, and connected with the right bank by a strong bridge. The counterpart to this "Old Camp," at the mouth of the Lippe was probably formed by that at the mouth of the Main, Mogontiacum, the modern Mentz, to all appearance a creation of Drusus ; at least the already mentioned cessions of territory imposed on the Chatti, as well as the constructions in the Taunus to be mentioned further on, show that Drusus clearly perceived the military importance of the line of the Main, and thus also that of its key on the left bank of the Rhine. If the legionary camp on the Aar was, as it would seem, instituted to keep the Raeti and Vindelici to their obedience (p. 18), it may be presumed to have been laid out about this time ; but then it had merely an outward connection with the Gallico-German military arrangements. The legionary camp at Strassburg hardly reaches back to so early a time. The line from Mentz to Wesel formed the basis of the Roman military dispositions. That Drusus and Tiberius had—apart from the Narbonese province which was then no longer imperial—the governorship of all Gaul as well as the command of all the

firmavit, with which is to be compared the mention by the same author of forts on the Maas. Bonn may reasonably have been at that time the station of the Rhine-fleet ; Boulogne was in later times still a fleet-station. Drusus might well have occasion to make the shortest and safest land-route between the two stations for the fleet available for transport, though the writer, probably bent on striking effect, awakens by his pointed mode of expression conceptions which cannot be in that form correct.

Rhenish legions, is an ascertained point; apart from these princes, the civil administration of Gaul may at that time perhaps have been separated from the command of the troops on the Rhine, but scarcely was the latter thus early divided into two co-ordinate commands.[1]

Correlative to these military arrangements on the left bank of the Rhine were those adopted on the right. In the first place the Romans took possession of the right bank itself. This step affected above all the Sugambri, in whose case certainly retaliation for the captured eagle and the crucified centurions contributed to it. The envoys sent to declare their submission, the most eminent men of the nation, were, at variance with the law of nations, treated as prisoners of war, and perished miserably in the Italian fortresses. Of the mass of the people, 40,000 were removed from their homes and settled in the north of Gaul, where they subsequently, perhaps, meet us under the name of the Cugerni. Only a small and harmless remnant of the powerful tribe was allowed to remain in their old abodes. Suebian bands were also transferred to Gaul, other tribes were pushed farther into the interior, such as the Marsi and doubtless also the Chatti; on the middle Rhine the native population of the right bank was everywhere dislodged or at any rate weakened. Along this bank of the Rhine, moreover, fortified posts, fifty in number, were instituted. In front of Mogontiacum the territory taken from the Chatti, thenceforth the canton of the Mattiaci near the modern Wiesbaden, was brought within the Roman lines, and the height of Taunus strongly

Positions on the right bank of the Rhine.

---

[1] As to the administrative partition of Gaul there is, apart from the separation of the Narbonensis, an utter absence of accounts, because it rested only on imperial ordinances, and nothing in reference to it came into the records of the senate. But the first information of the existence of separate Upper and Lower German commands is furnished by the campaigns of Germanicus, and the battle of Varus can hardly be understood under that assumption; here, doubtless, the *hiberna inferiora* appear, viz. that of Vetera (Velleius, ii. 120), and the counterpart to it, the *superiora*, can only have been formed by that of Mentz; but this was not under a colleague of Varus, but under his nephew, who was thus subordinate to him in command. Probably the partition only took place, in consequence of the defeat, in the last years of Augustus.

fortified.[1]   But above all the line of the Lippe was taken possession of from Vetera ; of the two military roads furnished at intervals of a day's march with forts, on the two banks of the river, the one on the right bank at least is as certainly the work of Drusus as the fortress of Aliso in the district of the sources of the Lippe, probably the present village of Elsen, not far from Paderborn,[2] is attested to have been so.   Moreover, there was the already mentioned canal from the mouth of the Rhine to the Zuider See, and a dyke drawn by Lucius Domitius Ahenobarbus through the marshy flat country between the Ems and the lower Rhine—the so-called " long bridges." Besides, there were detached Roman posts scattered through the whole region ; such are subsequently mentioned among the Frisians and the Chauci, and in this sense it may be correct that the Roman garrisons reached as far as the Weser and the Elbe.   Lastly, the army encamped in winter, no doubt, on the Rhine ; but in summer, even though no

---

[1] The *praesidium* constructed by Drusus *in monte Tauno* (Tacitus, *Ann.* i. 56), and the φρούριον ἐν Χάττοις παρ' αὐτῷ τῷ 'Ρήνῳ associated with Aliso (Dio, liv. 33), are probably identical, and the special position of the canton of the Mattiaci is evidently connected with the construction of Mogontiacum.

[2] That the " fort at the confluence of the Lupias and the Helison," in Dio, liv. 33, is identical with the oftener mentioned Aliso, and this must be sought on the upper Lippe, is subject to no doubt ; and that the Roman winter-camp at the sources of the Lippe (*ad caput Lupiae*, Velleius, ii. 205), the only one of the kind, so far as we know, on German ground, is to be sought just there, is at least very probable.   That the two Roman roads running along the Lippe, and their fortified places of bivouac, led at least as far as the region of Lippstadt, the researches of Hölzermann in particular have shown.   The upper Lippe has only one confluent of note, the Alme, and as the village of Elsen lies not far from where the Alme

falls into the Lippe, some weight may be here assigned to the similarity of name.   To the view, supported among others by Schmidt, which places Aliso at the confluence of the Glenne (and Liese) with the Lippe, the chief objection is that the camp *ad caput Lupiae* must then have been different from Aliso, and in general this point lies too far from the line of the Weser, while from Elsen the route leads directly through the Dören defile into the Werra valley.   Schmidt, who does not adhere to the identification of Aliso and Elsen, remarks generally (*Westfälische Zeitschrift für Gesch. und Alterthumskunde*, xx. p. 259), that the heights of Weser (not far from Elsen), and generally the left margin of the valley of the Alme, are the centre of a semicircle formed by the mountains in front, and this high-lying, dry region, allowing an exact look-out as far as the mountains, which covers the whole country of the Lippe and is itself covered in front by the Alme, is well adapted for the starting-point of a march towards the Weser.

expeditions properly so called were undertaken, uniformly in the conquered country, as a rule near Aliso.

The Romans, however, did not make mere military arrangements in the newly acquired domain. The Germans were urged, like other provincials, to have law administered to them by the Roman governor, and the summer expeditions of the general gradually developed into the usual judicial circuits of the governor. The accusation and defence of the accused took place in the Latin language ; the Roman advocates and legal assessors began, on the right as on the left side of the Rhine, their operations, sorely felt everywhere, but here deeply exasperating to the barbarians, who were unaccustomed to such things. Much was lacking to the full carrying out of the provincial organisation ; a formal assessment of taxation, a regulated levy for the Roman army, were not yet thought of. But as the new cantonal union had just been instituted in Gaul in connection with the divine adoration of the monarch there introduced, a similar arrangement was made also in the new Germany. When Drusus consecrated for Gaul the altar of Augustus at Lyons, the Germans last settled on the left bank of the Rhine, the Ubii, were not received into this union ; but in their chief place, which, as regards position, was for Germany nearly what Lyons was for the three Gauls, a similar altar for the Germanic cantons was erected, the priesthood of which was, in the year 9, administered by the young Cheruscan prince Segimundus, son of Segestes.

Organisation of the province Germany.

Political differences, however, in the imperial family broke down or interrupted the full military success. The discord between Tiberius and his stepfather led to the former resigning the command in the beginning of 748. The dynastic interest did not allow comprehensive military operations to be entrusted to other generals than princes of the imperial house ; and after the death of Agrippa and Drusus, and the retirement of Tiberius, there were no able generals in that house. Certainly in the ten years, when governors with the ordinary powers bore sway in Illyricum and in Germany, the military operations

Retirement of Tiberius from the chief command. 6.

there may not have undergone so complete an interruption as they appear to us to have done, seeing that tradition, with its courtly colouring, does not in its report deal out equal measure to campaigns conducted by, and to those conducted without, princes ; but the arrest laid on them was unmistakable, and this itself was a retrogression.   Ahenobarbus, who, in consequence of his alliance by marriage with the imperial house—his wife was the daughter of a sister of Augustus—had greater freedom of action than other officers, and who in his Illyrian governorship had crossed the Elbe without encountering resistance, afterwards as governor of Germany reaped no laurels there.   Not merely the exasperation, but the courage also, of the Germans was again rising, and in the year 2 the country appears again in revolt, the Cherusci and the Chauci under arms.   Meanwhile at the imperial court death had interposed, and the removal of the young sons of Augustus had reconciled the latter and Tiberius.

Tiberius once more commander in chief. Scarcely was this reconciliation sealed by his adoption as a son and proclaimed (4), when Tiberius resumed the work where it had been broken off, and once more in this and in the two following summers (5-6) led the armies over the Rhine.   It was a repetition of, and an advance upon, the earlier campaigns.   The Cherusci were brought back to allegiance in the first campaign, the Chauci in the second ; the Cannenefates, adjoining the Batavi, and not inferior in bravery, the Bructeri, settled in the region of the sources of the Lippe and on the Ems, and various other cantons, submitted, as did also the powerful Langobardi, here first mentioned, dwelling at that time between the Weser and Elbe.   The first campaign led over the Weser into the interior ; in the second at the Elbe itself the Roman legions confronted the Germanic general levy on the other bank.   From the year 4 to 5 the Roman army took up, apparently for the first time, its winter quarters on German soil at Aliso.   All this was attained without any considerable conflicts ; the circumspect conduct of the war did not break resistance, but made it impossible.   This general aimed, not

at unfruitful laurels, but at lasting success. The naval
expedition, too, was repeated ; like the first campaign
of Drusus, the last of Tiberius was distinguished by the
navigating of the North Sea. But the Roman fleet
this time advanced farther ; the whole coast of the
North Sea, as far as the promontory of the Cimbri, that
is, the extremity of Jutland, was explored by it, and it
then, sailing up the Elbe, joined the land-army stationed
on the latter. The emperor had expressly forbidden the
crossing of the river ; but the tribes beyond the Elbe—the
Cimbri just named, in what is now Jutland, the Charudes
to the south of them, the powerful Semnones between
the Elbe and the Oder—were brought at least into relation
to the new neighbours.

It might have been thought that the goal was reached. Campaign
But one thing was still wanting to the establishment of against
Maro-
the iron ring which was to surround the Great Germany ; boduus.
it was the establishment of a connection between the
middle Danube and the upper Elbe—the occupation of the
old home of the Boii, which with its mountain-cincture
planted itself like a gigantic fortress between Noricum
and Germany. The king Maroboduus, of noble Marcomanian lineage, but in his youth by prolonged residence
in Rome introduced to its firmer military and political
organisation, had after his return home—perhaps during
the first campaign of Drusus and the transmigration,
thereby brought about, of the Marcomani from the Main
to the upper Elbe—not merely raised himself to be prince
of his people, but had also moulded his rule not after the
loose fashion of the Germanic kings, but, one might say,
after the model of the Augustan. Besides his own
people, he ruled over the powerful tribe of the Lugii
(in what is now Silesia), and the body of his clients must
have extended over the whole region of the Elbe, as the
Langobardi and the Semnones are described as subject
to him. Hitherto he had observed entire neutrality in
presence of the other Germans as of the Romans. He
gave perhaps to the fugitive enemies of the Romans an
asylum in his country, but he did not actively mingle in

the strife, not even when the Hermunduri had settlements assigned to them by the Roman governor on Marcomanian territory (p. 31), and when the left bank of the Elbe became subject to the Romans. He did not submit to them, but he bore all these occurrences without interrupting, on that account, his friendly relations with the Romans. By this certainly not magnanimous and scarce even so much as prudent policy, he had gained this much, that he was the last to be attacked ; after the completely successful Germanic campaigns in the years 4 and 5 his turn came. From two sides—from Germany and Noricum —the Roman armies advanced against the Bohemian mountain-circle ; Gaius Sentius Saturninus, advanced up the Main, clearing the dense forests from Spessart to the Fichtelgebirge with axe and fire ; while Tiberius in person, starting from Carnuntum, where the Illyrian legions had encamped during the winter of the years 5-6, advanced against the Marcomani. The two armies, amounting together to twelve legions, were even in number so superior as almost to double that of their opponents, whose fighting force was estimated at 70,000 infantry and 4000 horsemen. The cautious strategy of the general seemed on this occasion also to have quite ensured success, when a sudden incident interrupted the farther advance of the Romans.

Dalmato-Pannonian insurrection.

The Dalmatian tribes and the Pannonians, at least of the region of the Save, for a short time obeyed the Roman governors ; but they bore the new rule with an ever increasing grudge, above all on account of the taxes, to which they were unaccustomed, and which were relentlessly exacted. When Tiberius subsequently asked one of the leaders as to the grounds of the revolt, he answered that it had taken place because the Romans set not dogs and shepherds, but wolves, to guard their flocks. Now the legions from Dalmatia were brought to the Danube, and the men capable of arms were called out, in order to be sent thither to reinforce the armies. These troops made a beginning, and took up arms not for, but against, Rome. Their leader was one of the Daesitiatae (around

Serajevo), Bato.   The example was followed by the
Pannonians, under the leadership of two Breuci, another
Bato and Pinnes.   All Illyricum rose with unheard of
rapidity and unanimity.   The number of the insurgent
forces was estimated at 200,000 infantry and 9000
horsemen.   The levy for the auxiliary troops, which
had taken place more especially among the Pannonians
to a considerable extent, had diffused more widely a
knowledge of Roman warfare, along with the Roman
language and even Roman culture.   Those who had
served as Roman soldiers formed now the nucleus of the
insurrection.[1]   The Roman citizens settled or sojourning
in large number in the insurgent regions, the merchants,
and above all, the soldiers, were everywhere seized and
slain.   The independent tribes, as well as those of the
provinces, entered into the movement.   The princes of
the Thracians, entirely devoted to the Romans, certainly
brought their considerable and brave bands to the aid of
the Roman generals ; but from the other bank of the
Danube the Dacians, and with them the Sarmatae, broke
into Moesia.   The whole wide region of the Danube
seemed to have conspired to put an abrupt end to the
foreign rule.

The insurgents were not disposed to await attack, but
planned an invasion of Macedonia, and even of Italy.
The danger was serious ; the insurgents might, by crossing the Julian Alps, stand in a few days once more before
Aquileia and Tergeste—they had not yet forgotten the
way thither—and in ten days before Rome, as the
emperor himself expressed it in the senate, to make
sure at all events of its assent to the comprehensive and
urgent military preparations.   In the utmost haste new
forces were raised, and the towns more immediately

---

[1] This and not more is what
Velleius says (ii. 110) : *in omnibus
Pannoniis non disciplinae* (=military
training) *tantummodo, sed linguae quoque notitia Romanae, plerisque etiam
litterarum usus et familiaris animo-
rum erat exercitatio.*   These are the
same phenomena as are met with in
the case of the Cheruscan princes,
only in increased measure ; and they
are quite intelligible when we bear in
mind the Pannonian and Breucian
alae and *cohortes* raised by Augustus.

threatened were provided with garrisons ; in like manner whatever troops could be dispensed with were despatched to the threatened points.   The first to arrive at the spot was the governor of Moesia, Aulus Caecina Severus, and with him the Thracian king Rhoemetalces ; soon other troops followed from the transmarine provinces.   But above all Tiberius was obliged, instead of penetrating into Bohemia, to return to Illyricum.   Had the insurgents waited till the Romans were engaged in the struggle with Maroboduus, or had the latter made common cause with them, the position might have been a very critical one for the Romans.   But the former broke loose too early, and the latter, faithful to his system of neutrality, condescended just at this time to conclude peace with the Romans on the basis of the *status quo*.   Thus Tiberius had, no doubt, to send back the Rhine-legions, because Germany could not possibly be denuded of troops, but he could unite his Illyrian army with the troops arriving from Moesia, Italy, and Syria, and employ it against the insurgents.   In fact the alarm was greater than the danger.   The Dalmatians, indeed, broke repeatedly into Macedonia and pillaged the coast as far as Apollonia ; but there was no invasion of Italy, and the fire was soon confined to its original hearth.

Nevertheless, the work of the war was not easy ; here, as everywhere, the renewed overthrow of the subjects was more laborious than the subjugation itself.   Never in the Augustan period was such a body of troops ever united under the same command ; already in the first year of the war the army of Tiberius consisted of ten legions along with the corresponding auxiliary forces, and in addition numerous veterans who had again joined of their own accord and other volunteers, together about 120,000 men ; later he had fifteen legions united under his banners.[1]   In the first campaign (6 A.D.) the contest was

---

[1] If we assume that of the twelve legions who were on the march against Maroboduus (Tacitus, *Ann.* ii. 46), as many as we find soon after in Germany, that is, five, went to form the army there, the Illyrian army of Tiberius numbered seven, and the number of ten (Velleius, ii. 113) may fairly be referred to the contingents from Moesia and Italy,

waged with very varying fortune ; the large places, like Siscia and Sirmium, were successfully protected against the insurgents, but the Dalmatian Bato fought as obstinately and in part successfully against the governor of Pannonia, Marcus Valerius Messalla, the orator's son, as his Pannonian namesake against Aulus Caecina governor of Moesia. The petty warfare above all gave much trouble to the Roman troops. Nor did the following year (7), in which along with Tiberius his nephew the young Germanicus appeared on the scene of war, put an end to the ceaseless conflicts. It was not till the third campaign (8) that the Romans succeeded in subduing in the first instance the Pannonians, chiefly, as it would seem, through the circumstance that their leader, gained over by the Romans, induced his troops all and sundry to lay down their arms at the river Bathinus, and surrendered his colleague in the supreme command, Pinnes, to the Romans, for which he was recognised by them as prince of the Breuci. Punishment indeed soon befell the traitor ; his Dalmatian namesake caught him and had him executed, and once more the revolt blazed up among the Breuci ; but it was speedily extinguished again, and the Dalmatian was confined to the defence of his own home. There Germanicus and other leaders of division had in this, as in the following year (9), to sustain vehement conflicts in the several cantons ; in the latter year the Pirustae (on the borders of Epirus) and the canton to which the leader himself belonged, the Daesitiatae, were subdued, one bravely defended stronghold being reduced after another. Once more in the course of the summer Tiberius himself took the field, and set in motion all his fighting force against the remains of the insurrection. Even Bato, shut up by the Roman army in the strong Andetrium (Much, above

that of fifteen to the contingents from Egypt or Syria, and to the further levies in Italy, whence the newly raised legions went no doubt to Germany, but those thereby relieved went to the army of Tiberius. Velleius (ii. 112) speaks inaccurately, at the very beginning of the war, of five legions brought up by A. Caecina and Plautius Silvanus *ex transmarinis provinciis ;* firstly, the transmarine troops could not be at once on the spot, and secondly, the legions of Caecina were of course the Moesian. Comp. my commentary on the *Mon. Ancyr.* 2d ed. p. 71.

Salonae), his last place of refuge, gave up the cause as lost. He left the town, when he could not induce the desperadoes to submit, and yielded himself to the victor, with whom he found honourable treatment; he was relegated as a political prisoner to Ravenna, where he died. Without their leader the troops still for a time continued the vain struggle, till the Romans captured the fort by assault—it is probably this day, the 3d August, that is recorded in the Roman calendar as the anniversary of the victory achieved by Tiberius in Illyricum.

Dacian war of Lentulus.
Retribution fell also on the Dacians beyond the Danube. Probably at this time, after the Illyrian war was decided in favour of Rome, Gnaeus Lentulus led a strong Roman army across the Danube, reached as far as the Marisus (Marosch) and emphatically defeated them in their own country, which was then for the first time trodden by a Roman army. Fifty thousand captive Dacians were made to settle in Thrace.

Men of later times termed the "Batonian war" of the years 6-9 the most severe which Rome had to sustain against an external foe since that of Hannibal. It inflicted severe wounds on the Illyrian land; in Italy the joy over the victory was boundless when the young Germanicus brought the news of the decisive success to the capital. The exultation did not last long; almost simultaneously with the news of this success there came to Rome accounts of a defeat, such as reached the ears of Augustus but once in his reign of fifty years—a defeat which was still more significant in its consequences than in itself.

Germanic rising.
The state of things in the province of Germany has been already set forth. The recoil which follows on any foreign rule with the inevitableness of a natural event, and which had just set in in the Illyrian land, was in preparation also among the cantons of the middle Rhine. The remnants of the tribes settled immediately on the Rhine were indeed quite discouraged; but those dwelling farther back, especially the Cherusci, Chatti, Bructeri, Marsi, were less injuriously affected and by no means

powerless.   As always in such cases, there was formed in every canton a party of the compliant friends of the Romans, and a national party preparing in secret a renewed rising.   The soul of the latter was a young man of twenty-six years, of the Cheruscan princely house, Arminius son of Sigimer ; he and his brother Flavus had received from the emperor Augustus the gifts of Roman citizenship and of equestrian rank,[1] and both had fought with distinction as officers in the last Roman campaigns under Tiberius ; the brother was still serving in the Roman army and had established a home for himself in Italy.   Naturally Arminius also was regarded by the Romans as a man specially to be trusted ; the accusations, which his better informed countryman Segestes brought forward against him, availed not to shake this confidence in view of the well-known hostility subsisting between the two.   Of the further preparations we have no knowledge ; that the nobility and especially the noble youth took the side of the patriots, was a matter of course, and found clear expression in the fact that Segestes's own daughter, Thusnelda, in spite of the prohibition of her father, married Arminius, while her brother Segimundus and Segestes's brother Segimer, as well as his nephew Sesithacus, played a prominent part in the insurrection.   It had not a wide range, far less than that of the Illyrian rising ; it can scarcely in strictness be called a Germanic revolt ; the Batavi, the Frisii, the Chauci on the coast took no part in it, as little such of the Suebian tribes as were under Roman rule, still less king Maroboduus ; in reality only those Germans rose who had some years previously leagued themselves against Rome, and against whom the offensive of Drusus was primarily directed.   The Illyrian rising doubtless promoted the ferment in Germany, but

---

[1] Velleius (ii. 118) says so ; *adsiduus militiae nostrae prioris comes, iure etiam civitatis Romanae eius equestres consequens gradus ;* which coincides with the *ductor popularium* of Tacitus, *Ann.* ii. 10.   Such officers must have been of no infrequent occurrence at this time ; thus, there fought in the third campaign of Drusus *inter primores Chumstinctus et Avectius tribuni ex civitate Nerviorum* (Liv. *Ep.* 141), and under Germanicus Chariovalda *dux Batavorum* (Tac. *Ann.* ii. 11).

there is no trace of any thread of connection between the two similar and almost contemporary insurrections; had such a connection subsisted the Germans would hardly have waited to strike till the Pannonian rising had been overpowered and the very last strongholds in Dalmatia were surrendering. Arminius was the brave and shrewd, and above all things fortunate, leader in the conflict of despair over the lost national independence— nothing less, but also nothing more.

Varus.

It was more the fault of the Romans than the merit of the insurgents, if the plan of the latter succeeded. So far, certainly, the Illyrian war had an effect on Germany. The able generals, and to all appearance also the experienced troops, had been moved from the Rhine to the Danube. The Germanic army was apparently not diminished, but the greatest part of it consisted of new legions formed during the war. Still worse was its position as to leaders. The governor, Publius Quinctilius Varus,[1] was, no doubt, the husband of a niece of the emperor, and a man of ill-acquired, but princely, wealth and of princely arrogance, but inert in body and obtuse in mind, and without any military gifts or experience— one of those many Romans in high station who, in consequence of an adherence to the old mixture of administrative functions with those of higher command, wore the general's scarf after the model of Cicero. He knew not how to spare nor yet to see through the new subjects; oppression and exaction were practised, as had been the wont of his earlier governorship over the patient Syria; the headquarters swarmed with advocates and clients; and in grateful humility the conspirators especially received judgment and justice at his hands, while the net was being drawn more and more closely around the arrogant praetor.

---

[1] The effigy of Varus is shown on a copper çoin of the African town Achulla, struck under his proconsulate of Africa in the year 747-8, B.C. 7-6 (L. Müller, *Num. de l'ancienne Afrique*, ii. p. 44, comp. p. 52). The base which once supported the statue erected to him by the town of Pergamus has again been brought to light by the excavations there; the subscription runs : ὁ δῆμος [ἐτίμησεν] Πόπλιον Κοινκτίλιον Σέξτου υἱὸν Οὐάρ[ου] πάσης ἀρετῆ[ς ἔνεκα].

The position of the army was what was then the normal one.   There were at least five legions in the province, two of which had their winter-quarters at Mogontiacum, three in Vetera or else in Aliso.   The latter had taken up their summer encampment in the year 9 on the Weser.   The natural route of communication from the upper Lippe to the Weser leads over the low chain of heights of the Osning and of the Lippe Forest, which separates the valley of the Ems from that of the Weser, through the Dören defile into the valley of the Werra, which falls into the Weser at Rehme, not far from Minden. Here therefore, approximately, the legions of Varus at that time were encamped.   As a matter of course this summer camp was connected with Aliso, the base of the Roman position on the right bank of the Rhine, by a road supplied with depots.   The good season of the year came to its close, and they were making ready for the return march, when the news came that a neighbouring canton was in revolt ; and Varus resolved, instead of leading back the army by that depot-route, to take a circuit and by the way to bring back the rebels to allegiance.[1]   So they set out ; the army consisted, after numerous reductions, of three legions and nine divisions of troops of the second class, together about 20,000 men.[2]   When the

[1] The report of Dio, the only one which hands down to us a somewhat connected view of this catastrophe, explains the course of it sufficiently, if we only take further into account —what Dio certainly does not bring into prominence — the general relation of the summer and winter camps, and thereby answer the question justly put by Ranke (*Weltgeschichte*, iii. 2, 275), how the whole army could have marched against a local insurrection.   The narrative of Florus by no means rests on sources originally different, as that scholar assumes, but simply on the dramatic accumulation of motives for action, such as is characteristic of all historians of this type.   The peaceful dispensing of justice by Varus and

the storming of the camp are both known to the better tradition, and that in their causal connection.   The ridiculous representation of the Germans breaking in at all the gates into the camp, while Varus is sitting on the judgment-seat and the herald is summoning the parties before him, is not tradition, but a picture manufactured from it.   That this is in utter antagonism to the description by Tacitus of the three bivouacs, as well as to sound reason, is obvious.

[2] The normal strength of the three *alae* and the six *cohortes* is not to be calculated exactly, inasmuch as among them there may have been double divisions (*miliariae*) ; but the army cannot have numbered much over 20,000 men.   On the other hand, there ap-

army had removed to a sufficient distance from its line of communication, and penetrated far enough into the pathless country, the confederates in the neighbouring cantons rose, cut down the small divisions of troops stationed among them, and broke forth on all sides from the defiles and woods against the army of Varus on its march. Arminius and the most notable leaders of the patriots had remained to the last moment at the Roman headquarters to make Varus secure. On the very evening before the day on which the insurrection burst forth they had supped in the general's tent with Varus; and Segestes, when announcing the impending outbreak of the revolt, had adjured the general to order the immediate arrest of himself as well as of the accused, and to await the justification of his charge by the facts. The confidence of Varus was not to be shaken. Arminius rode away from table to the insurgents, and was next day before the ramparts of the Roman camp. The military situation was neither better nor worse than that of the army of Drusus before the battle at Arbalo, and than had, under similar circumstances, often been the plight of Roman armies. The communications were for the moment lost; the army, encumbered with heavy baggage in a pathless country and at a bad rainy season in autumn, was separated by several days' march from Aliso; the assailants were beyond doubt far superior in number to the Romans. In such cases it is the solid quality of the troops that is decisive; and, if the decision here for once was unfavourable to the Romans, the result was doubtless mostly due to the inexperience of the young soldiers, and especially to the want of head and of courage in the general. After the attack took place the Roman army continued its march, now beyond doubt in the direction of Aliso, amidst constantly increasing pressure and increasing demoralisation. Even the higher officers failed in part to do their

pears no reason for assuming a material difference of the effective strength from the normal. The numerous detachments which are mentioned (Dio, lvi. 19) serve to account for the comparatively small number of the *auxilia*, which were always by preference employed for this duty.

duty ; one of them rode away from the field of battle with all the cavalry, and left the infantry to sustain the conflict alone.   The first to despair utterly was the general himself ; wounded in the struggle, he put himself to death before the matter was finally decided, so early indeed, that his followers still made an attempt to burn the dead body and to withdraw it from being dishonoured by the enemy. A number of the superior officers followed his example. Then, when all was lost, the leader that was left surrendered, and thereby put out of his own power what remained open to these last—an honourable soldier's death. Thus perished the Germanic army in one of the valleys of the mountain-range that bounds the region of Münster, in the autumn of the year 9 A.D.[1]   The eagles fell—all three

[1] As Germanicus, coming from the Ems, lays waste the territory between the Ems and Lippe, that is, the region of Münster, and not far from it lies the *Teutoburgiensis saltus*, where Varus's army perished (Tacitus, *Ann.* i. 61), it is most natural to understand this description, which does not suit the flat Münster region, of the range bounding the Münster region on the north-east, the Osning ; but it may also be deemed applicable to the Wiehen mountains somewhat farther to the north, parallel with the Osning, and stretching from Minden to the source of the Hunte.   We do not know at what point on the Weser the summer camp stood ; but in accordance with the position of Aliso near Paderborn, and with the connections subsisting between this and the Weser, it was probably somewhere near Minden.   The direction of the march on the return may have been any other excepting only the nearest way to Aliso ; and the catastrophe consequently occurred not on the military line of communication between Minden and Paderborn itself, but at a greater or less distance from it.   Varus may have marched from Minden somewhat in the direction of Osnabrück, then after the attack have attempted from thence to reach Paderborn, and have met with his end on this march in one of those two ranges of hills.   For centuries there have been found in the district of Venne at the source of the Hunte a surprisingly large number of Roman gold, silver, and copper coins, such as circulated in the time of Augustus, while later coins hardly occur there at all (comp. the proofs in Paul Höfer, *der Feldzug des Germanicus im Jahre* 16, Gotha, 1884, p. 82, f.) The coins thus found cannot belong to one store of coins on account of their scattered occurrence and of the difference of metals, nor to a centre of traffic on account of their proximity as regards time ; they look quite like the leavings of a great extirpated army, and the accounts before us as to the battle of Varus may be reconciled with this locality.   As to the year of the catastrophe there should never have been any dispute ; the shifting of it to the year 10 is a mere mistake.   The season of the year is in some measure determined by the fact that between the arrangement to celebrate the Illyrian victory and the arrival of the unfortunate news in Rome there lay only five days, and that arrangement probably had in view the victory of 3d Aug., though it did not immediately follow on the latter.   Accordingly the defeat must have taken place somewhere in Sep-

of them—into the enemy's hand.   Not a division cut its way through, not even those horsemen who had left their comrades in the lurch ; only a few who were isolated and dispersed were able to effect their escape.   The captives, especially the officers and the advocates, were fastened to the cross, or buried alive, or bled under the sacrificial knife of the German priests.   The heads cut off were nailed as a token of victory to the trees of the sacred grove.   Far and wide the land rose against the foreign rule ; it was hoped that Maroboduus would join the movement; the Roman posts and roads on the whole right bank of the Rhine fell without further trouble into the power of the victors. Only in Aliso, the brave commandant Lucius Caedicius, not an officer, but a veteran soldier, offered a resolute resistance, and his archers were enabled to make the encampment before the walls so annoying to the Germans, who possessed no weapons for distant fighting, that they converted the siege into a blockade.   When the last stores of the besieged were exhausted, and still no relief came, Caedicius broke out one dark night; and this remnant of the army, though burdened with numerous women and children, and suffering severe losses through the assaults of the Germans, in reality ultimately reached the camp at Vetera.   Thither also the two legions stationed in Mentz under Lucius Nonius Asprenas had gone on the news of the disaster.   The resolute defence of Aliso, and the rapid intervention of Asprenas, hindered the Germans from following up the victory on the left bank of the Rhine, and perhaps the Gauls from rising against Rome.

Tiberius
again on the
Rhine.
The defeat was soon compensated, in so far as the Rhine army was immediately not simply made up to its strength, but considerably reinforced.   Tiberius once more took up the supreme command, and though for the year following on the battle of Varus (10) the history of the war had no combats to record, it is probable that arrangements were then made for the occupation of the Rhine-

tember or October, which also accords with the circumstance that the
last march of Varus was evidently
the march back from the summer to
the winter camp.

frontier by eight legions, and simultaneously for the division of this command into that of the upper army, with Mentz as its headquarters, and that of the lower with the head-quarters at Vetera, an arrangement, as a whole, which thereupon remained normal for centuries. It could not but be expected that this increase of the army of the Rhine would be followed by the energetic resumption of operations on the right bank. The Romano-German conflict was not a conflict between two powers equal in the political balance, in which the defeat of the one might justify the conclusion of an unfavourable peace ; it was the conflict of a great civilised and organised state against a brave but, in a political and military aspect, barbarous nation, in which the ultimate result was settled from the first, and an isolated failure in the plan as sketched might as little produce any change as the ship gives up its voyage because a gust of wind drives it out of its course. But it was otherwise. Tiberius, doubtless, went across the Rhine in the following year (11), but this expedition did not resemble the former one. He remained during the summer on that side, and celebrated the emperor's birth-day there, but the army kept to the immediate neighbour-hood of the Rhine, and of expeditions on the Weser and on the Elbe there was nothing said. Evidently the object was only to show to the Germans that the Romans still knew how to find the way into their country, and per-haps also to make such arrangements on the right bank of the Rhine as the change of policy required.

The great command embracing both armies was re-tained, and retained accordingly in the imperial house. *Germani-cus on the Rhine.* Germanicus had already exercised it in the year 11 along with Tiberius ; in the following year (12), when the administration of the consulate detained him in Rome, Tiberius commanded alone on the Rhine ; with the begin-ning of the year 13 Germanicus took up the sole command. The state of things was regarded as one of war with the Germans ; but these were years of inaction.[1]

---

[1] Tacitus, *Ann.* I. 9, and Dio, lvi. 26, attest the continuance of the state of war ; but nothing at all is reported from the nominal campaigns

The fiery and ambitious hereditary prince bore with reluctance the constraint imposed on him, and we can understand how, as an officer, he should not forget the three eagles in the hands of the enemy, and how, as the son of Drusus, he should wish to re-erect his structure that had been destroyed. Soon the opportunity presented itself, and he took it. On the 19th August of the year 14, the emperor Augustus died. The first change in the throne of the new monarchy did not pass over without a crisis, and Germanicus had opportunity of proving by deeds to his father that he was disposed to maintain allegiance to him. But at the same time he found in it warrant for resuming, even unbidden, the long-wished-for invasion of Germany; he declared that he had by this fresh campaign to repress the not inconsiderable ferment that had been called forth among the legions upon the change of sovereign. Whether this was a real reason or a pretext we know not, and perhaps he did not himself know. The commandant of the Rhine army could not be debarred from crossing the frontier anywhere, and it always to a certain degree depended on himself how far he should proceed against the Germans. Perhaps too, he believed that he was acting in the spirit of the new ruler, who had at least as much claim as his brother to the name of conqueror of Germany, and whose announced appearance in the camp on the Rhine might, doubtless, be conceived of, as though he were coming to resume the conquest of Germany broken off at the bidding of Augustus.

Renewed offensive.

However this may be, the offensive beyond the Rhine began anew. Even in the autumn of the year 14,

---

of the summers of 12, 13, and 14, and the expedition of the autumn of 14 appears as the first undertaken by Germanicus. It is true that Germanicus had been proclaimed as Imperator probably even in the lifetime of Augustus (*Mon. Ancyr.* p. 17); but there is nothing to hinder our referring this to the campaign of the year 11, in which Germanicus commanded with proconsular power alongside of Tiberius (Dio, lvi. 25). In the year 12 he was in Rome for the administration of the consulate, which he retained throughout the year, and which was still at that time treated in earnest; this explains why Tiberius, as has now been proved (Hermann Schulz, *Quaest. Ovidianae*, Greifswald, 1883, p. 15), still went to Germany in the year 12, and resigned his Rhenish command only at the beginning of the year 13, on the celebration of the Pannonian victory.

Germanicus in person led detachments of all the legions at Vetera over the Rhine, and penetrated up the Lippe pretty far into the interior, laying waste the country far and wide, putting to death the natives, and destroying the temples, such as that of Tanfana held in high honour. Those assailed—chiefly Bructeri, Tubantes, and Usipes,—sought to prepare the fate of Varus for the crown-prince on his way home ; but the attack recoiled before the energetic bearing of the legions. As this advance met with no censure, but on the contrary, thanks and marks of honour were decreed to the general for it, he went farther. In the opening of the year 15 he assembled his main force, in the first instance on the middle Rhine, and advanced in person from Mentz against the Chatti as far as the upper confluents of the Weser, while the lower army, farther to the north, attacked the Cherusci and the Marsi. There was a certain justification for this proceeding in the fact that the Cherusci favourably disposed towards Rome, who had, under the immediate impression of the disaster of Varus, been obliged to join the patriots, were now again at open variance with the much stronger national party, and invoked the intervention of Germanicus. He was actually successful in liberating Segestes, the friend of the Romans, when hard pressed by his countrymen, and at the same time in getting possession of his daughter, the wife of Arminius. Segestes' brother Segimerus, once the leader of the patriots by the side of Arminius, submitted. The internal dissensions of the Germans once more paved the way for the foreign rule. In the very same year Germanicus undertook his main expedition to the region of the Ems ; Caecina marched from Vetera to the upper Ems, while he in person went thither with the fleet from the mouth of the Rhine ; the cavalry moved along the coast through the territory of the faithful Frisians. When reunited the Romans laid waste the country of the Bructeri and the whole territory between the Ems and Lippe, and thence made an expedition to the disastrous spot where, six years before, the army of Varus had perished, to erect a monument to their fallen comrades. On their farther advance the Roman cavalry were allured by Arminius and the exasperated hosts of the patriots into an ambush, and would have been destroyed had not the infantry come up and prevented greater mischief. More serious dangers attended the return homeward from the Ems, which followed at first the same routes as the march thither.

Retreat of Caecina. The cavalry arrived at the winter camp uninjured. Seeing that the fleet was not sufficient for conveying the infantry of four legions, owing to the difficulty of navigation—it was about the time of the autumnal equinox—Germanicus disembarked two of them and made them return along the shore ; but inadequately acquainted with the ebbing and flowing of the tide at this season of the year, they lost their baggage and ran the risk of being drowned *en masse*. The retreat of the four legions of Caecina from the Ems to the Rhine resembled exactly that of Varus ; indeed, the difficult, marshy country offered perhaps still greater difficulties than the defiles of the wooded hills. The whole mass of natives, with the two princes of the Cherusci, Arminius and his highly esteemed uncle Inguiomerus, at their head, threw themselves on the retreating troops in the sure hope of preparing for them the same fate, and filled the morasses and woods all around. But the old general, experienced in forty years' of war service, remained cool even in the utmost peril, and kept his despairing and famishing men firmly in hand. Yet even he might not perhaps have been able to avert the mischief but for the circumstance that, after a successful attack during the march, in which the Romans lost a great part of their cavalry and almost the whole baggage, the Germans, sure of victory and eager for spoil, in opposition to Arminius' advice, followed the other leader, and instead of further surrounding the enemy, attempted directly to storm the camp. Caecina allowed the Germans to come up to the ramparts, but then burst forth from all posterns and gates with such vehemence upon the assailants that they suffered a severe defeat, and in consequence of it the further retreat took place without material hindrance. Those at the Rhine had already given up the army as lost, and were on the point of casting off the bridge at Vetera, to prevent the Germans at least from penetrating into Gaul ; it was only the resolute remonstrance of a woman, the wife of Germanicus and daughter of Agrippa, which frustrated the desperate and disgraceful resolve.

The resumption of the subjugation of Germany thus began not quite successfully. The territory between the Rhine and Weser had indeed been again trodden and traversed, but the Romans had no decisive results to show, and the enormous loss in material, particularly in horses, was sorely felt, so that, as in the times of Scipio, the towns of Italy and of the western provinces took part in patriotic contributions to make up for what was lost.

For the next campaign (16) Germanicus changed his plan of warfare. He attempted the subjugation of Germany on the basis of the North Sea and the fleet, partly because the tribes on the coast, the Batavi, Frisians, and Chauci, adhered more or less to the Romans, partly in order to shorten the marches—in which much time was spent and much loss incurred—from the Rhine to the Weser and Elbe and back again. After he had employed this spring, like the previous one, for rapid advances on the Main and on the Lippe, he, in the beginning of summer, embarked his whole army at the mouth of the Rhine in the powerful transport-fleet of 1000 sail which had meanwhile been made ready, and actually arrived without loss at the mouth of the Ems, where the fleet remained. Thence he advanced, as may be conjectured, up the Ems as far as the mouth of the Haase, and then along the latter as far up as the Werra-valley, and through this to the Weser. By this means the carrying of the army, 80,000 strong, through the Teutoburg Forest, which was attended with great difficulties, particularly as to provisions, was avoided. A secure reserve for supplies was furnished in the camp beside the fleet, and the Cherusci on the right bank of the Weser were assailed in flank instead of in front. Here the Romans encountered the levy *en*

Campaign of the year 16.

masse of the Germans, again led by the two chiefs of the
patriot party, Arminius and Inguiomerus. What warlike
resources were at their disposal is shown by the fact that
on two occasions, one shortly after the other, in the
Cheruscan country—first on the Weser itself and then
somewhat farther inland[1]—they fought in the open field
against the whole Roman army, and in both hardly
contested the victory. The latter certainly fell to the
Romans, and of the German patriots a considerable
number were left on the fields of battle. No prisoners
were taken, and both sides fought with extreme exasperation. The second tropaeum of Germanicus spoke of
the overthrow of all the Germanic tribes between the
Rhine and Elbe ; the son placed this campaign of his
alongside of the brilliant campaigns of his father, and
reported to Rome that in the next campaign he should
have the subjugation of Germany complete. But Arminius
escaped, although wounded, and continued still at the
head of the patriots ; and an unforeseen mischief marred
the success won by arms. On the return home, which
the greater part of the legions made by sea, the transport-
fleet encountered the autumn storms of the North Sea.
The vessels were dashed on all sides upon the islands of
the North Sea, and as far as the British coasts. A great
portion were destroyed, and those that escaped had for
the most part to throw horses and baggage overboard,
and to be glad of saving their bare life. The loss of
vessels was, as in the times of the Punic war, equivalent
to a defeat. Germanicus himself, cast adrift alone with
the admiral's ship on the desolate shore of the Chauci,
was in despair at this misfortune, and on the point of
seeking his death in that ocean the assistance of which
he had at the beginning of this campaign invoked so

---

[1] The hypothesis of Schmidt (*West-
fäl. Zeitschrift*, xx. p. 301)—that the
first battle was fought on the Idis-
tavisian field somewhere near Bücke-
burg, and the second, on account of
the morasses mentioned on the occasion, perhaps on the Steinhudersee,
near the village of Bergkirchen, which
lies to the south of this—will not be
far removed from the truth, and may
at least help us to realise the matter.
In this, as in most of the accounts of
battles by Tacitus, we must despair
of reaching an assured result.

earnestly and so vainly. Doubtless afterwards the loss of men proved not to be quite so great as it had at first appeared, and some effective blows which the general, on his return to the Rhine, inflicted on the nearest barbarians, raised the sunken courage of the troops. But, taken as a whole, the campaign of the year 16, as compared with that of the preceding year, ended in more brilliant victories doubtless, but also in much more serious loss.

The recall of Germanicus was at the same time the abolition of the command-in-chief of the Rhenish army. The mere division of the command put an end to the conduct of the war as heretofore pursued ; the circumstance that Germanicus was not merely recalled, but obtained no successor, was tantamount to ordaining the defensive on the Rhine. Thus the campaign of the year 16 was the last which the Romans waged in order to subdue Germany and to transfer the boundary of the empire from the Rhine to the Elbe. That this was the aim of the campaigns of Germanicus is shown by their very course, and by the trophy that celebrated the frontier of the Elbe. The re-establishment, too, of the military works on the right bank of the Rhine, of the forts of the Taunus, as well as of the stronghold of Aliso and the line connecting it with Vetera, belonged only in part to such an occupation of the right bank as was in keeping with the restricted plan of operations after the battle of Varus ; in fact it had a far wider scope. But the designs of the general were not, or not quite, those of the emperor. It is more than probable that Tiberius from the outset allowed rather than sanctioned the enterprises of Germanicus on the Rhine, and it is certain that he wished to put an end to them by recalling him in the winter of 16-17. Beyond doubt, at the same time, a good part of what had been attained was given up, and in particular the garrison was withdrawn from Aliso. As Germanicus, even in the following year, found not a stone left of the memorial of victory erected in the Teutoburg Forest, so the results of his victories disappeared like a flash of lightning into the water, and none of his successors continued the building on this basis.

The altered situation.

Motives for the change of policy.   If Augustus gave up the conquered Germany as lost after the battle of Varus, and if Tiberius now, when the conquest had once more been taken in hand, ordered it to be broken off, we are well entitled to ask, What motives guided the two notable rulers in this course, and what was the significance of these important events for the general policy of the empire ?

The battle of Varus is an enigma, not in a military but in a political point of view—not in its course, but in its consequences. Augustus was not wrong when he demanded back his lost legions, not from the enemy nor from fate, but from the general ; it was a disaster such as unskilled leaders of division from time to time bring about for every state. We have difficulty in conceiving that the destruction of an army of 20,000 men without further direct military consequences should have given a decisive turn to the policy at large of a judiciously governed universal empire. And yet the two rulers bore that defeat with a patience as unexampled as it was critical and hazardous for the position of the government in relation to the army and to its neighbours ; they allowed the conclusion of peace with Maroboduus, which, beyond doubt, was meant to be in strictness a mere armistice, to become withal definitive, and made no further attempt to get the upper valley of the Elbe into their hands. It must have been no easy thing for Tiberius to see the collapse of the great structure begun in concert with his brother, and after the latter's death almost completed by himself ; the energetic zeal with which, as soon as he had again entered on the government, he took up the Germanic war which he had begun ten years ago, enables us to measure what this self-denial must have cost him. If, nevertheless, the self-denial was persevered in not merely by Augustus, but also after his death by Tiberius himself, there is no other reason to be found for it than that they recognised the plans pursued by them for twenty years for the changing of the boundary to the north as incapable of execution, and the subjugation and mastery of the region between the Rhine and the

Elbe appeared to them to transcend the resources of
the empire.

If the previous boundary of the empire ran from the
middle Danube up to its source and to the upper Rhine,
and thence down that river, it was, at all events, materially shortened and improved by being shifted to the
Elbe, which in its head-waters approaches the middle
Danube, and to its course throughout ; in which case,
probably, besides the evident military gain, there came
into view also the political consideration that the keeping
of the great commands as far as possible remote from
Rome and Italy was one of the leading maxims of the
Augustan policy, and an army of the Elbe would hardly
have played such a part in the further development of
Rome as the armies of the Rhine but too soon undertook.
The preliminary conditions to this end, the overthrow of
the Germanic patriot-party and of the Suebian king in
Bohemia, were no easy tasks ; nevertheless they had
already once stood on the verge of succeeding, and with
a right conduct of the war these results could not fail to
be reached. But it was another question whether, after the
institution of the Elbe frontier, the troops could be withdrawn from the intervening region ; this question had
been raised in a very serious way for the Roman government by the Dalmato-Pannonian war. If the mere impending movement of the Roman Danube-army into
Bohemia had called forth a popular rising in Illyricum,
that was only put down by the exertion of all their military resources after a four years' conflict, this wide region
might not be left to itself either at the time or for many
years to come. Similar, doubtless, was the state of the
case on the Rhine. The Roman public was wont, indeed,
to boast that the state held all Gaul in subjection by
means of the garrison at Lyons 1200 strong ; but the
government could not forget that the two great armies on
the Rhine not merely warded off the Germans, but also
had a very material bearing on the Gallic cantons that were
not at all distinguished by submissiveness. Stationed on
the Weser or even on the Elbe, they would not have ren-

The Elbe
frontier.

dered this service in equal measure; and to keep both the Rhine and the Elbe occupied was beyond their power.

And its abandon- ment. Thus Augustus might well come to the conclusion that with the strength of the army as it then stood—considerably increased indeed of late, but still far below the measure of what was really requisite—that great regulation of the frontier was not practicable ; the question was thus converted from a military one into one of internal policy, and especially into one of finance.   Neither Augustus nor Tiberius ventured to increase still further the expense of the army.   We may blame them for not doing so.   The paralysing double blow of the Illyrian and the Germanic insurrections with their grave disasters, the great age and the enfeebled vigour of the ruler, the increasing disinclination of Tiberius for initiating any fresh and great undertaking, and above all any deviation from the policy of Augustus, doubtless co-operated to induce this result, and did so, perhaps, to the injury of the state.   By the demeanour of Germanicus, not to be approved but easily to be explained, we perceive how keenly the soldiers and the youth felt the abandonment of the new province of Germany.   In the poor attempt to retain, at least nominally, the lost Germany with the help of the two German cantons on the left of the Rhine, and in the ambiguous and uncertain words with which Augustus himself in his account of the case lays or forgoes claim to Germany as Roman, we discern how perplexed was the attitude of the government towards public opinion in this matter.   The grasping at the frontier of the Elbe was a mighty, perhaps a too bold stroke, undertaken possibly by Augustus—who did not generally soar so high—only after years of hesitation, and doubtless not without the determining influence of the younger stepson who was in closest intercourse with him.   But to retrace too bold a step is, as a rule, not a mending of the mistake, but a second mistake. The monarchy had need of warlike honour unstained and of unconditional warlike success, in quite another way than the former burgomaster-government ; the absence of the numbers 17, 18, and 19—never filled up since the battle

of Varus—in the roll of regiments, was little in keeping with military prestige, and the peace with Maroboduus,
on the basis of the *status quo*, could not be construed by
the most loyal rhetoric into a success.   The assumption
that Germanicus began those far-reaching enterprises in
opposition to the strict orders of his government is forbidden by his whole political position ; but the reproach that
he made use of his double position, as supreme commander
of the first army of the Rhine and as future successor
to the throne, in order to carry out at his own hand his
politico-military plans, is one from which he can as little
be exempted as the emperor from the no less grave reproach
of having started back perhaps from the forming, or perhaps only from the clear expression and the sharp execution, of his own resolves.   If Tiberius at least allowed the
resumption of the offensive, he must have felt how much
was to be said for a more vigorous policy ; he may perhaps, as over-considerate people do, have left the decision,
so to speak, to destiny, till at length the repeated and
severe misfortunes of the crown-prince once more justified
the policy of despair.   It was not easy for the government
to bid an army halt which had brought back two of the
three lost eagles ; but it was done.   Whatever may have
been the real and the personal motives, we stand here at
a turning-point in national destinies.   History, too, has its
flow and its ebb ; here, after the tide of Roman sway over
the world has attained its height, the ebb sets in.   Northward of Italy the Roman rule had for a few years reached
as far as the Elbe ; since the battle of Varus its bounds
were the Rhine and the Danube.   A legend—but an old
one—relates that the first conqueror of Germany, Drusus,
on his last campaign at the Elbe, saw a vision of a
gigantic female figure of Germanic mould, that called
to him in his own language the word "Back !"   The word
was not spoken, but it was fulfilled.

Nevertheless the defeat of the Augustan policy, as
the peace with Maroboduus and the sufferance of the
Teutoburg disaster may well be termed, was hardly a victory of the Germans.   After the battle with Varus the

Germans
against
Germans.

hope must doubtless have passed through the minds of the best, that a certain union of the nation would accrue from the glorious victory of the Cherusci and their allies, and from the retiring of the enemy in the west as in the south.   Perhaps in these very crises the feeling of unity may have dawned on the Saxons and Suebians formerly confronting each other as strangers.   The fact that the Saxons sent from the battle-field the head of Varus to the king of the Suebians, can be nothing but the savage expression of the thought that the hour had come for all Germans to throw themselves in joint onset upon the Roman empire, and thus to secure the frontier and the freedom of their land, as they could alone be secured, by striking down the hereditary foe in his own home.   But the cultured man and the politic king accepted the gift of the insurgents only in order to forward the head to the emperor Augustus for burial ; he did nothing for, but also nothing against, the Romans, and persevered unshaken in his neutrality.   Immediately after the death of Augustus there were fears at Rome of the Marcomani invading Raetia, but apparently without cause ; and when Germanicus thereupon resumed the offensive against the Germans from the Rhine, the mighty king of the Marcomani looked on inactive.   This policy of finesse or of cowardice dug its own grave amidst a Germanic world fiercely excited, and drunk with patriotic successes and hopes.   The more remote Suebian tribes but loosely connected with the empire, the Semnones, Langobardi, and Gothones, declared off from the king, and made common cause with the Saxon patriots ; it is not improbable that the considerable forces, which were evidently at the disposal of Arminius and Inguiomerus in the conflicts with Germanicus, flowed to them in great part from these quarters.

Fall of Maro-boduus.

Soon afterwards, when the Roman attack was suddenly broken off, the patriots turned (17) to assail Maroboduus, perhaps to assail the kingly office in general, at least as the latter administered it on the Roman model.[1]

---

[1] The statement of Tacitus (*Ann.* ii. 45), that this was properly a war of the republicans against the monarchists, is probably not free from a

But even among themselves divisions had set in ; the two nearly related Cheruscan princes, who in the last struggles had led the patriots, if not victoriously, at any rate bravely and honourably, and had hitherto constantly fought shoulder to shoulder, no longer stood together in this war. The uncle Inguiomerus no longer tolerated his being second to his nephew, and at the outbreak of the war passed to the side of Maroboduus. Thus matters came to a decisive battle between Germans and Germans, nay, between the same tribes; for Suebi as well as Cherusci fought in both armies. Long the conflict wavered ; both armies had learned from the Roman tactics, and on both sides the passion and the exasperation were alike. Arminius did not achieve a victory properly so called, but his antagonist left to him the field of battle ; and, as Maroboduus seemed to have fared the worst, those who had hitherto adhered to him left him, and he found himself confined to his own kingdom. When he asked for Roman aid against his overpowerful countrymen, Tiberius reminded him of his attitude after the battle of Varus, and replied that now the Romans in turn would remain neutral. His fate was rapidly decided. In the very following year (18) he was surprised in his royal abode itself by a prince of the Gothones, Catualda, to whom he had formerly given personal offence, and who had thereupon revolted from him with the other non-Bohemian Suebi ; and, abandoned by his own people, he with difficulty made his escape to the Romans, who granted to him the asylum which he sought—he died many years afterwards, as a Roman pensioner, at Ravenna.

Thus the opponents as well as the rivals of Arminius had become refugees, and the Germanic nation looked to none else than to him. But this greatness was his danger and his destruction. His own countrymen, especially his own clan, accused him of going the way of Maroboduus and of desiring to be not merely the first, but also the

End of Arminius.

wish to transfer Hellenico - Roman views to the very different Germanic world. So far as the war had an ethico-political tendency, it would be called forth not by the *nomen regis*, as Tacitus says, but by the *certum imperium visque regia* of Velleius (ii. 108).

lord and the king of the Germans—whether with reason or not, and whether, if he wished this, he did not perhaps wish what was right, who can say ? The result was a civil war between him and these representatives of popular freedom ; two years after the banishment of Maroboduus he too, like Caesar, fell by the dagger of nobles of republican sentiments near to his person. His wife Thusnelda and his son born in captivity, Thumelicus, on whom he had never set eyes, marched at the triumph of Germanicus (26th May, 17) among the other Germans of rank, in chains to the Capitol ; the old Segestes was for his fidelity to the Romans provided with a place of honour, whence he might look on at the public entry of his daughter and his grandson. They all died within the Roman empire ; with Maroboduus the wife and son of his antagonist met in the exile of Ravenna. When Tiberius remarked at the recall of Germanicus that there was no need to wage war against the Germans, and that they would of themselves take care to do what was requisite for Rome, he knew his adversaries ; in this, at all events, history has pronounced him right. But to the high-spirited man who, at the age of six-and-twenty, had released his Saxon home from the Italian foreign rule, who thereafter had been general as well as soldier in a seven years' struggle for that freedom regained, who had staked not merely person and life, but also wife and child for his nation, to fall at the age of thirty-seven by an assassin's hand— to this man his people gave, what it was in their power to give, an eternal monument in heroic song.

CHAPTER II.

SPAIN.

THE accidents of external policy caused the Romans to establish themselves on the Pyrenaean peninsula earlier than in any other part of the transmarine mainland, and to institute there two standing commands. There, too, the republic had not, as in Gaul and Illyricum, confined itself to subduing the coasts of the Italian sea, but had rather from the outset, after the precedent of the Barcides, contemplated the conquest of the whole peninsula. With the Lusitanians (in Portugal and Estremadura) the Romans had fought from the time that they called themselves masters of Spain; the "more remote province" had been instituted, strictly speaking, against these tribes and simultaneously with the "nearer" one; the Callaeci (Gallicia) became subject to the Romans a century before the battle of Actium; shortly before that battle the subsequent dictator Caesar had, in his first campaign, carried the Roman arms as far as Brigantium (Corunna), and consolidated afresh the annexation of this region to the more remote province. Then, in the years between the death of Caesar and the sole rule of Augustus, there was unceasing warfare in the north of Spain; no fewer than six governors in this short time won triumphs there, and perhaps the subjugation of the northern slope of the Pyrenees was effected chiefly in this epoch.[1] The wars with the

[1] There triumphed over Spain— apart from the doubtless political triumph of Lepidus—in 718 Cn. Domitius Calvinus (consul in 714), in 720 C. Norbanus Flaccus (consul in 716), between 720 and 725 L. Marcius Philippus (consul in 716) and Appius Claudius Pulcher (consul in

36.
40.

34.
38, 34, 29.
38.

cognate Aquitanians on the north side of the mountains,
which fall within the same epoch, and the last of which
27. was victoriously ended in the year 727, must stand in
connection with these events.　On the reorganising of the
27. administrative arrangements in 727 the peninsula went
to Augustus, because there was a prospect of extensive
military operations there, and it needed a permanent garrison.　Although the southern third of the more remote
province, thenceforth named from the river Baetis (Guadalquivir) was soon given back to the government of the
senate,[1] by far the greater portion of the peninsula
remained constantly under imperial administration, including the greater part of the more remote province, Lusitania and Callaecia,[2] and the whole of the large nearer one.
Immediately after the institution of the new supreme control Augustus resorted in person to Spain, with a view, in
26, 25. his two years' stay (728, 729), to organise the new administration, and to direct the occupation of the portions
of the country not yet subject.　This he did from Tarraco
as his headquarters, and it was at that time that the
seat of government of the nearer province was transferred
from New Carthage to Tarraco, after which town this
province is thenceforth usually named.　While it appeared

38, 28. 716), in 726 C. Calvisius Sabinus
39, 26. (consul in 715), and in 728 Sex. Ap-
29. puleius (consul in 725).　The historians mention only the victory
achieved over the Cerretani (near
Puycerda in the eastern Pyrenees) by
Calvinus (Dio, xlviii. 42 ; comp.
Velleius, ii. 78, and the coin of Sabinus with *Osca*, Eckhel, v. 203).

[1] As Augusta Emerita in Lusi-
25. tania only became a colony in 729
(Dio, liii. 26), and this cannot well
have been left out of account in the
list of the provinces in which Augustus founded colonies (*Mon. Ancyr.* p.
119, comp. p. 222), the separation of
Lusitania and Hispania Ulterior must
not have taken place till after the
Cantabrian war.

[2] Callaecia was not merely occupied from the Ulterior province, but
must still in the earlier time of Augus-

tus have belonged to Lusitania, just
as Asturias also must have been at
first attached to this province.　Otherwise the narrative in Dio, liv. 5, is
not intelligible ; T. Carisius, the
builder of Emerita, is evidently the
governor of Lusitania, C. Furnius the
governor of the Tarraconensis.　With
this agrees the parallel representation
in Florus, ii. 33, for the *Drigaecini* of
the MSS. are certainly the βριγαικινοί,
whom Ptolemy, ii. 6, 29, adduces
among the Asturians.　Therefore
Agrippa, in his measurements, com-
prehends Lusitania with Asturia and
Callaecia (Plin. *H. N.* iv. 22, 118), and
Strabo (iii. 4, 20, p. 166) designates
the Callaeci as formerly termed Lusi-
tani.　Variations in the demarcation
of the Spanish provinces are mentioned by Strabo, iii. 4, 19, p.
166.

necessary on the one hand not to remove the seat of administration from the coast, the new capital on the other hand commanded the region of the Ebro and the communications with the north-west and the Pyrenees. Against the Astures (in the provinces of Asturias and Leon), and above all, the Cantabri (in the Basque country and the province of Santander), who obstinately held out in these mountains and overran the neighbouring cantons, a warfare attended by difficulties and heavy losses was prolonged—with interruptions, which the Romans called victories—for eight years, till at length Agrippa succeeded in breaking down the open resistance by destroying the mountain towns and transplanting their inhabitants to the valleys.

If, as the emperor Augustus says, from his time the coast of the ocean from Cadiz to the mouth of the Elbe obeyed the Romans, the obedience in this corner of it was far from voluntary and little to be trusted. Matters were still apparently far from having reached a proper pacification in north-western Spain. There is still mention in Nero's time of war-expeditions against the Asturians. A still clearer tale is told by the occupation of the country, as Augustus arranged it. Callaecia was separated from Lusitania and united with the Tarraconensian province, to concentrate in one hand the chief command in northern Spain. Not merely was this province then the only one which, without bordering on an enemy's country, obtained a legionary military command, but no fewer than three legions[1] were directed thither by Augustus—two to Asturia,

Military organisation in the North-west.

---

[1] These were the Fourth Macedonian, the Sixth Victrix, and the Tenth Gemina. The first of these went, in consequence of the shifting of quarters of the troops occasioned by the Britannic expedition of Claudius, to the Rhine. The two others, although in the meanwhile employed elsewhere on several occasions, were still, at the beginning of the reign of Vespasian, stationed in their old garrison-quarters, and with them, instead of the Fourth, the First Adiutrix newly instituted by Galba (Tacitus, *Hist.* i.

44). All three were on occasion of the Batavian war sent to the Rhine, and only one returned from it. For in the year 88 there were still several legions stationed in Spain (Plin. *Paneg.* 14; comp. *Hermes*, iii. 118), of which one was certainly the Seventh Gemina already, before the year 79, doing garrison-duty in Spain (*C. I. L.* ii. 2477); the second must have been one of those three, and was probably the First Adiutrix, as this soon after the year 88 takes part in the Danubian wars of Domitian, and is under

one to Cantabria ; and, in spite of the military pressure in Germany and in Illyricum, this occupying force was not diminished. The headquarters were established between the old metropolis of Asturia, Lancia, and the new Asturica Augusta (Astorga) in Leon that still at present bears its name. With this strong occupation of the north-west is probably connected the construction of roads undertaken there to a considerable extent in the earlier imperial period, although we are not able to demonstrate the connection in detail, seeing that the allocation of these troops in the Augustan age is unknown to us. Thus there was established by Augustus and Tiberius for the capital of Collaecia, Bracara (Braga), a connection with Asturica, that is, with the great headquarters, and not less with the neighbouring towns to the north, north - east, and south. Tiberius made similar constructions in the territory of the Vascones and in Cantabria.[1] Gradually the occupying force could be diminished, and under Claudius one legion, under Nero a second, could be employed elsewhere. But these were regarded only as drafted off, and still at the beginning of the reign of Vespasian the Spanish garrison had resumed its earlier strength ; it was reduced, in the strict sense, only by the Flavian emperors, by Vespasian to two, by Domitian to one legion. From thence down to the time of Diocletian a single legion, the Seventh Gemina, and a certain number of auxiliary contingents garrisoned Leon.

No province under the monarchy was less affected by outward or by inward wars than this land of the far west. While at this epoch the commanderships of the troops assumed, as it were, the positions of competing parties, the

Trajan stationed in upper Germany, which suggests the conjecture that it was one of the several legions brought in 88 from Spain to upper Germany, and on this occasion came away from Spain. In Lusitania no legions were stationed.

[1] The camp of the Cantabrian legion may have been at the place Pisoraca (Herrera on the Pisuerga, between Palencia and Santander), which alone is named on inscriptions of Tiberius and of Nero, and that as starting point of an imperial road (C. I. L. ii. 4883, 4884), just as the Asturian camp was at Leon. Augustobriga also (to the west of Saragossa) and Complutum (Alcalá de Henares to the north of Madrid) must have been centres of imperial roads, not on account of their urban importance, but as places of encampment for troops.

Spanish army played throughout a secondary part in that respect ; it was only as helper of his colleague that Galba entered into the civil war, and mere accident carried him to the first place. The force holding the northwest of the Peninsula, which even after its reduction still strikes us as comparatively strong, leads us to infer that this region had not been completely obedient even in the second and third centuries ; but we are unable to state anything definite as to the employment of the Spanish legion within the province which it held in occupation. The struggle against the Cantabrians had been waged with the help of vessels of war ; subsequently the Romans had no occasion to institute a permanent naval station there. It is not till the period after Diocletian that we find the Pyrenaean peninsula, like the Italian and the Graeco-Macedonian, without a standing garrison.

That the province of Baetica was, at least after the beginning of the second century, visited on various occasions from the opposite coast by the Moors—the pirates of Rif—we shall have to set forth in detail when we survey the affairs of Africa. We may presume that this serves to explain why, although in the senatorial provinces elsewhere imperial troops were not wont to be stationed, by way of exception Italica (near Seville) was provided with a division of the legion of Leon.[1] But it chiefly devolved on the command stationed in the province of Tingi (Tangier) to protect the rich south of Spain from these incursions. Still it happened that towns like Italica and Singili (not far from Antequera) were besieged by the pirates.

If preparation was anywhere made by the republic for the great all-significant work of the imperial period—the Romanising of the West—it was in Spain. Peaceful intercourse carried forward what the sword had begun ; Roman silver money was paramount in Spain long before it circulated elsewhere outside of Italy ; and the mines, the culture of the vine and olive, and the relations of

Incursions of the Moors.

Introduction of Italian municipal law.

---

[1] With this we may connect the fact that the same legion was, though only temporarily and with a detachment, on active service in Numidia.

traffic produced a constant influx of Italian elements to the coast, particularly in the south-west. New Carthage, the creation of the Barcides, and from its origin down to the Augustan age the capital of the Hither province and the first trading port of Spain, embraced already in the seventh century a numerous Roman population ; Carteia, opposite to the present Gibraltar, founded a generation before the age of the Gracchi, was the first transmarine civic community with a population of Roman origin iii. 4. (iii. 4) ; the old and renowned sister-town of Carthage, Gades, the modern Cadiz, was the first foreign town out of Italy, that adopted Roman law and Roman language iv. 543. (iv. 573). While thus along the greatest part of the coast of the Mediterranean the old indigenous as well as the Phoenician civilisation had already, under the republic, conformed to the ways and habits of the ruling people, in no province under the imperial period was Romanising so energetically promoted on the part of the ruling power as in Spain. First of all the southern half of Baetica, between the Baetis and the Mediterranean, obtained, partly already under the republic or through Caesar, 15, 14. partly in the years 739 and 740 through Augustus, a stately series of communities with full Roman citizenship, which here occupy not the coast especially, but above all the interior, headed by Hispalis (Seville) and Corduba (Cordova) with colonial rights, Italica (near Seville) and Gades (Cadiz) with municipal rights. In southern Lusitania, too, we meet with a series of equally privileged towns, particularly Olisipo (Lisbon), Pax Julia (Beja), and the colony of veterans founded by Augustus during his abode in Spain and made the capital of this province, Emerita (Merida). In the Tarraconensis the burgess-towns are found predominantly on the coast— Carthago Nova, Ilici (Elche), Valentia, Dertosa (Tortosa), Tarraco, Barcino (Barcelona) ; in the interior only the colony in the Ebro valley, Caesaraugusta (Saragossa), is conspicuous. In all Spain under Augustus there were numbered fifty communities with full citizenship ; nearly fifty others had up to this time received Latin rights,

and stood as to inward organisation on a par with the
burgess-communities. Among the rest the emperor
Vespasian likewise introduced the Latin municipal
organisation on occasion of the general imperial census
instituted by him in the year 74. The bestowal of
burgess-rights was neither then, nor generally in the
better imperial period, extended much further than it had
been carried in the time of Augustus ;[1] as to which
probably the chief regulative consideration was the
restricted right of levy in regard to those who were citizens
of the empire.

The indigènous population of Spain, which thus
became partly mixed up with Italian settlers, partly led
towards Italian habits and language, nowhere emerges so
as to be clearly recognised in the history of the imperial
period. Probably that stock, whose remains and whose
language maintain their ground up to the present day in
the mountains of Biscay, Guipuscoa, and Navarre, once
filled the whole peninsula, as the Berbers filled the region
of north Africa. Their language, different from the
Indo-Germanic, and destitute of flexion like that of the
Finns and Mongols, proves their original independence ;
and their most important memorials, the coins, in the
first century of the Roman rule in Spain embrace the
peninsula, with the exception of the south coast from
Cadiz to Granada, where the Phoenician language then
prevailed, and of the region northward of the mouth of
the Tagus and westward of the sources of the Ebro,
which was then probably to a large extent practically
independent, and certainly was utterly uncivilised. In
this Iberian territory the south-Spanish writing is clearly
distinguished from that of the north province ; but not
less clearly both are branches of one stock. The
Phoenician immigration here confined itself to still
narrower bounds than in Africa, and the Celtic mixture
did not modify the general uniformity of the national

Romanising of the Iberians.

---

[1] The expression used by Josephus
(*contra Ap.* ii. 4), that "the Iberians
were named Romans," can only be
referred to the bestowal of Latin rights
by Vespasian, and is an incorrect statement of one who was a stranger.

development in a way that we can recognise. But the conflicts of the Romans with the Iberians belong mainly to the republican epoch, and have been formerly described
ii. 209 f. (ii. 221 f.). After the already mentioned last passages of arms under the first dynasty, the Iberians vanish wholly out of sight. To the question, how far they became Romanised in the imperial period, the information that has come to us gives no satisfactory answer. That in the intercourse with their former masters they would have always occasion to make use of the Roman language, needs no proof; but under the influence of Rome the national language and the national writing disappear even from public use within their own communities. Already in the last century of the republic the native coinage, which at first was to a large extent allowed, had become in the main set aside; from the imperial period there is no Spanish civic coin with other than a Latin legend.[1]

Language.   Like the Roman dress, the Roman language was largely diffused even among those Spaniards who had not Italian burgess-rights, and the government favoured the *de facto* Romanising of the land.[2] When Augustus died the Roman language and habits prevailed in Andalusia, Granada, Murcia, Valencia, Catalonia, Aragon; and a good part of this is to be accounted for not by colonising but by Romanising. By the ordinance of Vespasian

---

[1] Probably the most recent monument of the native language, that admits of certainty as to its date, is a coin of Osicerda—which is modelled after the denarii with the elephant that were struck by Caesar during the Gallic war—with a Latin and Iberian legend (Zobel, *Estudio historico de la moneda antigua española*, ii. 11). Among the wholly or partially local inscriptions of Spain several more recent may be found; public sanction is not even probable in the case of any of them.

[2] There was a time when the communities of *peregrini* had to solicit from the senate the right to make Latin the language of business; but for the imperial period this no longer

held good. On the contrary, at this time probably the converse was of frequent occurrence. For example, the right of coining was allowed on the footing that the legend had to be Latin. In like manner public buildings erected by non-burgesses were described in Latin; thus an inscription of Ilipa in Andalusia (*C. I. L.* ii. 1087) runs: *Urchail Atitta f(ilius) Chilasurgun portas fornic(es) aedificand(a) curavit de s(ua) p(ecunia).* That the wearing of the toga was allowed even to non-Romans, and was a sign of a loyal disposition, is shown as well by Strabo's expression as to the Tarraconensis togata, as by Agricola's behaviour in Britain (Tacitus, *Agric.* 21).

previously mentioned the native language was restricted *de jure* to private intercourse. That it held its ground in this, is proved by its existence at the present day ; what is now confined to the mountains, which neither the Goths nor the Arabs ever occupied, must in the Roman period certainly have extended over a great part of Spain, especially the north-west. Nevertheless Romanising certainly set in very much earlier and more strongly in Spain than in Africa ; monuments with native writing from the imperial period can be pointed to in Africa in fair number, hardly at all in Spain ; and the Berber language at present still prevails over half of north Africa, the Iberian only in the narrow valleys of the Basques. It could not be otherwise, partly because in Spain Roman civilisation emerged much earlier and much more vigorously than in Africa, partly because the natives had not in the former as in the latter the free tribes to fall back upon.

The native communal constitution of the Iberians was not perceptibly to our view different from the Gallic. From the first Spain, like the Celtic country on either side of the Alps, was broken up into cantonal districts ; the Vaccaei and the Cantabri were hardly in any essential respect distinguished from the Cenomani of the Transpadana and the Remi of Belgica. The fact that on the Spanish coins struck in the earlier epoch of the Roman rule it is predominantly not the towns that are named, but the cantons,—not Tarraco but the Cassetani, not Saguntum but the Arsenses—shows, still more clearly than the history of the wars of the time, that in Spain too there once subsisted larger cantonal unions. But the conquering Romans did not treat these unions everywhere in like fashion. The Transalpine cantons remained even under Roman rule political commonwealths ; the Spanish were, like the Cisalpine, simply geographical conceptions. As the district of the Cenomani is nothing but a collective expression for the territories of Brixia, Bergomum, and so forth, so the Asturians consist of twenty-two politically independent communities, which to all appearance do not legally concern each other more than the towns of Brixia and Bergomum.[1]　Of these communities the Tarraconensian province numbered in the Augustan age 293, in the middle of the second century 275.　Here, therefore, the old canton-unions were broken up.　This course was hardly determined by the consideration that the compactness of the Vettones and the Cantabri seemed more hazardous for the unity of the empire than that of the Sequani and the Treveri ; the distinction doubtless was chiefly based on the diversity of the time and of the form of conquest.　The region on the Guadalquivir became Roman a century and a half earlier than the banks of the Loire and the Seine ; the time when the foundation of the Spanish organisation was laid was not so very far from the epoch at which the Samnite confederacy was dissolved.　There the spirit of the old republic prevailed ; in Gaul the freer and gentler view of Caesar.　The smaller and powerless districts, which after the dissolution of the unions became the pillars of political unity— the small cantons or clans—became changed in course of time, here as everywhere into towns.　The beginnings of urban development, even outside of the communities that attained Italian rights, go far back into the republican,

---

[1] These remarkable arrangements are clear, especially from the lists of Spanish places in Pliny, and have been well exhibited by Detlefsen (*Philologus*, xxxii., 606 f.).　The terminology no doubt varies.　As the designations *civitas*, *populus*, *gens*, belong to the independent community, they pertain *de jure* to these portions; thus, *e.g.* there is mention of the *X civitates* of the Autrigones, of the *XXII populi* of the Asturians, of the *gens Zoelarum* (*C. I. L.* ii. 2633), which is just one of these twenty-two tribes. The remarkable document which we possess concerning these Zoelae (*C. I. L.* ii. 2633) informs us that this *gens* was again divided into *gentilitates*, which latter are also themselves called *gentes*, as this same document and other testimonies (*Eph. Ep.* ii. p. 243) prove.　*Civis* is also found in reference to one of the Cantabrian *populi* (*Eph. Ep.* ii. p. 243).　But even for the larger canton, which indeed was once the political unit, there are no other designations than these, strictly speaking, retrospective and incorrect ; *gens* in particular is employed for it even in the technical style (*e.g.*, *C. I. L.* ii. 4233 *Intercat*[*iensis*] *ex gente Vaccaeorum*). That the commonwealth in Spain was based on those small districts, not on the cantons, is clear as well from the terminology itself as from the fact that Pliny in iii. 3, 18, places overagainst those 293 places the *civitates contributae aliis;* moreover it is shown by the official *at census accipiendos civitatium XXIII Vasconum et Vardulorum* (*C. I. L.* vi. 1463) compared with the *censor civitatis Remorum foederatae* (*C. I. L.* xi. 1855, comp. 2607).

perhaps into the pre-Roman, time; subsequently the general bestowal of Latin rights by Vespasian must have made this conversion general or very nearly so.[1] In reality there were among the 293 Augustan communities of the province of Tarraco 114, and among the 275 of the second century only twenty-seven, that were not urban communities.

Of the position of Spain in the imperial administration little is to be said. In the levy the Spanish provinces played a prominent part. The legions doing garrison-duty there were probably from the beginning of the principate raised chiefly in the country itself; when afterwards on the one hand the occupying force was diminished, and on the other hand the levy was more and more restricted to the garrison-district proper, Baetica, sharing in this respect the lot of Italy, enjoyed the dubious blessing of being totally excluded from military service. The auxiliary levy, to which especially the districts that lagged behind as regards urban development were subjected, was carried out on a great scale in Lusitania, Callaecia, Asturia, and not less in the whole of northern and inland Spain; Augustus, whose father had formed even his body-guard of Spaniards, recruited in none of the territories subject to him (setting aside Belgica) so largely as in Spain.

For the finances of the state this rich country was beyond doubt one of the most secure and most productive sources; but we have no detailed information transmitted to us.

The importance of the traffic of these provinces admits

Levy.

Trade and commerce.

---

[1] As the Latin communal constitution is unsuited for a community not organised as a town, those Spanish communities, which still after Vespasian's time lacked urban organisation, must either have been excluded from the bestowal of Latin rights or have had special modifications to meet their case. The latter may be regarded as having more probability. Inscriptions, even of the *gentes*, subsequent to Vespasian's time, show a Latin form of name, as *C. I. L.* ii. 2633, and *Eph. Ep.* ii. 322; and if isolated ones from this period should be found with non-Roman names, it must always be a question whether this is not simply due to actual negligence. Presumptive proofs of non-Roman communal organisation, comparatively frequent in the scanty inscriptions that certainly date before Vespasian (*C. I. L.* ii. 172, 1953, 2633, 5048), have not been met with by me in inscriptions that are certainly subsequent to Vespasian.

of being inferred in some measure from the careful provision of the government for the Spanish roads. Between the Pyrenees and Tarraco there have been found Roman milestones even from the last times of the republic, such as no other province of the West exhibits. We have already remarked that Augustus and Tiberius promoted road-making in Spain mainly for military reasons ; but the road formed by Augustus at Carthago Nova can only have been constructed on account of traffic, and it was traffic mainly that was served by the imperial highway named after him, and partly regulated partly constructed anew by him. This road, continuing the Italo-Gallic coast-road and crossing the Pyrenees at the Pass of Puycerda, went thence to Tarraco, then pretty closely followed the coast by way of Valentia as far as the mouth of the Jucar, but thence made right across the interior for the valley of the Baetis,[1] then ran from the arch of Augustus—which marked the boundary of the two provinces, and with which a new numbering of the miles began—through the province Baetica to the mouth of the river, and thus connected Rome with the ocean. This was certainly the only imperial highway in Spain. Afterwards the government did not do much for the roads of Spain ; the communes, to which these were soon in the main entrusted, appear, so far as we see, to have provided everywhere—apart from the tableland of the interior —communications to such an extent as was required by the state of culture in the province. For, mountainous as Spain is and not without steppes and waste land, it is yet one of the most productive countries of the earth, both through the abundance of the fruits of the soil and through its riches of wine and oil and metals. To this were early added manufactures, especially in iron wares and in woollen and linen fabrics. In the valuations under Augustus no Roman burgess-community, Patavium excepted, had such a number of rich people to show as the Spanish Gades

---

[1] The direction of the *via Augusta* is specified by Strabo (iii. 4, 9, p. 160) ; to it belong all the milestones which have that name, as well those from the region of Lerida (*C. I. L.* ii. 4920-4928) as those found between Tarragona and Valencia (*ibid.* 4949-4954), and lastly, the numerous ones *ab Iano Augusto, qui est ad Baetem,* or *ab arcu, unde incipit Baetica, ad oceanum.*

with its great merchants spread throughout the world ; and in keeping with this was the refined luxury of manners, the castanet-players who were here at home, and the Gaditanian songs, which circulated, like those of Alexandria, among the elegant Romans. The nearness of Italy, and the easy and cheap intercourse by sea, gave at this epoch, especially to the Spanish south and east coasts, the opportunity of bringing their rich produce to the first market of the world, and probably with no country in the world did Rome pursue so extensive and constant a traffic on a great scale as with Spain.

That Roman civilisation pervaded Spain earlier and more powerfully than any other province, is confirmed by evidence on various sides, especially in respect to religion and to literature.

It is true that in the territory that was still at a later period Iberian, and remained tolerably free from immigration—in Lusitania, Callaecia, Asturia—the native gods, with their singular names, ending mostly in -icus and -ecus, such as Endovellicus, Eaecus, Vagodonnaegus, and the like, maintained their ground still even under the principate at the old seats. But not a single votive stone has been found in all Baetica, which might not quite as well have been set up in Italy. And the same holds true of Tarraconensis proper, only that isolated traces are met with on the upper Douro of the worship of Celtic gods.[1] No other province shows an equally energetic Romanising in matters of ritual.

Religious rites.

Cicero mentions the Latin poets at Corduba only to censure them ; and the Augustan age of literature was still in the main the work of Italians, though individual provincials helped in it, and among others the learned librarian of the emperor, the philologue Hyginus, was born as a bondsman in Spain. But thenceforward the Spaniards undertook in it almost the part, if not of leader, at any rate of schoolmaster. The natives of Corduba, Mar-

The Spaniards in Latin literature.

---

[1] At Clunia there was found a dedication to the Mothers (*C. I. L.* ii. 2776)—the only Spanish example of this worship so widely diffused and so long continuing among the western Celts—at Uxama, one set up to the *Lugoves* (*ib.* 2818), a deity that recurs among the Celts of Aventicum.

cus Porcius Latro, the teacher and the model of Ovid, and his countryman and friend in youth, Annaeus Seneca,—both only about a decade younger than Horace, but for a considerable time employed in their native town as teachers of eloquence, before they transferred their activity in that character to Rome—were the true and proper representatives of the school-rhetoric that took the place of the republican freedom and sauciness of speech. Once, when the former could not avoid appearing in a real process, he came to a stand-still in his address, and only recovered his fluency when, to please the famous man, the court was transferred from the tribunal to the school-hall. Seneca's son, the minister of Nero and the fashionable philosopher of the epoch, and his grandson, the poet of the sentimental opposition to the principate, Lucanus, have an importance, as doubtful in literature as it is indisputable in history, which may in a certain sense be put to the account of Spain. In the early times of the empire, likewise, two other provincials from Baetica, Mela under Claudius, Columella under Nero, gained a place among the recognised didactic authors who cultivated style—the former by his short description of the earth, the latter by a thorough, in part poetical, picture of agriculture. If, in the time of Domitian, the poet Canius Rufus from Gades, the philosopher Decianus from Emerita, and the orator Valerius Licinianus from Bilbilis (Calatayud not far from Saragossa) are celebrated as literary notabilities by the side of Virgil and Catullus and by the side of the three stars of Corduba, this is certainly the fortune also of one likewise a native of Bilbilis, Valerius Martialis,[1] who himself yields to none among the poets of this epoch in elegance and plastic power, or yet in venality and emptiness, and we are justified in taking into account withal the fact of

[1] The choliambics (i. 61) run thus:—

Verona docti syllabas amat vatis,
Marone felix Mantua est,
Censetur Apona Livio suo tellus
Stellaque nec Flacco minus,
Apollodoro plaudit imbrifer Nilus,

Nasone Peligni sonant,
Duosque Senecas unicumque Lucanum
Facunda loquitur Corduba,
Gaudent iocosae Canio suo Gades,
Emerita Deciano meo:
Te, Liciniane, gloriabitur nostra,
Nec me tacebit Bilbilis.

their being fellow-countrymen ; yet the mere possibility of weaving such a garland of poets shows the importance of the Spanish element in the literature of the time. But the pearl of Spanish-Latin authorship is Marcus Fabius Quintilianus (35-95) from Calagurris on the Ebro. His father had already acted as a teacher of eloquence in Rome ; he himself was brought to Rome by Galba, and occupied, especially under Domitian, a distinguished position as tutor of the emperor's nephews. His text-book of rhetoric and, in some degree, of the history of Roman literature, is one of the most excellent which we possess from Roman antiquity, pervaded by fine taste and sure judgment, simple in feeling as in presentation, instructive without weariness, pleasing without effort, contrasting sharply and designedly with the fashionable literature that was so rich in phrases and so empty of ideas. It was in no small degree due to him that the tendency became changed at any rate, if not improved. Subsequently, amidst the general emptiness the influence of the Spaniards comes no further into prominence. What is, historically, of special moment in their Latin authorship is the complete clinging of these provincials to the literary development of the mother-country. Cicero, indeed, scoffs at the clumsiness and the provincialisms of the Spanish votaries of poetry ; and even Latro's Latin did not meet the approval of the equally genteel and correct Roman by birth, Messalla Corvinus. But after the Augustan age nothing similar is again heard of. The Gallic rhetors, the great African ecclesiastical authors have, as Latin writers, retained in some measure a foreign complexion ; no one would recognise the Senecas and Martial by their manner and style as belonging to one or to another land ; in hearty love to his own literature and in subtle understanding of it never has any Italian surpassed the teacher of languages from Calagurris.

CHAPTER III.

THE GALLIC PROVINCES.

LIKE Spain, southern Gaul had already in the time of the republic become a part of the Roman empire, yet neither so early nor so completely as the former country. The two Spanish provinces were instituted in the age of Hannibal, the province Narbo in that of the Gracchi ; and, while in the former case Rome took to itself the whole Peninsula, in the latter it was not merely content, down to the last age of the republic, with the possession of the coast, but even of this it directly took only the smaller and the more remote half. The republic was not wrong in designating what it so possessed as the town-domain of Narbo (Narbonne) ; the greater part of the coast, nearly from Montpellier to Nice, belonged to the city of Massilia. This Greek community was more a state than a city, and through its powerful position the equal alliance subsisting from of old with Rome obtained a real significance, such as had no parallel in any second allied city. It is true, nevertheless, that the Romans were for these neighbouring Greeks, still more than for the more remote Greeks of the East, shield as well as sword. The Massaliots had probably the lower Rhone as far up as Avignon in their possession ; but the Ligurian and the Celtic cantons of the interior were by no means subject to them, and the Roman standing camp at Aquae Sextiae (Aix) a day's march to the north of Massilia, was, quite in the true and proper sense, instituted for the permanent protection of the wealthy Greek mercantile city. It was one of the most momentous consequences of the Roman civil war, that along with the legitimate republic its most faithful ally, the city of Massilia, was politically annihilated, was converted from a state sharing rule into a community which continued free of the empire and Greek, but preserved its independence and its Hellenism in the modest proportions of a provincial middle-sized town. In a political aspect there is nothing more to be said of Massilia after its capture in the civil war ; the town was thenceforth for Gaul only what Neapolis was for Italy—the centre of Greek culture and Greek learning. Inasmuch as the greater part of the later province of Narbo only at that time came under direct Roman administration, it is to this epoch in particular that the erection of it in a certain measure belongs.

How the rest of Gaul came into the power of Rome has been already narrated (iv. 240 ff.) Before Caesar's Gallic war the rule of the Romans extended approximately as far as Toulouse, Vienne, and Geneva ; after it, as far as the Rhine throughout its course, and the coasts of the Atlantic Ocean on the north as on the west. This subjugation, it is true, was probably not complete, in the north-west perhaps not much less superficial than that of Britain (iv. 296). Yet we are informed of supplemental wars, in the main, merely as regards the districts of Iberian nationality. To the Iberians belonged not merely the southern but also the northern slope of the Pyrenees, with the country lying in front, Bearn, Gascony, and western Languedoc[1] ; and it has already been mentioned (p. 63) that when north-western Spain was sustaining the last conflicts with the Romans, there was also on the north

Last conflicts in the three Gauls. iv. 230 f.

iv. 283.

[1] The domain of Iberian coins reaches decidedly beyond the Pyrenees, though the interpretation of individual coin-legends, which are among others referred to Perpignan and Narbonne, is not certain. As all these coinings took place under Roman authorisation, this suggests the question whether this portion of the subsequent Narbonensis was not at an earlier date—namely before the founding of Narbo (636 U. C.)—under the governor of Hither Spain. There are no Aquitanian coins with Iberian legends any more than from north-western Spain, probably because the Roman supremacy, under whose protection this coinage grew up, did not, so long as the latter lasted, *i.e.* perhaps up to the Numantine war, embrace those regions.

118.

side of the Pyrenees, and beyond doubt in connection therewith, serious fighting, at first on the part of Agrippa 38. in the year 716, then on the part of Marcus Valerius Messalla, the well-known patron of the Roman poets, who 28, 27. in the year 726 or 727, and thus nearly at the same time with the Cantabrian war, vanquished the Aquitanians in a pitched battle in the old Roman territory not far from Narbonne.   In respect of the Celts nothing further is mentioned than that, shortly before the battle of Actium, the Morini in Picardy were overthrown ; and, although during the twenty years of almost uninterrupted civil war our reporters may have lost sight of the comparatively insignificant affairs of Gaul, the silence of the list of triumphs—here complete—shows at any rate that no further military undertakings of importance took place in the land of the Celts during this period.

Insurrections.

Subsequently, during the long reign of Augustus, and amidst all the crises—some of them very hazardous —of the Germanic wars, the Gallic provinces remained obedient.   No doubt the Roman government, as well as the Germanic patriot party, as we have seen, constantly had it in view that a decisive success of the Germans and their advance into Gaul would be followed by a rising of the Gauls against Rome ; the foreign rule cannot therefore at that time have stood by any means secure. Matters came to a real insurrection in the year 21 under Tiberius.   There was formed among the Celtic nobility a widely-ramified conspiracy to overthrow the Roman *Under Tiberius.* government.   It broke out prematurely in the far from important cantons of the Turones and the Andecavi on the lower Loire, and not merely the small garrison of Lyons, but also a part of the army of the Rhine at once took the field against the insurgents.   Nevertheless the most noted districts joined ; the Treveri, under the guidance of Julius Florus, threw themselves in masses into the Ardennes ; in the immediate neighbourhood of Lyons the Haedui and Sequani rose under the leadership of Julius Sacrovir.   The compact legions, it is true, gained the mastery over the rebels without much trouble ;

but the rising, in which the Germans in no way took part, shows at any rate the hatred towards the foreign rulers, which still at that time prevailed in the land and particularly among the nobility—a hatred which was certainly strengthened, but was not at first produced, by the pressure of taxes and the financial distress that are designated as causes of the insurrection.

It was a greater feat of Roman policy than that which enabled it to become master of Gaul, that it knew how to retain the mastery, and that Vercingetorix found no successor, although, as we see, there were not entirely wanting men who would gladly have walked in the same path. This result was attained by a shrewd combination of terrifying and of winning—we may add, of sharing. The strength and the proximity of the Rhine army was beyond question the first and the most effective means of preserving the Gauls in the fear of their master. If this army was maintained throughout the century at the same level, as will be set forth in the following section, it was so probably quite as much on account of their own subjects, as on account of neighbours who afterwards were by no means specially formidable. That even the temporary withdrawal of these troops imperilled the continuance of the Roman rule, not because the Germans might then cross the Rhine, but because the Gauls might renounce allegiance to the Romans, is shown by the rising after Nero's death, in spite of all its weakness; after the troops had marched off to Italy to make their general emperor, an independent Gallic empire was proclaimed in Treves, and those soldiers who were left were made bound to allegiance towards it. But although this foreign rule, like every such rule, rested primarily and mainly on superior power—on the ascendancy of compact and trained troops over the multitude—it by no means rested on this exclusively. The art of partition was here successfully applied. Gaul did not belong to the Celts alone ; not merely were the Iberians strongly represented in the south, but Germanic tribes were settled in considerable numbers on the Rhine, and were of

Gradual pacification of Gaul.

importance still more by their conspicuous aptitude for war, than by their number. Skilfully the government knew how to foster and to turn to useful account the antagonism between the Celts and the Germans on the left of the Rhine. But the policy of amalgamation and of reconciliation operated still more powerfully.

Policy of amalgamation.

What measures were taken with this view we shall explain in the sequel. Seeing that the cantonal constitution was spared, and even a sort of national representation was conceded, and the measures directed against the national priesthood were taken gradually, while the Latin language was from the beginning obligatory, and with that national representation there was associated the new worship of the emperor ; seeing that, on the whole, the Romanising was not undertaken in an abrupt way, but was cautiously and patiently pursued, the Roman foreign rule in the Celtic land ceased to be such, because the Celts themselves became, and desired to be, Romans. The extent to which the work had already advanced after the expiry of the first century of the Roman rule in Gaul is shown by the just mentioned occurrences after Nero's death, which, in their course as a whole, belong partly to the history of the Roman commonwealth, partly to its relations with the Germans, but must also be mentioned, at least by way of slight glance, in this connection. The overthrow of the Julio-Claudian dynasty emanated from a Celtic noble and began with a Celtic insurrection ; but this was not a revolt against the foreign rule like that of Vercingetorix or even of Sacrovir ; its aim was not the setting aside, but the transforming, of the Roman government. The fact that its leader reckoned descent from a bastard of Caesar one of the patents of nobility of his house, clearly expresses the half-national, half-Roman character of this movement. Some months later certainly, after the revolted Roman troops of Germanic descent and the free Germans had for the moment overpowered the Roman army, some Celtic tribes proclaimed the independence of their nation ; but this attempt proved a sad failure, not through the eventual interference of the government, but from the very opposition of the great majority of the Celtic cantons themselves, which could not, and did not, desire to fall away from Rome.

The Roman names of the leading nobles, the Latin legend on the coins of the insurrection, the travesty throughout of Roman arrangements, show most clearly that the deliverance of the Celtic nation from the yoke of the foreigners in the year 70 was no longer possible, just because there was such a nation no longer ; and the Roman rule might be felt, according to circumstances, as a yoke, but no longer as a foreign rule.   Had such an opportunity been offered to the Celts at the time of the battle of Philippi, or even under Tiberius, the insurrection would have run its course, not perhaps to another issue, but in streams of blood ; now it ran off into the sand. When, some decades after these severe crises, the Rhine army was considerably reduced, these crises had given the proof that the great majority of the Gauls were no longer thinking of separation from the Italians, and the four generations that had followed since the conquest had done their work.   Subsequent occurrences here were crises within the Roman world.   When that world threatened to fall asunder, the West as well as the East separated itself for some time from the centre of the empire ; but the separate state of Postumus was the work of necessity, not of choice, and the separation was merely *de facto ;* the emperors who bore sway over Gaul, Britain, and Spain, laid claim to the dominion of the whole empire quite as much as their Italian rival emperors.   Certainly traces enough remained of the old Celtic habits and also of the old Celtic unruliness.   As bishop Hilary of Poitiers, himself a Gaul, complains of the overbearing character of his countrymen, so the Gauls are, even in the biographies of the later Caesars, designated as stubborn and ungovernable and inclined to insubordination, so that in dealing with them tenacity and sternness of government appear specially requisite. But a separation from the Roman empire, or even a renouncing of the Roman nationality, so far as there was

Roman rule no longer felt as foreign.

any such at the time, was in these later centuries nowhere less thought of than in Gaul ; on the contrary, the development of the Romano-Gallic culture, of which Caesar and Augustus had laid the foundation, fills the later Roman period just as it fills the Middle Ages and more recent times.

Organisation of the three Gauls. The regulation of Gaul was the work of Augustus. In the adjustment of imperial affairs after the close of the civil wars the whole of Gaul, as it had been entrusted to Caesar or had been further acquired by him, came —with the exception merely of the region on the Roman side of the Alps, which had meanwhile been joined to Italy—under imperial administration. Immediately afterwards Augustus resorted to Gaul, and in the year 727 completed in the capital Lugudunum the census of the Gallic province, whereby the portions of the country brought to the empire by Caesar first obtained an organised land-register, and the payment of tribute was regulated for them. He did not stay long at that time, for Spanish affairs demanded his presence. But the carrying out of the new arrangement encountered great difficulties and, in various cases, resistance. It was not mere military affairs that gave occasion to Agrippa's stay in Gaul in the year 735, and that of the emperor himself during the years 738-741 ; and the governors or commanders on the Rhine belonging to the imperial house, Tiberius, stepson of Augustus, in 738, his brother Drusus, 742-745, Tiberius again, 745-747, 757-759, 763-765, his son Germanicus, 766-769, had all of them the task of carrying on the organisation of Gaul. The work of peace was certainly no less difficult and no less important than the passages of arms on the Rhine ; we perceive this in the fact that the emperor took in hand personally the laying of the foundation, and entrusted the carrying it out to the men in the empire who were most closely related .to him and highest in station. It was only in those years that the arrangements, established by Caesar amidst the pressure of the civil wars, received the shape which they thereafter in the main retained. They extended over the old as over the new province ;

[margin notes:]
27.
19.
16-13.
16.
12-9, 9-7,
A.D. 3-5,
9-11, 12-
15.

but Augustus gave up the old Roman territory, along
with that of Massilia, from the Mediterranean as far as
the Cevennes, as early as the year 732, to the senatorial 22.
government, and retained only New Gaul in his own
administration. This territory, still in itself very extensive, was then broken up into three administrative
districts, over each of which was placed an independent
imperial governor. This division attached itself to the
threefold partition of the Celtic country—already found
in existence by the dictator Caesar, and based on national
distinctions—into Aquitania inhabited by Iberians, the
purely Celtic Gaul, and the Celto-Germanic territory
of the Belgae ; doubtless too it was intended in this
administrative partition to lay some measure of stress on
these distinctions, which tended to favour the progress of
the Roman rule. This, however, was only approximately
carried out, and could not be practically realised otherwise.
The purely Celtic region between the Garonne and Loire
was attached to the too small Iberian Aquitania ; the
whole left bank of the Rhine, from the Lake of Geneva
to the Moselle, was joined with Belgica, although most
of these cantons were Celtic ; in general the Celtic
stock so preponderated that the united provinces could
be called "the three Gauls." Of the formation of the
two so-called "Germanies,"—nominally the compensation
for the loss or abeyance of a really Germanic province,
in reality the military frontier of Gaul—we shall speak in
the following section.

Matters of law and justice were arranged in an alto- Law and
gether different way for the old province of Gaul and for justice.
the three new ones ; the former was Latinised at once and
completely, in the latter the subsisting national state of
things was in the first instance merely regulated. This
contrast of administration, which reaches far deeper than
the formal diversity of the senatorial and imperial administration, was doubtless the primary and main occasion of
the diversity, still continuing at the present day in its
effects, between the regions of the Langue d'oc and
Provence and those of the Langue d'oui.

The Romanising of the south of Gaul had not in the republican period advanced so far as that of the south of Spain.
The eighty years lying between the two conquests were
not to be rapidly overtaken ; the military camps in Spain
were far stronger and more permanent than the Gallic;
the towns of Latin type were more numerous in the
former than in the latter. Here doubtless in the time of
the Gracchi and under their influence Narbo had been
founded, the first burgess-colony proper beyond the sea ;
but it remained isolated, and, though a rival of Massilia
in commercial intercourse, to all appearance by no means
equal to it in importance. But when Caesar began to
guide the destinies of Rome, here above all—in this land
of his choice and of his star—neglect was retrieved. The
colony of Narbo was strengthened, and was under Tiberius
the most populous city in all Gaul. Thereupon four new
burgess-communities were laid out, chiefly in the domain
ceded by Massilia (iv. 572), the most important among
them being, from a military point of view, Forum Julii
(Fréjus), the chief station of the new imperial fleet, and for
trade Arelate (Arles), at the mouth of the Rhone, which
soon—when Lyons rose and trade was tending more and
more towards the Rhone—outstripping Narbo, became the
true heir of Massilia and the great emporium of Gallo-
Italic commerce. What further he himself did, and what
his son did in the same sense, cannot be definitely distinguished, and historically little depends on the distinction ; here, if anywhere, Augustus was nothing but the
executor of Caesar's testament. Everywhere the Celtic
cantonal constitution gave way before the Italian community. The canton of the Volcae in the coast region,
formerly subject to the Massaliots, received through Caesar
a Latin municipal constitution on such a footing, that the
" praetors " of the Volcae presided over the whole district
embracing twenty-four townships,[1] until not long thereafter the old arrangement disappeared even in name, and

iv. 542.

---

[1] This is shown by the remarkable
inscription of Avignon (Herzog. *Gall.
Narb.* n. 403): *T. Carisius T. f.*
pr[aetor] Volcar[um] dat—the oldest
evidence for the Roman organisation
of the commonwealth in these regions.

instead of the canton of the Volcae came the Latin town of Nemausus (Nîmes). In a similar way the most considerable of all the cantons of this province, that of the Allobroges, who had possession of the country northward of the Isére and eastward of the middle Rhone, from Valence and Lyons to the mountains of Savoy and to the lake of Geneva, obtained, probably already through Caesar, a like urban organisation and Italian rights, till at length the emperor Gaius granted the Roman franchise to the town of Vienna. So in the province as a whole the larger centres were organised by Caesar, or in the first age of the empire, on the basis of Latin rights, such as Ruscino (Roussillon), Avennio (Avignon), Aquae Sextiae (Aix), Apta (Apt). Already at the close of the Augustan age the country along both banks of the lower Rhone was completely Romanised in language and manners ; the cantonal constitution throughout the province was probably set aside with the exception of slight remnants. The burgesses of the communities on whom the imperial franchise was conferred, and no less the burgesses in those of Latin rights, who had acquired for themselves and for their descendants the imperial franchise by entering the imperial army or by the holding of offices in their native towns, stood in law on a footing of complete equality with the Italians, and, like them, attained to offices and honours in the imperial service.

In the three Gauls, on the other hand, there were no towns of Roman and Latin rights, or rather there was only one such town[1] there, which on that account belonged to none of the three provinces or belonged to all—the town of Lugudunum (Lyons). On the extreme southern verge of imperial Gaul, immediately on the border of the municipally-organised province, at the confluence of the Rhone and the Saone, on a site equally well chosen from a military and from a commercial point of view, this settlement

Lugudunum.

---

[1] Noviodunum (Nyon on the lake of Geneva) alone perhaps in the three Gauls may be compared, as regards plan, with Lugudunum (iv. 254); but, as this community emerges later as civitas Equestrium (*Inscrip. Helvet.* 115), it seems to have been inserted among the cantons, which was not the case with Lugudunum.

43. had arisen in the year 711 during the civil wars, primarily in consequence of the expulsion of a number of Italians settled in Vienna.[1] Not having originated out of a Celtic canton,[2] and hence always with a territory of narrow limits, but from the outset composed of Italians and in possession of the full Roman franchise, it stood forth unique in its kind among the communities of the three Gauls—as respects its legal relations, in some measure resembling Washington in the North American Federation. This unique town of the three Gauls was at the same time the Gallic capital. The three provinces had not any common chief authority, and, of high imperial officials, only the governor of the middle or Lugudunensian province had his seat there ; but when emperors or princes stayed in Gaul they as a rule resided in Lyons. Lyons was, alongside of Carthage, the only city of the Latin half of the empire which obtained a standing garrison after the model of that of the capital.[3] The only mint for imperial money, which we can point to with certainty in the West for the earlier period of the empire, is that of Lyons. Here was the headquarters of the transit-dues which embraced all Gaul ; and to this as a centre the Gallic network of roads converged. But not merely had all government institutions, which were common to Gaul, their native seat in Lyons ; this Roman town became also, as we shall see further on, the seat of the

---

[1] The persons earlier driven forth from Vienna by the Allobroges (οἱ ἐκ Οὐιέννης τῆς Ναρβωνησίας ὑπὸ τῶν Ἀλλοβρίγων ποτὲ ἐκπεσόντες), in Dio, xlvi. 50, cannot well have been other than Roman citizens, for the foundation of a burgess-colony for their benefit is intelligible only on this supposition. The "earlier" expulsion probably stood connected with the rising of the Allobroges under Catugnatus in 693 (iv. 223). The explanation why the dispossessed were not brought back, but were settled elsewhere, is not forthcoming ; but various reasons prompting such a course may be conceived, and the fact itself is not thereby called in question. The re-

61.
iv. 213.

venues accruing to the city (Tacitus, *Hist.* i. 65) may have been conferred upon it possibly at the expense of Vienna.

[2] The ground belonged formerly to the Segusiavi (Plin. *H. N.* iv. 15, 107 ; Strabo, p. 186, 192), one of the small client-cantons of the Haedui (Caesar, *B. G.* vii. 75) ; but in the cantonal division it counts not as one of these, but stands for itself as μητρόπολις (Ptolem. ii. 8, 11, 12).

[3] This was the 1200 soldiers with whom, as Agrippa the king of the Jews says in Josephus (*Bell. Jud.* ii. 16, 4), the Romans held in subjection the whole of Gaul.

Celtic diet of the three provinces, and of all the political and religious institutions associated with it—of its temples and its yearly festivals. Thus Lugudunum rapidly rose into prosperity, helped onward by the rich endowment combined with its metropolitan position and by a site uncommonly favourable for commerce. An author of the time of Tiberius describes it as the second in Gaul after Narbo ; subsequently it takes a place there by the side of, or before, its sister on the Rhone, Arelate. On occasion of the fire, which in the year 64 laid a great part of Rome in ashes, the Lugudunenses sent to those burnt out a subsidy of 4,000,000 sesterces (£43,500), and when the same fate befel their own town next year in a still harder way, the whole empire paid its contribution to them, and the emperor sent a like sum from his privy purse. The town rose out of its ruins with more splendour than before ; and it has for almost two thousand years remained amidst all vicissitudes a great city up to the present day. In the later period of the empire, no doubt, it fell behind Treves. The town of the Treveri, named Augusta probably from the first emperor, soon gained the first place in the Belgic province ; if still in the time of Tiberius Durocortorum of the Remi (Rheims) is named the most populous place of the province and the seat of the governors, an author from the time of Claudius already assigns the primacy there to the chief place of the Treveri. But Treves became the capital of Gaul [1]—we may even say of the West—only through the remodelling of the imperial administration under Diocletian. After Gaul, Britain, and Spain were placed under one supreme administration, the latter had its seat in Treves : and thenceforth Treves was also, when the emperors stayed in Gaul, their regular residence, and, as a Greek of the fifth century says, the greatest city beyond the

---

[1] Nothing is so significant of the position of Treves at this time as the ordinance of the emperor Gratianus of the year 376 (*Cod. Theod.* xiii. 3, 11), that there should be given to the professors of rhetoric and of the grammar of both languages in all the capitals of the then subsisting seventeen Gallic provinces, over and above their municipal salary, a like addition from the state chest : but for Treves this was to be on a higher scale.

Alps.   But the epoch when this Rome of the north received its walls and its hot baths, which might well be named by the side of the city walls of the Roman kings and of the baths of the imperial capital, lies beyond the limits of our narrative.   Through the first three centuries of the empire Lyons remained the Roman centre of the Celtic land, and that not merely because it occupied the first place in population and wealth, but because it was, like no other in the Gallic north and but few in the south, a town founded from Italy, and Roman not merely as regards rights, but as regards its origin and its character.

The cantonal organisation of the three Gauls.

As the Italic town was the basis for the organisation of the south province, so the canton was for the northern, and predominantly indeed the canton of the Celtic formerly political, now communal, organisation.   The importance of the distinction between town and canton is not primarily dependent on its intrinsic nature ; even if it had been one of mere legal form, it would have separated the nationalities, and would have awakened and whetted, on the one hand, the feeling of their belonging to Rome, on the other hand, that of their being foreign to it.   The practical diversity of the two organisations may not be estimated as of much account for this period, since the elements of the communal organisation—the officials, the council, the burgess-assembly—were the same in the one case as in the other, and distinctions going deeper, such as perhaps formally subsisted, would hardly be tolerated long by Roman supremacy.   Hence the transition from the cantonal organisation to the urban was frequently effected of itself and without hindrance—we may even say, with a certain necessity, in the course of development.   In consequence of this the qualitative distinctions of the two legal forms come into little prominence in our traditional accounts.   Nevertheless, the contrast was certainly not a mere nominal one, but as regards the competence of the different authorities, judicature, taxation, levy, there subsisted diversities which were of importance, or at any rate seemed important, for administration, partly of themselves, partly in consequence of custom.

The quantitative distinction is definitely recognisable. The cantons, at least as they present themselves among the Celts and the Germans, are throughout tribes more than townships; this very essential element was peculiar to all Celtic territories, and was often covered over rather than obliterated even by the subsequent Romanising. Mediolanum and Brixia were indebted for their wide bounds and their lasting power essentially to the fact that they were, properly speaking, nothing but the cantons of the Insubres and the Cenomani. The facts, that the territory of the town of Vienna embraced Dauphiné and Western Savoy, and that the equally old and almost equally considerable townships of Cularo (Grenoble) and Genava (Geneva) were down to late imperial times in point of law villages of the colony of Vienna, are likewise to be explained from the circumstance that this was the later name of the tribe of the Allobroges. In most of the Celtic cantons one township so thoroughly preponderates that it is one and the same thing whether we name the Remi or Durocortorum, the Bituriges or Burdigala; but the converse also occurs, as *e.g.* among the Vocontii Vasio (Vaison) and Lucus, among the Carnutes Autricum (Chartres) and Cenabum (Orleans) balance each other; and it is more than questionable whether the privileges which, according to Italic and Greek organisation, attached as a matter of course to the ring-wall in contrast to the open field, stood *de jure*, or even merely *de facto*, on a similar footing among the Celts. The counterpart to this canton in the Graeco-Italic system was much less the town than the tribe; we have to liken the Carnutes to the Boeotians, Autricum and Cenabum to Tanagra and Thespiae. The specialty of the position of the Celts under the Roman rule as compared with other nations—the Iberians, for example, and the Hellenes—turns on this, that these larger unions continued to subsist as communities in the former case, while in the latter those constituent elements, of which they were composed, formed the communities. Older diversities of national development belonging to the pre-Roman epoch may have co-operated in the matter; it may pos-

sibly have been more easily practicable to take from the
Boeotians the joint diet of their towns than to break up
the Helvetii into three or four districts ; political unions
maintain their ground even after subjugation under a
central power, in cases where their dissolution would bring
about disorganisation.   Yet what was done in Gaul by
Augustus or, if it be preferred, by Caesar, was brought about
not by the force of circumstances, but chiefly by the free
resolution of the government, as it alone was in keeping
with the forbearance otherwise exercised towards the
Celts.   For there was, in fact, in the pre-Roman time and
even at the time of Caesar's conquest a far greater number of cantons than we find later ; in particular, it is
remarkable that the numerous smaller cantons attached
by clientship to a larger one did not in the imperial
period become independent, but disappeared.[1]   If subsequently the Celtic land appears divided into a moderate
number of considerable, and some of them even very large,
canton-districts, within which dependent cantons nowhere
make their appearance, this arrangement had the way no
doubt paved for it by the pre-Roman system of clientship, but was completely carried out only under the
Roman reorganisation.

Influence
of the
cantonal
constitu-
tion.

This continued subsistence and this enlargement of
the cantonal constitution must have been above all influential in determining the further political development of
Gaul.   While the Tarraconensian province was split up
into two hundred and ninety-three independent communi-

---

[1] In Caesar there appear doubtless,
taken on the whole, the same cantons
as are thereafter represented in the
Augustan arrangement, but at the
same time manifold traces of smaller

iv. 226. client-unions (comp. iv. 237); thus
as "clients" of the Haedui are
named the Segusiavi, the Ambivareti,
the Aulerci Brannovices, and the Bran-
novii (*B. G.* vii. 75), as clients of
the Treveri the Condrusi (*B. G.* iv.
6) as clients of the Helvetii the
Tulingi and Latobriges.   With the
exception of the Segusiavi, all these
are absent from the Lyons diet.   Such

minor cantons not wholly merged into
the leading places may have subsisted in great number in Gaul at the
time of the conquest.   If, according
to Josephus (*Bell. Jud.* ii. 16, 4),
three hundred and five Gallic cantons
and twelve hundred towns obeyed the
Romans ; these may be the figures that
were reckoned up for Caesar's successes
in arms ; if the small Iberian tribes in
Aquitania and the client-cantons in
the Celtic land were included in the
reckoning, such numbers might well
be the result.

ties (p. 72), the three Gauls numbered together, as we shall see, not more than sixty-four of them.   Their unity and their recollections remained unbroken ; the zealous adoration, which throughout the imperial period was paid among the Volcae to the fountain-god Nemausus, shows how even here, in the south of the land and in a canton transformed into a town, there was still a vivid sense of the traditional tie that bound them together. Communities with wide bounds, firmly knit in this way by inward ties, were a power.   Such as Caesar found the Gallic communities, with the mass of the people held in entire political as well as economic dependence, and an overpowerful nobility, they substantially remained under Roman rule ; exactly as in pre-Roman times the great nobles, with their train of dependents and bondsmen to be counted by thousands, played the part of masters each in his own home, so Tacitus describes the state of things in Tiberius's time among the Treveri.   The Roman government gave to the community comprehensive rights, even a certain military power, so that they under certain circumstances were entitled to erect fortresses and keep them garrisoned, as was the case among the Helvetii ; the magistrates could call out the militia, and had in that case the rights and the rank of officers.   This prerogative was not the same in the hands of the president of a small town of Andalusia, and of the president of a district on the Loire or the Moselle of the size of a small province. The large-hearted policy of Caesar the elder, to whom the outlines of this system must necessarily be traced back, here presents itself in all its grand extent.

But the government did not confine itself to leaving with the Celts their cantonal organisation ; it left, or rather gave, to them also a national constitution, so far as such a constitution was compatible with Roman supremacy.   As on the Hellenic nation, so Augustus conferred on the Gallic an organised collective representation, such as they in the epoch of freedom and of disorganisation had striven after, but had never attained. Under the hill crowned by the capital of Gaul, where

Diet of the three Gauls.

the Saone mingles its waters with those of the Rhone, on the 1st August of the year 742, the imperial prince Drusus, as representative of the government in Gaul, consecrated to Roma and to the Genius of the ruler the altar, at which thenceforth every year on this day the festival of these gods was to be celebrated by the joint action of the Gauls. The representatives of all the cantons chose from their midst year by year the "priest of the three Gauls," who on the emperor's day presented sacrifice to the emperor and conducted the festal games in connection with it. This representative council had not only a power of administering its own property by means of officials, who belonged to the chief circles of the provincial nobility, but also a certain share in the general affairs of the country. Of its immediate interference in politics there is, it is true, no other trace than that, in the serious crisis of the year 70, the diet of the three Gauls dissuaded the Treveri from rising against Rome ; but it had and used the right of bringing complaints as to the imperial and domestic officials acting in Gaul ; and it co-operated, moreover, if not in the imposition, at any rate in the apportionment of the taxes,[1] especially seeing that these were laid on not according to the several provinces but for Gaul in general. The imperial government certainly called into existence similar institutions in all the provinces, and not merely introduced in each of them the centralisation of sacred rites, but also—what the

---

[1] This is indicated not only by the inscription in Boissieu, p. 609, where the words *tot[i]us cens[us Galliarum]* are brought into connection with the name of one of the altar-priests, but also by the honorary inscription erected by the three Gauls to an imperial official *a censibus accipiendis* (Henzen, 6944). He appears to have conducted the revision of the land-register for the whole country, just as formerly Drusus did, while the valuation itself took place by commissaries for the individual districts. A *sacerdos Romae et Augusti* of the Tarraconensis is praised *ob curam tabulari censualis fideliter administratam* (C.

I. L. ii. 4248) ; thus doubtless the diets of all provinces were invested with the apportionment of the taxes. The imperial finance-administration of the three Gauls was at least, as a rule, so divided that the two western provinces (Aquitania and Lugudunensis) were placed under one procurator, Belgica and the two Germanies under another ; yet there were probably not legally fixed powers for this purpose. A regular taking part in the levy may not be inferred from the discussion held by Hadrian—evidently as an extraordinary step—with representatives of all the Spanish districts (*vita*, 12).

republic had not done—conferred on each one an organ for bringing requests and complaints before the government.   Yet Gaul had in this respect, as compared with all other parts of the empire, at least a privilege *de facto*, as indeed this institution is here alone found fully developed.[1]   For one thing, the united diet of the three provinces necessarily had a more independent position in presence of the legates and procurators of each of them, than, for example, the diet of Thessalonica in presence of the governor of Macedonia.   But then, in the case of institutions of this nature, far less depends on the measure of the rights conferred than on the weight of the bodies therein represented ; and the strength of the individual Gallic communities was transferred to the diet of Lyons, just as the weakness of the individual Hellenic communities to that of Argos.   In the development of Gaul under the emperors the diet of Lyons to all appearance promoted essentially that general Gallic homogeneity, which went there hand in hand with the Latinising.

The composition of the diet, which is known to us with tolerable accuracy,[2] shows in what way the question

Composition of the diet.

[1] For the *arca Galliarum*, the freedman of the three Gauls (Henzen, 6393), the *adlector arcae Galliarum*, *inquisitor Galliarum*, *iudex arcae Galliarum*, no other province, so far as I know, furnishes analogies ; and of these institutions, had they been general, the inscriptions elsewhere would certainly have preserved traces. These arrangements appear to point to a self-administering and self-taxing body (the *adlector*, the meaning of which term is not clear, occurs as an official in *collegia*, C. I. L. vi. 355 ; Orelli, 2406) ; probably this chest defrayed the doubtless not inconsiderable expenditure for the temple-buildings and for the annual festival. The *arca Galliarum* was not a state-chest.

[2] As the total number of the communities recorded on the altar at Lyons, Strabo (iv. 3, 2, p. 192) specifies sixty, and as the number of the Aquitanian communities in the Celtic portion north of the Garonne fourteen (iv. 1, 1, p. 177).   Tacitus (*Ann.* iii. 44) names as the total number of the Gallic cantons sixty-four, and so does, although in an incorrect connection, the scholiast on the *Aeneid*, i. 286.   A like total number is pointed to by the list given in Ptolemy from the second century, which adduces for Aquitania seventeen, for the Lugudunensis twenty-five, for the Belgica twenty-two cantons.   Of his Aquitanian cantons thirteen fall to the region between the Loire and Garonne, four to that between the Garonne and the Pyrenees. In the later one from the fifth century, which is well known under the name of *Notitia Galliarum*, twenty-six fall to Aquitania, twenty-four to the Lugudunensis (exclusive of Lyons), twenty-seven to Belgica.   All these numbers are presumably correct, each for its time.   Between the erection of the altar in 742 and the time of

12.

of nationalities was treated by the government. Of the sixty, afterwards sixty-four, cantons represented at the diet, only four fall to the Iberian inhabitants of Aquitania —although this region between the Garonne and the Pyrenees was divided among a very much larger number of, as a rule, small tribes—whether it was that the others were excluded altogether from representation, or that those four represented cantons were the meeting-places of canton-unions.[2] Afterwards, probably in the time of Trajan, the Iberian district was separated from the Lyons diet, and had an independent representation given to it.[2] On the other hand, the Celtic cantons in

Tacitus (for to this his statement is doubtless to be referred), four cantons may have been added, just as the shifting of the numbers from the second to the fifth century may be referred to individual changes still in good part demonstrable.

Considering the importance of these arrangements, it will not be superfluous to exhibit them in detail, at least for the two western provinces. In the purely Celtic middle province the three lists given by Pliny (first century), Ptolemy (second century), and the *Notitia* (fifth century), agree in twenty-one names : *Abrincates — Andecavi —Aulerci Cenomani—Aulerci Diablintes—Aulerci Eburovici—Baiocasses* (*Bodiocasses* Plin., *Vadicasii* Ptol.)— *Carnutes—Coriosolites* (beyond doubt the *Samnitae* of Ptolemy)—*Haedui — Lexovii — Meldae — Namnetes — Osismii —Parisii—Redones—Senones — Tricassini — Turones — Veliocasses* (*Rotomagenses*)—*Veneti—Unelli* (*Constantia*) ; in three more : *Caletae— Segusiavi — Viducasses*, Pliny and Ptolemy agree, while they are wanting in the *Notitia*, because in the meanwhile the *Caletae* were put together with the Veliocasses or the Rotomagenses, the Viducasses with the Baiocasses, and the Segusiavi were merged in Lyons. On the other hand, instead of the three that have disappeared, there appear two new ones that have arisen by division : *Aureliani* (Orleans), a branch from

the *Carnutes* (Chartres), and *Autessiodurum* (Auxerre), a branch from the *Senones* (Sens). There are left in Pliny two names, *Boi—Atesui ;* in Ptolemy one, *Arvii ;* in the *Notitia* one, *Saii.* For Celtic Aquitania the three lists agree in eleven names : *Arverni —Bituriges Cubi—Bituriges Vivisci* (*Burdigalenses*) — *Cadurci — Gabales —Lemovici—Nitiobriges* (*Aginnenses*) — *Petrucorii — Pictones — Ruteni — Santones ;* the second and third agree in the 12th of *Vellauni*, which must have dropped out in Pliny ; Pliny alone has (apart from the problematic *Aquitani*) two names more, *Ambilatri* and *Anagnutes ;* Ptolemy one otherwise unknown, *Datii ;* perhaps Strabo's number of fourteen is to be made up by two of these. The *Notitia* has, besides these eleven, other two, based on splitting up the *Albigenses* (Albi on the Tarn), and the *Ecolismenses* (Angoulême). The lists of the eastern cantons stand related in a similar way. Although subordinate differences emerge, which cannot be here discussed, the character and the continuity of the Gallic cantonal division are clearly apparent.

[1] The four represented tribes were the Tarbelli, Vasates, Auscii, and Convenae. Besides these Pliny enumerates in southern Aquitania no less than twenty-five tribes—most of them otherwise unknown—as standing on a legal equality with those four.

[2] Pliny and, presumably here too

that organisation, with which we have formerly become acquainted, were substantially all represented at the diet, and likewise the half or wholly Germanic,[1] so far as at the time of the institution of the altar they belonged to the empire.   That there was no place in this cantonal representation for the capital of Gaul was a matter of course.   Moreover, the Ubii do not appear at the diet of Lyons, but sacrifice at their own altar of Augustus : this was, as we saw (p. 35), a remnant, which was allowed to subsist, of the intended province of Germany.

While the Celtic nation in imperial Gaul was thus con- solidated in itself, it was also guaranteed in some measure against Roman influences by the course pursued as regards the conferring of the imperial franchise for this domain. The capital of Gaul no doubt was, and continued to be, a Roman burgess-colony, and this was essentially bound

Restricted Roman franchise of the Gauls admitted to citizenship.

following older sources of informa- tion, Ptolemy know nothing of this division ; but we still possess the un- couth verses of the Gascon farmer (Borghesi, *Opp.* viii. 544), who effected this change in Rome, beyond doubt in company with a number of his countrymen, although he has pre- ferred not to add that it was so :—

Flamen, item dumvir, quaestor pagi- q[ue] magister
Verus ad Augustum legato (sic) *munere functus*
pro novem optinuit populis seiungere Gallos :
urbe redux Genio pagi hanc dedicat aram.

The oldest trace of the administrative separation of Iberian Aquitania from the Gallic is the naming of the "district of Lactora" (Lectoure) alongside of Aquitania in an inscrip- tion from Trajan's time (*C. I. L.* v. 875 : *procurator provinciarum Lugu- duniensis et Aquitanicae, item Lac- torae*).   This inscription certainly of itself proves the diversity of the two territories rather than the formal severance of the one from the other ; but it may be otherwise shown that soon after Trajan the latter was

carried out.   For the fact that the separated district was originally divided into nine cantons, as these verses say, is confirmed by the name that thenceforth continued in use, *Novempopulana ;* but under Pius the district numbers already eleven com- munities (for the *dilectator per Aqui- tanicae XI populos*, Boissieu, *Lyon*, p. 246, certainly belongs to this con- nection), in the fifth century twelve, for the *Notitia* enumerates so many under the Novempopulana.   This increase is to be explained similarly to that discussed at p. 95, note 2. The division does not relate to the governorship ; on the contrary, both the Celtic and the Iberian Aquitania remained under the same legate.   But the Novempopulana obtained under Trajan its own diet, while the Celtic districts of Aquitania, after as before, sent deputies to the diet of Lyons.

[1] There are wanting some smaller Germanic tribes, such as the Baetasii and the Sunuci, perhaps for similar reasons with those of the minor Iberian ; and further, the Cannenefates and the Frisians, probably because it was not till later that these became subjects of the empire.   The Batavi were represented.

up with the peculiar position which it occupied and was intended to occupy in contradistinction to the rest of Gaul. But while the south province was covered with colonies and organised throughout according to Italian municipal law, Augustus did not institute in the three Gauls a single burgess-colony ; and probably even that municipal *ius,* which under the name of " Latin " formed an intervening stage between burgesses and non-burgesses, and afforded to its more notable holders burgess-rights in law for their persons and their descendants, was for a considerable time withheld from Gaul.   The personal bestowal of the franchise, partly, according to general enactments, on the soldiers sometimes at their entering on, sometimes at their leaving, service, partly out of special favour on individuals, might certainly fall to the lot also of the Gaul ; Augustus did not go so far as the republic went in prohibiting the Helvetian, for example, once for all from acquiring the Roman franchise, nor could he do so, after Caesar had in many cases given the franchise in this way to native Gauls.   But he took at least from burgesses proceeding from the three Gauls—with the exception always of the Lugudunenses—the right of candidature for magistracies, and therewith at the same time excluded them from the imperial senate.   Whether this enactment was made primarily in the interest of Rome or primarily in that of the Gauls, we cannot tell ; certainly Augustus wished to secure both points—to check on the one hand the intrusion of the alien element into the Roman system, and thereby to purify and elevate the latter, and on the other hand to guarantee the continued subsistence of the Gallic idiosyncrasy after a fashion, which precisely by its judicious reserve promoted the ultimate blending with the Roman character more surely than an abrupt obtrusion of foreign institutions would have done.

Admission of individual communities to Latin rights.

The emperor Claudius, himself born in Lyons and, as those who scoffed at him said, a true Gaul, set aside in great part these restrictions.   The first town in Gaul which certainly received Italian rights was that of the Ubii, where the altar of Roman Germany was constructed ;

there Agrippina, the subsequent wife of Claudius, was born in the camp of her father Germanicus, and she procured in the year 50 colonial rights, probably Latin, for her native place, the modern Cologne.   Perhaps at the same time, perhaps even earlier, the same privilege was procured for the town of the Treveri Augusta, the modern Treves.   Some other Gallic cantons, moreover, were in this way brought nearer to the Roman type, such as that of the Helvetii by Vespasian, and also that of the Sequani (Besançon) ; but Latin rights do not seem to have met with great extension in these regions.   Still less in the time of the earlier emperors was the full right of citizenship conferred in imperial Gaul on whole communities. But Claudius probably made a beginning by cancelling the legal restriction which excluded the Gauls that had attained to personal citizenship of the empire from the career of imperial officials ; this barrier was set aside in the first instance for the oldest allies of Rome, the Haedui, and soon perhaps generally.   By this step equality of position was essentially obtained.   For, according to the circumstances of this epoch, the imperial citizenship had hardly any special practical value for the circles that were by their position in life excluded from an official career, and was of easy attainment for wealthy *peregrini* of good descent, who wished to enter on this career and on that account had need of it ; but it was doubtless a slight keenly felt, when the official career remained in law closed against the Roman burgess from Gaul and his descendants. Setting aside of the restricted franchise.

While in the organising of administration the national character of the Celts was respected so far as was at all compatible with the unity of the empire, this was not the case as regards language.   Even if it had been practicable to allow the communities to conduct their administration in a language, of which the controlling imperial officials could only in exceptional cases be masters, it undoubtedly was not the design of the Roman government to erect this barrier between the rulers and the ruled.   Accordingly, among the coins struck in Gaul under Roman rule, Celtic and Latin language.

and monuments erected on behalf of any community, there has been found no demonstrably Celtic inscription. The use of the language of the country otherwise was not hindered ; we find as well in the southern province as in the northern monuments with Celtic inscription, written in the former case always with the Greek,[1] in the latter always with the Latin[2] alphabet ; and probably at least several of the former, certainly all of the latter, belong to the epoch of Roman rule. The fact that in Gaul, outside of the towns having Italian rights and the Roman camps, inscribed monuments occur at all in but small number, is in all probability to be accounted for mainly by supposing that the language of the country, treated as dialect, appeared just as unsuited for such employment as the unfamiliar imperial language, and hence the erection of memorial-stones did not become generally adopted here as in the Latinised regions ; the Latin probably may at that time in the greater part of Gaul have had nearly the same position, as it had subsequently in the earlier Middle ages over against the popular language of the time. The vigorous survival of the national language is most distinctly shown by the reproduction of the Gallic proper names in Latin, not seldom with the retention of non-Latin forms of sound. The facts that spellings like *Lousonna* and *Boudicca* with the non-Latin diphthong *ou* found their way even into Latin literature, that for the aspirated dental, the English *th*, there was even employed in Roman writing a special sign (Ð), that Epadatextorigus is written alongside of Epasnactus, and Ðirona along-

---

[1] Thus there was found in Nemausus a votive inscription written in the Celtic language, erected Ματρεβο Ναμαυσικαβο (*C. I. L.* xi. p. 383), *i.e.*, to the Mothers of the place.

[2] For example, we read on an altar-stone found in Néris-les-Bains, (Allier ; Desjardins, *Géographie de la Gaule romaine*, ii. 476) ; *Bratronos Nantonicn Epadatextorici Leucullo Suio rebelocitoi.* On another, which the Paris mariners' guild under Tiberius erected to Jupiter the highest and best (Mowat ; *Bull. épig. de la Gaule,* p. 25f.) the main inscription is Latin, but on the reliefs of the lateral surfaces, which appear to represent a procession of nine armed priests, there stand explanatory words appended : *Senani Useiloni* . . . and *Eurises,* which are not Latin. Such a mixture is also met with elsewhere, *e.g.*, in an inscription of Arrènes (Creuse, *Bull. épig. de la Gaule,* i. 38) ; *Sacer Peroco ieuru* (probably = *fecit*) *Duorico v(ot-um) s(olvit) l(ibens) m(erito).*

side of Sirona—make it almost a certainty that the Celtic language, whether in the Roman territory or beyond it, had in or before this epoch undergone a certain regulation in the matter of writing, and could already at that time be written as it is written in the present day.

Nor are evidences wanting of its continued use in Gaul. When the names of towns Augustodunum (Autun), Augustonemētum (Clermont), Augustobona (Troyes), and various similar ones arose, Celtic was necessarily still spoken even in middle Gaul. Arrian, under Hadrian, gives in his disquisition on cavalry, the Celtic expression for particular manœuvres borrowed from the Celts. Irenaeus, a Greek by birth, who towards the end of the second century acted as a clergyman in Lyons, excuses the defects of his style by saying that he lives in the country of the Celts, and is compelled constantly to speak in a barbarian language. In a juristic treatise from the beginning of the third century, in contrast to the rule of law that testamentary directions in general are to be drawn up in Latin or Greek, any other language, *e.g.*, Punic or Gallic, is allowed for *fidei commissa*. The emperor Alexander had his end announced to him by a Gallic fortune-teller in the Gallic language. Further, the church father Jerome, who had been himself in Ancyra as well as in Treves, assures us that the Galatians of Asia Minor and the Treveri of his time spoke nearly the same language, and compares the corrupt Gallic of the Asiatic with the corrupt Punic of the African. The Celtic language has maintained itself in Brittany, just as in Wales, to the present day ; but while the province no doubt obtained its present name from the insular Britons who, in the fifth century fled thither before the Saxons, the language was hardly imported for the first time with these, but was to all appearance handed down from one generation to another there for thousands of years. In the rest of Gaul naturally during the course of the imperial period Roman habits step by step gained ground ; but the Celtic idiom was put an end to here, not so much by the Germanic immigration as by the Christianising of Gaul, which did not,

Evidences of continued use of Celtic.

as in Syria and Egypt, adopt and make a vehicle of the language of the country that was set aside by the government, but preached the Gospel in Latin.

Romanising stronger in the East.

In the progress of Romanising, which in Gaul, apart from the southern province, continued to be left in substance to inward development, there is apparent a remarkable diversity between the eastern Gaul and the west and north—a difference, which turns doubtless in part, but not solely, on the contrast between the Germans and the Gauls. In the occurrences at and after Nero's fall this diversity comes into prominence even as exercising a political influence. The close contact of the eastern cantons with the camps on the Rhine and the recruiting of the Rhenish legions, which took place especially here, procured earlier and more complete entrance for Roman habits there than in the region of the Loire and the Seine. On occasion of those quarrels the Rhenish cantons—the Celtic Lingones and Treveri, as well as the Germanic Ubii or rather the Agrippinenses—went with the Roman town of Lugudunum and held firmly to the legitimate Roman government, while the insurrection, at least, as was observed, in a certain sense national, originated from the Sequani, Haedui, and Arverni. In a later phase of the same struggle we find under altered party-relations the same disunion—those eastern cantons in league with the Germans, while the diet of Rheims refuses to join them.

Native road-measurement.

While the Gallic land was thus in respect of language treated in the main just like the other provinces, we again meet with forbearance towards its old institutions in the regulations as to weights and measures. It is true that, alongside of the general imperial ordinance, which was issued in this respect by Augustus, the local observances continued in many places to subsist agreeably to the tolerant, or rather indifferent, attitude of the government in such things ; but it was only in Gaul that the local arrangement afterwards supplanted that of the empire. The roads in the whole Roman empire were measured and marked according to the unit of the Roman mile (1.48 kilom.), and up to the end of the second century this applied also to those provinces. But from Severus onward its place was taken in the three Gauls and the two Germanies by a mile correlated no doubt to the Roman, but yet different and with a Gallic name, the *leuga* (2.22 kilomètres), equal to one and a half Roman miles. Severus cannot possibly have wished in this matter to make a national concession to the Celts ; this is not in keeping either with the epoch or with that emperor in particular, who stood in an attitude of expressed hostility to these very provinces ; it must have been considerations of expediency that influenced him. These could only be based on the fact that the national road-measure, the *leuga* or else the double *leuga*, the German *rasta*, which latter corresponds to the French *lieue*, continued to subsist in these provinces after the introduction of the unit of road-measure to a much greater extent than was the case in other countries of the empire. Augustus must have extended the Roman mile formally to Gaul and placed the itineraries and the imperial highways on that footing, but must have in reality left to the country the old road-measurement ; and so it may have happened that the later administration found it less inconvenient to acquiesce in the double unit for postal traffic[1] than to continue to make use of a road-measure practically unknown in the country.

Of far greater significance is the attitude of the Roman government to the religion of the country ; in this beyond doubt the Gallic nationality found its most solid support. Even in the south province the worship of non-Roman deities must have held its ground long, much longer than, for example, in Andalusia. The great commercial town of Arelate, indeed, has no other dedications to show than to gods worshipped also in Italy ; but in Fréjus, Aix, Nîmes, and the whole coast region generally, the old Celtic divinities were in the imperial epoch not much less worshipped than in the interior of Gaul. In the Iberian part of Aquitania also we meet numerous traces of the

Religion of the country.

---

[1] The posting-books and itineraries do not fail to remark at Lyons and Toulouse that here the *leugae* begin.

indigenous worship altogether different from the Celtic.
All the images of gods, however, that have come to light
in the south of Gaul bear a stamp deviating less from the
usual type than the monuments of the north ; and, above
all, it was easier to manage matters with the national gods
than with the national priesthood, which meets us only in
imperial Gaul and in the British Islands,—the Druids (iv.
236). It would be vain labour to seek to give any conception of the internal character of the Druidic doctrine,
strangely composed of speculation and imagination ; only
some examples may be allowed to illustrate its singular
and fearful nature. The power of speech was symbolically
represented in a bald-headed, wrinkled, sunburnt old man,
who carries club and bow, and from whose perforated
tongue fine golden chains run to the ears of the man that
follows him—betokening the flying arrows and the crushing blows of the old man mighty in speech, to whom the
hearts of the multitude willingly listen. This was the
Ogmius of the Celts ; to the Greeks he appeared as
a Charon dressed up as Herakles. An altar found in
Paris shows us three images of the gods with annexed
inscription ; in the middle Jovis, on his left Vulcan, on
his right Esus "the horrid with his cruel altars," as a
Roman poet terms him, and yet a god of commerce and
of peaceful dealing ;[1] he is girded for labour like Vulcan,
and, as the latter carries hammer and tongs, so he hews
a willow tree with the axe. A frequently recurring deity,
probably named Cernunnos, is represented cowering with
crossed legs ; on its head it bears a stag's antlers, on
which hangs a neck chain, and holds in its lap a money-
bag ; before it stand cattle and goats—apparently, as if
it were meant to express the ground as the source of
riches. The enormous difference of this Celtic Olympus—
void of all chasteness and beauty and delighting in quaint
and fantastic mingling of things very earthly—from the
simply human forms of the Greek, and the simply human

iv. 225.

---

[1] The second Berne gloss on Lucan,
i. 445, which rightly makes Teutates
Mars, and seems also otherwise credible, says of him : *Hesum Mercurium
colunt, si quidem a mercatoribus
colitur.*

conceptions of the Roman, religion enables us to guess the barrier which stood between these conquered and their conquerors.   With this were connected, moreover, very serious practical consequences ; a comprehensive traffic in secret remedies and charms, in which the priests played at the same time the part of physicians, and in which, alongside of the conjuring and the blessing, human sacrifices occurred, and healing of the sick by the flesh of those thus slain.   That direct opposition to the foreign rule prevailed in the Druidism of this period cannot at least be proved ; but, even if this were not the case, it is easy to conceive that the Roman government, which elsewhere let alone all local peculiarities of worship with indifferent toleration, contemplated this Druidical system, not merely in its extravagances but as a whole, with apprehension. The institution of the Gallic annual festival in the purely Roman capital of the country, and with the exclusion of any link attaching it to the national cultus, was evidently a counter-move of the government against the old religion of the country, with its yearly council of priests at Chartres, the centre of the Gallic land.   Augustus, however, took no further direct step against Druidism than that of prohibiting any Roman citizen from taking part in the Gallic national cultus.   Tiberius in his more energetic way acted with decision, and prohibited altogether this priesthood with its retinue of teachers and healing practitioners ; but it does not quite speak for the practical success of this enactment that the same prohibition was issued afresh under Claudius : it is narrated of the latter that he caused a Gaul of rank to be beheaded, simply because he was convicted of having brought into application the charms customary in his own country for a good result in proceedings before the emperor.   That the occupation of Britain, which had been from of old the chief seat of these priestly actings, was in good part resolved on in order thereby to get at the root of the evil, will be fully set forth in the sequel (p. 185).   In spite of all this the priesthood still played an important part in the revolt which the Gauls attempted after the downfall of the Claudian dynasty ; the burning of the Capitol—so the Druids preached—announced the revolution in affairs, and the beginning of the dominion of the north over the south. But, although this oracle came subsequently to be fulfilled, it was not so through this nation and in favour of its priests. The peculiarities of the Gallic worship doubtless still exerted their effect even later ; when in the third century a distinctive Gallo-Roman empire came into existence for some time, Hercules played the first part on its coins partly in his Graeco-Roman form, partly as Gallic Deusoniensis or Magusanus. But of the Druids there is no further mention, except only so far as the sage women in Gaul down to the time of Diocletian passed under the name of Druidesses and uttered oracles, and the ancient noble houses still for long boasted of Druidic progenitors on their ancestral roll. The religion of the country fell into the background still more rapidly perhaps than the native language, and Christianity, as it pushed its way, hardly encountered in the former any serious resistance.

Economic condition

Southern Gaul, withdrawn more than any other province by its position from hostile assault, and, like Italy and Andalusia, a land of the olive and the fig, rose under the imperial government to great prosperity and rich urban development. The amphitheatre and the sarcophagus-field of Arles, the "mother of all Gaul," the theatre of Orange, the temples and bridges still standing erect to this day in and near Nîmes, are vivid witnesses of this down to the present time. Even in the northern provinces the old prosperity of the country was enhanced by the lasting peace, which, certainly with lasting pressure of taxation, accrued to the land by means of the foreign rule. " In Gaul," says a writer of the time of Vespasian, " the sources of wealth are at home, and flood the earth with their abundance."[1] Perhaps nowhere do equally

---

[1] Josephus, *Bell. Jud.* ii. 16, 4. There king Agrippa asks his Jews whether they imagined themselves to be richer than the Gauls, braver than the Germans, more sagacious than the Hellenes. With this all other testimonies accord. Nero hears of the revolt not unwillingly *occasione nata spoliandarum iure belli opulentissimarum provinciarum* (Suetonius, *Nero*, 40 ; Plut. *Galb.* 5) ; the booty taken from the insurgent army of

numerous and equally magnificent country-houses make
their appearance,—especially in the east of Gaul, on the
Rhine and its affluents ; we discern clearly the rich Gallic
nobility.   Famous is the testament of a man of rank
among the Lingones, who directs that there should be
erected for him a memorial tomb and a statue of Italian
marble or best bronze, and that, among other things, his
whole implements for hunting and fowling be burned
along with him.   This reminds us of the elsewhere mentioned hunting-parks enclosed for miles in the Celtic
country, and of the prominent part which the Celtic
hounds for the chase and Celtic huntsmanship play in the
Xenophon of Hadrian's time, who does not fail to add
that the hunting system of the Celts could not have been
known to Xenophon the son of Gryllos.   To this connection
belongs likewise the remarkable fact that in the Roman
army of the imperial period the cavalry was, properly
speaking, Celtic, not merely inasmuch as it was pre-
eminently recruited from Gaul, but also because the
manœuvres, and even the technical expressions, were in
good part derived from the Celts ; we see here how,
after the disappearance of the old burgess-cavalry under
the republic, the cavalry became reorganised by Caesar
and Augustus with Gallic men and in Gallic fashion.
The basis of this notable prosperity was agriculture,
towards the elevation of which Augustus himself worked
with energy, and which yielded rich produce in all Gaul,
apart perhaps from the steppe-region on the Aquitanian
coast.   The rearing of cattle was also lucrative, especially
in the north, particularly the rearing of swine and sheep,
which soon acquired importance for manufactures and
for export ; the Menapian hams (from Flanders) and
the Atrebatian and Nervian cloth-mantles (near Arras

Vindex is immense (Tac. *Hist.* i. 51).
Tacitus (*Hist.* iii. 46) calls the Haedui
pecunia dites et voluptatibus opulentos.
The general of Vespasian is not wrong
in saying to the revolted Gauls in
Tac. *Hist.* iv. 74 : *Regna bellaque per
Gallias semper fuere, donec in nostrum
ius concederetis; nos quamquam totiens*
*lacessiti iure victoriae id solum vobis
addidimus quo pacem tueremur, nam
neque quies gentium sine armis neque
arma sine stipendiis neque stipendia
sine tributis haberi queunt.* The
taxes doubtless pressed heavily, but
not so heavily as the old state of
feud and club-law.

and Tournay) went forth in later times to the whole empire.

Culture of the vine.

Of special interest was the development of the culture of the vine. Neither the climate nor the government was favourable to it. The "Gallic winter" remained long proverbial among the inhabitants of the southern lands ; as, indeed, it was on this side that the Roman empire extended farthest towards the north. But narrower limits were drawn for the Gallic cultivation of the vine by Italian commercial competition. Certainly the god Dionysos accomplished his conquest of the world on the whole slowly, and only step by step did the drink prepared from grain give way to the juice of the vine ; but it was a result of the prohibitive system that in Gaul beer maintained itself at least in the north as the usual spirituous drink throughout the whole period of the empire ; and even the emperor Julian, on his abode in Gaul, came into conflict with this pseudo-Bacchus.[1] The imperial government did not indeed go so far as the republic, which placed under police prohibition the culture of the vine

iii. 177 ; ii. 375.

and olive on the south coast of Gaul (iii. 175 ; ii. 398) ; but the Italians of their time were withal the true sons of their fathers. The flourishing condition of the two great emporia on the Rhine, Arles and Lyons, depended in no small degree on the market for Italian wine in Gaul ; by which fact we may measure what importance the culture of the vine must at that time have had for Italy. If one of the most careful administrators who held the imperial office, Domitian, issued orders that in all the provinces at least the half of the vines should be destroyed[2]—which,

---

[1] This epigram on "barley-wine" is preserved (*Anthol. Pal.* ix. 368):

Τίς πόθεν εἶς, Διόνυσε ; μὰ γὰρ τὸν
  ἀληθέα Βάκχον,
οὐ σ' ἐπιγιγνώσκω· τὸν Διὸς οἶδα μόνον.
κεῖνος νέκταρ ὄδωδε· σὺ δὲ τράγου· ἦ
  ῥά σε Κελτοὶ
τῇ πενίῃ βοτρύων τεῦξαν ἀπ'
  ἀσταχύων.
τῷ σε χρὴ καλέειν Δημήτριον, οὐ
  Διόνυσον,
πυρογένη μᾶλλον καὶ βρόμον, οὐ
  Βρόμιον.

On an earthen ring found in Paris (Mowat, *Bull. épig. de la Gaule*, ii. 110 ; iii. 133), which is hollow and adapted for the filling of cups, the drinker says to the host : *copo, conditu(m)* [*cnoditu* is a misspelling] *abes ; est reple(n)da*—"Host, thou hast more in the cellar ; the flask is empty ;" and to the barmaid : *ospita, reple lagona(m) cervesa*—"Girl, fill the flask with beer."

[2] Suetonius, *Dom.* 7. When it was

it is true, were not so carried out—we may thence infer that the diffusion of the vine-culture was at all events subjected to serious restriction on the part of the government. In the Augustan age it was still unknown in the northern part of the Narbonese province (iv. 227, note), and, though here too it was soon taken up, it yet appears to have remained through centuries restricted to the Narbonensis and southern Aquitania ; of Gallic wines the better age knows only the Allobrogian and the Biturigian, according to our way of speaking, the Burgundian and the Bordeaux.[1] It was only when the reins of the empire fell from the hands of the Italians, in the course of the third century, that this was changed, and the emperor Probus (276-282) at length threw the culture of the vine open to the provincials. Probably it was only in consequence of this that the vine gained a firm footing on the Seine as on the Moselle. " I have," writes the emperor Julian, " spent a winter " (it was the winter of 357-358) " in dear Lutetia, for so the Gauls term the little town of the Parisii, a small island lying in the river and walled all round. The water is there excellent and pure to look at and to drink ; the inhabitants have a pretty mild winter, and good wine is grown among them ; in fact, some even rear figs, covering them up in winter with wheaten straw as with a cloth." And not much later the poet of Bordeaux, in his pleasing description of the Moselle, depicts the vineyards as bordering that river on both banks, "just as my own vines wreathe for me the yellow Garonne."

iv. 217

The internal intercourse, as well as that with the neighbouring lands, especially with Italy, must have been very active, and the network of roads must have been much developed and fostered. The great imperial highway from Rome to the mouth of the Baetis, which has

Network of highways.

---

specified as a reason, that the higher prices of corn were occasioned by the conversion of agricultural land into vineyards, that was of course a pretext which calculated on the want of intelligence in the public.

[1] When Hehn still appeals (*Kulturpflanzen*, p. 76) for the vine-culture of the Arverni and the Sequani, beyond the Narbonensis, to Pliny, *H. N.* xiv. 1, 18, he follows discarded interpolations of the text. It is possible that the sterner imperial government in the three Gauls kept back the cultivation of the vine more than the lax senatorial rule in the Narbonensis.

been mentioned, under Spain (p. 74), was the main artery for the land traffic of the south province; the whole stretch, kept in repair in republican times from the Alps to the Rhone by the Massaliots, from thence to the Pyrenees by the Romans, was laid anew by Augustus. In the north the imperial highways led mainly to the Gallic capital or to the great camps on the Rhine; yet sufficient provision seems to have been made for other requisite communication.

Hellenism in south Gaul.

If the southern province in the olden time belonged intellectually to the Hellenic type, the decline of Massilia and the mighty progress of Romanism in southern Gaul produced, no doubt, an alteration in that respect; nevertheless this portion of Gaul remained always, like Campania, a seat of Hellenism. The fact that Nemausus, one of the towns sharing the heritage of Massilia, shows on its coins of the Augustan period Alexandrian numbering of the years and the arms of Egypt, has been not without probability referred to the settlement by Augustus himself of veterans from Alexandria in this city, which presented no attitude of opposition to Hellenism. It may, doubtless, also be brought into connection with the influence of Massilia, that to this province, at least as regards descent, belonged that historian, who—apparently in intentional contrast to the national-Roman type of history, and occasionally with sharp sallies against its most noted representatives, Sallust and Livy—upheld the Hellenic type, the Vocontian Pompeius Trogus, author of a history of the world beginning with Alexander and the kingdoms of the Diadochi, in which Roman affairs are set forth only within this framework, or by way of appendix. Beyond doubt in this he was only retaliating, which was strictly within the province of the literary opposition of Hellenism; still it remains remarkable that this tendency should find its Latin representative, and an adroit and fluent one, here in the Augustan age. From a later period Favorinus deserves mention, of an esteemed burgess-family in Arles, one of the chief pillars of polymathy in Hadrian's time; a philosopher with an Aristotelian and sceptical tendency, at the

same time a philologue and rhetorician, the scholar of
Dion of Prusa, the friend of Plutarch and of Herodes
Atticus, assailed polemically in the field of science by
Galen and in light literature by Lucian, sustaining lively
relations generally with the noted men of letters of the
second century, and not less with the emperor Hadrian.
His manifold investigations, among other matters, concerning the names of the companions of Odysseus that
were devoured by Scylla, and as to the name of the first
man who was at the same time a man of letters, make
him appear as the genuine representative of the erudite
dealing in trifles that was then in vogue; and his discourses
for a cultivated public on Thersites and the ague, as
well as his conversations in part recorded for us "on all
things and some others," give not an agreeable, but a
characteristic, picture of the literary pursuits of the time.
Here we have to call attention to what he himself reckoned
among the remarkable points of his career in life, that he
was by birth a Gaul and at the same time a Greek author.
Although the *literati* of the West frequently gave, as
occasion offered, specimens of their Greek, but few of
them made use of this as the proper language of their
authorship ; in this case its use would be influenced in
part by the scholar's place of birth.

South Gaul, moreover, had so far a share in the
Augustan bloom of literature, that some of the most
notable forensic orators of the later Augustan age,
Votienus Montanus († 27 A.D.), from Narbo—named the
Ovid of orators—and Gnaeus Domitius Afer (consul in
39 A.D.) from Nemausus, belonged to this province.
Generally, as was natural, Roman literature extended its
circulation also over this region ; the poets of Domitian's
time sent their free copies to friends in Tolosa and Vienna.
Pliny, under Trajan, is glad that his minor writings find
even in Lugudunum not merely favourable readers, but
booksellers who push their sale.   But we cannot produce
evidence for the south of any such special influence, as
Baetica exercised in the earlier, and northern Gaul in the
later, imperial period, on the intellectual and literary

Latin litera-
ture in the
south pro-
vince.

development of Rome. The fair land yielded richly wine and fruits ; but the empire drew from it neither soldiers nor thinkers.

Gaul proper was in the domain of science the promised land of teaching and of learning ; this presumably was due to the peculiar development and to the powerful influence of the national priesthood. Druidism was by no means a naive popular faith, but a highly developed and pretentious theology, which in the good church-fashion strove to enlighten, or at any rate control, all spheres of human thought and action, physics and metaphysics, law and medicine ; which demanded of its scholars unwearied study, it was said, for twenty years, and sought and found these its scholars pre-eminently in the ranks of the nobility. The suppression of the Druids by Tiberius and his successors must have affected in the first instance these schools of the priests, and have led to their being at least publicly abolished ; but this could only be done effectively when the national training of youth was brought face to face with the Romano-Greek culture, just as the Carnutic council of Druids was confronted with the temple of Roma in Lyons. How early this took place in Gaul, without question under the guiding influence of the government, is shown by the remarkable fact that in the formerly mentioned revolt under Tiberius the insurgents attempted above all to possess themselves of the town of Augustodunum (Autun), in order to get into their power the youths of rank studying there, and thereby to gain or to terrify the great families. In the first instance these Gallic Lycea may well have been, in spite of their by no means national course of training, a leaven of distinctively Gallic nationality ; it was hardly an accident that the most important of them at that time had its seat, not in the Roman Lyons, but in the capital of the Haedui, the chief among the Gallic cantons. But the Romano-Hellenic culture, though perhaps forced on the nation and received at first with opposition, penetrated, as gradually the antagonism wore off, so deeply into the Celtic character, that in time the scholars applied themselves to it more zealously than the teachers.   The training of a gentleman, somewhat after the manner in which it at present exists in England, based on the study of Latin and in the second place of Greek, and vividly reminding us in the development of the school-speech, with its finely cut points and brilliant phrases, of more recent literary phenomena springing from the same soil, became gradually in the West a sort of chartered right of the Gallo-Romans.   The teachers there were probably at all times better paid than in Italy, and above all were better treated. Quintilian already mentions with respect among the prominent forensic orators several Gauls ; and not without design Tacitus, in his fine dialogue on oratory, makes the Gallic advocate, Marcus Aper, the defender of modern eloquence against the worshippers of Cicero and Caesar. The first place among the universities of Gaul was subsequently taken by Burdigala, and indeed generally Aquitania was, as respects culture, far in advance of middle and northern Gaul ; in a dialogue written there at the beginning of the fifth century one of the speakers, a clergyman from Châlon-sur-Saône, hardly ventures to open his mouth before the cultivated Aquitanian circle.   This was the sphere of working of the formerly-mentioned professor Ausonius, who was called by the emperor Valentinian to be teacher of his son Gratian (born in 359), and who has in his miscellaneous poems raised a monument to a large number of his colleagues ; and, when his contemporary Symmachus, the most famous orator of this epoch, sought a private tutor for his son, he had one brought from Gaul in recollection of his old teacher who had his home on the Garonne.   By its side Augustodunum remained always one of the great centres of Gallic studies ; we have still the speeches which were made before the emperor Constantine, asking, and giving thanks for, the re-establishment of this school of instruction.

The representation in literature of this zealous scholastic activity is of a subordinate kind, and of slight value—declamations, which were stimulated especially by the later conversion of Treves into an imperial residence and the frequent sojourn of the court in the Gallic land, and occasional poems of a multifarious character.   The making of verses was, like the supply of speeches, a necessary function of the teaching office, and the public teacher of literature was at the same time a poet not exactly born, but bespoken.   At least the depreciation of poetry, which is characteristic of the otherwise similar Hellenic literature of the same epoch, did not prevail among these Occidentals.   In their verses the reminiscence of the school and the artifice of the pedant predominate,[1] and pictures of vivid and real feeling, as in the Moselle-trip of Ausonius, but rarely occur.   The speeches, which we are indeed in a position to judge of only by some late addresses delivered at the imperial palace, are models in the art of saying little in many words, and of expressing absolute loyalty with an equally absolute lack of thought. When a wealthy mother sent her son, after he had acquired the copiousness and ornateness of Gallic speech, onward to Italy to acquire also the Roman dignity,[2] this was certainly more difficult of acquisition for these Gallic rhetoricians than the pomp of words.   For the early Middle age such performances as these exercised decisive influence ; through them in the first Christian period Gaul became the seat proper of pious verses and withal the last refuge of scholastic literature, while the great mental movement within Christianity did not find its chief representatives there.

Construc-
tive and
plastic art.

In the sphere of the constructive and plastic arts the climate itself called forth various phenomena unknown, or known only in their germs, to the south proper.   Thus the heating of the air, which in Italy was usual only for

---

[1] One of the professorial poems of Ausonius is dedicated to four Greek grammarians :—

Sedulum cunctis studium docendi ;
Fructus exilis tenuisque sermo ;
Sed, quia nostro docuere in aevo,
    Commemorandi.

This mention is the more meritorious, seeing that he had learned nothing suitable from them :—

Obstitit nostrae quia, credo, mentis
Tardior sensus, neque disciplinis
Appulit Graecis puerilis aevi
    Noxius error.

Such thoughts have frequently found utterance, but seldom in Sapphic measure.

[2] *Romana gravitas,* Hieronymus, *Ep.* 125, p. 929, Vall.

baths, and the use of glass windows, which was likewise far from common there, were comprehensively brought into application in Gallic architecture. But we may perhaps speak of a development of art peculiar to this region, in so far as figures and, in progress of time, representations of scenes of daily life emerge in the Celtic territory with relatively greater frequency than in Italy, and replace the used-up mythological representations by others more pleasing. It is certainly almost in the sepulchral monuments alone that we are able to recognise this tendency to the real and the *genre*, but it doubtless prevailed in the practice of art generally. The arch of Arausio (Orange), from the early imperial period, with its Gallic weapons and standards ; the bronze statue of the Berlin museum found at Vetera, representing apparently the god of the place with ears of barley in his hair ; the Hildesheim silver-plate, probably proceeding in part from Gallic workshops, show a certain freedom in the adoption and transformation of Italian suggestions. The tomb of the Julii at St. Remy, near Avignon, a work of the Augustan age, is a remarkable evidence of the lively and spirited reception of Hellenic art in southern Gaul, as well in its bold architectural structure of two square storeys crowned by a peristyle with conic dome, as also in its reliefs which, in style most nearly akin to the Pergamene, present battle and hunting scenes with numerous figures, taken apparently from the life of the persons honoured, in picturesque animated execution. It is remarkable that the acme of this development is reached —by the side of the southern province—in the district of the Moselle and the Maas. This region, not placed so completely under Roman influence as Lyons and the headquarter-towns on the Rhine, and more wealthy and civilised than the districts on the Loire and the Seine, seems to have in some measure produced of itself this exercise of art. The tomb of a man of rank in Treves, well known under the name of the Igel Column, gives a clear idea of the tower-like monuments, crowned with pointed roof and covered on all sides with representations of the life of the deceased, that are here at home. Frequently we see on them the landlord, to whom his peasants present sheep, fish, fowls, eggs. A tomb-stone from Arlon, near Luxemburg, shows, besides the portraits of the two spouses, on the one side a cart and a woman with a fruit-basket, on the other a sale of apples above two men squatting on the ground. Another tombstone from Neumagen, near Treves, has the form of a ship; in this sit six mariners plying the oars; the cargo consists of large casks, alongside of which the merry-looking steersman seems—one might imagine—to be rejoicing over the wine which they contain. We may perhaps bring them into connection with the serene picture which the poet of Bordeaux has preserved to us of the Moselle valley, with its magnificent castles, its many vineyards, and its stirring doings of fishermen and of sailors, and find in it the proof that in this fair land, more than fifteen hundred years ago, there was already the pulsation of peaceful activity, serene enjoyment, and warm life.

CHAPTER IV.

ROMAN GERMANY AND THE FREE GERMANS.

THE two Roman provinces of Upper and Lower Germany Limitation of Roman Germany. were the result of that defeat of the Roman arms and of Roman policy under the reign of Augustus which has been already (p. 55 f.) described. The original province of Germany, which embraced the country from the Rhine to the Elbe, subsisted only twenty years, from the first campaign of Drusus, 742 U. C., down to the battle of 12. Varus and the fall of Aliso, 762 U. C.; but as, on the A.D. 9. one hand, it included the military camps on the left bank of the Rhine—Vindonissa, Mogontiacum, Vetera—and, on the other hand, even after that disaster, more or less considerable portions of the right bank remained Roman, the governorship and the command were not, in a strict sense, done away by that catastrophe, although they were, so to speak, placed in suspense. The internal organisation of the Three Gauls has been already set forth ; they embraced the whole country as far as the Rhine without distinction of descent—except that the Ubii, who had only been brought over to settle in Gaul during the last crises, did not belong to the sixty-four cantons, while the Helvetii, the Triboci, and generally the districts elsewhere held in occupation by the Rhenish troops, doubtless did so belong. The intention had been to gather together the German cantons between the Rhine and Elbe into a similar association under Roman supremacy, as had been constituted in the case of the Gallic cantons, and to bestow upon it, in the altar to Augustus of the Ubian town—the germ of the modern Cologne—an executive centre similar to that which the altar of Augustus at Lyons formed for Gaul ; for the more remote future the transference of the chief camp to the right bank of the Rhine, and the restoration of the left, at least in the main, to the governor of the Belgica, were doubtless in contemplation. But these projects came to an end with the legions of Varus ; the Germanic altar of Augustus on the Rhine became or remained the altar of the Ubii ; the legions permanently retained their standing quarters in the territory, which properly belonged to the Belgica, but—seeing that a separation of the military and civil administration was, according to the Roman arrangement, excluded—was placed, so long as the troops were stationed there, for administrative purposes also under the commandants of the two armies.[1] For, as was formerly stated, Varus was probably the last commandant of the united army of the Rhine ; on the increase of the army to eight legions, which was consequent upon that disaster, the division of it to all appearance also ensued. What we have to describe in this section therefore is not, strictly speaking, the circumstances of a Roman province, but the fortunes of a Roman army, and, as most closely connected therewith, the fortunes of the neighbouring peoples and adversaries, so far as these are interwoven with the history of Rome.

Upper and Lower Germany.

The two headquarters of the army of the Rhine were always Vetera near Wesel and Mogontiacum, the modern Mentz, both doubtless older than the division of the command, and one of the reasons for introducing that division. The two armies numbered in the first century

---

[1] This division of a province among three governors is without parallel elsewhere in Roman administration. The relation of Africa and Numidia offers doubtless an external analogy, but was politically conditioned by the position of the senatorial governor to the imperial military commandant, while the three governors of Belgica were uniformly imperial ; and it is not at all easy to see why the two Germanic ones had districts within the Belgica assigned to them instead of districts of their own. Nothing but the taking back of the frontier, while the hitherto subsisting name was retained—just as the Transdanubian Dacia continued subsequently to subsist in name as Cis - Danubian — explains this singular peculiarity.

four legions each, thus about 30,000 men[1]; at or between those two points lay the main bulk of the Roman
troops, besides one legion at Noviomagus (Nimeguen),
another at Argentoratum (Strassburg), and a third at Vindonissa (Windisch not far from Zürich) not far from the
Raetian frontier.   To the lower army belonged the not
inconsiderable fleet on the Rhine.   The boundary between
the upper and the lower army lay between Andernach and
Remagen near Brohl,[2] so that Coblenz and Bingen fell to
the upper, Bonn and Cologne to the lower military district.
On the left bank there belonged to the upper German
administrative circuit the districts of the Helvetii (Switzerland), the Sequani (Besançon), the Lingones (Langres),
the Rauraci (Basle), the Triboci (Alsace), the Nemetes
(Spires), and the Vangiones (Worms); to the more restricted lower German circuit belonged the district of the
Ubii, or rather the colony Agrippina (Cologne), those of
the Tungri (Tongern), the Menapii (Brabant), and the
Batavi, while the cantons situated farther to the west,
including Metz and Treves, were placed under the different governors of the three Gauls.   While this separation
has merely administrative significance, on the other hand
the varying extent of the two jurisdictions on the right

---

[1] The strength of the *auxilia* of the
upper army may be fixed for the epoch
of Domitian and Trajan with tolerable
certainty at about 10,000 men.   A
document of the year 90 enumerates
four *alae* and fourteen *cohortes* of this
army ; to these is to be added at least
one cohort (*I Germanorum*), which, it
can be shown, did garrison-duty there
as well in the year 82 as in the year
116 ; whether two *alae* which were
there in the year 82, and at least
three cohorts which were there in
116, and which are absent from the
list of the year 90, were doing garrison work there in 90 or not, is
doubtful, but most of them probably
were away from the province before
90 or only came into it after 90.   Of
those nineteen *auxilia* one was certainly
(*coh. I Damascenorum*), another perhaps (*ala I Flavia gemina*), a double

division.   At the minimum, therefore, the figure indicated above results as the normal state of the *auxilia*
of this army, and it cannot have been
materially exceeded.   But the *auxilia*
of lower Germany, whose garrisons
were less extended, may well have
been smaller in number.

[2] At the frontier bridge over the
rivulet Abrinca, now Vinxt, the old
boundary of the archdioceses of
Cologne and Treves, stood two altars, that on the side of Remagen
dedicated to the Boundaries, the
Spirit of the place, and Jupiter (*Finibus et Genio loci et Iovi optimo
maximo*) by soldiers of the 30th
lower German legion ; the other on
the side of Andernach, dedicated to
Jupiter, the Genius of the place, and
Juno, by a soldier of the 8th Upper
Germanic (Brambach, 649, 650).

bank coincides with the varying relations to their neighbours and the advancing or receding of the bounds of the Roman rule conditioned by those relations. With these neighbours confronting them, matters on the lower and on the upper Rhine were regulated in ways so diverse, and the course of events was so thoroughly different that here the provincial separation became historically of the most decisive importance. Let us look first at the development of things on the lower Rhine.

Lower Germany.

We have formerly described how far the Romans had subjugated the Germans on both banks of the Rhine. The Germanic Batavi had been peacefully united with the empire not by Caesar, but not long afterwards, perhaps by Drusus (p. 28). They were settled in the Rhine delta, that is on the left bank of the Rhine and on the islands formed by its arms, upwards as far at least as the Old Rhine, and so nearly from Antwerp to Utrecht and Leyden in Zealand and southern Holland, on territory originally Celtic—at least the local names are predominantly Celtic ; their name is still borne by the Betuwe, the lowland between the Waal and the Leck with the capital Noviomagus, now Nimeguen. They were, especially compared with the restless and refractory Celts, obedient and useful subjects, and hence occupied a distinctive position in the aggregate, and particularly in the military system, of the Roman empire. They remained quite free from taxation, but were on the other hand drawn upon more largely than any other canton in the recruiting ; this one canton furnished to the army 1000 horsemen and 9000 foot soldiers ; besides, the men of the imperial body-guard were taken especially from them. The command of these Batavian divisions was conferred exclusively on native Batavi. The Batavi were accounted indisputably not merely as the best riders and swimmers of the army, but also as the model of true soldiers, and in this case certainly the good pay of the Batavian body-guard, as well as the privilege of the nobles to serve as officers, considerably confirmed their loyalty. These Germans accordingly had taken no part either preparatory to, or consequent upon, the disaster of Varus; and if Augustus, under the first impression of the terrible news, discharged his Batavian guard, he soon became convinced of the groundlessness of his suspicion, and the troop was a short time afterwards reinstated.

On the other bank of the Rhine next to the Batavi, in the modern Kennemer district (North Holland beyond Amsterdam), dwelt the Cannenefates, closely related to them but less numerous; they are not merely named among the tribes subjugated by Tiberius, but were also treated like the Batavi in the furnishing of soldiers. The Frisians, adjoining these further on, in the coast district that is still named after them, as far as the lower Ems, submitted to Drusus and obtained a position similar to that of the Batavi. There was imposed on them instead of tribute simply the delivery of a number of bullocks' hides for the wants of the army; on the other hand they had to furnish comparatively large numbers of men for the Roman service. They were the most faithful allies of Drusus as afterwards of Germanicus, useful to him in constructing canals as well as especially after the unfortunate North Sea expeditions (p. 53). They were followed on the east by the Chauci, a widely extended tribe of sailors and fishermen along the coast of the North Sea on both sides of the Weser, perhaps from the Ems to the Elbe; they were brought into subjection to the Romans by Drusus at the same time with the Frisians, but not, like these, without resistance. All these Germanic coast tribes submitted either by agreement or at any rate without any severe struggle to the new rule, and as they had taken no part in the rising of the Cherusci, they still continued after the battle of Varus in their earlier relations to the Roman empire; even from the more remote cantons of the Frisians and the Chauci the garrisons were not at that time withdrawn, and the latter still furnished a contingent to the campaigns of Germanicus. On the renewed evacuation of Germany in the year 17 the poor and distant land of the Chauci, difficult of protection, seems certainly to have been given up; at least there are no later evidences

Cannene-fates.

Frisians.

Chauci.

of the continuance of the Roman dominion there, and some decades later we find them independent. But all the land westward of the lower Ems remained with the empire, whose boundary thus included the modern Netherlands. The defence of this part of the imperial frontier against the Germans not belonging to the empire was left in the main to the subject maritime cantons themselves.

Limes and desert-frontier on the lower Rhine.

Farther up the stream a different course was taken ; a frontier-road was here marked off, and the land lying between it and the Rhine was depopulated. With the frontier-road drawn at a greater or less distance from the Rhine, the *Limes*,[1] was associated the control of frontier-

---

[1] *Limes* (from *limus*, across) is a technical expression foreign to the state of things under our [German] law, and hence not to be reproduced in our language, derived from the fact that the Roman division of land, which excludes all natural boundaries, separates the squares, into which the ground coming under the head of private property is divided, by intermediate paths of a definite breadth ; these intermediate paths are the *limites*, and so far the word always denotes at once the boundary drawn by man's hand, and the road constructed by man's hand. The word retains this double signification even in application to the state (Rudorff, *Grom. Inst.* p. 289, puts the matter incorrectly) ; *limes* is not every imperial frontier, but only that which is marked out by human hands, and arranged at the same time for being patrolled and having posts stationed for frontier-defence (*Vita Hadriani*, 12 ; *locis in quibus barbari non fluminibus, sed limitibus dividuntur*), such as we find in Germany and in Africa. Therefore there are applied to the laying-out of this *limes* the terms that serve to designate the construction of roads, *aperire* (Velleius, ii. 121, which is not to be understood, as Müllenhoff, *Zeitschr. f. d. Alterth.*, new series, ii. p. 32, would have it, like our opening of a turnpike),

munire, agere (Frontinus, *Strat.* i. 3, 10 : *limitibus per* CXX *m. p. actis*). Therefore the *limes* is not merely a longitudinal line, but also of a certain breadth (Tacitus, *Ann.* i. 50 ; *castra in limite locat*). Hence the construction of the *limes* is often combined with that of the *agger*—that is, of the road-embankment (Tacitus, *Ann.* ii. 7 : *cuncta novis limitibus aggeribusque permunita*), and the shifting of it with the transference of frontier-posts (Tacitus, *Germ.* 29 : *limite acto promotisque praesidiis*). The Limes is thus the imperial frontier-road, destined for the regulation of frontier-intercourse, inasmuch as the crossing of it was allowed only at certain points corresponding to the bridges of the river boundary, and elsewhere forbidden. This was doubtless effected in the first instance by patrolling the line, and, so long as this was done, the *limes* remained a boundary road. It remained so too, when it was fortified on both sides, as was done in Britain and at the mouth of the Danube ; the Britannic wall is also termed *limes* (p. 187, note 2). Posts might also be stationed at the allowed points of crossing, and the intervening spaces of the frontier-roads might be in some way rendered impassable. In this sense the biographer of Hadrian says in the above-quoted passage that at the *limites* he *stipitibus magnis in*

intercourse, as the crossing of this road was forbidden altogether by night, and, as regards armed men, by day, and was permitted in the case of others, as a rule, only under special precautions for security and on payment of the prescribed transit-dues. Such a road was drawn opposite to the headquarters on the lower Rhine, in what is now Münster, by Tiberius after the disaster of Varus, at some distance from the Rhine, seeing that between it and the river stretched the "Caesian forest," the more precise position of which is not known. Similar arrangements must have been made at the same time in the valleys of the Ruhr and the Sieg as far as that of the Wied, where the province of the lower Rhine ended. This road did not necessarily require to be militarily occupied and arranged for defence, although of course the defence of the frontier and the fortification of it always aimed at making the frontier-road as far as possible secure. A chief means for protecting the frontier was the depopulation of the tract of land between the river and the road. "The tribes on the right bank of the Rhine," says a well-informed author of the time of Tiberius, "have been in part transferred by the Romans to the left bank, in part withdrawn of their own accord into the interior." This applied, in what is now the Münster country, to the Germanic stocks earlier settled there of the Usipes, Tencteri, Tubantes. In the campaigns of Germanicus these appear dislodged from the Rhine, but still in the region of the Lippe, afterwards, probably in consequence of those very expeditions, farther southward opposite to Mentz. Their old home lay thenceforth desolate, and formed the extensive pasture-country reserved for the herds of the

modum muralis saepis funditus iactis atque conexis barbaros separavit. By this means the frontier-road was converted into a frontier-barricade provided with certain passages through it, and such was the *limes* of upper Germany in the developed shape to be set forth in the sequel. We may add that the word is not used with this special import in the time of the republic; and beyond doubt this conception of the *limes* only originated with the institution of the chain of posts enclosing the state, where natural boundaries were wanting—a protection of the imperial frontier, which was foreign to the republic, but was the foundation of the Augustan military system, and above all, of the Augustan system of tolls.

lower Germanic army, on which in the year 58 first the Frisii and then the Amsivarii, wandering homeless, thought of settling, without being able to procure leave from the Roman authorities to do so. Farther to the south at least a portion of the Sugambri, who likewise were subjected in great part to the same treatment, remained settled on the right bank,[1] while other smaller tribes were wholly dislodged. The scanty population tolerated within the Limes were, as a matter of course, subjects of the empire, as is confirmed by the Roman levy taking place among the Sugambri.

Conflicts with the Frisii and Chauci under Claudius. In this way matters were arranged on the lower Rhine after the abandonment of the more comprehensive projects, and thus a not inconsiderable territory on the right bank was still held by the Romans. But various inconvenient complications arose in connection with it. Towards the end of the reign of Tiberius (28) the Frisians, in consequence of intolerable oppression in the levying of tribute in itself small, revolted from the empire, slew the people employed in levying it, and besieged the Roman commandant acting there, with the rest of the Roman soldiers and civilians sojourning in the territory, in the fortress of Flevum, where, previous to the extension of the Zuyder See that took place in the Middle Ages, lay the eastmost mouth of the Rhine, near the modern island Vlieland beside the Texel. The rising assumed such proportions that both armies of the Rhine marched in concert against the Frisians ; but still the governor Lucius Apronius accomplished nothing. The Frisians gave up the siege of the fortress, when the Roman fleet brought up the legions ; but it was difficult to get near the Frisians

---

[1] The Sugambri transplanted to the left bank are not subsequently mentioned under this name, and are probably the Cugerni dwelling below Cologne on the Rhine. But that the Sugambri on the right bank, whom Strabo mentions, were at least still in existence in the time of Claudius, is shown by the cohort named after this emperor, and thus certainly formed under him, doubtless of Sugambri (*C. I. L.* iii. p. 877); and they, as well as the four other probably Augustan cohorts of this name, confirm what Strabo also in a strict sense says, that these Sugambri belonged to the Roman empire. They disappeared doubtless, like the Mattiaci, only amidst the tempests of the migration of nations.

themselves in a country so much intersected; several Roman corps were destroyed in detail, and the Roman advanced guard was so thoroughly defeated that even the dead bodies of the fallen were left in the power of the enemy. The matter was not brought to a decisive action, nor yet to a true subjugation , Tiberius, the older he grew, became ever less inclined to larger enterprises, which gave to the general in command a position of power.   With this state of things was connected the fact that in the immediately succeeding years the neighbours of the Frisians, the Chauci, became very troublesome to the Romans ; in the year 41 the governor Publius Gabinius Secundus had to undertake an expedition against them, and six years later (47) they even pillaged far and wide the coast of Gaul with their light piratical vessels under the leadership of the Roman deserter Gannascus, by birth one of the Cannenefates.   Gnaeus Domitius Corbulo, nominated governor of Lower Germany by Claudius, put a stop with his fleet to these forerunners of the Saxons and Normans, and afterwards vigorously brought back the Frisians to obedience, by organising anew their commonwealth and stationing a Roman garrison among them.

Corbulo had the intention of chastising the Chauci also; at his instigation Gannascus was put out of the way— against a deserter he held himself entitled to take this course—and he was on the point of crossing the Ems and advancing into the country of the Chauci, when not only did he receive counter-orders from Rome, but the Roman government wholly and completely altered its attitude on the lower Rhine.   The emperor Claudius directed the governor to remove all Roman garrisons from the right bank.   We may well conceive that the imperial general with bitter words commended the good fortune of the free commanders of Rome in former days ; in this step certainly there was a conclusive admission of defeat, which had been but partially owned after the battle of Varus.   Probably this restriction of the Roman occupation of Germany, which was not occasioned by any pressure of immediate necessity, was called forth by the

The occupation of the right bank abandoned.

resolve just then adopted to occupy Britain, and finds its
justification in the fact that the troops were not sufficient
for accomplishing both objects at once.   That the order
was executed, and matters remained afterwards in that
position, is proved by the absence of Roman military inscriptions on the whole right bank of the lower Rhine.[1]
Only isolated points for crossing and sally-ports, such as,
in particular, Deutz opposite Cologne, formed exceptions
from this general rule.   The military road keeps here to
the left bank and strictly to the course of the Rhine,
while the traffic-route running behind it, cutting off the
windings, pursues the straight line of communication.
Here on the right bank of the Rhine there is no evidence
of Roman military roads, either through the discovery of
milestones or otherwise.

Its subse-
quent posi-
tion.

The withdrawal of the garrisons did not imply giving
up possession, strictly speaking, of the right bank in this
province.   It was looked upon by the Romans thenceforth
somewhat as the commandant of a fortress looks upon the
ground that lies under his cannon.   The Cannenefates and
at least a part of the Frisians[2] were afterwards subject, as
before, to the empire. We have already remarked that subsequently in the Münster country the herds of the legions still
pastured, and the Germans were not allowed to settle there.
But the government thenceforth relied — for the defence
of such border-territory on the right bank as still existed

---

[1] The fortress of Niederbiber, not
far from the point at which the Wied
falls into the Rhine, as well as that of
Arzbach, near Montabaur, in the region
of the Lahn, belong to upper Germany.   The special significance of
the former stronghold, the largest
fortress in upper Germany, turned
on the fact that it, in a military point
of view, closed the Roman lines on
the right bank of the Rhine.

[2] The levies (*Eph. Epigr.* v. p. 274)
require us to assume this, while the
Frisians, as they come forward in the
year 58 (Tacitus, *Ann.* xiii. 54)
rather appear independent; the elder
Pliny also (*H. N.* xxv. 3, 22) under
Vespasian names them, looking back

to the time of Germanicus, as *gens
tum fida*.   Probably this is connected
with the distinction between the
Frisii and *Frisiavones* in Pliny, *H. N.*
iv. 15, 101, and between the *Frisii
maiores* and *minores* in Tacitus, *Germ.*
34.   The Frisians that remained
Roman would be the western; the
free, the eastern; if the Frisians
generally reach as far as the Ems
(Ptolem. iii. 11, 7), those subsequently
Roman may have settled perhaps to
the westward of the Yssel.   We may
not put them elsewhere than on the
coast that still bears their name; the
designation in Pliny, iv. 17, 106,
stands isolated, and is beyond doubt
incorrect.

in this province—in the north on the Cannenefates and the Frisians, and farther up the stream substantially on the space left desolate ; and, if it did not directly forbid, at any rate did not give scope to Roman settlement there. The altar stone of a private person found at Altenberg (circuit of Mülheim), on the river Dhün, is almost the only evidence of Roman inhabitants in these regions. This is the more remarkable, as the prosperity of Cologne would, if special hindrances had not here stood in the way, have of itself carried Roman civilisation far and wide on the other bank. Often enough Roman troops may have traversed these extensive regions, perhaps even have kept the roads—which were here laid out in large number during the Augustan period—in some measure passable, and possibly laid out new ones ; sparse settlers, partly remains of the old Germanic population, partly colonists from the empire, may have settled here, similar to those that we shall soon find in the earlier imperial period on the right bank of the upper Rhine ; but the highways, like the possessions, lacked the stamp of durability. There was no wish to undertake here a labour of similar extent and difficulty to that which we shall become acquainted with further on in the upper province, or to provide here, as was done there, military defence and fortification for the frontier of the empire. Therefore the lower Rhine was crossed doubtless by Roman rule, but not, like the upper Rhine, also by Roman culture.

For the double task of keeping the neighbouring Gaul in obedience and of keeping the Germans of the right bank aloof from Gaul, the army of the lower Rhine would, even after abandoning the occupation of the region on the right of the river, have quite sufficed, and the peace without and within would not presumably have been interrupted, had not the downfall of the Julio-Claudian dynasty, and the civil or rather military war thereby called forth, exercised a momentous influence on these relations. The insurrection of the Celtic land under the leadership of Vindex was no doubt defeated by the two Germanic armies ; but Nero's fall nevertheless ensued, and when

The situation in Gaul and Germany after the fall of Nero.

the Spanish army as well as the imperial guard in Rome
appointed a successor to him, the armies of the Rhine did
the same ; and in the beginning of the year 69 the greater
portion of these troops crossed the Alps to settle the point
on the battle-fields of Italy, whether its ruler was to be
called Marcus or Aulus.   In May of the same year the
new emperor Vitellius followed, after arms had decided in
his favour, accompanied by the remainder of the good
soldiers inured to war.   The blanks in the garrisons of
the Rhine were no doubt filled up for the exigency by
recruits hastily levied in Gaul ; but the whole land knew
that they were not the old legions, and it soon became
apparent that these were not coming back.   If the new
ruler had had in his power the army that placed him on
the throne, at least a portion of them must have returned
to the Rhine immediately after the defeat of Otho in
April ; but the insubordination of the soldiers still more
than the new complication which soon set in with the proclamation of Vespasian as emperor in the East, retained
the German legions in Italy.

Prepara-
tions for
the insur-
rection.
Gaul was in the most fearful excitement.   The rising
of Vindex was, as we formerly remarked (p. 82), in itself
directed not against the rule of Rome but against the
rulers for the time being ; but it was none the less on that
account a warfare between the armies of the Rhine and
the levy *en masse* of the great majority of the Celtic cantons; and these were none the less subjected to pillage and
maltreatment resembling that of the conquered.   The tone
of feeling which subsisted between the provincials and the
soldiers was shown, for instance, by the treatment which
the canton of the Helvetii experienced as the troops
destined for Italy marched through it.   Because a courier
despatched by the adherents of Vitellius to Pannonia had
here been seized, the columns on the march from the one
side, and the Romans stationed as a garrison in Raetia
on the other, entered the canton, pillaged the villages far
and wide, particularly what is now Baden near Zürich,
chased those who had fled to the mountains out of their
lurking-places, and put them to death by thousands or

sold the captives under martial law. Although the capital Aventicum (Avenches, near Murten) submitted without resistance, the agitators of the army demanded that it should be razed, and all that the general granted was that the question should be referred not, forsooth, to the emperor, but to the soldiers of the great headquarters ; these sat in judgment on the fate of the town, and it was merely the turn of their caprice that saved the place from destruction. Outrages of this nature brought the provincials to extremities ; even before Vitellius left Gaul, a certain Mariccus, from the canton of the Boii, dependent on the Haedui, came forward a god on earth, as he said, and destined to restore the freedom of the Celts ; and people flocked in troops to his banner. But the exasperation in the Celtic country was not of so very great moment. The very rising of Vindex had most clearly shown how utterly incapable the Gauls were of releasing themselves from the Roman embrace.

But the tone of feeling of the Germanic districts reckoned as belonging to Gaul—in the modern Netherlands—of the Batavi, the Cannenefates, the Frisians, whose distinctive position has already been dwelt on, had a somewhat greater importance ; and it happened that, on the one hand, these very tribes had been exasperated to the utmost, and on the other, that their contingents were accidentally to be found in Gaul. The bulk of the Batavian troops, 8000 men, assigned to the 14th legion, had for a considerable time a place along with the latter in the army of the upper Rhine, and had then under Claudius, on occasion of the occupying of Britain, gone to that island, where this corps shortly before had, by its incomparable valour, gained the decisive battle under Paullinus for the Romans ; from this day onward it occupied indisputably the first place among all the divisions of the Roman army. When it was recalled on account of this very distinction by Nero, in order to go off with him to the war in the East, the revolution breaking out in Gaul had brought about a quarrel between the legion and its auxiliary troops ; the former, faithfully

Rising of the Batavian auxiliaries.

devoted to Nero, hastened to Italy ; the Batavi, on the
other hand, refused to follow.   Perhaps this was connected with the fact that two of their most noted officers,
Civilis   the brothers Paulus and Civilis, had, without any reason
and without respect to many years of faithful service and
honourable wounds, been shortly before put on trial as
suspected of high treason, and the former executed, the
latter placed in captivity.   After the downfall of Nero,
to which the revolt of the Batavian cohorts had materially
contributed, Galba released Civilis and sent the Batavians
back to their old headquarters in Britain.   While they, on
the march thither, were encamped among the Lingones
(Langres), the legions of the Rhine revolted from Galba
and proclaimed Vitellius emperor.   The Batavi, after considerable hesitation, ultimately joined the movement ; Vitellius
did not forgive them for this hesitation, but did not venture
directly to call to account the leader of the powerful corps.

Progress of   Thus the Batavians had marched with the legions of
the move-   lower Germany to Italy and had fought with their usual
ment.   valour in the battle of Betriacum for Vitellius, while their
old legionary comrades confronted them in the army of
Otho.   But the arrogance of the Germans exasperated
their Roman comrades in victory, however much these
acknowledged their valour in battle ; the very generals in
command did not trust them, and even made an attempt
to divide by detaching them—a course, which, in this war,
where the soldiers commanded and the generals obeyed,
was not capable of being carried out, and had almost cost
the general his life.   After the victory they were commissioned to accompany their hostile comrades of the 14th
legion to Britain ; but when matters came to a skirmish
between the two at Turin, the latter alone went to Britain,
and the Batavians to Germany.   Meanwhile Vespasian
had been proclaimed emperor in the East, and, while in
consequence of this Vitellius gave to the Batavian cohorts
marching orders for Italy as well as ordered new comprehensive levies among the Batavi, commissioners of Vespasian opened communications with the Batavian officers
to hinder this departure, and to provoke in Germany

itself a rising which should detain the troops there. Civilis entered into the suggestion. He resorted to his home, and gained easily the assent of his own people as well as the neighbouring Cannenefates and Frisians. The insurrection broke out among the former ; the camps of the two cohorts in the neighbourhood were surprised and the Roman posts seized ; the Roman recruits fought ill ; soon Civilis with his cohort—which he had caused to follow, ostensibly to employ it against the insurgents—threw himself openly into the movement, along with the three Germanic cantons renounced allegiance to Vitellius, and summoned the other Batavians and Cannenefates, who just then were breaking up from Mentz for the march to Italy, to join him.

All this was more a soldiers' rising than an insurrection *Its character.* of the province, or even a Germanic war. If at that time the Rhine legions were fighting with those of the Danube, and further with these and the army of the Euphrates, it was but in keeping that the soldiers of the second class, and above all their most distinguished troop, the Batavian, should enter independently into this divisional warfare. Any one who compares this movement among the cohorts of the Batavians and the Germans on the left of the Rhine with the insurrection of those on the right bank of the Rhine under Augustus, may not overlook the fact, that in the later rising the alae and cohorts took up the part of the general levy of the Cherusci ; and, if the perfidious officer of Varus released his nation from the Roman rule, the Batavian leader acted in the commission of Vespasian ; in fact, perhaps, on the secret directions of the governor of his province privately inclined towards Vespasian, and the rising in the first instance was directed simply against Vitellius. It is true that the position of things was such that this soldiers' revolt might change itself at any moment into a German war of the most dangerous kind. The same Roman troops who covered the Rhine against the Germans of the right bank were, in consequence of the corps-warfare, placed in an attitude of hostility to the Germans on the left bank; the parts were of such a nature, that it seemed almost easier to exchange them than to carry them out. Civilis himself may possibly have left it to depend on the sequel, whether the movement would end in a change of emperor or in the expulsion of the Romans from Gaul by the Germans.

State of the armies on the Rhine. The command of the two armies on the Rhine was held at this time, after the governor of lower Germany had been made emperor, by his former colleague in upper Germany, Hordeonius Flaccus, a gouty man advanced in years, without energy and without authority, either, moreover, in fact secretly holding to Vespasian, or at any rate very much suspected of such faithlessness by the legions, who zealously adhered to the emperor of their own making. It is characteristic of him and of his position that, to clear himself of the suspicion of treason, he gave orders that the government despatches on arrival should be sent unopened to the eagle-bearers of the legions, and these should read them in the first instance to the soldiers, before they forwarded them to their address. Of the four legions of the lower army which had primarily to do with the insurgents two, the 5th and the 15th, were stationed under the legate Munius Lupercus in the headquarters at Vetera; the 16th, under Numisius Rufus, in Novaesium (Neuss); the 1st, under Herennius Gallus, in Bonna (Bonn). Of the upper army, which then numbered only three legions,[1] one, the 21st, remained in its stated quarters Vindonissa, aloof from these events, if it had not rather been drawn off wholly to Italy; the two others, the 4th Macedonian and the 22d, were stationed at the headquarters Mentz, where Flaccus also was present; and in point of fact, his able legate Dillius Vocula exercised the chief command. The legions had throughout only half of their full complement, and most of the soldiers were half-invalids or recruits.

First conflicts. Civilis, at the head of a small number of regular troops, but of the collective levy of the Batavi, Cannene-

[1] The fourth upper German legion was sent in the year 58 to Asia Minor on account of the Armeno-Parthian war (Tacitus, *Ann.* xiii. 35).

fates, and Frisians, advanced from his home to the attack. In the first instance, on the Rhine he met with remnants of the Roman garrisons driven from the northern cantons and a division of the Roman Rhenish fleet ; when he attacked them, not merely did the ships' crews, consisting in great part of Batavians, go over to him, but also a cohort of the Tungri—it was the first revolt of a Gallic division ; such Italian soldiers as were present were slain or taken prisoners. This success brought at length the Germans on the right of the Rhine into the movement. What they had long vainly hoped for—the rising of the Roman subjects on the other bank—now came to be fulfilled, and as well the Chauci and the Frisians on the coast, as above all, the Bructeri on both sides of the upper Ems as far down as the Lippe, the Tencteri on the middle Rhine opposite to Cologne, and in lesser measure the tribes adjoining these on the south—Usipes, Mattiaci, Chatti—threw themselves into the struggle. When, on the orders of Flaccus, the two weak legions marched out from Vetera against the insurgents, these could already confront them with a numerous contingent drawn from beyond the Rhine ; and the battle ended, like the combat on the Rhine, with a defeat of the Romans through the defection of the Batavian cavalry, which belonged to the garrison of Vetera, and through the bad behaviour of the cavalry of the Ubii and of the Treveri.

Participation of the Germans on the right of the Rhine.

The insurgents and the Germans who flocked to them proceeded to invest and besiege the headquarters of the lower army. During this siege news of the events on the lower Rhine reached the other Batavian cohorts in the neighbourhood of Mentz ; they at once wheeled round towards the north. Instead of ordering them to be cut down, the weak-minded commander-in-chief allowed them to go, and when the commandant of the legion in Bonn sought to intercept them, Flaccus did not support him as he might have done and had even at first promised. So the brave Germans dispersed the Bonn legion and succeeded in joining Civilis—henceforth the compact core of his army, in which now the banners of the Roman cohorts

Siege of Vetera.

stood by the side of the animal-standards from the sacred groves of the Germans. But still the Batavian held, at least ostensibly, by Vespasian ; he swore in the Roman troops in Vespasian's name, and summoned the garrison of Vetera to join him in declaring for the latter. These troops, however, saw in this, probably with warrant, a mere attempt to overreach them, and repelled it as resolutely as they repelled the assailing hosts of the enemy, who soon found themselves compelled by the superiority of Roman tactics to change the siege into a blockade. But, as the leaders of the Roman army had been taken by surprise in these events, provisions were scarce and speedy relief was urgently called for. In order to bring it, Flaccus and Vocula set out with their whole force from Mentz, drew to themselves on the way the two legions from Bonna and Novaesium as well as the auxiliary troops of the Gallic cantons appearing at the word of command in large numbers, and approached Vetera.

Vocula. But instead of throwing at once the whole force from within and without on the besiegers, however great their superiority in numbers, Vocula pitched his camp at Gelduba (Gellep on the Rhine, not far from Krefeld) a long day's march distant from Vetera, while Flaccus lay farther back. The worthlessness of the so-called general and the ever increasing demoralisation of the troops, above all, the distrust towards the officers, which frequently went so far as to maltreat and attempt to kill them, can alone at least explain this halting. Thus the mischief gradually thickened on all sides. All Germany seemed desirous to take part in the war ; while the besieging army constantly obtained new contingents from that quarter, other bands passed over the Rhine, which in this dry summer was unusually low. partly in the rear of the Romans into the cantons of the Ubii and the Treveri to lay waste the valley of the Moselle, partly below Vetera into the region of the Maas and the Scheldt ; further bands appeared before Mentz and made pretext of besieging it. Then came the accounts of the catastrophe in Italy. On the news of the second battle at Betriacum in the autumn of the year 69 the Germanic legions gave up the cause of Vitellius as lost and took the oath, though reluctantly, to Vespasian, perhaps in the hope that Civilis, who had in fact inscribed the name of Vespasian on his banners, would then make his peace.   But the German swarms, who had meanwhile poured themselves over all northern Gaul, had not come to install the Flavian dynasty ; even if Civilis had ever wished this, he now had no longer the power.   He threw off the mask, and openly expressed—what indeed was long settled—that the Germans of north Gaul intended, with the help of their free countrymen, to shake off the Roman rule.

But the fortune of war changed.   Civilis attempted to surprise the camp of Gelduba ; the attack began success- fully, and the defection of the cohorts of the Nervii brought Vocula's little band into a critical position.   Then suddenly two Spanish cohorts fell on the rear of the Ger- mans ; what threatened to be a defeat was converted into a brilliant victory ; the flower of the assailing army remained on the field of battle.   Vocula indeed did not advance at once against Vetera, as he possibly might have done, but he penetrated into the besieged town some days later after a renewed vehement conflict with the enemy.   It is true that he brought no provisions ; and, as the river was in the power of the enemy, these had to be procured by the land-route from Novaesium, where Flaccus was encamped.   The first convoy passed through ; but the enemy, having meanwhile assembled again, attacked the second column with provisions on its way, and com- pelled it to throw itself into Gelduba.   Vocula went off thither to its support with his troops and a part of the old garrison of Vetera.   When they had arrived at Gelduba, the men refused to return to Vetera and to take upon themselves the further sufferings of the siege in prospect ; instead of this they marched to Novaesium, and Vocula, who knew that the remnant of the old garrison of Vetera was in some measure provisioned, had for good or evil to follow.

Relief of Vetera.

In Novaesium meanwhile mutiny had broken out. The soldiers had come to learn that a largess destined for them by Vitellius had reached the general, and compelled its distribution in the name of Vespasian. They had scarcely received it, when, in the wild carousing which ensued upon the largess, the old grudge of the soldiers broke out afresh ; they pillaged the house of the general who had betrayed the army of the Rhine to the general of the Syrian legions, slew him, and would have prepared the same fate for Vocula, if the latter had not escaped in disguise. Thereupon they once more proclaimed Vitellius emperor, not knowing that he was already dead. When this news came to the camp, the better part of the soldiers, and in particular the two upper German legions, began in some measure to reflect ; they again exchanged the effigy of Vitellius on their standards for that of Vespasian, and placed themselves under the orders of Vocula ; he led them to Mentz, where he remained during the rest of the winter 69-70. Civilis occupied Gelduba, and thereby cut off Vetera, which was most closely blockaded ; the camps of Novaesium and Bonna were still held.

Hitherto the Gallic land, apart from the few insurgent Germanic cantons in the north, had kept firmly by Rome. Certainly partisanship ran through the several cantons ; among the Tungri, for example, the Batavi had a strong body of adherents, and the bad behaviour of the Gallic auxiliary troops during the whole campaign may probably have been in part called forth by such a temper of hostility to the Romans. But even among the insurgents there was a considerable party favourably disposed to Rome ; a Batavian of note, Claudius Labeo, waged a partisan warfare not without success against his countrymen in his home and its neighbourhood, and the nephew of Civilis, Julius Briganticus, fell in one of these combats at the head of a band of Roman horse. All the Gallic cantons had without more ado complied with the injunction to send contingents ; the Ubii, although of Germanic descent, were in this war mindful simply of their Romanism, and they as well as the Treveri had offered brave and successful resistance to the Germans invading their territory.   It is easy to understand how this was so.   The position of things in Gaul was still much as it was in the days of Caesar and Ariovistus ; a liberation of their Gallic home from the Roman dominion by means of those hordes, which, in order to lend to Civilis the help of his country-men, were just then pillaging the valleys of the Moselle, Maas, and Scheldt, was tantamount to a surrender of the land to its Germanic neighbours ; in this war, which had grown out of a feud between two corps of Roman troops into a conflict between Rome and Germany, the Gauls were, properly speaking, nothing but the stake and the booty.   That the tone of feeling among the Gauls, in spite of all their well-founded general and special com-plaints as to the Roman government, was predominantly anti-Germanic, and that the materials for kindling such a national rising suddenly bursting into flame and reckless of consequences, as had spread through the people in an earlier time, were wanting in this Gaul now half-Romanised, events up to this time had most clearly shown. But amidst the constant misfortunes of the Roman army the courage of the Gauls hostile to the Romans gradually grew stronger, and their defection completed the catas-trophe.   Two Treveri of note, Julius Classicus, the com-mander of the Treverian cavalry, and Julius Tutor, com-mandant of the garrisons on the banks of the middle Rhine, Julius Sabinus one of the Lingones, descended, as he at least boasted, from a bastard of Caesar, and some other men of like mind from different cantons, professed in thoughtless Celtic fashion to discern that the destruc-tion of Rome was written in the stars and announced to the world by the burning of the Capitol (Dec. 69).

So they resolved to set aside the Roman rule and to set up a Gallic empire.   For this purpose they took the course of Arminius.   Vocula allowed himself to be really induced by falsified reports of these Roman officers to set out, with the contingents placed under their command and a part of the Mentz garrison, in the spring of 70 for the lower Rhine, in order with these troops and the legions of

The Gallic empire.

Bonna and Novaesium to relieve the hard-pressed Vetera. On the march from Novaesium to Vetera, Classicus and the officers in concert with him left the Roman army and proclaimed the new Gallic empire. Vocula led the legions back to Novaesium ; Classicus pitched his camp immediately in front of it. Vetera could not now hold out long ; the Romans could not but expect after its fall to find themselves confronted by the whole power of the enemy.

Capitulation of the Romans.

The Roman troops refused to face this prospect and entered into a capitulation with the revolted officers. In vain Vocula attempted once more to urge the ties of discipline and of honour ; the legions of Rome allowed a Roman deserter from the 1st legion to stab the brave general on the order of Classicus, and themselves delivered up the other chief officers in chains to the representative of the empire of Gaul, who thereupon made the soldiers swear allegiance to that empire. The same oath was taken at the hands of the perfidious officers by the garrison of Vetera, which, compelled by famine, at once surrendered, and likewise by the garrison of Mentz, where but a few individuals avoided disgrace by flight or death. The whole proud army of the Rhine, the first army of the empire, had surrendered to its own auxiliaries ; Rome had surrendered to Gaul.

End of the Gallic empire.

It was a tragedy, and at the same time a farce. The Gallic empire lapsed, as it could not fail to do. Civilis and his Germans were doubtless, in the first instance, well content that the quarrel in the Roman camp delivered the one as well as the other half of their foes into their hands ; but he had no thought of recognising that empire, and still less had his allies from the right bank of the Rhine.

As little would the Gauls themselves have anything to do with it—a result, to which certainly the split between the eastern districts and the rest of the country, which had already become apparent at the rising of Vindex, materially contributed. The Treveri and the Lingones, whose leading men had instigated that camp-conspiracy, stood by their leaders, but they remained

virtually alone ; only the Vangiones and Triboci joined
them.   The Sequani, into whose territory the Lingones
marched to induce their accession, drove them summarily
homeward.   The esteemed Remi, the leading canton in
Belgica, convoked the diet of the three Gauls, and,
although there was no lack there of orators on behalf of
political freedom, it resolved simply to dissuade the
Treveri from the revolt.   How the constitution of the
new empire would have turned out, had it been established,
it is difficult to say ; we learn only that Sabinus, the
great-grandson of Caesar's concubine, named himself
also Caesar, and in this capacity allowed himself to be
beaten by the Sequani ; whereas Classicus, who had not
such ascendency at his command, assumed the insignia
of Roman magistracy, and thus played perhaps the part
of republican proconsul.   In keeping with this there
exists a coin, which must have been struck by Classicus
or his adherents, exhibiting the head of Gallia, as the
coins of the Roman republic show that of Roma, and by
its side the symbol of the legion, with the genuinely
audacious legend of " fidelity " (*fides*).   At first, doubtless,
on the Rhine the imperialists, in concert with the
insurgent Germans, had full freedom.   The remnants
of the two legions that had capitulated in Vetera were
put to death, contrary to the terms of surrender and to
the will of Civilis ; the two from Novaesium and Bonna
were sent to Treves ; all the Roman camps on the
Rhine, large and small, with the exception of Mogontiacum, were burnt.   The Agrippinenses found themselves in the worst plight.   The imperialists had certainly
confined themselves to requiring from them the oath of
allegiance ; but the Germans in this case did not forget
that they were properly speaking, the Ubii.   A message
of the Tencteri from the right bank of the Rhine—this
was one of the tribes whose old home the Romans had
laid desolate and used as pasture-ground, and which had
in consequence of this been obliged to seek other abodes
—demanded the razing of this chief seat of the Germanic
apostates, and the execution of all their citizens of Roman

descent. This would probably have been resolved on had not Civilis, who was personally under obligation to them, as well as the German prophetess Veleda in the canton of the Bructeri, who had predicted this victory, and whose authority the whole insurgent army recognised, interceded on their behalf.

Advent of
the Ro-
mans.
The victors were not left long to contend over the booty. The imperialists certainly gave the assurance that the civil war in Italy had broken out, that all the provinces were overrun by the enemy, and Vespasian was probably dead ; but the heavy arm of Rome was soon enough felt. The newly confirmed government could despatch its best generals and numerous legions to the Rhine ; and certainly an imposing display of power was there needed. Annius Gallus took up the command in the upper, Petillius Cerialis in the lower province ; the latter, an impetuous and often incautious, but brave and capable officer, took the really serious action. Besides the 21st legion from Vindonissa, five came from Italy, three from Spain, one along with the fleet from Britain, and, in addition, a further corps from the Raetian garrison. This and the 21st legion were the first to arrive. The imperialists had possibly talked of blocking the passes of the Alps ; but nothing was done, and the whole country of the upper Rhine lay open as far as Mentz. The two Mentz legions had no doubt sworn allegiance to the Gallic empire, and at first offered resistance ; but, so soon as they perceived that a larger Roman army confronted them, they returned to obedience, and the Vangiones and Triboci immediately followed their example. Even the Lingones submitted—merely upon a promise of mild treatment—without striking a blow on the part of their 70,000 men capable of bearing arms.[1] The Treveri themselves had almost done the same ; but they were prevented from doing so by the nobility. The

[1] Frontinus, *Strat.* iv. 3, 14. In their territory the advancing troops must have constructed a reserve station and a depot ; according to tiles recently found near Mirabeau-sur-Bèze, about fourteen miles north-east of Dijon, men of at least five of the advancing legions had executed buildings here (*Hermes,* xix. 437).

two surviving legions of the lower Rhenish army that were stationed here had, on the first news of the approach of the Romans, torn the Gallic insignia from their standards, and withdrew to the Mediomatrici that had remained faithful (Metz), where they submitted to the mercy of the new general. When Cerialis arrived at the army, he found a good part of the work already done. The insurgent leaders exerted themselves, it is true, to the utmost—at that time by their orders the legionary legates delivered up at Novaesium were put to death—but in a military sense they were impotent, and their last political move—that of offering the Roman general himself the sovereignty of the Gallic empire—was worthy of the beginning. After a short combat Cerialis occupied the capital of the Treveri, the leaders and the whole council having taken refuge with the Germans. This was the end of the Gallic empire.

More serious was the struggle with the Germans. Civilis, with his whole fighting strength, the Batavi, the contingent of the Germans, and the refugee bands of the Gallic insurgents, suddenly assailed the much weaker Roman army in Treves itself. The Roman camp was already in his power, and the bridge of the Moselle occupied by him, when his men, instead of following up the victory which they had won, began prematurely to pillage, and Cerialis, compensating for his imprudence by brilliant valour, restored the combat and ultimately drove the Germans out from the camp and the town. There was no further success of importance. The Agrippinenses again joined the Romans, and killed the Germans, who were staying among them, in their houses; a whole Germanic cohort encamped there was shut up and burnt in its quarters. Whatsoever in Belgica still held to the Germans was brought back to obedience by the legion arriving from Britain; a victory of the Cannenefates over the Roman ships which had landed the legion, and other isolated successes of the brave Germanic bands, above all, of the more numerous and better managed Germanic ships, did not change the general position of the war

Last struggles of Civilis.

On the ruins of Vetera Civilis confronted the foe ; but
he had to give way to the Roman army, which had meanwhile been doubled, and at length, after an obstinate
resistance, had to leave his own home to the enemy.
As ever happens, discord ensued in the train of misfortune.   Civilis was no longer sure of his own men, and
sought and found protection from them among his
opponents.   Late in the autumn of the year 70 the
unequal struggle was decided ; the auxiliaries now on
their part surrendered to the burgess-legions, and the
priestess Veleda went as a captive to Rome.

Nature of
the Roman
task and
its issue.

When we look back on this war, one of the most
singular and most dreadful in all ages, we cannot but
own that hardly ever has an army had a task set before
it equally severe with that of the two Roman armies on
the Rhine in the years 69 and 70.   In the course of a
few months soldiers successively of Nero, of the senate,
of Galba, of Vitellius, and of Vespasian ; the only support
to the dominion of Italy over the two mighty nations
of the Gauls and the Germans, while the soldiers of the
auxiliaries were taken almost entirely, and those of the
legions in great part, from those very nations ; deprived
of their best men, mostly without pay, often starving, and
beyond all measure wretchedly led, they were certainly
expected to perform feats physically and morally super-
human.   They ill sustained the severe trial.   This was
less a war between two divisions of the army, like the
other civil wars of this terrible time, than a war of
soldiers, and above all of officers, of the second class
against those of the first, combined with a dangerous
insurrection and invasion of the Germans, and an incidental
and insignificant revolt of some Celtic districts.   In
Roman military history Cannae and Carrhae and the
Teutoburg Forest are glorious pages compared with the
double disgrace of Novaesium ; only a few individual
men, not a single troop, preserved a pure escutcheon
amidst the general dishonour.   The frightful disorganisation of the political and, above all, of the military system,
which meets us on the fall of the Julio-Claudian dynasty,

appears—more clearly even than in the leaderless battle of Betriacum—in those events on the Rhine, to which the history of Rome never before and never after exhibits a parallel.

The very extent and general diffusion of these misdeeds rendered a corresponding chastisement impossible. It deserves to be acknowledged that the new ruler, who happily had remained in person aloof from all these occurrences, in a genuine statesmanly fashion allowed the past to be past, and exerted himself only to prevent the repetition of similar scenes.   That the prominent culprits, whether from the ranks of the troops or from the insurgents, were brought to account for their crimes, was a matter of course ; we may measure the punishment by the fact that when five years afterwards one of the Gallic insurgent leaders was discovered in a lurking-place, in which his wife had up to that time kept him concealed, Vespasian gave him as well as her over to the executioner. But the renegade legions were allowed to share in the fighting against the Germans, and to atone for their guilt to some extent in the hot conflicts at Treves and at Vetera.   It is true, nevertheless, that the four legions of the lower Rhenish army were all dismissed, as was one of the two upper Rhenish legions that took part—one would gladly believe that the 22d was spared in honourable remembrance of its brave legate.   Probably a considerable number of the Batavian cohorts met with the same fate, and not less, apparently, the cavalry regiment of the Treveri, and perhaps several other specially prominent troops.   Still less than against the rebellious soldiers could proceedings be taken with the full severity of the law against the insurgent Celtic and German cantons ; that the Roman legions demanded the razing of the Treverian colony of Augustus—this time for the sake not of booty but of vengeance—is at least as intelligible as the destruction, desired by the Germans, of the town of the Ubii ; but as Civilis protected the one so Vespasian protected the other.   Even the Germans on the left of the Rhine had, on the whole, their previous position left

Consequences of the Batavian war.

to them. But probably—we are here without certain tradition—there was introduced in the levy and the employment of the *auxilia* an essential change, which diminished the danger involved in the auxiliary system. The Batavi retained freedom from taxation and a still privileged position as regards service ; a part of them, not altogether inconsiderable, had withal championed in arms the cause of the Romans. But the Batavian troops were considerably diminished, and, while hitherto—as it would appear of right—officers had been placed over them from their own nobility, and the same had been at least frequently done as respects the other Germanic and Celtic troops, the officers of the *alae* and *cohortes* were afterwards taken predominantly from the class from which Vespasian himself was descended—from the good urban middle class of Italy and of the provincial towns organised after the Italian fashion. Officers of the position of the Cheruscan Arminius, of the Batavian Civilis, of the Treverian Classicus do not henceforth recur. As little is the previous close association of troops levied from the same canton met with subsequently ; on the contrary, the men serve, without distinction as to their descent, in the most various divisions ; this was probably a lesson which the Roman military administration gathered from this war. It was another change, probably suggested by this war, that while hitherto the majority of the auxiliaries employed in Germany were taken from the Germanic and neighbouring cantons, thenceforth the Germanic auxiliary troops found preponderantly employment outside of their native country, just like the Dalmatian and Pannonian troops in consequence of the war with Bato. Vespasian was a soldier of sagacity and experience ; it is probably in good part a merit of his if we meet with no later example of revolt of the *auxilia* against their legions.

Later attitude of the Roman Germans on the lower Rhine.

That the insurrection, which we have just narrated, of the Germans on the left of the Rhine—although it, in consequence of the accidental completeness of the accounts preserved respecting it, alone gives us a clear insight into the political and military relations on the lower Rhine and in Gaul generally, and therefore deserved to be nar-rated in more detail—was yet called forth more by outward and accidental causes than by the inner necessity of things, is proved by the apparently complete quiet which now ensued there, and by the—so far as we can see—unin-terrupted *status quo* in this very region. The Roman Ger-mans were merged in the empire no less completely than the Roman Gauls ; of attempts at insurrection on the part of the former there is no further mention. At the close of the third century, the Franks invading Gaul by way of the lower Rhine included in their seizure the Batavian territory ; yet the Batavians maintained them-selves in their old though diminished settlements, as did like-wise the Frisians, even during the confusions of the great migration of peoples, and, so far as we know, preserved allegiance even to the decaying empire.

When we turn from the Romanised to the free Germans to the east of the Rhine, we find offensive action on their part not less brought to an end with their participation in that Batavian insurrection, than the attempts of the Romans to bring about an alteration of the frontier on a grand scale in those regions came to a close with the expeditions of Germanicus.

The free Germans on the lower Rhine.

Of the free Germans, those dwelling next to the Roman territory were the Bructeri on both banks of the middle Ems, and in the region of the sources of the Ems and Lippe ; for which reason they took part before all the other Germans in the Batavian insurrection. To their canton belonged the maiden Veleda, who sent forth her countrymen to the war against Rome and promised them the victory, whose utterance decided the fate of the town of the Ubii, and to whose high tower the captive senators and the captured admiral's ship of the Rhenish fleet were sent. The overthrow of the Batavi affected them also ; and perhaps, in addition, a special counterblow of the Romans since that virgin was subsequently led as a cap-tive to Rome. This disaster, as well as feuds with the neighbouring tribes, broke their power ; under Nero a king whom they did not wish was obtruded on them by

Bructeri.

force of arms on the part of their neighbours with the passive assistance of the Roman legate.

Cherusci. The Cherusci, in the region of the upper Weser, in the time of Augustus and Tiberius the leading canton in central Germany, is seldom mentioned after the death of Arminius, but always as sustaining good relations to the Romans. When the civil war, which must have continued to rage among them even after the fall of Arminius, had swept away the whole family of their princes, they requested from the Roman government the last of that house, Italicus, a brother's son of Arminius living in Italy, to be their ruler ; it is true that the return home of one who was brave but answered more to his name than to his lineage, kindled the feud afresh, and, when he was driven off by his own people, the Langobardi placed him once more on the tottering throne. One of his successors, king Chariomerus, so earnestly took the side of the Romans in Domitian's war with the Chatti, that he after its close, when driven away by the Chatti, fled to the Romans and invoked—although vainly—their intervention. Through those perpetual inward and outward feuds the Cheruscan people was so weakened that it henceforth disappears from active politics. The name of the Marsi is no longer met with at all after the expeditions of Germanicus. That the tribes dwelling farther to the east on the Elbe as well as all the more remote Germans took as little part in the struggles of the Batavians and their allies in the years 69 and 70, as these took in the German wars under Augustus and Tiberius may, considering the detailed character of the narrative, be described as certain. Where they meet us subsequently they never appear in a

Lango- hostile attitude to the Romans. That the Langobardi
bardi.   reinstated the Roman king of the Cherusci, has already
Semnones. been mentioned. Masuus, the king of the Semnones, and —what is remarkable—along with him the prophetess Ganna, who was held in high repute among this tribe famous for its special credulity, visited the emperor Domitian in Rome, and met with a friendly reception at his court. In the regions from the Weser to the Elbe

during these centuries various feuds may have raged, the balance of power may in various cases have shifted, various cantons may have changed their name or joined another combination ; as regards their relations to the Romans a permanent frontier-peace set in, after it came to be generally felt that these had positively abandoned the subjugation of this region. Even invasions from the far East cannot have materially disturbed it at this epoch ; for they could not but have reacted on the Roman guarding of the frontier, and we should not have lacked information had more serious crises occurred in this domain. All this is confirmed by the reduction of the army of the lower Rhine to half of its former amount, which occurred we know not exactly when, but within this epoch. The army of the lower Rhine, with which Vespasian had to fight, numbered four legions ; that of the time of Trajan presumably the same number, at least three ;[1] probably already under Hadrian, certainly under Marcus, there were not more than two—the 1st Minervian and the 30th of Trajan—stationed there.

Germanic affairs in the upper province developed themselves after another fashion. Of the Germans on the left of the Rhine who belonged to this province, the Triboci, Nemetes, Vangiones, there is nothing historically worth mentioning, except that they, for long settled among the Celts, shared the destinies of Gaul. Here too the Rhine always remained the chief line of defence for the Romans. All the standing camps of the legions were at all times on the left bank of the Rhine ; not even that of

Upper Germany.

---

[1] Under the legate Q. Acutius Nerva, who was probably the consul of the year 100, and so administered lower Germany after that year, there were stationed, according to inscriptions of Brohl (Brambach, 660, 662, 679, 680), in this province four legions, the 1st Minervia, 6th Victrix, 10th Gemina, 22d Primigenia. As each of these inscriptions names only two or three, the garrison may then have consisted only of three legions, if during the governorship of Acutius the 1st Minervia came in place of the 22d Primigenia drafted off elsewhere. But it is far more probable—seeing that all the legions were not always taking part in the detachments to the stone quarries at Brohl—that these four legions were doing garrison-duty at the same time in lower Germany. These four legions are probably just those that came to lower Germany on the reorganisation of the Germanic armies by Vespasian (p. 159 note), only that the 1st Minervia was put by Domitian in the place of the 21st, probably broken up by him.

Argentoratum was transferred to the right bank, when the whole region of the Neckar was Roman. But while in the lower province the Roman rule on the right bank of the Rhine was restricted in course of time, here on the other hand it was extended. The project of Augustus to connect the camps on the Rhine with those on the Danube by advancing the imperial frontier in an eastward direction—which, if it had been carried out, would have enlarged upper more than lower Germany—was perhaps never completely abandoned in this command, and was resumed subsequently, though on a more modest scale. Historical tradition does not give us the means of presenting a connected view of the operations continued with this object for centuries, the construction of roads and walls pertaining thereto, and the wars waged on this account ; and even the great military structure still existing, whose rise and progress—likewise embracing centuries —must include in itself a good part of that history, has hitherto not been investigated throughout, as it well might be, by the eyes of military experts. The hope that unified Germany would combine for the investigation of this its oldest historical monument, has not been fulfilled. We shall here attempt to put together what has hitherto been brought to light on the subject from the fragments of the Roman annals or of the Roman strongholds.

Mogonti-
acum.

On the right bank, not far from the northern end of the province, there stretches in front of the level or hilly country of the lower Rhine, in a direction from west to east, the range of the Taunus, which abuts on the Rhine opposite to Bingen. Parallel to this mountain-range, shut off on the other side by the spurs of the Odenwald, stretches the plain of the lower Main-valley, the true access to the interior of Germany, dominated by the key of the position at the point where the Main falls into the Rhine, Mogontiacum or Mentz, from the time of Drusus down to the end of Rome the stronghold out of which the Romans sallied to attack Germany from Gaul,[1] as it

---

[1] According to the ingenious de- *deutsche Zeitschrift*, iii. 307 ff), it is
cipherings of Zangemeister (*West-* established that a military road was

is at the present day the true barrier of Germany against France. Here the Romans, even after they had abandoned their rule in the region of the upper Rhine generally, retained not merely the *tête-de-pont* on the other bank, the *castellum Mogontiacense* (Castel), but also that plain of the Main itself in their possession ; and in this region a Roman civilisation might establish itself. This land Mattiaci. originally belonged to the Chatti, and a Chattan tribe, the Mattiaci, remained settled here even under Roman rule ; but, after the Chatti were compelled to cede this district to Drusus, it remained a part of the empire. The hot springs in the immediate neighbourhood of Mentz (aquae Mattiacae, Wiesbaden) were used by the Romans demonstrably in Vespasian's time, and doubtless long before : silver was worked here under Claudius ; the Mattiaci already furnished troops to the army at an early date like other subject districts. They took part in the general rising of the Germans under Civilis ; but, after they were vanquished, the earlier relations were re-established. From the end of the second century we find the community of the Taunensian Mattiaci under authorities organised after the Roman model.[1]

The Chatti, although thus driven away from the Chatti. Rhine, appear in the sequel as the most powerful among the tribes of inland Germany who came into contact with the Romans ; the lead which, under Augustus and Tiberius, had been possessed by the Cherusci on the middle Weser, passed, amidst the constant feuds with these their southern cognate neighbours, over to the latter. All the wars between Romans and Germans, of which we have any knowledge from the time after the death of Arminius down to the time when the migrations of the

already laid out under Claudius on the left bank of the Rhine from Mentz as far as the frontier of the upper German province.

[1] The full name *c(ivitas) M(attia-corum) Ta(unensium)* appears on the inscription of Castel in Brambach, *C. I. Rh.* 1330; it occurs frequently as *civitas Mattiacorum* or *civitas Taun-* *ensium*, with Duoviri, Aediles, De-curiones, Sacerdotales, Seviri; peculiar and characteristic of a frontier town are the *hastiferi civitatis Mattiacorum*, probably to be taken as a municipal militia (Brambach, 1336). The oldest dated document of this community is of the year 198 (Brambach, 956).

peoples began at the end of the third century, were waged against the Chatti ; as in the year 41 under Claudius by Galba, who became afterwards emperor ; and in the year 50 under the same emperor by Publius Pomponius Secundus, celebrated as a poet. These were the usual border incursions, and the Chatti had taken a part, but only a secondary one, in the great Batavian war (p. 133). But in the campaign which the Emperor Domitian undertook in the year 83 the Romans were the aggressors ; and this war led, not indeed to brilliant victories, but doubtless to a considerable and momentous pushing forward of the Roman frontier.[1]   At that time the frontier-line was arranged, as we find it thenceforth drawn ; and within that line, which in its most northern portion was not far removed from the Rhine, must have been included a great part of the Taunus and the region of the Main as far as above Friedberg. The Usipes, who, after their already-mentioned expulsion from the region of the Lippe, appear about the time of Vespasian in the neighbourhood of Mentz, and may have found new settlements to the east of the Mattiaci on the Kinzig or in the Fuldan district, were then annexed to the empire, and, at the same time with them, a number of smaller tribes thrown off by the Chatti. Thereupon, when in the year 88, under the governor Lucius Antonius Saturninus, the upper German

---

[1] The accounts of this war have been lost ; its time and place admit of being determined. As the coins give to Domitian the title *Germanicus* after the beginning of the year 84 (Eckhel, vi. 378, 397), the campaign falls in the year 83. Accordant with this is the levy of the Usipes, which falls on this same year, and their desperate attempt at flight (Tacitus, *Agr.* 28 ; comp. Martialis, vi. 60). It was an aggressive war (Suetonius, *Dom.* 6 : *expeditio sponte suscepta ;* Zonaras, xi. 19 ; λεηλατήσας τινὰ τῶν πέραν Ῥήνου τῶν ἐνσπόνδων). The shifting of the line of posts is attested by Frontinus, who took part in the war, *Strat.* ii. 11, 7 : *cum in finibus Cubiorum* (name unknown and probably corrupt) *castella poneret,* and i. 3, 10 : *limitibus per cxx. m. p. actis,* which is here brought into immediate connection with the military operations, and hence may not be separated from the Chattan war itself and referred to the *agri decumates,* which had for long been in the Roman power. The measure of 108 miles is very conceivable for the military line which Domitian planned at the Taunus (according to Cohausen's estimates, *Röm. Grenzwall,* p. 8, the later Limes from the Rhine round the Taunus as far as the Main is set down at 137 miles), but is much too small to admit of its being referred to the line of connection from thence to Ratisbon.

army rose against Domitian, the war was on the point of renewal ; the revolted troops made common cause with the Chatti ;[1] and it was only the interruption of the communications, when the ice broke up on the Rhine, that made it possible for the regiments which had remained faithful to settle matters with the revolters before the dangerous contingent arrived. It is stated that the Roman rule extended from Mentz towards the interior 80 *leugae*, and thus even beyond Fulda ;[2] and this

[1] The Germans (Suetonius, *Dom.* 6) could only be the Chatti, and their earlier allies, perhaps in the first instance just the Usipes and those sharing their fate. The insurrection broke out in Mentz, which alone was a double camp of two legions. Saturninus was assailed from Raetia by the troops of L. Appius Maximus Norbanus. For the epigram of Martial, ix. 84, cannot be understood otherwise, the more especially as his conqueror, of senatorial rank as he was, could not administer a regular command in Raetia and Vindelicia, and could only be led into this region by a case of war emerging, as indeed the *sacrilegi furores* clearly point to the insurrection. The tiles of this same Appius, which have been found in the provinces of upper Germany and Aquitania, do not warrant the making him legate of the Lugdunensis, as Asbach (*Westdeutsche Zeitschrift*, iii. 9), suggests, but must be referred to the epoch after the defeat of Antonius (*Hermes*, xix. 438). Where the battle was fought remains doubtful ; the region of Vindonissa most naturally suggests itself, to which point Saturninus may have gone to meet Norbanus. Had Norbanus encountered the insurgents only at Mentz, which in itself seems conceivable, these would have had the crossing of the Rhine in their power, and the contingent of the Germans could not have been hindered by the breaking-up of the Rhine from reinforcing them.

[2] The detached notice is found subjoined to the Veronese provincial list (*Notitia dignitatum*, ed. Seeck, p. 253) : *nomina civitatum trans Renum fluvium quae sunt; Usiphorum* (read *Usiporum*) — *Tuvanium* (read *Tubantum*) — *Nictrensium* — *Novarii* — *Casuariorum* : *istae omnes civitates trans Renum in formulam Belgicae primae redactae trans castellum Montiacese : nam lxxx. leugas trans Renum Romani possederunt. Istae civitates sub Gallieno imperatore a barbaris occupatae sunt.* That the Usipes afterwards dwelt in this region, is confirmed by Tacitus, *Hist.* iv. 37, *Germ.* 32 ; that they belonged to the empire in the year 83, but had perhaps been made subject only shortly before, is plain from the narrative, *Agr.* 28. The Tubantes and Chasuarii are placed by Ptolemy, ii. 11, 11, in the vicinity of the Chatti ; that they shared the fate of the Usipes is accordingly probable. No certain identification of the other two corrupt names has hitherto been found ; perhaps the Tencteri had a place here, or some of the small tribes named with these only in Ptolemy, ii. 11, 6. The notice in its original form named Belgica simply, as the province was only divided by Diocletian, and named it rightly in so far as the two Germanies belonged geographically to Belgica. The specified measurement carries us, if we follow the Kinzig valley to the north-east, beyond Fulda nearly to Hersfeld. Inscriptions have been found here far eastward beyond the Rhine, as far as the Wetterau ; Friedberg and Butzbach were military positions strongly garrisoned ; at Altenstadt between Friedberg and

account appears worthy of credit, if we take into consideration that the military frontier-line, which certainly seems not to have gone far above Friedberg, doubtless kept here also within the territorial boundary.

The region of the Neckar.

But not merely was the valley of the lower Main in front of Mentz brought within the military frontier-line; in south-western Germany also the boundary was pushed forward in a still greater degree. The region of the Neckar, once possessed by the Celtic Helvetii, then for long a debateable borderland between these and the advancing Germans, and therefore named the Helvetian desert, subsequently perhaps occupied partially by the Marcomani, before these retreated to Bohemia (p. 29), came on the regulation of the Germanic boundaries after the battle of Varus into the same position as the greater portion of the right bank of the lower Rhine. Here, too, there must have been a frontier-line already at that time marked off, within which Germanic settlements were not tolerated. Thereupon individual, mostly Gallic, immigrants, who had not much to lose, settled down, as on an unenclosed moor, in these fertile but little protected regions, which went at that time by the name of *agri decumates*.[1] This private occupation, which was, it may be conjectured, merely tolerated by the government, was followed by the formal taking possession of it probably under Vespasian. As already, about the year 74, a highway was carried from Strassburg on the right bank of the Rhine as far as Offenburg,[2] there must have been instituted about this

Büdingen there has been found an inscription of the year 242 (Brambach, *C. I. Rh.* 1410) pointing to protection of the frontier (*collegium iuventutis*).

[1] What the designation *agri decumates* (for the latter word is at any-rate to be connected with *agri*) occurring only in Tacitus, *Germ.* 29, means, is uncertain. It is possible that the territory regarded in the earlier imperial period certainly as property of the state or rather of the emperor, like the old *ager occupatorius* of the republic, might be used

by the first who took possession upon payment of the tenth; but neither is it linguistically proved that *decumas* can mean "liable for a tenth," nor are we acquainted with such arrangements in the imperial period. Moreover it should not be overlooked that the description of Tacitus refers to the time before the institution of the line of the Neckar; it does not suit the latter period any more than does the designation, which doubtless is not clear, but is at any rate certainly connected with the earlier legal relation.

[2] This has been proved by Zange-

time in this region a more earnest protection of the frontier than the mere prohibition of Germanic settlement furnished. What the father had begun the sons carried out. Perhaps even through the construction—whether by Vespasian, by Titus, or Domitian—of the "Flavian altars"[1] at the source of the Neckar, near the modern Rottweil— a settlement of which indeed we know nothing but the name—there was procured for the new upper Germany on the right of the Rhine a centre similar to what the Ubian altar was formerly intended to become for Great Germany, and soon afterwards the altar of Sarmizegetusa became for the newly-conquered Dacia. The first institu- tion of the frontier-defence, to be described further on, by which the Neckar valley was brought within the Roman line, is thus the work of the Flavii, chiefly, doubtless, of Domitian,[2] who thereby carried further the construction at the Taunus. The military road on the right of the Rhine from Mogontiacum by way of Heidelberg and Baden in the direction of Offenburg—the necessary consequence of this annexation of the Neckar region—was, as we now know,[3] constructed by Trajan in the year 100, and was a part of the more direct communication established by that emperor between Gaul and the line of the Danube. There was employment for the soldiers at these works, but hardly for their arms ; there were no Germanic tribes dwelling in the region of the Neckar, and still less can the narrow strip on the left bank of the Danube, which was thereby brought within the frontier line, have cost serious struggles. The nearest Germanic people of note there, the Hermunduri, had more friendly

meister (*Westdeutsche Zeitschrift*, iii. p. 246).

[1] The fact that here several altars were dedicated, while elsewhere at these central sanctuaries only one is mentioned, may be explained perhaps by the cultus of Roma falling into the background by the side of that of the emperors. If at the very outset several altars were erected, which is probable, perhaps one of the sons caused altars to be set up as well to his father and perhaps his brother as to his own Genius.

[2] That the transfer took place shortly before Tacitus wrote the Germania in the year 98, he himself states, and that Domitian was its author, follows from the fact that he does not name the author.

[3] This, too, has been documentarily established by Zangemeister (*Westdeutsche Zeitschrift*, iii. 237 f.).

dispositions towards the Romans than any other tribe had, and carried on lively commercial intercourse with them in the town of the Vindelici, Augusta ; of the fact that this advance met with no resistance from them, we shall find traces further on. Under the following reigns of Hadrian, Pius, and Marcus, further progress was made with these military arrangements.

The upper Germanic Limes.

We cannot historically follow out the mode in which the frontier-fence between the Rhine and the Danube— still in great part subsisting as regards its foundations at the present day—came into existence, but we are able to recognise not merely the course which it took but also the purpose which it served. The work was as to its nature and purpose different in upper Germany from what it was in Raetia. The upper German frontier-fence, with a length in all of about 250 Roman miles (228 English miles[1]) begins immediately at the northern boundary of the province, embraces, as has been already said, the Taunus and the plain of the Main as far as the district of Friedberg, and turns thence southward to the Main, which it meets at Grosskrotzenburg above Hanau. Following the Main thence as far as Wörth, it here takes the direction of the Neckar, which it reaches somewhat below Wimpfen and does not again leave. Afterwards in front of the southern half of this frontier-line a second was laid out, which follows the Main by way of Wörth as far as Miltenberg, and thence is led for the most part in a straight direction to Lorch between Stuttgart and Aalen. Here to the upper German frontier-fence is joined on the Raetian, only 120 miles (108 English) long ; it leaves the Danube at Kelheim above Ratisbon and runs thence, twice crossing the Altmuhl, in a curve westward likewise as far as Lorch.

[1] This measurement holds for the line of forts from Rheinbrohl to Lorch (Cohausen, *der Röm. Grenzwall*, p. 7 f.). For the earthen rampart there falls to be deducted the stretch of the Main from Miltenberg to Grosskrotzenburg, of about thirty Roman miles. In the case of the older line of the Neckar the rampart is considerably shorter, since, instead of that from Miltenberg to Lorch, here comes in the much shorter one of the Odenwald from Wörth to Wimpfen.

The upper Germanic Limes consists of a series of forts which are distant from each other, at the most, half a day's march (about nine English miles). Where the lines of connection between the forts are not closed by the Main or the Neckar, as stated above, there was introduced an artificial barrier, at first perhaps merely by a palisade,[1] afterwards by a continuous earthen rampart of moderate height, with a fosse outside and watch-towers built in at short intervals on the inner side.[2] The forts are not introduced into the rampart, but constructed immediately behind it at a distance seldom exceeding one-third of an English mile.

The Raetian frontier-fence was a mere barrier, produced by piling up quarry-stones ; there were no fosses or watch-towers, and the forts, constructed behind the Limes without regular succession and at unequal intervals (none nearer than two and a half to three miles), stand in no immediate connection with the barrier-line. As to the order in time of the constructions there is no definite testimony ; it is proved that the upper Germanic line of the Neckar was in existence under Pius,[3] that placed in front

The Raetian Limes.

---

[1] If, as is probable, the statement that Hadrian blocked the imperial frontier-roads by palisades against the barbarians (p. 122) relates in part and perhaps primarily to the upper Germanic, the wall, of which remains are extant, was not his work ; whether this may have carried palisades or not, no report would mention these and pass over the wall itself. Dio, lxix. 9, says that Hadrian revised the defence of the frontier throughout the empire. The designation of the pale [*Pfahl*] or pale-ditch [*Pfahlgraben*] cannot be Roman ; in Latin the stakes, which, driven into the wall of the camp, form a palisade-chain for it, are called not *pali*, but *valli* or *sudes*, just as the wall itself is never other than *vallum*. If the designation in use from of old for this purpose apparently along the whole line among the Germans was really borrowed from the palisades, it must have been of Germanic origin, and can only have proceeded from the time when this

wall stood before their eyes in its integrity and significance. Whether the "region" Palas which Ammianus mentions (xviii. 2, 15) is connected with this is doubtful.

[2] In such an one recently discovered between the forts of Schlossau and Hesselbach, 1850 yards from the former, about three miles from the latter, there has been found a votive inscription (*Korrespondenzblatt der Westdeutschen Zeitschrift*, 1 Jul. 1884), which the troop that built it—a detachment of the 1st cohort of the Sequani and Raurici under command of a centurion of the 22d legion, erected as thanksgiving *ob burgum explic(itum)*. These towers thus were *burgi*.

[3] The oldest dated evidence for these is two inscriptions of the garrison of Böckingen, opposite Heilbronn, on the left bank of the Neckar of the year 148 (Brambach, *C. I. Rh.* 1583, 1590).

of it from Miltenberg to Lorch under Marcus.[1]   The idea of
a frontier-bar was common to the two structures, otherwise
so different ; the preference in the one case for the piling
up of earth—whence the fosse for the most part resulted
of itself—in the other case, for layers of stone, probably
depended only on the diversity of the soil and of the
materials for building.   It was common to them, further,
that neither the one nor the other was constructed for the
defence, as a whole, of the frontier.   Not merely was the
hindrance, which the piling up of earth or stone presented
to the assailant, slight in itself ; but along the line we meet
everywhere with commanding positions, morasses lying in
the rear, a want of outlook towards the country in front,
and similar clear indications of the fact, that in the tracing
of it warlike purposes generally were not contemplated.
The forts are of course arranged for defence, each by itself,
but they are not connected by paved cross-roads ; and
so the individual garrison relied for support not on those
of the neighbouring forts, but on the rear-base, to which
the road led, whereby each was kept garrisoned.   Moreover, these garrisons were not dovetailed into a military
system of frontier defence ; they were rather fortified positions for a case of need than strategically chosen for the
occupation of the territory, as indeed the very extent of
the line itself, compared with the number of troops at
disposal, excludes the possibility of its defence as a
whole.[2]

---

[1] The oldest dated evidence for the
existence of this line is the inscription
of *vicus Aurelii* (Oehringen) of the
year 169 (Brambach, *C. I. Rh.* 1558),
doubtless only private, but certainly
not set up before the construction of
this fort belonging to the Miltenberg-
Lorch line ; little later is that of Jags-
thausen, likewise belonging to that
line, of the year 179 (*C. I. Rh.* 1618).
Accordingly *vicus Aurelii* might take
its name from Marcus, not from Caracalla, though it is attested of the latter
that he constructed various forts in
these regions and named them after
himself (Dio, lxxvi. 13).

[2] As to the distribution of the
upper German troops there is a want
of sufficient information, but not entirely of data on which to rest.   Of
the two headquarters in upper Germany, that of Strassburg can be shown
to have been after the construction of
the line of the Neckar occupied but
weakly, and was probably more an
administrative than a military centre
(*Westdeutsches   Correspondenzblatt*,
1884, p. 132).   On the other hand,
the garrison of Mentz always demanded
a considerable portion of the aggregate strength, all the more because it
was probably the only compact body

Thus these extensive military structures had not, like the Britannic wall, the object of checking the invasion of the enemy. The intention rather was, that, like the bridges over the river-frontier, so the roads on the land-frontier should be commanded by the forts, but in other respects, like the river as the water-boundary, so the wall on the landward should hinder the uncontrolled crossing of the frontier. Other uses might be combined with this ; the preference, often apparent, for the rectilineal direction points to its application for signals, and occasionally the structure may have been used directly for purposes of war. But the proper and immediate object of the structure was to prevent the crossing of the frontier. The fact, withal, that watch-posts and forts were erected, not on the Raetian but on the upper Germanic frontier, is

Object of these structures.

of troops on a large scale in all upper Germany. The other troops were distributed partly to the Limes, whose forts, according to Cohausen's estimate (*Röm. Grenzwall*, p. 335), were on an average five miles apart from one another, and so in all about fifty ; partly to the interior forts, especially on the line of the Odenwald from Gündelsheim to Wörth ; that the latter, at least in part, remained occupied even after the laying out of the outer Limes, is at least probable. Owing to the inequality in size of the forts still measurable, it is difficult to say what number of troops was required to make them capable of defence. Cohausen (*l. c.* p. 340) reckons to a middle-sized fort, including the reserve, 720 men. As the usual cohort of the legion as of the auxiliaries numbered 500 men, and the fort-buildings must necessarily have had regard to this fact, the garrison of the fort in the event of siege must be estimated on an average at least at this number. After the reduction the upper German army could not possibly have held the forts, even of the Limes alone, simultaneously in this strength. Much less could it, even before the reduction, have kept the lines between the forts even barely occupied with its 30,000 men (p.

119) ; and, if this was not possible, the simultaneous occupation of all the forts had in fact no object. To all appearance each fort was planned in such a way that, when duly garrisoned, it could be held ; but, as a rule—and on this frontier the state of peace was the rule—the individual fort was not on a war-footing, but only furnished with troops, in so far that posts might be stationed in the watch-towers, and the roads as well as the byways might be kept under inspection. The standing garrisons of the forts were, it may be conjectured, very much weaker than is usually assumed. We possess from antiquity but a single record of such a garrison ; it is of the year 155, and relates to the fort of Kutlowitza, to the north of Sofia (*Eph. Epigr.* iv. p. 524), for which the army of lower Moesia, and in fact the 11th legion, furnished the garrison. This troop numbered at that time, besides the centurion in command, only 76 men. The Raetian army was, at least before Marcus, still less in a position to occupy extensive lines ; it numbered then at the most 10,000 men, and had, besides the Raetian Limes, to supply also the line of the Danube from Ratisbon to Passau.

explained by their different relations to the neighbours, in the former case to the Hermunduri, in the latter to the Chatti. The Romans in upper Germany did not confront their neighbours as they confronted the Highlanders of Britain, in whose presence the province was always in a state of siege ; but the repulse of predatory invaders as well as the levying of the frontier-dues demanded at any rate ready and near military help. The upper German army, and in keeping with it the garrisons on the Limes, might be gradually reduced, but the Roman *pilum* could never be dispensed with in the land of the Neckar. It might, however, be dispensed with in presence of the Hermunduri, who, in Trajan's time, alone of all the Germans, were at liberty to cross the frontier of the empire without special control and to trade freely in the Roman territory, especially in Augsburg, and with whom, so far as we know, border-collisions never took place. There was thus at this period no occasion for a similar structure on the Raetian frontier ; the forts north of the Danube, which can be shown to have subsisted already in Trajan's time,[1] sufficed here for the protection of the frontier and the control of frontier-intercourse. This accords with the observation that the Raetian Limes, as it stands before our eyes, corresponds only with the more recent upper Germanic barrier-line perhaps laid out for the first time under Marcus. Then occasion for it was not wanting. The wars of the Chatti, as we shall see (p. 161), seized at this time also on Raetia ; the strengthening too of the garrison of the province might reasonably stand in connection with the erection of this Limes, which, however little it was arranged for military ends, was at any rate doubtless constructed with a view to its being a frontier-bar, though of less strong character.[2]

---

[1] This is proved by the document of Trajan of the year 107, found at Weissenburg.

[2] The investigations hitherto as to the Raetian Limes have but little cleared up the destination of this work ; this only is made out that it was less adapted than the analogous upper German one for military occupation. A weaker frontier-bar of that sort may reasonably, even before the Marcomanian war, have been chosen to face the Hermunduri ; nor does what Tacitus says of their intercourse in Augusta Vindelicum by any means exclude the existence at that time of a

In a military as well as a political sense the shifting of the frontier, or rather the strengthening of the frontier-fence, was effective and useful. While formerly the Roman chain of forts in upper Germany and Raetia probably went up the Rhine by way of Strassburg to Basel and along by Vindonissa to the lake of Constance, then from thence to the upper Danube, now the upper German headquarters were in Mentz and the Raetian in Ratisbon, and generally the two chief armies of the empire were brought considerably nearer to each other. The legionary camp of Vindonissa (Windisch near Zürich) became thereby superfluous. The army of the upper Rhine could, like the neighbouring one, be reduced after some time to the half of its former strength. The original number of four legions, which was only accidentally diminished to three during the Batavian war, subsisted, at all events, probably still under Trajan ;[1] but under Marcus the province was only occupied by two legions, the 8th and the 22d, of which the former was stationed at Strassburg, the second at the headquarters Mentz, while most of the troops, broken up into smaller posts, were stationed along the frontier-wall. Within the new line urban life flourished almost as on the left bank of the Rhine ; Sumelocenna (Rottenburg on the Neckar), Aquae (*civitas Aurelia Aquensis*, Baden), Lopodunum

Raetian Limes. Only in that case we should expect that it would not end at Lorch, but would join the line of the Neckar ; and in some measure it does this, inasmuch as at Lorch instead of the Limes comes the Rems, which falls into the Neckar at Canstatt.

[1] Of the seven legions which at Nero's death were stationed in the two Germanies (p. 132), Vespasian broke up five; there remained the 21st and the 22d, to which, thereupon, were added the seven or eight legions introduced for the suppression of the revolt, the 1st Adiutrix, 2d Adiutrix, 6th Victrix, 8th and 10th Gemina, 11th, 13th (?), and 14th. Of these, after the close of the war, the 1st Adiutrix was sent probably to Spain (p. 65, note), the 2d Adiutrix probably to Britain (p. 174, note 4), the 13th Gemina (if this came to Germany at all) to Pannonia ; the other seven remained, namely, in the lower province the 6th, 10th, 21st, and 22d (p. 147, note), in the upper the 8th, 11th, and 14th. To the latter was probably added in the year 88 the 1st Adiutrix, once more sent from Spain to upper Germany (p. 65 note). That under Trajan the 1st Adiutrix and the 11th were stationed in upper Germany is shown by the inscription of Baden-Baden (Brambach, *C. I. Rh.* 1666). The 8th and the 14th, it can be shown, both came with Cerialis to Germany, and both did garrison duty there for a considerable period.

(Ladenburg), had, if we except Cologne and Treves, to fear no comparison as respects Roman urban development with any town of Belgica. The rise of these settlements was chiefly the work of Trajan, who began his government with this act of peace;[1] "the Rhine Roman on both its banks" is what a Roman poet entreats speedily to send to Rome its yet unseen ruler. The great and fertile region, which was placed in this way under the protection of the legions, needed that protection and was worthy of it. Doubtless the battle of Varus marks the beginning of the ebb of Roman power, but only in so far as its advance was thereby ended, and the Romans thenceforth contented themselves in general with shielding more vigorously and continuously what was retained.

Germany under Marcus.

Down to the beginning of the third century the Roman power on the Rhine showed no indications of tottering. During the war with the Marcomani under Marcus all remained quiet in the lower province. If a legate of Belgica had at that time to call out the general levy against the Chauci, this was presumably a piratical expedition, such as often visited the north coast at this time, just as earlier and later. The surge of the great movement of peoples reached to the sources of the Danube and even as far as the region of the Rhine; but it did not shake the

---

[1] Traian was sent by Nerva in the year 96 or 97 as legate to Germany, probably to the upper, as at that time Vestricius Spurinna seems to have presided over the lower. Nominated here as co-regent in October of the year 97, he received the accounts of Nerva's death and of his nomination as the Augustus in February 98 at Cologne. He may have remained there during the winter and the following summer; in the winter 98-99 he was on the Danube. The words of Eutropius, viii. 2: *urbes trans Rhenum in Germania reparavit* (whence the often misused notice in Orosius, vii. 12, 2, has been copied), which can only be referred to the upper province, but naturally apply not to the legate, but to the Caesar or the Augustus, obtain a confirmation through the *civitas Ulpia s(altus ?) N(icerini ?) Lopodunum* of the inscriptions. The "restoration" may stand in contrast not to the institutions of Domitian, but to the irregular germs of urban arrangements in the Decumates-land before the shifting of the military frontier. There is no indication pointing to warlike events under Trajan; that he planned and gave his name (Ammianus, xvii. 1, 11) to a *castellum in Alamannorum solo*—according to the connection, on the Main not far from Mentz—is as little proof of such events as the circumstance that a later poet (Sidonius, *Carm.* vii. 115), mixing up old and new, makes Agrippina under him the terror of the Sugambri—that is, in his sense, of the Franks.

foundations there. The Chatti, the only considerable Germanic tribe on the upper German and Raetian border-fence, pushed forward in both directions, and were probably at that time even among the Germans invading Italy, as will be shown further on when we describe this war. At any rate the reinforcement of the Raetian army at that time ordained by Marcus, and its conversion into a command of the first class with legion and legates, can only have taken place in order to check the attacks of the Chatti, and proves that they did not treat them lightly as regards the future. The already-mentioned strengthening of the border-defence would likewise stand connected with this movement. These measures must have sufficed for the next generation.

Under Antoninus the son of Severus a new and more severe war once more (213) broke out in Raetia. This also was waged against the Chatti; but by their side a second people is named, which we here meet for the first time—the Alamanni. Whence they came, we know not. According to a Roman writing a little later they were a conflux of mixed elements; the appellation also seems to point to a league of communities, as well as the fact that afterwards the different tribes comprehended under this name stand forth—more than is the case among the other great Germanic peoples—in their separate character, and the Juthungi, the Lentienses, and other Alamannic peoples not seldom act independently. But that it is not the Germans of this region who here emerge allied under the new name and strengthened by the alliance, is shown as well by the naming of the Alamanni alongside of the Chatti, as by the mention of the unwonted skifulness of the Alamanni in equestrian combat. On the contrary it was certainly, in the main, hordes coming on from the East that lent new strength to the almost extinguished German resistance on the Rhine; it is not improbable that the powerful Semnones, in earlier times dwelling on the middle Elbe, of whom there is no further mention after the end of the second century, furnished a strong contingent to the Alamanni. The constantly increasing mis-

War with the Alamanni.

Severus
Antoninus. government in the Roman empire naturally contributed its share, although only in a secondary degree, to the shifting of power. The emperor took the field in person against the new foe ; in August of the year 213 he crossed the Roman frontier, and a victory over them on the Main was achieved or at least celebrated ; further forts were constructed ; the tribes of the Elbe and of the North Sea sent deputies to the Roman ruler, and wondered when in receiving them he wore their own dress, with silver-mounted jacket, and hair and beard coloured and arranged after the German fashion. But thenceforth the wars on the Rhine are incessant, and the aggressors are the Germans ; the neighbours formerly so pliant had as it were exchanged characters. Twenty years later the inroads of the barbarians on the Danube as on the Rhine were so constant and so

Alexander. serious, that the emperor Alexander had on their account to break off the less immediately dangerous Persian war and to resort in person to the camp of Mentz, not so much to defend the territory as to purchase peace from the Germans by large sums of money. The exasperation of the soldiers at this led to his murder (A.D. 235), and thereby to the fall of the Severian dynasty, the last that existed at all until the regeneration of the state.

Maxi-
minus. His successor Maximinus, a rough but brave Thracian who had risen from the position of a common soldier, compensated for the cowardly conduct of his predecessor by an energetic expedition into the heart of Germany. The barbarians did not yet venture to face a strong and well-led Roman army ; they retreated to their forests and morasses, and the brave emperor, following them even thither, fought in front of all hand to hand. From these conflicts, which were doubtless directed from Mentz primarily against the Alamanni, he could with right call himself Germanicus ; and even for the future the expedition of the year 236, for long the last great victory which the Romans gained on the Rhine, bore some fruit. Although the constant and bloody changes on the throne and the grave disasters in the East and on the Danube allowed the Romans no time to breathe, during the next

twenty years, if peace was not strictly preserved on the
Rhine a greater disaster did not occur.   It appears even
that one of the upper German legions was at that time
sent to Africa without its place being supplied, and so
upper Germany was held as tolerably secure.   But when
in the year 253 the different generals of Rome were once
more fighting each other for the imperial dignity, and the
Rhine-legions marched to Italy to fight out the cause of
their emperor Valerianus against the Aemilianus of the
Danube-army, this seems to have been the signal[1] for the
Germans pushing forward especially towards the lower
Rhine.[2]   These Germans were the Franks, who appear The
here for the first time, perhaps new opponents only in Franks.
name ; for, although the identification of them, already to
be met with in later antiquity, with tribes formerly named
on the lower Rhine—partly, the Chamavi settled beside
the Bructeri, partly the Sugambri formerly mentioned
subject to the Romans—is uncertain and at least inadequate, there is here greater probability than in the case of
the Alamanni that the Germans hitherto dependent on
Rome on the right bank of the Rhine, and the Germanic
tribes previously dislodged from the Rhine, took at that
time — under the collective name of the " Free "— the
offensive in concert against the Romans.

So long as Gallienus himself remained on the Rhine, Gallienus.
he, notwithstanding the small forces that were at his disposal, kept his opponents to some extent in check, prevented them from crossing the river, or drove out again
the intruders, although he doubtless ceded to one of the
Germanic leaders a portion of the desired territory on the

---

[1] Not merely the causal connection, but even the chronological succession of these important events is
obscure.   The account, relatively the
best, in Zosimus, i. 29, describes the
Germanic war as the cause why Valerian immediately on ascending the
throne in 253 made his son joint-ruler
with equal rights ; and Valerian bears
the title *Germanicus maximus* as
early as 256 (*C. I. L.* viii. 2380 ;
likewise in 259 *C. I. L.* xi. 826),

perhaps even if the coin in Cohen, n.
54, is to be trusted, the title *Germanicus maximus ter.*

[2] That the Germans, against whom
Gallienus had to fight, are to be
sought at least chiefly on the lower
Rhine, is shown by the residence of
his son in Agrippina, where he can
only have remained behind as nominal
representative of his father.   His
biographer also, c. 8, names the
Franks.

river-bank, under the condition of his acknowledging the Roman rule and defending his possession against his countrymen—which indeed almost amounted to a capitulation. But when the emperor, recalled by the still more dangerous position of affairs on the Danube, resorted thither and left behind as representative in Gaul his elder son still in boyhood, one of the officers, to whom he had intrusted the defence of the frontier and the guardianship of his son, Marcus Cassianius Latinius Postumus,[1] got

Postumus.

[1] It is difficult to form a conception of the degree of historical falsification which prevails in a portion of the Imperial Biographies; it will not be amiss to present here a specimen of it in the account of Postumus. He is here called (no doubt in an inserted document) *Iulius Postumus* (*Tyr.* 6), on the coins and inscriptions M. *Cassianius Latinius Postumus*, in the epitomised Victor, 32, Cassius Labienus Postumus. — He reigns seven years (*Gall.* 4); *Tyr.* 3, 5; the coins name his *tr. p. X.*, and Eutropius, ix. 10, gives him ten years. —His opponent is called *Lollianus*, according to the coins *Ulpius Cornelius Laelianus*, Laelianus in Eutropius ix. 9 (according to the one class of manuscripts, while the other follows the interpolation of the biographers) and in Victor (c. 33), *Aelianus* in the epitome of Victor.—Postumus and Victorinus rule jointly according to the biographer; but there are no coins common to both, and consequently these confirm the report in Victor and Eutropius that Victorinus was the successor of Postumus.—It is a peculiarity of this class of falsifications that they reach their culmination in the documents inserted. The Cologne epitaph of the two Victorini (*Tyr.* 7), *hic duo Victorini tyranni* (!) *siti sunt* criticises itself. The alleged commission of Valerian, whereby the latter communicates to the Gauls the nomination of Postumus, not only praises prophetically the gifts of Postumus as a ruler, but names also various impossible offices; a *Transrhenani limitis dux et Galliae prae-*ses at no time existed, and Postumus ἀρχὴν ἐν Κελτοῖς στρατιωτῶν ἐμπεπιστευμένος (Zosimus, i. 38) can only have been *praeses* of one of the two Germanies, or, if his command was an extraordinary one, *dux per Germanias*. Equally impossible is, in the same quasi-document, the *tribunatus Vocontiorum* of the son, an evident imitation of the tribunates, as they emerge in the *Notitia Dign.* of the time of Honorius. --Against Postumus and Victorinus, under whom the Gauls and the Franks fight, Gallienus marches with Aureolus, afterwards his opponent, and the later emperor Claudius; he himself is wounded by a shot from an arrow, but is victorious, without any change being produced by the victory. Of this war the other accounts know nothing. Postumus falls in the military insurrection instigated by the so-called Lollianus, while according to the report in Victor and Eutropius, Postumus becomes master of this Mentz insurrection, but then the soldiers kill him because he will not deliver up Mentz to them for plunder. As to the elevation of Postumus, by the side of the narrative which agrees in the main with the ordinary one, that Postumus had perfidiously set aside the son of Gallienus entrusted to his guardianship, stands another evidently invented to clear him, according to which the people in Gaul did this, and then offered the crown to Postumus. The tendency to eulogise one who had spared Gaul the fate of the Danubian lands and of Asia and had saved it from the Germans, comes

himself proclaimed by his men as emperor and besieged in Cologne Silvanus the guardian of the emperor's son. He was successful in capturing the town and in getting into his power his former colleague as well as the imperial boy, whereupon he had them both executed. But during this confusion the Franks burst over the Rhine, and not merely overflowed all Gaul, but penetrated also into Spain and indeed pillaged even the coast of Africa. Soon afterwards, when the capture of Valerian by the Persians had filled up the measure of misfortune, all the Roman land on the left bank of the Rhine in the upper province was lost, passing doubtless to the Alamanni, whose eruption into Italy in the last years of Gallienus necessarily presupposes this loss. He is the last emperor whose name is found on monuments on the right of the Rhine. His coins celebrate him on account of five great victories over the Germans, and not less are those of his successor in the Gallic rule, Postumus, full of the praise of the German victories of the deliverer of Gaul. Gallienus in his earlier years had taken up the struggle on the Rhine not without energy, and Postumus was even an excellent officer and would gladly have been a good regent ; but amidst the utter unruliness which then prevailed in the Roman state or rather in the Roman army, the talent and ability of the individual profited neither himself nor the commonwealth. A series of flourishing Roman towns was at that time laid desolate by the invading barbarians, and the right bank of the Rhine was for ever lost to the Romans.

The re-establishment of peace and order in Gaul was *Aurelianus.* primarily dependent on the cohesion of the empire generally ; so long as the Italian emperors stationed their troops in the Narbonensis to set aside the Gallic

here and everywhere (most obviously at *Tyr.* 5) to light ; with which is connected the fact that this report knows nothing of the loss of the right bank of the Rhine and of the expeditions of the Franks to Gaul, Spain, and Africa. It is further significant that the alleged progenitor of the Constantinian house is here provided with an honourable secondary part. This narrative, not confused but thoroughly falsified, must be completely set aside ; the reports on the one hand in Zosimus, on the other in the Latins drawing from a common source—Victor and Eutropius, short and confused as they are, can alone be taken into account.

rival, and the latter in turn made as though he would cross the Alps, effective operations against the Germans were of themselves excluded. It was only after that, about the year 272,[1] the then ruler of Gaul, Tetricus, weary of his ungrateful part, had himself brought about the submission of his troops to Aurelianus, the emperor recognised by the Roman senate, that the thought of warding off the Germans could be again entertained. The raids of the Alamanni, who had for almost ten years ravaged upper Italy as far down as Ravenna, had a stop put to them for long by the same able ruler who had brought Gaul back to the empire, and he emphatically defeated one of their tribes, the Juthungi, on the upper Danube. If his government had lasted he would doubtless have renewed the protection of the frontier also in Gaul ; after his speedy and sudden end (275) the Germans once more crossed the Rhine and devastated the country far and wide.

Probus.   His successor Probus (from 276), also an able soldier, not merely drove them out afresh—he is said to have taken from them seventy towns—but also advanced again on the aggressive, crossed the Rhine, and drove the Germans back over the Neckar. He did not, however, renew the lines of the earlier time,[2] but contented

---

[1] The rule of Postumus lasted ten years (p. 164, note 1). That the elder son of Gallienus was already dead in 259, we learn from the inscription of Modena, *C. I. L.* xi. 826 ; the revolt of Postumus thus falls certainly in or before this year. As the captivity of Tetricus cannot well be placed later than 272, immediately after the second expedition against Zenobia, and the three Gallic rulers reigned, Postumus for ten years, Victorinus for two (Eutropius, ix. 9), Tetricus for two (Victor, 35), this brings the revolt of Postumus to somewhere about 259 ; yet such numbers are frequently somewhat deranged. When the duration of the expeditions of the Germans into Spain under Gallienus is definitely stated at twelve years (Orosius, vii.

41, 2), this appears to be superficially reckoned according to the Chronicle of Jerome. The usual exact numbers are unattested and deceptive.

[2] According to the biographer, c. 14, 15, Probus brought the Germans of the right bank of the Rhine into dependence, so that they were tributary to the Romans and defended the frontier for them (*omnes jam barbari vobis arant, vobis jam serviunt et contra interiores gentes militant*) ; the right of bearing arms is left to them for the time, but the idea is, on further successes, to push forward the frontier and erect a province of Germania. Even as free fancies of a Roman of the fourth century—more they are not—these utterances have a certain interest.

himself with erecting and occupying at the more important positions of the Rhine *têtes de pont* on the other bank, —that is, he reverted nearly to such arrangements as had subsisted here before Vespasian.   At the same time the Franks were defeated by his generals in the northern province.   Great masses of the vanquished Germans were sent as forced settlers to Gaul, and above all to Britain.   In this way the frontier of the Rhine was won back and handed over to the later empire.   No doubt, like the rule on the right bank of the Rhine, peace on the left had passed away beyond recall.   The Alamanni stood in a threatening attitude opposite to Basel and Strassburg, the Franks opposite to Cologne.   By their side other tribes presented themselves.   The fact that the Burgundiones, once settled beyond the Elbe, advancing westward as far as the upper Main, threatened Gaul, is first mentioned under the emperor Probus ; a few years later the Saxons, in concert with the Franks, began their attacks by sea on the north coast of Gaul as on the Roman Britain.   But under the—for the most part— vigorous and capable emperors of the Diocletiano- Constantinian house, and even under their immediate successors, the Romans kept the threatening inundation of peoples within measured bounds.

To depict the Germans in their national development is not the task of the historian of the Romans ; for him they appear only as hindering or as destroying.   An interpenetration of the two nationalities, and a mixed culture thence resulting, such as the Romanised land of the Celts presented, Roman Germany has none to show ; or—so far as concerns our conception of it—it coincides with the Romano-Gallic all the more, since the Germanic territories on the left bank of the Rhine, which remained for a considerable time in the Roman possession, were pervaded throughout with Celtic elements, and even those on the right, deprived for the most part of their original population, obtained the majority of the new settlers from Gaul.   Communal centres, such as the Celtic system possessed in large number, were wanting to the German

Romanis-ing of the Germans.

element. Partly on that account, partly in consequence of outward circumstances, the Roman element was able, as has been already brought out (p. 102), to develop itself sooner and more fully in the Germanic east than in the Celtic regions. The encampments of the army of the Rhine, all of which fell within Roman Germany, were of essential influence in this respect. The larger of them obtained, partly through the traders who attached themselves to the army, partly, and above all, through the veterans who remained in their wonted quarters even after their discharge, an urban appendage—a town of huts (*canabae*), separate from the military quarters proper; everywhere, and particularly in Germany, towns proper grew in time out of these at the legionary camps and especially the headquarters. At their head stood the Roman town of the Ubii, originally the second largest camp of the army of the lower Rhine, then from the year 50 onward a Roman colony (p. 99), exercising the most important effect in elevating Roman civilisation in the region of the Rhine. Here the camp-town gave place to that of the Roman plantation; subsequently urban rights were obtained, without shifting the quarters of the troops, by the settlements belonging to the two great camps of the lower Rhine—Ulpia Noviomagus, in the land of the Batavi, and Ulpia Traiana, near Vetera— from Trajan, and in the third century by the military capital of upper Germany, Mogontiacum. No doubt these civil towns always retained a subordinate position by the side of the military centres of administration independent of them.

Roman Germanising. If we look beyond the limit where this narrative closes, we certainly find, instead of the Romanising of the Germans, in some measure a Germanising of the Romans. The last phase of the Roman state was marked by its becoming barbarian, and especially becoming Germanised; and the beginnings of the process reach far back. It commences with the peasantry in the colonate, passes on to the troop as modelled by the emperor Severus, seizes then on the officers and magistrates, and ends with the hybrid Romano-Germanic states of the Visigoths in Spain and Gaul, the Vandals in Africa, above all, with the Italy of Theoderic. For the understanding of this last phase there is certainly needed an insight into the political development of the one as of the other nation. Unfortunately, the enquiry into early German history is here at fault. It is true that the political arrangements into which these Germans entered as servants or joint rulers are well known, far better than the systematic history of the same epoch. But over the primitive condition of the Germans floats that gray morning-haze in which sharp outlines are lost. German heathenism, apart from the far north, perished before the time of which we have knowledge ; and the religious elements, which are never wanting in a national war, we know doubtless for the Sassanidae, but not for the Marcomani. The beginnings of the political development of the Germans are delineated for us in part by the picture of Tacitus—many-coloured, hampered by modelling itself on the ideas of a fading past, and but too often keeping silence as to elements of really decisive moment—while in part we must take them from the hybrid states which arose on formerly Roman soil and had Roman elements everywhere inwoven. Here our records seldom give us German technical terms, but substitute Latin descriptions which are plainly inadequate, and here, in general, we miss those sharply-defined ideas which our studies of classical history offer us in plenty. It is characteristic of our German nation that it has not been permitted to develop itself by German effort from German origins, and we may connect with this the fact that German scholarship has studied the beginnings and characters of other nations with more success than it has won in the study of its own.

CHAPTER V.

BRITAIN.

NINETY-SEVEN years elapsed from the time when Roman
troops had entered, subdued, and again abandoned the
great island in the north-western ocean, before the Roman
government resolved to repeat the voyage and permanently
to occupy Britain. Certainly Caesar's Britannic expedition
had not been, like his campaigns against the Germans, a
mere forward movement of defence. So far as his arm
reached, he had made the individual tribes subject to the
empire, and had regulated their annual tribute to it in
this case as in Gaul. The leading tribe, too, which was
to be firmly attached to Rome by its privileged position
and thereby to become the fulcrum of Roman rule, was
found ; the Trinovantes (Essex) were to take up on the
Celtic island the same part—more advantageous than
honourable—as the Haedui and the Remi on the
Gallic continent. The bloody feud between the prince
Cassivellaunus and the princely house of Camalodunum
(Colchester) had been the immediate cause of the Roman
invasion ; to reinstate this house Caesar had landed, and
the object was for the moment attained. Beyond doubt
Caesar never deceived himself as to the fact that the
tribute, as well as the protectorate, were in the first
instance mere words ; but these words were a programme
which could not but bring about, and was intended to
bring about, the permanent occupation of the island by
Roman troops.

Caesar himself did not get so far as permanently to

organise the affairs of the subject island ; and for his successors Britain was a perplexity. The Britons who had become subject to the empire certainly did not long pay—perhaps never paid at all—the tribute which was due. The protectorate over the dynasty of Camalodunum must have been still less respected, and had simply as its effect, that princes and scions of that house again and again appeared in Rome and invoked the intervention of the Roman government against neighbours and rivals. Thus king Dubnovellaunus, probably the successor of the prince of the Trinovantes confirmed by Caesar, came as a refugee to Rome to the emperor Augustus, and so, later, one of the princes of the same house came to the emperor Gaius.[1]

In fact the expedition to Britain was a necessary part of the heritage left by Caesar. Already during the Dual Rule Caesar the younger had projected such an expedition, and had only desisted from it on account of the more urgent necessity of procuring quiet in Illyricum, or on account of the strained relation with Antonius, which proved useful to the Parthians in the first instance as well as to the Britons. The courtly poets of the earlier years of Augustus celebrated variously in anticipation the Britannic conquest ; the programme of Caesar was thus accepted and adopted by his successor. When the monarchy was consolidated, all Rome thereupon expected that the close of the civil war would be followed by the

---

[1] To all appearance the political relations between Rome and Britain in the time before the conquest are to be regarded essentially as arising out of the restoration and guarantee (*B. G.* v. 22) of the principality of the Trinovantes by Caesar. That king Dubnovellaunus, who along with another quite unknown Britannic prince sought protection with Augustus, ruled chiefly in Essex, is shown by his coins (my *Mon. Ancyr.* 2d ed., p. 138 f.). We have to seek also mainly there the Britannic princes who sent to Augustus and recognised his supremacy (for such apparently we must take to be the meaning of Strabo, iv. 5, 3, p. 200 ; comp. Tacitus, *Ann.* ii. 24). Cunobelinus, according to the coins the son of king Tasciovanus, of whom history is silent, dying as it would seem in advanced years between 40 and 43, and thus contemporary in his government with the later years of Augustus and with Tiberius and Gaius, resided in Camalodunum (Dio, lx. 21) ; around him and his sons the preliminary history of the invasion turns. To what quarter Bericus, who came to Claudius (Dio, lx. 19), belonged we do not know, and other British dynasts may have followed the example of those of Colchester ; but these stand at the head.

Britannic expedition ; the complaints of the poets as to
the dreadful strife, but for which the Britons would long
since have been led in triumphal procession to the
Capitol, became transformed into the proud hope of
adding to the empire the new province of Britain. The

27. expedition was, moreover, repeatedly announced (727,
26. 728), yet Augustus, without formally abandoning the
undertaking, soon desisted from carrying it out ; and
Tiberius, faithful to his maxim, adhered in this question
also to the system of his father.[1] The worthless thoughts
of the last Julian emperor roamed doubtless also over
the ocean ; but serious things he was incapable of even
planning. It was the government of Claudius that first
took up the plan of the dictator afresh and carried it out.

The reasons for, and against, the occupation of Britain. What were the determining motives, on the one side
as on the other, may be at least partially discerned.
Augustus himself laid it down that the occupation of the
island was not necessary from a military point of view—
seeing that its inhabitants were not in a position to annoy
the Romans on the continent—and was not advantageous
for the finances ; that what could be drawn from Britain
flowed into the exchequer of the empire in the form of
import and export duties at the Gallic harbours ; that
at least a legion and some cavalry would be requisite
as garrison, and after deduction of its cost from the
tribute of the island not much would be left.[2] All this
was indisputably correct, but it was not the whole
truth. Experience showed later that a legion was far
from sufficient to hold the island. We must further take
into account, what the government certainly had no
occasion to say, that, considering the state of weakness
to which the Roman army had been brought by the
internal policy of Augustus, it could not but appear very

---

[1] Tacitus, *Agr.* 13, *consilium id
divus Augustus vocabat, Tiberius prae-
ceptum.*

[2] The exposition in Strabo, ii. 5, 8,
p. 115 ; iv. 5, 3, p. 200, gives
evidently the governmental version.
That, after annexation of the island,

the free traffic and therewith the
produce of the customs would decline,
must doubtless be taken as conced-
ing the proposition that the Roman
rule and the Roman tribute affected
injuriously the prosperity of the
subjects.

hazardous to banish a considerable fragment of it, once for all, to a distant island of the North Sea. There was presumably only the choice of keeping aloof from Britain or increasing the army on its account ; and with Augustus considerations of internal policy always outweighed those of an external character.

But yet the conviction of the necessity for subduing Britain must have predominated with Roman statesmen. Caesar's conduct would be inconceivable if we do not presuppose that conviction in his case. Augustus at first formally recognised, and never formally disowned, the aim proposed by Caesar, notwithstanding its inconvenience. It was precisely the governments that were the most far-seeing and most tenacious of purpose—those of Claudius, Nero, and Domitian—that laid the foundation for the conquest of Britain, or extended the work ; and, after it had taken place, it was never regarded in any such light as, let us say, the conquest by Trajan of Dacia and Mesopotamia. If the maxim of government, elsewhere adhered to almost inviolably, that the Roman empire had simply to fill, but not to extend, its bounds, was permanently set aside only in respect of Britain, the cause lies in the fact that the Celts could not be subdued in such a way as Rome's interest demanded, on the continent alone. This nation was to all appearance more connected than separated by the narrow arm of the sea which parts England and France ; the same names of peoples meet us on the one side and on the other ; the bounds of the individual states often reach over the Channel ; the chief seat of the priestly system, which here more than anywhere else pervaded the whole nationality, was from of old the islands of the North Sea. These islanders indeed were not able to wrest the continent of Gaul from the Roman legions ; but, if the conqueror of Gaul himself, and, later, the Roman government in Gaul, pursued other aims than in Syria and Egypt—if the Celts were to be annexed as members to the Italian nation—this task remained quite impracticable, so long as the subjugated and the free Celtic territories touched each other over the sea, and the enemy of the

Conviction of its necessity predominant.

Romans as well as the Roman deserter found an asylum in Britain.[1] In the first instance the subjugation of the southern coast sufficed for this purpose, although the effect was naturally the greater, the farther the free Celtic territory was pushed back.[2] The special regard of Claudius for his Gallic home and his knowledge of Gallic relations may also have played a part in the matter.

Occasion for the war. Cunobelinus.

What furnished occasion for the war was the fact that that very principality which sustained a certain dependence on Rome under the leadership of its king Cunobelinus — this was Shakespeare's Cymbeline — extended widely its rule,[3] and emancipated itself from the Roman protectorate. One of his sons—Adminius, who had revolted against his father, came to the emperor Gaius desiring protection, and upon his successor refusing to deliver up to the British ruler these his subjects, the war arose in the first instance against the father and the brothers of this Adminius. The real motive, of course, was the indispensable need for completing the conquest of a nation hitherto but half vanquished and keeping closely together.

Military arrangements for occupying the island.

That the occupation of Britain could not ensue without a contemporary increase of the standing army was also the view of those statesmen who gave occasion to it; three of the Rhine-legions and one from the Danube were destined thither,[4] but at the same time two newly instituted legions were assigned to the Germanic armies. An able

---

[1] Suetonius, *Claud.* 17, specifies as cause of the war: *Britanniam tunc tumultuantem ob non redditos transfugas ;* which O. Hirschfeld justly brings into connection with *Gai.* 44 : *Adminio Cunobellini Britannorum regis filio, qui pulsus a patre cum exigua manu transfugerat, in deditionem recepto.* By the *tumultuari* are doubtless meant at least projected expeditions for pillage to the Gallic coast. The war was certainly not waged on account of Bericus (Dio, lx. 19).

[2] Mona was in like manner afterwards *receptaculum perfugarum* (Tacitus, *Ann.* xiv. 29).

[3] Tacitus, *Ann.* xii. 37 : *pluribus gentibus imperitantem.*

[4] The three legions of the Rhine were the 2d Augusta, the 14th, and the 20th ; from Pannonia came the 9th Spanish. The same four legions were still stationed there at the beginning of the government of Vespasian ; the latter called away the 14th for the war against Civilis, and it did not return to Britain, but, in its stead, probably the 2d Adiutrix. This was presumably transferred under Domitian to Pannonia ; under Hadrian the 9th was broken up and replaced by the 6th Victrix. The two other legions, the 2d Augusta and the 20th, were stationed in England from the beginning to the end of the Roman rule.

soldier, Aulus Plautius, was selected as leader of this expedition, and at the same time as first governor of the province ; it departed for the island in the year 43. The soldiers showed themselves reluctant, more doubtless because of the banishment to the distant island than from fear of the foe.   One of the leading men, perhaps the soul of the undertaking, Narcissus, the emperor's cabinet-secretary, wished to instil into them courage ; they did not allow the slave to utter a word for their shouts of scoffing, but did withal as he wished and embarked.

The occupation of the island was not attended by any special difficulty.   The natives stood, in a political as in a military point of view, at the same low stage of development which Caesar had previously found in the island. Kings or queens reigned in the several cantons, which had no outward bond of conjunction and were at perpetual feud with one another.   The men were doubtless possessed of bodily strength, endurance, and bravery—despising death ; and were in particular expert horsemen.   But the Homeric war-chariot, which was still a reality here, and on which the princes of the land themselves wielded the reins, as little held its ground against the compact squadrons of Roman cavalry as the foot soldier without coat of mail and helmet, defended only by the small shield, was with his short javelin and his broad sword a match in close combat for the short Roman knife, or even for the heavy *pilum* of the legionary, and sling-bullet and arrow of the light Roman troops.   To the army of about 40,000 well-trained soldiers the natives could oppose no corresponding defensive force.   The disembarkation did not even encounter resistance ; the Britons had accounts as to the reluctant temper of the troops and no longer expected the landing.   King Cunobelinus had died shortly before ; the opposition was led by his two sons Caratacus and Togodumnus.   The invading army had its march at once directed to Camalodunum,[1] and in a rapid course of victory

Course of the occupation.

---

[1] The identification, based only on dubious emendations, of the Boduni and Catuellani in Dio. lx. 20, with tribes of similar name in Ptolemy, can- not be correct ; these first conflicts must have taken place between the coast and the Thames.

it reached as far as the Thames ; here a halt was made,
chiefly perhaps to give the emperor the opportunity of
plucking the easy laurels in person.   So soon as he
arrived, the river was crossed ; the British levy was beaten,
on which occasion Togodumnus met his death ; Camalodunum itself was taken.   His brother Caratacus, it is
true, obstinately continued the resistance, and gained for
himself, in victory or defeat, a proud name with friend and
foe ; nevertheless, the progress of the Romans was not to
be checked.   One prince after another was beaten and
deposed—the triumphal arch of Claudius names eleven
British kings as conquered by him ; and what did not
succumb to the Roman arms yielded to the Roman
largesses.   Numerous men of rank accepted the possessions
which the emperor conferred on them at the expense of
their countrymen ; various kings also submitted to the
modest position of vassals, as indeed Cogidumnus the
king of the Regni (Chichester) and Prasutagus the king of
the Iceni (Norfolk) bore rule for a series of years as dependent princes.   But in most districts of the island, which
had hitherto been monarchically governed throughout, the
conquerors introduced their communal constitution, and
gave what was still left to be administered into the hands
of the local men of rank—a course which brought in its
train wretched factions and internal quarrels.   Even under
the first governor the whole level country as far as the
Humber seems to have come into Roman power ; the
Iceni, for example, had already submitted to him.   But it
was not merely with the sword that the Romans made
way for themselves.   Veterans were settled at Camalodunum immediately after its capture ; thus the first town
of Roman organisation and Roman burgess-rights, the
" Claudian colony of victory," was founded in Britain,
destined to be the capital of the country.   Immediately
afterwards began also the profitable working of the British
mines, particularly of the productive lead-mines ; there are
British leaden bars from the sixth year after the invasion.
Evidently with like rapidity the stream of Roman merchants and artisans poured itself over the field newly

opened up ; if Camalodunum received Roman colonists, Roman townships, which soon obtained legally urban organisation, were formed elsewhere in the south of the island as a mere result of freedom of traffic and of immigration, particularly at the hot springs of Sulis (Bath), in Verulamium (St. Albans to the north-west of London), and above all in the natural emporium of trading on a great scale—Londinium at the mouth of the Thames.

The advance of the foreign rule asserted itself everywhere, not merely in new taxes and levies, but perhaps still more in commerce and trade. When Plautius after four years of administration was recalled, he entered Rome in triumph, the last citizen who attained such honour, and honours and orders were lavished on the officers and soldiers of the victorious legions ; triumphal arches were erected to the emperor in Rome, and thereafter in other towns, on account of victory achieved " without any losses whatever ;" the crown-prince born shortly before the invasion received, instead of his grandfather's name, that of Britannicus. We may discern in these matters the unmilitary age disused to victories with loss, and the extravagance in keeping with political dotage ; but, if the invasion of Britain has not much significance from a military standpoint, testimony must withal be borne to the leading men that they set about the work in an energetic and persistent fashion, and that the painful and dangerous time of transition from independent to foreign rule in Britain was an unusually short one.

After the first rapid success, it is true, there were developed difficulties and even dangers, which the occupation of the island brought not merely to the conquered but also to the conquerors.

They were masters of the level country, but not of the mountains or of the sea. The west above all gave trouble to the Romans. No doubt in the extreme south-west, in what is now Cornwall, the old nationality maintained itself, probably more because the conquerors concerned themselves but little about this remote corner than because it directly rebelled against them. But the Silures in the

Resistance in West Britain.

Mona.

south of the modern Wales, and their northern neighbours the Ordovici, perseveringly defied the Roman arms ; the island Mona (Anglesey), adjacent to the latter, was the true focus of national and religious resistance. It was not the character of the ground alone that hindered the advance of the Romans ; what Britain had been for Gaul, that the large island Ivernia was now for Britain, and especially for this west coast ; the freedom on the one side of the channel did not allow the foreign rule to take firm root in the other. We clearly recognise in the laying out of the legionary camps that the invasion was here arrested. Under the successor of Plautius the camp for the 14th legion was laid out at the confluence of the Tern with the Severn near Viroconium (Wroxeter, not far from Shrewsbury) ;[1] presumably about the same time, to the south of it, that of Isca (Caerleon = *Castra legionis*) for the 2d ; to the north that of Deva (Chester = *Castra*) for the 20th ; these three camps shut off the region of Wales towards the south, north, and west, and protected thus the pacified land against the mountains that remained free. Into this region the last prince of Camalodunum, Caratacus, threw himself, after his home had become Roman. He was defeated by the successor of Plautius, Publius Ostorius Scapula, in the territory of the Ordovici, and soon afterwards delivered up by the terrified Brigantes, with whom he had taken refuge, to the Romans (51), and conducted with all his adherents to Italy. In surprise he asked, when he saw the proud city, how the masters of such palaces could covet the poor huts of his native country. But with this the west was by no means subdued ; the Silures above all persevered in obstinate

---

[1] Tacitus, *Ann.* xii. 31 (*P. Ostorius*) *cuncta castris ad . . ntonam* (MSS. read *castris antonam*) *et Sabrinam fluvios cohibere parat.* So the passage is to be restored, only that the name of the river Tern not elsewhere given in tradition cannot be supplied. The only inscriptions found in England of soldiers of the 14th legion, which left England under Nero, have come to light at Wroxeter,
the so-called " English Pompeii." The epitaph of a soldier of the 20th has also been found there. The camp described by Tacitus was perhaps common at first to the two legions, and the 20th did not go till afterwards to Deva. That the camp at Isca was laid out immediately after the invasion is plain from Tacitus, *Ann.* xii. 32, 38.

resistance, and the fact that the Roman general announced his purpose of extirpating them to the last man did not contribute to make them more submissive. The enterprising governor, Gaius Suetonius Paullinus, attempted Paullinus some years later (61) to bring into Roman power the chief seat of resistance, the island of Mona, and in spite of the furious opposition with which he was met, and in which the priests and the women took the lead, the sacred trees, beneath which many a Roman captive had bled, fell under the axes of the legionaries. But out of the occupation of this last asylum of the Celtic priesthood there was developed a dangerous crisis in the subject territory itself; and the governor was not destined to complete the conquest of Mona.

In Britain, too, the alien rule had to stand the test of Boudicca. national insurrection. What was undertaken by Mithradates in Asia Minor, by Vercingetorix among the Celts of the continent, by Civilis among the subject Germans, was attempted among the insular Celts by a woman, the wife of one of those vassal-princes confirmed by Rome, the Queen of the Iceni, Boudicca. Her deceased husband had, to secure the future of his wife and his daughters, bequeathed his sovereignty to the emperor Nero, and divided his property between the latter and his own relatives. The emperor took the legacy and, in addition, what was not meant for him; the princely cousins were put in chains, the widow was scourged, the daughters maltreated in more shameful fashion. Then came other wrongs at the hands of the later Neronian government. The veterans settled in Camalodunum chased the earlier possessors from house and homestead as it pleased them, without the authorities interfering to check them. The presents conferred by the emperor Claudius were confiscated as revocable gifts. Roman ministers, who at the same time trafficked in money, drove in this way the Britannic communities, one after the other, to bankruptcy. The moment was favourable. The governor Paullinus, more brave than cautious, was just then, as we have said, with the flower of the Roman army in the remote island of

Mona, and this attack on the most sacred seat of the national religion exasperated men's minds as much as it paved the way for insurrection. The old vehement Celtic faith, which had given the Romans so much trouble, burst forth once more, for the last time, in a mighty flame. The weakened and far separated camps of the legions in the west and in the north afforded no protection to the whole south-east of the island with its flourishing Roman towns.

Attack on Camalo- dunum. Above all, the capital, Camalodunum, was utterly defenceless ; there was no garrison. The walls were not completed, although the temple of their imperial founder, the new god Claudius, was so. The west of the island, probably kept down by the legions stationed there, seems not to have taken part in the rising, and as little the non-subject north ; but, as frequently occurred in Celtic revolts, in the year 61 on a concerted signal all the rest of the subject territory rose in a moment against the foreigners, the Trinovantes, driven out of their capital, taking the lead. The second commander, who at the time represented the governor, the procurator Decianus Catus, had at the last moment sent what soldiers he had to its protection ; they were 200 men. They defended themselves with the veterans and the other Romans capable of arms for two days in the temple ; then they were overpowered, and all that was Roman in the town perished. The like fate befell the chief emporium of Roman trade, Londinium, and a third flourishing Roman city, Verulamium (St. Albans, north-west of London), as well as the foreigners scattered over the island ; it was a national Vesper like that of Mithradates, and the number of victims—alleged to be 70,000—was not less. The procurator gave up the cause of Rome as lost, and fled to the continent. The Roman army, too, became involved in the disaster. A number of scattered detachments and garrisons succumbed to the assaults of the insurgents. Quintus Petillius Cerialis, who held the command in the camp of Lindum, marched on Camalodunum with the 9th legion ; he came too late to save it, and, assailed by an enormous superiority of force, lost in the battle all his infantry ; the camp was stormed by the Brigantes. The same fate well-nigh overtook the general-in-chief. Hastily returning from the island of Mona, he called to him the 2d legion stationed at Isca ; but it did not obey the command, and with only about 10,000 men Paullinus had to take up the unequal struggle against the numberless and victorious army of the insurgents. If ever soldiers made good the errors of their leader it was on the day when this small band—chiefly the thenceforth celebrated 14th legion—achieved, doubtless to its own surprise, a full victory, and once more established the Roman rule in Britain. Little was wanting to bring the name of Paullinus into association with that of Varus. But success decides, and here it remained with the Romans.[1] The guilty commandant of the legion that remained aloof anticipated the court-martial, and threw himself upon his sword. The queen Boudicca drank the cup of poison. The otherwise brave general was not indeed brought to trial, as seemed to be at first the intention of the government, but was soon under a suitable pretext recalled.

The subjugation of the western portions of the island was not continued at once by the successors of Paullinus. The able general Sextus Julius Frontinus first under Vespasian forced the Silures to recognise the Roman

Subjugation of West Britain.

---

[1] A worse narrative than that of Tacitus concerning this war, *Ann.* xiv. 31-39, is hardly to be found even in this most unmilitary of all authors. We are not told where the troops were stationed, and where the battles were fought ; but we get, instead, signs and wonders enough and empty words only too many. The important facts, which are mentioned in the life of Agricola, 31, are wanting in the main narrative, especially the storming of the camp. That Paullinus coming from Mona should think not of saving the Romans in the southeast, but of uniting his troops, is intelligible ; but not why, if he wished to sacrifice Londinium, he should march thither on that account. If he really went thither, he can only have appeared there with a personal escort, without the corps which he had with him in Mona—which indeed has no meaning. The bulk of the Roman troops, as well those brought back from Mona as those still in existence elsewhere, can, after the extirpation of the 9th legion, only have been stationed on the line Deva—Viroconium—Isca ; Paullinus fought the battle with the two legions stationed in the first two of these camps, the 14th and the (incomplete) 20th. That Paullinus fought because he was obliged to fight, is stated by Dio, lxii. 1-12, and although his narrative cannot be otherwise used to correct that of Tacitus, this much seems required by the very state of the case.

rule ; his successor Gnaeus Julius Agricola, after obstinate conflicts with the Ordovici, effected what Paullinus had not achieved, and occupied in the year 78 the island of Mona. Afterwards there is no mention of active resistance in these regions ; the camp of Viroconium could probably about this time be dispensed with, and the legion thereby set free could be employed in northern Britain. But the other two legionary camps still remained on the spot down to the time of Diocletian, and only disappeared in the later arrangements of the troops. If political considerations may have contributed to this (p. 190), yet the resistance of the west was probably continued even later, perhaps supported by communications with Ivernia. Moreover, the complete absence of Roman traces in the interior of Wales, and the Celtic nationality maintaining itself there up to the present day, tell in favour of this view.

Subjugation of Northern Britain.

In the north the camp of the 9th Spanish legion in Lindum (Lincoln) formed the centre of the Roman position to the east of Viroconium. In closest contact with this camp in north England was the most powerful principality of the island, that of the Brigantes (Yorkshire) ; it had not properly submitted, but the queen, Cartimandus, sought to keep peace with the conquerors and showed herself compliant to them. The party hostile to the Romans had attempted to break loose here in the year 50, but the attempt had been quickly suppressed. Caratacus, beaten in the west, had hoped to be able to continue his resistance in the north, but the queen delivered him, as already stated, to the Romans. These internal dissensions and domestic quarrels must have partly influenced the rising against Paullinus, in which we find the Brigantes in a leading position, and which fell with all its weight upon this very legion of the north. Meanwhile the Roman party of the Brigantes, however, was influential enough to obtain the restoration of the government of Cartimandus after the insurrection was defeated. But some years afterwards the patriotic party there, supported by the tidings of revolt from Rome, which during the civil war after the downfall of Nero filled all the west, brought about a new rising of the Brigantes against the foreign rule, at the head of which stood Cartimandus's former husband, set aside and scorned by her—the veteran warrior Venutius. It was only after prolonged conflicts that the mighty people was subdued by Petillius Cerialis, the same who had fought unsuccessfully under Paullinus against these same Britons, now one of the most noted generals of Vespasian, and the first governor of the island nominated by him. The gradually slackening resistance of the west made it possible to combine one of the three legions hitherto stationed there with that stationed in Lindum, and to advance the camp itself from Lindum to the chief place of the Brigantes, Eburacum (York). But, so long as the west offered serious resistance, nothing further was done in the north for the extension of the Roman bounds ; at the Caledonian forest, says an author of the time of Vespasian, the Roman arms were arrested for thirty years.

It was Agricola who first, after his work was over in the west, energetically set himself to the subjugation also of the north. First of all, he created for himself a fleet, without which the provisioning of the troops in these mountains, which afforded few supplies, would have been impossible. Supported by this fleet he reached, under Titus (80), as far as the estuary of the Tava (Frith of Tay), into the region of Perth and Dundee, and employed the three following campaigns in gaining an exact knowledge of the wide districts between this frith and the previous Roman boundary on the two seas, in breaking everywhere the local resistance, and in constructing intrenchments at the fitting places ; with reference to which, in particular, the natural line of defence which is formed by the two friths running deeply into the land, of Clota (Clyde) near Glasgow, and Bodotria (Forth) near Edinburgh, was selected for a basis. This advance called the whole Highlands under arms ; but the mighty battle which the united Caledonian tribes offered to the legions between the two friths of Forth and Tay at the Graupian

Agricola.

mountains ended with the victory of Agricola. According to his view the subjugation of the island, once begun, had to be also completed, nay, even extended to Ivernia ; and in favour of that course there might be urged, with respect to Roman Britain, what the occupation of the island had brought about with respect to Gaul. Moreover, with an energetic carrying out of the occupation of the islands as a whole, the expenditure of men and money for the future would probably be reduced.

Caledonia abandoned. The Roman government did not follow these counsels. How far personal and spiteful motives may have co-operated in the recall of the victorious general in the year 85, who for that matter had remained longer in office than was usually the case elsewhere, must be left undetermined. The coincidence of the last victories of the general in Scotland and the first defeats of the emperor in the region of the Danube was certainly in a high degree annoying. But for the putting a stop to the operations in Britain,[1] and for the calling away, which apparently then ensued, of one of the four legions with which Agricola had executed his campaigns to Pannonia, a quite sufficient explanation is furnished by the military position of the state at that time—the extension of the Roman rule to the right bank of the Rhine in upper Germany and the outbreak of the dangerous wars in Pannonia. This, indeed, does not explain why, withal, an end should be put to the pressing forward towards the north, and northern Scotland as well as Ireland should be left to themselves.

Probable grounds for this policy. That thenceforth the government desisted not on account of accidents of the situation for the moment, but once for all, from pushing forward the frontier of the empire, and amidst all change of persons adhered to this course, we are taught by the whole later history of the island, and taught especially by the laborious and costly wall-structures to be mentioned immediately. Whether the completion of the conquest was renounced by them in the true interest of the state, is another question. That the imperial

---

[1] Tacitus, *Hist.* i. 2, sums up the result in the words *perdomita Britannia et statim missa.*

finances would only suffer loss by this extension of the
bounds was even now urged, quite as much as it formerly
was against the occupation of the island itself ; but could
not be decisive of the matter.[1]   In a military point of
view the occupation was capable of being carried out, as
Agricola had conceived it, beyond doubt without material
difficulty.   But the consideration might turn the scale, that
the Romanising of the regions still free would have to encounter great difficulty on account of the diversity of race.
The Celts in England proper belonged throughout to those
of the continent ; national name, faith, language, were common to both.   As the Celtic nationality of the continent
had found a support in the island, on the other hand the
Romanising of Gaul necessarily carried its influence over
to England, and to this especially Rome owed the fact
that Britain became Romanised with so surprising rapidity.
But the natives of Ireland and Scotland belonged to
another stock and spoke another language ; the Briton
understood their Gaelic probably as little as the German
understood the language of the Scandinavians.   The
Caledonians—with the Iverni the Romans hardly came
into contact—are described throughout as barbarians of
the wildest type.   On the other hand, the priest of the
oak (Derwydd, *Druida*) exercised his office on the Rhone
as in Anglesey, but not in the island of the west nor in
the mountains of the north.   If the Romans had waged
the war chiefly to bring the domain of the Druids entirely
into their power, this aim was in some measure attained.
Beyond doubt at another time all these considerations
would not have induced the Romans to renounce the
sea-frontier on the north when brought so near to them,
and at least Caledonia would have been occupied.   But
the Rome of that time was no longer able to leaven
further regions with Roman habits ; the productive power
and the progressive spirit of the people had disappeared

---

[1] The imperial finance-official under
Pius, Appian (*proem.* 5), remarks that
the Romans had occupied the best
part (τὸ κράτιστον) of the British
islands οὐδὲν τῆς ἄλλης δεόμενοι, οὐ
γὰρ εὔφορος αὐτοῖς ἐστὶν οὐδ᾿ ἦν
ἔχουσιν.   This was the answer of the
governmental staff to Agricola and
such as shared his opinion.

from it.   At least that sort of conquest, which cannot be enforced by decrees and marches, would have hardly succeeded, had they attempted it.

Fortifying of the northern frontier.
Their aim therefore was to arrange the northern frontier appropriately for defence, and to this object their military works were thenceforth directed.   Eburacum remained the military centre.   The wide territory occupied by Agricola was retained and furnished with forts, which served as advanced posts for the headquarters in rear ; probably the greatest part of the non-legionary troops were employed for this purpose.   The construction of connected lines of fortification followed later.   The first of the kind proceeded from Hadrian, and is also remarkable, in so far as it still in a certain sense subsists to the
The wall of Hadrian.
present day, and is more completely known than any other of the great military structures of the Romans. It is, strictly taken, a military road protected on both sides by fortifications, leading from sea to sea for a length of about seventy miles, westward to the Solway Frith, and eastward to the mouth of the Tyne.   The defence on the north is formed by a huge wall, originally at least 16 feet high and 8 feet thick, built on the two outer sides of square stones, filled up between with rubble and mortar, in front of which stretched a no less imposing fosse, 9 feet in depth and 34 feet or more in breadth at the top. Towards the south the road is protected by two parallel earthen ramparts, even now 6 to 7 feet high, between which is drawn a fosse 7 feet deep, with a margin raised to the south, so that the structure from rampart to rampart has a total breadth of 24 feet.   Between the stone-wall and the earthen ramparts on the road itself lie the camp-stations and watch-houses, viz. at the distance of about four miles from one another the cohort-camps, constructed as forts, independently capable of defence, with gates opening towards all the four sides ; between every two of these a smaller structure of a similar kind with sally-ports to the north and south ; between every two of the latter four smaller watch-houses within call of each other. This structure of grand solidity, which must have required

as garrison 10,000 to 12,000 men, formed thenceforth the basis of military operations in the north of England. It was not a frontier-wall in the proper sense ; on the contrary, not merely did the posts that had already from Agricola's time been pushed forward far beyond it continue to subsist by its side, but subsequently the line, about a half shorter, from the Frith of Forth to the Frith of Clyde, already occupied by Agricola with a chain of posts, was fortified in a similar but weaker way, first under Pius, then in a more comprehensive manner under Severus—as it were, as an advanced post for Hadrian's wall.[1] In point of construction this line was different from that of Hadrian only so far as it was limited to a considerable earthen wall, with fosse in front and road behind, and so was not adapted for defence toward the south ; moreover, it too included a number of smaller camps. At this line the Roman imperial roads terminated,[2] and, although there were Roman posts even beyond this—the most northerly

The wall of Antoninus.

[1] The opinion that the northern wall took the place of the southern is as widely spread as it is untenable ; the cohort-camps on Hadrian's wall, as shown to us by the inscriptions of the second century, still subsisted in the main unchanged at the end of the third (for to this epoch belongs the relative section of the *Notitia*). The two structures subsisted side by side, after the more recent was added ; the mass of monuments at the wall of Severus also shows evidently that it continued to be occupied up to the end of the Roman rule in Britain.

The building of Severus can only be referred to the northern structure. In the first place, the structure of Hadrian was of such a nature that any sort of restoration of it could not possibly be conceived as a new building, as is said of the wall of Severus ; while the structure of Pius was a mere earthen rampart (*murus cespiticius, Vita,* c. 5), and such an assumption in its case creates less difficulty. Secondly, the length of Severus's wall 32 miles (Victor, *Epit.* 20 ; the impossible number 132 is an error of our MSS. of Eutropius, viii. 19— where Paulus has preserved the correct number ; which error has been then taken over by Hieronymus, *Abr.* 2221 ; Orosius, vii. 17, 7 ; and Cassiodorus on the year 207), does not suit Hadrian's wall of 80 miles ; but the structure of Pius, which, according to the data of inscriptions, was about 40 miles long, may well be meant, as the terminal points of the structure of Severus on the two seas may very well have been different and situated closer. Lastly, if, according to Dio, lxxvi. 12, the Caledonians dwell to the north and the Maeates to the south of the wall which divides the island into two parts, the dwelling-places of the latter are indeed not otherwise known (comp. lxxv. 5), but cannot possibly, even according to the description which Dio gives of their district, be placed to the south of Hadrian's wall, and those of the Caledonians have extended up to the latter. Thus what is here meant is the line from Glasgow to Edinburgh.

[2] *A limite id est a vallo* is the expression in the *Itinerarium,* p. 464.

point, at which the tombstone of a Roman soldier has been found, is Ardoch, between Stirling and Perth—the limit of the expeditions of Agricola, the Frith of Tay, may be regarded as subsequently still the limit of the Roman empire.

Wars in the 2d and 3d centuries. We know more of these imposing defensive works than of the application that was made of them, and generally of the later events on this distant scene of warfare. Under Hadrian a severe disaster occurred here, to all appearance a sudden attack on the camp of Eburacum, and the annihilation of the legion stationed there,[1] the same 9th legion which had fought so unsuccessfully in the war with Boudicca. Probably this was occasioned, not by a hostile inroad, but by the revolt of the northern tribes that passed as subjects of the empire, especially of the Brigantes. With this we shall have to connect the fact that the wall of Hadrian presents a front towards the south as well as towards the north; evidently it was destined also for the purpose of keeping in check the superficially subdued north of England. Under Hadrian's successor Pius also conflicts took place here, in which the Brigantes again took part; yet more exact information cannot be got.[2] The first serious attack upon this imperial boundary, and the first demonstrable crossing of the wall—doubtless that of Pius—took place under Marcus, and further attacks under Commodus; as indeed Commodus is the first emperor who assumed the surname of victory Britannicus, after the able general Ulpius Marcellus had routed the barbarians. But the sinking

---

[1] The chief proof of this lies in the disappearance of this legion, that undoubtedly took place soon after the year 108 (*C. I. L.* vii. 241), and the substitution for it of the 6th Victrix. The two notices which point to this incident (Fronto, p. 217 Naber: *Hadriano imperium obtinente quantum militum a Britannis caesum?* Vita, 5, *Britanni teneri sub Romana dicione non poterant*), as well as the allusion in Juvenal, xiv. 196: *castella Brigantum*, point to a revolt, not to an inroad.

[2] If Pius, according to Pausanias, viii. 43, 4, ἀπετέμετο τῶν ἐν Βριτταννίᾳ Βριγάντων τὴν πολλήν, ὅτι ἐπεσβαίνειν καὶ οὗτοι σὺν ὅπλοις ἦρξαν ἐς τὴν Γενουνίαν μοῖραν (unknown; perhaps, as O. Hirschfeld suggests, the town of the Brigantes, Vinovia) ὑπηκόους Ῥωμαίων, it follows from this, not that there were Brigantes also in Caledonia, but that the Brigantes in the north of England at that time ravaged the settled land of the Britons, and therefore a part of their territory was confiscated.

of the Roman power was henceforth just as apparent here
as on the Danube and on the Euphrates. In the turbulent
early years of Severus's reign the Caledonians had broken
their promise not to interfere with the Roman subjects,
and, resting on their support, their southern neighbours,
the Maeates, had compelled the Roman governor Lupus
to ransom captive Romans with large sums. For this
the heavy arm of Severus lighted on them not long before
his death; he penetrated into their own territory and compelled them to cede considerable tracts,[1] from which indeed,
after the old emperor had died in 211 at the camp of
Eburacum, his sons at once of their own accord withdrew
the garrisons, to be relieved of their burdensome defence.

From the third century hardly anything is told us of
the fate of the island. Since none of the emperors down
to Diocletian and his colleagues derived the name of conqueror from the island, there were probably no more
serious conflicts in that quarter ; and, although in the
region lying between the walls of Pius and of Hadrian
the Roman system doubtless never gained a firm footing,
yet at least the wall of Hadrian seems to have rendered
even then the service for which it was intended, and the
foreign civilisation seems to have developed in security
behind it. In the time of Diocletian we find the district
between the two walls evacuated, but the Hadrianic wall
occupied still as before, and the rest of the Roman army
in cantonments between it and the headquarters Eburacum,
to ward off the predatory expeditions, thenceforth often
mentioned, of the Caledonians, or—as they are now usually
called—the " tattooed " (*picti*), and the Scots streaming
in from Ivernia.

*Cale-
donians
and Scots.*

The Romans possessed a standing fleet in Britain ;
but, as the marine always remained the weak side of
Roman warlike organisation, the British fleet was temporarily of importance only under Agricola.

Fleet.

If, as is probable, the government had reckoned on

---

[1] That he had the design of bringing the whole north under the Roman
power (Dio, lxxvi. 13) is not very
compatible either with the cession
(*l.c.*) or with the building of the
wall, and is doubtless as fabulous as
the Roman loss of 50,000 men without
the matter even coming to a battle.

Garrison
and admi-
nistration
in the 2d
and 3d
centuries. being able to take back the greater part of the troops sent to the island, after it had been occupied, this hope was not fulfilled ; only one of the four legions sent thither was, as we have seen, recalled under Domitian; the three others must have been indispensable, for no attempt was ever made to shift them.   To these fall to be added the auxiliaries, who were called out apparently in larger proportion than the burgess-troops for the far from inviting service in the remote island of the North Sea.   In the battle at the Graupian Mount in 84 there fought, besides the four legions, 8000 infantry and 3000 horsemen of the auxiliary soldiers.   For the time of Trajan and Hadrian, when of these there were stationed in Britain six *alae* and twenty-one cohorts, together about 15,000 men, we shall have to estimate the whole British army at about 30,000 men.   Britain was from the outset a field of command of the first rank, inferior to the two Rhenish commands and to the Syrian perhaps in rank, but not in importance, towards the end of the second century probably the most highly esteemed of all the governorships.   It was owing only to the great distance that the British legions appear in the second rank amidst the rival armies of the earlier imperial period ; in the soldiers' war after the extinction of the Antonine house they fought in the first rank. But it was one of the consequences of the victory of Severus that the governorship was divided.   Thenceforth the two legions of Isca and Deva were placed under the legate of the upper province, the legion of Eburacum and the troops at the walls—consequently the main body of the auxiliaries—under the legate of the lower province.[1] Probably the transference of the whole garrison to the north, which, as was above remarked, would doubtless have been appropriate on mere military grounds, was not carried out—partly because it would have put three legions into the hands of one governor.

Taxation
and levy.   That financially the province cost more than it brought in (p. 172), can accordingly excite no surprise.   For the military strength of the empire, on the other hand, Britain

[1] The division results from Dio, lv. 23.

was of considerable account ; the balance of proportion between taxation and levy must have had its application also to the island, and the British troops were reckoned alongside of the Illyrian as the flower of the army. At the very beginning seven cohorts were raised from the natives there, and these were constantly increased onward to the time of Hadrian ; after the latter had brought in the system of recruiting the troops as far as possible from their garrison-districts, Britain appears to have furnished the supply, at least in great part, for its strong garrison. There was an earnest and brave spirit in the people ; they bore willingly the taxes and the levy, but not the arrogance and brutality of the officials.

As a basis for the internal organisation of Britain, the cantonal constitution existing there at the time of the conquest offered itself, which differed, as we have already remarked, from that of the Celts of the continent essentially only in the fact that the several tribes of the island, apparently all of them, were under princes (iv. 233). But this organisation seems not to have been retained, and the canton (*civitas*) to have become in Britain as in Spain a geographical conception ; at least we can hardly otherwise explain the facts that the Britannic tribes, taken in the strict sense, disappear as soon as they fall under Roman rule, and of the individual cantons after their subjugation there is virtually no mention at all. Probably the several principalities, as they were subdued and annexed, were broken up into smaller communities ; this was facilitated by the fact that there did not exist on the island, as there did on the continent, a cantonal constitution organised without a monarchic head. With this is doubtless connected the circumstance that, while the Gallic cantons possessed a common capital and in it a political and religious collective representation, nothing similar is stated as to Britain. The province was not without a *concilium* and a common *cultus* of the emperor ; but, if the altar of Claudius in Camalodunum[1] had been even approximately

Communal organisation.

iv. 222.

---

[1] To it doubtless the epigram of Seneca applies (vol. iv. p. 69, Bäh- rens): *oceanusque tuas ultra se respicit aras.* The temple too, which accord-

what that of Augustus was in Lugudunum, something
would doubtless have been heard of it. The free and
great political remodelling, which was given to the Gallic
country by Caesar and confirmed by his son, no longer
fits into the framework of the later imperial policy.

We have already mentioned the founding, nearly contemporary with the invasion of Britain, of the colony
Camalodunum (p. 176), as it has also been already noticed
that the Italian urban constitution was early introduced
into a series of British townships. Herein, too, Britain
was treated more after the model of Spain than after that
of the Celtic continent.

Prosperity. The internal condition of Britain must, in spite of the
general faults of the imperial government, have been, at
least in comparison with other regions, not unfavourable.
If the people in the north knew only hunting and pastur-
ing, and the inhabitants there as well as those adjoining
them were always ready for feud and rapine, the south
developed itself in an undisturbed state of peace, especially
by means of agriculture, and along with it by cattle-rear-
ing and the working of mines, to a moderate prosperity.
The Gallic orators of Diocletian's time praise the wealth
of the fertile island, and often enough the Rhine-legions
received their corn from Britain.

Roads. The network of roads in the island, which was uncommonly developed, and for which in particular Hadrian did
much in connection with the building of his wall, was of
course primarily subservient to military ends ; but alongside of, and in fact taking precedence over the legionary
camps Londinium occupies in that respect a place which
brings clearly into view its leading position in traffic. Only
in Wales were these imperial roads solely in the immediate
neighbourhood of the Roman camps, from Isca to Nidum

ing to the satire of the same Seneca
(viii. 3), was erected to Claudius
during his lifetime in Britain, and the
temple certainly identical therewith of
the god Claudius in Camalodunum
(Tacitus, *Ann*. xiv. 31), is probably to
be taken not as a sanctuary for the
town itself, but after the analogy of the
shrines of Augustus at Lugudunum and
Tarraco. The *delecti sacerdotes*, who
*specie religionis omnes fortunas effun-
debant*, are the well-known provincial
priests and purveyors of spectacles.

(Neath) and from Deva to the point of crossing to Mona.

In respect of Romanisation, Britain seems to have been Roman manners and culture. very similar to northern and central Gaul. The national deities, the Mars Belatucadrus or Cocidius, the goddess Sulis treated as equivalent to Minerva, after whom the modern city of Bath was named, still received much worship on the island even in the Latin language. The language and manners that penetrated thither from Italy were yet more an exotic growth on the island than on the continent; still towards the close of the first century the families of note there shunned as well the Latin language as the Latin dress. The great urban centres, the seats proper of the new culture, were more weakly developed in Britain; we do not precisely know what English town served as seat for the *concilium* of the province and for the common worship of the emperor, or in which of the three legion-camps the governor of the province resided; if, as it seems, the civil capital of Britain was Camalodunum, and the military capital Eburacum,[1] the latter can as little measure itself with Mentz as the former with Lyons. The ruined sites even of places of note, of the Claudian veteran-town Camalodunum, and the populous mercantile town Londinium, and not less the camps of the legions for several hundred years, at Deva, Isca, Eburacum, present inscribed stones only in trifling number; towns of name with Roman rights like the colony Glevum (Gloucester), and the *municipium* Verulamium, have hitherto yielded not a single one; the custom of setting up memorial-stones, on the results of which we are for such questions largely dependent, never really prevailed in Britain. In the interior of Wales and in other less accessible districts no Roman monuments at all have come to light. But there exist withal

---

[1] The command stationed here was, at least in later times, without question the most important among the Britannic; and there is also mention here (for it is beyond doubt Eburacum that is in view) of a *Palatium* (*Vita Severi*, 22). The *praetorium*, situated probably on the coast below Eburacum (*Itin. Ant.* p. 466), may have been the summer seat of the governor.

clear traces of the stirring commerce and traffic brought
into prominence by Tacitus, such as the numerous drink-
ing-cups which have come out of the ruins of London, and
the London network of roads. If Agricola exerted himself to transplant municipal emulation in the embellishment of one's native city by buildings and monuments
to Britain, as it had been transferred from Italy to Africa
and Spain, and to induce the islanders of note to adorn
the markets of their home and to erect temples and
palaces, as this was usual elsewhere, he was but in a slight
degree successful as regards the public buildings. But it
was otherwise as regards private economics ; the stately
country-houses constructed and embellished in Roman
fashion, of which now nothing is left but the mosaic pave-
ments, are found in southern Britain—so far north as the
region of York[1]—as frequently as in the land of the Rhine.
The higher scholastic training of youth penetrated gradually
from Gaul into Britain. It is specified among Agricola's
administrative successes that the Roman tutor began to
find his way into the leading houses of the island. In
Hadrian's time Britain is described as a region conquered
by the Gallic schoolmasters, and " even Thule speaks of
hiring a professor for itself." These schoolmasters were
in the first instance Latin, but Greeks also came ; Plutarch
tells of a conversation which he held at Delphi with a
Greek teacher of languages from Tarsus returning home
from Britain. If in modern England, apart from Wales
and its borders, the old native language has disappeared,
it has given way not to the Angles or to the Saxons, but to
the Roman idiom ; and, as usually happens in border-lands,
in the later imperial period no one stood more faithfully by
Rome than the man of Britain. It was not Britain that
gave up Rome, but Rome that gave up Britain. The last
that we learn of the island is the urgent entreaty of the
population addressed to the emperor Honorius for protection against the Saxons, and his answer, that they might
help themselves as best they could.

[1] None have been found to the
north of Aldborough and Easingwold
(both somewhat north of York). See
Bruce, *The Roman Wall*, p. 61.

CHAPTER VI.

THE DANUBIAN LANDS AND THE WARS ON THE DANUBE.

As the frontier on the Rhine was the work of Caesar, so the frontier on the Danube was the work of Augustus. When he came to the helm, the Romans were in the Italian peninsula hardly masters of the Alps, and in the Greek peninsula hardly masters of the Haemus (Balkan) and of the coast districts along the Adriatic and the Black Sea ; nowhere did their territory reach the mighty stream which separates southern from northern Europe. As well northern Italy as the Illyrian and Pontic commercial towns, and still more the civilised provinces of Macedonia and Thrace, were constantly exposed to the predatory expeditions of the rude and restless neighbouring tribes. When Augustus died there were substituted for the one province of Illyricum, which had barely attained to independent administration, five great Roman administrative districts, Raetia, Noricum, Lower Illyria or Pannonia, Upper Illyria or Dalmatia, and Moesia ; and the Danube became in its whole course, if not everywhere the military, at any rate the political, frontier of the empire. The comparatively easy subjugation of these wide territories, as well as the grave insurrection of the years 6-9, and the abandonment, thereby occasioned, of the formerly cherished purpose of shifting the boundary-line from the upper Danube to Bohemia and to the Elbe, have been formerly described It remains that we should set forth the development of these provinces in the time after Augustus and the relations of the Romans to the tribes dwelling beyond the Danube.

Late civilis-
ation in
Raetia.
The destinies of Raetia were so closely interwoven
with those of the upper German province that we might
refer for them to the earlier narrative.   Roman civilisation
here, taken as a whole, underwent but little development.
The highlands of the Alps with the valleys of the upper
Inn and the upper Rhine embraced a weak and peculiar
population, probably the same as had once possessed the
eastern half of the north-Italian plain, perhaps akin to
the Etruscans.   Driven back thence by the Celts, and
perhaps also by the Illyrici, it held its ground in the
northern mountains.   While the valleys opening to the
south, like that of the Adige, were attached to Italy, these
offered to the southerns little room and still less incite-
ment for settlement and founding of towns.   Farther
northward on the plateau between the lake of Constance
and the Inn, which was occupied by the Celtic tribes of
the Vindelici, there would doubtless have been room and
place for Roman culture; but apparently in this region,
which could not become, like the Norican, an immediate
continuation of Italy, and which, like the adjacent so-
called Decumates-land, was probably in the first instance
of value for the Romans merely as separating them from
the Germans, the policy of the earlier imperial period
had rather repressed culture.   We have already indicated
(p. 18) that immediately after the conquest there were
thoughts of depopulating the district.   Alongside of this
lies the fact, that in the earlier imperial period no
community with Roman organisation originated here.
It is true that the founding of Augusta Vindelicorum,
the modern Augsburg, was a necessary part of the
laying out of the great road which was carried, simultaneously with the conquest itself, by the elder Drusus
through the high Alps to the Danube (pp. 19, 20); but
this rapidly flourishing place was, and remained for above
a century, a market-village, till at length Hadrian in this
respect left the path prescribed by Augustus and made
the land of the Vindelici share in the Romanising of
the north.   The bestowal of Roman urban rights on the
chief place of the Vindelici by Hadrian may be connected

with the fact that, nearly about the same time, the military frontier was pushed forward on the upper Rhine, and Roman towns arose in the former Decumates - land ; nevertheless in Raetia ever afterwards Augusta remained the only larger centre of Roman civilisation. The military arrangements exercised an influence in keeping it back. The province was from the first under imperial administration, and could not be left without a garrison ; but special considerations, as we have formerly shown, compelled the government to send to Raetia simply troops of the second class, and, though these were not inconsiderable in number, the smaller headquarters of *alae* and *cohortes* could not have exercised a civilising and town-forming effect like the camp of the legion. Under Marcus certainly, in consequence of the Marcomanian war, the Raetian headquarters, Castra Regina, the modern Ratisbon, was occupied by a legion ; but even this place appears to have remained in the Roman time a mere military settlement, and hardly to have stood on a line in urban development with the camps of second rank on the Rhine, such as *e.g.* Bonna.

That the frontier of Raetia was already in Trajan's time pushed forward from Ratisbon westward some distance beyond the Danube, has already been observed (p. 158) ; and it has been there also shown that this territory was probably annexed to the empire without applying force of arms, similarly with the Decumates-land. It was likewise already mentioned that the fortifying of this territory was perhaps connected with the incursions of the Chatti extending thus far under Marcus, as also that these and subsequently the Alamanni in the third century visited as well this country in front as Raetia itself, and ultimately under Gallienus wrested it from the Romans.

The Rae-tian Limes.

The neighbouring province of Noricum was doubtless in the provincial arrangement treated similarly to Raetia, but in other respects had a different development. In no direction was Italy so open for land-traffic as towards the north-east ; the commercial relations of Aquileia, as well through Friuli with the upper Danube and with the iron-

The Italis-ing of Noricum.

works of Noreia, as over the Julian Alps with the valley of the Save, here paved the way for the Augustan extension of the frontier as nowhere else in the region of the Danube. Nauportus (Upper Laybach) beyond the pass was a Roman trading village already in the time of the republic ; Emona (Laybach), a Roman burgess - colony, afterwards formally incorporated with Italy, but substantially belonging to Italy from the time of its foundation by Augustus. Hence, as has already been noticed (p. 18), the mere proclamation was probably enough for the conversion of this " kingdom " into a Roman province. The population, originally doubtless Illyrian, afterwards in good part Celtic, shows no trace of that adherence to the national ways and language which we perceive among the Celts of the west. Roman language and Roman manners must have found early entrance here; and by the emperor Claudius the whole territory, even the northern portion separated by the Tauern chain from the valley of the Drave, was organised in accordance with the Italian municipal constitution. While in the neighbouring lands of Raetia and Pannonia the monuments of Roman language are either wanting or appear withal only at the larger centres, the valleys of the Drave, the Mur, and the Salzach and their affluents are filled far up into the mountains with evidences of the Romanising which here took deep hold. Noricum adjoined, and was as it were a part of, Italy; in the levy for the legions and for the guard, so long as the Italians were here at all preferred, this preference was extended to no other province so fully as to this.

As respects military occupation what applies to Raetia applies also to Noricum. For the reasons already developed there were in Noricum, during the first two centuries of the empire, only forts of *alae* and *cohortes*. Carnuntum (Petronell, near Vienna), which in the Augustan age belonged to Noricum, was, when the Illyrian legions were sent thither, annexed for that very reason to Pannonia. The smaller Norican encampments on the Danube, and even the camp of Lauriacum (near Enns), instituted by Marcus for the legion sent by him to this province, were of no importance for the urban development. The large townships of Noricum, such as Celeia (Cilli), in the valley of the Sann, Aguontum (Lienz), Teurnia (not far from Spital), Virunum (Zollfeld, near Klagenfurt), in the north Juvavum (Salzburg), originated purely out of civil elements.

Illyricum, that is the Roman territory between Italy and Macedonia, was in the republican time united, as to its lesser portion, with the Graeco-Macedonian governorship, as to its greater, administered as a land adjacent to Italy, and, after the institution of the governorship of Cisalpine Gaul, as a portion of the latter. The territory coincides to a certain degree with the widely diffused stock from which the Romans named it ; it is the same whose scanty remnant still at the present day, at the southern end of its formerly far-extended possessions, has preserved its own nationality and its old language under the name of Skipetars, which they assign to themselves, or, as their neighbours call them, the Arnauts or Albanians. It is a member of the Indo-Germanic family, and within it doubtless most closely akin to the Greek branch, as is in keeping with its local relations ; but it stands by the side of the Greek at least as independent as the Latin and the Celtic. This nation in its original extent filled the coast of the Adriatic Sea from the mouth of the Po through Istria, Dalmatia, and Epirus, as far as Acarnania and Aetolia, and also in the interior upper Macedonia, as well as the modern Servia and Bosnia and the Hungarian territory on the right bank of the Danube ; it bordered thus on the east with the Thracian tribes, on the west with the Celtic, from which latter Tacitus expressly distinguishes them. It is a vigorous type of a southern kind, with black hair and dark eyes, very different from the Celts, and still more from the Germans ; sober, temperate, intrepid, proud people, excellent soldiers, but little accessible to civic organisation, shepherds more than agriculturists. They did not attain any great political development. On the Italian coast they were confronted

The Illyrian stock.

probably, in the first instance, by the Celts ; the probably Illyrian tribes there, especially the Veneti, became, through rivalry with the Celts, at an early date pliant subjects of the Romans.

Its relations with Rome.

ii. 196.

At the end of the sixth century of the city the founding of Aquileia and the subjugation of the peninsula of Istria (ii. 207 f.) farther narrowed their limits. Along the east coast of the Adriatic Sea the more important islands and the southern harbours of the mainland had long been occupied by the bold Hellenic mariners. When thereupon in Scodra (Scutari), to a certain extent in olden time as now the central point of the Illyrian land, the rulers began to develop a power of their own, and especially to make war upon the Greeks at sea, Rome, even before the Hannibalic war, struck them down with a strong hand, and took the whole coast under its protectorate

ii. 74 f.

ii. 303.

(ii. 77 f.), which soon, after the ruler of Scodra had shared war and defeat with king Perseus of Macedonia, brought about the complete dissolution of this principality (ii. 321). At the end of the sixth century of the city, and in the first half of the seventh, after long years of conflict, the coast between Istria and Scodra was also occupied by

iii. 172.

the Romans (iii. 180 f.). In the interior the Illyrians were little touched by the Romans during the republican period ; but instead the Celts, advancing from the west, must have brought under their power a good portion of originally Illyrian territory, such as Noricum, afterwards preponderantly Celtic. The Latobici also in the modern Carniola were Celts ; and in the whole territory between the Save and Drave, just as in the Raab valley, the two great stocks were settled promiscuously, when Caesar Augustus subjected the southern districts of Pannonia to the Roman rule. Probably this strong admixture of Celtic elements contributed its part, along with the level character of the ground, to the early decline of the Illyrian nation in the Pannonian districts. Into the southern half, on the other hand, of the regions inhabited by Illyrians there penetrated of the Celts only the Scordisci, whose establishment on the lower Save

as far as Morava, and raids as far as the vicinity of
Thessalonica, have been formerly mentioned (iii. 184 f.). iii. 176 f.
But the Greeks here gave place to them in some measure ;
the sinking of the Macedonian power, and the desolation
of Epirus and Aetolia, must have favoured the extension
of the Illyrian neighbours. Bosnia, Servia, above all
Albania, were in the imperial period Illyrian, and Albania
is so still.

It has already been mentioned that Illyricum was, The pro-
vince of Il-
lyricum.
according to the design of the dictator Caesar, to be
constituted as a special governorship, and this design
came into execution on the partition of the provinces
between Augustus and the senate ; that this governorship, at first committed to the senate, passed to the
emperor on account of the need for waging war there ;
that Augustus divided this governorship and rendered
effective the rule, which hitherto on the whole had been
but nominal, over the interior both in Dalmatia and in
the region of the Save ; and, lastly, that he subdued, after
a severe struggle of four years, the mighty national
insurrection which broke out among the Dalmatian as
among the Pannonian Illyrians in the year 6. It remains
that we relate the further fortunes, in the first instance,
of the southern province.

After the experience attained in the insurrection it Dalmatia
and its
Italian civi-
lisation.
seemed requisite not merely to employ the forces raised in
Illyricum abroad rather than as hitherto in their native
country, but also to keep in subordination the Dalmatians
as well as the Pannonians by a command of the first rank.
This rapidly fulfilled its object. The resistance, which the
Illyrici under Augustus opposed to the unwonted foreign
rule, expended its rage in the one violent storm ; afterwards our reports record no similar movement, even of
but a partial kind. For the southern or, according to the
Roman expression, the Upper Illyricum—the province
Dalmatia, as it was usually called from the time of the
Flavii—a new epoch began with the government of the
emperors. The Greek merchants had indeed founded on
the coast lying nearest to them the two great emporia of

Apollonia (near Valona) and Dyrrachium (Durazzo) ;
for that very reason this portion had already under the
republic been consigned to Greek administration. But
farther northward the Hellenes had settled only on the
adjacent islands Issa (Lissa), Pharos (Lesina), Black-Cor-
cyra (Curzola), and thence maintained intercourse with
the natives particularly along the coast of Narona and in
the townships adjacent to Salonae. Under the Roman
republic the Italian traders, who here entered upon the
heritage of the Greek, had settled in the chief ports Epi-
taurum (Ragusa Vecchia), Narona, Salonae, Iader (Zara),
in such numbers that they could play a not unimportant
part in the war of Caesar and Pompeius. But it was only
through Augustus that these townships received strengthening by the settlement of veterans there, and—what was
the main thing—urban rights ; and at the same time partly
the energetic suppression of the piratic retreats still existing in the islands, partly the subjugation of the interior
and the pushing forward of the Roman frontier towards
the Danube, tended to benefit especially these Italians
settled on the east coast of the Adriatic Sea. Above all
the capital of the country, the seat of the governor and of
Salonae. the whole administration, Salonae rapidly flourished and
far outstripped the older Greek settlements Apollonia and
Dyrrachium, although to the latter town there were sent
likewise under Augustus Italian colonists, not indeed
veterans but dispossessed Italians, and the town was
erected as a Roman burgess-community. It may be conjectured that in the prosperity of Dalmatia and the arrested
development of the Illyro-Macedonian coast the distinction
between the imperial and the senatorial government played
an essential part — as regards better administration, as
well as a privileged position with the real holder of
power. With this, moreover, may be connected the fact,
that the Illyrian nationality held its ground better in the
sphere of the Macedonian governorship than in that of the
Dalmatian ; in the former it still lives at the present day ;
and in the imperial period—apart from the Greek Apollonia and the Italian colony of Dyrrachium—while the two

languages of the empire were made use of, in the interior
that of the people must have continued to be the Illyrian.
In Dalmatia, on the other hand, the coasts and the islands,
so far as they were at all adapted thereto—the inhospitable stretch to the north of the Iader necessarily was left
behind in the development—were communalised after the
Italian organisation, and soon the whole coast spoke Latin,
somewhat as it speaks at the present day Venetian.

The advance of civilisation into the interior had to
encounter local difficulties. The considerable streams of
Dalmatia form waterfalls more than water-ways; and
even the establishment of land-routes meets unusual difficulties from the nature of its mountain-network. The
Roman government made earnest exertions to open up the
country. Under the protection of the legionary camp of
Burnum in the valley of the Kerka and in that of Cettina
under the protection of the camp of Delminium—which
camps must have been here too the channels of civilisation
and of Latinising—the cultivation of the soil developed
itself after the Italian fashion, as also the planting of the
vine and the olive, and in general Italian organisation and
habits. On the other hand, beyond the watershed between the Adriatic Sea and the Danube the valleys less
favourable for agriculture from the Kulpa to the Drin
remained during the Roman period in a primitive state,
similar to that exhibited by Bosnia at the present day.
The emperor Tiberius certainly had various roads made
by the soldiers of the Dalmatian camps from Salonae into
the valleys of Bosnia; but the later governments apparently allowed the difficult task to drop. On the coast
and in the districts adjoining the coast Dalmatia soon
needed no further military protection; Vespasian could
already withdraw the legions from the valleys of the Kerka
and the Cettina and employ them elsewhere.

Amidst the decay of the empire in the third century
Dalmatia suffered comparatively little; indeed, Salonae
probably only reached at that time its greatest prosperity.
This, it is true, was occasioned partly by the fact that the
regenerator of the Roman state, the emperor Diocletian,

Civilisation in the interior.

Prosperity under Diocletian.

was by birth a Dalmatian, and allowed his efforts aimed at the decapitalising of Rome to redound chiefly to the benefit of the capital of his native land; he built alongside of it the huge palace, from which the modern capital of the province takes the name Spalato, within which it has for the most part found a place, and the temples of which now serve it as cathedral and as baptistery.[1] Diocletian, however, did not make Salonae a great city for the first time, but, because it was such, chose it for his private residence ; commerce, navigation, and trade must at that time in these waters have been concentrated chiefly at Aquileia and at Salonae, and the city must have been one of the most populous and opulent towns of the west. The rich iron mines of Bosnia were largely worked at least in the later imperial period ; the forests of the province likewise yielded abundant and excellent timber; even of the flourishing textile industry of the land a reminiscence is still preserved in the priestly "Dalmatica." Altogether the civilising and Romanising of Dalmatia form one of the most peculiar and most significant phenomena of the imperial period. The boundary between Dalmatia and Macedonia was at the same time the political and linguistic demarcation of the West and East. As the spheres of rule of Caesar and Marcus Antonius came into contact at Scodra, so did those of Rome and Byzantium after the partition of the empire in the fourth century. Here the Latin province of Dalmatia bordered with the Greek province of Macedonia ; and the younger sister stands here alongside of the elder, vigorous in aspiration and excelling in energy of effort.

Pannonia down to Trajan.

While the southern Illyrian province and its peaceful government soon ceased to be prominent in a historical aspect, northern Illyricum, or as it is usually called, Pannonia, forms in the imperial period one of the great military and thereby also political centres. In the army of the Danube the Pannonian camps have the leading position like the Rhenish in the west, and the Dalmatian and the Moesian attach themselves to them, and subordinate

---

[1] The baptistery is perhaps the tomb of the emperor.

themselves under them, in like manner as the legions of Spain and Britain were subordinate to those of the Rhine. Roman civilisation stands and continues here under the influence of the camps, which did not remain in Pannonia as in Dalmatia only for some generations, but were permanent. After the subduing of the insurrection of Bato, the regular garrison of the province amounted at first to three, afterwards apparently only to two, legions ; and the further development was conditioned by their standing quarters and the shifting of these forward. When Augustus after the first war against the Dalmatians had selected Siscia, at the point where the Kulpa falls into the Save, as his chief stronghold, after Tiberius had subdued Pannonia at least as far as the Drave, the camps were pushed forward to the latter, and at least one of the Pannonian headquarters was thenceforth found at Poetovio (Pettau), on the borders of Noricum. The reason why the Pannonian army remained wholly or in part in the valley of the Drave can only have been the same as led to the construction of the Dalmatian legionary camps ; they needed troops here to keep in obedience their subjects as well in the neighbouring Noricum as above all in the region of the Drave itself. On the Danube watch was kept by the Roman fleet, which is already mentioned in the year 50, and presumably originated on the erection of the province. There was not yet perhaps a legionary camp on the river itself under the Julio-Claudian dynasty,[1] in connection

---

[1] That there were no legions stationed on the Danube itself in the year 50, follows from Tacitus, *Ann.* xii. 29 ; otherwise it would not have been necessary to send a legion thither to receive the accession of the Suebi. The laying out also of the Claudian Savaria suits better, if the town was then Norican, than if it already belonged to Pannonia ; and, as the assignment of this town to Pannonia coincides certainly as to time with the like severance of Carnuntum and with the transference of the legion thither, all this may probably have taken place only in the period after Claudius. The small number also of inscriptions of Italici found in the camps of the Danube (*Eph. Ep.* v. p. 225) points to their later origin. Certainly there have been found in Carnuntum some epitaphs of soldiers of the 15th legion which, from their outward form and from the absence of cognomen, appear to be older (Hirschfeld, *Arch. Epigraph. Mittheilungen*, v. 217). Such determinations of date cannot claim full certainty, where a decade is concerned ; nevertheless it must be conceded that the former arguments also furnish no full proofs, and the translocation may have begun earlier,

with which we may note that the state of the Suebi immediately adjoining the province in front was at that time immediately dependent on Rome, and sufficed in some measure to protect the frontier. Then, as with the camps of Dalmatia, Vespasian apparently did away also with the camps on the Drave and transferred them to the Danube itself; thenceforth the great headquarters of the Pannonian army were the formerly Norican (p. 198) Carnuntum (Petronell, to the east of Vienna), and along with it Vindobona (Vienna).

Urban development.

Civil development, such as we meet in Noricum and on the coast of Dalmatia, shows itself likewise in Pannonia only at some districts situated on the Norican frontier, and in part belonging originally to Noricum; Emona and the upper valley of the Save stand on an equality with Noricum, and if Savaria (Stein, on the Anger) received the Italian municipal constitution at the same time with the Norican towns, that place must doubtless, so long as Carnuntum was a Norican town, have belonged also to Noricum. It was only after the troops were stationed on the Danube that the government set to work to give urban organisation to the country behind. In the western territory originally Norican, Scarbantia (Oedenburg, on the Neusiedler See) obtained urban rights under the Flavii, while Vindobona and Carnuntum became of themselves camp-towns. Between the Save and Drave Siscia and Sirmium received urban rights under the Flavii, as on the Drave Poetovio (Pettau) under Trajan, Mursa (Eszeg) under Hadrian colonial rights—to mention here only the chief places. That the population, predominantly Illyrian but in good part also Celtic, opposed no energetic resistance to the Romanising, has already been mentioned; the old language and the old habits disappeared where the Romans came, and kept their ground only in the more remote districts. The districts—wide, but far from inviting for settlement—to the east of

possibly under Nero. For the construction or extension of this camp by Vespasian we have the evidence of the inscription, attesting such a structure, of Carnuntum, dating from the year 73 (Hirschfeld, *l. c.*).

the river Raab and to the north of the Drave as far as the
Danube were probably reckoned even from the time of
Augustus as belonging to the empire, but perhaps in a
way not much differing from Germany before the battle
of Varus ; urban development neither then nor later found
a true soil here, and in a military point of view this region
was for a long time occupied but little or not at all. This
state of matters changed in some measure only in consequence of the incorporation of Dacia under Trajan ; the
pushing forward of the Pannonian camps towards the east
frontier of the province, to which that step gave occasion,
and the further internal development of Pannonia, will be
better described in connection with the wars of Trajan.

The last portion of the right bank of the Danube—the
mountain-land on the two sides of the Margus (Morava),
and the flat country stretching along between the Haemus
and the Danube—was inhabited by Thracian tribes ; and
it appears necessary in the first instance to cast a glance
at this great stock as such. It runs parallel in a certain
sense to the Illyrian. As the Illyrians once filled the
regions from the Adriatic Sea to the middle Danube, so
the Thracians were formerly settled to the east of them,
from the Aegean Sea as far as the mouths of the Danube,
and not less on the one hand upon the left bank of the
Danube, particularly in the modern Transylvania, on the
other hand beyond the Bosporus, at least in Bithynia
and as far as Phrygia. Herodotus is not wrong in calling
the Thracians the greatest of the peoples known to him
after the Indians. Like the Illyrian, the Thracian stock
attained to no full development, and appears more as hard-
pressed and dispossessed than as having any historically
memorable course of its own. But, while the language
and habits of the Illyrians have been preserved—though
in a form worn down in the course of centuries—to the
present day, and we with some right transfer the image
of the Palikars from more recent history to that of the
Roman imperial period, the same does not hold good
of the Thracian stock. There is manifold and sure
attestation that the tribes of the territory, which in conse-

*The Thra-
cian stock.*

quence of the Roman provincial division has ultimately
retained the name Thracian, as well as the Moesians between the Balkan and the Danube, and not less the Getae
or Daci on the other bank of the Danube, all spoke one
and the same language. This language had in the Roman
empire a position similar to that of the Celts and of the
Syrians. The historian and geographer of the Augustan
age, Strabo, mentions the likeness of language among the
peoples named ; in botanical writings of the imperial
period the Dacian appellations of a number of plants are
specified.[1] When his contemporary, the poet Ovid, had
opportunity given to him in the far-off Dobrudscha to
reflect on his too dissolute course of life, he used his leisure
to learn Getic, and became almost a poet of the Getae :—

> *Ah pudet! et Getico seripsi sermone libellum . . . .*
> *Et placui (gratare mihi) coepique poetae*
> *Inter inhumanos nomen habere Getas.*

But while the Irish bards, the Syrian missionaries, and
the mountain valleys of Albania secured a certain continued duration for other idioms of the imperial period, the
Thracian disappeared amidst the fluctuations of peoples in
the region of the Danube and the overpowerful influence
of Constantinople, and we cannot even determine the
place which belongs to it in the pedigree of nations. The
descriptions of manners and customs of particular tribes
belonging to it, as to which various notices have been preserved, yield no individual traits valid for the race as a
whole, and for the most part bring into relief merely singu-
larities such as appear among all peoples at a low stage
of culture. But they were and remained a soldier-people,
not less useful as horsemen than for light infantry, from
the times of the Peloponnesian war and of Alexander
down to that of the Roman Caesars, whether they might

---

[1] We know whole sets of Thracian, Getic, Dacian names of places and persons. Remarkable in a linguistic point of view is a group of personal names compounded with—*centhus* : *Bithicenthus, Zipacenthus, Disacenthus, Tracicenthus, Linicenthus* (*Bull. de Corr. Hell.* vi. 179), of which the first two also frequently occur isolated in their other half (*Bithus, Zipa*). A similar group is formed by the compounds with—*poris*, such as *Mucaporis* (as Thracian, *Bull. l. c.*, as Dacian in numerous cases), *Cetriporis, Rhaskyporis, Bithoporis, Dirdiporis*.

range themselves against them or subsequently fight for them. Their wild but grand mode of worshipping the gods may perhaps be conceived as a trait peculiar to this stock—the mighty outburst of the joy of spring and youth, the nocturnal mountain-festivals of torch-swinging maidens, the intoxicating sense-confusing music, the flowing of wine and the flowing of blood, the giddy festal whirl frantic with the simultaneous excitement of all sensuous passions. Dionysos, the glorious and the terrible, was a Thracian god ; and whatever of the kind was specially prominent in the Hellenic and the Roman *cultus*, was connected with Thracian or Phrygian customs.

While the Illyrian tribes in Dalmatia and Pannonia, after the overthrow of the great insurrection in the last years of Augustus, did not again invoke the decision of arms against the Romans, the same did not hold true of the Thracian stock ; the often-shown spirit of independence and the wild bravery of this nation did not fail it even in its decline. In Thrace, south of the Haemus, the old principate remained under Roman supremacy. The native ruling house of the Odrysae, with their residence Bizye (Wiza), between Adrianople and the coast of the Black Sea, was already in the earlier period the most prominent among the princely families of Thrace ; after the triumviral period there is no further mention of other Thracian kings than of those of this house, so that the other princes appear to have been made vassals or superseded under Augustus, and only members of this family were thenceforth invested with the Thracian kingly office. This was done, probably, because during the first century, as will be shown further on, there were no Roman legions stationed on the lower Danube ; Augustus expected the frontier at the mouth of the Danube to be protected by the Thracian vassals. Rhoemetalces, who in the second half of the reign of Augustus ruled all Thrace as a Roman vassal-king,[1] and his children and grandchildren therefore

The Thracian principate.

[1] Tacitus, *Ann.* ii. 64, says this expressly. Of free Thracians, viewed from the Roman stand-point, there were at that time none ; but the Thracian mountains, and especially the Rhodope of the Bessi, maintained even in the state of peace an attitude as regards the princes installed by

played in this country nearly the same part as Herod and his descendants in Palestine ; unconditional devotedness towards the lord-paramount, a decided inclination to Roman habits, hostility to their own countrymen who clung to the national independence, mark the attitude of the Thracian ruling house. The great Thracian insurrection of the years 741-743, of which we have formerly spoken (p. 24), was directed in the first instance against this Rhoemetalces and his brother and co-regent Cotys who perished in it, and, as he at that time was indebted to the Romans for reinstatement into his dominion, so he some years afterwards rendered to them his thanks when, on occasion of the rising of the Dalmatians and the Pannonians, to which his Dacian kinsmen adhered, he kept faithfully to the Romans, and bore an essential part in its overthrow. His son Cotys was more Roman, or rather Greek, than Thracian ; he traced back his pedigree to Eumolpus and Erichthonius, and gained the hand of a kinswoman of the imperial house, the great granddaughter of the triumvir Antonius ; and not merely did the Greek and Latin poets of his time address him in song, but he himself was also a poet and not a Getic poet.[1] The last of the Thracian kings, Rhoemetalces, son of the early deceased Cotys, was reared in Rome, and, like the Herodian Agrippa, a youthful playmate of the emperor Gaius.

Province of Thrace.

But the Thracian nation by no means shared the Roman leanings of the ruling house, and the government gradually became convinced in Thrace as in Palestine that the tottering vassal-throne, only maintained by constant interference of the protecting power, was of use neither for them nor for the country, and that the introduction of direct administration was in every respect to be preferred. The emperor Tiberius made use of the quarrels that arose in the Thracian royal house to send to Thrace in the

Rome, that could hardly be designated as subjection ; they acknowledged the king doubtless, but obeyed him, as Tacitus says (*l.c.* and iv. 46, 51), only when it suited them.

[1] We have still a Greek epigram, dedicated to Cotys by Antipater of Thessalonica (*Anthol. Planud.* iv. 75), the same poet who celebrated also the conqueror of the Thracians, Piso (p. 24), and a Latin epistle in verse addressed to Cotys by Ovid (*ex Ponto*, ii. 9).

year 19 a Roman governor, Titus Trebellenus Rufus, under cover of exercising guardianship over the princes that were minors. Yet this occupation was not accomplished without resistance, ineffectual doubtless, but serious on the part of the people, who, particularly in the mountain-valleys, troubled themselves little about the rulers appointed by Rome, and whose forces, led by their family-chiefs, hardly felt themselves to be soldiers of the king, and still less soldiers of Rome. The sending of Trebellenus called forth in the year 21 a rising, in which not merely did the most noted Thracian tribes take part, but which threatened to assume greater proportions ; messengers of the insurgents went over the Haemus to enkindle the national war in Moesia, and perhaps still further. Meanwhile the Moesian legions appeared in right time to relieve Philippopolis, which the insurgents besieged, and to suppress the movement. But, when some years later (25) the Roman government ordered levies in Thrace, the men refused to serve beyond the bounds of their own country. When no regard was paid to this refusal, the whole mountains rose and a struggle of despair ensued, in which the insurgents, constrained at length by hunger and thirst, threw themselves in great part on the swords of the enemy or on their own, and preferred to renounce life rather than their time-honoured freedom. The direct government continued in the form of exercising wardship in Thrace up to the death of Tiberius ; and, if the emperor Gaius at the commencement of his reign gave back the rule to the Thracian friend of his youth just as to the Jewish, a few years after, in the year 46, the government of Claudius definitely put an end to it. This final annexation of the kingdom, and conversion of it into a Roman province, also encountered an equally hopeless and equally obstinate resistance. But with the introduction of direct administration the resistance was broken. The governor, at first of equestrian, and from Trajan's time of senatorial, rank, never had a legion ; the garrison sent into the country, though it was not stronger than 2000 men, along with a small squadron stationed at Perinthus, was sufficient, in connection with the precautionary measures otherwise taken by the government, to keep down the Thracians. The laying out of military roads was begun immediately after the annexation ; we find that the buildings requisite in the state of the country for the accommodation of travellers at the posting stations were already, in the year 61, erected by the government and opened to traffic. Thrace was thenceforth an obedient and important province of the empire ; hardly any other furnished so numerous men for all parts of the war-forces, especially for the cavalry and the fleet, as this old home of gladiators and of mercenary soldiers.

Moesia.

The serious conflicts which the Romans had to sustain with the same nation on the so-called " Thracian shore " [Ripa Thraciae], in the region between the Balkan and the Danube, and which led to the institution of the Moesian command, form an essential constituent part of the regulation of the northern frontier in the Augustan age, and have been already described in their connection (p. 13 f.) Of resistance similar to that offered by the Thracians to the Romans nothing is reported from Moesia ; the tone of feeling there may not have been different, but in the level country and under the pressure of the legions encamped at Viminacium the resistance did not emerge openly.

Hellenism and Romanism in Thrace.

Civilisation came to the Thracian tribes, as to the Illyrian, from two sides ; that of the Hellenes from the coast and from the Macedonian frontier, the Latin from the Dalmatian and Pannonian frontier. Of the former it will be more appropriate to treat when we attempt to describe the position of the European Greeks under the imperial rule ; here it suffices generally to bring out the fact that not merely did that rule protect the Greek element, where it found it, and the whole coast, even that subject to the governor of Moesia, always remained Greek; but that the province of Thrace, whose civilisation was begun in earnest only by Trajan, and was throughout a work of the imperial period, was not guided into a Roman path, but became Hellenised. Even the northern slopes of the Haemus, although administratively belonging to

Moesia, were comprehended in this Hellenising ; Nicopolis on the Jantra and Marcianopolis, not far from Varna, both foundations of Trajan, were organised after a Greek model.

Of the Latin civilisation of Moesia the same holds true as of that of the adjoining Dalmatian and Pannonian interior ; only, as was natural, it emerges so much the later, weaker, and more impure, the farther remote it is from its starting-point. It followed predominantly here the encampments of the legions, and with these advanced eastward, starting from the probably oldest camps of Moesia at Singidunum (Belgrade) and Viminacium (Kostolatz).[1] It is true that, in keeping with the character of its armed apostles, it kept at a very low stage in upper Moesia, and left room enough for the play of the primitive conditions. Viminacium obtained Italian urban rights from Hadrian. Lower Moesia, between the Balkan and the Danube, in the earlier imperial period, remained probably throughout in the condition which the Romans found subsisting there ; not till the legion-camps on the lower Danube were founded at Novae, Durostorum, and Troesmis, which, as will be set forth further on (p. 227), probably did not take place till the beginning of the second century, did this part of the right bank of the Danube become a seat of so much Italian civilisation as was compatible with camp-arrangements. Thenceforth civil settlements arose here too—particularly on the Danube

And in Moesia.

---

[1] It is one of the most seriously felt blanks of the Roman imperial history that the standing quarters of the two legions, which formed under the Julio-Claudian emperors the garrison of Moesia, the 4th Scythica and the 5th Macedonica (at least these were stationed there in the year 33 ; *C. I. L.* iii. 1698) cannot hitherto be pointed out with certainty. Probably they were Viminacium and Singidunum in what was afterwards upper Moesia. Among the legion-camps of lower Moesia, of which that of Troesmis in particular has numerous monuments to show, none appear to be older than Hadrian's time ; the remains of the upper-Moesian are hitherto so scanty that they at least do not hinder our carrying back their origin a century further. When the king of Thrace in the year 18 takes arms against the Bastarnae and Scythians (Tacitus, *Ann.* ii. 65), this could not have been put forward even as a pretext, had lower-Moesian legionary camps been already at that time in existence. This very narrative shows that the warlike power of this vassal-prince was not inconsiderable, and that the setting aside of an uncompliant king of Thrace demanded caution.

itself, between the great standing camps, the towns constituted after the Italian model, Ratiaria, not far from Widin, and Oescus at the confluence of the Iskra with the Danube—and gradually the region approached the level of the Roman culture then subsisting, though of itself on its decline.   In the construction of highways in lower Moesia the rulers displayed manifold activity after the time of Hadrian, from whom the oldest milestones hitherto found there date.

Hermunduri. If we turn from the survey of the Roman rule, as it took shape from Augustus onward in the lands on the right bank of the Danube, to the relations and the inhabitants of the left, what we should have to remark as to the most westerly region has already in the main been said in the description of upper Germany ; and in particular it has been noticed (p. 158) that the Germans next adjoining Raetia, the Hermunduri, were of all the neighbours of the Romans the most peaceful, and, so far as is known to us, never fell into conflict with them.

Marcomani. We have already stated that the people of the Marcomani, or, as the Romans usually term them in earlier times, the Suebi, after it had in the Augustan age found new settlements in the old land of the Boii, the modern Bohemia, and had acquired through king Maroboduus a more fixed political organisation, remained indeed an onlooker during the Romano-German wars, but was preserved through the intervention of the Rhenish Germans from the threatened Roman invasion.   We have also pointed out that, indirectly, the renewed abandonment of the Roman offensive on the Rhine overthrew this too neutral state. The position of paramount power, which the Marcomani under Maroboduus had gained over the more remote peoples in the region of the Elbe, was thereby lost ; and the king himself died as an exile on Roman soil (p. 61). The Marcomani and their eastern neighbours of kindred stock, the Quadi in Moravia, fell under Roman clientship, in so far as in their case, nearly as in that of Armenia, the pretenders contending for the mastery leaned in part for support on the Romans, and these claimed, and according to circumstances also exercised, the right of investiture. The prince of the Cotones, Catualda, who had in the first instance overthrown Maroboduus, could not maintain himself long as his successor, especially as Vibilius king of the neighbouring Hermunduri took part against him ; he too had to pass over into Roman territory, and like Maroboduus to invoke the imperial favour. Tiberius then induced a Quadian of rank Vannius to take his place ; for the numerous train of the two banished kings, which was not allowed to remain on the right bank of the Danube, Tiberius procured settlements on the left in the March valley,[1] and procured for Vannius recognition on the part of the Hermunduri friendly with Rome. After a thirty years' rule the latter was overthrown in the year 50 by his two nephews Vangio and Sido, who revolted against him, and gained for themselves the neighbouring peoples, the Hermunduri in Franconia, the Lugii in Silesia. The Roman government, which Vannius solicited for support, remained true to the policy

Vannius.

---

[1] That the *regnum Vannianum* (Plin. *H. N.* iv. 12, 81), the Suebian state (Tacitus, *Ann.* xii. 29 ; *Hist.* iii. 5, 21), must be referred, not merely, as might appear from Tacitus, *Ann.* ii. 63, to the dwellings of the people that went over with Maroboduus and Catualda, but to the whole territory of the Marcomani and Quadi, is shown clearly by the second report, *Ann.* xii. 29, 30, since here, as opponents of Vannius alongside of his own insurgent subjects, there appear the peoples bordering on Bohemia to the west and north, the Hermunduri and Lugii. As boundary towards the east Pliny *l.c.* designates the region of Carnuntum (*Germanorum ibi confinium*) more exactly the river Marus or Duria, which separates the Suebi and the *regnum Vannianum* from their eastern neighbours, whether we may refer the *dirimens eos* with Müllenhoff (*Sitzungsberichte der Berliner Akademie* 1883, p. 871) to the Jazyges, or, as is more natural, to the Bastarnae. In reality both doubtless bordered, the Jazyges on the south, the Bastarnae on the north, with the Quadi of the March valley. Accordingly the Marus is the March, and the demarcation is formed by the small Carpathians that stretch between the March and the Waag. If thus those retainers were settled *inter flumen Marum et Cusum*, then the Cusus not elsewhere mentioned is, provided the statement is correct, not the Waag, or even, as Müllenhoff supposed, the Eipel falling into the Danube below Gran, but an affluent of the Danube westward of the March, perhaps the Gusen near Linz. The narrative in Tacitus xii. 29, 30, also requires the territory of Vannius to have reached to the west even beyond the March. The subscription to the first book of the *Meditations* of the emperor Marcus ἐν Κουάδοις πρὸς τῷ Γρανούᾳ, proves doubtless that then the state of the Quadi stretched as far as the river Gran ; but this state is not coincident with the *regnum Vannianum*.

of Tiberius; it granted to the overthrown king the right of asylum, but did not interfere, especially as the successors, who shared the territory between them, readily acknowledged the Roman supremacy. The new prince of the Suebi, Sido, and his co-ruler Italicus, perhaps the successor of Vangio, fought in the battle, which decided between Vitellius and Vespasian, with the Roman army of the Danube on the side of the Flavians. In the great crises of the Roman rule on the Danube under Domitian and Marcus we shall again meet their successors. The Suebi of the Danube did not belong to the Roman empire; coins probably struck by them show doubtless Latin inscriptions, but not the Roman standard, to say nothing of the image of the emperor; taxes proper and levies for Rome did not here take place. But, in the first century particularly, the Suebian state in Bohemia and Moravia was included within the sphere of Roman power; and, as was already observed, this was not without its influence on the stationing of the Roman frontier-guard.

Jazyges.   In the plain between the Danube and Theiss eastward from the Roman Pannonia, and between this and the Thracian Daci, there was inserted a section of the people —probably belonging to the Medo-Persian stock—the Sarmatae, who living nomadically as a nation of shepherds and horsemen filled in great part the wide east-European plain; these were the Jazyges, named the "emigrants" (μετανάσται) in distinction from the chief stock which remained behind on the Black Sea. The designation shows that they only advanced at a comparatively late period into these regions; perhaps their immigration falls to be included among the assaults, under which about the time of the battle of Actium the Dacian kingdom of Burebista broke down (p. 11). They meet us here at first under the emperor Claudius; the Jazyges supplied the Suebian king Vannius with the cavalry for his wars. The Roman government was on its guard against the alert and predatory bands of horsemen, but did not otherwise sustain hostile relations to them. When the legions of the Danube marched to Italy in the year 70 to place Vespasian on the throne, they declined the contingent of cavalry offered by the Jazyges, and in fitter fashion carried with them only a number of the men of chief rank, in order that these should meanwhile be pledges for quiet on the denuded frontier.

More serious and continuous watch was needed farther down on the lower Danube. There, beyond the mighty stream, which was now the boundary of the empire, were settled in the plains of Wallachia and the modern Transylvania the Daci ; in the eastern flat country, in Moldavia, Bessarabia, and onward, in the first instance, the Germanic Bastarnae, and then Sarmatian tribes, such as the Roxolani, a people of horsemen like the Jazyges, at first between the Dnieper and Don (iii. 295), then advancing along the sea-shore. In the first years of Tiberius the vassal prince of Thrace strengthened his troops to ward off the Bastarnae and Scythians; in the latter years of Tiberius it was urged among other proofs of his government more and more neglecting everything, that he suffered the inroads of the Dacians and the Sarmatae to pass unpunished. How matters went on in the last years of Nero on either side of the mouths of the Danube is approximately shown by the accidentally preserved report of the governor of Moesia at that time, Tiberius Plautius Silvanus Aelianus. The latter "brought upwards of 100,000 men dwelling beyond the Danube, with their wives and children, and their princes or kings over the river, so that they became liable to pay tribute. He suppressed a movement of the Sarmatae before it came to an outbreak, although he had given away a great part of his troops for the carrying on of war in Armenia (to Corbulo). A number of kings hitherto unknown or at feud with the Romans he brought over to the Roman bank, and compelled them to prostrate themselves before the Roman standards. To the kings of the Bastarnae and Roxolani he sent back their sons, who had been made captive or recovered from the enemy, to those of the Dacians their captive brothers,[1] and took hostages from several of them. Thereby the state of peace for the province

Daci.

iii. 281.

---

[1] *Regibus Bastarnarum et Roxolanorum filios, Dacorum fratrum cap-* *tos aut hostibus ereptos remisit* (Orelli, 750) is miswritten; it must run *fratres,*

was confirmed as well as further extended. He induced also the king of the Scythians to desist from the siege of the town Chersonesus (Sebastopol) beyond the Borysthenes. He was the first who, by great consignments of corn from this province, made bread cheaper in Rome." We perceive here clearly as well the agitated vortex of peoples on the left bank of the Danube under the Julio-Claudian dynasty, as also the strong arm of the imperial power, which even beyond the stream sought to protect the Greek towns on the Dnieper and in the Crimea, and was able also in some measure to do so, as will be further set forth when we describe the state of Greek affairs.

Inadequacy of Roman forces. The forces, however, which Rome had here at her disposal, were more than inadequate. The insignificant garrison of Asia Minor, and the fleet, likewise small on the Black Sea, were of account at most for the Greek inhabitants of its northern and western coasts. A very difficult task was assigned to the governor of Moesia, who with his two legions had to protect the bank of the Danube from Belgrade to the mouth; and the aid of the far from obedient Thracians was under the circumstances an additional danger. Especially towards the mouth of the Danube there was wanting a sufficient bulwark against the barbarians now pressing on with increasing weight. The withdrawal on two occasions of the Danubian legions to Italy in the troubles after Nero's death provoked still more at the mouth of the Danube, than on the lower Rhine, incursions of the neighbouring peoples, at first of the Roxolani, then of the Dacians, then of the Sarmatae, that is, probably the Jazyges. There were severe conflicts ; in one of these engagements, apparently with the Jazyges, the brave governor of Moesia, Gaius Fonteius Agrippa, fell. Nevertheless, Vespasian did not proceed to increase the army of the Danube ;[1] the necessity of strengthening the Asiatic garrisons must have appeared still more urgent,

---

or at anyrate *fratrum filios.* In like manner afterwards *per quae* is to be read for *per quem* and *rege* instead of *regem.*

[1] In Pannonia there were stationed about the year 70 two legions, the 13th Gemina and the 15th Apollinaris, in room of which latter during its participation in the Armenian war for some time the 7th Gemina came in

and the economy specially enjoined at that time forbade any increase of the army as a whole. He contented himself with pushing forward the great camps of the army of the Danube to the frontier of the empire, as the pacification of the interior allowed, and the relations subsisting at the frontier, as well as the breaking up of the Thracian troops brought about by the annexation of Thrace, imperatively required. Thus the Pannonian camps were brought away from the Drave, opposite to the Suebian kingdom, to Carnuntum and Vindobona (p. 206), and the Dalmatian from the Kerka and the Cettina to the Moesian bank of the Danube,[1] so that the governor of Moesia thenceforth disposed of double the number of legions.

A shifting of the proportions of power to the disadvantage of Rome set in under Domitian,[2] or rather the consequences of the insufficient frontier-defence were then reaped. According to the little we know of the matter,

Dacian war of Domitian.

(*C. I. L.* iii. p. 482). Of the two legions added later, 1st Adiutrix and 2d Adiutrix, the first still at the beginning of the reign of Trajan lay in upper Germany (p. 159, note 1), and can only have come to Pannonia under Trajan; the second stationed under Vespasian in Britain can only have come to Pannonia under Domitian (p. 174, note 4). The Moesian army numbered after the union with the Dalmatian under Vespasian probably but four legions, consequently as many as the two armies together previously—the later upper-Moesian, 4th Flavia and 7th Claudia, and the later lower-Moesian, 1st Italica and 5th Macedonica. The positions shifted by the marching to and fro of the year of the four emperors (Marquardt, *Staatsverw.* ii. 435), which temporarily brought these legions to Moesia, need not deceive us. The subsequent third lower-Moesian legion, the Eleventh, was still under Trajan stationed in upper Germany.

[1] Josephus, *Bell. Iud.* vii. 4, 3: πλείοσι καὶ μείζοσι φυλακαῖς τὸν τόπον διέλαβεν, ὡς εἶναι τοῖς βαρβάροις τὴν διάβασιν τελέως ἀδύνατον. By this seems meant the transference of the two Dalmatian legions to Moesia.

Whither they were transferred we do not know. According to the Roman custom elsewhere it is more probable that they were stationed in the environs of the previous headquarters Viminacium than in the remote region of the mouths of the Danube. The camp there probably originated only at the division of the Moesian command and at the erection of the independent province of lower Moesia under Domitian.

[2] The chronology of the Dacian war is involved in much uncertainty. That it had begun already before the war with the Chatti (83), we learn from the Carthaginian inscription (*C. I. L.* viii. 1082) of a soldier decorated three times by Domitian, in the Dacian, in the German, and again in the Dacian war. Eusebius puts the outbreak of the war, or rather the first great conflict, in the year Abr. 2101 or 2102 = A.D. 85 (more exactly 1 Oct. 84—30 Sept. 85) or 86, the triumph in the year 2106 = 90; these numbers indeed have no claim to complete trustworthiness. With some probability the triumph is placed in the year 89 (Henzen, *Acta Arval.* p. 116).

the change of affairs hinged, quite like the similar one in Caesar's time, upon a single Dacian man ; what king Burebista had planned, king Decebalus seemed destined

Decebalus. to execute. How much the real moving-spring lay in his personality, is shown by the story that the Dacian king Duras, in order to bring the right man into the right place, retired from his office in favour of Decebalus. That Decebalus first of all organised in order to strike, is shown by the reports as to his introduction of Roman discipline into the Dacian army, and his enlisting people of capacity among the Romans themselves, and even by the condition proposed by him to the Romans after the victory, that they should send him the necessary workmen to instruct his people in the arts of peace as of war. On what a great scale he set to work is shown by the connections which he formed, westward and eastward, with the Suebi and the Jazyges, and even with the Parthians. The assailants were the Dacians. The governor of the province of Moesia, who first went to oppose them, Oppius Sabinus, lost his life on the field of battle. A number of smaller camps were conquered ; the larger were threatened, the possession of the province itself was at stake. Domitian in person resorted to the army, and his representative—he himself was no general and remained in the background—the commandant of the guard, Cornelius Fuscus, led the army over the Danube ; but he paid for the incautious proceeding by a severe defeat, and he too, the second in supreme command, fell before the enemy. His successor, Julianus, a capable officer, defeated the Dacians in their own territory in a great battle near Tapae, and was on the way to achieve lasting results. But, while the struggle with the Dacians was in suspense, Domitian had threatened the Suebi and Jazyges with war, because they had omitted to send to him a contingent against the former ; the messengers, who came to excuse this, he caused to be executed.[1] Here too misfortune

---

[1] The fragment, Dio, lxvii. 7, 1, Dind., stands in the sequence of the Ursinian excerpts before lxvii. 5, 1, 2, 3, and belongs also in the order of events to a time before the negotiation with the Lugii. Comp. *Hermes*, iii. 115.

pursued the Roman arms. The Marcomani achieved a victory over the emperor himself; a whole legion was surrounded by the Jazyges and cut down. Shaken by this defeat, Domitian, in spite of the advantages gained by Julianus over the Dacians, hastily concluded with these a peace, which did not indeed prevent him from conferring the crown upon the representative of Decebalus in Rome, Diegis, just as if the latter were a vassal of the Romans, or from marching as victor to the Capitol, but which in reality was equivalent to a capitulation. What Decebalus, on the advance of the Roman army into Dacia, had scoffingly offered—to dismiss to his home uninjured every man for whom a yearly payment of two asses was promised to him—became almost true : in the peace the incursions into Moesia were bought off with a fixed sum to be paid yearly.

Here a change had to be effected. Domitian, who was doubtless a good administrator of the empire, but obtuse to the demands of military honour, was followed after the short reign of Nerva by the emperor Trajan, who, first and above all a soldier, not merely tore in pieces that agreement, but also took measures that similar things should not recur. The war against the Suebi and Sarmatae, which was still being continued at Domitian's death (96), was happily ended, as it would seem, under Nerva in the year 97. The new emperor went, even before he held his entrance into the capital of the empire, from the Rhine to the Danube, where he stayed in the winter 98-99, but not to attack the Dacians at once, but to prepare for the war : to this time belongs the construction—joining itself on to the roads formed in upper Germany—of the road completed on the right bank of the Danube in the region of Orsova in the year 100 (p. 153). For the war against the Dacians, in which, as in all his campaigns, he commanded in person, he did not set out till the spring of 101. He crossed the Danube below Viminacium, and advanced against the not far distant capital of the king, Sarmizegetusa. Decebalus with his allies—the Buri and other tribes dwelling to the

Dacian war of Trajan.

northward took part in this struggle—offered resolute resistance, and it was only by vehement and bloody conflicts that the Romans cleared their way ; the number of the wounded was so great that the emperor put his own wardrobe at the disposal of the physicians. But victory did not waver ; one stronghold after another fell ; the sisters of the king, the captives from the former war, the standards taken from the armies of Domitian, fell into the hands of the Romans ; for the king, intercepted by Trajan himself and by the brave Lusius Quietus, nothing was left but complete surrender (102). Trajan demanded nothing less than the renunciation of the sovereign power and the entrance of the Dacian kingdom into the clientship of Rome. The deserters, the arms, the engines of war, the workmen once supplied for these by Rome, had to be delivered up, and the king personally to kneel before the victor ; he divested himself of the right to make war and peace, and promised military service ; the fortresses were either razed or delivered to the Romans, and in these, above all in the capital, there remained a Roman garrison. The strong bridge of stone, which Trajan caused to be thrown over the Danube at Drobetae (opposite Turnu Severinului), secured the communication even in the bad season of the year, and gave to the Dacian garrisons a reserve-support in the near legions of upper-Moesia.

Second Dacian war. But the Dacian nation, and above all the king himself, did not know the art of accommodating themselves to dependence, as the kings of Cappadocia and Mauretania had understood it ; or rather they had merely taken upon them the yoke in the hope of ridding themselves of it again on the first opportunity. The signs of this were soon apparent. A portion of the arms to be delivered up was kept back ; the fortresses were not given over as had been stipulated ; an asylum was still granted, moreover, to Roman deserters ; portions of territory were wrested from the Jazyges at enmity with the Dacians, or perhaps the occurrence of violations of the frontier on their part was not taken patiently ; a lively and

suspicious intercourse was maintained with the more remote natives still free. Trajan could not but be convinced that his work was but half done ; and, rapid in
resolution as he was, he, without entering upon further
negotiations, declared war once more against the king
three years after the conclusion of peace (105). Gladly
would the latter have avoided it ; but the demand that
he should give himself a captive spoke too clearly. Nothing was left but a struggle of despair, and all were not
ready for this ; a great part of the Dacians submitted
without resistance. The appeal to the neighbouring
peoples to enter jointly into measures for warding off
the danger that threatened even their freedom and their
national existence sounded without effect ; Decebalus
and the Dacians that remained faithful to him stood alone
in this war. The attempts to make away with the
imperial general by means of deserters, or to purchase
tolerable terms by the release of a high officer taken
prisoner, likewise broke down. The emperor marched
once more as victor into the enemy's capital, and Decebalus, who up to the last moment had struggled with fate,
put himself to death when all was lost (107). This time
Trajan made an end ; the war concerned no longer the
freedom of the people, but its very existence. The native
population were driven out from the best part of the land,
and these districts were reoccupied with a non-national
population brought in from the mountains of Dalmatia,
for the mines, and otherwise preponderantly, as it would
appear, from Asia Minor. In several regions, no doubt,
the old population yet remained, and even the language
of the country maintained its ground.[1] These Dacians,
as well as the sections dwelling beyond the bounds, still
gave trouble to the Romans—subsequently, for example,
under Commodus and Maximinus ; but they stood
isolated, and dwindled away. The danger with which
the vigorous Thracian race had several times threatened

---

[1] Arrian, *Tact.* 44, mentions among
the changes which Hadrian introduced
into the cavalry, that he allowed to
the several divisions their national

battle-cries : Κελτικοὺς μὲν τοῖς Κελτοῖς ἱππεῦσιν, Γετικοὺς δὲ τοῖς Γέταις,
Ῥαιτικοὺς δὲ ὅσοι ἐκ Ῥαίτων.

the Roman rule could not be allowed to recur, and this end Trajan attained. The Rome of Trajan was no longer that of the age of Hannibal ; but it was still dangerous to have conquered the Romans.

Trajan's column.

The stately column which six years afterwards was erected to the emperor by the imperial senate in the new Forum Trajanum of the capital, and which still adorns it at the present day, is an evidence, to which we possess nothing parallel, of the extent to which the traditional history of the Roman imperial period has suffered havoc. Throughout its height of exactly one hundred Roman feet it is covered with separate representations to the number of one hundred and twenty-four—a chiselled picture-book of the Dacian wars, to which almost everywhere we lack the text. We see the watch-towers of the Romans with their pointed roofs, their palisaded court, their upper gallery, their fire-signals ; the town on the bank of the Danube-stream, whose river-god looks on at the Roman warriors, as they march under their standards along the bridge of boats ; the emperor himself in his council of war, and then sacrificing at the altar before the walls of the camp. It is narrated that the Buri allied with the Dacians dissuaded Trajan from the war in a Latin sentence written on a huge mushroom ; we fancy that we recognise this mushroom placed as a load on a sumpter-animal, jumping from which a barbarian, lying on the ground with his club, points out the mushroom with his finger to the advancing emperor. We see the pitching of the camp, the felling of trees, the fetching of water, the laying of the bridge. The first captive Dacians, easily recognisable by their long-sleeved frocks and their wide trousers, with their hands bound behind their back, and with their long bushy hair grasped by the soldiers, are brought before the emperor. We see the combats, the men hurling spears, the slingers, the sickle-bearers, the archers on foot, the heavy-mailed horsemen also bearing the bow, the dragon-banners of the Dacians, the officers of the enemy adorned with the round cap as the token of their rank, the pine-wood, into which the Dacians carry their wounded, the cut-off heads of the barbarians deposited before the emperor. We see the Dacian village on piles in the middle of the lake, against the round huts of which, with their pointed roof, the burning torches are flying. Women and children sue the emperor for mercy. The wounded are cared for and bound up ; badges of honour are distributed to officers and soldiers. Then the conflict proceeds ; the hostile entrenchments, partly of wood, partly stone walls, are assailed ; the besieging-train advances, the ladders are brought up, the storming-column makes its assault under cover of the *testudo*. Lastly, the king with his train lies at the feet of Trajan ; the dragon-banners are in the hands of the Romans ; the troops in exultation salute the emperor ; Victoria stands before the piled-up arms of the enemy and inscribes the slab recording the victory. Then follow the pictures of the second war, of similar character on the whole to those of the first series. Worthy of notice is one great representation, which, after the king's stronghold has been burnt, appears to show the princes of the Dacians sitting round a kettle and, one after the other, emptying the poison-cup; another, where the head of the brave Dacian king is brought on a tray to the emperor ; and lastly, the closing picture, the long series of the conquered with their women, children, and flocks marching away from their home. The emperor himself wrote the history of this war—as Frederick the Great wrote that of the Seven Years' War—and many others after him ; all this is lost to us, and as nobody would venture to invent the history of the Seven Years' War from Menzel's pictures, there is left to us only, along with a glimpse into half intelligible details, the painful feeling of a stirring and great historical catastrophe faded for ever and lost even to remembrance.

The defence of the frontier in the region of the Danube was not shifted to such a degree, as might well be expected, in consequence of the conversion of Dacia into a Roman province ; a change, in the strict sense, of the line of defence did not take place, but the new province

Military position on the Danube after Trajan.

was treated on the whole as an eccentric position, which was only connected directly with the Roman territory towards the south along the Danube itself, on the other three sides projected into the barbarian land.   The plain of the Theiss, stretching between Pannonia and Dacia continued in the hands of the Jazyges ; there have been found remains of old walls, which led from the Danube over the Theiss away to the Dacian mountains, and bounded the region of the Jazyges to the north, but of the time and the authors of these entrenchments nothing certain is known.   Bessarabia also is intersected by a double barrier-line which, running from the Pruth to the Dniester, ends at Tyra, and—according to the inadequate reports hitherto before us on the subject—appears to proceed from the Romans.[1]   If this was the case, then Moldavia and the south half of Bessarabia as well as the whole of Wallachia were incorporated in the Roman empire.   But, though this may have been done nominally, the Roman rule hardly extended effectively to these lands ; at least there is, up to the present time, an utter absence of sure proofs of Roman settlement either in eastern Wallachia or in Moldavia and Bessarabia.   At any rate, the Danube here remained, much more than the Rhine in Germany, the limit of Roman civilisation and the proper basis of frontier-defence.   The positions on it were considerably reinforced.   It was a fortunate circumstance for Rome that, while the surge of peoples rose on the Danube, it sank on the Rhine, and the troops that could be there dispensed with were disposable elsewhere.

Commands increased to five.

Although under Vespasian probably not more than six legions were stationed on the Danube, their number was subsequently raised by Domitian and Trajan to ten ; the two chief commands of Moesia and Pannonia hitherto

---

[1] The walls, which, three mètres in height and two mètres in thickness, with broad outer fosse and many remains of forts, stretch in two almost parallel lines, partly—to the length of ninety-four miles—from the left bank of the Pruth by way of Tabak and Tatarbunar to Dniester-Liman, between Akerman and the Black Sea ; partly—to the length of sixty-two miles—from Leowa on the Pruth to the Dniester below Bendery (Petermann, *Geograph. Mittheilungen*, 1857, p. 129), may perhaps be also Roman ; but there has not been as yet any exact settlement of this point.

subsisting were withal divided, the first under Domitian, the second under Trajan, and, as the Dacian was super-added, the whole number of the commanderships on the lower Danube was fixed at five. At the outset, indeed, they seem to have cut off the corner which this stream forms below Durostorum (Silistria)—the modern Dobrudscha—and from the place now called Rassowa, where the river approaches within thirty miles of the sea, in order then to bend almost at a right angle to the north, to have substituted for the river-line a fortified road after the manner of the British (p. 187), which reached the coast at Tomis.[1] This corner, however, was, at least from the time of Hadrian, embraced within the Roman frontier-fortification ; for from that time we find lower Moesia, which before Trajan had probably possessed no larger standing garrisons at all, furnished with the three legionary camps of Novae (near Svischtova), Durostorum (Silistria), and Troesmis (Iglitza, near Galatz), of which the last lies in front of that very angle of the Danube. Against the Jazyges the position was strengthened by adding to the

---

[1] According to von Vincke's estimate (*Monatsberichte über die Verhandlungen der Gesellschaft für Erdkunde in Berlin* in the years 1839-40, p. 197 f. ; comp. in von Moltke's *Briefe über Zustände in der Turkei*, the letter of 2d Nov. 1837), as well as according to the delineations and plans of Dr. C. Schuchhardt communicated to me, three barriers were here constructed. The south-most and probably oldest is a simple earthen wall with (singularly) a fosse in front of it towards the south ; whether of Roman origin may be doubtful. The two other lines are an earthen wall, even now at many places as high as three mètres, and a lower wall, once lined with stones, which often run close beside each other and elsewhere again are miles apart. We might hold them as the two lines of defence of a fortified road, though in the eastern half the earthen wall, in the more southern half the stone-wall, is the more northerly, and they cross in the middle. At one spot the earthen wall (here more southerly) forms the rear of a fort constructed behind the stone-wall. The earthen wall is covered on the north side by a deep, on the south side by a shallow, fosse ; each fosse is closed off by a bank. A fosse lies also in front of the stone-wall to the north. Behind the earthen wall, and mostly resting on it, are found forts distant from each other seven hundred and fifty mètres ; others at irregular distances of the like kind behind the stone-wall. All the lines keep behind the Karasu-lakes as the natural basis of defence ; from the point where this ceases, they are carried as far as the sea with slight regard to the character of the ground. The town Tomis lies outside of the wall and to the north of it ; but its fortress-walls are put in connection with the barrier-fortification by a special wall.

upper Moesian camps at Singidunum and Viminacium the lower Pannonian at the confluence of the Theiss with the Danube near Acumincum. Dacia itself was then but weakly garrisoned. The capital, now a colony of Trajan, Sarmizegetusa, lay not far from the chief crossings over the Danube in upper Moesia ; here and on the middle Marisus, as well as beyond it in the districts of the gold mines, the Romans chiefly settled ; the one legion serving as garrison since Trajan's time in Dacia obtained its headquarters, at least soon afterwards, in this region at Apulum (Karlsburg). Farther to the north Potaissa (Thorda) and Napoca (Klausenburg) were probably also at once taken possession of by the Romans, but it was only gradually that the great Pannono-Dacian military centres pushed farther towards the north. The transference of the lower Pannonian legion from Acumincum to Aquincum, the modern Buda, and the occupation of this commanding military position, fall not later than Hadrian, and probably under him ; probably at the same time one of the upper Pannonian legions came to Brigetio (opposite to Comorn). Under Commodus all settlement was prohibited along the northern frontier of Dacia for a breadth of nearly five miles, which must stand connected with the frontier regulations to be subsequently mentioned after the Marcomanian war. At that time also the fortified lines may have originated, which barred this frontier similarly to the upper Germanic. Under Severus one of the legions previously in lower Moesia was brought to Potaissa (Thorda) on the Dacian north frontier.

Dacia an advanced position.

But even after these transferences Dacia remained an advanced position on the left bank, covered by mountains and defences, with reference to which it might well be doubtful whether it did more to promote or to impede the general defensive attitude of the Romans. Hadrian, in fact, had thought of giving up this territory, and so regarded its incorporation as a mistake ; after the step had once been taken, there certainly preponderated the consideration, if not of the lucrative gold mines of the country, at any rate of the Roman civilisation rapidly developing itself in the region of the Marisus. But he caused at least the superstructure of the stone bridge of the Danube to be removed, as his apprehension of its being used by the enemy outweighed his consideration for the Dacian garrison. The later period released itself from this anxiety ; but the eccentric position of Dacia in relation to the rest of the frontier-defence remained.

The sixty years after the Dacian wars of Trajan were for the Danube lands a time of peace and of peaceful development. No doubt there was never entire quiet, particularly at the mouths of the Danube, and even the hazardous expedient of purchasing the security of the frontier from the adjoining restless neighbours, just as was done with Decebalus, by the bestowal of yearly gratuities was further employed ;[1] yet the remains of antiquity show at this very time everywhere the flourishing of urban life, and. not a few communities, particularly of Pannonia, name as their founder Hadrian or Pius. But upon this stillness followed a storm such as the empire had not yet sustained, and which, although properly but a frontier-war, by its extension over a series of provinces and by its duration for thirteen years shook the empire itself.

The war named after the Marcomani was not kindled by any single personage of the type of Hannibal or Decebalus. As little did aggressions on the part of the Romans provoke this war ; the emperor Pius injured no neighbour, either powerful or humble, and set on peace almost more than its just value. The realm of Maroboduus and of Vannius had thereafter, perhaps in consequence of the partition under Vangio and Sido (p. 216), become divided into the kingdom of the Marcomani in what is now Bohemia and that of the Quadi in Moravia and upper Hungary. Conflicts with the Romans do not appear to have occurred here ; the vassal-relation of the princes of the Quadi was even formally recognised under the reign of Pius by the confirmation

Marcom-
anian war.

---

[1] *Vita Hadriani* 6: *cum rege Roxo- lanorum qui de imminutis stipendiis querebatur cognito negotio pacem com- posuit.*

asked for. Shiftings of peoples, which lay beyond the Roman horizon, were the proximate cause of the great war. Soon after the death of Pius († 161) masses of Germans, especially Langobardi from the Elbe, but also Marcomani and other bodies of men, appeared in Pannonia, apparently to gain new abodes on the right bank. Pressed hard by the Roman troops who were despatched against them, they sent the prince of the Marcomani, Ballomarius, and with him a representative of each of the ten tribes taking part, to renew their request for assignation of land. But the governor abode by his decision and compelled them to go back over the Danube.

Its beginning. This was the beginning of the great Danubian war.[1] The governor of upper Germany, Gaius Aufidius Victorinus, the father-in-law of Fronto known in literature, had already, about the year 162, to repel an assault of the Chatti, which likewise may have been occasioned by tribes from the Elbe pressing on their rear. Had equally energetic steps been taken, greater mischief might have been averted. But just then the Armenian war had begun, into which the Parthians soon entered; though the troops were not actually sent away from the threatened frontier to the east, for which there is at least no evidence,[2] there was at any rate a want of men to take up the second war at once with energy. This temporising severely avenged itself. Just when people were triumphing in Rome over the kings of the east, on the Danube the Chatti, the Marcomani, the Quadi, the Jazyges burst

---

[1] *Vita Marci* 14: *gentibus quae pulsae a superioribus barbaris fugerant nisi reciperentur bellum inferentibus.* Dio, in Petrus Patricius, *fr.* 6, says: Λαγγιβάρδων καὶ Ὀβίων (otherwise unknown) ἑξακισχιλίων Ἴστρον περαιωθέντων τῶν περὶ Βίνδικα (perhaps already then *praef. praetorio*, in which case the guard would be marched out on account of this occurrence), ἱππέων ἐξελασάντων καὶ τῶν ἀμφὶ Κάνδιδον πεζῶν ἐπιφθασάντων εἰς παντελῆ φυγὴν οἱ βάρβαροι ἐτράποντο· ἐφ᾽ οἷς οὕτω πραχθεῖσιν ἐν δέει καταστάντες ἐκ πρώτης ἐπιχειρήσεως οἱ βάρβαροι πρέσ-

βεις παρὰ Αἴλιον Βάσσον τὴν Παιονίαν διέποντα στέλλουσι Βαλλομάριόν τε τὸν βασιλέα Μαρκομάνων καὶ ἑτέρους δέκα, κατ᾽ ἔθνος ἐπιλεξάμενοι ἕνα· καὶ ὅρκοις τὴν εἰρήνην οἱ πρέσβεις πιστωσάμενοι οἴκαδε χωροῦσιν. That this incident falls before the outbreak of the war, is shown by its position; *fr.* 7 of Patricius is an excerpt from Dio, lxxi. 11, 2.

[2] The Moesian army gave away soldiers to the Armenian war (Hirschfeld, *Arch. epig. Mitth.* vi. 41); but here the frontier was not endangered.

as with a thunderclap into the Roman territory. Raetia, Noricum, the two Pannonias, Dacia, were inundated at the same moment; in the Dacian mine-district we can still follow the traces of this irruption. What devastations they then wrought in those regions, which for long had seen no enemy, is shown by the fact that several years afterwards the Quadi gave back first 13,000, then 50,000, and the Jazyges even 100,000 Roman captives. Nor did the matter end with the injury done to the provinces. There happened what had not occurred for three hundred years and begun to be accounted as impossible—the barbarians broke through the wall of the Alps and invaded Italy itself; from Raetia they destroyed Opitergium (Oderzo); bands from the Julian Alps invested Aquileia.[1] Defeats of individual Roman divisions must have taken place in various cases; we learn only that one of the commandants of the guard, Victorinus, fell before the enemy, and the ranks of the Roman armies were sorely thinned. *Invasion of Italy.*

This grave attack befell the state at a most unhappy moment. No doubt the Oriental war was ended; but in its train a pestilence had spread throughout Italy and the west, which swept men away more continuously than the war, and in more fearful measure. When the troops were concentrated, as was necessary, the victims of the pestilence were all the more numerous. As dearth always accompanies pestilence, so on this occasion there appeared with it failure of crops and famine, and severe financial distress; the taxes did not come in, and in the course of the war the emperor saw himself under the necessity of alienating by public auction the jewels of his palace. *Pestilence.*

There was lack of a fitting leader. A military and political task so extensive and so complicated could, as things stood in Rome, be undertaken by no commissioned general, but only by the ruler himself. Marcus had, with a correct and modest knowledge of his shortcomings, on *Verus and Marcus.*

---

[1] The participation of the Germans on the right of the Rhine is attested by Dio, lxxi. 3, and only thereby are the measures explained which Marcus adopted for Raetia and Noricum. The position of Oderzo also speaks for the view that these assailants came over the Brenner.

ascending the throne, placed by his side with equal rights
his younger adopted brother Lucius Verus, on the benevo-
lent assumption that the jovial young man—as he was
a vigorous fencer and hunter—would also grow into an
able general.   But the worthy emperor did not possess
the sharp glance of one who knows men ; the choice had
proved as unfortunate as possible ; the Parthian war just
ended had shown the nominal general to be personally
dissolute, and as an officer incapable.   The joint regency of
Verus was nothing but an additional calamity, which indeed
was obviated by his death, that ensued not long after the
outbreak of the Marcomanian war (169).   Marcus, by his
leanings more reflective than inclined to practical life,
and not at all a soldier, nor in general a strong personality, undertook the exclusive and personal conduct of
the requisite operations.   He may, in doing so, have made
mistakes enough in detail, and perhaps the long duration
of the struggle is partly traceable to this ; but the unity
of supreme command, his clear insight into the object for
which the war was waged, the tenacity of his statesmanly
action, above all the rectitude and firmness of the man
administering his difficult office with self-forgetful faith-
fulness, ultimately broke the dangerous assault.   This
was a merit all the higher, as the success was due more
to character than to talent.

Progress of
the war.

The character of the task set before the Romans is
shown by the fact that the government, despite the want
of men and money in the first year of this war, had the
walls of the capital of Dalmatia, Salonae, and of the
capital of Thrace, Philippopolis, restored by its soldiers
and at its expense ; certainly these were not isolated
arrangements.   They had to prepare themselves to see the
men of the north everywhere investing the great towns
of the empire ; the terrors of the Gothic expeditions were
already knocking at the gates, and were perhaps for this
time averted only by the fact that government saw them
coming.   The immediate superintendence of the military
operations, and the regulation, demanded by the state of the
case, of the relations to the frontier-peoples and reformation

of the existing arrangements on the spot, might neither be omitted nor left to his unprincipled brother or individual leaders. In fact, the position of matters was changed as soon as the two emperors arrived at Aquileia, in order to set out thence with the army to the scene of war. The Germans and Sarmatians, far from united in themselves, and without common leading, felt themselves unequal to such a counter-blow. The masses of invaders everywhere retreated ; the Quadi sent in their submission to the imperial generals, and in many cases the leaders of the movement directed against the Romans paid for this reaction with their lives. Lucius thought that the war had demanded victims enough, and advised a return to Rome ; but the Marcomani persevered in haughty resistance, and the calamity which had come upon Rome, the hundred thousands of captives dragged away, the successes achieved by the barbarians, imperatively demanded a more vigorous policy and the offensive continuance of the war. The son-in-law of Marcus, Tiberius Claudius Pompeianus, as an extraordinary measure took the command in Raetia and Noricum ; his able lieutenant, the subsequent emperor, Publius Helvius Pertinax, cleared the Roman territory without difficulty with the first auxiliary legion called up from Pannonia. In spite of the financial distress two new legions were formed, particularly from Illyrian soldiers, in the raising of which no doubt many a previous highway-robber was made a defender of his country ; and, as was already stated (pp. 161, 198), the hitherto slight frontier-guard of these two provinces was reinforced by the new legion-camps of Ratisbon and Enns. The emperors themselves went to the upper Pannonian camps. It was above all of consequence to restrict the area within which the fire of war was raging. The barbarians coming from the north, who offered their aid, were not repelled, and fought in Roman pay, so far as they did not—as also occurred—break their word and make common cause with the enemy. The Quadi, who sued for peace and for the confirmation of the new king Furtius, had the latter readily granted to them, and nothing demanded of them but the

giving back of the deserters and the captives. Success in
some measure attended the attempt to restrict the war to
the two chief opponents, the Marcomani and the Jazyges
from of old allied with them. Against these two peoples
it was carried on in the following years with severe conflicts and not without defeat. We know only isolated
details, which do not admit of being brought into set
connection. Marcus Claudius Fronto, to whom had been
entrusted the commands of upper Moesia and Dacia
united as an extraordinary measure, fell about the year
171 in conflict against Germans and Jazyges. The commandant of the guard, Marcus Macrinius Vindex, likewise
fell before the enemy. They and other officers of high
rank obtained in these years honorary monuments in Rome
at the column of Trajan, because they had met death in
defence of their fatherland. The barbaric tribes, who had
declared for Rome, again partially fell away—such as the
Cotini and above all the Quadi, who granted an asylum
to the fugitive Marcomani and drove out their vassal-
king Furtius, whereupon the emperor Marcus set a price
of 1000 gold pieces on the head of his successor Ario-
gaesus.

Its issue ;
and second
war.

Not till the sixth year of the war (172) does the
complete conquest of the Marcomani seem to have been
achieved, and Marcus to have thereupon assumed the
well-deserved title of victory, Germanicus. Then followed
the overthrow of the Quadi ; lastly in 175 that of the
Jazyges, in consequence of which the emperor received
the further surname of Conqueror of the Sarmatae.
The terms which were laid down for the conquered
tribes show that Marcus designed not to punish but to
subdue. The Marcomani and the Jazyges, probably also
the Quadi, were required to evacuate a border-strip along
the river to the breadth of ten, subsequently modified to
five, miles. In the strongholds on the right bank of
the Danube were placed Roman garrisons, which, among
the Marcomani and Quadi alone, amounted together to
not less than 20,000 men. All the subdued had to
furnish contingents to the Roman army ; the Jazyges, for

example, 8000 horsemen. Had the emperor not been recalled by the insurrection of Syria, he would have driven the latter entirely from their country, as Trajan drove the Dacians. That Marcus intended to treat the revolted Transdanubians after this model, was confirmed by the further course of events. Hardly was that hindrance removed, when the emperor went back to the Danube and began, just like Trajan, in 178 the second definitive war. The ground put forward for thus declaring war is not known ; the aim is doubtless correctly specified to the effect that he purposed to erect two new provinces, Marcomania and Sarmatia. To the Jazyges, who must have shown themselves submissive to the designs of the emperor, their burdensome imposts were for the most part remitted, and, in fact, for intercourse with their kinsmen dwelling to the east of Dacia the Roxolani, right of passage through Dacia was granted to them under fitting supervision—probably just because they were already regarded as Roman subjects. The Marcomani were almost extirpated by sword and famine. The Quadi in despair wished to migrate to the north, and to seek settlements among the Semnones ; but even this was not allowed to them, as they had to cultivate the fields in order to provide for the Roman garrisons. After fourteen years of almost uninterrupted warfare, he who was a warrior-prince against his will reached his goal, and the Romans were a second time face to face with the acquisition of the upper Elbe ; now, in fact, all that was wanting was the announcement of the wish to retain what was won. Thereupon he died—not yet sixty years of age— in the camp of Vindobona on 17th March 180.

We must not merely acknowledge the resoluteness and tenacity of the ruler, but must also admit that he did what right policy enjoined. The conquest of Dacia by Trajan was a doubtful gain, although in this very Marcomanian war the possession of Dacia not only removed a dangerous element from the ranks of the antagonists of Rome, but probably also had the effect of preventing the host of peoples on the lower Danube, the Bastarnae, Roxo-

Results of the Marcomanian war.

lani, and others, from interfering in the war. But after the mighty onset of the Transdanubians to the west of Dacia had made their subjugation a necessity, this could only be accomplished in a definitive way by embracing Bohemia, Moravia, and the plain of the Theiss within the Roman line of defence, although these regions were probably accounted, like Dacia, as having only the position of advanced posts, and the strategical frontier-line was certainly meant to remain the Danube.

Conclusion of peace by Commodus.

The successor of Marcus, the emperor Commodus, was present in the camp when his father died, and as he had already for several years nominally shared the throne with his father, he entered with the latter's death at once into possession of unlimited power. Only for a brief time did the nineteen years' old successor allow the men who had enjoyed his father's confidence—his brother-in-law Pompeianus, and others who had borne with Marcus the heavy burden of the war—to rule in his spirit. Commodus was in every respect the opposite of his father ; not a scholar, but a fencing-master ; as cowardly and weak in character, as his father was resolute and tenacious of purpose; as indolent and forgetful of duty, as his father was active and conscientious. He not merely gave up the idea of incorporating the territory won, but voluntarily granted even to the Marcomani conditions such as they had not ventured to hope for. The regulation of the frontier-traffic under Roman control, and the obligation not to injure their neighbours friendly to the Romans, were matters of course; but the garrisons were withdrawn from their country, and there was retained only the prohibition of settlement on the border-strip. The payment of taxes and the furnishing of recruits were doubtless stipulated for, but the former were soon remitted, and the latter were certainly not furnished. A similar settlement was made with the Quadi ; and the other Transdanubians must have been similarly dealt with. Thereby the conquests made were given up, and the work of many years of warfare was in vain ; if no more was wished for, a similar arrangement of things might have been reached much earlier. Nevertheless the

Marcomanian war secured in these regions the supremacy of Rome for the sequel, in spite of the fact that Rome let slip the prize of victory. It was not by the tribes that had taken part in it that the blow was dealt, to which the Roman world-power succumbed.

Another permanent consequence of this war was con- The nected with the removals, to which it gave occasion, of the colonate. Transdanubians over into the Roman empire. Of themselves such changes of settlement had occurred at all times ; the Sugambri, transplanted under Augustus to Gaul, the Dacians sent to Thrace, were nothing but new subjects or communities of subjects added to those formerly existing, and probably not much different were the 3000 Naristae, whom Marcus allowed to exchange their settlements westward of Bohemia for such settlements within the empire, while the like request was refused to the otherwise unknown Astingi on the Dacian north frontier. But the Germans settled by him not merely in the land of the Danube, but in Italy itself at Ravenna, were neither free subjects nor strictly non-free persons ; these were the beginnings of the Roman villanage, the colonate, the influence of which on the agricultural economy of the whole state is to be set forth in another connection. That Ravennate settlement, however, had no permanence ; the men rose in revolt and had to be conveyed away, so that the new colonate remained restricted primarily to the provinces, particularly to the lands of the Danube.

The great war on the middle Danube was once more The ad-followed by sixty years' time of peace, the blessings of vancing which could not be completely neutralised by the internal Northmen. misgovernment that was constantly increasing during its course. No doubt various isolated accounts show that the frontier, especially the Dacian, which was most exposed, remained not without trouble ; but above all, the stern military government of Severus did its duty here, and at least Marcomani and Quadi appear even under his immediate successors in unconditional dependence, so that the son of Severus could cite a prince of the Quadi before him and lay his head at his feet. The conflicts occurring at this epoch on the lower Danube were of subordinate importance. But probably at this period a comprehensive shifting of peoples from the north-east towards the Black Sea took place, and the Roman frontier-guard on the lower Danube had to confront new and more dangerous opponents. Up to this time the antagonists of the Romans there had been chiefly Sarmatian tribes, among whom the Roxolani came into closest contact with them ; of Germans there were settled here at that time only the Bastarnae, who had been long at home in this region. Now the Roxolani disappear, merged possibly among the Carpi apparently akin to them, who thenceforth were the nearest neighbours of the Romans on the lower Danube, perhaps in the valleys of the Seret and Pruth.

Goths. By the side of the Carpi came, likewise as immediate neighbours of the Romans at the mouth of the Danube, the people of the Goths. This Germanic stock migrated, according to the tradition which has been preserved to us, from Scandinavia over the Baltic towards the region of the Vistula, and from this to the Black Sea ; in accordance with this the Roman geographers of the second century know them at the Vistula, and Roman history from the first quarter of the third at the north-west coast of the Black Sea. Thenceforth they appear here constantly on the increase ; the remains of the Bastarnae retired before them to the right bank of the Danube under the emperor Probus, the remains of the Carpi under the emperor Diocletian, while beyond doubt a great part of the former as of the latter mingled among the Goths and joined them. On the whole this catastrophe may be designated as that of the Gothic war only in the sense in which that which set in under Marcus is called the war of the Marcomani ; the whole mass of peoples set in movement by the stream of migration from the north-east to the Black Sea took part in it ; and took part all the more, seeing that these attacks took place just as much by land over the lower Danube as by water from the north coasts of the Black Sea, in an inextricable complication of landward and maritime piracy. Not unsuitably, therefore, the learned

Athenian who fought in this war and has narrated it, prefers to term it the Scythian, as he includes under this name—which, like the Pelasgian, forms the despair of the historian—all Germanic and non-Germanic enemies of the empire. What is to be told of these expeditions will here be brought together, so far as the confusion of tradition, which is only too much in keeping with the confusion of these fearful times, allows.

The year 238—a year also of civil war, when there were four emperors—is designated as that in which the war against those here first named Goths began.[1] As the coins of Tyra and Olbia cease with Alexander († 235), these Roman possessions situated beyond the boundary of the empire had doubtless become some years earlier a prey to the new enemy. In that year they first crossed the Danube, and the most northerly of the Moesian coast towns, Istros, was the first victim. Gordianus, who emerged out of the confusions of this time as ruler, is designated as conqueror of the Goths; it is more certain that the Roman government at any rate under him, if not already earlier, agreed to buy off the Gothic incursions.[2] As was natural, the Carpi demanded the same as the emperor had granted to the inferior Goths; when the demand was not granted, they invaded the Roman territory in the

Gothic wars.

[1] The alleged first mention of the Goths in the biography of Caracalla, c. 10, rests on a misunderstanding. If really a senator allowed himself the malicious jest of assigning to the murderer of Geta the name Geticus, because he on his march from the Danube to the east had conquered some Getic hordes (*tumultuariis proeliis*), he meant Dacians, not the Goths, scarcely at that time dwelling there and hardly known to the Roman public, whose identification with the Getae was certainly only a later invention.—We may add that the statement that the emperor Maximinus (235-238) was the son of a Goth settled in the neighbouring Thrace, carries us still further back; yet not much weight is to be attached to it.

[2] Petrus Patricius *fr.* 8. The administration of the legate of lower Moesia here mentioned, Tullius Menophilus, is fixed by coins certainly to the time of Gordian, and with probability to 238-240 (Borghesi, *Opp.* ii. 227). As the beginning of the Gothic war and the destruction of Istros are fixed by Dexippus (*vita Max. et Balb.* 16) at 238, it is natural to bring into connection with these events the undertaking of tribute; at any rate it was then renewed. The vain sieges of Marcianopolis and Philippopolis by the Goths (Dexippus, *fr.* 18, 19) may have followed on the capture of Istros. Jordanes, *Get.* 16, 92, puts the former under Philippus, but is in chronological questions not a valid witness.

year 245. The emperor Philippus—Gordianus was at that time already dead—repulsed them, and energetic action with the combined strength of the great empire would probably here have checked the barbarians.

Decius.

But in these years the murderer of an emperor reached the throne as surely as he found in turn his own murderer and successor ; it was just in the imperilled regions of the Danube that the army proclaimed against the emperor Philippus first Marinus Pacatianus, and, after he was set aside, Traianus Decius, which latter in fact vanquished his antagonist in Italy, and was acknowledged as ruler. He was an able and brave man, not unworthy of the two names which he bore, and entered, so soon as he could, resolutely into the conflicts on the Danube ; but what the civil war waged in the meanwhile had destroyed, could no longer be retrieved. While the Romans were fighting with one another the Goths and the Carpi had united, and had under the Gothic prince Cniva invaded Moesia denuded of troops. The governor of the province, Trebonianus Gallus, threw himself with his force into Nicopolis on the Haemus, and was here besieged by the Goths ; these at the same time pillaged Thrace and besieged its capital, the great and strong Philippopolis ; indeed they reached as far as Macedonia, and invested Thessalonica, where the governor Priscus found this just a fitting moment to have himself proclaimed as emperor. When Decius arrived to combat at once his rival and the public foe, the former was doubtless without difficulty set aside, and success also attended the relief of Nicopolis, where 30,000 Goths are said to have fallen. But the Goths, retreating to Thrace, conquered in turn at Beroë (Alt-Zagora), threw the Romans back on Moesia, and reduced Nicopolis there as well as Anchialus in Thrace and even Philippopolis, where 100,000 men are said to have come into their power. Thereupon they marched northwards to bring into safety their enormous booty. Decius projected the plan of inflicting a blow on the enemy at the crossing of the Danube. He stationed a division under Gallus on the bank, and hoped to be able to throw the Goths upon this, and to cut off their retreat. But at Abrittus, a place on the Moesian frontier, the fortune of war, or else the treachery of Gallus, decided against them. Decius perished with His death. his son, and Gallus, who was proclaimed as his successor, began his reign by once more assuring to the Goths the annual payments of money (251).[1] This utter defeat of Roman arms as of Roman policy, the fall of the emperor, the first who lost his life in conflict with the barbarians— a piece of news which deeply moved men's minds even in this age demoralised by its familiarity with misfortune— the disgraceful capitulation following thereon, placed in fact the integrity of the empire at stake. Serious crises on the middle Danube, threatening probably the loss of Dacia, must have been the immediate consequence. Once more this was averted; the governor of Pannonia, Marcus Aemilius Aemilianus, a good soldier, achieved an important success of arms, and drove the enemy over the frontier. But Nemesis bore sway. The consequence of this victory, achieved in the name of Gallus, was, that the army renounced allegiance to the betrayer of Decius and chose their general as his successor. Once more therefore civil war took precedence of frontier-defence; and, while Aemilianus no doubt vanquished Gallus in Italy but soon afterwards succumbed to his general Valerianus (254), Dacia was lost for the empire—how, and Loss of to whom, we know not.[2] The last coin struck by this Dacia. province, and the latest inscription found there, are of the year 255, the last coin of the neighbouring Viminacium in upper Moesia of the following year; in the first years of Valerianus and Gallienus therefore the barbarians occupied the Roman territory on the left bank

[1] The reports of these occurrences in Zosimus, i. 21-24, Zonaras, xii. 20, Ammianus, xxxi. 5, 16, 17 (which accounts, down to that concerning Philippopolis, are fixed as belonging to this time by the fact that the latter recurs in Zosimus), although all fragmentary or in disorder, may have flowed from the report of Dexippus, of which *fr.* 16, 19, are preserved, and may be in some measure combined. The same source lies at the bottom of the imperial biographies and Jordanes; but both have disfigured and falsified it to such a degree that use can be made of their statements only with great caution. Victor, *Caes.* 29, is independent.

[2] Perhaps the irruption of the Marcomani in Zosimus, i. 29, refers to this.

of the Danube, and certainly also pressed across to the right.

Before we pursue further the development of affairs on the lower Danube, it appears necessary to cast a glance at piracy, as it was then in vogue in the eastern half of the Mediterranean, and the maritime expeditions of the Goths and their allies originating from it.

Piracy on the Black Sea.

That the Roman fleet could at no time be dispensed with on the Black Sea, and piracy there was probably never extirpated, was implied in the very nature of the Roman rule as it had taken shape on its coasts. The Romans were in firm possession only from about the mouths of the Danube as far as Trapezus. It is true that on the one hand Tyra at the mouth of the Dniester and Olbia on the bay at the mouth of the Dnieper, on the other side the Caucasian harbours in the regions of the modern Suchum-Kaleh, Dioscurias and Pityus, were Roman. The intervening Bosporan kingdom in the Crimea also stood under Roman protection, and had a Roman garrison subject to the governor of Moesia. But on these shores, for the most part far from inviting, there were only those posts formerly held either as old Greek settlements or as Roman fortresses ; the coast itself was desolate or in the hands of the natives filling the interior, who, comprehended under the general name of Scythians, mostly of Sarmatian descent, never were, or were to become, subject to the Romans ; it was enough if they did not directly lay hands on the Romans or their clients. Accordingly, it is not to be wondered at, that even in the time of Tiberius the pirates of the east coast not merely made the Black Sea insecure, but also landed and levied contributions on the villages and towns of the coast. If, under Pius or Marcus, a band of the Costoboci dwelling on the north-western shore fell upon the inland town Elateia situated in the heart of Phocis, and came to blows under its walls with the citizens, this event, which certainly only by accident stands forth for us as isolated, shows that the same phenomena which preceded the downfall of the government of the senate were now renewed, and even with the imperial power maintaining itself outwardly unshaken not merely individual piratical ships, but squadrons of pirates cruised in the Black and even in the Mediterranean seas. The decline of the government, clearly discernible after the death of Severus, and above all after the end of the last dynasty, manifested itself then, as was natural, especially in the further decay of marine police. The accounts, in detail far from trustworthy, mention already in the time before Decius the appearance of a great fleet of pirates in the Aegean Sea ; then under Decius the plundering of the Pamphylian coast and of the Graeco-Asiatic islands ; under Gallus maraudings ot pirates in Asia Minor as far as Pessinus and Ephesus.[1] These were predatory expeditions. These comrades plundered the coasts far and wide, and made even, as we see, bold raids into the interior ; but nothing is mentioned of the destruction of towns, and the pirates shunned coming into collision with Roman troops ; the attack was chiefly directed against such regions as had no troops stationed in them.

Under Valerian these expeditions assume a different character. The nature of the raids varies so much from the earlier, that the raid, in itself not specially important, of the Borani against Pityus under Valerian could be designated by intelligent reporters precisely as the beginning of this movement,[2] and that the pirates were

Maritime expeditions of the Goths and allies.

---

[1] Ammianus, xxxi. 5, 15 ; *duobus navium milibus perrupto Bosporo et litoribus Propontidis Scythicarum gentium catervae transgressae ediderunt quidem acerbas terra marique strages: sed amissa suorum parte maxima reverterunt ;* whereupon the catastrophe of the Decii is narrated, and into this is inwoven the further notice : *obsessae Pamphyliae civitates* (to which must belong the siege of Side in Dexippus himself, fr. 23), *insulæ populatæ complures*, as also the siege of Cyzicus. If in this retrospect all is not confused—which cannot well be assumed to be the case with Ammianus—this falls before those naval expeditions which begin with the

siege of Pityus, and are more a part of the migration of peoples than piratical raids. The number of the ships might indeed be transferred hither by error of memory from the expedition of the year 269. To the same connection belongs the notice in Zosimus, i. 28, as to the Scythian expeditions into Asia and Cappadocia as far as Ephesus and Pessinus. The account as to Ephesus in the biography of Gallienus, c. 6, is the same, but transposed as to time.

[2] In the case of Zosimus himself we should not expect complete understanding of the matter ; but his voucher Dexippus, who was a contemporary and took part in the matter, knew

for a long time called in Asia by the name of this tribe not otherwise known to us. These expeditions proceed no longer from the old native dwellers beside the Black Sea, but from the hordes pressing behind them. What had hitherto been piracy begins to form a portion of that migratory movement of peoples to which the advance of the Goths on the lower Danube belongs. The peoples taking part in it are very varied and in part little known ; in the later expeditions the Germanic Heruli, then dwelling beside the Maeotis, appear to have played a leading part. The Goths also took part, but, so far as sea-voyages are concerned—and tolerably exact reports of these are before us—not in a prominent manner ; strictly speaking, these expeditions are more correctly termed Scythian than Gothic. The maritime centre of these aggressions was the mouth of the Dniester, the port of Tyra.[1] The Greek towns of the Bosporus, abandoned through the bankruptcy of the imperial power, without protection to the hordes pressing onward, and expecting to be besieged by them, consented, half under compulsion, half voluntarily, to convey in their vessels, and by their mariners, the inconvenient new neighbours over to the nearest Roman possessions on the north coast of Pontus—for which these neighbours themselves lacked the needful means and the needful skill. It was thus that the expedition against Pityus was brought about. The Borani were landed and. confident of success, sent back the ships. But the resolute commander of Pityus, Successianus, repelled the attack ; and the assailants, fearing the arrival of the other Roman garrisons, hastily withdrew, for which they had difficulty in procuring the necessary transports. But the

---

well why he termed the Bithynian expedition the δευτέρα ἔφοδος (Zos. i. 35) ; and even in Zosimus we discern clearly the contrast, intended by Dexippus, between the expedition of the Borani against Pityus and Trapezus and the traditional piratic voyages. In the biography of Gallienus the Scythian expedition to Cappadocia, narrated at c. 11, under

the year 264, must be that to Trapezus, just as the Bithynian therewith connected must be that which Zosimus terms the second ; here indeed everything is confused.

[1] This is said by Zosimus, i. 42, and follows also from the relation of the Bosporans to the first (i. 32), and that of the first to the second expedition (i. 34).

plan was not given up ; in the next year they came back, and, as the commandant had meanwhile been changed, the fortress surrendered. The Borani, who this time had To Trapezus. retained the Bosporan vessels and had them manned by pressed mariners and Roman captives, possessed themselves of the coast far and wide, and reached as far as Trapezus. Into this well fortified and strongly garrisoned town all had fled, and the barbarians were not in a position for a real siege. But the leadership of the Romans was bad, and the military discipline so on the decline that not even the walls were occupied ; so the barbarians scaled them by night, without encountering resistance, and in the great and rich city enormous booty, including a number of ships, fell into their hands. They returned successful from the far distant land to the Maeotis.

Excited by this success, a second expedition of other To Bithynia. but neighbouring Scythian bands was in the following winter directed against Bithynia. It is significant of the unsettled state of things that the instigator of this movement was Chrysogonus, a Greek of Nicomedia, and that he was highly honoured by the barbarians for its successful result. This expedition was undertaken—as the necessary number of ships was not to be procured—partly by land partly by water ; it was only in the neighbourhood of Byzantium that the pirates succeeded in possessing themselves of a considerable number of fishing-boats, and so they arrived along the Asiatic coast at Chalcedon, whose strong garrison on this news ran off. Not merely this town fell into their hands, but also along the coast Nicomedia, Chios, Apamea ; in the interior Nicaea and Prusa ; Nicomedia and Nicaea they burnt down, and reached the river Rhyndacus. Thence they sailed home, laden with the treasures of the rich land and of its considerable cities.

The expedition against Bithynia had already been To Greece. undertaken in part by land ; all the more were the attacks that were directed against European Greece composed of piratical expeditions by land and sea. If Moesia and

Thrace were not permanently occupied by the Goths, they yet came and went there as if they were at home, and roved from thence far into Macedonia. Even Achaia expected under Valerian invasion from this side; Thermopylae and the Isthmus were barricaded, and the Athenians set to work to restore their walls that had lain in ruins since the siege by Sulla. The barbarians did not come then, nor by this route. But under Gallienus a fleet of five hundred sail, this time chiefly Heruli, appeared before the port of Byzantium, which, however, had not yet lost its capacity of defence; the ships of the Byzantines successfully repulsed the robbers. These sailed onward, showed themselves on the Asiatic coast before Cyzicus not formerly attacked, and arrived from thence by way of Lemnos and Imbros at Greece proper. Athens, Corinth, Argos, Sparta, were pillaged and destroyed. It was always something that, as in the times of the Persian wars, the citizens of the destroyed Athens, two thousand in number, laid an ambush for the retiring barbarians, and, under the leadership of their equally learned and brave captain, Publius Herennius Dexippus, of the old and noble family of the Kerykes, with support of the Roman fleet, inflicted a notable loss on the pirates. On the return home, which took place in part by the land route, the emperor Gallienus attacked them in Thrace at the river Nestus and put to death a considerable number of their men.[1]

The imperial government of the Gothic period.

In order completely to survey the measure of misfortune, we must take into account that in this empire going to shreds, and above all in the provinces overrun by the enemy, one officer after another grasped at the crown, which hardly any longer existed. It is not worth the trouble to record the names of these ephemeral

[1] The report of Dexippus as to this expedition is given in extract by Syncellus, p. 717 (where ἀνελόντος must be read for ἀνελόντες), Zosimus, i. 39, and the biographer of Gallienus, c. 13. *Fr.* 22 is a portion of his own narrative. In the continuator of Dio, on whom Zonaras depends, the event is placed under Claudius, through error or through falsification, which grudged this victory to Gallienus. The biography of Gallienus narrates the incident apparently twice, first shortly in c. 6 under the year 262; then better, under or after 265, in c. 13.

wearers of the purple ; it marks the situation that, after the devastation of Bithynia by the pirates, the emperor Valerian omitted to send thither an extraordinary commandant, because every general was, not without reason, regarded by him as a rival. This co-operated to produce the almost thoroughly passive attitude of the government in presence of this sore emergency. Yet, on the other hand, undoubtedly a good part of this irresponsible passiveness is to be traced to the personality of the rulers : Valerian was weak and aged, Gallienus vehement and dissolute, and neither the one nor the other was equal to the guidance of the vessel of the state in a storm. Marcianus, to whom Gallienus after the invasion of Achaia had committed the command in these regions, operated not without success ; but the matter did not gain any real turn for the better so long as Gallienus occupied the throne.

After the murder of Gallienus (268), perhaps on the news of it, the barbarians, again led by the Heruli, but this time with united forces, undertook an assault on the imperial frontier, such as there had not been hitherto, with a powerful fleet, and probably at the same time by land from the Danube.[1] The fleet had much to suffer from storms in the Propontis ; then it divided, and the Goths advanced partly against Thessaly and Greece, partly against Crete and Rhodes ; the chief mass resorted to Macedonia and thence penetrated into the interior, beyond doubt in combination with the bands that had marched into Thrace. But the emperor Claudius, who marched

Gothic victories of Claudius.

---

[1] In our traditional accounts this expedition appears as a pure sea-voyage, undertaken with (probably) 2000 ships (so the biography of Claudius ; the numbers 6000 and 900, between which the tradition in Zosimus, i. 42, wavers, are probably both corrupt) and 320,000 men. It is, however, far from credible that Dexippus, to whom these statements must be traced back, can have put the latter figure in this way. On the other hand, considering the direction of the expedition, in the first instance against Tomis and Marcianopolis, it is more than probable that in it the procedure described by Zos. i. 34 was followed, and a portion marched by land ; and under this supposition even a contemporary might well estimate the number of assailants at that figure. The course of the campaign, particularly the place of the decisive battle, shows that they had by no means to do merely with a fleet.

up in person with a strong force, brought relief at length to the Thessalonians oft besieged but now reduced to extremity ; he drove the Goths before him up the valley of the Axius (Vardar) and onward over the mountains to upper Moesia ; after various conflicts, with changing fortune of war, he achieved here in the Morava valley near Naissus a brilliant victory, in which 50,000 of the enemy are said to have fallen.   The Goths retired broken up, first in the direction towards Macedonia, then through Thrace to the Haemus, in order to put the Danube between themselves and the enemy.   A quarrel in the Roman camp, this time between infantry and cavalry, had almost given them once more a respite ; but, when it came to fighting, the cavalry could not bear to leave their comrades in the lurch, and so the united army was once more victorious.   A severe pestilence, which raged in all the years of distress, but especially then in those regions, and above all in the armies, did great injury doubtless to the Romans—the emperor Claudius himself succumbed to it—but the great army of the Northmen was utterly extirpated, and the numerous captives were incorporated in the Roman armies or made serfs.   The hydra of military revolutions, too, was in some measure subdued ; Claudius, and after him Aurelian, were masters in the empire after another fashion than could be said of Gallienus.   The renewal of the fleet, towards which a beginning had been made under Gallienus, would not be wanting.   The Dacia of Trajan was, and remained, lost ; Aurelian withdrew the posts still holding out there, and gave to the possessors dislodged or inclined for emigration new dwellings on the Moesian bank.   But Thrace and Moesia, which for a time had belonged more to the Goths than to the Romans, returned under Roman rule, and at least the frontier of the Danube was once more fortified.

Renewed fortifying of the Danube-frontier.

Character of the Gothic wars.

We may not assign to these Gothic and Scythian expeditions by land and by sea, which fill up the twenty years 250-269, such significance, as if the hordes moving forth had been minded to take permanent possession of the countries which they traversed.   Such a plan cannot be shown to have existed even for Moesia and Thrace, to say nothing of the more remote coasts ; hardly, moreover, were the assailants numerous enough to undertake invasions proper. As the bad government of the last rulers, and above all the untrustworthiness of the troops, far more than the superior power of the barbarians, called forth the flooding of the territory by land and sea robbers, so the re-establishment of internal order and the energetic demeanour of the government of themselves brought its deliverance. The Roman state could not yet be broken if it did not break itself. But still it was a great work to rally the government again as Claudius had done it. We know somewhat less even of him than of most regents of this time, as the probably fictitious carrying back of the Constantinian pedigree to him has repainted his portrait after the tame pattern of perfection ; but this very association, as well as the numberless coins struck in his honour after his death, show that he was regarded by the next generation as the deliverer of the state, and in this it cannot have been mistaken. These Scythian expeditions were at all events a prelude of the later migration of peoples ; and the destruction of cities, which distinguishes them from the ordinary piratic voyages, took place at that time to such an extent that the prosperity as well as the culture of Greece and Asia Minor never recovered from it.

On the re-established frontier of the Danube Aurelian consolidated the victory achieved, inasmuch as he conducted the defensive once more offensively, and, crossing the Danube at its mouth, defeated beyond it not only the Carpi, who thenceforth stood in client-relation to the Romans, but also the Goths under king Canabaudes. His successor Probus took, as was already stated, the remains of the Bastarnae, hard pressed by the Goths, over to the Roman bank, just as Diocletian in the year 295 took the remnant of the Carpi. This points to the fact that beyond the river the empire of the Goths was consolidating; but they came no further. The border-fortresses were reinforced ; counter-Aquincum (*contra Aquincum*, Pesth) was constructed in the year 294. The piratic expeditions did not

The Danubian wars to the end of the 3d century.

entirely disappear.   Under Tacitus hordes from the
Maeotis appeared in Cilicia.   The Franks, whom Probus
had settled on the Black Sea, procured for themselves
vessels, and sailed home to their North Sea, after plundering by the way on the Sicilian and African coasts.   By
land, too, there was no cessation of arms, as indeed all the
numerous Sarmatian victories of Diocletian, and a part of
his Germanic, would fall to the regions of the Danube ;
but it was only under Constantine that matters again came
to a serious war with the Goths, which had a successful
issue.   The preponderance of Rome was re-established
after the Gothic victory of Claudius as firmly as before.

Illyrising of the military force and of the govern- ment.
The war-history which we have just unfolded did not
fail to react with general and lasting effect upon the internal organisation of the Roman political and military
system.   It has already been pointed out that the corps
of the Rhine, holding in the early imperial period the
leading position in the army, yielded their primacy already
under Trajan to the legions of the Danube.   While under
Augustus six legions were stationed in the region of the
Danube and eight in that of the Rhine, after the Dacian
wars of Domitian and Trajan in the second century the
Rhine-camps numbered only four, the camps of the Danube
ten, and after the Marcomanian war even twelve, legions.
Inasmuch as since Hadrian's time the Italian element,
apart from the officers, had disappeared from the army,
and, taken on the whole, every regiment was recruited in
the district in which it was quartered, the most of the
soldiers of the Danubian army, and not less the centurions
who rose from the ranks, were natives of Pannonia, Dacia,
Moesia, Thrace.   The new legions formed under Marcus
proceeded from Illyricum, and the extraordinary supplemental levies which the troops then needed were probably
likewise taken chiefly from the districts in which the
armies were stationed.   Thus the primacy of the Danubian armies, which the war of the three emperors in the
time of Severus established and increased, was at the same
time a primacy of Illyrian soldiers ; and this reached a
very emphatic expression in the reform of the guard under

Severus. This primacy did not, properly speaking, affect the higher spheres of government, so long as the position of officer still coincided with that of imperial official, although the equestrian career was accessible to the common soldier through the intervening link of the centurionate at all times, and thus the Illyrians early found their way into that career ; as indeed, already, in the year 235, a native Thracian, Gaius Julius Varus Maximinus, in the year 248 a native Pannonian, Trajanus Decius, had in this way attained even to the purple. But when Gallienus, in a distrust certainly but too well justified, excluded the class of senators from serving as officers, what had hitherto held good as to the soldiers became necessarily extended to the officers also. It was thus simply a matter of course that the soldiers belonging to the army of the Danube, and mostly springing from Illyrian districts, played thenceforth the first part also in government, and, so far as the army made the emperors, these were likewise as to the majority Illyrians. Thus Gallienus was followed by Claudius the Dardanian, Aurelianus from Moesia, Probus from Pannonia, Diocletianus from Dalmatia, Maximianus from Pannonia, Constantius from Dardania, Galerius from Serdica ; as to the last named, an author writing under the Constantinian dynasty brings into prominence their descent from Illyricum, and adds that they, with little culture but good preliminary training by labour in the field and service in war, had been excellent rulers. Such service as the Albanians for a long time rendered to the Turkish empire, their predecessors likewise rendered to the Roman imperial state, when this had arrived at similar disorder and similar barbarism. Only, the Illyrian regeneration of the Roman imperial order may not be conceived of as a national reorganisation ; it was simply the propping up, by soldiers, of an empire utterly reduced through the misgovernment of rulers of gentler birth. Italy had wholly ceased to be military ; and history does not acknowledge the ruler's right without the warrior's power.

CHAPTER VII.

GREEK EUROPE.

Hellenism and Panhellenism. WITH the general intellectual development of the Hellenes the political development of their republics had not kept equal pace, or rather the luxuriant growth of the former had—just as too full a bloom bursts the calyx that contains it—not allowed any individual commonwealth to acquire the extent and stability which are preliminary conditions for the thorough formation of a state. The petty-state-system of individual cities or city-leagues could not but be stunted in itself or fall a prey to the barbarians. Panhellenism alone guaranteed alike the continued existence of the nation and its further development in presence of the alien races dwelling around it. It was realised by the treaty which king Philip of Macedonia, the father of Alexander, concluded in Corinth with the states of Hellas. This was, in name, a federal agreement, in fact, the subjection of the republics to the monarchy, but a subjection, which took effect only as regards external relations, seeing that the absolute generalship in opposition to the national foe was transferred by almost all towns of the Greek mainland to the Macedonian general, while in other respects freedom and autonomy were left to them ; and this was, as circumstances stood, the only possible realisation of Panhellenism and the form regulating in substance the future of Greece. It subsisted in presence of Philip and Alexander, though the Hellenic idealists were reluctant, as they always were, to acknowledge the realised ideal as such. Then, when the kingdom of Alexander fell to pieces, all was over, as with Panhellenism itself, so also with the union of the Greek towns under the monarchic supremacy ; and these wore out their last mental and material power in centuries of aimless striving, distracted between the alternating rule of the too powerful monarchies, and vain attempts, under cover of their quarrels, to restore the old particularism.

When at length the mighty republic of the west Hellas and Rome. entered into the conflict, hitherto in some measure balanced, of the monarchies of the east, and soon showed itself more powerful than each of the Greek states there striving with one another, the Panhellenic policy became renewed as the position of supremacy became fixed. Neither the Macedonians nor the Romans were Hellenes in the full sense of the word ; it is indeed the sad feature of Greek development that the Attic naval empire was more a hope than a reality, and the work of union could not emanate from the bosom of the nation itself. While in a national respect the Macedonians stood nearer to the Greeks than the Romans did, the commonwealth of Rome had politically far more of elective affinity to the Hellenic than the Macedonian hereditary kingdom. But—what is the chief matter—the attractive power of the Greek spirit was probably felt more permanently and deeply by the Roman burgesses than by the statesmen of Macedonia, just because the former stood at a greater distance from it than the latter. The desire to become at least internally Hellenised, to become partakers of the manners and the culture, of the art and the science of Hellas, to be—in the footsteps of the great Macedonian—shield and sword of the Greeks of the East, and to be allowed further to civilise this East not after an Italian but after a Hellenic fashion—this desire pervades the later centuries of the Roman republic and the better times of the empire with a power and an ideality which are almost no less tragic than that political toil of the Hellenes failing to attain its goal. For both sides strove after the impossible : to Hellenic Pan-hellenism there was refused duration, and to Roman Hellenism solid intrinsic worth. Nevertheless it has essentially influenced the policy of the Roman republic as well as that of the emperors. However much the Greeks, particularly in the last century of the republic, showed the Romans that their labour of love was a forlorn one, this made no change either in the labour or in the love.

The Greeks of Europe had been comprehended by the Roman republic under a single governorship named after the chief country Macedonia. When this was administratively dissolved at the beginning of the imperial period, there was at the same time conferred on the whole Greek name a religious bond of union, which attached itself to the old Delphic Amphictiony introduced for the sake of " a peace of God " and then misused for political ends. Under the Roman republic it had been in the main brought back to the original foundations ; Macedonia as well as Aetolia, both of which had intruded as usurpers, were again eliminated, and the Amphictiony once more embraced not all, but most, of the tribes of Thessaly and of Greece proper. Augustus caused the league to be extended to Epirus and Macedonia, and thereby made it in substance the representative of the Hellenic land in the wider sense alone suited to this epoch. A privileged position in this union alongside of the time-honoured Delphi was occupied by the two cities of Athens and Nicopolis, the former the capital of the old, the latter, according to Augustus's design, that of the new imperial, Hellenic body.[1] This new Amphictiony has a certain

The Amphictiony of Augustus.

---

[1] The organisation of the Delphic Amphictiony under the Roman republic is especially clear from the Delphic inscription, *C. I. L.* iii. p. 987 (comp. *Bull. de Corr. Hell.* vii. 427 ff.). The union was formed at that time of seventeen tribes with—together—twenty-four votes, all of them belonging to Greece proper or Thessaly; Aetolia, Epirus, Macedonia were wanting. After the remodelling by Augustus (Pausanias, x. 8) this organisation continued to subsist in other respects, except only that by restriction of the disproportionately numerous Thessalian votes those of the tribes hitherto represented were reduced to eighteen ; to these were now added Nicopolis in Epirus with six, and Macedonia likewise with six votes. Moreover the six votes of Nicopolis were to be given on each occasion, just as this continued to be the case, for the two of Delphi and the one of Athens ; whereas the other votes were given by the groups, so that, *e.g.* the one vote of the Peloponnesian Dorians alternated between Argos, Sicyon, Corinth, and Megara. The Amphictionies were even now not a collective representation of the European Hellenes, in so far as the

resemblance to the diet of the three Gauls (p. 93); just like the altar of the emperor at Lyons for this diet, the temple of the Pythian Apollo was the religious centre of the Greek provinces. But, while to the former withal a directly political activity was conceded, the Amphictions of this epoch, in addition to the religious festivals proper, simply attended to the administration of the Delphic sanctuary and of its still considerable revenues.[1] If its president in later times ascribed to himself " Helladarchy," this rule over Greece was simply an ideal conception.[2] But the official conserving of the Greek nationality remained always a token of the attitude which the new imperialism occupied towards it, and of its Philhellenism, far surpassing that of the republic.

Hand in hand with the ritual union of the European Greeks went the administrative breaking up of the Graeco-Macedonian governorship of the republic. It did not depend on the partition of the imperial administration between emperor and senate, as this whole territory and not less the adjacent Danubian regions were assigned in the original partition to the senate ; as little did military considerations here intervene, seeing that the whole peninsula up to the frontier of Thrace was—as protected partly by this region, partly by the garrisons on the Danube—always reckoned to belong to the pacified interior. If the Peloponnesus and the Attico-Boeotian

Province of Achaia.

---

tribes earlier excluded in Greece proper, a portion of the Peloponnesians, and the Aetolians not attached to Nicopolis, were not represented in it.

[1] The stated meetings in Delphi and at Thermopylae continued (Pausanias, vii. 24, 3 ; Philostratus, *Vita Apoll.* iv. 23), and of course also the carrying out of the Pythian games, along with the conferring of the prizes by the *collegium* of the Amphictiones (Philostratus, *Vitae Soph.* ii. 27); the same body has the administration of the " interest and revenues " of the temple (inscription of Delphi, *Rhein. Mus. N. F.* ii. 111), and fits up from it, for example at Delphi, a

library (Lebas, ii. 845) or puts up statues there.

[2] The members of the college of the Ἀμφικτίονες, or, as they were called at this epoch, Ἀμφικτύονες, were appointed by the several towns in the way previously described, sometimes from time to time (iteration : *C. I. Gr.* 1058), sometimes for life (Plutarch, *An seni,* 10), which probably depended on whether the vote was constant or alternating (Wilamowitz). Its president was termed in earlier times ἐπιμελητὴς τοῦ κοινοῦ τῶν Ἀμφικτύονων (Delphic inscriptions, *Rhen. Mus. N. F.* ii. 111 ; *C. I. Gr.* 1713), subsequently Ἑλλαδάρχης τῶν Ἀμφικτυόνων (*C. I. Gr.* 1124).

mainland obtained at that time its own proconsul and was separated from Macedonia—which perhaps Caesar may have already designed—it may be presumed that in that course, along with the general tendency not to magnify the senatorial governorships the dominant consideration was that of separating the purely Hellenic domain from what was half-Hellenic. The boundary of the province of Achaia was at first Oeta, and, even after the Aetolians were subsequently attached to it,[1] it did not go beyond the Achelous and Thermopylae.

The Greek towns under the Roman republic.

These arrangements concerned the country as a whole. We turn now to the position which was given to the several urban communities under the Roman rule.

The original design of the Romans—to attach the whole of the Greek urban communities to their own commonwealth, in a way similar to what had been done with the Italian—had undergone essential restrictions, in consequence of the resistance which these arrangements met with, especially in consequence of the insurrection of the

iii. 45.

Achaean league in the year 608 (iii. 47), and of the falling away of most of the Greek towns to king Mithra-

iii. 297.

dates in the year 666 (iii. 313). The city-leagues, the foundation of all development of power in Hellas as in Italy, and at first accepted by the Romans, were all of them—particularly the most important, the Peloponnesian, or, as it called itself, the Achaean—broken up, and

---

[1] The original bounds of the province are indicated by Strabo, xvii. 3, 25, p. 840, in the enumeration of the senatorial provinces : Ἀχαία μέχρι Θετταλίας καὶ Ἀιτωλῶν καὶ Ἀκαρνάνων καὶ τινων Ἡπειρωτικῶν ἐθνῶν ὅσα τῇ Μακεδονίᾳ προσώριστο, in which case the remaining part of Epirus appears to be assigned to the province of Illyricum (reckoned here by Strabo —erroneously as regards his time —among the senatorial). To take μέχρι inclusively is—apart from considerations of fact—unsuitable for this very reason, because according to the closing words the regions previously named " are assigned to Macedonia."

Subsequently we find the Aetolians annexed to Achaia (Ptolem. iii. 14). That Epirus also for a time belonged to it, is possible, not so much on account of the statement in Dio, liii. 12, which cannot be defended either for Augustus's time or for that of Dio, but because Tacitus on the year 17 (*Ann.* ii. 53) reckons Nicopolis to Achaia. But at least from the time of Trajan Epirus with Acarnania forms a procuratorial province of its own (Ptolem. iii. 13 ; *C. I. L.* iii. 536 ; Marquardt, *Staatsalth.* v. 1, 331). Thessaly and all the country northward of Oeta constantly remained with Macedonia.

the several cities were admonished to regulate their own public affairs. Moreover certain general rules were laid down by the leading power for the several communal constitutions, and according to this scheme these were reorganised in an anti-democratic sense. It was only within these limits that the individual community retained autonomy and a magistracy of its own. It retained also its own courts ; but the Greek stood at the same time *de jure* under the rods and axes of the praetor, and at least could be sentenced—on account of any offence which admitted of being regarded as rebellion against the leading power—by the Roman officials to a money-fine or banishment, or even capital punishment.[1] The communities taxed themselves ; but they had throughout to pay to Rome a definite sum, on the whole, apparently, not on a high scale. Garrisons were not assigned, as formerly in the Macedonian period, to the towns, for the troops stationed in Macedonia were in a position, should need arise, to move also into Greece. But a graver blame than that falling on the memory of Alexander through the destruction of Thebes rests on the Roman aristocracy for the razing of Corinth. The other measures, odious and exasperating as in part they were, particularly as imposed by foreign rule, might, taken as a whole, be unavoidable and have in various respects a salutary operation ; they were the inevitable palinode of the original Roman policy— in part truly impolitic—of forgiving and forgetting towards the Hellenes. But in the treatment of Corinth mercantile selfishness had after an ill-omened fashion shown itself more powerful than all Philhellenism.

Amidst all this, the fundamental idea of Roman

---

[1] Nothing gives a clearer idea of the position of the Greeks in the last century of the Roman republic than the letter of one of these governors to the Achaean community of Dyme (*C. I. Gr.* 1543). Because this community had given to itself laws that ran counter to the freedom granted in general to the Greeks (ἡ ἀποδεδομένη κατὰ κοινὸν τοῖς Ελλησιν ἐλευθερία) and to the organisation given by the Romans to the Achaeans (ἡ ἀποδοθεῖσα τοῖς Ἀχαιοῖς ὑπὸ Ῥωμαίων πολιτεία ; probably with the co-operation of Polybius, Pausan. viii. 30, 9), whereupon at all events tumults had arisen, the governor informs the community that he had caused the two ringleaders to be executed, and that a less guilty third person was exiled to Rome.

Freed com-
munities
under the
Roman re-
public.
policy—to confederate the Greek towns with the Italian—
was never forgotten; just as Alexander never wished to rule
Greece like Illyria and Egypt, so his Roman successors
never completely applied the subject-relation to Greece,
and even in the republican period essentially fell short
of urging the strict rights of the war forced upon the
Romans. Especially was this the case in dealing with
Athens. No Greek city from the standpoint of Roman
policy erred so gravely against Rome as this; its demeanour in the Mithradatic war would, had its case been
that of any other commonwealth, have inevitably led to
its being razed. But from the Philhellenic standpoint,
doubtless, Athens was the masterpiece of the world, and
for the genteel world of other lands similar leanings and
memories were associated with it, as for our cultivated
circles are connected with Pforta and Bonn. This consideration then, as formerly, prevailed. Athens was never
placed under the fasces of the Roman governor, and never
paid tribute to Rome; it always had a sworn alliance
with Rome, and granted aid to the Romans only in an extraordinary and, at least as to form, voluntary fashion. The
capitulation after the Sullan siege brought about doubtless
a change in the constitution of the community, but the
alliance was renewed,—in fact, even all extraneous possessions were given back, including the island of Delos itself,
which, when Athens passed over to Mithradates, had
broken off and constituted itself an independent commonwealth, and had been, by way of punishment for its fidelity
towards Rome, pillaged and destroyed by the Pontic
fleet.[1]

Sparta was treated with similar consideration, and that
doubtless in good part on account of its great name.
Some other towns of the freed communities to be afterwards named had this position already under the repub-

---

iii. 297,
300.

ii. 309

[1] Comp. iii. 312, 316. The Delian
excavations of recent years have furnished the proofs that the island, after
the Romans had once given it to
Athens (ii. 329), remained constantly
Athenian, and constituted itself, doubtless in consequence of the defection
of the Athenians from Rome, as a
community of the "Delians" (*Eph.
epig.* v. p. 604), but already six
years after the capitulation of Athens
was again Athenian (*Eph. epig.* v.
184 f.; Homolle, *Bull. de corr. Hell.*
viii. p. 142).

lic. Probably such exceptions occurred in every Roman province; but this was from the outset peculiar to the Greek territory, that precisely its two most noted cities were beyond the range of the subject-relation, which accordingly affected only the smaller commonwealths.

Even for the subject Greek cities alleviations were introduced already under the republic. The city-leagues, at first prohibited, gradually and very soon revived, especially the smaller and powerless ones, like the Boeotian;[1] with the becoming familiarised to foreign rule the oppositional tendencies disappeared which had brought about their abolition, and their close connection with the time-hallowed *cultus* carefully spared must have further told in their favour, as indeed it has already been observed that the Roman republic restored and protected the Amphictiony in its original non-political functions. Towards the end of the republican period the government seems even to have allowed the Boeotians to enter into a collective union with the small regions adjacent to the north and the island of Euboea.[2]

City-leagues under the republic.

[1] Whether the κοινὸν τῶν 'Αχαιῶν, which naturally does not occur in the republican period proper, was reconstituted already at the end of it or not till after the introduction of the imperial provincial organisation, is doubtful. Inscriptions like the Olympian one of the proquaestor Q. Ancharius Q. f. (*Arch. Zeitung*, 1878, p. 38, n. 114) speak rather in favour of the former supposition; yet it cannot with certainty be designated as pre-Augustan. The oldest sure evidence for the existence of this union is the inscription set up by it to Augustus in Olympia (*Arch. Zeitung*, 1877, p. 36, n. 33). Perhaps these were arrangements of the dictator Caesar, and in connection with the governor of "Greece,"—probably the Achaia of the imperial period—to be met with under him (Cicero, *Ad fam.* vi. 6, 10).—We may add that certainly also under the republic, according to the discretion of each governor for the time being, several communi-ties might meet for a definite object by deputies and adopt resolutions; as the κοινόν of the Siceliots thus decreed a statue to Verres (Cicero, *Verr.* i. 2, 46, 114), similar things must have occurred in Greece also under the republic. But the regular provincial diets with their fixed officers and priests were an institution of the imperial period.

[2] This is the κοινὸν Βοιωτῶν Εὐβοέων Λοκρῶν Φωκέων Δωριέων of the remarkable inscription probably set up shortly before the battle of Actium (*C. I. Att.* iii. 568). We cannot possibly with Dittenberger (*Arch. Zeitung*, 1876, p. 220) refer to this league the notice of Pausanias (vii. 16, 10), that the Romans "not many years" after the destruction of Corinth had compassion on the Hellenes, and had again allowed them the provincial unions (σύνεδρια κατὰ ἔθνος ἑκάστοις τὰ ἀρχαῖα); this applies to the minor individual leagues.

The copestone of the republican epoch was the atonement for the sack of Corinth made by the greatest of all Romans and of all Philhellenes, the dictator Caesar

iv. 544. (iv. 574), and the renewal of the star of Hellas in the form of an independent community of Roman citizens, the new "Julian Honour."

Achaia under the emperors. These were the relations which the imperial government at its outset found existing in Greece, and in these paths it went forward. The communities freed from the immediate interference of the provincial government and from the payment of tribute to the empire, with which the colonies of Roman burgesses in many respects stood on a level, comprehended far the largest and best part of the

Freed towns and Roman colonies. province of Achaia : in the Peloponnesus, Sparta, with its territory diminished no doubt, but yet once more embracing the northern half of Laconia,[1] still the counterpart of Athens as well in its petrified, old-fashioned institutions as in its at least outwardly preserved organisation and bearing ; further, the eighteen communities of the free Laconians, the southern half of the Laconian region, once Spartan subjects, organised by the Romans as an independent cities-league after the war against Nabis, and, like Sparta, invested with freedom by Augustus ;[2] lastly, in the region of the Achaeans not only Dyme, which had been already furnished by Pompeius with pirate-colonists, and then had received new Roman settlers from Caesar,[3] but above all Patrae, which Augustus, on account of its

---

[1] To it belonged not merely the neighbouring Amyclae, but also Cardamyle (by gift of Augustus, Pausan. iii. 26, 7), Pherae (Pausan. iv. 30, 2), Thuria (*ib.* iv. 31, 1), and for a time also Corone (*C. I. Gr.* 1258; comp. Lebas-Foucart, ii. 305) on the Messenian gulf; and further the island of Cythera (Dio, liv. 7).

[2] In the republican period this district appears as τὸ κοινὸν τῶν Λακεδαιμονίων (Foucart on Lebas, ii. p. 110); Pausanias (iii. 21, 6) is therefore wrong when he makes it only released from Sparta by Augustus. But they term themselves Ἐλευ-

θερολάκωνες only from the time of Augustus, and the bestowal of their freedom is therefore justly traced to him.

[3] There are coins of this city with the legend *c[olonia] I[ulia] D[ume]* and the head of Caesar, others with the legend *c[olonia] I[ulia] A[ugusta] Dum[e]* and the head of Augustus along with that of Tiberius (Imhoof-Blumer, *Monnaies grecques*, p. 165). That Augustus assigned Dyme to the colony of Patrae, is probably an error of Pausanias (vii. 17, 5) ; it remains indeed possible that Augustus in his later years ordained this union.

position favourable for commerce, transformed from a declining hamlet,—partly by drawing together the small surrounding townships, partly by settlement of numerous Italian
veterans—into the most populous and most flourishing
city of the peninsula, and constituted as a Roman burgess-
colony, under which was also placed Naupactus (the
Italian Lepanto) on the opposite Locrian coast.   On the
Isthmus Corinth, as it had formerly become a victim to
the advantages of its site, had now after its restoration
rapidly risen, similarly to Carthage, and had become the
richest in industry and in population of the cities of
Greece, as well as the regular seat of government.   As
the Corinthians were the first Greeks who had recognised
the Romans as countrymen by admission to the Isthmian
games (ii. 79), so this town now, although a Roman bur- ii. 75.
gess-community, took charge of this high Greek national
festival.   On the mainland there belonged to the freed
districts not merely Athens, with its territory embracing
all Attica and numerous islands of the Aegean Sea, but
also Tanagra and Thespiae, at that time the two most considerable towns of the Boeotian country, as also Plataeae ;[1]
in Phocis Delphi, Abae, Elateia, as well as the most considerable of the Locrian towns, Amphissa.   What the
republic had begun Augustus completed in the arrangement just set forth, which was at least in its main outlines
settled by him and was afterwards in substance maintained.   Although the communities of the province subject to the proconsul preponderated, certainly as to number,
and perhaps also as to the aggregate population, yet in
a genuinely Philhellenic spirit the towns of Greece most
distinguished by material importance or by great memories
were set free.[2]

---

[1] This is shown, at least for the
time of Pius, by the African inscription *C. I. L.* viii. 7059 (comp. Plutarch, *Arist.* 21).   The accounts of
authors as to the freed communities
give no guarantee at all for the completeness of the list.   Probably Elis
also belonged to them, which was not
affected by the catastrophe of the

Achaeans, and even subsequently
dated still by Olympiads, not by the
era of the province ; besides, it is
incredible that the town of the Olympic
festival should not have had the best
of legal rights.

[2] This is pointedly expressed by
Aristides in the panegyric on Rome
p. 224 Jebb : διατελεῖτε τῶν μὲν

Nero's liberation of Greece.

The last emperor of the Claudian house, one of the race of spoiled poets and so far at all events a born Philhellene, went further than Augustus had gone in this direction. In gratitude for the recognition which his artistic contributions had met with in the native land of the Muses Nero, like Titus Flamininus formerly (ii. 262)— and that once more in Corinth at the Isthmian games— declared the Greeks collectively to be rid of Roman government, free from tribute, and, like the Italians, subject to no governor. At once there arose throughout Greece movements, which would have been civil wars, if these people could have achieved anything more than brawling ; and after a few months Vespasian re-established the provincial constitution,[1] so far as it went, with the dry remark that the Greeks had unlearned the art of being free.

ii. 247.

Rights of the freed towns.

The legal position of the communities set free remained in substance the same as under the republic. They retained, so far as Roman burgesses were not in question, the full control of justice ; only, the general enactments as to appeals to the emperor on the one hand and to the senatorial authorities on the other seem to have also included the free towns.[2] Above all, they retained full self-determination and self-administration. Athens, for example, exercised in the imperial period the right of

Ἑλλήνων ὥσπερ τροφέων ἐπιμελόμενοι . . . τοὺς μὲν ἀρίστους καὶ πάλαι ἡγεμόνας (Athens and Sparta) ἐλευθέρους καὶ αὐτονόμους ἀφεικότες αὐτῶν, τῶν δ᾽ ἄλλων μετρίως . . . ἐξηγούμενοι, τοὺς δὲ βαρβάρους πρὸς τὴν ἑκάστοις αὐτῶν οὖσαν φύσιν παιδεύοντες.

[1] But the Hellenic literati remained grateful to their colleague and patron. In the Apollonius-romance (v. 41) the great sage from Cappadocia refuses Vespasian the honour of his company, because he had made the Hellenes slaves, just as they were on the point of again speaking Ionic or Doric, and writes to him various *billets* of delectable coarseness. A man of Soloi, who broke his neck and then became alive again, and on

this occasion saw all that Dante beheld, reported that he had met with Nero's soul, into which the agents of the world-judgment had driven flaming nails, and were employed in turning it into a viper ; but a heavenly voice had interposed, and ordered them to transform the man—on account of his Philhellenism when on earth—into a less repulsive animal (Plutarch, *De sera num. vind.*, at the end).

[2] At least in the ordinance of Hadrian regarding the deliveries of oil to the community incumbent on the Athenian landowners (*C. I. A.* iii. 18), the decision was indeed given to the *Boule* and the *Ekklesia*, but appeal to the emperor or the proconsul was allowed.

coinage, without even putting the emperor's head on its coins, and even on Spartan coins of the first imperial period it is frequently wanting. In Athens even the old reckoning by *drachmae* and *oboli* continued ; only that, it is true, the local Attic *drachma* of this period was nothing but small money current on the spot, and as to value circulated as *obolus* of the Attic imperial *drachma* or of the Roman *denarius*. Even the formal exercise of the right of war and peace was in individual treaties granted to such states.[1] Numerous institutions quite at variance with the Italian municipal organisation remained in existence, such as the annual change of the members of council and the daily allowance-moneys of these and the jurymen, which, at least at Rhodes, were still paid in the imperial period. As a matter of course, the Roman government nevertheless exercised continuously a regulative influence over the constitution even of the freed communities. Thus, for example, the Athenian constitution was, whether at the end of the republic or by Caesar or Augustus, modified in such a way that the right of bringing a proposal before the burgesses belonged no longer to every burgess, but, as according to the Roman arrangement, only to definite officials ; and among the great number of officials, who were mere figures, the conduct of business was placed in the hands of a single one—the *Strategos*. Certainly in this way various further reforms were carried out, the presence of which, in dependent as in independent Greece, we everywhere discern, without being able to determine the time and occasion of the reform. Thus the right, or rather the wrong, of asylums, which, as survivals of a lawless period, had now become pious retreats for bad debtors and criminals, was certainly, if not set aside, at least restricted in this province also. The institution of *proxenia*—originally an appropriate arrangement, that may be compared to our foreign consulates, but politically dangerous through the bestowal of full civil rights and

---

[1] What Strabo reports (xiv. 3, 3, p. 665) of the Lycian cities-league, in his time autonomous—that it had not the right of war and peace and that of alliance, except when the Romans allowed it or it operated for their advantage—may probably be, without ceremony, held to relate also to Athens.

often also of the privilege of exemption from taxes on the friendly foreigner, especially considering the extent to which it was granted—was set aside by the Roman government, apparently only at the beginning of the imperial period ; in room of which thereupon came, after the Italian fashion, the empty city-patronate, which did not come into contact with the system of taxation. Lastly, the Roman government, as wielding supreme sovereignty over these dependent republics just as over the client-princes, always regarded it as its right, and exercised the power, to cancel the free constitution in case of misuse, and to take the town into its own administration. But partly the sworn agreement, partly the powerlessness of these nominally allied states, gave to these treaties a greater stability than is discernible in the relation to the client-princes.

Diets of the Greek cities.

While the freed communities of Achaia retained their previous legal position under the empire, Augustus conferred on those communities of the province, in which freedom was not granted or possessed, a new and better legal position. As he had given to the Greeks of Europe a common centre in the reorganised Delphic Amphictiony, he allowed also all the towns of the province of Achaia, so far as they were placed under Roman administration, to constitute themselves as a collective union, and to meet annually in Argos, the most considerable town of non-free Greece, as a national assembly.[1] Thereby not merely

[1] At all events the hitherto known presidents of the κοινὸν τῶν Ἀχαιῶν, whose home is made out, are from Argos, Messene, Corone in Messenia (Foucart-Lebas, ii. 305), and there have been hitherto found among them not merely no citizens of the freed communities, such as Athens and Sparta, but also none of those belonging to the confederation of the Boeotians and allies (p. 259). Perhaps this κοινόν was legally restricted to the territory, which the Romans called the republic of Achaia—that is, that of the Achaean league at its overthrow—and the Boeotians and allies were united with the κοινόν proper of the Achaeans into that wider league, whose existence and diets in Argos are vouched for by the inscriptions of Acraephia mentioned in the next note. We may add that alongside of this κοινόν of the Achaeans there subsisted a still narrower one of the district of Achaia in the proper sense, whose representatives met in Aegium (Pausanias, vii. 24, 4), just as the κοινὸν τῶν Ἀρκάδων (*Arch. Zeit.* 1879, p. 139, n. 274), and numerous others. If, according to Pausanias, v. 12, 6, οἱ πάντες Ἕλληνες set up statues in Olympia to Trajan, and αἱ ἐς τὸ Ἀχαικὸν

was the Achaean league, dissolved after the Achaean war, reconstituted, but also the enlarged Boeotian union formerly mentioned (p. 259) was engrafted on it.   Probably it was just by the laying together of these two domains that the demarcation of the province of Achaia was brought about.   The new union of the Achaeans, Boeotians, Locrians, Phocians, Dorians, and Euboeans,[1] or, as it is usually designated like the province, the union of the Achaeans, presumably had rights neither more nor less than the other provincial diets of the empire.   A certain control of the Roman officials must have been intended in the case, and for that reason the towns not placed under the proconsul, like Athens and Sparta, must have been excluded from it.   This diet withal, like all similar ones, must have found the centre of its activity chiefly in the common *cultus* embracing the whole land.   But, while in the other provinces this *cultus* of the land preponderantly attached itself to Rome, the diet of Achaia was rather a focus of Hellenism, and was perhaps meant to be so.   Already under the Julian emperors it regarded itself as the true representative of the Greek nation, and assigned to its president the name of Helladarch, to itself even that of "the Panhellenes."[2]   The assembly thus

---

τελοῦσαι πόλεις to Hadrian, and no misunderstanding has here crept in, the latter dedication must have taken place at the diet of Aegium.

[1] So (only that the Dorians are wanting ; comp. p. 259, note 2) the union is termed on the inscription of Acraephia (Keil, *Syll. Inscr. Boeot.* n. 31).   But this very document, along with the contemporary one, *C. I. Gr.* 1625, furnishes a proof that the union under the emperor Gaius, instead of this doubtless strictly official appellation, designated itself also on the one hand as union of the Achaeans, on the other as τὸ κοινὸν τῶν Πανελλήνων, or ἡ σύνοδος τῶν Ἑλλήνων, also τὸ τῶν Ἀχαιῶν καὶ Πανελλήνων συνέδριον.   This grandiloquence is nowhere so glaringly prominent as in those Boeotian petty country-towns ; but even in Olympia,

where the union especially set up its memorials, it names itself for the most part no doubt τὸ κοινὸν τῶν Ἀχαιῶν, but shows often enough the same tendency ; *e.g.* when τὸ κοινὸν τῶν Ἀχαιῶν II. Αἴλιον Ἀρίστωνα . . . σύνπαντες οἱ"Ελληνες ἀνέστησαν (*Arch. Zeit.* 1880, p. 86, n. 344).   So too in Sparta, οἱ"Ελληνες set up a statue to Caesar Marcus ἀπὸ τοῦ κοινοῦ τῶν Ἀχαιῶν (*C. I. Gr.* 1318).

[2] In Asia, Bithynia, lower Moesia, the president of the Greek towns belonging to the province is also called Ἑλλαδάρχης, without more being thereby expressed than the contrast with the non-Greeks.   But, as the name of Hellenes is employed in Greece in a certain contrast to the strictly correct one of Achaeans, this is certainly suggested by the same tendency which was most clearly

deviated from its provincial basis, and its modest administrative functions fell into the background.

The Panhellenion of Hadrian in Athens. These Panhellenes therefore took to themselves this name by an abuse of language, and were simply tolerated by the government. But as Hadrian created a new Athens, so he created also a new Hellas. Under him the representatives of all the autonomous or non-autonomous towns of the province of Achaia were allowed to constitute themselves in Athens as united Greece, as the Panhellenes.[1] The national union, often dreamed of and never attained in better times, was thereby created, and what youth had wished for old age possessed in imperial fulness. It is true that the new Panhellenion did not obtain political prerogatives; but there was no lack of what imperial favour and imperial gold could give. There arose in Athens the temple of the new Zeus Panhellenios, and brilliant popular festivals and games were connected with this foundation, the carrying out of which pertained to the *collegium* of the Panhellenes, and primarily to the priest of Hadrian as the living god who founded them. One of the acts, which these performed every year, was the offering of sacrifice to Zeus the Deliverer at Plataeae, in memory of the Hellenes that fell there in

---

marked in the Panhellenes of Argos. Thus we find στρατηγὸς τοῦ κοινοῦ τῶν Ἀχαιῶν καὶ προστάτης διὰ βίου τῶν Ἑλλήνων (*Arch. Zeit.* 1877, p. 192, n. 98), or on another document of the same man προστάτης διὰ βίου τοῦ κοινοῦ τῶν Ἀχαιῶν (Lebas-Foucart, n. 305); an ἄρξας τοῖς Ἕλλησιν σύνπασιν (*Arch. Zeit.* p. 195, n. 106) στρατηγὸς ἀσυνκρίτως ἄρξας τῆς Ἑλλάδος (*ib.* 1877, p. 40, n. 42) στρατηγὸς καὶ Ἑλλαδάρχης (*ib.* 1876, n. 8, p. 226), all likewise on inscriptions of the κοινὸν τῶν Ἀχαιῶν. That in this κοινόν, though it may perhaps be deemed to refer merely to the Peloponnesus (p. 264, note), the Panhellenic tendency none the less asserted itself, may well be conceived.

[1] The Hadrianic Panhellenes name themselves τὸ κοινὸν συνέδριον τῶν Ἑλλήνων τῶν εἰς Πλατηὰς συνιόντων (Thebes: Keil, *Syll. Inscr. Boeot.* n. 31, comp. Plutarch, *Arist.* 19, 21); κοινὸν τῆς Ἑλλάδος (*C. I. Gr.* 5852); τὸ Πανελλήνιον (*ib.*). Its president is termed ὁ ἄρχων τῶν Πανελλήνων (*C. I. A.* iii. 681, 682; *C. I. Gr.* 3832, comp. *C. I. A.* iii. 10: ἀ[ρτ]-άρχων τοῦ ἱερωτάτου ἀ[γῶνος τοῦ Π]αν[ελ]ληνίου), the individual deputy Πανέλλην (*e.g. C. I. A.* iii. 534; *C. I. Gr.* 1124). Alongside of these in the period subsequent to Hadrian the κοινὸν τῶν Ἀχαιῶν and its στρατηγὸς or Ἑλλαδάρχης still occur, who are probably to be distinguished from those just mentioned, although the latter now sets up his honorary decrees not merely in Olympia, but also in Athens (*C. I. A.* 18; second example in Olympia, *Arch. Zeit.* 1879, p. 52).

battle against the Persians, on the anniversary of the battle, the 4th Boedromion : this marks its tendency.[1] Still more clearly was this shown in the fact that the Greek towns outside of Hellas, which appeared worthy of the national fellowship, had ideal certificates of Hellenism issued to them by the assembly in Athens.[2]

While the imperial rule in its whole wide range encountered the devastations of a twenty years' civil war, and in many places its consequences were never entirely healed, probably no domain was so severely affected by them as the Greek peninsula. Fate had so arranged, that the three great decisive battles of this epoch—Pharsalus, Philippi, Actium—were fought on its soil or on its coast ; and the military operations, which with both parties led up to these battles, had here above all demanded their sacrifices of human life and human happiness. Even Plutarch was told by his great-grand-father how the officers of Antonius had compelled the citizens of Chaeronea, when they no longer possessed slaves or beasts of burden, to drag their last grain on their own shoulders to the nearest port to be shipped for the army ; and how thereupon, just as the second convoy was about to depart, the accounts of the battle of Actium arrived as glad news of relief. The first thing that Caesar did after the victory was to distribute the enemy's stores of grain that had fallen into his power among the famishing population of Greece. This heaviest measure

The decay of Hellas.

---

[1] That the remark of Dio of Prusa, *Or.* xxxviii. p. 148 R., as to the dispute of the Athenians and the Lacedaemonians ὑπὲρ τῆς προπομπείας, refers to the festival at Plataeae, is evident from (Lucian) Ἔρωτες 18, ὡς περὶ προπομπείας ἀγωνιούμενοι Πλαταιᾶσιν. The sophist Irenaeus also wrote περὶ τῆς Ἀθηναίων προπομπείας (Suidas, *s. v.*), and Hermogenes, *de ideis*, ii. p. 373. Walz gives as the topic spoken of Ἀθηναῖοι καὶ Λακεδαιμόνιοι περὶ τῆς προπομπείας κατὰ τὰ Μηδικὰ (communication from Wilamowitz).

[2] Two of these are preserved, for

Cibyra in Phrygia (*C. I. Gr.* 5882), issued from the κοινὸν τῆς Ἑλλάδος by a δόγμα τοῦ Πανελληνίου ; and for Magnesia on the Maeander (*C. I. Att.* iii. 16). In both the good Hellenic descent of the corporations concerned is brought out along with their other services to the Hellenes. Characteristic are also the letters of recommendation, with which these Panhellenes furnish a man who had merited well of their commonwealth to the community of his home Aezani in Phrygia, to the emperor Pius, and to the Hellenes in Asia generally (*C. I. Gr.* 3832, 3833, 3834).

of suffering fell upon a specially weak power of resistance. Already, more than a century before the battle of Actium, Polybius had stated that unfruitfulness in marriage and diminution of the population had in his time come over all Greece, without any diseases or severe wars befalling the land. Now these scourges had emerged in fearful fashion ; and Greece remained desolate for all time to come. Plutarch thinks that throughout the Roman empire the population had fallen off in consequence of the devastating wars, but most of all in Greece, which was not now in a position to furnish from the better circles of the citizens the 3000 hoplites, with which once the smallest of the Greek districts, Megara, had fought at Plataeae.[1] Caesar and Augustus had attempted to remedy this depopulation, which alarmed even the government, by the despatch of Italian colonists, and, in fact, the two most flourishing towns of Greece were these very colonies ; the later governments did not repeat such consignments. The background to the charming Euboean peasant-idyll of Dio of Prusa is formed by a depopulated town, in which numerous houses stand empty, flocks are fed at the council-hall and at the city register-house, two-thirds of the territory lie untilled for want of hands ; and when the narrator reports this as falling within his own experience, he therewith assuredly describes not unaptly the circumstances of numerous small Greek country towns in the time of Trajan. " Thebes in Boeotia," says Strabo in the Augustan age, " is now hardly to be termed even a goodly village, and the same holds true of all the Boeotian towns, with the exception of Tanagra and Thespiae." But not merely did men dwindle away as regards number ; the type also declined. " There are doubtless still beautiful women," says one of the finest observers about the end of the first

---

[1] Beyond doubt Plutarch in these words (*de defectu orac.* 8) does not mean to say that Greece was not able at all to furnish 3000 men capable of arms, but that, if burgess-armies of the old sort were to be formed, they would not be in a position to set on foot 3000 " hoplites." In this sense the expression may well be correct, so far as correctness can be expected at all in the case of general complaints of this sort. The number of communities of the province amounted nearly to a hundred.

century,[1] " but beautiful men one sees no longer ; the Olympian victors of more recent times appear, compared with
the older, inferior and common, partly no doubt owing to
the fault of the artists, but chiefly because they are just
what they are." The bodily training of the youth had
been carried in this promised land of ephebi and athletes
to such an extent, as if the very aim of the communal
constitution were to rear the boys as gymnasts and the men
as boxers ; but, if no province possessed so many artists
for the ring, none supplied so few soldiers to the imperial
army. Even from the instruction of the Athenian youth—
which in the olden time embraced spear-throwing, shooting
with the bow, the use of missiles, the marching out and
pitching of the camp—this playing at soldiers on the part
of the boys now disappears. The Greek towns of the
empire were virtually not taken account of in the levy,
whether because their recruits appeared physically incapable, or because this element appeared dangerous in
the army; it was an imperial pleasantry that the caricature of Alexander, Severus Antoninus, reinforced the
Roman army for the conflict with the Persians by some
companies of Spartiates.[2] Whatever was done for internal
order and security must have emanated from the individual communities, as Roman troops were not stationed
in the province ; Athens, for example, maintained a garrison in the island of Delos, and probably a division of
militia lay also in the citadel.[3] In the crises of the third
century the general levy of Elateia (p. 242) and that of
Athens (p. 246) valiantly repulsed the Costoboci and the
Goths ; and, after a worthier fashion than the grandchildren
of the combatants of Thermopylae in Caracalla's Persian
war, in the Gothic the grandchildren of the victors of
Marathon inscribed their names for the last time in the
annals of ancient history. But, though such incidents

---

[1] [Dio, *Orat.* xxi. 501 R.]

[2] This is told to us by Herodian,
iv. 8, 3, c. 9, 4, and we have the
inscriptions of two of these Spartiates,
Nicocles, ἐστρατευμένος δὶς κατὰ
Περσῶν (*C. I. Gr.* 1253), and Dios-

coras, ἀπελθὼν εἰς τὴν εὐτυχεστάτην
συμμαχίαν (= expeditio) τὴν κατὰ
Περσῶν (*C. I. Gr.* 1495).

[3] The φρόυριον (*C. I. A.* iii. 826)
cannot well be understood otherwise.

must preclude us from treating the Greeks of this epoch absolutely as a decayed rabble, yet the decline of the population as regards number and vigour steadily continued even during the better imperial period, until, from the end of the second century, the diseases which severely visited these lands, likewise the inroads of land and sea pirates who particularly affected the east coast, and lastly, the collapse of the imperial power in the time of Gallienus, raised the chronic suffering into an acute catastrophe.

Greek tone of feeling. The decay of Hellas, and the feelings which it called forth among the best men, come before us after a striking manner in the appeal which one of these, the Bithynian Dio, addressed about the time of Vespasian to the Rhodians. These were not unjustly regarded as the most excellent of the Hellenes. In no city were the lower population better cared for, and nowhere did that care bear more the stamp of giving not alms but work. When, after the great civil war, Augustus made all private debts irrecoverable at law in the East, the Rhodians alone rejected the dangerous favour. Although the great epoch of Rhodian commerce was over, there were still in Rhodes numerous flourishing branches of business and wealthy houses.[1] But many evils had invaded the place, and the philosopher demands that they be done away, not so much, as he says, for the sake of the Rhodians, as for the sake of the Hellenes in common. "Once upon a time the honour of Hellas rested on many, and many increased its renown—you, the Athenians, the Lacedaemonians, Thebes, Corinth for a time, at a remote period Argos. But now the others are as nothing; for some are totally decayed and destroyed, others conduct them-

---

[1] "You have no want of means," says Dio (*Or.* xxxi. p. 566), "and there are thousands upon thousands here, for whom it would be advantageous to be less rich;" and further on (p. 620), "you are richer than any one else in Hellas. Your ancestors possessed not more than you do. The island has not become worse; you draw the profit of Caria and a part of Lycia; a number of towns are tributary to you; the city is always receiving rich gifts from numerous citizens." He further states that new expenses had not been added, but the earlier outlays for army and fleet had almost fallen into abeyance; they had to supply annually at Corinth (and so to the Roman fleet) but one or two small vessels.

selves as you know, and are dishonoured and destroyers of their old renown.   You are surviving ; you alone are still somewhat and are not utterly despised ; for, after the way in which those go to work, all Hellenes would long ago have sunken more deeply than the Phrygians and the Thracians.   As when a great and noble family is reduced to a single survivor, and the sin which this last of the house commits brings all his ancestors into dishonour, so you stand in Hellas.   Believe not that you are the first of the Greeks ; you are the only ones.   If we look at those pitiful scoundrels, the great destinies of the past become themselves inconceivable ; the stones and ruins of cities show more clearly the pride and the greatness of Hellas than these descendants not even worthy of Mysian ancestors ; and better than with towns inhabited by such as these has it fared with those cities which lie in ruins, for their memory remains in honour and their well-acquired renown unstained—better burn the carcase than allow it to lie rotting." [1]

We shall not disparage this noble spirit of a scholar who measured the petty present by the great past, and, as could not fail to be the case, looked at the one with indignant eyes and at the other in the transfigured glory of what had been, if we point out the fact that the good old Hellenic habits were at that time and even long afterwards not merely to be found in Rhodes, but were in many respects still everywhere alive.   The inward independence, the well warranted self-esteem of the nation that was still standing at the head of civilisation had not disappeared in the Hellenes even of this age, amidst all the pliancy of subjection and all the humility of parasitism. The Romans borrowed the gods from the old Hellenes and the form of administration from the Alexandrines ; they sought to master the Greek language and to Hellenise their own in measure and style.   The Hellenes even of the imperial period did not pursue a like course ; the national deities of Italy, like Silvanus and the Lares, were not adored in Greece, and it never entered into the mind

The good old manners.

[1] [Dio, *Orat.* xxxi. 649, 650.]

of any Greek urban community to introduce at home the political organisation which their Polybius celebrates as the best. So far as the knowledge of Latin was a condition for the career of the higher as of the lower magistracies, the Greeks who entered upon this career acquired it ; for, though practically it only occurred to the emperor Claudius to withdraw the Roman franchise from the Greeks who did not understand Latin, certainly the real execution of the rights and duties connected with it was possible only for one who was master of the imperial language. But, apart from public life, Latin was never so learned in Greece as Greek in Rome. Plutarch, who, as an author, joined as it were in marriage the two halves of the empire, and whose parallel biographies of famous Greeks and Romans recommended themselves and were effective above all by this juxtaposition, understood not very much more of Latin than Diderot of Russian, and at least, as he himself says, did not master the language ; the Greek literati having a real command of Latin were either officials, like Appian and Dio Cassius, or neutrals, like king Juba.

Really Greece was far less changed in itself than in its external position. The government of Athens was truly bad, but even in the time of Athenian greatness it had not been at all exemplary. "There is," says Plutarch, "the same national type, the same disorders, earnest and jest, charm and malice, as among their ancestors." This epoch, too, still exhibits in the life of the Greek people individual features which are worthy of its civilising leadership. The gladiatorial games, which spread from Italy everywhere, especially to Asia Minor and to Syria, found admission to Greece latest of all lands ; for a considerable period they were confined to the half-Italian Corinth, and when the Athenians, in order not to be behind that city, introduced them also among themselves without listening to the voice of one of their best men, who asked them whether they would not first set up an altar to the God of compassion, several of the noblest turned indignantly away from the city of their fathers that so dishonoured itself. In

no country of the ancient world were slaves treated with
such humanity as in Hellas; it was not the law, but custom
that forbade the Greek to sell his slaves to a non-Greek
master, and so banished from this region the slave-trade
proper.   Only here in the imperial period do we find the
non-free people provided for in the burgess-feasts and in
largesses of oil to the burgesses.[1]   Only here could one
who was not free, like Epictetus under Trajan, in his more
than modest outward existence in the Epirot Nicopolis,
hold intercourse with respected men of senatorial rank,
after the manner of Socrates with Critias and Alcibiades,
so that they listened to his oral instructions as disciples
to the master, and took notes of, and published, his conversations.   The alleviations of slavery by the imperial
law are essentially traceable to the influence of Greek
views, *e.g.* with the emperor Marcus, who looked up tc
that Nicopolitan slave as his master and model.

The author of a dialogue preserved among those of
Lucian gives an unsurpassed description of the demeanour
of the polished Athenian citizen, amidst his narrow circumstances, overagainst the genteel and rich travelling public
of doubtful culture or else undoubted coarseness ; how
the rich foreigner has been weaned from appearing in the
public bath with a host of attendants, as if he were not
otherwise certain of his life in Athens and there were no
peace in the land ; and how he was weaned from showing
himself on the street with his purple dress by people making
the friendly inquiry whether it was not that of his mamma.
He draws a parallel between Roman and Athenian
existence ; in the former the burdensome banquets and
the still more burdensome brothels, the inconvenient
convenience of the swarms of menials and the domestic
luxury, the troubles of a dissolute life, the torments of
ambition, all the superfluity, the multifariousness, the

*Parallel be-
tween Ro-
man and
Athenian
life.*

---

[1] At the popular festivals, which
in Tiberius's time a rich man gave at
Acraephia in Boeotia, he invited the
grown-up slaves, and his wife the
female slaves, as guests along with the
free (*C. I. Gr.* 1625). In an endowment for the distribution of oil at
the fencing - institute (γυμνάσιον) of
Gytheion in Laconia it is ordained
that on six days in the year the
slaves should also partake in it
(Lebas-Foucart n. 243*a*).   Similar
largesses occur in Argos (*C. I. Gr.*
1122, 1123).

unrest of the doings of the capital; in the latter the charm
of poverty, the free talk in the friendly circle, the leisure
for intellectual enjoyment, the possibility of peace and of
joy in life—" How couldest thou," one Greek in Rome
asks another, "leave the light of the sun, Hellas, and its
happiness and its freedom for the sake of this crowd ? "
In this fundamental keynote all the more finely and purely
organised natures of this epoch are agreed ; the very best
Hellenes would rather not exchange with the Romans.
There is hardly anything equally pleasing in the literature
of the imperial period with the already mentioned Euboean
idyll of Dio ; it depicts the existence of two families
of hunters in the lonely forest, whose property consists
of eight goats, a cow without a horn, and a fine calf, four
sickles and three hunting-spears, who know nothing either
of gold or of taxes, and who, when placed before the
raging burgess-assembly of the city, are by the latter dismissed at length unmolested to joy and to freedom.

Plutarch.   The real embodiment of this poetically transfigured
conception of life is Plutarch of Chaeronea, one of the
most charming, most fully informed, and withal most
effective writers of antiquity.   Sprung from a family of
means in that small Boeotian country-town, and introduced to the full Hellenic culture, first at home and then
at Athens and at Alexandria ; familiar, moreover, with
Roman affairs through his studies and manifold personal
relations, as well as by his travels in Italy, he disdained to
enter into the service of the state or to adopt the professional career after the usual manner of gifted Greeks ;
he remained faithful to his home, enjoying domestic life,
in the finest sense of the word, with his excellent wife and
his children, and with his friends, male and female ; con-
tenting himself with the offices and honours which his own
Boeotia was able to offer to him, and with the moderate
property which he had inherited.   In this Chaeronean
the contrast between the Hellenes and the Hellenised
finds expression ; such a type of Greek life was not
possible in Smyrna or in Antioch ; it belonged to the
soil like the honey of Hymettus.   There are men enough

of more powerful talents and of deeper natures, but hardly any second author has known in so happy a measure how to reconcile himself serenely to necessity, and how to impress upon his writings the stamp of his tranquillity of spirit and his blessedness of life.

The self-mastery of Hellenism cannot manifest itself in the field of public life with the purity and beauty which it presents in the quiet homestead, after which history happily does not inquire any more than it inquires after history. When we turn to public affairs, there is more to be told of misrule than of rule, both as regards the Roman government and the Greek autonomy. There was no want of goodwill on the part of the former, in so far as Roman Philhellenism dominated the imperial period even much more decidedly than the republican. It expresses itself everywhere in great matters as in small, in the prosecution of the Hellenising of the Eastern provinces and the recognition of a double official language for the empire, as well as in the courteous forms in which the government dealt, and enjoined its officials to deal, even with the pettiest Greek community.[1] Nor did the emperors fail to favour this province with gifts and buildings ; and, though most things of this sort came to Athens, Hadrian at any rate constructed a great aqueduct for the benefit of Corinth, and Pius the hospital at Epidaurus. But the considerate treatment of the Greeks in general, and the special kindness which was shown by the imperial government to Hellas proper, because it was accounted in a certain sense as, like Italy, " motherland," did not redound

[1] In answer to one of the numerous complaints, with which the towns of Asia Minor plagued the government on account of their disputes as to titles and rank, Pius tells the Ephesians (Waddington, *Aristide*, p. 51), that he was glad to hear that the Pergamenes had given to them the new title ; that the Smyrnaeans had doubtless merely by accident omitted it, and would certainly in future be ready to do what was correct, if they —the Ephesians—would accord to them their right titles. To a small Lycian town, which applied to the proconsul for the confirmation of a resolution adopted by it, the latter replied (Benndorf, *Lykische Reise*, i. 71), that excellent ordinances require only praise, not confirmation ; the latter is implied in the case. The rhetorical schools of this epoch furnished also the draughtsmen for the imperial chancery; but this alone mattered little. It belonged to the essence of the principate not to accentuate outwardly the subject-relation, and especially not against the Greeks.

Misgovernment of the provincial administration.

to the true benefit either of the government or of the country. The annual changes of the chief magistrates, and the remiss control of the central position, made all the senatorial provinces, so far as rule by governors went, feel rather the oppression than the blessing of unity of administration, and doubly so in proportion to their smallness and their poverty. Even under Augustus himself these evils prevailed to such a degree that it was one of the first acts of the reign of his successor to take Greece as well as Macedonia into his own power,[1] as it was alleged, temporarily, but in fact for the whole duration of his reign. It was very constitutional, but perhaps not quite so wise on the part of the emperor Claudius, when he came to power, that he re-established the old arrangement. Thenceforward the matter remained on this footing, and Achaia was administered by magistrates not nominated, but chosen by lot, till this form of administration fell altogether into abeyance.

Misgovernment of the free towns. But the case was far worse with the communities of Greece exempted from the rule of the governor. The design of favouring these commonwealths—by freeing them from tribute and levy, and not less by the slightest possible restriction of the rights of the sovereign state— led at least in many cases to the opposite result. The intrinsic falseness of the institutions avenged itself. No doubt among the less privileged or better administered communities the communal autonomy may have fulfilled its aim ; at least we do not learn that Sparta, Corinth, Patrae fared specially ill in this respect. But Athens was **Administration of Athens.** not made for self-administration, and affords the disheartening picture of a commonwealth pampered by the supreme power, and financially as well as morally ruined. By rights it ought to have found itself in a flourishing

---

[1] A formal alteration of the tax-organisation does not follow of itself from this change, and is not hinted at in Tacitus, *Ann.* i. 76 ; if the arrangement was made because the provincials complained of the pressure of taxation (*onera deprecantes*), better governors might help the provinces by suitable redistribution, and eventually by procuring remission. That the furtherance of the imperial postal service was felt specially in this province as an oppressive burden is shown by the edict of Claudius from Tegea (*Ephem. ep.* v. p. 69).

condition. If the Athenians were unsuccessful in uniting the nation under their hegemony, this city was the only one in Greece, as in Italy, which carried out completely the union of its territory : no city of antiquity elsewhere possessed a domain of its own, such as was Attica, of about 700 square miles, double the size of the island of Rügen. But even beyond Attica they retained what they possessed, as well after the Mithradatic war by favour of Sulla, as after the Pharsalian battle, in which they had taken the side of Pompeius, by the favour of Caesar—he asked them only how often they would still ruin themselves and trust to be saved by the renown of their ancestors. To the city there still belonged not merely the territory, formerly possessed by Haliartus, in Boeotia (ii. 329), but also on ii. 309 their own coast Salamis, the old starting-point of their dominion of the sea, and in the Thracian Sea the lucrative islands Scyros, Lemnos, and Imbros, as well as Delos in the Aegean ; it is true this island, after the end of the republic, was no longer the central emporium of trade with the East, now that the traffic had been drawn away from it to the ports of the west coast of Italy, and this was an irreparable loss for the Athenians. Of the further grants, which they had the skill to draw by flattery from Antonius, Augustus, against whom they had taken part, took from them certainly Aegina and Eretria in Euboea, but they were allowed to retain the smaller islands of the Thracian Sea, Icus, Peparethus, Sciathus, and further Ceos confronting the promontory of Sunium ; and Hadrian, moreover, gave to them the best part of the great island Cephallenia in the Ionian Sea. It was only by the emperor Severus, who bore them no good will, that a portion of these extraneous possessions was withdrawn from them. Hadrian further granted to the Athenians the delivery of a certain quantity of grain at the expense of the empire, and by the extension of this privilege, hitherto reserved for the capital, acknowledged Athens, as it were, as another imperial metropolis. Not less was the blissful institute of alimentary endowments, which Italy had enjoyed since Trajan's time, extended by Hadrian to Athens, and the

capital requisite for this purpose certainly presented to
the Athenians from his purse. An aqueduct, which he
likewise dedicated to his Athens, was only completed
after his death by Pius. To this falls to be added the
conflux of travellers and of students, and the endowments
bestowed on the city in ever increasing number by Roman
grandees and by foreign princes.

Yet the community was in constant distress. The
right of citizenship was dealt with not merely in the way
everywhere usual of giving and taking, but was made
formally and openly a matter of traffic, so that Augustus
interfered to prohibit the evil. Once and again the
council of Athens resolved to sell this or that one of its
islands; and not always was there found a rich man ready
to make sacrifices like Julius Nicanor, who, under
Augustus, bought back for the bankrupt Athenians the
island of Salamis, thereby earning from its senate the
honorary title of the "new Themistocles," as well as,
seeing that he also made verses, that of the "new Homer,"
and—together with the noble councillors—from the public
well-merited derision. The magnificent buildings with
which Athens continued to embellish herself were obtained
without exception from foreigners, among others from the
rich kings Antiochus of Commagene and Herod of
Judaea, but above all from the emperor Hadrian, who laid
out a complete "new town" (*novae Athenae*) on the Ilisus,
and—besides numberless other buildings, including the
already mentioned Panhellenion—worthily brought to
completion the wonder of the world, seven centuries after
it had been begun, the gigantic building, commenced by
Pisistratus, of the Olympieion, with its 120 columns partly
still standing, the largest of all that are erect at the present
day. This city itself was without money, not merely for
its harbour-walls, which now certainly might be dispensed
with, but even for its harbour. In Augustus's time the
Piraeus was a small village of a few houses, only visited
for the sake of the masterpieces of painting in the halls of
the temples. There was hardly any longer commerce or
industry in Athens ; or rather for the citizens as a body

as well as individually there was but a single flourishing trade—begging.

Nor did the matter end with financial distress.   The Street-riots. world doubtless had peace, but not the streets and squares of Athens.   Even under Augustus an insurrection in Athens assumed such proportions that the Roman government had to take steps against the free city ;[1] and though this event stands isolated, riots on the street on account of the price of bread and on other trifling occasions belonged in Athens to the order of the day.   The prospect must not have been much better in numerous other free towns, of which there is less mention.   To give criminal justice absolutely into the hands of such a burgess-body could hardly be justified ; and yet it belonged *de jure* to the communities admitted to international federation, like Athens and Rhodes.   When the Athenian Areopagus in the time of Augustus refused to release from punishment on the intercession of a Roman of rank a Greek condemned for forgery, it must have been within its right ; but when the Cyzicenes under Tiberius imprisoned Roman burgesses, and under Claudius the Rhodians even nailed a Roman burgess to the cross, these were formal violations of law, and a similar occurrence under Augustus cost the Thessalians their autonomy.   Arrogance and aggression are not excluded by absence of power—are not seldom even ventured on by weak clients.   With all respect for great memories and sworn treaties, these free states could not but appear to every conscientious government not much less than an infringement ot the general order of the empire, like the still more time-hallowed right of asylum in the temples.

Ultimately the government acted with decision, and Cor- placed the free towns, as regards their economy, under the rectores. superintendence of officials of imperial nomination, who, at all events in the first instance, are described as extra-

---

[1] The Athenian insurrection under Augustus is certainly attested by the notice derived from Africanus in Eusebius, *ad ann. Abr.* 2025 (whence Orosius, vi. 22, 2).   The riots against the *strategoi* are often mentioned ; Plutarch, *Q. sympos.* viii. 3, *init.* ; (Lucian), *Demonax*, 11, 64 ; Philostratus, *Vit. soph.* i. 23, ii. 8, 11.

ordinary commissioners " for the correction of evils prevailing in the free towns," and thence subsequently bear the designation " Correctores " as their title. The germs of this office may be traced back to the time of Trajan ; we find them as standing officials in Achaia in the third century. These officials, appointed by the emperor, and acting alongside of the proconsuls, occur in no part of the Roman empire so early, and are in no case found so early permanent, as in Achaia, which half consisted of free cities.

Clinging to memories of the past.

The self-esteem of the Hellenes, well-warranted in itself and fostered by the attitude of the Roman government, and perhaps still more by that of the Roman public— the consciousness of intellectual primacy—called into life among them a *cultus* of the past, which was compounded of a faithful clinging to the memories of greater and happier times and a quaint reverting of matured civilisation to its in part very primitive beginnings.

Religion.

To foreign worships, if we keep out of view the service of the Egyptian deities already earlier naturalised by trading intercourse, particularly that of Isis, the Greeks in Hellas proper sustained throughout the attitude of declining them ; if this held least true in the case of Corinth, Corinth was also the least Greek town of Hellas. The old religion of the country was not protected by hearty faith, from which this age had long since broken off ;[1] but the habits of home and the memory of the past clung to it by preference, and therefore it was not merely retained with tenacity, but it even became—in good part by the process of erudite retouching—always more rigid and more antique as time went on, always more a distinctive possession of such as made it a study.

Pedigrees.

It was the same with the worship of pedigrees, in which the Hellenes of this age performed uncommon feats, and left the most aristocratic of the Romans far behind them. In Athens the family of the Eumolpidae played a

---

[1] The magistrate even of culture, that is the freethinker, is advised to attach the largesses which he makes to the religious festivals ; for the multitude is strengthened in its faith, when it sees that the men of rank in the city lay some stress on the worship of the gods, and can expend something upon it (Plutarch, *Praec. ger. reip.* 30).

prominent part at the reorganisation of the Eleusinian festival under Marcus. His son Commodus conferred on the head of the clan of the Kerykes the Roman franchise, and from him descended the brave and learned Athenian, who, almost like Thucydides, fought with the Goths and then described the Gothic war (p. 246). A contemporary of Marcus, the professor and consular Herodes Atticus, belonged to this same clan, and his court-poet sings of him, that the red shoe of the Roman patriciate well befitted the high-born Athenian, the descendant of Hermes and of Cecrops's daughter Herse, while one of his panegyrists in prose celebrates him as Aeacides, and at the same time as a descendant of Miltiades and Cimon. But even Athens was far outbidden in this respect by Sparta; on several occasions we meet with Spartiates who boast of descent from the Dioscuri, Herakles, Poseidon, and of the priesthood of these ancestors hereditary for forty generations and more in their house. It is significant of this nobility, that it in the main presents itself only with the end of the second century; the heraldic draughtsmen who projected these genealogical tables cannot have been very punctilious as to vouchers either in Athens or in Sparta.

The same tendency appears in the treatment of the language or rather of the dialects. While at this time in the other Greek-speaking lands and also in Hellas the so-called common Greek, debased in the main from the Attic dialect, predominated in ordinary intercourse, not merely did the written language of this epoch strive to set aside prevalent faults and innovations, but in many cases dialectic peculiarities were again taken up in opposition to common usage, and here, where it was least of all warranted, the old particularism was in semblance brought back. On the statues which the Thespians set up to the Muses in the grove of Helicon, there were inscribed in good Boeotian the names Orania and Thalea, while the epigrams belonging to them, composed by a poet of Roman name, called them in good Ionic Uranie and Thaleie, and the non-learned Boeotians, if they knew

Language; archaism and barbarism.

them, like all other Greeks called them Urania and Thaleia. By the Spartans especially incredible things were done in this way, and not seldom more was written for the shade of Lycurgus than for the Aelii and Aurelii living at the time.[1] Moreover, the correct use of the language at this period appears gradually losing ground even in Hellas ; archaisms and barbarisms often stand peacefully side by side in the documents of the imperial period. The population of Athens, much mixed with foreigners, has at no time specially distinguished itself in this respect,[2] and, although the civic documents keep themselves comparatively pure, yet from the time of Augustus the gradually increasing corruption of language here also makes itself felt. The strict grammarians of the time filled whole books with the linguistic slips with which the much celebrated rhetorician Herodes Atticus just mentioned and the other famous school-orators of the second century were chargeable,[3] quite apart from the quaint artificiality and the affected point of their discourse. But barbarism proper as regards language and writing set in in Athens and all Greece, just as in Rome, with Septimius Severus.[4]

---

[1] A model sample is the inscription (Lebas - Foucart, ii. p. 142 n., 162 *j.*) of Μ[ᾶρκορ] Αὐρ[ήλιορ] Ζεύξιπ-πορ ὁ καὶ Κλέανδρορ Φιλομούσω, a contemporary therefore of Pius and Marcus, who was ἱερεὺς Λευκιππίδων καὶ Τυνδαριδᾶν, of the Dioscuri and their wives, the daughters of Leukippos, but—in order that with the old the new might not be wanting—also ἀρχιερέος τῶ Σεβαστῶ καὶ τῶν θείων προγόνων ὠτῶ. He had in his youth, moreover, been βουαγὸρ μικκιχιδδομένων, literally herd-leader of the little ones, namely, director of three-year old boys—the "herds" of boys of Lycurgus began with the seventh year, but his successors had overtaken what was wanting, and embraced in the "herd" and provided with "leaders" all from one year old onward. This same man was victorious (νεικάαρ = νικήσας) κασσηρατοριν, μωαν καὶ λωαν :

what this means, may be known perhaps to Lycurgus.

[2] " Inland Attica," says an inhabitant of it in Philostratus, *Vitae Soph.* ii. 7, " is a good school for one who would learn to speak ; the inhabitants of the city of Athens on the other hand, who hire out lodgings to the young people flocking thither from Thrace and Pontus and other barbarian regions, allow their language to be corrupted by these more than they impart to them good speaking. But in the interior, whose inhabitants are not mixed with barbarians, the pronunciation and language are good."

[3] Karl Keil (Pauly, *Realencycl.* i² p. 2100) points to τινός for ἧς τινός and τὰ χωρία γέγοναν in the inscription of the wife of Herodes (*C. I. L.* vi. 1342).

[4] Dittenberger, *Hermes,* i. 414.

The bane of Hellenic existence lay in the limitation The public career.
of its sphere ; high ambition lacked a corresponding
aim, and therefore the low and degrading ambition flourished luxuriantly. Even in Hellas there was no lack of
native families of great wealth and considerable influence.[1]
The country was doubtless on the whole poor, but there Great families.
were houses of extensive possessions and old-established
prosperity. In Sparta, for example, that of Lachares
occupied, from Augustus down at least to the time of
Hadrian, a position which in point of fact was not far
removed from that of a prince. Antonius had caused
Lachares to be put to death for exaction. Thereupon his
son Eurycles was one of the most decided partisans of
Augustus, and one of the bravest captains in the decisive
naval battle, who had almost made the conquered general
personally a captive ; he received from the victor, among
other rich gifts as private property, the island of Cythera
(Cerigo). Later he played a prominent and hazardous
part not merely in his native land, over which he must
have exercised a permanent presidency, but also at the
courts of Jerusalem and Caesarea, to which the respect
paid to a Spartiate by the Orientals contributed not a
little. For that reason brought to trial several times at
the bar of the emperor, he was at length condemned and
sent into exile ; but death seasonably withdrew him from
the consequences of the sentence, and his son Lacon came
into the property, and substantially also, though in a more
cautious form, into the position of power of his father.
The family of the often-mentioned Herodes had a similar

Here, too, may be adduced what the stupid champion of Apollonius makes his hero write to the Alexandrian professors (*Ep.* 34), that he has left Argos, Sicyon, Megara, Phocis, Locris, in order that he might not, by staying longer in Hellas, become utterly a barbarian.

[1] Tacitus (on the year 62, *Ann.* xv. 20) characterises one of these rich and influential provincials, Claudius Timarchides from Crete, who is all powerful in his sphere (*ut solent praevalidi provincialium et opibus nimiis ad iniurias minorum elati*), and has at his disposal the diet and consequently also the decree of thanks—a due accompaniment very desirable for the departing proconsul in view of possible actions of reckoning (*in sua potestate situm an proconsulibus, qui Cretam obtinuissent, grates agerentur*). The opposition proposes that this decree of thanks be refused, but does not succeed in bringing the proposal to a vote. From another side Plutarch (*Praec. ger. reip.* c. 19, 3) depicts these Greeks of rank.

standing in Athens ; we can trace it going back through four generations to the time of Caesar, and confiscation was decreed, just as over the Spartan Eurycles, over the grandfather of Herodes on account of his exorbitant position of power in Athens. The enormous landed estates which the grandson possessed in his poor native country, the extensive spaces applied for the sake of erecting tombs for his boy-favourites, excited the indignation even of the Roman governors. It may be presumed that there were powerful families of this sort in most districts of Hellas, and, while they as a rule decided matters at the diet of the province, they were not without connections and

The career of state-offices.

influence even in Rome. But although those legal bars, which excluded the Gaul and the Alexandrian even after obtaining the franchise from the imperial senate, hardly stood in the way of those Greeks of rank, but on the contrary the political and military career which offered itself to the Italian likewise stood open in law to the Hellenes, these in point of fact entered only at a late period and to a limited extent into the service of the state ; partly, doubtless, because the Roman government of the earlier imperial period reluctantly admitted the Greeks as foreigners, partly because these themselves shunned the translation to Rome that was associated with entrance on this career, and preferred to be the first at home instead of one the more among the many senators. It was the great-grandson of Lachares, Herclanus, who first in the time of Trajan entered the Roman senate ; and in the family of Herodes probably his father was the first to do so about the same time.[1]

Personal service of the emperor.

The other career, which only opened up in the imperial period—the personal service of the emperor—gave doubtless in favourable circumstances riches and influence, and was earlier and more frequently pursued by the

---

[1] Herodes was ἐξ ὑπάτων (Philostratus, *Vit. Soph.* i. 25, 5, p. 526), ἐτέλει ἐκ πατέρων ἐς τοὺς δισυπάτους (*ib.* ii. *init.* p. 545). Otherwise nothing is known of consulships of his ancestors ; but certainly his grandfather Hipparchus was not a senator. Possibly the question is even only as to cognate ascendants. The family did not receive the Roman franchise under the Julii (comp. *C. I. A.* iii. 489), but only under the Claudii.

Greeks ; but, as most, and the most important, of these positions were associated with service as officers, there seems to have been for a considerable time a *de facto* preference of Italians for these places, and the direct way was here also in some measure barred to Greeks. In subordinate positions Greeks were employed at the imperial court from the first and in great numbers, and they often in circuitous ways attained to trust and influence ; but such persons came more from the Hellenised regions than from Hellas itself, and least of all from the better Hellenic houses. For the legitimate ambition of the young man of ancestry and estate there was, if he was a Greek, but limited scope in the Roman empire.

There remained to him his native land, and in its case to be active for the common weal was certainly a duty and an honour. But the duties were very modest and the honours more modest still. " Your task," Dio says further to his Rhodians, " is a different one from that of your ancestors. They could develop their ability on many sides, aspire to government, aid the oppressed, gain allies, found cities, make war and conquer ; of all this you can no longer do aught. There is left for you the conduct of the household, the administration of the city, the bestowal of honours and distinctions with choice and moderation, a seat in council and in court, sacrifice to the gods and celebration of festivals ; in all this you may distinguish yourselves above other towns. Nor are these slight matters : the decorous bearing, the care for the hair and beard, the sedate pace in the street, so that the foreigners accustomed to other things may by your side unlearn their haste, the becoming dress, even, though it may seem ridiculous, the narrow and neat purple-border, the calmness in the theatre, the moderation in applause—all this forms the honour of your town ; therein more than in your ports and walls and docks appears the good old Hellenic habit ; and thereby even the barbarian, who knows not the name of the city, perceives that he is in Greece and not in Syria or Cilicia." All this was to the point ; but, if it was no longer required now of the citizen

[margin note:] Municipal administration.

to die for the city of his fathers, the question was at any rate not without warrant, whether it was still worth the trouble to live for that city. There exists a disquisition by Plutarch as to the position of the Greek municipal official in his time, wherein he discusses these relations with the fairness and circumspection characteristic of him. The old difficulty of conducting the good administration of public affairs by means of majorities of the citizens—uncertain, capricious, often bethinking them more of their own advantage than of that of the commonwealth—or even of the very numerous council-board—the Athenian numbered in the imperial period first 600, then 700, later 750 town-councillors—subsisted now, as formerly : it is the duty of the capable magistrate to prevent the " people " from inflicting wrong on the individual burgess, from appropriating to themselves unallowably private property, from distributing among them the municipal property —tasks which are not rendered the easier by the fact that the magistrate has no means for the purpose but judicious admonition and the art of the demagogue, that it is further suggested to him not to be too punctilious in such things, and, if at a city festival a moderate largess to the burgesses is proposed, not to spoil matters with the people on account of such a trifle. But in other respects the circumstances had entirely changed, and the official must learn to adapt himself to things as they are. First of all he has to keep the powerlessness of the Hellenes present at every moment to himself and to his fellow-citizens. The freedom of the community reaches so far as the rulers allow it, and anything more would doubtless be evil. When Pericles put on the robes of office, he called to himself not to forget that he was ruling over free men and Greeks ; to-day the magistrate has to say to himself that he rules under a ruler, over a town subject to proconsuls and imperial procurators, that he can and may be nothing but the organ of the government, that a stroke of the governor's pen suffices to annul any one of his decrees. Therefore it is the first duty of a good magistrate to place himself on a good understanding with

Plutarch's view of its duties.

the Romans, and, if possible, to form influential connections in Rome, that these may benefit his native place. It is true that the upright man warns urgently against servility ; in case of need the magistrate ought courageously to confront the bad governor, and the resolute championship of the community in such conflicts at Rome before the emperor appears as the highest service. In a significant way he sharply censures those Greeks who— quite as in the times of the Achaean league—call for the intervention of the Roman governor in every local quarrel, and urgently exhorts them rather to settle the communal affairs within the community than by appeal to give themselves into the hands, not so much of the supreme authority, as of the pleaders and advocates that practise before it. All this is judicious and patriotic, as judicious and patriotic as was formerly the policy of Polybius, which is expressly referred to. At this epoch of complete world-peace, when there was neither a Greek nor a barbarian war anywhere, when civic commands, civic treaties of peace and alliances belonged solely to history, the advice was very reasonable to leave Marathon and Plataeae to the schoolmasters, and not to heat the heads of the Ecclesia by such grand words, but rather to content themselves with the narrow circle of the free movement still allowed to them. The world, however, belongs not to reason but to passion. The Hellenic burgess could still even now do his duty towards his fatherland ; but for the true political ambition striving after what was great, for the passion of Pericles and Alcibiades, there was in this Hellas—apart perhaps from the writing-desk—nowhere any room ; and in the vacant space there flourished the poisonous herbs which, wherever high effort is arrested in the bud, harden and embitter the human heart.

Therefore Hellas was the motherland of the degenerate, Games. empty ambition which was perhaps the most general, and certainly among the most pernicious, of the many sore evils of the decaying ancient civilisation. Here in the first rank stood the popular festivals with their prize competitions. The Olympic rivalries well beseemed the youthful people of the Hellenes ; the general gymnastic festival of the Greek tribes and towns, and the chaplet plaited from the branches of the olive for the ablest runner according to the decision of the " Hellas-judges," were the innocent and simple expression of the young nation as a collective unity. But their political development had soon carried them beyond this early dawn. Already in the days of the Athenian naval league, or at least of the monarchy of Alexander, that festival of the Hellenes was an anachronism, a childs' play continued in the age of manhood ; the fact, that the possessor of that olive wreath passed at least with himself and his fellow-citizens as holder of the national primacy, had nearly as much significance, as if in England the victors in the students' boat races were to be placed on a level with Pitt and Beaconsfield. The extension of the Hellenic nation by colonising and Hellenising found, amidst its ideal unity and real disruption, its true expression in this dreamy realm of the olive-wreath ; and the materialist policy of the time of the Diadochi thereupon gave itself, as was meet, but little trouble on the subject. But when the imperial period after its fashion took up the Panhellenic idea, and the Romans entered into the rights and duties of the Hellenes, then Olympia remained or became the true symbol for the Roman "All-Hellas"; at any rate the first Roman Olympic victor appears under Augustus, and in the person of no less than Augustus's stepson, the subsequent emperor Tiberius.[1] The far from pure marriage-alliance, which Allhellenism entered into with the demon of play, converted these festivals into an institution as powerful and lasting as it was injurious in general, and especially for Hellas. The whole Hellenic and Hellenising world took part therein,

---

[1] The first Roman Olympionices, of whom we know, is Ti. Claudius Ti. f. Nero, beyond doubt the subsequent emperor, with the four-in-hand (*Arch. Zeit.* 1880, p. 53) ; this victory falls probably in Ol. 195 (A.D. 1), not in Ol. 99 (A.D. 17), as the list of Africanus states (Euseb. i. p. 214, Schöne). In this year the conqueror was rather his son Germanicus, likewise with the four-in-hand (*Arch. Zeit.* 1879, p. 36). Among the eponymous Olympionicae, the victors in the stadium, no Roman is found ; this wounding of the Greek national feeling seems to have been avoided.

sending deputies to them and imitating them ; everywhere similar festivals destined for the whole Greek world sprang from the soil, and the zealous participation of the masses at large, the general interest felt in the individual competitors, the pride not merely of the victor but of his adherents and of his native land, made people almost forget what in the strict sense were the things contended for.

Not merely did the Roman government allow free scope to this rivalry in gymnastic and other competitions, but the empire took part in them ; the right solemnly to fetch home the victor to his native city did not in the imperial period depend on the pleasure of the burgesses concerned, but was conferred on the individual agonistic institutes by imperial charter,[1] and in this case also the yearly pension ($\sigma\acute{\iota}\tau\eta\sigma\iota\varsigma$) assigned to the victor was charged upon the imperial exchequer, and the more important agonistic institutes were treated directly as imperial institutions. This interest in games seized all the provinces as well as the empire itself ; but Greece proper was always the ideal centre of such contests and victories. Here was their home on the Alpheus ; here the seat of the oldest imitations, of the Pythia, Isthmia, and Nemea, still belonging to the great times of the Hellenic name and glorified by its classic poets, and no less of a number of more recent but richly equipped similar festivals, the Euryclea, which the just-mentioned lord of Sparta had founded under Augustus, the Athenian Panathenaea, the Panhellenia, endowed by Hadrian with imperial munificence and likewise celebrated at Athens. It might be matter for wonder that the whole world of the wide empire seemed to revolve round these gymnastic festivals, but not that the Hellenes above all got intoxicated over this rare cup of enchantment, and that the life of political quiet, which their best men recommended to them, was in

Universal interest in them.

---

[1] An agonistic institute thus privileged is termed ἀγὼν ἱερός, *certamen sacrum* (that is, with pensioning : Dio, li. 1), or ἀγὼν εἰσελαστικός, *certamen iselasticum* (comp. among others, Plin. *ad Trai.* 118, 119 ; *C. I. L.* x. 515). The Xystarchia too is, at least in certain cases, conferred by the emperor (Dittenberger, *Hermes*, xii. 17 f.). Not without warrant these institutes called themselves " world-games " (ἀγὼν οἰκουμενικός).

the most injurious way disturbed by the wreaths and the statues and the privileges of the festal victors.

Municipal ambition. Civic institutions took a similar course, certainly in the empire as a whole, but again more especially in Hellas. When great aims and an ambition still existed there, in Hellas, just as in Rome, the pursuit of public offices and public honours had formed the centre of political emulation, and had called forth, along with much that was empty, ridiculous, mischievous, also the ablest and noblest services. Now the kernel had vanished and the husk remained ; in Panopeus, in the Phocian territory, the houses were roofless, and the citizens dwelt in huts, but it was still a city, indeed a state, and in the procession of the Phocian communities the Panopeans were not wanting. These towns, with their magistracies and priesthoods, with their laudatory decrees proclaimed by herald and their seats of honour in the public assemblies, with the purple dress and the diadem, with statues on foot and on horseback, drove a trade in vanity and money-jobbing worse than the pettiest paltry prince of modern times with his orders and titles. There would not be wanting even amidst these incidents real merit and honourable gratitude ; but generally it was a trade of giving and taking, or, to use Plutarch's language, an affair as between a courtesan and her customers. As at the present day private munificence in the positive degree procures an order, in the superlative a patent of nobility, so it then procured the priestly purple and the statue in the market place ; and it is not with impunity that the state issues a spurious coinage of its honours.

Its honours and their evils. As regards the scale of conducting such proceedings and the grossness of their forms the doings of the present day fall considerably behind those of the ancient world, as is natural, seeing that the seeming autonomy of the community, not sufficiently restrained by the idea of the State, bore unhindered sway in this domain, and the decreeing authorities throughout were the burgesses or the councils of petty towns. The consequences were pernicious on both sides ; the municipal offices were given away more according to the ability to pay than according to the aptitude of the candidates; the banquets and largesses made the recipients none the richer, and often impoverished the donor; to the increased aversion for labour and the decay in the means of good families, this evil habit contributed its full share. The economy of the communities themselves also suffered severely under the spreading evil of adulation. No doubt the honours, with which the community thanked the individual benefactor, were measured in great part by the same rational principle of cheapness which governs at the present day similar decorative favours; and, when that was not the case, the benefactor frequently found himself ready, for example, personally to pay for the statue to be erected in his honour. But the same did not apply to the marks of honour which the community showed to foreigners of rank, above all to the governors and the emperors, and to the members of the imperial house. The tendency of the time to set value even on meaningless and enforced homage did not dominate the imperial court and the Roman senators so much as the circles of ambition in the petty town, but yet it did so in a very perceptible way; and, as a matter of course, the honours and the homage grew withal in the course of time through misuses to which they were put, and, further, in the same proportion as the worthlessness of the personages governing or taking part in the government. In this respect, as might be conceived, the supply of honours was always stronger than the demand for them, and those who correctly valued such marks of homage, in order to remain spared from it, were compelled to decline them, which seems to have been done often enough in individual cases,[1] but seldom with consistency—for Tiberius, the small number

---

[1] The emperor Gaius declines, in his letter to the diet of Achaiā, the "great number" of statues adjudged to him, and contents himself with the four of Olympia, Nemea, Delphi, and the Isthmus (Keil, *Inscr. Boeot.* n. 31). The same diet resolves to set up a statue to the emperor Hadrian in each of its towns, of which the base of that set up at Abea in Messenia has been preserved (*C. I. Gr.* 1307). Imperial authorisation for such erections was required from the first.

of statues erected to him may perhaps be recorded among his titles to honour. The disbursements for honorary memorials, which often went far beyond the simple statue, and for honorary embassies,[1] were a cancer, and became ever more so, in the municipal economy of all the provinces. But none perhaps expended uselessly sums so large in proportion to its slender ability to furnish them as the province of Hellas, the motherland of municipal honours as of rewards for the festal victor, and unexcelled at this period in one pre-eminence—that of menial humility and abject homage.

Trade and intercourse. That the economic circumstances of Greece were not favourable, scarce needs to be specially set forth in detail. The land, taken on the whole, was but of moderate fertility, the agricultural portions of limited extent, the culture of the vine on the mainland not of prominent importance, that of the olive more so. As the quarries of the famous marble—the shining white Attic and the green Carystian—belonged, like most others, to the domanial possessions, the working of them by imperial slaves tended little to benefit the population.

The most assiduous of the Greek districts from an industrial point of view was that of the Achaeans, where the manufacture of woollen stuffs, that had long existed, maintained its ground, and in the well-peopled town of Patrae numerous looms worked up the fine flax of Elis into clothing and head-dresses. Art and art-handiwork still continued chiefly in the hands of the Greeks; and of the masses in particular of Pentelic marble, which the imperial period made use of, no small portion must have been worked up on the spot. But it was predominantly abroad that the Greeks practised both; of the export of Greek art-products formerly so important there is little mention at this period. The city of the two seas, Corinth

---

[1] At the revision of the town-accounts of Byzantium, Pliny found that annually 12,000 sesterces (£125) were set down for the conveyance of new-year's good wishes by a special deputation to the emperor, and 3000 sesterces (£32) for the same to the governor of Moesia. Pliny instructs the authorities to send these congratulations thenceforth only in writing, which Trajan approves (*Ep. ad Trai.* 43, 44).

—the metropolis common to all Hellenes, constantly swarming with foreigners, as a rhetorician describes it— had the most stirring traffic. In the two Roman colonies of Corinth and Patrae, and, moreover, in Athens constantly filled by strangers seeing and learning, was concentrated the larger banking-business of the province, which, in the imperial period, as in the republican, lay largely in the hands of Italians settled there. In places too of the second rank, as in Argos, Elis, Mantinea in the Peloponnesus, the Roman merchants who were settled formed societies of their own, standing alongside of the burgesses. In general trade and commerce were at a low ebb in Achaia, particularly since Rhodes and Delos had ceased to be emporia for the carrying traffic between Asia and Europe, and the latter had been drawn to Italy. Piracy was restrained, and even the land-routes were tolerably secure[1]; but withal the old happy times did not return. The desolation of the Piraeus has been already mentioned; it was an event when one of the great Egyptian corn ships once strayed thither. Nauplia, the port of Argos, the most considerable coast town of the Peloponnesus after Patrae, lay likewise desolate.[2]

[1] That the land-routes of Greece were specially unsafe, we do not learn; as to what was the nature of the insurrection in Achaia under Pius (*Vita*, 5, 4), we are quite in the dark. If the robber-chief generally—and not precisely the Greek one —plays a prominent part in the light literature of the epoch, this vehicle is common to the bad romance-writers of all ages. The Euboean desert of the more polished Dio was not a robber's nest, but it was the wreck of a great landed estate, whose possessor had been condemned on account of his wealth by the emperor, and which thenceforth lay waste. Moreover it is here apparent—as indeed needs no proof, at least for those who are non-scholars—that this history is just as true as most which begin by stating that the narrator himself had it from the person concerned; if the confiscation were his-

torical, the possession would have come to the exchequer, not to the town, which the narrator accordingly takes good care not to name.

[2] The naive description of Achaia by an Egyptian merchant of Constantius's time may find a place here: —" The land of Achaia, Greece, and Laconia has much of learning, but is inadequate for other things needful; for it is a small and mountainous province, and cannot furnish much corn, but produces some oil and the Attic honey, and can be praised more on account of the schools and eloquence, but not so in most other respects. Of towns it has Corinth and Athens. Corinth has much commerce, and a fine building, the amphitheatre; but Athens has old pictures (*historias antiquas*), and a work worth mentioning, the citadel, where many statues stand and wonderfully set forth the war-deeds of the forefathers

Roads. It is in accordance with this state of things that virtually nothing was done for the roads of this province in the imperial period ; Roman milestones have been found only in the immediate vicinity of Patrae and of Athens, and even these belong to the emperors of the end of the third and of the fourth century ; evidently the earlier governments renounced the idea of restoring communications here. Hadrian alone undertook at least to make the equally important and short land-connection between Corinth and Megara—by way of the wretched pass of the " Scironian cliffs "—into a practicable road by means of huge embankments thrown into the sea.

Piercing of the Isthmus.

The long-discussed plan of piercing the Corinthian isthmus, which the dictator Caesar had conceived, was subsequently attempted, first by the emperor Gaius and then by Nero. The latter even, on occasion of his abode in Greece, personally took the first step towards the canal, and caused 6000 Jewish captives to work at it for a series of months. In connection with the cutting operations resumed in our own day, considerable remains of these buildings have been brought to light, which show that the works were tolerably far advanced when they were broken off, probably not in consequence of the revolution that broke out some time afterwards in the West, but because here, just as with the similar Egyptian canal, in consequence of the difference of level that was erroneously assumed to exist between the two seas, there were apprehensions of the destruction of the island of Aegina and of further mischief on the completion of the canal. No doubt had this canal been completed, it would have shortened the course of traffic between Asia and Italy, but it would not have tended specially to benefit Greece itself.

Epirus. It has already been remarked (p. 256) that the regions

(*ubi multis statuis stantibus mirabile est videre dicendum antiquorum bellum*). Laconia is said alone to have the marble of Croceae to show, which people call the Lacedaemonian." The barbarism of expression is to be set down to the account, not of the writer, but of the much later translator.

to the north of Hellas, Thessaly, and Macedonia, and at least from Trajan's time Epirus, were in the imperial period separated administratively from Greece. Of these the small Epirot province, which was administered by an imperial governor of the second rank, never recovered from the devastation to which it had been subjected in the course of the third Macedonian war (ii. 329). The mountainous and poor interior possessed no city of note and a thinly-scattered population. Augustus had endeavoured to raise the not less desolated coast by the construction of two towns—by the completion of the colony of Roman citizens already resolved on by Caesar in Buthrotum over against Corcyra, which, however, attained no true prosperity, and by the founding of the Greek town Nicopolis, just at the spot where the headquarters had been stationed before the decisive battle of Actium, at the southernmost point of Epirus, about an hour and a half north of Prevesa, according to the design of Augustus, at once a permanent memorial of the great naval victory and the centre of a newly flourishing Hellenic life. This foundation was new in its kind as Roman.[1] The words of a contemporary Greek poet, which we quote below, simply express what Augustus here did ; he united the whole surrounding territory, southern Epirus, the opposite region of Acarnania with the island of Leucas, and even a portion of Aetolia into one urban domain, and transferred the inhabitants still left in the decaying townships there existing to the new city of Nicopolis, opposite to which on the Acarnanian shore the old temple of the Actian Apollo was magnificently renewed and enlarged.

A Roman city had never been founded in this way ; this was the *synoekismos* of the successors of Alexander. Quite in the same way had king Cassander constituted

(margin notes:) ii. 309. — Nicopolis. — Its character and privileges.

---

[1] Λευκάδος ἀντί με Καῖσαρ, ἰδ' Ἀμ-
βρακίης ἐριβώλου,
Θυρρείου τε πέλειν, ἀντί τ' Ἀνακ-
τορίου,
Ἀργεος Ἀμφιλόχου τε, καὶ ὁππόσα
ῥαίσατο κύκλῳ

ἄστε' ἐπιθρώσκων δουρομανὴς πό-
λεμος,
εἴσατο Νικόπολιν, θείην πόλιν· ἀντι
δε νίκης
φοῖβος ἄναξ ταύτην δέχνυται Ἀκ-
τιάδος.
Anthol. Gr. ix. 553.

the Macedonian towns Thessalonica and Cassandreia,
Demetrius Poliorcetes the Thessalian town Demetrias,
and Lysimachus the town of Lysimachia on the Thracian
Chersonese out of a number of surrounding townships
divested of their independence. In keeping with the
Greek character of the foundation Nicopolis was, according
to the intention of its founder, to become a Greek city on
a great scale.[1] It obtained freedom and autonomy like
Athens and Sparta, and was intended, as already stated,
to wield the fifth part of the votes in the Amphictiony
representing all Hellas, and to do so, like Athens, without
alternating with other towns (p. 254). This new Actian
shrine of Apollo was erected quite after the model of
Olympia, with a quadriennial festival, which even bore
the name of " Olympia " alongside of its own, had equal
rank and equal privileges, and even its Actiads as the
former had its Olympiads;[2] the town of Nicopolis stood
related to it like the town of Elis to the Olympian
temple.[3] Everything properly Italian was carefully
avoided in the erection of the town as well as in the
religious arrangements, however natural it might be to
mould after the Roman fashion the "city of victory" so
intimately associated with the founding of the empire.
Whoever considers the arrangements of Augustus in

[1] When Tacitus, *Ann.* v. 10,
names Nicopolis a *colonia Romana*,
the statement is one liable to be misunderstood, but not exactly incorrect;
but that of Pliny (*H. N.* iv. 1, 5),
*colonia Augusti Actium cum . . .
civitate libera Nicopolitana*, is erroneous, as Actium was as little a town
as Olympia.

[2] Ὁ ἀγὼν Ὀλύμπιος τὰ Ἄκτια,
Strabo, vii. 7, 6, p. 325; Ἀκτιάς,
Josephus, *Bell. Jud.* i. 20, 4;
Ἀκτιονίκης oftener. As the four
great Greek national festivals are, as
is well known, termed ἡ περίοδος,
and the victor crowned in all four
περιοδονίκης, so in *C. I. Gr.* 4472
τῆς περιόδου is appended also to the
games of Nicopolis, and the former
περίοδος is designated as the ancient

(ἀρχαία). As competitive games are
frequently called ἰσολύμπια, so we find
also ἀγὼν ἰσάκτιος (*C. I. Gr.* 4472),
or *certamen ad exemplar Actiacae religionis* (Tacitus, *Ann.* xv. 23).

[3] Thus a Nicopolite terms himself
ἄρχων τῆς ἱερᾶς Ἀκτιακῆς βουλῆς
(Delphi, *Rhein. Mus.* N. F. ii. 111),
as in Elis the expression is used:
ἡ πόλις Ἠλείων καὶ ἡ Ὀλυμπικὴ βουλή
(*Arch. Zeit.* 1876, p. 57; similarly
ibid. 1877, pp. 40, 41 and elsewhere).
Moreover the Spartans, as the only
Hellenes that took part in the victory
at Actium, obtained the conduct
(ἐπιμέλεια) of the Actian games
(Strabo, vii. 7, 6 p. 325): their
relation to the βουλή Ἀκτιακή of
Nicopolis we do not know.

Hellas in this connection, and especially this remarkable corner-stone, will not be able to resist the conviction that Augustus believed that a reorganisation of Hellas under the protection of the Roman principate was practicable, and wished to carry it out. The locality at least was well chosen for it, as at that time, before the foundation of Patrae, there was no larger city on the whole Greek west coast. But what Augustus may have hoped for at the commencement of his sole rule, he did not attain, and perhaps even subsequently abandoned, when he gave to Patrae the form of a Roman colony. Nicopolis remained, as the extensive ruins and the numerous coins show, comparatively populous and flourishing ;[1] but its citizens do not appear to have taken a prominent part in commerce and manufactures or otherwise. Northern Epirus, which, like the adjoining Illyricum bordering on Macedonia, was in greater part inhabited by Albanian tribes and was not placed under Nicopolis, continued during the imperial period in its primitive condition, which still subsists in some measure at the present day. "Epirus and Illyricum," says Strabo, "are in great part a desert ; where men are found, they dwell in villages and in ruins of earlier towns ; even the oracle of Dodona,"—laid waste in the Mithradatic war by the Thracians (iii. 312),—"is extinct like everything else."[2]

iii. 296.

Thessaly, in itself a purely Hellenic district as well as Aetolia and Acarnania, was in the imperial period separated administratively from the province of Achaia

Thessaly.

---

[1] The description of its decay in the time of Constantius (*Paneg.* 11, 9) is an evidence to the opposite effect for the earlier times of the empire.

[2] The excavations at Dodona have confirmed this ; all the articles found belong to the pre-Roman period except some coins. Certainly a restoration of the building took place, the time of which cannot be determined ; perhaps it was quite late. When Hadrian, who is named Ζεὺς Δωδωναῖος (*C. I. Gr.* 1822), visited Dodona (Dürr, *Reisen Haarians*, p. 56) he did so as an archaeologist. A consultation of the oracle during the imperial period is only reported— and that not after the most trustworthy manner—in the case of the emperor Julian (Theodoretus, *Hist. Eccl.* iii. 21).

and placed under the governor of Macedonia. What holds true of northern Greece applies also to Thessaly. The freedom and autonomy which Caesar had allowed generally to the Thessalians, or rather had not withdrawn from them, seem to have been withdrawn, on account of misuse, from them by Augustus, so that subsequently Pharsalus alone retained this legal position;[1] Roman colonists were not settled in the district. It retained its separate diet in Larisa, and civic self-administration was left with the Thessalians, as with the dependent Greeks in Achaia. Thessaly was far the most fertile region of the whole peninsula, and still exported grain in the fourth century; nevertheless Dio of Prusa says that even the Peneus flows through waste land; and in the imperial period money was coined in this region only to a very small extent. Hadrian and Diocletian exerted themselves to restore the roads of the country, but they alone, so far as we see, of the Roman emperors did so.

Macedonia. Macedonia, as a Roman administrative district under the empire, was materially curtailed as compared with the Macedonia of the republic. Certainly, like the latter, it reached from sea to sea, inasmuch as the coast as well of the Aegean Sea from the region of Thessaly belonging to Macedonia as far as the mouth of the Nestus (Mesta), as of the Adriatic from the Aous[2] as far as the Drilon (Drin), was reckoned to this district; the latter territory, not properly Macedonian but Illyrian

---

[1] The ordinance of Caesar is attested by Appian, *B. C.* ii. 88, and Plutarch, *Caes.* 48, and it very well accords with his own account, *B. C.* iii. 80; whereas Pliny, *H. N.* iv. 8, 29, names only Pharsalus as a free town. In Augustus' time a Thessalian of note, Petraeos (probably the partisan of Caesar, *B. C.* iii. 35), was burnt alive (Plutarch, *Praec. ger. reip.* 19), doubtless not by a private crime, but according to resolution of the diet, and so the Thessalians were brought before the tribunal of the emperor (Suetonius, *Tib.* 8). Presumably the two incidents and likewise the loss of freedom stand connected.

[2] In the time of the republic Scodra seems to have belonged to Macedonia (iii. 181); in the imperial period this and Lissus are Dalmatian towns, and the mouth of the Drin forms the boundary on the west. iii. 173

land, but already in the republican period assigned to
the governor of Macedonia (iii. 44), remained with the iii. 42.
province also during the time of the empire.   But we
have already stated that Greece south of Oeta was
separated from it.   The northern frontier towards Moesia
and the east frontier towards Thrace remained indeed
in so far unaltered, as the province in the imperial period
reached as far as the Macedonia proper of the republic
had reached, viz. on the north almost as far as the vale
of the Erigon, eastward as far as the river Nestus ; but
while in the time of the republic the Dardani and the
Thracians, and all the tribes of the north and north-east
adjoining the Macedonian territory, had to do with this
governor in their circumstances of peaceful or warlike
contact, and in so far it could be said that the Macedonian
boundary reached as far as the Roman lances, the
Macedonian governor of the imperial period bore sway
only over the district assigned to him, which no longer
bordered on neighbours half or wholly independent.
As the defence of the frontier was transferred in the
first instance to the kingdom of the Thracians which
had come under allegiance to Rome, and soon to the
governor of the new province Moesia, the governor of
Macedonia was from the outset relieved of his command.
There was hardly any fighting on Macedonian soil under
the empire ; only the barbarian Dardani on the upper
Axius (Vardar) still at times pillaged the peaceful
neighbouring province.   There is no report, moreover,
from this province of any local revolts.

From the more southerly Greek districts this—the Nation
most northerly—stood aloof as well in its national basis alities.
as in the stage of its civilisation.   While the Macedonians
proper on the lower course of the Haliacmon (Vistritza)
and the Axius (Vardar), as far as the Strymon, were an
originally Greek stock, whose diversity from the more
southern Hellenes had no further significance for the
present epoch, and while the Hellenic colonisation
embraced within its sphere both coasts—on the west
with Apollonia and Dyrrachium, on the east in particular

with the townships of the Chalcidian peninsula—the interior of the province, on the other hand, was filled with a confused mass of non-Greek peoples, which must have differed from the present state of things in the same region more as to elements than as to results. After the Celts who had pushed forward into this region, the Scordisci, had been driven back by the generals of the Roman republic, the interior of Macedonia fell to the share especially of Illyrian stocks in the west and north, of Thracian in the east. Of both we have already spoken previously; here they come into consideration only so far as the Greek organisation, at least the urban, was probably introduced—as in the earlier,[1] so also in the imperial period—among these stocks only in a very limited measure. On the whole, an energetic impulse of urban development never pervaded the interior of Macedonia; the more remote districts hardly reached—at least as in a real sense—beyond the village-system.

Greek polity.
The Greek polity itself was not a spontaneous growth in this monarchical country, as it was in Hellas proper, but was introduced by the princes, who were more Hellenes than their subjects. What shape it had is little known; yet the civic presidency of politarchs uniformly recurring in Thessalonica, Edessa, Lete, and not met with elsewhere, leads us to infer a perceptible, and indeed in itself probable, diversity of the Macedonian urban constitution from that elsewhere usual in Hellas. The Greek cities, which the Romans found existing, retained their organisation and their rights; Thessalonica, the most considerable of them, also freedom and autonomy. There existed a league and a diet (κοινόν) of the Macedonian towns, similar to those in Achaia and Thessaly. It deserves mention, as an evidence of the continued working of the memories of the

---

[1] The towns founded in these regions outside of Macedonia proper bear quite the character of colonies proper; *e.g.* that of Philippi in the Thracian land, and especially that of Derriopus in Paeonia (Liv. xxxix. 53), for which latter place also the dis- tinctively Macedonian politarchs have epigraphic attestation (inscription of the year 197 A.D., τῶν περὶ ᾿Αλέξ-ανδρον Φιλίππου ἐν Δερρίοπῳ πολι-ταρχῶν, Duchesne and Bayet, *Mission au mont Athos*, p. 103).

old and great times, that still in the middle of the third century after Christ the diet of Macedonia and individual Macedonian towns issued coins on which, in place of the head and the name of the reigning emperor, came those of Alexander the Great.   The pretty numerous colonies of Roman burgesses which Augustus established in Macedonia, Byllis not far from Apollonia, Dyrrachium on the Adriatic, on the other coast Dium, Pella, Cassandreia, in the region of Thrace proper Philippi, were all of them older Greek towns, which obtained merely a number of new burgesses and a different legal position, and were called into life primarily by the need of providing quarters in a civilised and not greatly populous province for Italian soldiers who had served their time, and for whom there was no longer room in Italy itself.   The granting of Italian rights certainly took place only to gild for the veterans their settlement abroad.   That it was never intended to draw Macedonia into the development of Italian culture is evinced, apart from all else, by the fact that Thessalonica remained Greek and the capital of the country.   By its side flourished Philippi, properly a mining town, constituted on account of the neighbouring gold mines, favoured by the emperors as the seat of the battle which definitively founded the monarchy, and on account of the numerous veterans who took part in it and subsequently settled there.   A Roman, not colonial, municipal constitution was obtained already in the first period of the empire by Stobi, the already mentioned most northerly frontier-town of Macedonia towards Moesia, at the confluence of the Erigon with the Axius, in a commercial as in a military point of view an important position, and which, it may be conjectured, had already in the Macedonian time attained to Greek polity.

In an economic point of view little was done on the part of the state for Macedonia under the emperors ; at least there is no appearance of any special care on their part for this province, which was not put under their own administration.   The military road already constructed under the republic right across the country from

Dyrrachium to Thessalonica, one of the most important arteries of intercourse in the whole empire, called forth renewed effort, so far as we know, only from emperors of the third century, and first from Severus Antoninus ; the towns adjacent to it, Lychnidus on the Ochrida-lake and Heraclea Lyncestis (Bitolia), were never of much account. Yet Macedonia was, economically, better situated than Greece. It far excelled it in fertility ; as still at present the province of Thessalonica is relatively well cultivated and well peopled, so in the description of the empire from the time of Constantius, at all events when Constantinople was already in existence, Macedonia is reckoned among the specially wealthy districts. If for Achaia and Thessaly our documents concerning the Roman levy are absolutely silent, Macedonia on the other hand was drawn upon, in particular for the imperial guard, to a considerable extent, more strongly than the most of the Greek districts—on which, no doubt, the familiarity of the Macedonians with regular war-service and their excellent qualifications for it, and probably also the relatively small development of the urban system in this province, had an important bearing. Thessalonica, the metropolis of the province, and its most populous and most industrial town at this time, represented likewise under various forms in literature, has also secured to itself an honourable place in political history by the brave resistance which its citizens opposed to the barbarians in the terrible times of the Gothic invasions (p. 248).

Thrace.　　If Macedonia was a half-Greek, Thrace was a non-Greek land. Of the great but for us vanished Thracian stock we have formerly (p. 207) spoken. Into its domain Hellenism came simply from without ; and it will not be superfluous in the first instance to glance back and to set forth how often Hellenism had previously knocked at the gates of the most southerly region which this stock possessed, and which we still name after it, and how little it had hitherto penetrated into the interior, in order to make clear what was left for Rome here to overtake and what it did overtake.   Philip, the father of Alexander, first *Philip and* subjected Thrace, and founded not merely Calybe in the *Alexander.* neighbourhood of Byzantium, but also in the heart of the land the town which thenceforth bore his name.   Alexander, here too the precursor of Roman policy, arrived at and crossed the Danube, and made this stream the northern boundary of his empire ; the Thracians in his army played by no means the least part in the subjugation of Asia. After his death the Hellespont seemed as though it would become one of the great centres of the new formation of states, and the wide domain from thence to the Danube [1] as though it would become the northern half of a Greek empire, and would promise for the capital of Lysimachus, the former governor of Thrace—the town of Lysimachia, *Lysima-* newly established in the Thracian Chersonese—a like *chus.* future as for the capitals of the marshals of Syria and Egypt.   But this result was not attained ; the independence of this kingdom did not survive the fall of its first ruler (281 B.C., 473 U.C.).   In the century which elapsed from that time to the establishment of the ascendancy of Rome in the East, attempts were made, sometimes by the Seleucids, sometimes by the Ptolemies, sometimes by the Attalids, to bring the European possessions of Lysimachus under their power, but all of them without lasting result. The empire of Tylis in the Haemus, which the Celts not *Empire of* long after the death of Alexander, and nearly at the same *Tylis.* time with their permanent settlement in Asia Minor, had founded in the Moeso-Thracian territory, destroyed the seed of Greek civilisation within its sphere, and itself succumbed during the Hannibalic war to the assaults of the Thracians, who extirpated these intruders to the last man.   Thenceforth there was not in Thrace any leading power at all ; the relations subsisting between the Greek coast-towns and the princes of the several tribes, which would probably correspond approximately to those before

---

[1] That for Lysimachus the Danube was the boundary of the empire, is evident from Pausanias, i. 9, 6.

Alexander's time, are illustrated by the description which Polybius gives of the most important of these towns : " Where the Byzantines had sowed, there the Thracian barbarians reaped, and against these neither the sword nor money is of avail ; if the citizens kill one of the princes, three others thereupon invade their territory, and, if they buy off one, five more demand the like annual payment."

Later Macedonian rulers.

The efforts on the part of the later Macedonian rulers to gain once more a firm footing in Thrace, and in particular to bring under their power the Greek towns of the south coast, were opposed by the Romans, partly in order to keep down the development of Macedonia's power generally, partly in order not to allow the important " royal road " leading to the East—that along which Xerxes marched to Greece and the Scipios marched against Antiochus—to fall in all its extent into Macedonian hands.   Already, after the battle at Cynoscephalae, the frontier-line was drawn nearly such as it thenceforth remained.   The two last Macedonian rulers made several attempts, either directly to establish themselves in Thrace or to attach to themselves its individual rulers by treaties ; the last Philip even gained over Philippopolis once more, and put into it a garrison, which, it is true, the Odrysae soon drove out afresh.   Neither he nor his son succeeded in placing matters on a permanent footing ; and the independence conceded by Rome to the Thracians after the breaking up of Macedonia destroyed whatever Hellenic germs might still be left there.   Thrace itself became— in part already in the republican, and more decidedly in the imperial period—a Roman vassal-principality, and then in 46 a Roman province (p. 211) ; but the Hellenising of the land had not passed beyond the fringe of Greek colonial towns, which in the earliest period had been established round this coast, and in course of time had sunk rather than risen.   Powerful and permanent as was the hold of Macedonian civilisation on the East, as weak and perishable was its contact with Thrace ; Philip and Alexander themselves appear to have reluctantly undertaken, and to have but lightly valued, their settlements in this land.[1] Till far into the imperial period the land remained with the natives; the Greek towns that were still left along the coast, almost all on the decline, remained without any Greek land in their rear.

This belt of Hellenic towns stretching from the Macedonian frontier to the Tauric Chersonese was of very unequal texture. In the south it was close and compact from Abdera onward to Byzantium on the Dardanelles; yet none of these towns held a prominent position in later times with the exception of Byzantium, which through the fertility of its territory, its productive tunny fisheries, its uncommonly favourable position for trade, its industrial diligence, and the energy of its citizens—heightened merely and hardened by its exposed situation—was enabled to defy even the worst times of Hellenic anarchy. Far more scantily had the settlements developed themselves on the west coast of the Black Sea; among those subsequently belonging to the Roman province of Thrace Mesembria alone was of some importance; among those subsequently Moesian Odessus (Varna) and Tomis (Küstendje). Beyond the mouths of the Danube and the boundary of the Roman empire, on the northern shore of the Pontus, there lay amidst the barbarian land Tyra[2] and Olbia; further on, the old and great Greek mercantile cities in what is now the Crimea—Heraclea or Chersonesus and Panticapaeum—formed a stately copestone.

Greek towns in Thrace and on the Black Sea.

All these settlements enjoyed Roman protection, after the Romans had become generally the leading power on the Graeco-Asiatic continent; and the strong arm, which often came down heavily on the Hellenic land proper, prevented here at least disasters like the destruction of Lysimachia. The protection of these Greeks devolved in

Under Roman protection.

[1] Calybe near Byzantium arose according to Strabo (vii. 6, 2, p. 320) φιλίππου τοῦ 'Αμύντου τοὺς πονηροτάτους ἐνταῦθα ἱδρύσαντος. Philippopolis is alleged even according to the account of Theopompus (fr. 122 Müller) to have been founded as Πονηρόπολις, and to have received

VOL. I.

colonists corresponding with that description. However little these reports deserve trust, they yet in their coincidence express the Botany-Bay character of these foundations.

[2] Yet the northern Bessarabian line, which perhaps is Roman, reaches as far as Tyra (p. 226).

the republican period partly on the governor of Macedonia, partly on the governor of Bithynia, after this became Roman; Byzantium subsequently remained with Bithynia.[1] We may add that in the imperial period, after the erection of the governorship of Moesia and subsequently of that of Thrace, the supplying of protection devolved on these.

Protection and favour were granted by Rome to these Greeks from the first; but neither the republic nor the earlier imperial period made efforts for the extension of Hellenism.[2] After Thrace had become Roman, it was divided into land-districts;[3] and almost down to the end of the first century there is no record of the laying out of a town there, with the exception of two colonies of Claudius and Vespasian—Apri in the interior not far from

---

[1] That Byzantium was still in Trajan's time under the governor of Bithynia, follows from Plin. *ad Trai.* 43. From the congratulations of the Byzantines to the legates of Moesia we cannot infer their having belonged to this governorship, which from their situation was hardly possible; the relations to the governor of Moesia may be explained from the commercial connections of the city with the Moesian ports. That Byzantium was in the year 53 under the senate, and so did not belong to Thrace, is plain from Tacitus, *Ann.* xii. 62. Cicero (*in Pis.* 35, 86; *de prov. cons.* 4, 6) does not attest its having belonged to Macedonia under the republic, since the town was then free. This freedom seems, as in the case of Rhodes, to have been often given and often taken away. Cicero, *l.c.*, ascribes freedom to it; Pliny in the year 53 it is tributary; Pliny (*H. N.* iv. 11, 46) adduces it as a free city; Vespasian withdraws its freedom (Suetonius, *Vesp.* 8).

[2] This is proved by the absence of coins of the Thracian inland towns, which could be assigned by metal and style to the older period. That a number of Thracian, especially Odrysian, princes coined in part even at a very early period, proves only that

they ruled over places on the coast with a Greek or half-Greek population. A similar judgment must be formed as to the tetradrachms of the "Thracians," which stand quite isolated (Sallet, *Num. Zeitschrift,* iii. 241).—The inscriptions also found in the interior of Thrace are throughout of Roman times. The decree of a town not named found at Bessapara, now Tatar Bazarjik, to the west of Philippopolis, by Dumont (*Inscr. de la Thrace,* p. 7), is indeed assigned to a good Macedonian time, but only from the character of the writing, which is perhaps deceptive.

[3] The fifty strategies of Thrace (Plin. *H. N.* iv. 11, 40; Ptolem. iii. 11, 6) are not military districts, but, as is apparent with special clearness in Ptolemy, land-districts, which correspond with the tribes (στρατηγία Μαιδική, Βεσσική κ. τ. λ.) and form a contrast to the towns. The designation στρατηγός has, just like *praetor,* lost subsequently its original military value. Here perhaps the analogy of Egypt, which likewise was divided into urban domains under urban magistrates and into land-districts under *strategoi,* served primarily as a basis. A στρατηγὸς Ἀστικῆς περὶ Πέρινθον from the Roman period occurs in *Eph. epigr.* ii. p. 252.

Perinthus, and Deultus on the most northern coast.[1]
Domitian began by introducing the Greek urban constitution into the interior, at first for the capital of the country,
Philippopolis.   Under Trajan a series of other Thracian
townships obtained like civic rights ; Topirus not far
from Abdera, Nicopolis on the Nestus, Plotinopolis on the
Hebrus, Pautalia near Köstendil, Serdica now Sofia,
Augusta Traiana near Alt-Zagora, a second Nicopolis on
the northern slope of Haemus,[2] besides, on the coast, Traianopolis at the mouth of the Hebrus ; further, under
Hadrian Adrianopolis, the modern Adrianople.   All these
towns were not colonies of foreigners but polities of Greek
organisation, composed after the model set up by Augustus
in the Epirot Nicopolis ; it was a civilising and Hellenising of the province from above downwards.   A Thracian
diet existed thenceforth in Philippopolis just as in the
properly Greek provinces.   This last offshoot of Hellenism
was not the weakest.   The country was rich and charming—a coin of the town Pautalia praises the fourfold
blessing of the ears of grain, of the grapes, of the silver,
and of the gold ; and Philippopolis as well as the beautiful
valley of the Tundja were the home of rose-culture and
of rose-oil—and the vigour of the Thracian type was not
broken.   Here was developed a dense and prosperous
population ; we have already mentioned the largeness of
the levy in Thrace, and few territories stand on an equality
with Thrace at this epoch in the activity of the urban
mints.   When Philippopolis succumbed in the year 251

*Philippo-
polis and
other towns
with civic
rights.*

---

[1] In Deultus, the *colonia Flavia Pacis
Deultensium*, veterans of the eighth
legion, were provided for (*C. I. L.* vi.
3828). Flaviopolis on the Chersonese,
the old Coela, was certainly not a
colony (Plin. iv. 11, 47), but belongs
to the peculiar settlement of the imperial menials on this domanial possession (*Eph. epigr.* v. p. 83).

[2] This town Νικόπολις ἡ περὶ Αἶμον
of Ptolem. iii. 11, 7, Νικόπολις πρὸς
Ἴστρον of the coins, the modern Ni-
kup on the Jantra, belongs to lower
Moesia geographically, and, as the
names of governors on the coins show,

since Severus also administratively ; but
not merely does Ptolemy adduce it in
Thrace, but the places where the Hadrianic terminal stones (*C. I. L.* iii. 749,
comp. p. 992) are found, appear to
assign it likewise to Thrace.   As this
Greek inland town fitted neither the
Latin town-communities of lower
Moesia nor the κοινόν of the Moesian
Pontus, it was assigned at the first
organising of the relations to the κοινόν
of the Thracians.   Subsequently it
must, no doubt, have been attached
to one or the other of those Moesian
groups.

to the Goths (p. 240), it is said to have numbered 100,000 inhabitants. The energetic part taken by the Byzantines in favour of the emperor of the Greek East, Pescennius Niger, and the several years' resistance which the town even after his defeat opposed to the victor, show the resources and the courage of these Thracian townsmen. If the Byzantines here, too, succumbed and lost even for a season their civic rights, the time, for which the rise of the Thracian land paved the way, was soon to set in, when Byzantium should become the new Hellenic Rome and the chief capital of the remodelled empire.

Lower Moesia.

In the neighbouring province of lower Moesia a similar development took place, although on a smaller scale. The Greek coast-towns, the metropolis of which, at least in the Roman period, was Tomis, were, probably on the constituting of the Roman province of Moesia, grouped as the "Five-cities-league of the left shore of the Black Sea," or as it was also called, " of the Greeks," that is, the Greeks of this province. Later there was annexed to this league, as a sixth town, that of Marcianopolis, constructed by Trajan not far from the coast on the Thracian frontier, and organised, like the Thracian towns, after the Greek model.[1]

Tomis and the Pontic Pentapolis.

[1] The κοινὸν τῆς Πενταπόλεως is found on an inscription of Odessus, *C. I. Gr.* 2056 *c.*, which may fairly belong to the earlier imperial period, the Pontic Hexapolis, on two inscriptions of Tomis probably of the second century A.D. (Marquardt, *Staatsverw.* i.[2] p. 305; Hirschfeld, *Arch. epigr. Mitth.* vi. 22). The Hexapolis in any case, and in accordance therewith probably also the Pentapolis, must have been brought into harmony with the Roman provincial boundaries, that is, must have included in it the Greek towns of lower Moesia. These are also found, if we follow the surest guides,—the coins of the imperial period. There were six mints (apart from Nicopolis, p. 282, note) in lower Moesia : Istros, Tomis, Callatis, Dionysopolis, Odessus, and Marcianopolis, and, as the last town was founded by Trajan, the Pentapolis is

thereby explained. Tyra and Olbia hardly belonged to it ; at least the numerous and loquacious monuments of the latter town nowhere show any link of connection with this city-league. It is called κοινὸν τῶν Ἑλλήνων on an inscription of Tomis, printed in the Athenian *Pandora* of 1st June 1868 [and in *Anc. Gr. Inscr. in the British Museum*, ii. n. 175] : Ἀγαθῇ τύχη. Κατὰ τὰ δόξαντα τῇ κρατήστη βουλῇ καὶ τῷ λαμπροτάτω δήμω τῆς λαμπροτάτης μητροπόλεως καὶ ά τοῦ εὐωνύμου πόντου Τόμεως τὸν Ποντάρχην Αὐρ. Πρείσκιον Ἀννιανὸν ἄρξαντα τοῦ κοινοῦ τῶν Ἑλλήνων καὶ τῆς μητρ[ο]-πόλεως τὴν ά ἀρχὴν ἀγνῶς, καὶ ἀρχιερα-σάμενον, τὴν δὲ ὅπλων καὶ κυνηγεσίων ἐνδόξως φιλοτειμίαν μὴ διαλιπόντα, ἀλλὰ καὶ βουλευτὴν καὶ τῶν πρωτευόντων φλαβίας Νέας πόλεως, καὶ τὴν ἀρχιέρειαν σύμβιον αὐτοῦ Ἰουλίαν Ἀπολαύστην πάσης τειμῆς χάριν.

We have already observed that the camp-towns on the
bank of the Danube, and generally the townships
called into life by Rome in the interior, were instituted
after the Italian model ; lower Moesia was the only
Roman province intersected by the linguistic boundary,
inasmuch as the Tomitanian cities-league belonged to the
Greek, the Danubian towns, like Durostorum and Oescus
to the Latin, linguistic domain.   In other respects essentially the same holds true of this Moesian cities-league, as
was remarked regarding Thrace.   We have a description
of Tomis from the last years of Augustus, doubtless by
one banished thither for punishment, but certainly true in
substance.   The population consists for the greater part
of Getae and Sarmatae ; they wear, like the Dacians on
Trajan's column, skins and trousers, long waving hair and
unshorn beard, and appear in the street on horseback
and armed with the bow, with the quiver on their shoulder,
and the knife in their girdle.   The few Greeks who are
found among them have adopted the barbarian customs,
including the trousers, and are able to express themselves
as well or better in Getic than in Greek ; he is lost, who
cannot make himself intelligible in Getic, and no man
understands a word of Latin.   Before the gates rove
predatory bands of the most various peoples, and their
arrows not seldom fly over the protecting city-walls ; he
who ventures to till his field does it at the peril of his life,
and ploughs in armour—at anyrate about the time of
Caesar's dictatorship; on occasion of the raid of Burebista,
the town had fallen into the hands of the barbarians, and
a few years before that exile came to Tomis, during the
Dalmato-Pannonian insurrection, the fury of war had once
more raged over this region.   The coins and the inscriptions of that city accord well with these accounts, in so far
as the metropolis of the " left-Pontic cities-league " in the
pre-Roman period coined no silver, which several other of
these towns did ; and, in general, coins and inscriptions
from the time before Trajan occur only in an isolated way.
But in the second and third centuries it was remodelled
and may be termed a foundation of Trajan with very

much the same warrant as Marcianopolis, which likewise quickly attained to considerable development. The barrier formerly mentioned (p. 227) in the Dobrudscha served at the same time as a protecting wall for the town of Tomis. Behind this wall commerce and navigation were flourishing. There was in the town a society of Alexandrian merchants with its own chapel of Serapis;[1] in municipal liberality and municipal ambition the town was inferior to no Greek town of middle size ; it was still even now bilingual, but in such a way that, alongside of the Greek language always retained on the coins, here on the border, where the two languages of the empire came into contact, the Latin is also often employed even in public monuments.

Tyra.

Beyond the imperial frontier, between the mouths of the Danube and the Crimea, the Greek merchant had made few settlements on the coast ; there were here only two Greek towns of note, both founded in remote times by Miletus, Tyra at the mouth of the river of the same name, the modern Dniester, and Olbia on the bay into which the Borysthenes (Dnieper) and the Hypanis (Bug) fall. The forlorn position of these Hellenes amidst the barbarians pressing around them, in the time of the Diadochi as well as during the earlier rule of the Roman

iii. 282.

republic, has already been described (iii. 297). The emperors brought help. In the year 56, that is, in the exemplary beginning of Nero's government, Tyra was annexed to the province of Moesia. Of the more remote

Olbia.

Olbia we possess a description from the age of Trajan ;[2]

---

[1] This is shown by the remarkable inscription in Allard (*La Bulgarie orientale*, Paris, 1863, p. 263) : Θεῷ μεγάλῳ Σαράπ[ιδι καὶ] τοῖς συννάοις θεοῖς [καὶ τῷ αὐ]τοκράτορι T. Αἰλίῳ Ἀδριαν[ῷ Ἀ]ντωνείνῳ Σεβαστῷ Εὐσεβ-[εῖ] καὶ M. Ἀυρηλίῳ Οὐήρῳ Καίσαρι Καρπίων Ἀνουβίωνος τῷ οἴκῳ τῶν Ἀλεξανδρέων τὸν βωμὸν ἐκ τῶν ἰδίων ἀνέθηκεν ἔτους κγ' [μηνὸς] φαρμουθὶ ά ἐπὶ ἱερέων [Κ]ορνούτου τοῦ καὶ Σαραπίωνος [Πολύ]-μνου τοῦ καὶ Λον[γείνου]. The mariner's guild of Tomis meets us several times in the inscriptions of the town.

[2] Olbia, constantly assailed in war and often destroyed, suffered, according to the statement of Dio (*Borysth.* p. 75, n.), about 150 years before his time, *i.e.* somewhat before the year 100 A.D., and so probably in the expedition of Burebista (iv. 305), its last and most severe conquest (τὴν τελευταίαν καὶ μεγίστην ἅλωσιν). Εἷλον δὲ, Dio continues, καὶ ταύτην Γέται καὶ τὰς ἄλλας τὰς ἐν τοῖς ἀριστεροῖς τοῦ Πόντου πόλεις μέχρι Ἀπολλωνίας (Sozopolis or Sizebolu, the last Greek town of note on the Pontic west coast);

the town was still bleeding from its old wounds ; the
wretched walls enclosed equally wretched houses, and the
quarter then inhabited filled but a small portion of the old
considerable city-circuit, of which individual towers that
were left stood far off in the desolate plain ; in the
temples there was no statue of the gods which did not
bear traces of the hands of the barbarians ; the inhabitants
had not forgotten their Hellenic character, but they
dressed and fought after the manner of the Scythians,
with whom they were daily in conflict. Just as often as
by Greek names, they designated themselves by Scythian,
i.e. by those of Sarmatian stocks akin to the Iranians ;[1]
in fact, in the royal house itself Sauromates was a common name. These towns were indebted doubtless for
their very continued existence less to their own power
than to the good-will or rather the self-interest of the
natives. The tribes settled on this coast were neither in
a position to carry on foreign trade from emporia of their
own, nor could they dispense with it ; in the Hellenic
coast-towns they bought salt, articles of clothing and
wine, and the more civilised princes protected in some
measure the strangers against the attacks of the barbarians
proper. The earlier rulers of Rome must have had
scruples at undertaking the difficult protection of this
remote settlement ; nevertheless Pius, when the Scythians
once more besieged them, sent to them Roman auxiliary
troops, and compelled the barbarians to offer peace and furnish hostages. The town must have been incorporated

ὅθεν δὴ καὶ σφόδρα ταπεινὰ τὰ πράγ-
ματα κατέστη τῶν ταύτῃ Ἑλλήνων,
τῶν μὲν οὐκέτι συνοικισθεισῶν πόλεων,
τῶν δὲ φαύλως καὶ τῶν πλείσ-
των βαρβάρων εἰς αὐτὰς συρρυέντων.
The young citizen of rank with a
marked Ionic physiognomy, with
whom Dio then meets, who has slain
or captured numerous Sarmatians, and
though not acquainted with Phocy-
lides, knows Homer by heart, wears
mantle and trousers after the Scythian
fashion, and a knife in his girdle.
The townsmen all wear long hair and
a long beard, and only one has shorn

both, which is suspected in him as a
token of servile attitude towards the
Romans. Thus a century later matters
there looked quite such as Ovid describes them at Tomis.

[1] Quite commonly the father has a
Scythian name and the son a Greek,
or conversely ; *e.g.* an inscription of
Olbia set up under or after Trajan
(*C. I. Gr.* 2074) records six *strategoi*,
M. Ulpius Pyrrhus son of Arseuaches,
Demetrios son of Xessagaros, Zoilos
son of Arsakes, Badakes son of Ra-
danpson, Epikrates son of Koxuros,
Ariston son of Vargadakes.

directly with the empire by Severus, from whom onward
Olbia struck coins with the image of the Roman rulers.
As a matter of course this annexation extended only to
the town-territories themselves, and it never was intended
to bring the barbarian dwellers around Tyra and Olbia
under the Roman sceptre.   It has already been remarked
(p. 239) that these towns were the first which, presumably under Alexander († 235), succumbed to the incipient
Gothic invasion.

Bosporus.   If the Greeks had but sparingly settled on the mainland to the north of the Black Sea, the great peninsula
projecting from this coast, the Tauric Chersonesus—the
modern Crimea—had for long been in great part in their
hands.   Separated by the mountains, which the Taurians
occupied, the two centres of the Greek settlement upon it
were, at the western end the Doric free town of Heraclea
or Chersonesus (Sebastopol), at the eastern the principality
of Panticapaeum or Bosporus (Kertch).   King Mithradates had at the summit of his power united the two, and
here established for himself a second northern empire (iii.
298), which then, after the collapse of his power, was left
as the only remnant of it to his son and murderer Pharnaces.   When the latter, after the war between Caesar and
Pompeius, attempted to regain his father's dominion in
Asia Minor, Caesar had vanquished him (iv. 439), and
declared him to have forfeited also the Bosporan empire.

Asander. In the meanwhile Asander, the governor left there by
Pharnaces, had renounced allegiance to the king in the
hope of acquiring the kingdom for himself by this service
rendered to Caesar.   When Pharnaces after his defeat
returned to his Bosporan kingdom, he at first indeed
repossessed himself of his capital, but ultimately was
worsted, and fell bravely fighting in the last battle—as a
soldier at least, not unequal to his father.   The succession
was contested between Asander, who was in fact master
of the land, and Mithradates of Pergamus, an able officer
of Caesar, whom the latter had invested with the Bosporan principality ; both sought at the same time to lean
for support on the dynasty heretofore ruling in the

Bosporus and on the great Mithradates, inasmuch as Asander married Dynamis, the daughter of Pharnaces, while Mithradates, sprung from a Pergamene burgess-family, asserted that he was an illegitimate son of the great Mithradates Eupator—whether it was that this rumour determined the selection, or that it was put into circulation in order to justify it. As Caesar himself was called in the first instance to attend to more important tasks, arms decided between the legitimate and the illegitimate Caesarian, and once more in favour of the latter ; Mithradates fell in combat, and Asander remained master in the Bosporus. In the outset—without doubt, because he had not the confirmation of the lord-paramount—he avoided assuming the name of king, and contented himself with the title of archon, borne by the older princes of Panticapaeum ; but he soon procured, probably even from Caesar himself, the confirmation of his rule and the royal title.[1]　At his death (737-738 U.C.) he left his kingdom to his wife Dynamis. So strong was still the power of hereditary succession and of the name of Mithradates, that both a certain Scribonianus, who first attempted to occupy Asander's place, and after him king Polemon of Pontus, to whom Augustus promised the Bosporan kingdom, conjoined with the taking up of the dominion a marriage-alliance with Dynamis ; moreover, the former asserted that he was himself a grandson of Mithradates, while king Polemon, soon after the death of Dynamis, married a granddaughter of Antonius, and consequently a kinswoman of the imperial house. After his early death—he fell in conflict with the Aspurgiani on the Asiatic coast—his children under age did not succeed him ; and even with his grandson of the same name, whom the emperor Gaius reinstated, notwithstanding his boyish age, in the

(margin: 17-16.)

(margin: Polemon.)

---

[1] As Asander reckoned his archonship probably from the very time of his revolt from Pharnaces, and so from the summer of 707, and assumes the royal title already in the fourth year of his reign, this year may warrantably be put in the autumn 709-710, and the confirmation have thus been the work of Caesar. Antonius cannot well have bestowed it, as he only came to Asia at the end of 712; still less can we think of Augustus, whom the pseudo-Lucian (*Macrob.* 15) names, interchanging father and son.

(margin: 47.)

(margin: 45-4.)

(margin: 42.)

year 38, into the two principalities of his father, the Bosporan kingdom did not long remain. In his place the emperor Claudius called a real or alleged descendant of Mithradates Eupator, and in this house, apparently, the principality thenceforth continued.[1]

The Eupatorids.

Extent of the Bosporan rule.

While in the Roman state elsewhere the dependent principality disappears after the end of the first dynasty, and from Trajan's time the principle of direct government is carried out through the whole extent of the Roman empire, the Bosporan kingdom subsisted under Roman supremacy down to the fourth century. It was only after the centre of gravity of the empire was shifted to Constantinople that this state became merged in the empire at large,[2] in order to be soon thereafter abandoned by it and to become, at least in greater part, the prey of the Huns.[3]

[1] Mithradates, whom Claudius in the year 41 made king of Bosporus, traced back his descent to Eupator (Dio, lx. 8 ; Tacitus, *Ann.* xii. 18), and he was followed by his brother Cotys (Tacitus, *l.c.*). Their father was called Aspurgus (*C. I. Gr.* ii. p. 95), but need not on that account have been an Aspurgian (Strabo, xi. 2, 19, p. 415). Of a subsequent change of dynasty there is no mention ; king Eupator in the time of Pius (Lucian, *Alex.* 57 ; *vita Pii*, 9) points to the same house. Probably, we may add, these later Bosporan kings, as well as the immediate successors of Polemon not even known to us by name, stood in relations of affinity to the Polemonids, as indeed the first Polemon himself had as his wife a granddaughter of Eupator. The Thracian royal names, such as Cotys and Rhascuporis, which are common in the Bosporan royal house, connect themselves doubtless with the son-in-law of Polemon, the Thracian king Cotys. The appellation Sauromates, which frequently occurs after the end of the first century, has doubtless arisen through intermarriage with Sarmatian princely houses, but, of course, does not prove that those who bore it were themselves Sarmatians. If Zosimus, i. 31, blames the petty and unworthy

princes who attained to government after the extinction of the old royal family, for the fact that the Goths under Valerian could carry out their piratical expeditions in Bosporan ships, this may be correct, and in the first instance Pharnaces may be meant, of whom there are coins from the years 254 and 255. But even these, too, are marked with the image of the Roman emperor, and later there are again found the old family names (all the Bosporan kings are Tiberii Julii), and the old surnames, such as Sauromates and Rhascuporis. Taken as a whole, the old traditions as well as the Roman protectorate were still at that time here retained.

[2] The last Bosporan coin is of the year 631, of the Achaemenid era, A.D. 335 ; this is certainly connected with the installation, which falls in this very year, of Hanniballianus, the nephew of Constantine I., as "king," although this kingdom embraced chiefly the east of Asia Minor and had as its capital Caesarea in Cappadocia. After this king and his kingdom had perished in the bloody catastrophe after Constantine's death, the Bosporus was placed directly under Constantinople.

[3] The Bosporus was still in Roman possession in the year 366 (Ammi-

The Bosporus, however, in reality was and continued to be more a town than a kingdom, and had more similarity with the town-districts of Tyra and Olbia than with the kingdoms of Cappadocia and Numidia. Here, too, the Romans protected only the Hellenic town Panticapaeum, and did not aim at enlargement of the bounds and subjugation of the interior any more than in Tyra and Olbia. To the domain of the prince of Panticapaeum belonged the Greek settlements of Theudosia on the peninsula itself, and Phanagoria (Taman) on the opposite Asiatic coast, but not Chersonesus[1]—or at least only somewhat as Athens belonged to the province of the governor of Achaia. The town had obtained autonomy from the Romans, and saw in the prince its immediate protector, not its sovereign ; as a free town, too, in the imperial period, it never coined with the stamp either of king or emperor. On the mainland, not even the town which the Greeks called Tanais—a stirring emporium at the mouth of the Don, but hardly a Greek foundation—stood permanently under subjection to the Roman vassal-princes.[2] Of the more or less barbarian tribes on the peninsula itself, and on the European and Asiatic coast southward from Tanais,

anus, xxvi. 10, 6) ; soon afterwards the Greeks on the north shore of the Black Sea must have been left to themselves, until Justinian reoccupied the peninsula (Procopius, *Bell. Goth.* iv. 5). In the interval Panticapaeum perished under the assaults of the Huns.

[1] The coins of the town Chersonesus from the imperial period have the legend Χερσονήσου ἐλευθέρας, once even βασιλευούσης, and neither name nor head of king or emperor (A. v. Sallet, *Zeitschrift für Num.* i. 27 ; iv. 273). The independence of the town evidences itself also in the fact that it coins in gold no less than the kings of the Bosporus. As the era of the town appears correctly fixed at the year 36 B.C. (*C. I. Gr.* n. 8621), in which freedom was conferred upon it presumably by Antonius, the gold coin of the "ruling city" dated from

the year 109 was struck in 75 A.D.

[2] According to Strabo's representation (xi. 2, 11, p. 495) the rulers of Tanais stand independently by the side of those of Panticapaeum, and the tribes to the south of the Don depend sometimes on the latter, sometimes on the former ; when he adds that several of the Panticapaean princes ruled as far as Tanais, and particularly the last, Pharnaces, Asander, Polemon, this seems more exception than rule. In the inscription quoted in the next note the Tanaites stand among the subject stocks, and a series of Tanaitic inscriptions confirms this for the time from Marcus to Gordian ; but the Ἕλληνες καὶ Ταναεῖται alongside of the ἄρχοντες Ταναειτῶν and of the frequently mentioned Ἑλληνάρχαι confirm the view that the town even then remained non-Greek.

probably only the nearest stood in a fixed relation of dependence.[1]

Military position of the Bosporus.
The territory of Panticapaeum was too extensive and too important, especially for mercantile intercourse, to be left like Olbia and Tyra to the administration of changing municipal officials and a far distant governor; therefore it was entrusted to hereditary princes—a course further recommended by the circumstance that it might not seem advisable to transfer directly to the empire the relations which this region sustained to the surrounding tribes. The rulers of the Bosporan house, in spite of their Achaemenid pedigree and their Achaemenid mode of reckoning time, felt themselves thoroughly as Greek princes, and traced back their origin, after the good Hellenic fashion, to Herakles and the Eumolpids. The dependence of these Greeks on Rome—the royal in Panticapaeum, as the republican in Chersonesus—was implied in the nature of things, and they never thought of rising against the protecting arm of the empire; if once, under the emperor Claudius, the Roman troops had to march against an insubordinate prince of the Bosporus,[2] yet withal this

---

[1] In the only vivid narrative from the Bosporan history which we possess, that of Tacitus, *Ann.* xii. 15-31, concerning the two rival brothers, Mithradates and Cotys, the neighbouring tribes, the Dandaridae, Siracae, Aorsi, are under rulers of their own not legally dependent on the Roman prince of Panticapaeum.—As to titles, the older Panticapaean princes are wont to call themselves archons of the Bosporus, that is, of Panticapaeum, and of Theudosia, and kings of the Sindi and of all the Maitae and other non-Greek tribes. In like manner what is, so far as I know, the oldest among the royal inscriptions of the Roman epoch names Aspurgos, son of Asandrochos (Stephani, *Comptes rendus de la comm. pour* 1866, p. 128), as βασιλεύοντα παντὸς Βοσπόρου, Θεοδοσίης καὶ Σίνδων καὶ Μαϊτῶν καὶ Τορετῶν Ψησῶν τε καὶ Ταναειτῶν, ὑποτάσαντα Σκύθας καὶ Ταύρους. No inference as to the extent of the territory may be drawn

from the simplified title.—In the inscriptions of the later period there is found once under Trajan the doubtless adulatory title βασιλεὺς βασιλέων μέγας τοῦ παντὸς Βοσπόρου (*C. I. Gr.* 2123). The coins generally, from Asander onward, know no title but βασιλεύς, while yet Pharnaces calls himself βασιλεὺς βασιλέων μέγας. Beyond doubt this was the effect of the Roman sovereignty, with which a vassal-prince placed over other princes was not very compatible.

[2] This was the king Mithradates, installed by Claudius in the year 41, who some years afterwards was deposed and replaced by his brother Cotys; he lived afterwards in Rome, and perished in the confusions of the four-emperor-year (Plutarch, *Galba*, 13, 15). The state of the matter, however, is not clear either from the hints in Tacitus, *Ann.* xii. 15 (comp. Plin. *H. N.* vi. 5, 17), or from the report (confused by the interchange

region itself, amidst the fearful confusion in the middle of the third century, which especially affected it, never broke away from the empire even when it was falling to pieces.[1] The prosperous merchant-towns, permanently in need of military protection amidst a flux of barbaric peoples, held to Rome as the advanced posts to the main army. The garrison was doubtless chiefly raised in the land itself, and to create and manage it was beyond doubt the main task of the king of the Bosporus. The coins, which were struck on occasion of the investiture of such a king, exhibit doubtless the curule chair and the other honorary presents usual at such investiture, but also by their side shield, helmet, sword, battle-axe, and war-horse; it was no peaceful office which this prince undertook. The first of them, whom Augustus appointed, fell in conflict with the barbarians, and of his successors, *e.g.* king Sauromates, son of Rhoemetalces, fought in the first years of Severus with the Siracae and the Scythians—perhaps it was not quite without reason that he stamped his coins with the feats of Herakles. By sea, too, he had to be active, especially in keeping down the piracy which never ceased in the Black Sea (p. 242); that Sauromates likewise is credited with having brought the Taurians to order and chastised piracy. Roman troops, however, were also

of the two, Mithradates of Bosporus, and Mithradates of Iberia) in Petrus Patricius *fr.* 3. The Chersonese tales in the late Constantinus Porphyrogenitus, *de adm. imp.* c. 53, do not, of course, come into account. The bad Bosporan king Sauromates, Κρισκωνόρου (not Ρησκοπόρου) υἱός, who with the Sarmatians wages war against the emperors Diocletian and Constantius, as well as against the Chersonese faithful to the empire, has evidently arisen from a confusion of names between the Bosporan king and people; and just as historical as the variation on the history of David and Goliath, is the despatch of the mighty king of the Bosporans, Sauromates, by the small Chersonesite Pharnaces. The kings' names alone, *e.g.* besides those named, the Asander, who comes in after the

extinction of the family of the Sauromatae, suffice. The civic privileges and the localities of the city, for the explanation of which these *mirabilia* are invented, certainly deserve attention.

[1] There are no Bosporan gold or pseudo-gold coins without the head of the Roman emperor, and this is always that of the ruler recognised by the Roman senate. In the years 263 and 265, when in the empire elsewhere after the captivity of Valerian Gallienus was officially regarded as sole ruler, two heads here appear on the coins, is perhaps due only to want of information; yet the Bosporans may at that time have made another choice amid the many pretenders. The names are at this time not appended, and the effigies are not to be certainly distinguished.

stationed in the peninsula, perhaps a division of the Pontic fleet, certainly a detachment of the Moesian army ; their presence even in small numbers showed to the barbarians that the dreaded legionary stood behind these Greeks. In another way still the empire protected them ; at least in the later period there were regularly paid from the imperial chest to the princes of the Bosporus sums of money, of which they stood in need, in so far as the buying off of the hostile incursions by stated annual payments probably became a standing practice here—in what was not directly territory of the empire—still earlier than elsewhere.[1]

Position of this vassal-prince.

That the centralisation of the government had its application also in reference to this prince, and he stood to the Roman Caesar on a footing not much different from that of the burgomaster of Athens, is in various ways apparent ; it deserves mention that king Asander and the queen Dynamis struck gold coins with their name and their effigy, whereas king Polemon and his immediate successors, while retaining the right of coining gold, seeing that this territory as well as the adjoining barbarians were for long accustomed exclusively to gold currency, were induced to furnish their gold pieces with the name and the image of the reigning emperor. In like manner from Polemon's time the prince of this land was at the same time the chief priest for life of the emperor and of the imperial house. In other respects the administration and the court retained the forms introduced under Mithradates after the model of the Persian grand monarchy, although the chief secretary (ἀρχιγραμματεύς) and the chief chamberlain (ἀρχικοιτωνείτης) of the court of Panticapaeum stood related to the leading court-officers of the great kings, as the enemy of the Romans Mithradates Eupator to his descendant Tiberius Julius Eupator, who, on account of his claim to the Bosporan throne, appeared as a suitor at Rome at the bar of the emperor Pius.

[1] This we may be allowed to believe at the hands of the Scythian Toxaris in the dialogue placed among those of Lucian (c. 44) ; for the rest he narrates not merely μύθοις ὅμοια, but a very myth, of whose kings Leucanor and Eubiotes the coins, as may well be conceived, have no knowledge.

This northern Greece remained valuable for the empire on account of its commercial relations. Though these at this epoch were doubtless less important than in earlier times,[1] yet the mercantile intercourse continued very lively. In the Augustan period the tribes of the steppes brought slaves and skins,[2] the merchants of civilisation articles of clothing, wine, and other luxuries to Tanais; in a still higher degree Phanagoria was the depôt for the exports of the natives, Panticapaeum for the imports of the Greeks. Those troubles in the Bosporus in the Claudian age were a severe blow for the merchants of Byzantium. That the Goths began their piratic voyages in the third century by pressing the Bosporan vessels to lend them involuntary aid, has been already mentioned (p. 244). It was doubtless in consequence of this traffic, indispensable for the barbarian neighbours themselves, that the citizens of Chersonesus maintained their ground even after the withdrawal of the Roman garrisons, and were able subsequently— when in Justinian's time the power of the empire once more asserted itself in this direction—to return as Greeks into the Greek empire.

Trade and commerce in the Bosporus.

[1] As respects the export of grain, the notice in the report of Plautius (p. 218), deserves attention.

[2] From the offer of a township of the Siracae (on the Sea of Azoff) hard pressed by the Roman troops to deliver 10,000 slaves (Tacitus, *Ann.* xii. 17), it may be allowable to infer a lively import of slaves from these regions.

CHAPTER VIII.

ASIA MINOR.

THE great peninsula which is washed on three sides by the three seas, the Black, the Aegean, and the Mediterranean, and which is connected towards the east with the Asiatic continent proper, will, so far as it belongs to the frontier-territory of the empire, be dealt with in the next section, which treats of the region of the Euphrates and the relations between the Romans and Parthians. Here we have to set forth the peaceful relations, more especially of the western districts, under the imperial government.

The natives and the colonists.

The original, or at any rate pre-Greek, population of these wide regions held its ground in many places to a considerable extent down to the imperial period. The greatest part of Bithynia certainly belonged to the formerly' discussed Thracian stock ; Phrygia, Lydia, Cilicia, Cappadocia, show very manifold and not easily unravelled survivals of older linguistic epochs, which in various forms reach down to the Roman period ; strange names of gods, men, and places meet us everywhere. But, so far as our view reaches—and it is but seldom allowed to penetrate here very deeply—these elements appear only losing ground and waning, essentially as a negation of civilisation or—what seems to us here at least to coincide with it—Hellenising. We shall return at the fitting place to the individual groups of this category ; so far as concerns the historical development of Asia Minor in the imperial period there were but two active nationalities, the two which were the last immigrants, the Hellenes in the beginnings of the historical period, and the Celts during the troublous times of the Diadochi.

The history of the Hellenes of Asia Minor, so far as it forms a part of Roman history, has already been set forth. In the remote age, when the coasts of the Mediterranean were first navigated and settled, and the world began to be apportioned among the progressive nations at the expense of those left behind, the flood of Hellenic emigration had poured no doubt over all the shores of the Mediterranean Sea, but yet nowhere—not even towards Italy and Sicily,—in so broad a stream as over the Aegean Sea rich in islands, and the adjacent charming coast of anterior Asia rich in harbours. Thereafter the west-Asiatic Greeks themselves had taken an active part, above all the rest, in the further conquest of the world, and had helped to settle from Miletus the coasts of the Black, and from Phocaea and Cnidus those of the Western, Sea. In Asia Hellenic civilisation doubtless laid hold of the inhabitants of the interior, the Mysians, Lydians, Carians, Lycians ; and even the Persian great power remained not unaffected by it. But the Hellenes themselves possessed nothing but the fringe of coast, including at the utmost the lower course of the larger rivers and the islands. They were not able here to gain continental conquests and a power of their own by land overagainst the powerful native princes ; moreover the interior of Asia Minor, highlying and in great part but little capable of cultivation, was not so attractive for settlement as the coasts, and the communications of the latter with the interior were difficult. Essentially in consequence of this, the Asiatic Hellenes attained still less than the European to inward union and to great power of their own, and early learned submissiveness in presence of the lords of the continent. The national Hellenic idea first came to them from Athens ; they became its allies only after the victory, and did not remain so in the hour of danger. What Athens had

Hellenic and Hellenistic culture.

wished to provide, and had not been able to furnish
for these clients of the nation, was accomplished by
Alexander; Hellas he was obliged to conquer, Asia
Minor saw in the conqueror simply its deliverer.

Formation of new centres.

Alexander's victory in fact not merely made Asiatic
Hellenism secure, but opened up for it a wide, almost
boundless, future; in the process of continental settlement,
which, in contrast to the merely littoral, marked this second
stage of Hellenic world-conquest, Asia Minor took part to
a considerable extent. Yet of the great centres for the
newly formed states there was none that came to the
old Greek towns of the coast.[1]   The new period required
new formations in general, and above all, new towns, to
serve at once as Greek royal residences and as centres
of populations hitherto non-Greek, that were to be brought
to Greek habits. The great political development
moves around the towns of royal foundation and of royal
name, Thessalonica, Antioch, Alexandria. With their
masters the Romans had to contend; the possession of
Asia Minor they gained almost throughout, as a man
gets an estate from relations or friends, by bequest in a
testament; and, however heavy was the burden at times
of Roman government on the regions thus acquired,
there was not added here the sting of foreign rule.
Doubtless the Achaemenid Mithradates confronted the
Romans in Asia Minor with a national opposition, and
the Roman misrule drove the Hellenes into his arms;
but the Hellenes themselves never undertook anything
similar. Therefore there is little to be told of this great,
rich, and important possession in a political respect; and
all the less, inasmuch as what has been remarked in the
previous section concerning the national relations of the
Hellenes generally to the Romans holds good in substance
also for those of Asia Minor.

The provinces of Asia Minor.

The Roman administration of Asia Minor was never
organised in a systematic way, but the several territories

---

[1] Had the state of Lysimachus
endured it would probably have been
otherwise. His foundations, Alexandria in the Troad and Lysimachia,
Ephesos-Arsinoe strengthened by the
transference of the inhabitants of
Colophon and Lebedos, tended in
the direction indicated.

were, just as they came to the empire, established without material change of their limits as Roman administrative districts. The states which king Attalus III. of Pergamus bequeathed to the Romans, formed the province of Asia ; those of king Nicomedes, which likewise fell to them by inheritance, formed the province of Bithynia ; the territory taken from Mithradates Eupator formed the province of Pontus united with Bithynia. Crete was occupied by the Romans on occasion of the great war with the pirates ; Cyrene, which may also be mentioned here, was taken over by them according to the last will of its ruler. The same legal title gave to the republic the island of Cyprus ; to which was here added the need for the suppression of piracy. This had also laid a basis for the formation of the governorship of Cilicia ; the land was annexed to Rome completely by Pompeius at the same time with Syria, and the two were administered jointly during the first century. Possession of all these lands was already acquired by the republic. In the imperial period a number of territories were added, which had formerly belonged but indirectly to the empire : in 729 U. C. the kingdom of Galatia, with which there had been united a part of Phrygia, Lycaonia, Pisidia, and Pamphylia ; in 747 U. C. the lordship of king Deiotarus, son of Castor, which embraced Gangra in Paphlagonia and probably also Amasia and other neighbouring places ; in 17 A. D. the kingdom of Cappadocia ; in 43 the territory of the confederation of the Lycian towns ; in 63 the north-east of Asia Minor from the valley of the Iris to the Armenian frontier ; Lesser Armenia and some smaller principalities in Cilicia probably by Vespasian. Thereby the direct imperial administration was carried out throughout Asia Minor. As dependent principalities, there remained only the Tauric Bosporus, of which we have already spoken, and Great Armenia, of which the next section will treat.

When, on the introduction of the imperial government, the administrative partition was made between it and that of the senate, the whole territory of Asia Minor, so far as it was at that time directly under the empire, fell to

25.

7.

Senatorial and imperial government.

the latter body; the island of Cyprus, which at first had come under imperial administration, was likewise transferred, a few years later, to the senate. Thus arose the four senatorial governorships of Asia, Bithynia and Pontus, Cyprus, Crete and Cyrene. Only Cilicia, as part of the Syrian province, was placed at first under imperial administration. But the territories that subsequently came to be directly administered as parts of the empire were here, as throughout the empire, placed under imperial governors; thus even under Augustus there was formed from the inland districts of the Galatian kingdom the province of Galatia, and the coast district of Pamphylia was assigned to another governor, under which latter Lycia was also placed under Claudius. Moreover Cappadocia became an imperial governorship under Tiberius. Cilicia also naturally remained, when it obtained governors of its own, under imperial administration. Apart from the fact that Hadrian exchanged the important province of Bithynia and Pontus for the unimportant Lycio-Pamphylian one, this arrangement remained in force, until towards the end of the third century the senatorial share in administration generally was, with the exception of some slight remnants, superseded. The frontier was in the first period of the empire formed throughout by the dependent principalities; after their annexation the imperial frontier did not, apart from Cyrene, touch any of these administrative districts, excepting only the Cappadocian, so far as to this at that time was apportioned also the north-eastern border-district as far as Trapezus;[1] and even this

[1] Nowhere have the boundaries of the vassal states and even of the provinces changed more than in the north-east of Asia Minor. Direct imperial administration was introduced here for the districts of king Polemon, to which Zela, Neocaesarea, Trapezus belonged, in the year 63; for Lesser Armenia, we do not know exactly when, probably at the beginning of the reign of Vespasian. The last vassal king of Lesser Armenia, of whom there is mention, was the Herodian Aristobulus (Tacitus, *Ann.* xiii. 7, xiv. 26; Josephus, *Ant.* xx. 8, 4), who still possessed it in the year 60; in the year 75 the district was Roman (*C. I. L.* iii. 306), and probably one of the legions garrisoning Cappadocia from Vespasian's time was stationed from the first in the Lesser-Armenian Satala. Vespasian combined the regions mentioned, as well as Galatia and Cappadocia, into one large governorship. At the end of the reign of Domitian we find Galatia and Cappadocia separated and the north-eastern provinces

governorship bordered not with the foreign land proper, but in the north with the dependent tribes on the Phasis, and farther on with the vassal-kingdom of Armenia, which belonged *de jure* and in more than one sense *de facto* to the empire.

In order to gain a conception of the condition and the development of Asia Minor in the first three centuries of our era, so far as this is possible in the case of a country as to which we have no direct historical tradition, we must, looking to the conservative character of the Roman provincial government, begin with the older territorial divisions and the previous history of the several regions.

The province of Asia was the old kingdom of the Attalids, the west of Asia Minor as far north as the Bithynian and as far south as the Lycian frontier ; the eastern districts at first separated from it, the Great Phrygia, had already in the republican period been again attached to it (iii. 288), and the province thenceforth reached as far as the country of the Galatians and the Pisidian mountains. Rhodes too and the other smaller islands of the Aegean Sea belonged to this province. The original Hellenic settlement had, besides the islands and the coast proper, occupied also the lower valleys of the larger rivers ; Magnesia on the Sipylus, in the valley of the Hermus, the other Magnesia and Tralles in the valley of the Maeander, had already before Alexander been founded as Greek towns, or had at any rate become such ; the Carians, Lydians, Mysians, became early at least half Hellenes. The Greek rule, when it set in, found not much to do in the coast districts ; Smyrna, which centuries before had been destroyed by the barbarians of the

Asia.

iii. 274.

The coast-towns.

attached to Galatia. Under Trajan at first the whole district is once more in one hand, subsequently (*Eph. Ep. V.* n. 1345) it is divided in such a way that the north-east coast belongs to Cappadocia. On that footing it remained, at least in so far that Trapezus and so also Lesser Armenia were thenceforth constantly under this governor. Consequently—apart from a short interruption under Domitian —the legate of Galatia had nothing to do with the defence of the frontier, and this, as was implied in the nature of the case, was always combined with the command of Cappadocia and of its legions.

interior, rose at that time from its ruins, in order speedily to become one of the first stars in the brilliant belt of the cities of Asia Minor ; and if the rebuilding of Ilion at the sepulchral mound of Hector was more a work of piety than of policy, the laying out of Alexandria on the coast of the Troas was of enduring importance. Pergamus in the valley of the Caicus flourished as the court-residence of the Attalids.

The interior.

In the great work of Hellenising the interior of this province in keeping with the intentions of Alexander, all the Hellenic governments, Lysimachus, the Seleucids, the Attalids vied with each other. The details of the foundations have disappeared from our tradition still more than the warlike events of the same epoch ; we are left dependent mainly on the names and the surnames of the towns ; but even these suffice to make known to us the general outlines of this activity continuing for centuries, and yet homogeneous and throughout conscious of its aim. A series of inland townships, Stratonicea in Caria, Peltae, Blaundus, Docimeium, Cadi in Phrygia, the Mysomacedonians in the district of Ephesus, Thyatira, Hyrcania, Nacrasa in the region of the Hermus, the Ascylaces in the district of Adramytium, are designated in documents or other credible testimonies as cities of the Macedonians ; and these notices are of a nature so accidental, and the townships in part so unimportant, that the like designation certainly extended to a great number of other settlements in this region ; and we may infer an extensive settling of Greek soldiers in the districts indicated, probably connected with the protection of anterior Asia against the Galatians and Pisidians. If, moreover, the coins of the considerable Phrygian town Synnada combine with the name of their city that ot the Ionians and the Dorians as well as that of the common Zeus (Ζεὺς πάνδημος), one of the Alexandrids must have summoned the Greeks in common to settle there ; and the summons was certainly not confined to this single town. The numerous towns, chiefly of the interior, the names of which are traceable to the royal houses of the Seleucids or the Attalids, or

which have otherwise Greek names, need not here be
adduced ; there are found in particular among the towns
certainly founded or reorganised by the Seleucids several
that were in later times the most flourishing and most
civilised in the interior, *e.g.* in southern Phrygia Laodicea,
and above all Apamea, the old Celaenae on the great
military road from the west coast of Asia Minor to the
middle Euphrates, already in the Persian period the entrepôt for this traffic, and under Augustus, next to Ephesus,
the most considerable city of the province of Asia.
Although every case of assigning a Greek name is not to
be connected with a settlement by Greek colonists, we
may be allowed at any rate to reckon a considerable
portion of these townships among Greek colonies. But
even the urban settlements of non-Greek origin, which the
Alexandrids found in existence, turned of themselves into
the paths of Hellenising, as indeed the residence of the
Persian governor, Sardes, was organised even by Alexander
himself as a Greek commonwealth.

This urban development was completed when the Romans entered upon the rule of interior Asia ; they themselves did not make special exertions to promote it. That a great number of the urban communities in the eastern half of the province reckon their years from that of the city 670, is due to the fact that then, after the close of the Mithradatic war, these districts were brought by Sulla under direct Roman administration (iii. 328) ; these townships did not receive city-rights only then for the first time. Augustus occupied the town of Parium on the Hellespont and the already-mentioned Alexandria in Troas with veterans of his army, and assigned to both the rights of Roman burgess - communities ; the latter was thenceforth in Greek Asia an Italian island like Corinth in Greece and Berytus in Syria. But this was nothing but a provision for soldiers ; of the foundation of towns proper in the Roman province of Asia under the emperors there is little mention. Among the not numerous towns named after emperors there it is only perhaps in the case of Sebaste and Tiberiopolis, both in Phrygia, and of

Its position under the Romans.

84.

iii. 312.

Hadrianoi on the Bithynian frontier, that no older name
of the city can be pointed out.   Here, in the mountain-
region between Ida and Olympus, dwelt Cleon in the time
of the triumvirate, and a certain Tilliborus under Hadrian,
both half robber-chiefs, half popular princes, of whom the
former even played a part in politics ; in this asylum of
criminals the foundation of an organised urban community
by Hadrian was at all events a benefit.   Otherwise in
this province, with its five hundred urban communities,
the province richest in cities of the whole state, not much
more was left to be done in the way of foundation ; there
was room at the most perhaps for division, that is, for
detaching such hamlets as developed themselves *de facto*
into urban communities, from the earlier communal union
and making them independent, as we can point to a case
of the kind in Phrygia under Constantine I.   But from
Hellenising proper the sequestered districts were still far
remote when the Roman government began ; especially
in Phrygia the language of the country, perhaps similar in
character to the Armenian, held its ground.   If from the
absence of Greek coins and of Greek inscriptions we may
not with certainty infer the absence of Hellenising,[1] yet
the fact that the Phrygian coins belong almost throughout
to the Roman imperial period, and the Phrygian inscriptions as regards the great majority to the later times of
the empire, points to the conclusion that, so far as Hellenic habits found their way at all into the regions of the
province of Asia that were remote and difficult of access
to civilisation, they did so in the main only under the
emperors.   For direct interference on the part of the
imperial administration this process, accomplishing itself
in silence, gave little opportunity, and traces of such interference we are not able to show.   Asia, it is true, was a

[1] Urban coining and setting up of
inscriptions are subject to so manifold
conditions that the want or the abundance of the one or the other do not
per se warrant inferences as to the
absence or the intensity of a definite
phase of civilisation.   For Asia Minor in particular we must take note
that it was the promised land of municipal vanity, and our memorials, including even the coins, have for by
far the greatest part been called forth
by the fact that the government of
the Roman emperors allowed free
scope to this vanity.

senatorial province, and we may here bear in mind that with the government of the senate all initiative fell into abeyance.

Syria, and still more, Egypt, became merged in their capitals ; the province of Asia and Asia Minor generally had no single town to show like Antioch and Alexandria, but their prosperity rested on the numerous middle-sized towns. The division of the towns into three classes, which are distinguished as to the right of voting at the diet, as to the apportionment of the contributions to be furnished by the whole province, even as to the number of town-physicians and town-teachers to be appointed,[1] is eminently peculiar to these regions. The urban rivalries, which appear in Asia Minor so emphatic and in part so childish, occasionally even so odious—as, for example, the war between Severus and Niger in Bithynia was properly a war of the two rival capitals Nicomedia and Nicaea— belong to the character of Hellenic polities in general, but especially of those in Asia Minor. We shall mention further on the emulation as to temples of the emperors ; in a similar way the ranking of the urban deputations at the common festivals in Asia Minor was a vital question— Magnesia on the Maeander calls itself on the coins the " seventh city of Asia "—and above all the first place was one so much desired, that the government ultimately agreed to admit several first cities. It fared similarly with the designation of " metropolis." The proper metropolis of the province was Pergamus, the residence of the Attalids and the seat of the diet. But Ephesus, the *de facto* capital of the province, where the governor was obliged to enter on his office, and which boasts of this " right of reception at landing" on its coins ; Smyrna, in constant rivalship with its Ephesian neighbour, and, in defiance of the legitimate right of the Ephesians to

Urban rivalries.

[1] "The ordinance," says the jurist Modestinus, who reports it (Dig. xxvii. 1, 6, 3) "interests all provinces, although it is directed to the people of Asia." It is suitable, in fact, only where there are classes of towns, and the jurist adds an instruc- tion how it is to be applied to provinces otherwise organised. What the biographer of Pius, c. 11, reports as to the distinctions and salaries granted by Pius to the rhetoricians, has nothing to do with this enactment.

primacy, naming itself on coins "the first in greatness and beauty ;" the very ancient Sardis, Cyzicus, and several others strove after the same honorary right. With these their wranglings, on account of which the senate and the emperor were regularly appealed to—the " Greek follies," as men were wont to say in Rome—the people of Asia Minor were the standing annoyance and the standing laughing-stock of the Romans of mark.[1]

Bithynia.   Bithynia did not stand on a like level with the Attalid kingdom.   The older Greek colonising had here confined itself merely to the coast.   In the Hellenistic epoch at first the Macedonian rulers, and later the native dynasty which walked entirely in their steps, had—along with a regulation of the places on the coast, which perhaps on the whole amounted to a changing of their names—also opened up in some measure the interior, in particular by the two successful foundations of Nicaea (Isnik) and Prusa on Olympia (Broussa) ; of the former it is stated that the first settlers were of good Macedonian and Hellenic descent.   But in the intensity of the Hellenising the kingdom of Nicomedes was far behind that of the citizen prince of Pergamus; in particular the eastern interior can have been but little settled before Augustus.   This was otherwise in the time of the empire. In the Augustan age a successful robber-chief, who became a convert to order, reconstructed on the Galatian frontier the utterly decayed township Gordiou Kome, under the name of Juliopolis ; in the same region the towns Bithynion-Claudiopolis and Crateia-Flaviopolis probably attained Greek civic rights in the course of the first century.

---

[1] Dio of Prusa, in his address to the citizens of Nicomedia and of Tarsus, excellently lays it down that no man of culture would have such empty distinctions for himself, and that the greedy quest of the towns for titles was altogether inconceivable ; how it is the sign of the true petty-townsman to cause a display of such attestations of rank on his behalf; how the bad governor always screens himself under this quarrelling of towns, as Nicaea and Nicomedia never act together. "The Romans deal with you as with children, to whom one presents trifling toys ; you put up with bad treatment in order to obtain a name ; they name your town the first in order to treat it as the last. By this you have become a laughing-stock to the Romans, and they call your doings 'Greek follies'" (Ἑλληνικὰ ἁμαρτήματα).

Generally in Bithynia Hellenism took a mighty upward impulse under the imperial period, and the tough Thracian stamp of the natives gave a good foundation for it. The fact that, among the inscribed stones of this province known in great number, not more than four belong to the pre-Roman epoch, cannot well be explained solely from the circumstance that urban ambition was only fostered under the emperors. In the literature of the imperial period a number of the best authors and the least carried away by exuberant rhetoric, such as the philosopher Dio of Prusa, the historian Memnon of Heraclea, Arrianus of Nicomedia, Cassius Dio of Nicaea, belong to Bithynia.

The eastern half of the south coast of the Black Sea, Pontus. the Roman province of Pontus, had as its basis that portion of the kingdom of Mithradates, of which Pompeius took direct possession immediately after the victory. The numerous smaller principalities, which Pompeius at the same time gave away in the interior of Paphlagonia and thence eastward to the Armenian frontier, were, after a shorter or longer subsistence, on their annexation partly attached to the same province, partly joined to Galatia or Cappadocia. The former kingdom of Mithradates had been far less affected than the western regions either by the older or by the younger Hellenism. When the Romans took possession directly or indirectly of this territory, there were, strictly speaking, no towns of Greek organisation there; Amasia, the old capital of the Pontic Achaemenids, and still their burial-place, was not such; the two old Greek coast-towns, Amisus and Sinope that once commanded the Black Sea, had become royal residences, and Greek polity would hardly be given to the few townships laid out by Mithradates, *e.g.* Eupatoria (iv. 152). But here, as was already shown in detail (iv. 151 f.), iv. 146. the Roman conquest was at the same time the Hellenising; Pompeius organised the province in such a way as to make the eleven chief townships of it into towns, and to distribute the territory among them. Certainly these artificially created towns with their immense districts— that of Sinope had along the coast an extent of 70 miles, and bordered on the Halys with that of Amisus—resembled more the Celtic cantons than the Hellenic and Italian urban communities proper. But at any rate Sinope and Amisus were then reinstated in their old positions, and other towns in the interior, such as Pompeiopolis, Nicopolis, Megalopolis, the later Sebasteia, were called into life. Sinope obtained from the dictator Caesar the rights of a Roman colony, and beyond doubt also Italian settlers (iv. 574). More important for the Roman administration was Trapezus, an old colony of Sinope ; the town, which in the year 63 was joined to the province of Cappadocia (p. 324, note), was both the station of the Roman Black Sea fleet and in a certain measure the base of operations for the military corps of this province, which was the only corps in all Asia Minor.

iv. 544.

Inland Cappadocia was in the Roman power after the erection of the provinces of Pontus and Syria ; of its annexation in the beginning of the reign of Tiberius, which was primarily occasioned by the attempt of Armenia to release itself from the Roman suzerainty, we shall have to give an account in the following section. The court, and those immediately connected with it, had become Hellenised (iii. 59), somewhat as the German courts of the eighteenth century adapted themselves to French habits. The capital, Caesarea, the ancient Mazaca, like the Phrygian Apamea, an intermediate station for the great traffic between the ports of the west coast and the lands of the Euphrates, and in the Roman period, as still at the present day, one of the most flourishing commercial cities of Asia Minor, was, at the instigation of Pompeius, not merely rebuilt after the Mithradatic war, but probably also furnished at that time with civic rights after the Greek type. Cappadocia itself was at the beginning of the imperial period hardly more Greek than Brandenburg and Pomerania under Frederick the Great were French. When the country became Roman, it was divided, according to the statements of the contemporary Strabo, not into city-districts, but into ten prefectures, of which only two had towns, the already-mentioned capital and Tyana ;

Cappadocia.

iii. 57.

and this arrangement was here on the whole not more changed than in Egypt, though individual townships subsequently received Greek civic rights ; *e.g.* the emperor Marcus made the Cappadocian village, in which his wife had died, into the town Faustinopolis. It is true that the Cappadocians now spoke Greek ; but the students from Cappadocia had much to endure abroad on account of their uncouth accent, and of their defects in pronunciation and modulation ; and, if they learned to speak after an Attic fashion, their countrymen found their language affected.[1] It was only in the Christian period that the comrades in study of the emperor Julian, Gregory of Nazianzus and Basil of Caesarea, gave a better sound to the Cappadocian name.

The Lycian cities in their secluded mountain-land did not open their coast for Greek settlement, but did not on that account debar themselves from Hellenic influence. Lycia was the only district of Asia Minor in which early civilising did not set aside the native language, and which, almost like the Romans, entered into Greek habits without becoming externally Hellenised. It is characteristic of their position, that the Lycian confederation as such joined the Attic naval league and paid its tribute to the Athenian leading power. The Lycians not merely practised their art after Hellenic models, but probably also regulated their political organisation early in the same way. The conversion of the cities-league, once subject to Rhodes, but which had become independent after the third Macedonian war (ii. 325) into a Roman province, which was ordained by the emperor Claudius on account of the endless quarrels among the allies, must have furthered the progress of Hellenism ; in the course of the imperial period the Lycians thereupon became completely Greeks.

Lycia.

ii. 307.

The Pamphylian coast-towns, like Aspendus and Perga,

Pamphylia and Cilicia.

---

[1] Pausanias of Caesarea in Philostratus (*Vitae soph.* ii. 13) places before Herodes Atticus his faults : παχείᾳ τῇ γλώττῃ καὶ ὡς Καππαδόκαις ξύνηθες, ξυγκρούων μὲν τὰ σύμφωνα τῶν στοι- χείων, συστέλλων δὲ τὰ μηκυνόμενα καὶ μηκύνων τὰ βραχέα. *Vita Apoll.* i. 7 ; ἡ γλῶττα Ἀττικῶς εἶχεν, οὐδ' ἀπήχθη τὴν φωνὴν ὑπὸ τοῦ ἔθνους.

Greek foundations of the oldest times, subsequently left
to themselves, and attaining under favourable circumstances prosperous development, had either conserved, or
moulded specially on their own part, the oldest Hellenic
character in such a way that the Pamphylians might be
regarded as an independent nation in language and writing
not much less than the neighbouring Lycians.   Then,
when Asia was gained for the Hellenes, they found
gradually their way back into the common Greek civilisation, and so also into the general political organisation.
The rulers in this region and on the neighbouring Cilician
coast were in the Hellenistic period partly the Egyptians,
whose royal house gave its name to different townships
in Pamphylia and Cilicia, partly the Seleucids, after whom
the most considerable town of west Cilicia was named
Seleucia on the Calycadnus, partly the Pergamenes, of
whose rule Attalia (Adalia) in Pamphylia testifies.

Pisidia and
Isauria.

On the other hand the tribes in the mountains of
Pisidia, Isauria, and western Cilicia substantially maintained their independence down to the beginning of the
imperial period.   Here hostilities never ceased.   Not
merely by land had the civilised governments continued
troubles with the Pisidians and their comrades, but these
pursued still more zealously than robbery by land the
trade of piracy, particularly from western Cilicia, where
the mountains immediately approach the sea.   When, on
the decline of the Egyptian naval power, the south coast
of Asia Minor became entirely an asylum of the pirates,
the Romans interfered and erected the province of Cilicia,
which embraced also, or was at any rate intended to
embrace, the Pamphylian coast, for the sake of suppressing
piracy.   But what they did showed more what ought to
have been done than that anything was really accomplished ; the intervention took place too late and too
fitfully.   Though a blow was once struck against the
corsairs, and Roman troops penetrated even into the
Isaurian mountains, and broke up the pirates' strongholds
iv. 44.   far into the interior (iv. 47), the Roman republic did
not attain true permanent establishment in these districts

reluctantly annexed by it. Here everything was left for the empire to do. Antonius, when he took in hand the East, entrusted an able Galatian officer, Amyntas, with the subjugation of the refractory Pisidian region,[1] and, when the latter proved his quality,[2] he made him king of Galatia, —the region of Asia Minor which was best organised in a military point of view, and most ready for action—and at the same time extended his government from thence as far as the south coast, and so as to include Lycaonia, Pisidia, Isauria, Pamphylia, and western Cilicia, while the civilised east half of Cilicia was left with Syria. Even when Augustus, after the battle of Actium, entered upon rule in the East, he left the Celtic prince in his position. The latter made essential progress as well in the suppression of the bad corsairs harbouring in the lurking places of western Cilicia, as also in the extirpation of the brigands, killed one of the worst of these robber-chiefs, Antipater, the ruler of Derbe and Laranda in southern Lycaonia, built for himself a residence in Isauria, and not merely drove the Pisidians out from the adjoining Phrygian territories, but invaded their own land, and took Cremna in the heart of it. But some years after (729 U.C.) 25. he lost his life on an expedition against one of the west Cicilian tribes, the Homonadenses ; after he had taken most of the townships and their prince had fallen, he perished through a plot directed against him by the wife of the latter. After this disaster Augustus himself undertook the difficult business of pacifying the interior of Asia

---

[1] Amyntas was placed over the Pisidians as early as 715 before Antonius returned to Asia (Appian, *B.C.* v. 75), doubtless because these had once more undertaken one of their predatory expeditions. From the fact that he first ruled there is explained the circumstance that he built for himself a residence in Isaura (Strabo, xii. 6, 3, p. 569). Galatia went in the first instance to the heirs of Deiotarus (Dio, xlviii. 33). It was not till the year 718 that Amyntas obtained Galatia, Lycaonia, and Pamphylia (Dio, xlix. 32).

[2] That this was the cause why these regions were not placed under Roman governors is expressly stated by Strabo (xiv. 5, 5, p. 671), who was near in time and place to the matters dealt with : ἐδόκει πρὸς ἄπαν τὸ τοιοῦτο (for the suppression of the robbers and pirates) βασιλεύεσθαι μᾶλλον τοὺς τόπους ἢ ὑπὸ τοῖς Ῥωμαίοις ἡγεμόσιν εἶναι τοῖς ἐπὶ τὰς κρίσεις πεμπομένοις, οἳ μήτ᾽ ἀεὶ παρεῖναι ἔμελλον (on account of the travelling on circuit) μήτε μεθ᾽ ὅπλων (which at all events were wanting to the later legate of Galatia).

39.

36.

Minor. If in doing so he, as was already observed (p. 324), assigned the small Pamphylian coast-district to a governor of its own and separated it from Galatia, this was evidently done because the mountain-land lying between the coast and the Galato-Lycaonian steppe was so little under control that the administration of the coast region could not well be conducted from Galatia. Roman troops were not stationed in Galatia ; yet the levy of the warlike Galatians must have meant more than in the case of most provincials. Moreover, as western Cilicia was then placed under Cappadocia, the troops of this dependent prince had to take part in the work. The Syrian army carried out the chastisement in the first place of the Homonadenses ; the governor, Publius Sulpicius Quirinius, advanced some years later into their territory, cut off their supplies, and compelled them to submit *en masse*, whereupon they were distributed to the surrounding townships and their former territory was laid waste. The Clitae, another stock settled in western Cilicia nearer to the coast, met with similar chastisements in the years 36 and 52 ; as they refused obedience to the vassal - prince placed over them by Rome, and pillaged land and sea, and as the so-called rulers of the land could not dispose of them, the imperial troops were on both occasions brought in from Syria to subdue them. These accounts have been accidentally preserved ; numerous similar incidents have certainly been lost to remembrance.

Pisidian colonies.

But Augustus attempted the pacification of this region also by way of settlement. The Hellenistic governments had, so to speak, isolated it; not merely retained or seized a footing everywhere on the coast, but also founded in the north-west a series of towns—on the Phrygian frontier Apollonia, alleged to have been founded by Alexander himself, Seleucia Siderus and Antiochia, both from the time of the Seleucids, further in Lycaonia, Laodicea Katakekaumene, and the capital of this district which doubtless originated at the same time, Iconium. But in the mountain-land proper no trace of Hellenistic settlement is found, and still less did the Roman senate apply

itself to this difficult task.   Augustus did so ; and only
here in the whole Greek coast we meet a series of colonies
of Roman veterans evidently intended to acquire this
district for peaceful settlement.   Of the older settlements
just mentioned, Antiochia was supplied with veterans
and reorganised in Roman fashion, while there were newly
laid out in southern Lycaonia Parlais, in Pisidia itself
the already - mentioned Cremna, as well as further to
the south Olbasa and Comama.   The later governments
did not continue with equal energy the work so begun ;
yet under Claudius the " iron Seleucia " of Pisidia was
made the " Claudian ; " while in the interior of western
Cilicia Claudiopolis, and not far from it, perhaps at the
same time, Germanicopolis were called into life, and
Iconium, in the time of Augustus a small place, was
brought to considerable development.   The newly-founded
towns remained indeed unimportant, but still notably
restricted the field of the free inhabitants of the mountains, and general peace must at length have made its
triumphal entrance also here.   As well the plains and
mountain-terraces of Pamphylia as the mountain-towns
of Pisidia itself, *e.g.* Selga and Sagalassus, were during the
imperial period well peopled and the territory carefully
cultivated ; the remains of mighty aqueducts and singularly large theatres, all of them structures of the Roman
imperial period, show, it is true, only mechanical skill, but
bear traces of a peaceful prosperity richly developed.

The government, it is true, never quite mastered Isaurians.
brigandage in these regions, and if in the earlier period
of the empire its ravages were kept in moderate bounds,
the bands once more emerge as a warlike power in the
troubles of the third century.   They now pass under the
name of Isaurians, and have their chief seat in the mountains of Cilicia, from whence they plunder land and sea.
They are mentioned first under Severus Alexander.   That
under Gallienus they proclaimed their robber-chief emperor, is probably a fable ; but certainly under the
emperor Probus such an one, by name Lydius, who for
long had pillaged Lycia and Pamphylia, was subdued in

the Roman colony Cremna, which he had occupied, after a long and obstinate siege by a Roman army. In later times we find a military cordon drawn round their territory, and a special commanding general appointed for the Isaurians. Their savage valour even procured for those of them, who chose to take service at the Byzantine court, for a time a position there such as the Macedonians had possessed at the court of the Ptolemies ; in fact one from their ranks, Zeno, died as emperor of Byzantium.[1]

Galatia. Lastly, the region of Galatia, at a remote period the chief seat of the Oriental rule over anterior Asia, and preserving in the famed rock-sculptures of the modern Boghazköi, formerly the royal town of Pteria, reminiscences of an almost forgotten glory, had in the course of centuries become in language and manners a Celtic island amidst the waves of eastern peoples, and remained so in internal organisation even under the empire. The three Celtic tribes, which, on the great migration of the nation about the time of the war between Pyrrhus and the Romans, had arrived in the heart of Asia Minor, and there, like the Franks in the East during the middle ages, had consolidated themselves into a firmly knit soldier-state, and after prolonged roving had taken up their definitive abode on either side of the Halys, had long since left behind the times when they issued forth thence to pillage Asia Minor, and were in conflict with the kings of Asia and Pergamus, provided that they did not serve them as mercenaries. They too were shattered before the superior power of the ii. 273. Romans (ii. 290), and became not less subject to them in Asia than their countrymen in the valley of the Po and on the Rhone and Seine. But in spite of their sojourn of several hundred years in Asia Minor, a deep gulf still separated these Occidentals from the Asiatics. It was not merely that they retained their native language and

---

[1] Amidst the great unnamed ruins of Sarajik, in the upper valley of the Limyrus, in eastern Lycia (comp. Ritter, *Erdkunde*, xix. p. 1172), stands a considerable temple-shaped tomb, certainly not older than the third century after Christ, on which mutilated parts of men—heads, arms, legs —are produced in relief, as emblems we might imagine, as the coat of arms of a civilised robber-chief (communication from Benndorf).

their nationality, that still each of the three cantons was
governed by its four hereditary princes, and the federal
assembly, to which deputies were sent by all in common,
presided in the sacred oak-grove as supreme authority
over the Galatian land (ii. 232) ; nor was it that continued ii. 219.
rudeness as well as warlike valour distinguished them
to advantage as well as to disadvantage from their
neighbours ; such contrasts between culture and barbarism existed elsewhere in Asia Minor, and the
superficial and external Hellenising—such as neighbourhood, commercial relations, the Phrygian cultus
adopted by the immigrants, and mercenary service
brought in their train—must have set in not much later
in Galatia than *e.g.* in the neighbouring Cappadocia.
The contrast was of a different kind ; the Celtic and
the Hellenic invasion came into competition in Asia
Minor, and to the distinction of nationality was added
the spur of rival conquest. This was brought clearly
to light in the Mithradatic crisis ; by the side of the
command of Mithradates to murder the Italians went the
massacre of the whole Galatian nobility (iii. 322), and, iii. 306.
in keeping therewith, the Romans in the wars against
the Oriental liberator of the Hellenes had no more faithful
ally than the Galatians of Asia Minor (iv. 56, 149). iv. 53, 143.

For that reason the success of the Romans was theirs The Gala-
also, and the victory gave to them for a time a leading tian king-
position in the affairs of Asia Minor. The old tetrarchate dom.
was done away, apparently by Pompeius. One of the new
cantonal princes, who had approved himself most in the
Mithradatic wars, Deiotarus, attached to himself, besides
his own territory, Lesser Armenia and other portions
of the former Mithradatic empire, and became an inconvenient neighbour to the other Galatian princes, and the
most powerful among the dynasts of Asia Minor
(iv. 149). After the victory of Caesar, to whom he iv. 143.
occupied an attitude of hostility, and whose favour he
was unable to gain even by help rendered against
Pharnaces, the possessions gained by him with or without
consent of the Roman government were for the most

part again withdrawn ; the Caesarian Mithradates of
Pergamus, who on the mother's side was sprung from
the Galatian royal house, obtained the most of what
Deiotarus lost, and was even placed by his side in
Galatia itself.   But, after the latter had shortly afterwards met his end in the Tauric Chersonese (p. 313),
and Caesar himself had not long afterwards been
murdered, Deiotarus reinstated himself unbidden in
possession of what he had lost, and, as he knew how
to submit to the Roman party predominant on each
occasion in the East as well as how to change it at the
40. right time, he died at an advanced age in the year 714
as lord of all Galatia.   His descendants were portioned
off with a small lordship in Paphlagonia ; his kingdom,
further enlarged towards the south by Lycaonia and all
the country down to the coast of Pamphylia, was
36. transferred, as was already said, in the year 718 by
Antonius to Amyntas, who seems to have conducted the
government already in the last years of Deiotarus as his
secretary and general, and, as such, had before the battle
of Philippi effected the transition from the republican
generals to the triumvirs.   His further fortunes have
been already told.   Equal to his predecessor in sagacity
and bravery, he served first Antonius, and then Augustus
as chief instrument for the pacification of the territory
not yet subject in Asia Minor, till he there met his
25. death in the year 729.   With him ended the Galatian
kingdom, and it was converted into the Roman province
of Galatia.

The inhabi-
tants.
Its inhabitants were called Gallograeci among the
Romans even in the last age of the republic ; they were,
adds Livy, a mixed people, as they were called, and
degenerate.   A good portion of them must have
descended from the older Phrygian inhabitants of these
regions.   Of still more weight is the fact, that the zealous
worship of the gods in Galatia and the priesthood there
have nothing in common with the ritual institutions of
the European Celts ; not merely was the Great Mother,
whose sacred symbol the Romans of Hannibal's time

asked and received from the Tolistobogi, of a Phrygian type, but her priests belonged in part at least to the Galatian nobility. Nevertheless, even in the Roman province of Galatia the internal organisation was predominantly Celtic. The fact that even under Pius the strict paternal power foreign to Hellenic law subsisted in Galatia, is a proof of this from the sphere of private law. In public relations there were in this country still only the three old communities of the Tectosages, the Tolistobogi, the Trocmi, who perhaps appended to their names those of the three chief places, Ancyra, Pessinus, and Tavium, but were essentially nothing but the well-known Gallic cantons, which also indeed were not without their chief place. If among the Celts of Asia the conception of the community as town gains the predominance earlier than among the European,[1] and the name Ancyra more quickly dispossesses that of the Tectosages than in Europe the name Burdigala dispossesses that of the Bituriges, and there Ancyra even as foremost place of the whole country calls itself the "mother-city" (μητρόπολις), this certainly shows—what could not in fact be otherwise—the influence of Greek neighbourhood and the incipient process of assimilation, the several phases of which the superficial information that survives to us does not allow us to follow out. The Celtic names keep their hold down to the time of Tiberius ; afterwards they appear only isolated in the houses of rank.

That the Romans after the erection of the province—as in Gaul they allowed only the Latin language—allowed in Galatia alongside of this only the Greek in business-dealings, was a matter of course. What course was taken earlier we know not, as we do not meet with pre-Roman written monuments in this country at all. As the language of conversation the Celtic maintained its ground with

Language under the Romans.

---

[1] The famous list of services rendered to the community of Ancyra of the time of Tiberius (*C. I. Gr.* 4039) designates the Galatian communities usually by ἔθνος, sometimes by πόλις. The former appellation subsequently disappears ; but in the full title, *e.g.* of the inscription, *C. I. Gr.* 4011, from the second century, Ancyra always bears the name of the people : ἡ μητρόπολις τῆς Γαλατίας Σεβαστὴ Τεκτοσάγων Ἄγκυρα.

tenacity also in Asia ;[1] yet the Greek gradually gained
the upper hand.   In the fourth century Ancyra was one
of the chief centres of Greek culture ; " the small towns
in Greek Galatia," says the man of letters, Themistius,
who had grown gray in addressing the cultivated public,
" cannot indeed cope with Antioch ; but the people
appropriate to themselves culture more zealously than
the genuine Hellenes, and, wherever the philosopher's
cloak appears, they cling to it like the iron to the
magnet."   Yet the national language may have preserved
itself in the lower circles down even to this period,
particularly beyond the Halys among the Trocmi
evidently much later Hellenised.[2]   It has already been
mentioned (p. 101) that, according to the testimony
of the far-travelled church-father Jerome, still at the
end of the fourth century the Asiatic Galatian spoke
the same language, although corrupt, which was then
spoken in Treves.   That as soldiers the Galatians, though
sustaining no comparison with the Occidentals, were
yet far more useful than the Greek Asiatics, is attested
as well by the legion which king Deiotarus raised from
his subjects after the Roman model, and which Augustus
took over with the kingdom and incorporated with the
Roman army under its previous name, as by the fact,
that in the Oriental recruiting of the imperial period
the Galatians were drawn upon by preference just as the
Batavians were in the West.[3]

The Greek islands.

To the extra-European Hellenes belong further the
two great islands of the eastern Mediterranean, Crete

[1] According to Pausanias, x. 36, 1,
among the Γαλάται ὑπὲρ Φρυγίας
φωνῇ τῇ ἐπιχωρίῳ σφίσιν the scarlet
berry is termed ὗς ; and Lucian,
Alex. 51, tells of the perplexities of
the soothsaying Paphlagonian, when
questions were proposed to him
Συριστὶ ἢ Κελτιστὶ and people conversant with this language were not
just at hand.

[2] If in the list mentioned at p. 314,
note, from the time of Tiberius the
largesses are given but seldom to three
peoples, mostly to two peoples or two

cities, the latter are, as Perrot correctly
remarks (*de Galatia*, p. 83), Ancyra
and Pessinus, and Tavium of the
Trocmi is in the matter of largesses
postponed to them.   Perhaps there
was at that time among these no
township which could be treated as
a town.

[3] Cicero (*ad Att.* vi. 5, 3) writes
of his army in Cilicia : *exercitum
infirmum habebam, auxilia sane bona,
sed ea Galatarum, Pisidarum, Lyci-
orum : haec enim sunt nostra robora.*

and Cyprus, as well as the numerous islets of the sea
between Greece and Asia Minor ; the Cyrenaic Pentapolis
also on the opposite African coast is so separated by the
surrounding desert from the interior that it may be in
some measure ranked along with those Greek islands.
These constituent elements, however, of the enormous
mass of lands united under the sceptre of the emperors
do not add essentially new features to the general
historical conception.   The minor islands, Hellenised
earlier and more completely than the continent, belong
as regards their essential character more to European
Greece than to the colonial field of Asia Minor ; as
indeed we have already several times mentioned the
Hellenic model - state, Rhodes, in connection with the
former.   The islands are chiefly noticed at this epoch,
inasmuch as it was usual in the imperial period to banish
men of the better classes to them by way of punishment.
They chose, where the case was specially severe, rocks like
Gyarus and Donussa ; but Andros, Cythnus, Amorgos,
once flourishing centres of Greek culture, were now places
of punishment, while in Lesbos and Samos not seldom
Romans of rank and even members of the imperial house
voluntarily took up a somewhat lengthened abode.   Crete
and Cyprus, whose old Hellenism had under the Persian
rule or in complete isolation lost contact with home,
organised themselves—Cyprus as a dependency of Egypt,
the Cretan towns as autonomous—in the Hellenistic and
later in the Roman epochs according to the general forms
of Greek polity.   In the Cyrenaic towns the system of
the Lagids prevailed ; we find in them not merely, as in
the strictly Greek towns, Hellenic burgesses and *metoeci*,
but alongside of them, as with the Egyptians in Alexandria, the " peasants," that is the native Africans, and
among the *metoeci* the Jews form, as they do likewise in
Alexandria, a numerous and privileged class.

    To the Greeks in common the Roman imperial Leagues of
government never granted a constitution.   The Augustan the Hel-
Amphictiony was restricted, as we saw (p. 254), to the AsiaMinor.
Hellenes in Achaia, Epirus, and Macedonia.   If the Had-

rianic Panhellenes in Athens acted as though they were representative of all the Hellenes, they yet encroached on the other Greek provinces only in so far as they decreed, so to speak, honorary Hellenism to individual towns in Asia (p. 267) ; and the fact that they did so, just shows that the extraneous communities of Greeks were by no means included among those Panhellenes. If in Asia Minor there is mention of representation or representatives of the Hellenes, what is meant by this in the provinces of Asia and Bithynia organised completely after the Hellenic manner, is the diet and the president of the diet of these provinces, in so far as these proceed from the deputies of the towns belonging to each of them, and all of these towns are Greek polities ;[1] while in the non-Greek province of Galatia the representatives of the Greeks sojourning there, placed alongside of the Galatian diet, are designated as " presidents of the Greeks."[2]

Land-diets and land festivals.

To the confederation of towns the Roman government in Asia Minor had no occasion to oppose special obstacles. In Roman as in pre-Roman times nine towns of the Troad performed in common religious functions and celebrated common festivals.[3] The diets of the different

[1] Decrees of the ἐπὶ τῆς ᾽Ασίας ῞Ελληνες, *C. I. A.* 3487, 3957 ; a Lycian honoured ὑπὸ τοῦ κο[ινο]ῦ τῶν ἐπὶ τῆς ᾽Ασίας ῾Ελλήνων καὶ ὑπὸ τῶν ἐ[ν Πα]μφυλίᾳ πόλεων, Benndorf, *Lyk. Reise*, i. 122 ; letters to the Hellenes in Asia, *C. I. Gr.* 3832, 3833 ; ὦ ἄνδρες ῞Ελληνες in the address to the diet of Pergamus, Aristides, p. 517.— An ἄρξας τοῦ κοινοῦ τῶν ἐν Βιθυνίᾳ ῾Ελλήνων, Perrot, *Expl. de la Galatie*, p. 32 ; letter of the emperor Alexander to the same, *Dig.* xlix. 1, 25.— Dio, li. 20 : τοῖς ξένοις, ῞Ελληνας σφᾶς ἐπικαλέσας, ἑαυτῷ τινα, τοῖς μὲν ᾽Ασιανοῖς ἐν Περγάμῳ, τοῖς δὲ Βιθυνοῖς ἐν Νικομηδείᾳ τεμενίσαι ἐπέτρεψε.

[2] Besides the Galatarchs (Marquardt, *Staatsverw.* i. 515) we meet in Galatia even under Hadrian Helladarchae (*Bull. de corr. Hell.* vii. 18), who can only be taken here like the Hellenarchs in Tanais (p. 315, note 2).

[3] The συνέδριον τῶν ἐννέα δήμων (Schliemann, *Troia*, 1884, p. 256) calls itself elsewhere ᾽Ιλιεῖς καὶ πόλεις αἱ κοινωνοῦσαι τῆς θυσίας καὶ τοῦ ἀγῶνος καὶ τῆς πανηγύρεως (*ib.* p. 254). Another document of the same league from the time of Antigonus is given in Droysen, *Hellenismus*, ii. 2, 382 ff. So too other κοινά are to be taken, which refer to a narrower circle than the province, such as the old one of the thirteen Ionic cities, that of the Lesbians (Marquardt, *Staatsverw.* i. p. 516), that of the Phrygians on the coins of Apamea. These have also had their magisterial presidents, as indeed there has recently been found a Lesbiarch (Marquardt, *l.c.*), and likewise the Moesian Hellenes were under a Pontarch (p. 308). Yet it is not improbable that, where the archonship is named, the league is more than a mere festal association ; the

provinces of Asia Minor, which were here as in the whole
empire called into existence as a fixed institution by
Augustus, were not different in themselves from those of
the other provinces. Yet this institution developed itself,
or rather changed its nature, here in a peculiar fashion.
With the immediate purpose of these annual assemblies of
the civic deputies of each province[1]—to bring its wishes
to the knowledge of the governor or the government, and
generally to serve as organ of the province—was here first
combined the celebration of the annual festival for the
governing emperor and the imperial system generally.
Augustus in the year 725 allowed the diets of Asia and
Bithynia to erect temples and show divine honour to him
at their places of assembly, Pergamus and Nicomedia.
This new arrangement soon extended to the whole empire,
and the blending of the ritual institution with the administrative became a leading idea of the provincial organisation of the imperial period. But as regards pomp of
priests and festivals and civic rivalries, this institution
nowhere developed itself so much as in the province of
Asia and, analogously, in the other provinces of Asia
Minor ; and nowhere, consequently, has there subsisted
alongside of, and above, municipal ambition a provincial
ambition of the towns still more than of the individuals,
such as in Asia Minor dominates the whole public life.

The high priest (ἀρχιερεύς) of the new temple appointed
from year to year in the province is not merely the most
eminent dignitary of the province, but throughout its bounds
the year is designated after him.[2] The system of festivals
and games after the model of the Olympic festival, which
spread more and more as we saw among all the Hellenes,

Provincial priests and Asiarchs.

Lesbians as well as the Moesian Pentapolis may have had a special diet,
over which these officers presided.
On the other hand the κοινὸν τοῦ
Ὑργαλέου πεδίου (Ramsay, *Cities and
bishoprics of Phrygia*, p. 10), which
stands alongside of several δῆμοι, is a
quasi-community destitute of civic
rights.

[1] The composition of the diets of
Asia Minor is most clearly apparent

in Strabo's account of the Lyciarchy
(xiv. 3, 3, p. 664) and in the narrative of Aristides (*Or.* 26, p. 344) as
to his election to one of the Asiatic
provincial priesthoods.

[2] See examples for Asia, *C. I. Gr.*
3487; for Lycia, Benndorf, *Lyk. Reise*,
i. p. 71. But the Lycian federal
assembly designates the years not by
the Archiereus but by the Lyciarch.

was associated in Asia Minor predominantly with the festivals and games of the provincial worship of the emperor. The conduct of these fell to the president of the diet, in Asia to the Asiarch, in Bithynia to the Bithyni-árch, and so on ; and not less he had chiefly to bear the costs of the annual festival, although a portion of these, like the remaining expenses of this equally brilliant and loyal worship, was covered by voluntary gifts and endowments, or was apportioned among the several towns. Hence these presidentships were only accessible to rich people ; the prosperity of the town Tralles is indicated by the fact, that it never wanted Asiarchs—the title remained even after the expiry of the official year—and the repute of the Apostle Paul in Ephesus is indicated by his connection with different Asiarchs there. In spite of the expense this was an honorary position much sought after, not on account of the privileges attached to it, *e.g.* of exemption from trusteeship, but on account of its outward splendour ; the festal entrance into the town, in purple dress and with chaplet on the head, preceded by a procession of boys swinging their vessels of incense, was in the horizon of the Greeks of Asia Minor what the olive-branch of Olympia was among the Hellenes. On several occasions this or that Asiatic of quality boasts of having been not merely himself Asiarch but descended also from Asiarchs. If this cultus was at the outset confined to the provincial capitals, the municipal ambition, which in the province of Asia in particular assumed incredible proportions, very soon broke through those limits. Here already in the year 23 a second temple was decreed by the province to the then reigning emperor Tiberius as well as to his mother and to the senate, and after long quarrelling of the towns was, by decree of the senate, erected at Smyrna. The other larger towns followed the example on later occasions.[1] If hitherto the province had had

[1] Tacitus, *Ann.* iv. 15, 55. The town which possesses a temple dedicated by the diet of the province (the κοινὸν τῆς ᾿Ασίας κ. τ. λ.) bears on that account the honorary predicate of the "(imperial) temple-keeper" (νεωκόρος); and, if one of them has several to show, the number is appended. In this institution one may clearly discern how the imperial worship ob-

only one president and one chief priest, as only one
temple, now not merely had as many chief priests to be
appointed as there were provincial temples, but also,
seeing that the conduct of the temple-festival and the
execution of the games pertained not to the chief priest
but to the land-president, and the rival great towns were
chiefly concerned about the festivals and games, there
was given to all the chief priests at the same time the
title and the right of presidency, so that at least in Asia
the Asiarchy and the chief priesthood of the provincial
temples coincided.[1]   Therewith the diet and the civil

tained its full elaboration in Asia
Minor.   In reality the *neocorate* is
general, applicable to any deity and
any town ; titularly, as an honorary
surname of the town, it meets us with
vanishing exceptions only in the imperial cultus of Asia Minor—only
some Greek towns of the neighbouring provinces, such as Tripolis in
Syria, Thessalonica in Macedonia,
participated in it.

[1] However little the original diversity of the presidency of the diet and
the provincial chief-priesthood for the
cultus of the emperor can be called
in question, yet not merely in the case
of the former does the magisterial
character of the president, still clearly
recognisable in Hellas, whence the
organisation of the κοινά generally
proceeds, fall completely into the
shade in Asia Minor, but here in
fact, where the κοινόν has several
ritual centres, the Ἀσιάρχης and the
ἀρχιερεὺς τῆς Ἀσίας seem to have
amalgamated.   The president of the
κοινόν never bears in Asia Minor the
title of στρατηγός, which sharply em-
phasises the civil office, and ἄρξας τοῦ
κοινοῦ (p. 344, note) or τοῦ ἔθνους
(*C. I. Gr.* 4380 ᵏ⁴, p. 1168) is rare ;
the compounds Ἀσιάρχης, Λυκιάρχης,
analogous to the Ἑλλαδάρχης of
Achaia, are already in Strabo's time
the usual designation.   That in the
minor provinces, like Galatia and
Lycia, the Archon and the Archiereus
of the province remained separate, is
certain.   But in Asia the existence of

Asiarchs for Ephesus and Smyrna is
established by inscriptions (Marquardt,
Staatsverw. i. 514), while yet according to the nature of the institution
there could only be one Asiarch for
the whole province.   Here, too, the
Agonothesia of the Archiereus is attested (Galen on Hippocrates *de part.*
18, 2, p. 567, Kühn : παρ᾽ ἡμῖν ἐν
Περγάμῳ τῶν ἀρχιερέων τὰς καλουμένας
μονομαχίας ἐπιτελούντων), while it is
the very essence of the Asiarchate.
To all appearance the rivalries of the
towns have here led to the result,
that, after there were several temples
of the emperor dedicated by the province in different towns, the Agonothesia was taken from the real president of the diet, and, instead, the
titular Asiarchate and the Agonothesia
were committed to the chief priest of
each temple.   In that case the Ἀσιάρχης
καὶ ἀρχιερεὺς ιγ´ πόλεων is explained on
the coins of the thirteen Ionic towns
(Mionnet, iii. 61, 1), and on Ephesian
inscriptions the same Ti. Julius Re-
ginus may be named sometimes Ἀσι-
αρχης β´ ναῶν τῶν ἐν Εφέσῳ (Wood,
Inscr. from the great theatre, p. 18),
sometimes ἀρχιερεὺς β´ ναῶν τῶν ἐν
Ἐφέσῳ (*ib.* n. 8. 14, similarly 9).—
Only in this way, too, are the institutions of the fourth century to be comprehended.   Here a chief priest appears in every province, in Asia with
the title of Asiarch, in Syria with
that of Syriarch, and so forth.   If
the amalgamation of the Archon and
the Archiereus had already begun

functions, from which the institution had its origin, fell into the background ; the Asiarch was soon nothing more than the provider of a popular festival annexed to the divine worship of the former and present emperors, on which account indeed his wife—the Asiarchess—might and zealously did take part in the celebration.

Superin-
tendence of
worship
by the pro-
vincial
priests. A practical importance, increased in Asia Minor by the high estimation in which this institution was held, may have attached to the provincial chief-priesthood for the worship of the emperors through the religious superintendence associated with it. After the diet had once resolved on the worship of the emperors, and the government had given its consent, action on the part of the towns followed as a matter of course ; in Asia already under Augustus at least all the chief places of judicial circuit had their Caesareum and their emperors' festival.[1] It was the right and duty of the chief priest to watch over the execution of these provincial and municipal decrees and the practice of the cultus in his district ; what this might mean, is elucidated by the fact, that the autonomy of the free city of Cyzicus in Asia was set aside under Tiberius for this among other reasons, that it had allowed the decree for building the temple of the god Augustus to remain unfulfilled—perhaps just because it as a free town was not under the diet. It is probable that this superintendence, although it primarily concerned the emperor-worship, extended to the affairs of religion in general.[2] Then, when the old and the new faith began to contend in the empire for the mastery, it was probably, in the first instance, through the provincial chief priesthood that the contrast between them was

earlier in the province of Asia, nothing was more natural than now, on the diminution of the provinces, to combine them everywhere in this way.

[1] *C. I. Gr.* 3902^b.

[2] Dio of Prusa, *Or.* 35, p. 66 R., names the Asiarchs and the analogous archons (he designates clearly their *Agonothesia*, and to it also point the corrupt words τοὺς ἐπωνύμους τῶν δύο ἠπείρων τῆς ἑσπέρας ὅλης, for which

probably we should read τῆς ἑτέρας ὅλης) τοὺς ἁπάντων ἄρχοντας τῶν ἱερέων. There is, as is well known, an almost constant absence in the designation of the provincial priests of express reference to the worship of the emperors ; there was good reason for that absence, if they were expected to play in their spheres the part of the Pontifex Maximus in Rome.

converted into conflict. These priests, appointed from the provincials of mark by the diet of the province, were by their traditions and by their official duties far more called and inclined than were the imperial magistrates to animadvert on neglect of the recognised worship, and, where dissuasion did not avail, as they had not themselves a power of punishment, to bring the act punishable by civil law to the notice of the local or imperial authorities and to invoke the aid of the secular arm—above all, to force the Christians to comply with the demands of the imperial cultus. In the later period the regents adhering to the old faith even expressly enjoin these chief priests personally, and through the priests of the towns placed under them, to punish contraventions of the existing religious arrangements, and assign to them exactly the part which under the emperors of the new faith is taken by the metropolitan and his urban bishops.[1] Probably here it was not the heathen organisation that copied the Christian institutions ; but, conversely, the conquering Christian church that took its hierarchic

---

[1] Maximinus for this purpose placed military help at the disposal of the chief priest of the individual province (Eusebius, *Hist. Eccl.* viii. 14, 9) ; and the famous letter of Julian (*Ep.* 49, comp. *Ep.* 63) to the Galatarch of the time gives a clear view of his obligations. He is to superintend the whole religious matters of the province ; to preserve his independence in contradistinction to the governor, not to dance attendance upon him, not to allow him to appear in the temple with military escort, to receive him not in front of, but in, the temple, within which he is lord and the governor a private man. Of the subsidies which the government has settled on the province (30,000 bushels of corn and 60,000 sextarii of wine), he is to expend the fifth part on the poor persons who become clients of the heathen priests, and to employ the rest otherwise on charitable objects ; in every town of the province, if possible, with the aid of private persons, to call into existence hospitals (ξενοδοχεῖα), not merely for heathens, but for everybody, and no longer to allow the Christians the monopoly of good works. He is to urge all the priests of the province by example and exhortation generally to maintain a religious walk, to avoid the frequenting of theatres and taverns, and in particular to frequent the temples diligently with their family and their attendants, or else, if they should not amend their ways, to depose them. It is a pastoral letter in the best form, only with the address altered, and with quotations from Homer instead of the Bible. Clearly as these arrangements bear on their face the stamp of heathenism already collapsing, and certainly as in this extent they are foreign to the earlier epoch, the foundation at any rate—the general superintendence of the chief priest of the province over matters of worship—by no means appears as a new institution.

weapons from the arsenal of the enemy. All this applied, as we have already observed, to the whole empire ; but the very practical consequences of the provincial regulation of the imperial cultus—the exercise of religious superintendence and the persecution of persons of another faith—were drawn pre-eminently in Asia Minor.

System of religion.
Alongside of the cultus of the emperors the worship of the gods proper found its favoured abode in Asia Minor, and all its extravagances in particular there found a refuge. The mischief of asylums and of miraculous cures had here its seat in a quite special sense. Under Tiberius the limitation of the former was enjoined by the Roman senate ; the god of healing, Asklepios, nowhere performed more and greater wonders than in his much-loved city of Pergamus, which worshipped him as Zeus Asklepios, and owed to him a good part of its prosperity in the imperial period. The most active wonder-workers of the time of the empire—the subsequently canonised Cappadocian Apollonius of Tyana and the Paphlagonian serpent-man Alexander of Abonuteichos —belonged to Asia Minor. If the general prohibition of associations was carried out, as we shall see, with special strictness in Asia Minor, the reason must doubtless be sought mainly in the religious conditions which gave special occasion to the abuse of such unions there.

Public safety.
The public safety was left to depend in the main on the land itself. In the earlier imperial period, apart from the Syrian command which included eastern Cilicia, there was stationed in all Asia Minor simply a detachment of 5000 auxiliary troops, which served as a garrison in the province of Galatia,[1] along with a fleet of 40 ships ; this command was destined partly to keep in check the restless Pisidians, partly to cover the north-eastern

[1] This troop, according to its position in Josephus, *Bell. Jud.* ii. 16, 4, between the provinces of Asia and Cappadocia not provided with garrisons, can only be referred to Galatia. Of course it furnished also the detachments, which were stationed in the dependent territories on the Caucasus, at that time—under Nero—apparently also those stationed on the Bosporus itself, in which, it is true, also the Moesian corps took part (p. 318).

frontier of the empire, and to watch over the coast of the Black Sea as far as the Crimea. Vespasian raised this troop to the status of an army corps of two legions and placed their staffs in the province of Cappadocia on the upper Euphrates. Besides these forces destined to guard the frontier there were not then any garrisons of note in anterior Asia ; in the imperial province of Lycia and Pamphylia, *e.g.* there lay a single cohort of 500 men, in the senatorial provinces, at the most, individual soldiers told off from the imperial guard or from the neighbouring imperial provinces for special purposes.[1] If this testifies, on the one hand, most emphatically to the internal peace of these provinces, and clearly brings before our eyes the enormous contrast of the citizens of Asia Minor with the constantly unsettled capitals of Syria and Egypt, it explains, on the other hand, the subsistence, already noticed in another connection, of brigandage in a country mountainous throughout and in the interior partly desolate, particularly on the Myso-Bithynian frontier and in the mountain valleys of Pisidia and Isauria. There was no civic militia proper in Asia Minor. In spite of the flourishing of gymnastic institutes for boys, youths, and men, the Hellenes of this period in Asia remained as unwarlike as in Europe.[2] They restricted Eirenarchs. themselves to creating for the maintenance of public safety civic peace-masters (Eirenarchs), and placing at their disposal a number of civic *gens d'armes*, partly mounted mercenaries of small repute, but which must yet have been useful, since the emperor Marcus did not disdain, in the sorely felt want of tried soldiers during the Marcomanian war, to incorporate these town-soldiers of Asia Minor among the imperial troops.[3]

---

[1] Praetorian *stationarius Ephesi*, *Eph. epigr.* iv. n. 70. A soldier *in statione Nicomedensi*, Plin. *ad Trai.* 74. A legionary centurion in Byzantium, *ib.* 77, 78.

[2] In the municipal matters of Asia Minor everything occurs except what relates to arms. The Smyrnaean στρατηγὸς ἐπὶ τῶν ὅπλων is of course

a reminiscence equally with the cultus of Herakles ὁπλοφύλαξ (*C. I. Gr.* 3162).

[3] The Eirenarch of Smyrna sends out these *gens d'armes* to arrest Polycarp : ἐξῆλθον διωγμῖται καὶ ἱππεῖς μετὰ τῶν συνήθων αὐτοῖς ὅπλων, ὡς ἐπὶ λῃστὴν τρέχοντες (*Acta mart.*, ed. Ruinart, p. 39). That they had

Adminis-
tration of
justice.

The administration of justice on the part as well of the civic authorities as of the governors left at this epoch much to be desired ; yet the emergence of the imperial rule marks a turn in it for the better. The interference of the supreme power had under the republic confined itself to the penal control of the public officials, and exercised this, especially in later times, feebly and factiously, or rather not at all. Now not merely were the reins drawn tighter in Rome, inasmuch as the strict superintendence of its own officers was inseparable from the unity of military government, and even the imperial senate was induced to watch more sharply over the administration of its mandatories ; but it became now possible to set aside the miscarriages of the provincial courts by way of the newly introduced appeal, or else, where an impartial trial could not be expected in the province, to carry the process to Rome before the bar of the emperor.[1] Both of these steps applied also to the senatorial provinces, and were to all appearance predominantly felt as a benefit.

The con-
stitution of
towns in
Asia Minor.

As in the case of the Hellenes of Europe, so in Asia Minor the Roman province was essentially an aggregate

not the armour of soldiers proper, is also elsewhere remarked (*Ammian.* xxvii. 9, 6 : *adhibitis semiermibus quibusdam* — against the Isaurians — *quos diogmitas apellant*). Their employment in the Marcomanian war is reported by the biographer of Marcus, c. 26 : *armavit et diogmitas*, and by the inscription of Aezani in Phrygia, *C. I. Gr.* 3031 *a* 8 = Lebas-Wadding-ton, 992 : παρασχὼν τῷ κυρίῳ Καίσαρι σύμμαχον διωγμείτην παρ᾽ ἑαυτοῦ.

[1] In Cnidus (*Bull. de corr. Hell.* vii.

13, 12. 62), in the year 741-742 U. C., some apparently respectable burgesses had during three nights assailed the house of one with whom they had a personal feud ; in repelling the attack one of the slaves of the besieged house had killed one of the assailants by a vessel thrown from the window. The occupants of the besieged house were thereupon accused of manslaughter, but, as they had public opinion against

them, they dreaded the civic tribunal and desired the matter to be decided by the verdict of the emperor Augustus. The latter had the case investigated by a commissioner, and acquitted the accused, of which he informed the authorities in Cnidus, with the remark that they would not have handled the matter impartially, and directed them to act in accordance with his verdict. This was certainly, as Cnidus was a free town, an encroachment on its sovereign rights, as also in Athens appeal to the emperor and even to the proconsul was in Hadrian's time allowable (p. 262, note 2). But any one who considers the state of things as to justice in a Greek town of this epoch and of this position, will not doubt that, while such encroachment gave doubtless occasion to various unjust decisions, it much more frequently prevented them.

of urban communities. Here, as in Hellas, the traditional received forms of democratic polity were in general retained, *e.g.* the magistrates continued to be chosen by the burgesses, but everywhere the determining influence was placed in the hands of the wealthy, and no free play was allowed to the pleasure of the multitude any more than to serious political ambition. Among the limitations of municipal autonomy it was peculiar to the towns of Asia Minor, that the already mentioned Eirenarch, the police-master of the city, was subsequently nominated by the governor from a list of ten names proposed by the council of the city. The government-trusteeship of civic finance-administration—the imperial appointment of one not belonging to the city itself as a guardian of property (*curator rei publicae*, λογιστής), whose consent the civic authorities had to procure in the more important dealings with property—was never generally ordained, but only for this or that city according to need ; in Asia Minor, however, in keeping with the importance of its urban development, it was introduced specially early, *i.e.* from the beginning of the second century, and on a specially comprehensive scale. At least in the third century here, as elsewhere, other important decrees of the communal administration had to be laid before the governor to be confirmed. The Roman government did not insist anywhere, and least of all in the Hellenic lands, on uniformity of municipal constitution ; in Asia Minor there prevailed great variety, according, it may be conjectured, in many cases with the pleasure of the individual burgess-bodies, although for the communities belonging to the same province the law organising each province prescribed general rules. Whatever institutions of this sort may be looked upon as diffused in Asia Minor, and predominantly peculiar to the land, bear no political character, but are merely significant as regards social relations, such as the unions spread over all Asia Minor, partly of the older, partly of the younger citizens, the Gerusia and the Neoi, clubs for the two classes of age with corresponding places of gymnastic exercise and

Logistae.

Gerusia, Neoi.

festivals.[1] Of autonomous communities there were from the outset far fewer in Asia Minor than in Hellas proper ; and, in particular, the most important towns of Asia Minor never had this doubtful distinction, or at any rate early lost it, such as Cyzicus under Tiberius (p. 348), Samos through Vespasian. Asia Minor was just old subject-territory and, under its Persian as under its Hellenic rulers, accustomed to monarchic organisation ; here less than in Hellas did useless recollections and vague hopes carry men away beyond the limited municipal horizon of the present, and there was not much of this sort to disturb the peaceful enjoyment of such happiness in life as was possible under the existing circumstances.

Urban life.   Of this happiness of life there was abundance in Asia Minor under the Roman imperial government. "No province of them all," says an author living in Smyrna under the Antonines, "has so many towns to show as ours, and none such towns as our largest. It has the advantage of a charming country, a favourable climate, varied products, a position in the centre of the empire, a girdle of peaceful people all round, good order, rarity of crime, gentle treatment of slaves, consideration and

[1] The Gerusia often mentioned in inscriptions of Asia Minor has nothing but the name in common with the political institution founded by Lysimachus in Ephesus (Strabo, xiv. 1, 21, p. 640 ; Wood, *Ephesus, inscr. from the temple of Diana*, n. 19) ; its character in Roman times is indicated partly by Vitruvius, ii. 8, 10 ; *Croesi (domum) Sardiani civibus ad requiescendum aetatis otio seniorum collegio gerusiam dedicaverunt*, partly by the inscription recently found in the Lycian town Sidyma (Benndorf, *Lyk. Reise*, i. 71), according to which council and people resolve, as the law requires, to institute a Gerusia, and to elect to it 50 Buleutae and 50 other citizens, who then appoint a gymnasiarch for the new Gerusia. This gymnasiarch, who meets us elsewhere, as well as the Hymnode of the Gerusia (Menadier, *qua condic. Ephesii usi* sint, p. 51), are, among the office-bearers of this body known to us, the only ones characteristic of its nature. Analogous, but of less estimation, are the *collegia* of the νέοι, which also have their own gymnasiarchs. To the two overseers of the places of gymnastic exercise for the grown-up citizens the gymnasiarchs of the Ephebi form the contrast (Menadier, p. 91). Common repasts and festivals (to which the Hymnodes has reference) were of course not wanting, particularly in the case of the Gerusia. It was not a provision for the poor, nor yet a *collegium* reserved for the municipal aristocracy ; but characteristic for the mode of civil intercourse among the Greeks, with whom the gymnasium was nearly what the citizens' assembly-rooms are in our small towns.

goodwill from the rulers." Asia was called, as we have already said, the province of the five hundred towns ; and, if the arid interior, in part fitted only for pasture, of Phrygia, Lycaonia, Galatia, and Cappadocia was even at that time but thinly peopled, the rest of the coast was not far behind Asia. The enduring prosperity of the regions capable of cultivation in Asia Minor did not extend merely to the cities of illustrious name, such as Ephesus, Smyrna, Laodicea, Apamea ; wherever a corner of the country, neglected under the desolation of the fifteen hundred years which separate us from that time, is opened up to investigation, there the first and the most powerful feeling is that of astonishment, one might almost say of shame, at the contrast of the wretched and pitiful present with the happiness and splendour of the past Roman age.

On a secluded mountain-top not far from the Lycian coast, where according to the Greek fable dwelt the Chimaera, lay the ancient Cragus, probably built only of beams and clay tiles, and having for that reason no trace of it left excepting the Cyclopian fortress-walls at the foot of the hill. Below the summit spreads a pleasant fertile valley with fresh Alpine air and southern vegetation, surrounded by mountains rich in woods and game. When under the emperor Claudius Lycia became a province, the Roman government transferred the mountain-town—the "green Cragus" of Horace—to this plain; in the market-place of the new town, Sidyma, the remains still stand of the tetrastyle temple then dedicated to the emperor, and of a stately colonnade, which a native of the place who had acquired means as a physician built in his early home. Statues of the emperors and of deserving fellow-citizens adorned the market ; there were in the town a temple to its protecting gods, Artemis and Apollo, baths, gymnastic institutions (γυμνάσια) for the older as for the younger citizens ; from the gates along the main road, which led steeply down the mountain side to the harbour Calabatia, there stretched on both sides rows of stone sepulchral monuments, more stately and more costly

Cragus-Sidyma.

than those of Pompeii, and for the most part still erect, while the houses presumably built, like those of the ancient city, from perishable materials, have disappeared. We may draw an inference as to the position and habits of the former inhabitants from a municipal decree recently found there, probably drawn up under Commodus, as to constituting the club for the elder citizens; it was composed of a hundred members, taken one half from the town-council and the other from the rest of the citizens, including not more than three freedmen and one person of illegitimate birth, all the rest begotten in lawful wedlock and belonging in part to demonstrably old and wealthy burgess-houses. Some of these families attained to Roman citizenship, one even to the senate of the empire. But even abroad this senatorial house, as well as different physicians of Sidyma employed in other lands and even at the imperial court, remained mindful of their home, and several of them closed their lives there; one of these distinguished denizens has put together the legends of the town and the prophecies concerning it in a compilation not exactly excellent, but very learned and very patriotic, and caused these memorabilia to be publicly exhibited. This Cragus-Sidyma did not vote among towns of the first class at the diet of the small Lycian province, was without a theatre, without honorary titles, and without those general festivals which in the world, as it then was, marked a great town; was even, according to the conception of the ancients, a small provincial town and thoroughly a creation of the Roman imperial period. But in the whole Vilajet Aïdin there is at the present day no inland place which can be even remotely placed by the side of this little mountain-town, such as it was, as regards civilised existence. What still stands vividly to-day before our eyes in this secluded village has disappeared, with the exception of slight remains, or even without a trace, in an untold number of other towns under the devastating hand of man. The coinage of the imperial period, freely given to the towns in copper, allows us a certain glance at this abundance; no province can even

remotely vie with Asia in the number of mints and the
variety of the representations.

No doubt this merging of all interests in the petty Defects of
town of one's birth was not without its reverse side in municipal
Asia Minor, any more than among the European Greeks. administration.
What was said of their communal administration holds
good in the main also here. The urban finance-system,
which knows itself to be without right control, lacks
steadiness and frugality and often even honesty ; as to
buildings — sometimes the resources of the town are
exceeded, sometimes even what is most needful is left
undone ; the humbler citizens become accustomed to the
largesses of the town-chest, or of men of wealth, to free oil
in the baths, to public banquets and popular recreations out
of others' pockets ; the good houses become used to the
clientage of the multitude, with its abject demonstrations
of homage, its begging intrigues, its divisions ; rivalries
exist, as between town and town (p. 329), so in every town
between the several circles and the several houses ; the
government in Asia Minor dares not to introduce the
formation of poor-clubs and of voluntary fire-brigades, such
as everywhere existed in the west, because the spirit of
faction here at once takes possession of every association.
The calm sea easily becomes a swamp, and the lack of
the great pulsation of general interest is clearly discernible
also in Asia Minor.

Asia Minor, especially in its anterior portion, was one of Prosperity.
the richest domains of the great Roman state.   It is true
that the misgovernment of the republic, the disasters of
the Mithradatic time thereby produced, thereafter the evil
of piracy, and lastly the many years of civil war which
had financially affected few provinces so severely as these,
had doubtless so utterly disorganised the means of the
communities and of individuals there, that Augustus
resorted to the extreme expedient of striking off all
claims of debt ; all the Asiatics, with the exception of
the Rhodians, made use of this dangerous remedy.   But
the peaceful government which again set in made up for
much.   Not everywhere—the islands of the Aegean Sea,

for example, never thereafter revived—but in most places, already when Augustus died, the wounds as well as the remedies were forgotten ; and in this state the land remained for three centuries down to the epoch of the Gothic wars. The sums at which the towns of Asia Minor were assessed, and which they themselves, certainly under control of the governor, had to allocate and raise, formed one of the most considerable sources of income for the imperial exchequer. How the burden of taxation stood related to the ability of the taxed to pay, we are unable to ascertain ; but permanent overburdening in the strict sense is not compatible with the circumstances in which we find the land down to the middle of the third century. The remissness of the government, still more perhaps than its intentional forbearance, may have kept within bounds the fiscal restriction of traffic and the application of a tax-screw which was inconvenient not merely for the taxed. In great calamities, particularly on occasion of the earthquakes which under Tiberius fearfully devastated twelve flourishing cities of Asia, especially Sardis, and under Pius a number of Carian and Lycian towns and the islands of Cos and Rhodes, private and above all imperial help was rendered with great liberality, and bestowed upon the natives of Asia Minor the full blessing of a great state—the collective guarantee of all for all. The construction of roads, which the Romans had taken in hand on the first erection of the province of Asia iii. 56. by Manius Aquillius (iii. 59), was seriously prosecuted during the imperial period in Asia Minor only where larger garrisons were stationed, particularly in Cappadocia and the neighbouring Galatia, after Vespasian had instituted a legionary camp on the middle Euphrates.[1] In the other provinces not much was done for it, partly, doubtless, in consequence of the laxity of the senatorial government ; wherever roads were here constructed on the part of the state, it was done on imperial ordinance.[2]

---

[1] The milestones begin here with Vespasian (*C. I. L.* iii. 306), and are thenceforth numerous, particularly from Domitian down to Hadrian.

[2] This is most clearly shown by the road-constructions executed in the senatorial province of Bithynia under Nero and Vespasian by the imperial

This prosperity of Asia Minor was not the work of a government of superior insight and energetic activity. The political institutions, the incitements of trade and commerce, the initiative in literature and art belong throughout Asia Minor to the old free towns or to the Attalids. What the Roman government gave to the land, was essentially the permanence of a state of peace, the toleration of inward prosperity, the absence of that governing wisdom which regards every sound pair of arms and every saved piece of money as rightfully subservient to its immediate aims—negative virtues of personages far from prominent, but often more conducive to the common weal than the great deeds of the self-constituted guardians of mankind.

The prosperity of Asia Minor was in beautiful equipoise, dependent as much on agriculture as on industry and commerce. The favours of nature were bestowed in richest measure, especially on the regions of the coast ; and there are many evidences with how laborious diligence, even under more difficult circumstances, every at all useable piece of ground was turned to account, *e.g.* in the rocky valley of the Eurymedon in Pamphylia by the citizens of Selga. The products of the industry of Asia Minor are too numerous and too manifold to be dwelt upon in detail ;[1] we may mention that the immense pas-

Trade and commerce.

---

procurator (*C. I. L.* iii. 346 ; *Eph. v.n.* 96). But even in the case of the roads constructed in the senatorial provinces of Asia and Cyprus the senate is never named, and the same may be assumed for them. In the third century here, as everywhere, the construction even of the imperial highways was transferred to the communes (Smyrna : *C. I. L.* iii. 471 ; Thyatira, *Bull. de corr. Hell.* i. 101 ; Paphos, *C. I. L.* iii. 218).

[1] The Christians of the little town of Corycus in the Rough Cilicia were wont, contrary to the general custom, to append regularly in their tomb-inscriptions the station in life. On the epitaphs recovered there by Langlois and recently by Duchesne (*Bull. de*

corr. *Hell.* vii. 230 ff.), there are found a writer (νοτάριος), a wine-dealer (οἰνέμπορος), two oil-dealers (ἐλεοπώλης), a green-grocer (λαχανοπώλης), a fruit-dealer (ὀπωροπώλης), two retail dealers (κάπηλος), five goldsmiths (αὐράριος thrice, χρυσόχοος twice), one of whom is also presbyter, four coppersmiths (χαλκότυπος once, χαλκεύς thrice),two instrument-makers (ἀρμενοράφος), five potters (κεραμεύς), of which one is designated as workgiver (ἐργοδότης), another is at the same time presbyter, a clothes-dealer (ἱματιοπώλης), two linen - dealers (λινοπώλης), three weavers (ὀθονιακός), a worker in wool (ἐρεουργός), two shoemakers (καλιγάριος, καλτάριος), a skinner (ἰνιοράφος, doubtless for ἡνιοράφος,

tures of the interior, with their flocks of sheep and goats, made Asia Minor the headquarters of woollen manufactures and of weaving generally—it suffices to recall the Milesian and the Galatian, that is, the Angora, wool, the Attalic gold - embroideries, the cloths prepared in the workshops of Phrygian Laodicea after the Nervian, that is the Flemish, style. It is well-known that an insurrection had almost broken out in Ephesus because the goldsmiths dreaded injury to their sale of sacred images from the new Christian faith. In Philadelphia, a considerable town of Lydia, we know the names of two out of the seven districts : they are those of the wool-weavers and the shoemakers. Probably there is here brought to light what in the case of the other towns is hidden under older and more genteel names, that the more considerable towns of Asia included throughout not merely a multitude of labourers, but also a numerous manufacturing population.

The money-dealing and traffic were in Asia Minor dependent chiefly on its own products. The great foreign import and export trade of Syria and Egypt was in the main excluded, though from the eastern lands various articles were introduced into Asia Minor, *e.g.* a considerable number of slaves through the Galatian traders.[1] But, if the Roman merchants were to be found here apparently in every large and small town, even at places like Ilium and Assus in Mysia, Prymnessus and Traianopolis in Phrygia, in such numbers that their associations were in the habit of taking part along with the town's burgesses in public acts ; if in Hierapolis, in the interior of Phrygia, a manufacturer (ἐργαστής) caused it to be inscribed on his tomb that he had in his lifetime sailed seventy-two times round Cape Malea to Italy, and a Roman poet describes the merchant of the capital who hastens to the port, in

---

pellio), a mariner (ναύκληρος), a midwife (ἰατρινή) ; further a joint tomb of the highly reputable money-changers (σύσστεμα τῶν εὐγενεστάτων τραπεζιτῶν). Such was the look of things there in the fifth and sixth centuries.

[1] This traffic attested for the fourth century (Ammianus, xxii. 7, 8 ; Claudianus in Eutrop. i. 59) is beyond doubt older. Of another nature is the fact, that, as Philostratus states (*Vita Apoll.* viii. 7, 12), the non-Greek inhabitants of Phrygia sold their children to the slave-dealers.

order not to let his business-friend from Cibyra, not far
distant from Hierapolis, fall into the hands of rivals,
there is thus opened up a glimpse into a stirring manufacturing and mercantile life not merely at the seaports.
Language also testifies to the constant intercourse with
Italy ; among the Latin words that became current in
Asia Minor not a few proceed from such intercourse, as
indeed in Ephesus even the guild of the wool-weavers
gives itself a Latin name.[1]   Teachers of all sorts and
physicians came especially from this quarter to Italy and
the other lands of the Latin tongue, and not merely
gained often considerable wealth, but also brought it back
to their native place ; among those to whom the towns of
Asia Minor owe buildings or endowments, the physicians
who had become rich,[2] and literati, occupy a prominent
position.   Lastly, the emigration of the great families to
Italy affected Asia Minor less and later than the West ; it
was easier for people from Vienna and Narbo to transplant
themselves to the capital of the empire than from the

---

[1] Συνεργασία τῶν λαναρίων (Wood,
Ephesus, city, n. 4). On the inscriptions of Corycus (p. 359) Latin descriptions of artisans abound. The stair
is called γράδος in the Phrygian inscriptions, *C. I. Gr.* 3900, 3902 *i.*

[2] One of these is Xenophon son of
Heraclitus of Cos, well known from
Tacitus (*Ann.* xii. 61, 67) and Pliny,
H. N. xxix. 1, 7, and from a series of
monuments of his native place (*Bull.
de corr. Hell.* v. 468). As physician-
in-ordinary (ἀρχιατρός, which title first
occurs here) to the emperor he acquired such influence that he combined with his medical activity the
position of imperial cabinet-secretary
for Greek correspondence (ἐπὶ τῶν
Ἑλληνικῶν ἀποκριμάτων ; comp. Suidas *s. v.* Διονύσιος 'Αλεξανδρεύς), and
he procured not merely for his brother
and uncle the Roman franchise and
posts as officers of equestrian rank,
and for himself, besides the horse of
a knight and the rank of officer, the
decoration of the golden chaplet and
the spear on occasion of the triumph
over Britain, but also for his native

place freedom from taxation. His
tomb stands on the island, and his
grateful countrymen set up statues to
him and to his, and struck in memory
of him coins with his effigy. He it
is who is alleged to have put an end
to Claudius, when dead - sick, by
further poisoning, and accordingly, as
equally valuable to him and to his successor, he is termed on his monuments not merely, as usual, "friend
of the emperor" (φιλοσέβαστος), but
specially friend of Claudius (φιλο-
κλαύδιος) and of Nero (φιλονέρων ; so
according to certain restoration).
His brother, whom he followed in
this position, drew a salary of 500,000
sesterces (£5000), but assured the
emperor that he had only taken the
position to please him, as his town-
practice brought in to him 100,000
sesterces more.   In spite of the enormous sums which the brothers had
expended on Naples in particular, as
well as on Cos, they left behind
an estate of 30,000,000 sesterces
(£325,000).

Greek towns; nor was the government in the earlier period quite inclined to bring the municipals of mark from Asia Minor to the court, and to introduce them into the Roman aristocracy.

Literary activity.

If we leave out of view the marvellous period of early bloom, in which the Ionic epos and the Aeolic lyric poetry, the beginnings of historical composition and of philosophy, of plastic art and of painting, had their rise on these shores, in science as in the practice of art the great age of Asia Minor was that of the Attalids, which faithfully cherished the memory of that still greater epoch. If Smyrna showed divine honours to its citizen Homer, struck coins for him and named them after him, there was thus expressed the feeling, which dominated all Ionia and all Asia Minor, that divine art had come down to earth in Hellas generally, and in Ionia in particular.

Instruction.

How early and to what extent elementary instruction was an object of public care in these regions is clearly shown by a decree of the town Teos in Lydia[1] concerning it. According to this, after the gift of capital by a rich citizen had provided the town with means, there was to be instituted in future, alongside of the inspector of gymnastics (γυμνασιάρχης), also the honorary office of a school-inspector (παιδονόμος). Further, there were to be appointed three paid teachers of writing with salaries, according to the three classes respectively, of 600, 550, and 500 drachmae, in order that all the free boys and girls might be instructed in writing; likewise two gymnastic masters, each with a salary of 500 drachmae; a teacher of music with a salary of 700 drachmae, who should instruct the boys of the last two years at school and the youths that had left school in playing the lute and the cithara; a boxing master with 300 drachmae, and a teacher for archery and throwing of the spear with a pay of 250 drachmae. The teachers of writing and music are to hold a public examination of the scholars annually in the town-hall. Such was the Asia Minor of the time of the Attalids; but

---

[1] The document is given by Dittenberger, n. 349. Attalus II. made a similar endowment in Delphi (*Bull. de corr. Hell.* v. 157).

the Roman republic did not continue their work. It did not cause its victories over the Galatians to be immortalised by the chisel, and the Pergamene library went shortly before the battle of Actium to Alexandria ; many of the best germs perished in the devastation of the Mithradatic and the civil wars. It was only in the time of the empire that the care of art, and above all of literature, revived at least outwardly with the prosperity of Asia Minor. To a primacy proper, such as was possessed by Athens as a university-town, by Alexandria in the sphere of scientific research, and by the frivolous capital of Syria for the drama and the *ballet*, none of the numerous cities of Asia Minor could lay claim in any direction whatever ; but general culture was probably nowhere more widely diffused and more influential. It must have been very early the custom in Asia to grant to teachers and physicians exemption from the civic offices and functions that involved expense ; to this province was directed the edict of the emperor Pius (p. 329), which, in order to set limits to an exemption that was evidently very burdensome for the city finances, prescribes maximal numbers for it : *e.g.* allows towns of the first class to grant this immunity to the extent of ten physicians, five instructors in rhetoric, and five in grammar.

The position of Asia Minor as occupying the first rank in the literary world of the imperial period was based on the system of the rhetors, or, according to the expression later in use, the sophists of this epoch—a system which we moderns cannot easily realise. The place of written works, which pretty nearly ceased to have any significance, was taken by the public discourse, somewhat of the nature of our modern university and academic addresses, eternally producing itself anew and preserved only by way of exception, once heard and applauded, and then for ever forgotten. The contents were furnished frequently by the occasion of the birthday of the emperor, the arrival of the governor, or any analogous event, public or private ; still more frequently without any occasion they talked at large on everything, which was not practical and not instructive.

Addresses of the sophists.

The political address had no existence for this age at all, not even in the Roman senate. The forensic speech was no longer for the Greeks the goal of oratory, but stood alongside of the speech for speaking's sake as a neglected and plebeian sister, to which a master of that art might occasionally condescend. From poetry, philosophy, history, there was borrowed whatever admitted of being dealt with by way of common-place, while these all themselves, little cultivated in general, least of all in Asia Minor, and still less esteemed, languish by the side of the pure art of words and beneath its infection. The great past of the nation is regarded by these orators, so to speak, as their special property ; they reverence and treat Homer in some measure as the Rabbins do the books of Moses, and even in religion they study the most zealous orthodoxy. These discourses are sustained by all the allowed and unallowed resources of the theatre, by the art of gesticulation and of modulation of the voice, by the magnificence of the orator's costume, by the artifices of the virtuoso and the methods of partisanship, by competition, by the *claque.* To the boundless self-conceit of these word-artists corresponds the lively sympathetic interest of the public— which is but little inferior to that felt for race-horses—and the expression given to this sympathy quite after the fashion of the theatre ; and the frequency with which such exhibitions were brought before the cultured in the larger places entitles them, just like the theatre, to rank everywhere among the customary doings of urban life. If perhaps our understanding of this extinct phenomenon may be somewhat helped by connecting it with the impression called forth in our most susceptible great cities by the discourses of their learned bodies, as they fall due, there is yet wholly wanting in the modern state of things what was by far the main matter in the ancient world— the didactic element, and the connection of the aimless public discourse with the higher instruction of youth. If the latter at present, as we say, educates the boy of the cultured class to be a professor of philology, it educated him then to be a professor of eloquence, and, in fact, of this

sort of eloquence. For the school-training conduced more
and more to equip the boy for holding just such discourses,
as we have now described, on his own part, if possible, in
two languages ; and, whoever had finished the course with
profit, applauded in similar performances the recollection
of his own time at school.

This production embraced East and West, but Asia Minor
stood in the van and led the fashion. When in the age of
Augustus the school-rhetoric gained a footing in the Latin
instruction of the youth of the capital, its chief pillars
alongside of Italians and Spaniards were two natives of
Asia Minor, Arellius Fuscus and Cestius Pius. At that
same place, where the grave forensic address maintained
its ground in the better imperial period by the side of
this parasite, an ingenious advocate of the Flavian age
points to the enormous gulf which separates Nicetes of
Smyrna and the other rhetoricians applauded in Ephesus
and Mytilene from Aeschines and Demosthenes. By far
the most, and most noted, of the famous rhetors of this sort
are from the coast of western Asia. We have already
observed how much the supply of schoolmasters for the
whole empire told upon the finances of the towns of Asia
Minor. In the course of the imperial period the number
and the estimation of these sophists were constantly on
the increase, and they gained ground more and more in
the west. The cause of this lies partly doubtless in the
changed attitude of the government, which in the second
century—especially after the Hadrianic epoch exhibiting
not so much a Hellenising as a bad cosmopolitan type—
stood less averse to Greek and Oriental habits than
in the first ; but chiefly in the ever increasing general
diffusion of higher culture, and the rapidly enlarging
number of institutes for the higher instruction of youth.
The sophistic system thus belongs, at all events especially,
to Asia Minor, and particularly to the Asia Minor of the
second and third centuries ; only there may not be found
in this literary primacy any special peculiarity of these
Greeks and of this epoch, or even a national characteristic.
The sophistic system appears everywhere alike, in Smyrna

Asia Minor
leads the
fashion.

and Athens as in Rome and Carthage ; the masters of eloquence were sent out like patterns of lamps, and the manufacture was organised everywhere in the same way, Greek or Latin, according to desire, the supply being raised in accordance with the need. But no doubt those Greek districts, which took precedence in prosperity and culture, furnished this article of export of the best quality and in greatest quantity ; this holds true of Asia Minor for the times of Sulla and Cicero no less than for those of Hadrian and the Antonines.

Here, however, all is not shadow. Those same regions possess, not indeed among the professional sophists, but yet among the *literati* of a different type, who are still found there in comparatively large numbers, the best representatives of Hellenism which this epoch has at all Galenus. to show, the teacher of philosophy, Dio of Prusa in Bithynia, under Vespasian and Trajan, and the medical man Galenus of Pergamus, imperial physician in ordinary at the courts of Marcus and Severus. What is particularly pleasing in the case of Galen is the polished manner of the man of the world and the courtier, in connection with a general and philosophical culture, such as is frequently conspicuous in the physicians of this period.[1]

Dio of Prusa. In purity of sentiment and clear grasp of the position of things, the Bithynian Dio is nowise inferior to the scholar of Chaeronea ; in plastic power, in elegance and apt vigour of speech, in earnest meaning underlying lightness of form, in practical energy, he is superior to him. The best of his writings—the fancies of the ideal Hellene before the invention of the city and of money ; the appeal to the Rhodians, the only surviving representatives of genuine

---

[1] A physician of Smyrna, Hermogenes, son of Charidemus (*C. I. Gr.* 3311), wrote not merely 77 volumes of a medical tenor, but, in addition, as his epitaph tells, historical writings : on Smyrna, on the native country of Homer, on the wisdom of Homer, on the foundation of cities in Asia, in Europe, on the islands, itineraries of Asia and Europe, on stratagems, chronological tables on the history of Rome and of Smyrna. A physician of the imperial household, Menecrates (*C. I. Gr.* 6607), whose descent is not specified, founded, as his Roman admirers attest, the new logical and at the same time empiric medicine (ἰδίας λογικῆς ἐναργοῦς ἰατρικῆς κτίστης) in his writings, which ran to 156 volumes.

Hellenism ; the description of the Hellenes of his time in the solitude of Olbia as in the luxury of Nicomedia and of Tarsus; the exhortations to the individual as to an earnest conduct of life, and to all as to their keeping together in unity—form the best evidence that even of the Hellenism of Asia Minor in the time of the empire the word of the poet holds good : " The sun even in setting is ever the same."

END OF VOL. I.

THE PROVINCES

OF THE

ROMAN EMPIRE

FROM CAESAR TO DIOCLETIAN

BY

THEODOR MOMMSEN

TRANSLATED

WITH THE AUTHOR'S SANCTION AND ADDITIONS

BY

WILLIAM P. DICKSON, D.D., LL.D.

PROFESSOR OF DIVINITY IN THE UNIVERSITY OF GLASGOW

VOL. II

CONTENTS

CHAPTER IX.

THE EUPHRATES FRONTIER AND THE PARTHIANS.

THE only great state with which the Roman empire The empire of Iran. bordered was the empire of Iran,[1] based upon that nationality which was best known in antiquity, as it is in the present day, under the name of the Persians, consolidated politically by the old Persian royal family of the Achaemenids and its first great-king Cyrus, united religiously by the faith of Ahura Mazda and of Mithra. No one of the ancient peoples of culture solved the problem of national union equally early and with equal completeness. The Iranian tribes reached on the south as far as the Indian Ocean, on the north as far as the Caspian Sea ; on the north-east the steppes of inland Asia formed the constant battle-ground between the settled Persians and the nomadic tribes of Turan. On the east mighty mountains formed a boundary separating them from the Indians. In western Asia three great nations early encountered one another, each pushing

---

[1] The conception that the Roman and the Parthian empires were two great states standing side by side, and indeed the only ones in existence, dominated the whole Roman East, particularly the frontier-provinces. It meets us palpably in the Apocalypse of John, in which there is a juxta-position as well of the rider on the white horse with the bow and of the rider on the red horse with the sword (vi. 2, 3) as of the Megistanes and the Chiliarchs (vi. 15, comp. xviii. 23, xix. 18). The closing catastrophe, too, is conceived as a subduing of the Romans by the Parthians bringing back the emperor Nero (ix. 14, xvi. 12) and Armageddon, whatever may be meant by it, as the rendezvous of the Orientals for the collective attack on the West. Certainly the author, writing in the Roman empire, hints these far from patriotic hopes more than he expresses them.

forward on its own account: the Hellenes, who from Europe grasped at the coast of Asia Minor, the Aramaic peoples, who from Arabia and Syria advanced in a northern and north-eastern direction and substantially filled the valley of the Euphrates, and lastly, the races of Iran, not merely inhabiting the country as far as the Tigris, but even penetrating to Armenia and Cappadocia, while primitive inhabitants of other types in these far-extending regions succumbed under these leading powers and disappeared. In the epoch of the Achaemenids, the culminating point of the glory of Iran, the Iranian rule went far beyond this wide domain proper to the stock on all sides, but especially towards the west. Apart from the times, when Turan gained the upper hand over Iran and the Seljuks and Mongols ruled over the Persians, foreign rule, strictly so called, has only been established over the flower of the Iranian stocks twice, by Alexander the Great and his immediate successors and by the Arabian Abbasids, and on both occasions only for a comparatively short time; the eastern regions—in the former case the Parthians, in the latter the inhabitants of the ancient Bactria—not merely threw off again the yoke of the foreigner, but dislodged him also from the cognate west.

The rule of the Parthians.

When the Romans in the last age of the republic came into immediate contact with Iran as a consequence of the occupation of Syria, they found in existence the Persian empire regenerated by the Parthians. We have formerly had to make mention of this state on several occasions; this is the place to gather together the little that can be ascertained regarding the peculiar character of the empire, which so often exercised a decisive influence on the destinies of the neighbouring state. Certainly to most questions, which the historical inquirer has here to put, tradition has no answer. The Occidentals give but occasional notices, which may in their isolation easily mislead us, concerning the internal condition of their Parthian neighbours and foes; and, if the Orientals in general have hardly understood how to fix and to

preserve historical tradition, this holds doubly true of the
period of the Arsacids, seeing that it was by the later
Iranians regarded, together with the preceding foreign
rule of the Seleucids, as an unwarranted usurpation
between the periods of the old and the new Persian rule
—the Achaemenids and the Sassanids ; this period of five
hundred years is, so to speak, eliminated by way of
correction[1] from the history of Iran, and is as if non-
existent.

The standpoint, thus occupied by the court-historio-
graphers of the Sassanid dynasty, is more the legitimist-
dynastic one of the Persian nobility than that of Iranian
nationality.   No doubt the authors of the first imperial
epoch describe the language of the Parthians, whose
home corresponds nearly to the modern Chorasan, as
intermediate between the Median and the Scythian, that
is, as an impure Iranian dialect; accordingly they were
regarded as immigrants from the land of the Scythians,
and in this sense their name is interpreted as " fugitive
people," while the founder of the dynasty, Arsaces, is
declared by some indeed to have been a Bactrian, but by
others a Scythian from the Maeotis.   The fact that their
princes did not take up their residence in Seleucia on the
Tigris, but pitched their winter quarters in the immediate
neighbourhood at Ctesiphon, is traced to their wish not
to quarter Scythian troops in the rich mercantile city.
Much in the manners and arrangements of the Parthians
is alien from Iranian habits, and reminds us of the
customs of nomadic life ; they transact business and eat
on horseback, and the free man never goes on foot.   It
cannot well be doubted that the Parthians, whose name
alone of all the tribes of this region is not named in the
sacred books of the Persians, stand aloof from Iran
proper, in which the Achaemenids and the Magians are at
home.   The antagonism of this Iran to the ruling family
springing from an uncivilised and half foreign district,

The Parthians Scythian.

---

[1] This holds true even in some
measure for the chronology.   The
official historiography of the Sassanids reduces the space between
the last Darius and the first Sassanid
from 558 to 266 years (Nöldeke,
Tabari, p. 1).

and to its immediate followers—this antagonism, which the Roman authors not unwillingly took over from their Persian neighbours—certainly subsisted and fermented throughout the whole rule of the Arsacids, till it at length brought about their fall. But the rule of the Arsacids may not on that account be conceived as a foreign rule. No privileges were conceded to the Parthian stock and to the Parthian province. It is true that the Parthian town Hecatompylos is named as residence of the Arsacids; but they chiefly sojourned in summer at Ecbatana (Hamadan), or else at Rhagae like the Achaemenids, in winter, as already stated, in the camp-town of Ctesiphon, or else in Babylon on the extreme western border of the empire. The hereditary burial-place continued in the Parthian town Nisaea; but subsequently Arbela in Assyria served for that purpose more frequently. The poor and remote native province of the Parthians was in no way suited for the luxurious court-life, and the important relations to the West, especially of the later Arsacids. The chief country continued even now to be Media, just as under the Achaemenids. Although the Arsacids might be of Scythian descent, not so much depended on what they were as on what they desired to be; and they regarded and professed themselves throughout as the successors of Cyrus and of Darius. As the seven Persian family-princes had set aside the false Achaemenid, and had restored the legitimate rule by the elevation of Darius, so needs must other seven have overthrown the Macedonian foreign yoke and placed king Arsaces on the throne. With this patriotic fiction must further be connected the circumstance that a Bactrian nativity instead of a Scythian was assigned to the first Arsaces. The dress and the etiquette at the court of the Arsacids were those of the Persian court; after king Mithradates I. had extended his rule to the Indus and Tigris, the dynasty exchanged the simple title of king for that of king of kings which the Achaemenids had borne, and the pointed Scythian cap for the high tiara adorned with pearls; on the coins the king carries the bow like Darius. The aristocracy, too, that came into the land with the Arsacids and doubtless became in many ways mixed with the old indigenous one, adopted Persian manners and dress, mostly also Persian names ; of the Parthian army which fought with Crassus it is said that the soldiers still wore their hair rough after the Scythian fashion, but the general appeared after the Median manner with the hair parted in the middle and with painted face.

The political organisation, as it was established by the first Mithradates, was accordingly in substance that of the Achaemenids. The family of the founder of the dynasty is invested with all the lustre and with all the consecration of ancestral and divinely-ordained rule ; his name is transferred *de jure* to each of his successors and divine honour is assigned to him ; his successors are therefore called sons of God,[1] and besides brothers of the sun-god and the moon-goddess, like the Shah of Persia still at the present day ; to shed the blood of a member of the royal family even by mere accident is a sacrilege —all of them regulations, which with few abatements recur among the Roman Caesars, and are perhaps borrowed in part from those of the older great-monarchy. *The regal office.*

Although the royal dignity was thus firmly attached to the family, there yet subsisted a certain choice as to the king. As the new ruler had to belong as well to the college of the "kinsmen of the royal house" as to the council of priests, in order to be able to ascend the throne, an act must have taken place, whereby, it may be presumed, these same colleges themselves acknowledged the new ruler.[2] By the "kinsmen" are doubtless to be *Megistanes.*

---

[1] The viceroys of Persis are called in their title constantly "Zag Alohin" (at least the Aramaean signs correspond to these words, which were presumably in pronunciation expressed in the Persian way), son of God (Mordtmann, *Zeitschrift für Numismatik*, iv. 155 f.), and to this corresponds the title θεοπάτωρ on the Greek coins of the great-kings. The designation "God" is also found, as with the Seleucids and the Sassanids.

—Why a double diadem is attributed to the Arsacids (Herodian, vi. 2, 1) is not cleared up.

[2] Τῶν Παρθναίων συνέδριόν φησιν (Ποσειδώνιος) εἶναι, says Strabo, xi. 9, 3, p. 515, διττόν, τὸ μὲν συγγενῶν, τὸ δὲ σόφων καὶ μάγων, ἐξ ὧν ἀμφοῖν τοὺς βασιλεῖς καθίστασθαι (καθίστησιν in MSS.) ; Justinus, xvii. 3, 1, *Mithridates rex Parthorum . . . propter crudelitatem a senatu Parthico regno pellitur.*

understood not merely the Arsacids themselves, but the
"seven houses" of the Achaemenid organisation, princely
families, to which according to that arrangement equality
of rank and free access to the great-king belonged, and
which must have had similar privileges under the Arsacids.[1]
These families were at the same time holders of hereditary
crown offices,[2] e.g. the Surên—the name is like the name
Arsaces, a designation at once of person and of office—
the second family after the royal house, as crown-masters,
placed on each occasion the tiara on the head of the new
Arsaces.   But as the Arsacids themselves belonged to
the Parthian province, so the Surên were at home in
Sacastane (Seistân) and perhaps Sacae, thus Scythians ;
the Carên likewise descended from western Media, while
the highest aristocracy under the Achaemenids was
purely Persian.

Satraps.   The administration lay in the hands of the under-
kings or satraps ; according to the Roman geographers
of Vespasian's time the state of the Parthians consisted
of eighteen "kingdoms."   Some of these satrapies were
appanages of a second son of the ruling house ; in
particular the two north-western provinces, the Atro-
patenian Media (Aderbijan) and Armenia, so far as it
was in the power of the Parthians, appear to have been
entrusted for administration to the prince standing next
to the ruler for the time.[3]   We may add that prominent

---

[1] In Egypt, whose court ceremonial,
as doubtless that of all the states of the
Diadochi, is based on that ordained by
Alexander, and in so far upon that of
the Persian empire, the like title seems
to have been conferred also personally
(Franz, C. I. Gr. iii. 270). That
the same occurred with the Arsacids,
is possible.   Among the Greek-speaking subjects of the Arsacid state the
appellation μεγιστᾶνες seems in the
original stricter use to denote the
members of the seven houses ; it is
worthy of notice that megistanes and
satrapae are associated (Seneca, Ep.
21 ; Josephus, Arch. xi. 3, 2 ; xx.
2, 3). The circumstance that in
court mourning the Persian king does

not invite the megistanes to table
(Suetonius, Gai. 5) suggests the conjecture that they had the privilege
of taking meals with him.   The title
τῶν πρώτων φίλων is also found
among the Arsacids just as at the
Egyptian and Pontic courts (Bull. de
corr. Hell. vii. p. 349).

[2] A royal cup-bearer, who is at
the same time general, is mentioned
in Josephus, Arch. xiv. 13, 7 = Bell.
Jud. i. 13, 1. Similar court offices are
of frequent occurrence in the states
of the Diadochi.

[3] Tacitus, Ann. xv. 2, 31. If,
according to the preface of Agathangelos (p. 109, Langlois), at the
time of the Arsacids the oldest and

among the satraps were the king of the province of
Elymais or of Susa, to whom was conceded a specially
powerful and exceptional position, and next to him the
king of Persis, the ancestral land of the Achaemenids.
The form of administration, if not exclusive, yet prepon-
derant and conditioning the title, was in the Parthian
empire—otherwise than in the case of the Caesars—that
of vassal - kingdom, so that the satraps entered by
hereditary right, but were subject to confirmation by the
great-king.[1] To all appearance this continued downwards, so that smaller dynasts and family chiefs stood
in the same relation to the under-kings as the latter
occupied to the great-king.[2] Thus the office of great-
king among the Parthians was limited to the utmost in
favour of the high aristocracy by the accompanying
subdivision of the hereditary administration of the land.
With this it is quite in keeping, that the mass of the
population consisted of persons half or wholly non-free,[3]
and emancipation was not allowable.   In the army
which fought against Antonius there are said to have
been only 400 free among 50,000.   The chief among
the vassals of Orodes, who as his general defeated

ablest prince bore rule over the
country, and the three standing next
to him were kings of the Armenians,
of the Indians, and of the Massagetae,
there is here perhaps at bottom the
same arrangement.   That the Partho-
Indian empire, if it was combined
with the main land, was likewise regarded as an appanage for the second
son, is very probable.

[1] These are doubtless meant by
Justinus (xli. 2, 2), *proximus maiestati
regum praepositorum ordo est ; ex hoc
duces in bello, ex hoc in pace rectores
habent.*   The native name is preserved
by the gloss in Hesychius, βίσταξ ὁ
βασιλεὺς παρὰ Πέρσαις. If in Ammianus, xxiii. 6, 14, the presidents of
the Persian *regiones* are called *vitaxae*
(read *vistaxae*), *id est magistri equitum
et reges et satrapae,* he has awkwardly
referred what is Persian to all Inner
Asia (comp. *Hermes,* xvi. 613) ; we
may add that the designation "leaders

of horsemen " for these viceroys may
relate to the fact that they, like the
Roman governors, united in themselves the highest civil and the
supreme military power, and the
army of the Parthians consisted preponderantly of cavalry.
[2] This we learn from the title
σατράπης τῶν σατραπῶν, attributed to
one Gotarzes in the inscription of
Kermanschahân in Kurdistan (*C. I.
Gr.* 4674).   It cannot be assigned
to the Arsacid king of the same
name as such ; but perhaps there
may be designated by it, as Olshausen
(*Monatsbericht der Berliner Akademie,*
1878, p. 179) conjectures, that position which belonged to him after
his renouncing of the great - kingdom
(Tacitus, *Ann.* xi. 9).
[3] Still later a troop of horse in the
Parthian army is called that "of the
free :" Josephus, *Arch.* xiv. 13, 5 =
Bell. Jud. i. 13, 3.

Crassus, marched to the field with a harem of 200 wives and a baggage train of 1000 sumpter-camels; he himself furnished to the army 10,000 horsemen from his clients and slaves. The Parthians never had a standing army, but at all times the waging of war here was left to depend on the general levy of the vassal-princes and of the vassals subordinate to these, as well as of the great mass of the non-free over whom these bore sway.

The Greek towns of the Parthian empire.
Certainly the urban element was not quite wanting in the political organisation of the Parthian empire. It is true that the larger townships, which arose out of the distinctive development of the East, were not urban commonwealths, as indeed even the Parthian royal residence, Ctesiphon, is named in contrast to the neighbouring Greek foundation of Seleucia a village; they had no presidents of their own and no common council, and the administration lay here, as in the country districts, exclusively with the royal officials. But a portion— comparatively small, it is true—of the foundations of the Greek rulers had come under Parthian rule. In the provinces of Mesopotamia and Babylonia by nationality Aramaean the Greek town-system had gained a firm footing under Alexander and his successors. Mesopotamia was covered with Greek commonwealths; and in Babylonia, the successor of the ancient Babylon, the precursor of Bagdad, and for a time the residence of the Greek kings of Asia—Seleucia on the Tigris—had by its favourable commercial position and its manufactures risen to be the first mercantile city beyond the Roman bounds, with more, it is alleged, than half a million of inhabitants. Its free Hellenic organisation, on which beyond doubt its prosperity above all depended, was not touched even by the Parthian rulers in their own interest, and the city preserved not merely its town council of 300 elected members, but also the Greek language and Greek habits amidst the non-Greek East. It is true that the Hellenes in these towns formed only the dominant element; alongside of them lived numerous Syrians, and, as a third constituent, there were associated

with these the not much less numerous Jews, so that the population of these Greek towns of the Parthian empire, just like that of Alexandria, was composed of three separate nationalities standing side by side. Between these, just as in Alexandria, conflicts not seldom occurred, as *e.g.* at the time of the reign of Gaius under the eyes of the Parthian government the three nations came to blows, and ultimately the Jews were driven out of the larger towns.

In so far the Parthian empire was the genuine counterpart to the Roman. As in the one the Oriental viceroyship is an exceptional occurrence, so in the other is the Greek city; the general Oriental aristocratic character of the Parthian government is as little injuriously affected by the Greek mercantile towns on the west coast as is the civic organisation of the Roman state by the vassal kingdoms of Cappadocia and Armenia. While in the state of the Caesars the Romano-Greek urban commonwealth spreads more and more, and gradually becomes the general form of administration, the foundation of towns— the true mark of Helleno-Roman civilisation, which embraces the Greek mercantile cities and the military colonies of Rome as well as the grand settlements of Alexander and the Alexandrids—suddenly breaks off with the emergence of the Parthian government in the East, and even the existing Greek cities of the Parthian empire wane in the further course of development. There, as here, the rule more and more prevails over the exceptions.

The religion of Iran with its worship—approximating Religion. to monotheism—of the " highest of the gods, who has made heaven and earth and men and for these everything good," with its absence of images and its spirituality, with its stern morality and truthfulness, with its influence upon practical activity and energetic conduct of life, laid hold of the minds of its confessors in quite another and deeper way than the religions of the West ever could ; and, while neither Zeus nor Jupiter maintained their ground in presence of a developed civilisation, the faith among the

Parsees remained ever young till it succumbed to another gospel—that of the confessors of Mohammed—or at any rate retreated before it to India. It is not our task to set forth how the old Mazda-faith, which the Achaemenids professed, and the origin of which falls in prehistoric time, was related to that which the sacred books of the Persians having their origin probably under the later Achaemenids —the Avestâ—announce as the doctrine of the wise Zarathustra ; for the epoch, when the West is placed in contact with the East, only the later form of religion comes under consideration. Perhaps the Avestâ took first shape in the east of Iran, in Bactria, but it spread thence to Media and from there it exercised its influence on the West. But the national religion and the national state were bound up with one another in Iran more closely than even among the Celts. It has already been noticed that the legitimate kingship in Iran was at the same time a religious institution, that the supreme ruler of the land was conceived as specially called to the government by the supreme deity of the land, and even in some measure divine. On the coins of a national type there appears regularly the great fire-altar, and hovering over it the winged god Ahura Mazda, alongside of him in lesser size, and in an attitude of prayer, the king, and over-against the king the imperial banner. In keeping with this, the ascendency of the nobility in the Parthian empire goes hand in hand with the privileged position of the clergy. The priests of this religion, the Magians, appear already in the documents of the Achaemenids and in the narratives of Herodotus, and have, probably with right, always been regarded by the Occidentals as a national Persian institution. The priesthood was hereditary, and at least in Media, presumably also in other provinces, the collective body of the priests was accounted, somewhat like the Levites in the later Israel, as a separate portion of the people. Even under the rule of the Greeks the old religion of the state and the national priesthood maintained their place. When the first Seleucus wished to found the new capital of his empire, the already mentioned Seleucia, he caused the Magians to fix day and hour for it, and it was only after those Persians, not very willingly, had cast the desired horoscope, that the king and his army, in accordance with their indication, accomplished the solemn laying of the foundation-stone of the new Greek city. Thus by his side stood the priests of Ahura Mazda as counsellors, and they, not those of the Hellenic Olympus, were interrogated in public affairs, so far as these concerned divine things. As a matter of course this was all the more the case with the Arsacids. We have already observed that in the election of king, along with the council of the nobility, that of the priests took part. King Tiridates of Armenia, of the house of the Arsacids, came to Rome attended by a train of Magians, and travelled and took food according to their directions, even in company with the emperor Nero, who gladly allowed the foreign wise men to preach their doctrine and to conjure spirits for him. From this certainly it does not follow that the priestly order as such exercised an essentially determining influence on the management of the state; but the Mazda-faith was by no means re-established only by the Sassanids; on the contrary, amidst all change of dynasties, and amidst all its own development, the religion of the land of Iran remained in its outline the same.

The language of the land in the Parthian empire was the native language of Iran. There is no trace pointing to any foreign language having ever been in public use under the Arsacids. On the contrary, it is the Iranian land-dialect of Babylonia and the writing peculiar to this— as both were developed before, and in, the Arsacid period under the influence of the language and writing of the Aramaean neighbours—which are covered by the appellation Pahlavi, *i.e.* Parthava, and thereby designated as those of the empire of the Parthians. Even Greek did not become an official language there. None of the rulers bear even as a second name a Greek one; and, had the Arsacids made this language their own, we should not have failed to find Greek inscriptions in their empire. Language.

Certainly their coins show down to the time of Claudius exclusively,[1] and predominantly even later, Greek legends, as they show also no trace of the religion of the land, and in standard attach themselves to the local coinage of the Roman east provinces, while they retain the division of the year as well as the reckoning by years just as these had been regulated under the Seleucids. But this must rather be taken as meaning that the great-kings themselves did not coin at all,[2] and these coins, which in fact served essentially for intercourse with the western neighbours, were struck by the Greek towns of the empire in the name of the sovereign. The designation of the king on these coins as "friend of Greeks" ($\phi\iota\lambda\acute{\epsilon}\lambda\lambda\eta\nu$), which already meets us early,[3] and is constant from the time of Mithradates I., *i.e.* from the extension of the state as far as the Tigris, has a meaning only, if it is the Parthian Greek city that is speaking on these coins. It may be conjectured that a secondary position was conceded in public use to the Greek language in the Parthian empire alongside of the Persian, similar to that which it possessed in the Roman state by the side of Latin. The gradual disappearance of Hellenism under the Parthian rule may be clearly followed on these urban coins, as well in the emergence of the native language alongside and instead of the Greek, as in the debasement of language which becomes more and more prominent.[4]

Extent of the Parthian empire.

As to extent the kingdom of the Arsacids was far inferior, not merely to the great state of the Achaemenids,

[1] The oldest known coin with Pahlavi writing was struck in Claudius's time under Vologasus I. ; it is bilingual, and gives to the king in Greek his full title, but only the name Arsaces, in Iranian merely the native individual name shortened (*Vol.*).

[2] Usually this is restricted to the large silver money, and the small silver and most of the copper are regarded as of royal coinage. But by this view a singular secondary part in coinage is assigned to the great-king. More correctly perhaps the former coinage is conceived of as predominantly destined for dealings abroad, the latter as predominantly for internal intercourse ; the diversities subsisting between the two kinds are also explained in this way.

[3] The first ruler that bears it is Phraapates about 188 B.C. (Percy Gardner, *Parthian Coinage*, p. 27).

[4] Thus there stands on the coins of Gotarzes (under Claudius) Γωτέρζης βασιλεὺς βασιλέων υἱὸς κεκαλουμένος Ἀρταβάνου. On the later ones the Greek legend is often quite unintelligible.

but also to that of their immediate predecessors, the state of the Seleucids. Of its original territory they possessed only the larger eastern half; after the battle with the Parthians, in which king Antiochus Sidetes, a contemporary of the Gracchi, fell, the Syrian kings did not again seriously attempt to assert their rule beyond the Euphrates; but the country on this side of the Euphrates remained with the Occidentals.

Both coasts of the Persian Gulf, even the Arabian, were in possession of the Parthians, and the navigation was thus completely in their power; the rest of the Arabian peninsula did not obey either the Parthians or the Romans ruling over Egypt. *Arabia.*

To describe the struggle of the nations for the possession of the Indus valley, and of the regions bordering on it, to the west and east, so far as the wholly fragmentary tradition allows of a description at all, is not the task of our survey; but the main lines of this struggle, which constantly goes by the side of that waged for the Euphrates valley, may the less be omitted in this connection, as our tradition does not allow us to follow out in detail the circumstances of Iran to the east in their influence on western relations, and it hence appears necessary at least to realise for ourselves its outlines. Soon after the death of Alexander the Great, the boundary between Iran and India was drawn by the agreement of his marshal and coheir Seleucus with Chandragupta, or in Greek Sandracottos, the founder of the empire of the Indians. According to this the latter ruled not merely over the Ganges-valley in all its extent and the whole north-west of India, but in the region of the Indus, at least over a part of the upland valley of what is now Cabul, further over Arachosia or Afghanistan, presumably also over the waste and arid Gedrosia, the modern Beloochistan, as well as over the delta and mouths of the Indus; the documents hewn in stone, by which Chandragupta's grandson, the orthodox Buddha-worshipper Asoka, inculcated the general moral law on his subjects, have been found, as in all this widely extended domain, *The region of the Indus.*

so particularly in the region of Peshawur.[1]   The Hindoo Koosh, the Parapanisus of the ancients, and its continuation to the east and west, thus separated with their mighty chain—pierced only by few passes—Iran and India.   But this agreement did not long subsist.

Bactro-Indian empire.   In the earlier period of the Diadochi the Greek rulers of the kingdom of Bactra, which took a mighty impulse on its breaking off from the Seleucid state, crossed the frontier-mountains, brought a considerable part of the Indus valley into their power, and perhaps established themselves still farther inland in Hindostan, so that the centre of gravity of this empire was shifted from western Iran to eastern India, and Hellenism gave way to an Indian type.   The kings of this empire were called Indian, and bore subsequently non-Greek names ; on the coins the native Indian language and writing appear by the side, and instead, of the Greek, just as in the Partho-Persian coinage the Pahlavi comes up alongside of the Greek.

Indo-Scythians.   Then one nation more entered into the arena ; the Scythians, or, as they were called in Iran and India, the Sacae, broke off from their ancestral settlements on the Jaxartes and crossed the mountains southward.   The Bactrian province came at least in great part into their power, and at some time in the last century of the Roman republic they must have established themselves in the

---

[1] While the kingdom of Darius, according to his inscriptions, includes in it the Gâdara (the Gandhâra of the Indians, Γανδαρῖτις of the Greeks on the Cabul river) and the Hîdu (the dwellers by the Indus), the former are in one of the inscriptions of Asoka adduced among his subjects, and a copy of his great edict has been found in Kapurdi Giri, or rather in Shahbaz Garhi (Yusufzai-district), nearly 27 miles north-west of the point where the Cabul river falls into the Indus at Attock.   The seat of the government of these north-west provinces of Asoka's kingdom was (according to the inscription *C. I. Indicar.* i. p. 91) Takkhasilâ, Τάξιλα of the Greeks, some 40 miles E.S.E. of Attock, the seat of government for the south-western provinces was Ujjênî ('Οζήνη).   The eastern part of the Cabul valley thus belonged at any rate to Asoka's empire.   It is not quite impossible that the Khyber pass formed the boundary ; but probably the whole Cabul valley belonged to India, and the boundary to the south of Cabul was formed by the sharp line of the Suleiman range, and farther to the south-west by the Bolan pass.   Of the later Indo-Scythian king Huvishka (Ooerke of the coins), who seems to have resided on the Yamunâ in Mathurâ, an inscription has been found at Wardak not far northward from Cabul (according to information from Oldenberg).

modern Afghanistan and Beloochistan.   On that account
in the early imperial period the coast on both sides of the
mouth of the Indus about Minnagara is called Scythian,
and in the interior the district of the Drangae lying to the
west of Candahar bears subsequently the name "land of
the Sacae," Sacastane, the modern Seistân.   This immigration of the Scythians into the provinces of the Bactro-
Indian empire doubtless restricted and injured it, somewhat as the Roman empire was affected by the first
migrations of the Germans, but did not destroy it ; under
Vespasian there still subsisted a probably independent
Bactrian state.[1]

Under the Julian and Claudian emperors the Parthians
seem to have been the leading power at the mouth of the
Indus.   A trustworthy reporter from the Augustan age
specifies that same Sacastane among the Parthian provinces, and calls the king of the Saco-Scythians an
under-king of the Arsacids ; as the last Parthian province
towards the east he designates Arachosia with the capital
Alexandropolis, probably Candahar.   Soon afterwards,
indeed, in Vespasian's time, Parthian princes rule in Minnagara.   This, however, was for the empire on the river
Indus more a change of dynasty than an annexation
proper to the state of Ctesiphon.   The Parthian prince
Gondopharus, whom the Christian legend connects with St.
Thomas, the apostle of the Parthians and Indians,[2] certainly
ruled from Minnagara as far up as Peshawur and Cabul ;
but these rulers use, like their superiors in the Indian
empire, the Indian language alongside of the Greek, and
name themselves great-kings like those of Ctesiphon ; they
appear to have been not the less rivals to the Arsacids,
on account of their belonging to the same princely house.[3]

Partho-Indian empire.

---

[1] The Egyptian merchant named
in note 3 makes mention, c. 47, of
"the warlike people of the Bactrians,
who have their own king." At that
time, therefore, Bactria was separated
from the Indus-empire that was under
Parthian princes.   Strabo, too (xi.
11, 1, p. 516) treats the Bactro-Indian
empire as belonging to the past.

[2] Probably he is the Kaspar—in
older tradition Gathaspar—who appears among the holy three kings
from the East (Gutschmid, *Rhein.
Mus.* xix. 162).

[3] The most definite testimony to
the Parthian rule in these regions is
found in the description of the coasts
of the Red Sea drawn up by an

This Parthian dynasty was then followed in the Indian empire after a short interval by what is designated in Indian tradition as that of the Sacae or that of king Kanerku or Kanishka, which begins with 78 A.D. and subsisted at least down to the third century.[1]   They

Egyptian merchant under Vespasian, c. 38: " Behind the mouth of the Indus in the interior lies the capital of Scythia Minnagara; but this is ruled by the Parthians, who constantly chase away one another" (ὑπὸ Πάρθων συνεχῶς ἀλλήλους ἐνδιωκόντων). The same is repeated in a somewhat confused way, c. 41; it might here appear as if Minnagara lay in India itself above Barygaza, and Ptolemy has already been led astray by this; but certainly the writer, who speaks as to the interior only from hearsay, has only wished to say that a large town Minnagara lay inland not far from Barygaza, and much cotton was brought thence to Barygaza. The numerous traces also of Alexander, which occur according to the same authority in Minnagara, can be found only on the Indus, not in Gujerat. The position of Minnagara on the lower Indus not far from Hyderabad, and the existence of a Parthian rule there under Vespasian, appear hereby assured. — With this we may be allowed to combine the coins of king Gondopharus or Hyndopherres, who in a very old Christian legend is converted to Christianity by St. Thomas, the apostle of the Parthians and Indians, and in fact appears to belong to the first period of the Roman empire (Sallet, *Num. Zeitschr.* vi. 355; Gutschmid, *Rhein. Mus.* xix. 162); of his brother's son Abdagases (Sallet, *ib.* p. 365), who may be identical with the Parthian prince of this name in Tacitus, *Ann.* vi. 36, at any rate bears a Parthian name; and lastly of king Sanabarus, who must have reigned shortly after Hyndopherres, perhaps was his successor. Here belongs also a number of other coins marked with Parthian names, Arsaces, Pacorus, Vonones. This coinage attaches itself decidedly to that of

the Arsacids (Sallet, *ib.* p. 277); the silver pieces of Gondopharus and of Sanabarus—of the others the coins are almost solely copper—correspond exactly to the Arsacid drachmae. To all appearance these belong to the Parthian princes of Minnagara; the appearance here of Indian legend alongside of the Greek, as of Pahlavi writing among the late Arsacids, suits this view.   These, however, are not coins of satraps, but, as the Egyptian indicates, of great-kings rivalling those of Ctesiphon; Hyndopherres names himself in very corrupt Greek βασιλεὺς βασιλέων μέγας αὐτοκράτωρ, and in good Indian " Maharajah Rajadi Rajah."   If, as is not improbable, under the Mambaros or Akabaros, whom the Periplus, c. 41, 52, designates as ruler of the coast of Barygaza, there lurks the Sanabarus of the coins, the latter belongs to the time of Nero or Vespasian, and ruled not merely at the mouths of the Indus, but also over Gujerat.   Moreover, if an inscription found not far from Peshawur is rightly referred to king Gondopharus, his rule must have extended up thither, probably as far as Cabul.—The fact that Corbulo in the year 60 sent the embassy of the Hyrcanians who had revolted from the Parthians—in order that they might not be intercepted by the latter—to the coast of the Red Sea, whence they might reach their home without setting foot on Parthian territory (Tacitus, *Ann.* xv. 25), tells in favour of the view that the Indus valley at that time was not subject to the ruler of Ctesiphon.

[1] That the great kingdom of the Arsacids of Minnagara did not subsist much beyond the time of Nero, is probable from the coins.   It is questionable what rulers followed them. The Bactro-Indian rulers of Greek

belong to the Scythians, whose immigration was formerly mentioned, and on their coins the Scythian language takes the place of the Indian.[1] Thus in the region of the Indus, after the Indians and the Hellenes, Parthians and Scythians bore sway in the first three centuries of our era. But even under the foreign dynasties a national Indian type of state was established and held its ground, and opposed a not less permanent barrier to the development of the Partho-Persian power in the East than did the Roman state in the West.

Towards the north and north-east Iran bordered with Turan. As the western and southern shores of the Caspian Sea and the upper valleys of the Oxus and Jaxartes offered an appropriate seat for civilisation, so the steppe round the Sea of Aral and the extensive plain stretching behind it belonged by right to the roving peoples. There were among those nomads probably individual tribes

Asiatic
Scythians.

names belong predominantly, perhaps all of them, to the pre-Augustan epoch; and various indigenous names, *e.g.* Maues and Azes, fall in point of language and writing (*e.g.* the form of the ω Ω) before this time. On the other hand the coins of the kings Kozulokadphises and Oemokadphises, and those of the Sacian kings, Kanerku and his successors, while all are clearly characterised as belonging to one coinage by the gold stater of the weight of the Roman aureus, which does not previously occur in the Indian coinage, are to all appearance later than Gondopharus and Sanabarus. They show how the state of the Indus valley assumed a national Indian type in ever increasing measure in contrast to the Hellenes as well as to the Iranians. The reign of these Kadphises will thus fall between the Indo-Parthian rulers and the dynasty of the Sacae, which latter begins with A.D. 78 (Oldenberg, in Sallet's *Zeitschr. für Num.* viii. 292). Coins of these Sacian kings, found in the treasure of Peshawur, name in a remarkable way Greek gods in a mutilated form, Ηρακιλο, Σαραπο, alongside of the national Βονδο. The

latest of their coins show the influence of the oldest Sassanid coinage, and might belong to the second half of the third century (Sallet, *Zeitschr. für Num.* vi. 224).

[1] The Indo-Greek and the Indo-Parthian rulers, just as the Kadphises, make use on their coins to a large extent of the indigenous Indian language and writing alongside of the Greek : the Sacian kings on the other hand never used the Indian language and Indian alphabet, but employ exclusively the Greek letters, and the non-Greek legends of their coins are beyond doubt Scythian. Thus on Kanerku's gold pieces there sometimes stands βασιλεὺς βασιλέων Κανήρκου, sometimes ραο ναναραο κανηρκι κορανο, where the first two words must be a Scythian form of the Indian Rajâdi Rajah, and the two following contain the personal and the family name (Gushana) of the king (Oldenberg, *l.c.* p. 294). Thus these Sacae were foreign rulers in India in another sense than the Bactrian Hellenes and the Parthians. Yet the inscriptions set up under them in India are not Scythian but Indian.

kindred to the Iranians ; but these have no part in the
Iranian civilisation, and it is this element which determines
the historical position of Iran, that it forms the bulwark
of the peoples of culture against those hordes, who, as
Scythians, Sacae, Huns, Mongols, Turks, appear to have
no other destiny in the world's history than that of anni-
hilating culture.   Bactria, the great bulwark of Iran
against Turan, sufficed for this defence during a considerable time under its Greek rulers in the epoch after
Alexander ; but we have already mentioned that subsequently, although it did not perish, it no longer availed to
prevent the Scythians from pressing onward towards the
south.   With the decay of the Bactrian power the same
task was transferred to the Arsacids.   How far they
responded to it it is difficult to say.   In the first period of
the empire the great-kings of Ctesiphon seem to have
driven back the Scythians or to have brought them into
subjection in the northern provinces as well as to the
south of the Hindoo Koosh ; they wrested from them
again a portion of the Bactrian territory.   But it is doubtful what limits were here fixed, and whether they were at
all lasting.   There is frequent mention of wars between
the Parthians and Scythians.   The latter, here in the first
instance dwellers around the Sea of Aral, the forefathers
of the modern Turkomans, are regularly the aggressors,
inasmuch as they partly by crossing over the Caspian
Sea invade the valleys of the Cyrus and the Araxes,
partly issuing from their steppes pillage the rich plains of
Hyrcania and the fertile oasis of Margiana (Merv).   The
border-regions agreed to buy off the levy of arbitrary
contributions by tributes, which were regularly called up
at fixed terms, just as at present the Bedouins of Syria
levy the *kubba* from the farmers there.   The Parthian
government thus, at least in the earlier imperial period,
was as little able as the Turkish government of the present
day to secure here to the peaceful subject the fruits of his
toil, and to establish a durable state of peace on the frontier.   Even for the imperial power itself these border-
troubles remained an open sore ; often they exercised an

influence on the wars of succession of the Arsacids as well
as on their disputes with Rome.

We have set forth in its due place how the attitude
of the Parthians to the Romans came to be shaped and
the boundaries of the two great powers to be established.
While the Armenians had been rivals of the Parthians,
and the kingdom on the Araxes set itself to play the
part of great-king in anterior Asia, the Parthians had in
general maintained friendly relations with the Romans
as the foes of their foes.   But, after the overthrow of
Mithradates and Tigranes, the Romans had, particularly
through the arrangements made by Pompeius, taken up
a position which was hardly compatible with serious and
lasting peace between the two states.   In the south
Syria was now under direct Roman rule, and the Roman
legions kept guard on the margin of the great desert
which separates the lands of the coast from the valley of
the Euphrates.   In the north Cappadocia and Armenia
were vassal-principalities of Rome.   The tribes bordering
on Armenia to the northward, the Colchians, Iberians,
Albanians, were thereby necessarily withdrawn from
Parthian influence, and were, at least according to the
Roman way of apprehending the matter, likewise Roman
dependencies.   The lesser Media or Atropatene (Aderbijân), adjoining Armenia to the south-east, and separated
from it by the Araxes, had maintained, despite the
Seleucidae, its ancient native dynasty reaching back
to the time of the Achaemenids, and had even asserted
its independence ; under the Arsacids the king of this
region appears, according to circumstances, as a vassal
of the Parthians or as independent of these by leaning
on the Romans.   The determining influence of Rome
consequently reached as far as the Caucasus and the
western shore of the Caspian Sea.   This involved an
overlapping of the limits indicated by the national
relations.   The Hellenic nationality had doubtless so
far gained a footing on the south coast of the Black
Sea and in the interior of Cappadocia and Commagene,
that here the Roman ascendency found in it a base of

support ; but Armenia, even under the long years of
Roman rule, remained always a non-Greek land, knit
to the Parthian state with indestructible ties, by community
of language and of faith, the numerous intermarriages of
people of rank, and similarity of dress and of armour.[1] The
Roman levy and the Roman taxation were never extended
to Armenia ; at most the land defrayed the raising and
the maintenance of its own troops, and the provisioning
of the Roman troops stationed there. The Armenian
merchants formed the channel for the exchange of goods
over the Caucasus with Scythia, over the Caspian Sea
with east Asia and China, down the Tigris with Babylonia
and India, towards the west with Cappadocia ; nothing
would have been more natural than to include the
politically dependent land in the domain of Roman
tribute and customs ; yet this step was never taken.

The incongruity between the national and the political
connections of Armenia forms an essential element in the
conflict—prolonged through the whole imperial period—
with its eastern neighbour. It was discerned doubtless
on the Roman side that annexation beyond the Euphrates
was an encroachment on the family-domain of Oriental
nationality, and was not any increase proper of power
for Rome. But the ground or, if the phrase be preferred,
the excuse for the continuance of such encroachment
lay in the fact that the subsistence side by side of great
states with equal rights was incompatible with the system
of Roman policy, we may even say with the policy of
antiquity in general. The Roman empire knew as limit,
in the strict sense, only the sea or a land-district un-
armed. To the weaker but yet warlike commonwealth
of the Parthians the Romans always grudged a position
of power, and took away from it what these in their turn

---

[1] Arrian, who, as governor of
Cappadocia, had himself wielded
command over the Armenians (*contra
Al.* 29), always in the *Tactica* names
the Armenians and Parthians together
(4, 3, 44, 1, as respects the heavy
cavalry, the mailed κοντοφόροι and
the light cavalry, the ἀκροβολισταί
or ἱπποτοξόται ; 34, 7 as respects the
wide hose) ; and, where he speaks of
Hadrian's introduction of barbaric
cavalry into the Roman army, he
traces the mounted archers back to
the model of "the Parthians or
Armenians" (44, 1).

could not forego ; and therefore the relation between Rome and Iran through the whole imperial period was one of perpetual feud, interrupted only by armistices, concerning the left bank of the Euphrates.

In the treaties concluded with the Parthians by Lucullus (iv. 71) and Pompeius (iv. 127) the Euphrates was recognised as the boundary, and so Mesopotamia was ceded to them. But this did not prevent the Romans from receiving the rulers of Edessa among their clients, and from laying claim to a great part of northern Mesopotamia at least for their indirect rule, apparently by extending the limits of Armenia towards the south (iv. 146). On that account, after some delay, the Parthian government began the war against the Romans, in the form of declaring it against the Armenians. The answer to this was the campaign of Crassus, and, after the defeat at Carrhae (iv. 351 f.), the bringing back of Armenia under Parthian power ; we may add, the resumption of their claims on the western half of the Seleucid state, the carrying out of which, it is true, proved at that time unsuccessful (iv. 356). During the whole twenty years of civil war, in which the Roman republic perished and ultimately the principate was established, the state of war between the Romans and Parthians continued, and not seldom the two struggles became intermixed. Pompeius had, before the decisive battle, attempted to gain king Orodes as ally ; but, when the latter demanded the cession of Syria, Pompeius could not prevail on himself to deliver up the province which he had personally made Roman. After the catastrophe he had nevertheless resolved to do so ; but accidents directed his flight not to Syria, but to Egypt, where he met his end (iv. 446). The Parthians appeared on the point of once more breaking into Syria ; and the later leaders of the republicans did not disdain the aid of the public foe. Even in Caesar's lifetime Caecilius Bassus, when he raised the banner of revolt in Syria, had at once called in the Parthians. They had followed this call ; Pacorus, the son of Orodes, had defeated Caesar's lieuten-

The Parthians during the civil wars.
iv. 67, 122.

iv. 140.

iv. 335 f.

iv. 339.

iv. 424.

ant and liberated the troops of Bassus besieged by him in
44. Apamea (709). For this reason, as well as in order to
take revenge for Carrhae, Caesar had resolved to go in
the next spring personally to Syria and to cross the
Euphrates ; but his death prevented the execution of
this plan. When Cassius thereupon took arms in Syria,
he entered into relations with the Parthian king ; and in
42. the decisive battle at Philippi (712) Parthian mounted
archers joined in fighting for the freedom of Rome.
When the republicans succumbed, the great-king, in the
first instance, maintained a quiet attitude ; and Antonius,
while designing probably to execute the plans of the
dictator, had at first enough to do with the settlement
of the East. The collision could not fail to take place ;
the assailant this time was the Parthian king.

41. In 713 when Caesar the son fought in Italy with the
generals and the wife of Antonius, and the latter tarried
inactive in Egypt beside queen Cleopatra, Orodes responded to the pressure of a Roman living with him
in exile, Quintus Labienus, and sent the latter, a son of
the dictator's embittered opponent Titus Labienus, and
41. formerly an officer in the army of Brutus, as well as (713)
his son Pacorus with a strong army over the frontier.
The governor of Syria, Decidius Saxa, succumbed to
the unexpected attack ; the Roman garrisons, formed in
great part of old soldiers of the republican army, placed
themselves under the command of their former officer ;
Apamea and Antioch, and generally all the towns of
Syria, except the island-town of Tyre which could not
be subdued without a fleet, submitted ; on the flight to
Cilicia Saxa, in order not to be taken prisoner, put
himself to death. After the occupation of Syria Pacorus
turned against Palestine, Labienus towards the province
of Asia ; here too the cities far and wide submitted or
were forcibly vanquished, with the exception of the
Carian Stratonicea. Antonius, whose attention was
claimed by the Italian complications, sent no succour
to his governors, and for almost two years (from the end
41, 39. of 713 to the spring of 715) Syria and a great part of

The Par-
thians in
Syria and
Asia Minor.

Asia Minor were commanded by the Parthian generals and by the republican imperator Labienus—*Parthicus*, as he called himself with shameless irony, not the Roman who vanquished the Parthians, but the Roman who with Parthian aid vanquished his countrymen.

Only after the threatened rupture between the two holders of power was averted, Antonius sent a new army under the conduct of Publius Ventidius Bassus, to whom he entrusted the command in the provinces of Asia and Syria. The able general encountered in Asia Labienus alone with his Roman troops, and rapidly drove him out of the province. At the boundary between Asia and Cilicia, in the passes of the Taurus, a division of Parthians wished to rally their fugitive allies ; but they too were beaten before they could unite with Labienus, and thereupon the latter was caught on his flight in Cilicia and put to death. With like good fortune Ventidius gained by fighting the passes of the Amanus on the border of Cilicia and Syria ; here Pharnapates, the best of the Parthian generals, fell (715). Thus was Syria delivered from the enemy. Certainly in the following year Pacorus once more crossed the Euphrates ; but only to meet destruction with the greatest part of his army in a decisive engagement at Gindarus, north-east of Antioch (9th June 716). It was a victory which counterbalanced in some measure the day of Carrhae, and one of permanent effect ; for long the Parthians did not again show their troops on the Roman bank of the Euphrates.

If it was in the interest of Rome to extend her conquests towards the East, and to enter on the inheritance of Alexander the Great there in all its extent, the circumstances were never more favourable for doing so than in the year 716. The relations of the two rulers to each other had become re-established seasonably for that purpose, and even Caesar at that time had probably a sincere wish for an earnest and successful conduct of the war by his co-ruler and brother-in-law. The disaster of Gindarus had called forth a severe dynastic crisis among the Parthians. King Orodes, deeply agitated by

Driven out by Ventidius Bassus.

39.

38.

Position of Antonius.

38.

the death of his eldest and ablest son, resigned the government in favour of his second son Phraates. The latter, in order the better to secure for himself the throne, exercised a reign of terror, to which his numerous brothers and his old father himself, as well as a number of the high nobles of the kingdom, fell victims ; others of them left the country and sought protection with the Romans, among them the powerful and respected Monaeses. Never had Rome in the East an army of equal numbers and excellence as at this time : Antonius was able to lead over the Euphrates no fewer than 16 legions, about 70,000 Roman infantry, about 40,000 auxiliaries, 10,000 Spanish and Gallic, and 6000 Armenian horsemen ; at least half of them were veteran troops brought up from the West, all ready to follow anywhere their beloved and honoured leader, the victor of Philippi, and to crown the brilliant victories, which had been already achieved not by but for him over the Parthians, with still greater successes under his own leadership.

His aims.   In reality Antonius had in view the erection of an Asiatic great-kingdom after the model of that of Alexander. As Crassus before his invasion had announced that he would extend the Roman rule as far as Bactria and India, so Antonius named the first son, whom the Egyptian queen bore to him, by the name of Alexander. He appears to have directly intended, on the one hand, to bring—excluding the completely Hellenised provinces of Bithynia and Asia—the whole imperial territory in the East, so far as it was not already under dependent petty princes, into this form ; and on the other hand, to make all the regions of the East once occupied by Occidentals subject to himself in the form of satrapies. Of eastern Asia Minor the largest portion and the military primacy were assigned to the most warlike of the princes there, the Galatian Amyntas (I. 335). Alongside of the Galatian prince stood the princes of Paphlagonia, the descendants of Deiotarus, dispossessed from Galatia ; Polemon, the new prince in Pontus, and the husband of Pythodoris the granddaughter of Antonius ;

and moreover, as hitherto, the kings of Cappadocia and Commagene. Antonius united a great part of Cilicia and Syria, as well as of Cyprus and Cyrene, with the Egyptian state, to which he thus almost restored its limits as they had been under the Ptolemies ; and as he had made queen Cleopatra, Caesar's mistress, his own or rather his wife, so her illegitimate child by Caesar, Caesarion, already earlier recognised as joint ruler of Egypt,[1] obtained the reversion of the old kingdom of the Ptolemies, and her illegitimate son by Antonius, Ptolemaeus Philadelphus, obtained that of Syria. To another son, whom she had borne to Antonius, the already mentioned Alexander, Armenia was for the present assigned as a payment to account for the rule of the East conceived as in reserve for him. With this great-kingdom organised after the Oriental fashion [2] he thought to combine the principate over the West. He himself did not assume the name of king, on the contrary bore in presence of his countrymen and the soldiers only those titles which also belonged to Caesar. But on imperial coins with a Latin legend Cleopatra is called queen of kings, her sons by Antonius at least kings ; the coins show the head of his eldest son along with that of his father, as if the hereditary character were a matter of course ; the marriage and the succession of the legitimate and the illegitimate children are treated by him, as was the usage with the great-kings of the

---

[1] Caesar's illegitimate son Πτολε-μαῖος ὁ καὶ Καῖσαρ θεὸς φιλοπάτωρ φιλομήτωρ, as his royal designation runs (*C. I. Gr.* 4717), entered on the joint rule of Egypt in the Egyptian year 29 Aug. 711/2, as the era shows (Wescher, *Bullett. dell' Inst.* 1866, p. 199 ; Krall, *Wiener Studien,* v. 313). As he came in place of Ptolemaeus the younger, the husband and brother of his mother, the setting aside of the latter by Cleopatra, of which the particulars are not known, must have taken place just then, and have furnished the occasion to proclaim him as king of Egypt. Dio also, xlvii. 31, places his nomination in the summer of 712 before the

battle of Philippi. It was thus not the work of Antonius, but sanctioned by the two rulers in concert at a time when it could not but be their object to meet the wishes of the queen of Egypt, who certainly had from the outset ranged herself on their side.

[2] This is what Augustus means when he says that he had brought again to the empire the provinces of the East in great part distributed among kings *(Mon. Ancyr.* 5, 41 : *provincias omnis, quae trans Hadri-anum mare vergunt ad orientem, Cyrenasque, iam ex parte magna regibus eas possidentibus . . . reci-peravi).*

42.

East, or, as he himself said, with the divine freedom of his ancestor Herakles :[1] the said Alexander and his twin sister were named by him, the former Helios, the latter Selene, after the model of those same great-kings, and, as once upon a time the Persian king bestowed on the refugee Themistocles a number of Asiatic cities, so he bestowed on the Parthian Monaeses, who went over to him, three cities of Syria. In Alexander too the king of the Macedonians and the king of kings of the East went in some measure side by side, and to him too the bridal bed in Susa was the reward for the camp-tent of Gaugamela ; but the Roman copy shows in its exactness a strong element of caricature.

Prepara-
tions for the
Parthian
war.

Whether Antonius apprehended his position in this way, immediately on his taking up the government in the East, cannot be decided ; it may be conjectured that the creation of a new Oriental great-kingdom in connection with the Occidental principate ripened in his mind gradually, and that the idea was only thought out completely, after, in the year 717, on his return from Italy to Asia, he had once more entered into relations with the last

37.

---

[1] The decorum, which was as characteristic of Augustus as its opposite was of his colleague, did not fail him here. Not merely in the case of Caesarion was the paternity, which the dictator himself had virtually acknowledged, afterwards officially denied ; the children also of Antonius by Cleopatra, where indeed nothing was to be denied, were regarded doubtless as members of the imperial house, but were never formally acknowledged as children of Antonius. On the contrary the son of the daughter of Antonius by Cleopatra, the subsequent king of Mauretania Ptolemaeus, is called in the Athenian inscription, C. I. A. iii. 555, grandson of Ptolemaeus ; for Πτολεμαίου ἔκγονος cannot well in this connection be taken otherwise. This maternal grandfather was invented in Rome, that they might be able officially to conceal the real one. Any one who prefers—as O. Hirschfeld proposes

—to take ἔκγονος as great-grandson, and to refer it to the maternal great-grandfather, comes to the same result ; for then the grandfather is passed over, because the mother was in the legal sense fatherless.—Whether the fiction, which is in my view more probable, went so far as to indicate a definite Ptolemaeus, possibly to prolong the life of the last Lagid who died in 712, or whether they were content with inventing a father without entering into particulars, cannot be decided. But the fiction was adhered to in this respect, that the son of Antonius's daughter obtained the name of the fictitious grandfather. The circumstance that in this case preference was given to the descent from the Lagids over that from Massinissa may probably have been occasioned more by regard to the imperial house, which treated the illegitimate child as belonging to it, than by the Hellenic inclination of the father.

42.

queen of the Lagid house not to be again broken off. But his temperament was not equal to such an enterprise. One of those men of military capacity, who knew how, in presence of the enemy, and especially in a position of difficulty, to strike prudently and boldly, he lacked the will of the statesman, the sure grasp and resolute pursuit of a political aim. Had the dictator Caesar assigned to him the problem of subduing the East, he would probably have solved it : the marshal was not fitted to be the ruler. After the expulsion of the Parthians from Syria, almost two years (summer of 716 to summer of 718) elapsed with- out any step being taken towards the object aimed at. Antonius himself, inferior also in this respect that he grudged to his generals important successes, had removed the conqueror of Labienus and of Pacorus, the able Ven- tidius, immediately after this last success, and taken the chief command in person in order to pursue and to miss the pitiful honour of occupying Samosata, the capital of the small Syrian dependent state, Commagene ; annoyed at this, he left the East, in order to negotiate in Italy with his father-in-law as to the future arrangements, or to enjoy life with his young spouse Octavia. His governors in the East were not inactive. Publius Canidius Crassus advanced from Armenia towards the Caucasus, and there subdued Pharnabazus king of the Iberians, and Zober king of the Albanians. Gaius Sossius took in Syria the last town still adhering to the Parthians, Aradus ; he further re-established in Judaea the rule of Herodes, and caused the pretender to the throne installed by the Par- thians, the Hasmonean Antigonus, to be put to death. The consequences of the victory on Roman territory were thus duly drawn, and the recognition of Roman rule was enforced as far as the Caspian Sea and the Syrian desert. But Antonius had reserved for himself the begin- ning of the warfare against the Parthians, and he came not.

When at length, in 718, he escaped from the arms, not of Octavia, but of Cleopatra, and set the columns of the army in motion, a good part of the appropriate season

38, 36.

36.
Parthian
war of
Antonius

of the year had already elapsed. Still more surprising than this delay was the direction which Antonius chose. All aggressive wars of the Romans against the Parthians, earlier and later, took the route for Ctesiphon, the capital of the kingdom and at the same time situated on its western frontier, and so the natural and immediate aim of operations for armies marching downward on the Euphrates or on the Tigris. Antonius too might, after he had reached the Tigris through northern Mesopotamia, nearly along the route which Alexander had traversed, have advanced down the river upon Ctesiphon and Seleucia. But instead of this he preferred to go in a northerly direction at first towards Armenia, and from that point, where he united his whole military resources and reinforced himself in particular by the Armenian cavalry, to the table-land of Media Atropatene (Aderbijân). The allied king of Armenia may possibly have recommended this plan of campaign, seeing that the Armenian rulers at all times aspired to the possession of this neighbouring land, and King Artavazdes of Armenia might hope now to subdue the satrap of Atropatene of the same name, and to add the latter's territory to his own. But Antonius himself cannot possibly have been influenced by such considerations. He may have rather thought that he should be able to push forward from Atropatene into the heart of the enemy's country, and might regard the old Persian court-residences of Ecbatana and Rhagae as the goal of his march. But, if this was his plan, he acted without knowledge of the difficult ground, and altogether underrated his opponents' power of resistance, besides which the short time available for operations in this mountainous country and the late beginning of the campaign weighed heavily in the scale. As a skilled and experienced officer, such as Antonius was, could hardly deceive himself on such points, it is probable that special political considerations influenced the matter. The rule of Phraates was tottering, as we have said ; Monaeses, of whose fidelity Antonius held himself assured, and whom he hoped perhaps to put into Phraates's place, had returned in accordance with the wish of the Parthian king to his native country ;[1] Antonius appears to have reckoned on a rising on his part against Phraates, and in expectation of this civil war to have led his army into the interior of the Parthian provinces. It would doubtless have been possible to await the result of this design in the friendly Armenia, and, if operations thereafter were requisite, to have at least the full summer-time at his disposal in the following year ; but this waiting was not agreeable to the hasty general. In Atropatene he encountered the obstinate resistance of the powerful and half independent under-king, who resolutely sustained a siege in his capital Praaspa or Phraarta (southward from the lake of Urumia, presumably on the lower course of the Jaghatu) ; and not only so, but the hostile attack brought, as it would seem, to the Parthians internal peace. Phraates led on a large army to the relief of the assailed city. Antonius had brought with him a great siege-train, but impatiently hastening forward, he had left this behind in the custody of two legions under the legate Oppius Statianus. Thus he on his part made no progress with the siege ; but king Phraates sent his masses of cavalry under that same Monaeses to the rear of the enemy, against the corps of Statianus laboriously pursuing its march. The Parthians cut down the covering force, including the general himself, took the rest prisoners, and destroyed the whole train of 300 waggons. Thereby the campaign was lost.

The Armenian, despairing of the success of the campaign, collected his men and went home. Antonius did not immediately abandon the siege, and even defeated the royal army in the open field, but the alert horsemen escaped without substantial loss, and it was a victory without effect. An attempt to obtain from the king at

Progress of the struggle.

---

[1] It is in itself credible that Antonius concealed the impending invasion from Phraates as long as possible, and therefore, when sending back Monaeses, declared himself ready to conclude peace on the basis of the restitution of the lost standards (Plutarch, 37 ; Dio, xlix. 24 ; Florus, ii. 20 [iv. 10]). But he knew presumably that this offer would not be accepted, and in no case can he have been in earnest with those proposals ; beyond doubt he wished for the war and the overthrow of Phraates.

least the restitution of the old and the newly lost eagles, and thus to conclude peace, if not with advantage, at least with honour, failed ; the Parthian did not give away his sure success so cheaply.   He only assured the envoys of Antonius that, if the Romans would give up the siege, he would not molest them on their return home.   This neither honourable nor trustworthy promise of the enemy would hardly have induced Antonius to break up.   It was natural to take up quarters for the winter in the enemy's country, seeing that the Parthian troops were not acquainted with continuous military service, and presumably most of their forces would have gone home at the commencement of winter.   But a strong basis was lacking, and supplies in the exhausted land were not secured ; above all Antonius himself was not capable of such a tenacious conduct of the war.   Consequently he abandoned the machines, which the besieged immediately burnt ; and entered on the difficult retreat, either too early or too late.   Fifteen days' march (300 Roman miles) through a hostile country separated the army from the Araxes, the border river of Armenia, whither in spite of the ambiguous attitude of the ruler the retreat could alone be directed.   A hostile army of 40,000 horsemen, in spite of the given promise, accompanied the returning force, and, with the marching off of the Armenians, the Romans had lost the best part of their cavalry.   Provisions and draught animals were scarce, and the season of the year far advanced.   But in the perilous position Antonius recovered his energy and his martial skill, and in some measure also his good fortune in war ; he had made his choice, and the general as well as the troops solved the task in a commendable way.   Had they not had with them a former soldier of Crassus, who, having become a Parthian, knew most accurately every step of the way, and, instead of conducting them back through the plain by which they had come, guided them by mountain paths, which were less exposed to cavalry attacks—apparently over the mountains about Tabreez—the army would hardly have reached its goal ; and had not Monaeses, paying off in his way his debt of thanks to Antonius, informed him in right time of the false assurances and the cunning designs of his countrymen, the Romans would doubtless have fallen into one of the ambushes which on several occasions were laid for them.

The soldierly nature of Antonius was often brilliantly conspicuous during these troublesome days, in his dexterous use of any favourable moment, in his sternness towards the cowardly, in his power over the minds of the soldiers, in his faithful care for the wounded and the sick. Yet the rescue was almost a miracle; already had Antonius instructed a faithful attendant in case of extremity not to let him fall alive into the hands of the enemy. Amidst constant attacks of the artful enemy, in weather of wintry cold, without adequate food and often without water, they reached the protecting frontier in twenty-seven days, where the enemy desisted from following them. The loss was enormous; there were reckoned up in those twenty-seven days eighteen larger engagements, and in a single one of them the Romans counted 3000 dead and 5000 wounded. It was the very best and bravest that those constant assaults on the vanguard and on the flanks swept away. The whole baggage, a third of the camp-followers, a fourth of the army, 20,000 foot soldiers, and 4000 horsemen had perished in this Median campaign, in great part not through the sword, but through famine and disease. Even on the Araxes the sufferings of the unhappy troops were not yet at an end. Artavazdes received them as a friend, and had no other choice; it would doubtless have been possible to pass the winter there. But the impatience of Antonius did not tolerate this; the march went on, and from the ever increasing inclemency of the season and the state of health of the soldiers, this last section of the expedition from the Araxes to Antioch cost, although no enemy hampered it, other 8000 men. No doubt this campaign was a last flash of what was brave and capable in the character of Antonius; but it was politically his overthrow all the more, as at the same time Caesar by the successful termination of the

Difficulties of the retreat.

Sicilian war gained the dominion in the West and the confidence of Italy for the present and all the future.

Last years of Antonius in the East. The responsibility for the miscarriage, which Antonius in vain attempted to deny, was thrown by him on the dependent kings of Cappadocia and Armenia, and on the latter so far with justice, as his premature marching off from Praaspa had materially increased the dangers and the losses of the retreat.   For the plan of the campaign, however, it was not he who was responsible, but Antonius ;[1] and the failure of the hopes placed on Monaeses, the disaster of Statianus, the breaking down of the siege of Praaspa, were not brought about by the Armenian. Antonius did not abandon the subjugation of the East, 35. but set out next year (719) once more from Egypt.   The circumstances were still even now comparatively favourable.   A friendly alliance was formed with the Median king Artavazdes ; he had not merely fallen into variance with his Parthian suzerain, but was indignant above all at his Armenian neighbour, and, considering the well-known exasperation of Antonius against the latter, he might reckon on finding a support in the enemy of his enemy. Everything depended on the firm accord of the two possessors of power—the victory-crowned master of the West and the defeated ruler in the East ; and, on the news that Antonius proposed to continue the war, his legitimate wife, the sister of Caesar, resorted from Italy to the East to bring up to him new forces, and to strengthen anew his relations to her and to her brother. If Octavia was magnanimous enough to offer the hand of reconciliation to her husband in spite of his relations to the Egyptian queen, Caesar must—as was further confirmed by the commencement, which just then took place, of the war on the north-east frontier of Italy—have been still ready at that time to maintain the subsisting relation.

[1] The account of the matter given by Strabo, xi. 13, 4, p. 524, evidently after the description of this war compiled by Antonius's comrade in arms Dellius, and, it may be conjectured, at his bidding (comp. *ib.* xi. 13, 3 ; Dio, xlix. 39), is a very sorry attempt to justify the beaten general.   If Antonius did not take the nearest route to Ctesiphon, king Artavazdes cannot be brought in for the blame of it as a false guide ; it was a military, and doubtless still more a political, miscalculation of the general in chief.

The brother and sister subordinated their personal interests magnanimously to those of the commonwealth. But loudly as interest and honour called for the acceptance of the offered hand, Antonius could not prevail on himself to break off the relation with the Egyptian queen ; he sent back his wife, and this was at the same time a rupture with her brother, and, as we may add, an abandonment of the idea of continuing the war against the Parthians. Now, ere that could be thought of, the question of mastery between Antonius and Caesar had to be settled. Antonius accordingly returned at once from Syria to Egypt, and in the following year undertook nothing further towards the execution of his plans of Oriental conquest ; only he punished those to whom he assigned the blame of the miscarriage. He caused Ariarathes the king of Cappadocia to be executed,[1] and gave the kingdom to an illegitimate kinsman of his, Archelaus. The like fate was intended for the Armenian. If Antonius in 720 appeared in Armenia, as he said, 34. for the continuance of the war, this had simply the object of getting into his power the person of the king, who had refused to go to Egypt. This act of revenge was ignobly executed by way of surprise, and was not less ignobly celebrated by a caricature of the Capitoline triumph exhibited in Alexandria. At that time the son of Antonius, destined for lord of the East, as was already stated, was installed as king of Armenia, and married to the daughter of the new ally, the king of Media ; while the eldest son of the captive king of Armenia executed some time afterwards by order of queen Cleopatra, Artaxes, whom the Armenians had proclaimed king instead of his father, took refuge with the Parthians. Armenia and Media Atropatene were thus in the power of Antonius or allied with him ; the continuance of the Parthian war was announced doubtless, but remained postponed till after the overcoming of the western rival. Phraates on his

[1] The fact of the deposition and execution, and the time, are attested by Dio, xlix. 32, and Valerius Maximus, ix. 15, ext. 2 ; the cause or the pretext must have been connected with the Armenian war.

part advanced against Media, at first without success, as
the Roman troops stationed in Armenia afforded help to
the Medians ; but when Antonius, in the course of his
armaments against Caesar, recalled his forces from that
quarter, the Parthians gained the upper hand, vanquished
the Medians, and installed in Media, as well as also in
Armenia, the king Artaxes, who, in requital for the execution of his father, caused all the Romans scattered in the
land to be seized and put to death.   That Phraates did
not turn to fuller account the great feud between Antonius
and Caesar, while it was in preparation and was being
fought out, was probably due to his being once more
hampered by the troubles breaking out in his own land.
These ended in his expulsion, and in his going to the
Scythians of the East.   Tiridates was proclaimed as
great-king in his stead.   When the decisive naval battle
was fought on the coast of Epirus, and thereupon the
overthrow of Antonius was completed in Egypt, this new
great-king sat on his tottering throne in Ctesiphon, and
at the opposite frontier of the empire the hordes of Turan
were making arrangements to reinstate the earlier ruler,
in which they soon afterwards succeeded.

First
arrange-
ments of
Augustus
in the East.

The sagacious and clear-seeing man, to whom it fell to
liquidate the undertakings of Antonius and to settle the
relations of the two portions of the empire, needed moderation quite as much as energy.   It would have been the
gravest of errors to enter into the ideas of Antonius as to
conquering the East, or even merely making further conquests there.   Augustus perceived this ; his military
arrangements show clearly that, while he viewed the possession of the Syrian coast as well as that of Egypt as an
indispensable complement to the empire of the Mediterranean, he attached no value to inland possessions there.
Armenia, however, had now been for a generation Roman,
and could, in the nature of the circumstances, only be
Roman or Parthian ; the country was by its position, in a
military point of view, a sally-port for each of the great
powers into the territory of the other.   Augustus had no
thought of abandoning Armenia and leaving it to the

Parthians ; and, as things stood, he could hardly think of doing so.   But, if Armenia was retained, the matter could not end there ; the local relations compelled the Romans further to bring under their controlling influence the basin of the river Cyrus, the territories of the Iberians on its upper, and of the Albanians on its lower course—that is, the inhabitants of the modern Georgia and Shirvan, skilled in combat on horseback and on foot—and not to allow the domain of the Parthian power to extend to the north of the Araxes beyond Atropatene.   The expedition of Pompeius had already shown that the settlement in Armenia necessarily led the Romans on the one hand as far as the Caucasus, on the other as far as the western shore of the Caspian Sea.   The initial steps were everywhere taken.   The legates of Antonius had fought with the Iberians and Albanians ; Polemon, confirmed in his position by Augustus, ruled not merely over the coast from Pharnacea to Trapezus, but also over the territory of the Colchians at the mouth of the Phasis.   To this general state of matters fell to be added the special circumstances of the moment, which most urgently suggested to the new monarch of Rome not merely to show his sword in presence of the Orientals, but also to draw it.   That king Artaxes, like Mithradates formerly, had given orders to put to death all the Romans within his bounds, could not be allowed to remain unrequited.   The exiled king of Media also had now sought help from Augustus, as he would otherwise have sought it from Antonius.   Not. merely did the civil war and the conflict of pretenders in the Parthian empire facilitate the attack, but the expelled ruler Tiridates likewise sought protection with Augustus, and declared himself ready as a Roman vassal to accept his kingdom in fief from the latter.   The restitution of the Romans who had fallen into the power of the Parthians at the defeats of Crassus and of the Antonians, and of the lost eagles, might not in themselves seem to the ruler worth the waging of war ; the restorer of the Roman state could not allow this question of military and political honour to drop.

Policy open
to him.

The Roman statesman had to reckon with these facts ; considering the position, which Antonius took in the East, the policy of action was imperative generally, and doubly so from the preceding miscarriages. Beyond doubt it was desirable soon to undertake the organisation of matters in Rome, but for the undisputed monarch there subsisted no stringent compulsion to do this at once. He found himself after the decisive blows of Actium and Alexandria on the spot and at the head of a strong and victorious army ; what had to be done some day was best done at once. A ruler of the stamp of Caesar would hardly have returned to Rome without having restored the protectorate in Armenia, having obtained recognition for the Roman supremacy as far as the Caucasus and the Caspian Sea, and having settled accounts with the Parthians. A ruler of caution and energy would have now at once organised the defence of the frontier in the East, as the circumstances required ; it was from the outset clear that the four Syrian legions, together about 40,000 men, were not sufficient to guard the interests of Rome simultaneously on the Euphrates, on the Araxes, and on the Cyrus, and that the militia of the dependent kingdoms only concealed, and did not cover, the want of imperial troops. Armenia by political and national sympathy held more to the Parthians than to the Romans ; the kings of Commagene, Cappadocia, Galatia, Pontus, were inclined doubtless on the other hand more to the Roman side, but they were untrustworthy and weak. Even a policy keeping within bounds needed for its foundation an energetic stroke of the sword, and for its maintenance the near arm of a superior Roman military power.

Inadequate
measures.

Augustus neither struck nor protected ; certainly not because he deceived himself as to the state of the case, but because it was his nature to execute tardily and feebly what he perceived to be necessary, and to let considerations of internal policy exercise a more than due influence on the relations abroad. The inadequacy of the protection of the frontier by the client states of Asia Minor he well perceived ; and in connection therewith, already in the

year 729, after the death of king Amyntas who ruled all 25.
the interior of Asia Minor, he gave to him no successor,
but placed the land under an imperial legate. Presumably
the neighbouring more important client-states, and particularly Cappadocia, were intended to be in like manner
converted after the decease of the holders for the time
into imperial governorships. This was a step in advance,
in so far as thereby the militia of these countries was incorporated with the imperial army and placed under
Roman officers ; these troops could not exercise a serious
pressure on the insecure border-lands or even on the neighbouring great-state, although they now counted among
those of the empire. But all these considerations were
outweighed by regard to the reduction of the numbers of
the standing army and of the expenditure for the military
system to the lowest possible measure.

Equally insufficient, in presence of the relations of the
moment, were the measures adopted by Augustus on his
return home from Alexandria. He gave to the dispossessed king of the Medes the rule of the Lesser Armenia,
and to the Parthian pretender Tiridates an asylum in
Syria, in order through the former to keep in check the
king Artaxes who persevered in open hostility against
Rome, by the latter to press upon king Phraates. The
negotiations instituted with the latter regarding the restitution of the Parthian trophies of victory were prolonged
without result, although Phraates in the year 731 had 23.
promised their return in order to obtain the release of a
son who had accidentally fallen into the power of the
Romans.

It was only when Augustus went in person to Syria Augustus
in the year 734, and showed himself in earnest, that the 20.]   in
Orientals submitted. In Armenia, where a powerful Syria.
party had risen against king Artaxes, the insurgents
threw themselves into the arms of the Romans and
sought imperial investiture for Artaxes's younger brother
Tigranes, brought up at the imperial court and living in
Rome. When the emperor's stepson Tiberius Claudius
Nero, then a youth of twenty-two years, advanced with

a military force into Armenia, king Artaxes was put to death by his own relatives, and Tigranes received the imperial tiara from the hand of the emperor's representative, as fifty years earlier his grandfather of the same name had received it from Pompeius (iv. 127). Atropatene was again separated from Armenia and passed under the sway of a ruler likewise brought up in Rome, Ariobarzanes, son of the already-mentioned Artavazdes ; yet the latter appears to have obtained the land not as a Roman but as a Parthian dependency. Concerning the organisation of matters in the principalities on the Caucasus we learn nothing ; but as they are subsequently reckoned among the Roman client-states, probably at that time the Roman influence prevailed here also. Even king Phraates, now put to the choice of redeeming his word or fighting, resolved with a heavy heart on the surrender—keenly as it did violence to the national feelings of his people—of the few Roman prisoners of war still living and the standards won.

Mission of Gaius Caesar to the East.   Boundless joy saluted this bloodless victory achieved by this prince of peace. After it there subsisted for a considerable time a friendly relation with the king of the Parthians, as indeed the immediate interests of the two great states came little into contact. In Armenia, on the other hand, the Roman vassal-rule, which rested only on its own basis, had a difficulty in confronting the national opposition. After the early death of king Tigranes his children, or the leaders of the state governing under their name, joined this opposition. Against them another ruler Artavazdes was set up by the friends of the Romans ; but he was unable to prevail against the stronger opposing party. These Armenian troubles disturbed also the relation to the Parthians ; it was natural that the Armenians antagonistic to Rome should seek to lean on these, and the Arsacids could not forget that Armenia had been formerly a Parthian appanage for the second son. Bloodless victories are often feeble and dangerous. Matters went so far that the Roman government, in the year 748, commissioned the same Tiberius, who, fourteen years before had installed Tigranes as vassal-king of Armenia, to enter it once more with a military force and to regulate the state of matters in case of need by arms. But the quarrels in the imperial family, which had interrupted the subjugation of the Germans (I. 35), interfered also here and had the same bad effect. Tiberius declined his stepfather's commission, and in the absence of a suitable princely general the Roman government for some years looked on, inactive for good or evil, at the doings of the anti-Roman party in Armenia under Parthian protection. At length, in the year 753, not merely 1. was the same commission given to the elder adopted son of the emperor, Gaius Caesar, at the age of twenty, but the subjugation of Armenia was to be, as the father hoped, the beginning of greater things; the Oriental campaign of the crown-prince of twenty was, we might almost say, to continue the expedition of Alexander. Literati commissioned by the emperor or in close relations to the court, the geographer Isidorus, himself at home at the mouth of the Euphrates, and king Juba of Mauretania, the representative of Greek learning among the princely personages of the Augustan circle, dedicated—the former his information personally acquired in the East, the latter his literary collections on Arabia—to the young prince, who appeared to burn with the desire of achieving the conquest of that land—over which Alexander had met his death—as a brilliant compensation for a miscarriage of the Augustan government which a considerable time ago had there occurred. In the first instance for Armenia this mission was just as successful as that of Tiberius. The Roman crown-prince and the Parthian great-king Phraataces met personally on an island of the Euphrates ; the Parthians once more gave up Armenia, the imminent danger of a Parthian war was averted, and the understanding, which had been disturbed, was at least outwardly re-established. Gaius appointed Ariobarzanes, a prince of the Median princely house, as king over the Armenians, and the suzerainty of Rome was once more confirmed. The Armenians, however, opposed to Rome did not submit without resistance ; matters came not merely to the marching in of the legions, but even to fighting. Before the walls of the Armenian stronghold Artageira the young crown-prince received from a Parthian officer through treachery the wound (2 A.D.) of which he died after months of sickness. The intermixture of imperial and dynastic policy punished itself anew. The death of a young man changed the course of great policy ; the Arabian expedition so confidently announced to the public fell into abeyance, after its success could no longer smooth the way of the emperor's son to the succession. Further undertakings on the Euphrates were no longer thought of ; the immediate object—the occupation of Armenia and the re-establishment of the relations with the Parthians—was attained, however sad the shadows that fell on this success through the death of the crown-prince.

Mission of Germanicus to [20. the East. The success had no more endurance than that of the more brilliant expedition of 734. The rulers of Armenia installed by Rome were soon hard pressed by those of the counter-party with the secret or open participation of the Parthians, and supplanted. When the Parthian prince Vonones, reared in Rome, was called to the vacant Parthian throne, the Romans hoped to find in him a support ; but on that very account he had soon to vacate it, and in his stead came king Artabanus of Media, an energetic man, sprung on the mother's side from the Arsacids, but belonging to the Scythian people of the Daci, and brought up in native habits (about 10 A.D.) Vonones was then received by the Armenians as ruler, and thereby these were kept under Roman influence. But the less could Artabanus tolerate his dispossessed rival as a neighbour prince ; the Roman government must, in order to sustain a man in every respect unfitted for his position, have applied armed force against the Parthians as against his own subjects. Tiberius, who meanwhile had come to reign, did not order an immediate invasion, and for the moment the anti-Roman party in Armenia was victorious ; but it was not his intention to abandon the important border-land. On the contrary, the annexation, probably long resolved on, of the kingdom of Cappadocia was carried out in the year 17 ; the old Archelaus, who had occupied the throne there from the year 718, was summoned to Rome and was there in- 36. formed that he had ceased to reign.   Likewise the petty, but on account of the fords of the Euphrates important, kingdom of Commagene came at that time under immediate imperial administration.   Thereby the direct frontier of the empire was pushed forward as far as the middle Euphrates.   At the same time the crown-prince Germanicus, who had just commanded with great distinction on the Rhine, went with extended full powers to the East, in order to organise the new province of Cappadocia and to restore the sunken repute of the imperial authority.

This mission also attained its end soon and easily. And its Germanicus, although not supported by the governor of results. Syria, Gnaeus Piso, with such a force of troops as he was entitled to ask and had asked, went nevertheless to Armenia, and by the mere weight of his person and of his position brought back the land to allegiance.   He allowed the incapable Vonones to fall, and, in accordance with the wishes of the chief men favourable to Rome, appointed as ruler of the Armenians a son of that Polemon whom Antonius had made king in Pontus, Zeno, or, as he was called as king of Armenia, Artaxias ; the latter was, on the one hand, connected with the imperial house through his mother queen Pythodoris, a granddaughter of the triumvir Antonius, on the other hand, reared after the manner of the country, a vigorous huntsman and a brave carouser at the festal board.   The great-king Artabanus also met the Roman prince in a friendly way, and asked only for the removal of his predecessor Vonones from Syria, in order to check the intrigues concocted between him and the discontented Parthians.   As Germanicus responded to this request and sent the inconvenient refugee to Cilicia, where he soon afterwards perished in an attempt to escape, the best relations were established between the two great states.   Artabanus wished even to meet personally with

Germanicus at the Euphrates, as Phraataces and Gaius had done ; but this Germanicus declined, doubtless with reference to the easily excited suspicion of Tiberius. In truth the same shadow of gloom fell on this Oriental expedition as on the last preceding one ; from this too the crown-prince of the Roman empire came not home alive.

Artabanus and Tiberius.

For a time the arrangements made did their work. So long as Tiberius bore sway with a firm hand, and so long as king Artaxias of Armenia lived, tranquillity continued in the East ; but in the last years of the old emperor, when he from his solitary island allowed things to take their course and shrank back from all interference, and especially after the death of Artaxias (about 34), the old game once more began. King Artabanus, exalted by his long and prosperous government and by many successes achieved against the border peoples of Iran, and convinced that the old emperor would have no inclination to begin a heavy war in the East, induced the Armenians to proclaim his own eldest son, Arsaces, as ruler ; that is, to exchange the Roman suzerainty for the Parthian. Indeed he seemed directly to aim at war with Rome ; he demanded the estate left by his predecessor and rival Vonones, who had died in Cilicia, from the Roman government, and his letters to it as undisguisedly expressed the view that the East belonged to the Orientals, as they called by the right name the abominations at the imperial court, of which people in Rome ventured only to whisper in their most intimate circles. He is said even to have made an attempt to possess himself of Cappadocia. But he had miscalculated on the old lion. Tiberius was even at Capreae formidable not merely to his courtiers, and was not the man to let himself, and in himself Rome, be mocked with impunity. He sent

Mission of Vitellius.

Lucius Vitellius, the father of the subsequent emperor, a resolute officer and skilful diplomatist, to the East with plenary power similar to that which Gaius Caesar and Germanicus had formerly had, and with the commission in case of need to lead the Syrian legions over the

Euphrates.   At the same time he applied the often tried means for giving trouble to the rulers of the East by insurrections and pretenders in their own land.   To the Parthian prince, whom the Armenian nationalists had proclaimed as ruler, he opposed a prince of the royal house of the Iberians, Mithradates, brother of the Armenian king Pharasmanes, and directed the latter, as well as the prince of the Albanians, to support the Roman pretender to Armenia with military force.   Large bands of the Transcaucasian Sarmatae, warlike and easy of access to every wooer, were hired with Roman money for the inroads into Armenia.   The Roman pretender succeeded in poisoning his rival through bribed courtiers, and in possessing himself of the country and of the capital Artaxata.   Artabanus sent in place of the murdered prince another son Orodes to Armenia, and attempted also on his part to procure Transcaucasian auxiliaries ; but only few made good their way to Armenia, and the bands of Parthian horsemen were not a match for the good infantry of the Caucasian peoples and the dreaded Sarmatian mounted archers.   Orodes was vanquished in a hard pitched battle, and himself severely wounded in single combat with his rival.   Then Artabanus in person set out for Armenia.   But now Vitellius also put in motion the Syrian legions, in order to cross the Euphrates and to invade Mesopotamia, and this brought the long fermenting insurrection in the Parthian kingdom to an outbreak.   The energetic and, with successes, more and more rude demeanour of the Scythian ruler, had offended many persons and interests, and had especially estranged from him the Mesopotamian Greeks and the powerful urban community of Seleucia, from which he had taken away its municipal constitution, democratic after a Greek type.   Roman gold fostered the movement which was in preparation.   Discontented nobles had already put themselves in communication with the Roman government, and besought from it a genuine Arsacid.   Tiberius had sent the only surviving son of Phraates, of the same name with his father, and—after the old man, accustomed to Roman habits, had succumbed to his exertions while still in Syria—in his stead a grandson of Phraates, likewise living in Rome, by name Tiridates. The Parthian prince Sinnaces, the leader of these plots, now renounced allegiance to the Scythian and set up the banner of the Arsacids. Vitellius with his legions crossed the Euphrates, and in his train the new great-king by grace of Rome. The Parthian governor of Mesopotamia, Ornospades, who had once as an exile shared under Tiberius in the Pannonian wars, placed himself and his troops at once at the disposal of the new ruler ; Abdagaeses, the father of Sinnaces, delivered over the imperial treasure ; very speedily Artabanus found himself abandoned by the whole country, and compelled to take flight to his Scythian home, where he wandered about in the forests without settled abode, and kept himself alive with his bow, while the tiara was solemnly placed on the head of Tiridates in Ctesiphon by the princes who were, according to the Parthian constitution, called to crown the ruler.

Tiridates superseded. But the rule of the new great-king sent by the national foe did not last long. The government, conducted less by himself, young, inexperienced, and incapable, than by those who had made him king, and chiefly by Abdagaeses, soon provoked opposition. Some of the chief satraps had remained absent even from the coronation festival, and again brought forth the dispossessed ruler from his banishment ; with their assistance and the forces supplied by his Scythian countrymen Artabanus returned, and already in the following year (36) the whole kingdom, with the exception of Seleucia, was again in his power, Tiridates was a fugitive, and was compelled to demand from his Roman protectors the shelter which could not be refused to him. Vitellius once more led the legions to the Euphrates ; but, as the great-king appeared in person and declared himself ready for all that was asked, provided that the Roman government would stand aloof from Tiridates, peace was soon concluded. Artabanus not merely recognised Mithradates as king of Armenia, but presented also to the effigy of the Roman emperor the homage which was wont to be required of vassals, and furnished his son Darius as a hostage to the Romans. Thereupon the old emperor died ; but he had lived long enough to see this victory, as bloodless as complete, of his policy over the revolt of the East.

What the sagacity of the old man had attained was undone at once by the indiscretion of his successor. Apart from the fact that he cancelled judicious arrangements of Tiberius, re-establishing, *e.g.* the annexed kingdom of Commagene, his foolish envy grudged the dead emperor the success which he had gained ; he summoned the able governor of Syria as well as the new king of Armenia to Rome to answer for themselves, deposed the latter, and, after keeping him for a time a prisoner, sent him into exile. As a matter of course the Parthian government took action for itself, and once more seized possession of Armenia which was without a master.[1] Claudius, on coming to reign in the year 41, had to begin afresh the work that had been done. He dealt with it after the example of Tiberius. Mithradates, recalled from exile, was reinstated, and directed with the help of his brother to possess himself of Armenia. The fraternal war then waged among the three sons of king Artabanus III. in the Parthian kingdom smoothed the way for the Romans. After the murder of the eldest son, Gotarzes and Vardanes contended over the throne for years ; Seleucia, which had already renounced allegiance to the father, defied him and subsequently his sons throughout seven years ; the peoples of Turan also interfered, as they always did, in this quarrel of princes of Iran. Mithradates was able, with the help of the troops of his brother and

The East under Gaius.

---

[1] The account of the seizure of Armenia is wanting, but the fact is clearly apparent from Tacitus, *Ann.* xi. 9. To this connection probably belongs what Josephus, *Arch.* xx. 3, 3, tells of the design of the successor of Artabanus to wage war against the Romans, from which Izates the satrap of Adiabene vainly dissuades him. Josephus names this successor, probably in error, Bardanes. The immediate successor of Artabanus III. was, according to Tacitus, *Ann.* xi. 8, his son of the same name, whom along with his son thereupon Gotarzes put out of the way ; and this Artabanus IV. must be here meant.

of the garrisons of the neighbouring Roman provinces, to overpower the Parthian partisans in Armenia and to make himself again master there;[1] the land obtained a Roman garrison. After Vardanes had come to terms with his brother and had at length reoccupied Seleucia, he seemed as though he would march into Armenia; but the threatening attitude of the Roman legate of Syria withheld him, and very soon the brother broke the agreement and the civil war began afresh. Not even the assassination of the brave and, in combat with the peoples of Turan, victorious Vardanes put an end to it; the opposition party now turned to Rome and besought from the government there the son of Vonones, the prince Meherdates then living in Rome, who thereupon was placed by the emperor Claudius before the assembled senate at the disposal of his countrymen and sent away to Syria with the exhortation to administer his new kingdom well and justly, and to remain mindful of the friendly protectorate of Rome (49). He did not reach the position in which these exhortations might be applied. The Roman legions, which escorted him as far as the Euphrates, there delivered him over to those who had called him—the head of the powerful princely family of the Carên and the kings Abgarus of Edessa and Izates of Adiabene. The inexperienced and unwarlike youth was as little equal to the task as all the other Parthian rulers set up by the Romans; a number of his most noted adherents left him so soon as they learned to know him, and went to Gotarzes; in the decisive battle the fall of the brave Carên turned the scale. Meherdates was taken prisoner and not even executed,

---

[1] The statement of Petrus Patricius (*fr.* 3 Müll.) that king Mithradates of Iberia had planned revolt from Rome, but in order to preserve the semblance of fidelity, had sent his brother Cotys to Claudius, and then, when the latter had given information to the emperor of those intrigues, had been deposed and replaced by his brother, is not compatible with the assured fact that in Iberia, at least from the year 35 (Tacitus, *Ann.* vi. 32) till the year 60 (Tacitus, *Ann.* xiv. 26), Pharasmanes, and in the year 75 his son Mithradates (*C. I. L.* iii. 6052) bore rule. Beyond doubt Petrus has confused Mithradates of Iberia and the king of the Bosporus of the same name (I. 316, note 1), and here at the bottom lies the narrative, which Tacitus, *Ann.* xii. 18, presupposes.

but only, after the Oriental fashion, rendered incapable of government by mutilation of the ears.

Nothwithstanding this defeat of Roman policy in the Parthian kingdom, Armenia remained with the Romans, so long as the weak Gotarzes ruled over the Parthians. But so soon as a more vigorous hand grasped the reins of sovereignty, and the internal conflicts ceased, the struggle for that land was resumed. King Vologasus, who after the death of Gotarzes and the short reign of Vonones II. succeeded this his father in the year 51,[1] ascended the throne, exceptionally, in full agreement with his two brothers Pacorus and Tiridates. He was an able and prudent ruler—we find him even as a founder of towns, and exerting himself with success to divert the trade of Palmyra towards his new town Vologasias on the lower Euphrates—averse to quick and extreme resolutions, and endeavouring, if possible, to keep peace with his powerful neighbour. But the recovery of Armenia was the leading political idea of the dynasty, and he too was ready to make use of any opportunity for realising it.

This opportunity seemed now to present itself. The Armenian court had become the scene of one of the most revolting family tragedies which history records. The old king of the Iberians, Pharasmanes, undertook to eject his brother Mithradates, the king of Armenia, from the throne and to put his own son Rhadamistus in his place. Under the pretext of a quarrel with his father Rhadamistus appeared at the court of his uncle and father-in-law, and entered into negotiations with Armenians of repute in that sense. After he had secured a body of adherents, Pharasmanes, in the year 52, under frivolous pretexts involved his brother in war, and brought the country into his own or rather his son's

---

[1] If the coins, which, it is true, for the most part admit of being distinguished only by resemblance of effigy, are correctly attributed, those of Gotarzes reach to Sel. 362 Daesius = A.D. 51 June, and those of Volo- gasus (we know none of Vonones II.) begin with Sel. 362 Gorpiaeus = A.D. 51 Sept. (Percy Gardner, *Parthian Coinage*, pp. 50, 51), which agrees with Tacitus, *Ann.* xii. 14, 44.

power. Mithradates placed himself under the protection of the Roman garrison of the fortress of Gorneae.[1] Rhadamistus did not venture to attack this ; but the commandant, Caelius Pollio, was well known as worthless and venal. The centurion holding command under him resorted to Pharasmanes to induce him to recall his troops, which the latter promised, but did not keep his word. During the absence of the second in command Pollio compelled the king—who doubtless guessed what was before him—by the threat of leaving him in the lurch, to deliver himself into the hands of Rhadamistus. By the latter he was put to death, and with him his wife, the sister of Rhadamistus, and their children, because they broke out in cries of lamentation at the sight of the dead bodies of their parents. In this way Rhadamistus attained to sovereignty over Armenia. The Roman government ought neither to have looked on at such horrors, of which its officers shared the guilt, nor to have tolerated that one of its vassals should make war on another. Nevertheless the governor of Cappadocia, Julius Paelignus, acknowledged the new king of Armenia. Even in the council of the governor of Syria, Ummidius Quadratus, the opinion preponderated that it might be matter of indifference to the Romans whether the uncle or the nephew ruled Armenia ; the legate, sent to Armenia with a legion, received only instructions to maintain the *status quo* till further orders. Then the Parthian king, on the assumption that the Roman government would not be zealous to take part for king Rhadamistus, deemed the moment a fit one for resuming his old claims upon Armenia. He invested his brother Tiridates with Armenia, and the Parthian troops marching in possessed themselves, almost without striking a blow, of the two capitals, Tigranocerta and Artaxata, and of the whole land. When Rhadamistus made an attempt to retain the price of his deeds of blood, the Armenians themselves drove him out of the land. The Roman garrison appears

---

[1] Gorneae, called by the Armenians Garhni, as the ruins (nearly east of Erivân) are still at present named. (Kiepert.)

to have left Armenia after the giving over of Gorneae ;
the governor recalled the legion put upon the march
from Syria, in order not to fall into conflict with the
Parthians.

When this news came to Rome (at the end of 54) Corbulo sent to Cappa- docia.
the emperor Claudius had just died, and the ministers
Burrus and Seneca practically governed for his young
successor, seventeen years old. The procedure of
Vologasus could only be answered by a declaration of
war. In fact the Roman government sent to Cappadocia,
which otherwise was a governorship of the second rank
and was not furnished with legions, by way of exception
the consular legate Gnaeus Domitius Corbulo. He had
come rapidly into prominence as brother-in-law of the
emperor Gaius, had then under Claudius been legate
of lower Germany in the year 47 (I. 125), and was
thenceforth regarded as one of the able commanders, not
at that time numerous, who energetically maintained the
stringency of discipline—in person a Herculean figure,
equal to any fatigue, and of unshrinking courage in
presence not of the enemy merely but also of his own
soldiers. It appeared to be a sign of things becoming
better that the government of Nero gave to him the first
important command which it had to fill. The incapable
Syrian legate of Syria, Quadratus, was not recalled, but
was directed to put two of his four legions at the disposal
of the governor of the neighbouring province. All the
legions were brought up to the Euphrates, and orders
were given for the immediate throwing of bridges over
the stream. The two regions bordering immediately on
Armenia to the westward, Lesser Armenia and Sophene,
were assigned to two trustworthy Syrian princes, Aristobulus, of a lateral branch of the Herodian house, and
Sohaemus, of the ruling family of Hemesa, and both were
placed under Corbulo's command. Agrippa, the king of
the remnant of the Jewish state still left at that time, and
Antiochus, king of Commagene, likewise received orders
to march.

At first, however, no fighting took place. The reason

Character
of his
troops.

lay partly in the state of the Syrian legions; it was a bad testimonial of poverty for the previous administration, that Corbulo was compelled to describe the troops assigned to him as quite unserviceable. The legions levied and doing garrison duty in the Greek provinces had always been inferior to the Occidentals; now the enervating power of the East with the long state of peace and the laxity of discipline completely demoralised them. The soldiers abode more in the towns than in the camps; not a few of them were unaccustomed to carry arms, and knew nothing of pitching camps and of service on the watch; the regiments were far from having their full complement and contained numerous old and useless men; Corbulo had, in the first instance, to dismiss a great number of soldiers, and to levy and train recruits in still larger numbers. The exchange of the comfortable winter quarters on the Orontes for those in the rugged mountains of Armenia, and the sudden introduction of inexorably stern discipline in the camp, brought about various ailments and occasioned numerous desertions. In spite of all this the general found himself, when matters became serious, compelled to ask that one of the better legions of the West might be sent to him. Under these circumstances he was in no haste to bring his soldiers to face the enemy; nevertheless it was political considerations that preponderantly influenced him in this course.

The aims
of the war.

If it had been the design of the Roman government to drive out the Parthian ruler at once from Armenia, and to put in his place not indeed Rhadamistus, with whose blood-guiltiness the Romans had no occasion to stain themselves, but some other prince of their choice, the military resources of Corbulo would probably have at once sufficed, since king Vologasus, once more recalled by internal troubles, had led away his troops from Armenia. But this was not embraced in the plan of the Romans; they wished, on the contrary, rather to acquiesce in the government of Tiridates there, and only to induce and, in case of need, compel him to an acknow-

ledgment of the Roman supremacy ; only for this object
were the legions, in case of extremity, to march.   This in
reality came very near to the cession of Armenia to the
Parthians.   What told in favour of this course, and what
prevented it, has formerly been set forth (p. 34 f.).   If Armenia were now arranged as a Parthian appanage for
a second son, the recognition of the Roman suzerainty
was little more than a formality, strictly taken, nothing
but a screen for military and political honour.   Thus the
government of the earlier period of Nero, which, as is well
known, was equalled by few in insight and energy, intended to get rid of Armenia in a decorous way ; and
that need not surprise us.   In fact they were in this case
pouring water into a sieve.   The possession of Armenia
had doubtless been asserted and brought to recognition
within the land itself, as among the Parthians, through
Tiberius in the year 20 B.C., then by Gaius in the year 2,
by Germanicus in the year 18, and by Vitellius in the
year 36.   But it was just these extraordinary expeditions
regularly repeated and regularly crowned with success,
and yet never attaining to permanent effect, that justified
the Parthians, when in the negotiations with Nero they
maintained that the Roman suzerainty over Armenia was
an empty name—that the land was, and could be, none
other than Parthian.   For the vindication of the Roman
supreme authority there was always needed, if not the
waging of war, at least the threat of it ; and the constant
irritation thereby produced made a lasting state of peace
between the two neighbouring great powers impossible.
The Romans had, if they were to act consistently, only
the choice between either bringing Armenia and the left
bank of the Euphrates in general effectively under their
power by setting aside the mere mediate government, or
leaving the matter to the Parthians, so far as was compatible with the supreme principle of the Roman government to acknowledge no frontier-power with equal rights.
Augustus and the rulers after him had so far decidedly
declined the former alternative, and they ought therefore
to have taken the second course.   But this too they had

at least attempted to decline, and had wished to exclude the Parthian royal house from the rule over Armenia, without being able to do so. This the leading statesmen of the earlier Neronian period must have regarded as an error, since they left Armenia to the Arsacids, and restricted themselves to the smallest conceivable measure of rights thereto. When the dangers and the disadvantages, which the retention of this region only externally attached to the empire brought to the state, were weighed against those which the Parthian rule over Armenia involved for the Romans, the decision might, especially in view of the small offensive power of the Parthian kingdom, well be found in the latter sense. But under all the circumstances this policy was consistent, and sought to attain in a clearer and more rational way the aim pursued by Augustus.

Negotiations with Vologasus. From this standpoint we understand why Corbulo and Quadratus, instead of crossing the Euphrates, entered into negotiations with Vologasus ; and not less why the latter, informed doubtless of the real designs of the Romans, agreed to submit to the Romans in a similar way with his predecessor, and to deliver to them as a pledge of peace a number of hostages closely connected with the royal house. The return tacitly agreed on for this was that the rule of Tiridates over Armenia should be tolerated, and that a Roman pretender should not be set up. So some years passed in a *de facto* state of peace. But when Vologasus and Tiridates did not agree to apply to the Roman government for the investing of the latter with Armenia,[1] Corbulo took the offensive against Tiridates in the year 58. The very policy of withdrawal and concession, if it was not to appear to friend and foe as weakness, needed a foil, and so either a formal and solemn recognition of the Roman supremacy or, better still, a victory won by arms.

---

[1] Even after the attack Tiridates complained *cur datis nuper obsidibus redintegrataque amicitia . . . vetere Armeniae possessione depelleretur,* and Corbulo presented to him, in case of his turning as a suppliant to the emperor, the prospect of a *regnum stabile* (Tacitus, *Ann.* xii. 37). Elsewhere too the refusal of the oath of fealty is indicated as the proper ground of war (Tacitus, *Ann.* xii. 34).

In the summer of the year 58 Corbulo led an army, Corbulo in
Armenia. tolerably fit for fighting, of at least 30,000 men, over the Euphrates. The reoganisation and the hardening of the troops were completed by the campaign itself, and the first winter-quarters were taken up on Armenian soil. In the spring of 59[1] he began the advance in the direction of Artaxata. At the same time Armenia was invaded from the north by the Iberians, whose king Pharasmanes, to cover his own crimes, had caused his son Rhadamistus to be executed, and now further endeavoured by good services to make his guilt be forgotten ; and not less by their neighbours to the north-west, the brave Moschi, and on the south by Antiochus, king of Commagene. King Vologasus was detained by the revolt of the Hyrcanians on the opposite side of the kingdom, and could or would not interfere directly in the struggle. Tiridates offered a courageous resistance, but he could do nothing against the crushing superiority of force. In vain he sought to throw himself on the lines of communication of the Romans, who obtained their necessary supplies by way of the Black Sea and the port of Trapezus. The strong-holds of Armenia fell under the attacks of the Roman assailants, and the garrisons were cut down to the last man. Defeated in a pitched battle under the walls of Artaxata, Tiridates gave up the unequal struggle, and went to the Parthians. Artaxata surrendered, and here, in the heart of Armenia, the Roman army passed the

---

[1] The report in Tacitus, *Ann.* xiii. 34-41, embraces beyond doubt the campaigns of 58 and 59, since Tacitus under the year 59 is silent as to the Armenian campaign, while under the year 60, *Ann.* xiv. 23 joins on immediately to xiii. 41, and evidently describes merely a single campaign ; generally, where he condenses in this way, he as a rule anticipates. That the war cannot have begun only in 59, is further confirmed by the fact that Corbulo observed the solar eclipse of 30th April 59 on Armenian soil (Plin. *H. N.* ii. 70, 180); had he not entered the country till 59, he could hardly have crossed the enemy's frontier so early in the year. The narrative of Tacitus, *Ann.* xiii. 34-41, does not in itself show an intercalation of a year, but with his mode of narrating it admits the possibility that the first year was spent in the crossing of the Euphrates and the settling in Armenia, and so the winter mentioned in *c.* 35 is that of the year 58-9, especially as in view of the character of the army such a beginning to the war would be quite in place, and in view of the short Armenian summer it was militarily convenient thus to separate the marching into the country and the conduct proper of the war.

winter. In the spring of 60 Corbulo broke up from thence, after having burnt down the town, and marched right across the country to its second capital Tigranocerta, above Nisibis, in the basin of the Tigris. The terrors of the destruction of Artaxata preceded him ; serious resistance was nowhere offered ; even Tigranocerta voluntarily opened its gates to the victor, who here in a well-calculated way allowed mercy to prevail. Tiridates still made an attempt to return and to resume the struggle, but was repulsed without special exertion. At the close of the summer of 60 all Armenia was subdued, and stood at the disposal of the Roman government.

Tigranes, king of Armenia.

It is intelligible that people in Rome now put Tiridates out of account. The prince Tigranes, a great-grandson on the father's side of Herod the Great, on the mother's of king Archelaus of Cappadocia, related also to the old Marenian royal house on the female side, and a nephew of one of the ephemeral rulers of Armenia in the last years of Augustus, brought up in Rome, and entirely a tool of the Roman government, was now (60) invested by Nero with the kingdom of Armenia, and at the emperor's command installed by Corbulo in its rule. In the country there was left a Roman garrison, 1000 legionaries, and from 3000 to 4000 cavalry and infantry of auxiliaries. A portion of the border land was separated from Armenia and distributed among the neighbouring kings, Polemon of Pontus and Trapezus, Aristobulus of Lesser Armenia, Pharasmanes of Iberia and Antiochus of Commagene. On the other hand the new master of Armenia advanced, of course with consent of the Romans, into the adjacent Parthian province of Adiabene, defeated Monobazus the governor there, and appeared desirous of wresting this region also from the Parthian state.

Negotiations with the Parthians.

This turn of affairs compelled the Parthian government to emerge from its passiveness ; the question now concerned no longer the recovery of Armenia, but the integrity of the Parthian empire. The long-threatened collision between the two great states seemed inevitable. Vologasus in an assembly of the grandees of the empire

confirmed Tiridates afresh as king of Armenia, and sent
with him the general Monaeses against the Roman usurper
of the land, who was besieged by the Parthians in Tigranocerta, which the Roman troops kept in their possession. Vologasus in person collected the Parthian main
force in Mesopotamia, and threatened (at the beginning
of 61) Syria. Corbulo, who, after Quadratus's death, held
the command for a time in Cappadocia as in Syria, but
had besought from the government the nomination of
another governor for Cappadocia and Armenia, sent provisionally two legions to Armenia to lend help to Tigranes,
while he in person moved to the Euphrates in order to
receive the Parthian king. Again, however, they came
not to blows, but to an agreement. Vologasus, well
knowing how dangerous was the game which he was
beginning, declared himself now ready to enter into the
terms vainly offered by the Romans before the outbreak
of the Armenian war, and to allow the investiture of his
brother by the Roman emperor. Corbulo entered into the
proposal. He let Tigranes drop, withdrew the Roman
troops from Armenia, and acquiesced in Tiridates establish-
ing himself there, while the Parthian auxiliary troops likewise withdrew ; on the other hand, Vologasus sent an
embassy to the Roman government, and declared the
readiness of his brother to take the land in fee from
Rome.

These measures of Corbulo were of a hazardous kind,[1]
and led to a bad complication. The Roman general may
possibly have been, still more thoroughly than the statesmen in Rome, impressed by the uselessness of retaining
Armenia ; but, after the Roman government had installed
Tigranes as king of Armenia, he could not of his own
accord fall back upon the conditions earlier laid down,
least of all abandon his own acquisitions and withdraw the
Roman troops from Armenia. He was the less entitled
to do so, as he administered Cappadocia and Armenia

*The Par-
thian war
under Nero.*

---

[1] From the representation of Tacitus, *Ann.* xv. 6, the partiality and
the perplexity are clearly seen. He
does not venture to express the surrender of Armenia to Tiridates, and
only leaves the reader to infer it.

merely *ad interim*, and had himself declared to the government that he was not in a position to exercise the
command at once there and in Syria; whereupon the
consular Lucius Caesennius Paetus was nominated as
governor of Cappadocia and was already on the way
thither.   The suspicion can hardly be avoided that Corbulo grudged the latter the honour of the final subjugation
of Armenia, and wished before his arrival to establish a
definitive solution by the actual conclusion of peace with
the Parthians.   The Roman government accordingly
declined the proposals of Vologasus and insisted on the
retention of Armenia, which, as the new governor who
arrived in Cappadocia in the course of the summer of 61
declared, was even to be taken under direct Roman
administration.   Whether the Roman government had
really resolved to go so far cannot be ascertained; but
this was at all events implied in the consistent following
out of their policy.   The installing of a king dependent
on Rome was only a prolongation of the previous untenable state of things; whoever did not wish the cession
of Armenia to the Parthians had to contemplate the conversion of the kingdom into a Roman province.   The
war therefore took its course; and on that account one of
the Moesian legions was sent to the Cappadocian army.

Measures
of Paetus.   When Paetus arrived, the two legions assigned to him
by Corbulo were encamped on this side of the Euphrates
in Cappadocia; Armenia was evacuated, and had to be
reconquered.   Paetus set at once to work, crossed the
Euphrates at Melitene (Malatia), advanced into Armenia,
and reduced the nearest strongholds on the border.   The
advanced season of the year, however, compelled him soon
to suspend operations and to abandon for this year the intended reoccupation of Tigranocerta; nevertheless, in order
to resume his march at once next spring, he, after Corbulo's
example, took up his winter-quarters in the enemy's
country at Rhandeia, on a tributary of the Euphrates, the
Arsanias, not far from the modern Charput, while the
baggage and the women and children had quarters not far
from it in the strong fortress of Arsamosata.   But he had

underrated the difficulty of the undertaking. One, and that the best of his legions, the Moesian, was still on the march, and spent the winter on this side of the Euphrates in the territory of Pontus ; the two others were not those whom Corbulo had taught to fight and conquer, but the former Syrian legions of Quadratus, not having their full complement, and hardly capable of use without thorough reorganisation. He had withal to confront not, like Corbulo, the Armenians alone, but the main body of the Parthians ; Vologasus had, when the war became in earnest, led the flower of his troops from Mesopotamia to Armenia, and judiciously availed himself of the strategical advantage that he commanded the inner and shorter lines. Corbulo might, especially as he had bridged over the Euphrates and constructed *tetes de pont* on the other bank, have at least hampered, or at any rate requited this marching off by a seasonable incursion into Mesopotamia ; but he did not stir from his positions and he left it to Paetus to defend himself, as best he could, against the whole force of his foes. The latter was neither himself military nor ready to accept and follow military advice, not even a man of resolute character; arrogant and boastful in onset, despairing and pusillanimous in presence of misfortune.

Thus there came what could not but come. In the spring of 62 it was not Paetus who assumed the aggressive, but Vologasus ; the advanced troops who were to bar the way of the Parthians were crushed by the superior force ; the attack was soon converted into a siege of the Roman positions pitched far apart in the winter camp and the fortress. The legions could neither advance nor retreat ; the soldiers deserted in masses ; the only hope rested on Corbulo's legions lying inactive far off in northern Syria, beyond doubt at Zeugma. Both generals shared in the blame of the disaster: Corbulo on account of the lateness of his starting to render help,[1] although, when

Capitulation of Rhandeia.

---

[1] This is said by Tacitus himself, *Ann.* xv. 10: *nec a Corbulone properatum, quo gliscentibus periculis etiam subsidii laus augeretur,* in naive unconcern at the severe censure which this praise involves. How partial is the tone of the whole account resting on Corbulo's despatches, is shown among other things by the circumstance that Paetus is reproached in

he did recognise the whole extent of the danger, he hastened his march as much as possible ; Paetus, because he could not take the bold resolution to perish rather than to surrender, and thereby lost the chance of rescue that was near—in three days longer the 5000 men whom Corbulo was leading up would have brought the longed-for help. The conditions of the capitulation were free retreat for the Romans and evacuation of Armenia, with the delivering up of all fortresses occupied by them, and of all the stores that were in their hands, of which the Parthians were urgently in need. On the other hand Vologasus declared himself ready, in spite of this military success, to ask Armenia as a Roman fief for his brother from the imperial government, and on that account to send envoys to Nero.[1] The moderation of the victor may have rested on the fact that he had better information of Corbulo's approach than the enclosed army ; but more probably the sagacious man was not concerned to renew the disaster of Crassus and bring Roman eagles again to Ctesiphon. The defeat of a Roman army—he knew— was not the overpowering of Rome; and the real concession, which was involved in the recognition of Tiridates, was not too dearly purchased by the compliance as to form.

Conclusion of peace.

The Roman government once more declined the offer of the Parthian king and ordered the continuance of the war. It could not well do otherwise ; if the recognition of Tiridates was hazardous before the recommencement of war, and hardly capable of being accepted after the Parthian declaration of war, it now, as a consequence of the capitulation of Rhandeia, appeared directly as its

one breath with the inadequate pro- visioning of the camp (xv. 8) and with the surrender of it in spite of copious supplies (xv. 16), and the latter fact is inferred from this, that the retiring Romans preferred to de- stroy the stores which, according to the capitulation, were to be delivered to the Parthians. As the exaspera- tion against Tiberius found its ex- pression in the painting of Germani- cus in fine colours, so did the exas-

peration against Nero in the picture of Corbulo.

[1] The statement of Corbulo that Paetus bound himself on oath in presence of his soldiers and of the Parthian deputies to send no troops to Armenia till the arrival of Nero's answer, is declared by Tacitus, *Ann.* xv. 16, unworthy of credit ; it is in keeping with the state of the case, and nothing was done to the con- trary.

ratification. From Rome the resumption of the struggle against the Parthians was energetically promoted. Paetus was recalled ; Corbulo, in whom public opinion, aroused by the disgraceful capitulation, saw only the conqueror of Armenia, and whom even those who knew exactly and judged sharply the state of the matter could not avoid characterising as the ablest general and one uniquely fitted for this war, took up again the governorship of Cappadocia, and at the same time the command over all the troops available for this campaign, who were further reinforced by a seventh legion brought up from Pannonia ; accordingly all the governors and princes of the East were directed to comply in military matters with his orders, so that his official authority was nearly equivalent to that which had been assigned to the crown-princes Gaius and Germanicus for their missions to the East. If these measures were intended to bring about a serious reparation of the honour of the Roman arms they missed their aim. How Corbulo looked at the state of affairs, is shown by the very agreement which he made with the Parthian king not long after the disaster of Rhandeia ; the latter withdrew the Parthian garrisons from Armenia, the Romans evacuated the fortresses constructed on Mesopotamian territory for the protection of the bridges. For the Roman offensive the Parthian garrisons in Armenia were just as indifferent as the bridges of the Euphrates were important ; whereas, if Tiridates was to be recognised as a Roman vassal-king in Armenia, the latter certainly were superfluous and Parthian garrisons in Armenia impossible. In the next spring (63) Corbulo certainly entered upon the offensive enjoined upon him, and led the four best of his legions at Melitene over the Euphrates against the Partho-Armenian main force stationed in the region of Arsamosata. But not much came of the fighting ; only some castles of Armenian nobles opposed to Rome were destroyed. On the other hand, this encounter led also to agreement. Corbulo took up the Parthian proposals formerly rejected by his government, and that, as the further course of things showed, in the sense that Armenia became once for all a Parthian appanage for the second son, and the Roman government, at least according to the spirit of the agreement, consented to bestow this crown in future only on an Arsacid. It was only added that Tiridates should oblige himself to take from his head the royal diadem publicly before the eyes of the two armies in Rhandeia, just where the capitulation had been concluded, and to deposit it before the effigy of the emperor, promising not to put it on again until he should have received it from his hand, and that in Rome itself. This was done (63). By this humiliation there was no change in the fact that the Roman general, instead of waging the war intrusted to him, concluded peace on the terms rejected by his government.[1] But the statesmen who formerly took the lead had meanwhile died or retired, the personal government of the emperor was installed in their stead, and the solemn act in Rhandeia and the spectacle in prospect of the investiture of the Parthian prince with the crown of Armenia in the capital of the empire failed not to produce their effect on the public, and above all on the emperor in person. The peace was ratified and fulfilled. In the year 66 the Parthian prince appeared according to promise in Rome, escorted by 3000 Parthian horsemen, bringing as hostages the children of his three brothers as well as those of Monobazus of Adiabene. Falling on his knees he saluted his liege lord seated on the imperial throne in the market-place of the capital, and here the latter in presence of all the people bound the royal chaplet round his brow.

Tiridates in Rome.

The East under the Flavians.

The conduct on both sides, cautious, and we might

---

[1] As, according to Tacitus, *Ann.* xv. 25 (comp. Dio, lxii. 22), Nero dismissed graciously the envoys of Vologasus, and allowed them to see the possibility of an understanding if Tiridates appeared in person, Corbulo may in this case have acted according to his instructions; but this was rather perhaps one of the turns added in the interest of Corbulo. That these events were brought under discussion in the trial to which he was subjected some years after, is probable from the statement that one of the officers of the Armenian campaign became his accuser. The identity of the cohort-prefect, Arrius Varus, in Tacitus, *Ann.* xiii. 9, and of the primipilus, *Hist.* iii. 6, has been without reason disputed; comp. on *C. I. L.* v. 867.

almost say peaceful, of the last nominally ten years' war, and its corresponding conclusion by the actual transfer of Armenia to the Parthians, while the susceptibilities of the mightier western empire were spared, bore good fruit. Armenia, under the national dynasty recognised by the Romans, was more dependent on them than formerly under the rulers forced upon the country. A Roman garrison was left at least in the district of Sophene, which most closely bordered on the Euphrates.[1] For the re-establishment of Artaxata the permission of the emperor was sought and granted, and the building was helped on by the emperor Nero with money and workmen. Between the two mighty states separated from each other by the Euphrates at no time has an equally good relation subsisted as after the conclusion of the treaty of Rhandeia in the last years of Nero and onward under the three rulers of the Flavian house. Other circumstances contributed to this. The masses of Transcaucasian peoples, perhaps allured by their participation in the last wars, during which they had found their way to Armenia as mercenaries, partly of the Iberians, partly of the Parthians, began then to threaten especially the western Parthian provinces, but at the same time the eastern provinces of the Roman empire. Probably in order to check them, immediately after the Armenian war in the year 63, the annexation was ordained of the so-called kingdom of Pontus, *i.e.* the south-east corner of the coast of the Black Sea, with the town of Trapezus and the region of the Phasis. The great Oriental expedition, which this emperor was just on the point of beginning when the catastrophe overtook him (68), and for which he already had put the flower of the troops of the West on the march, partly to Egypt, partly along the Danube, was meant no doubt to push forward the imperial frontier in other directions;[2] but its proper aim was the passes of the

[1] In Ziata (Charput) there have been found two inscriptions of a fort, which one of the legions led by Corbulo over the Euphrates, the 3d Gallica, constructed there by Cor-bulo's orders in the year 64 (*Eph. epigr.* v. p. 25).

[2] Nero intended *inter reliqua bella,* an Ethiopian one (Plin. vi. 29, comp. 184). To this the sending

Caucasus above Tiflis, and the Scythian tribes settled on the northern slope, in the first instance the Alani.[1] These were just assailing Armenia on the one side and Media on the other. So little was that expedition of Nero directed against the Parthians that it might rather be conceived of as undertaken to help them ; overagainst the wild hordes of the north a common defensive action was at any rate indicated for the two civilised states of the West and East. Vologasus indeed declined with equal friendliness the amicable summons of his Roman colleague to visit him, just as his brother had done, at Rome, since he had no liking on his part to appear in the Roman forum as a vassal of the Roman ruler ; but he declared himself ready to present himself before the emperor when he should arrive in the East, and the Orientals doubtless, though not the Romans, sincerely mourned for Nero. King Vologasus addressed to the senate officially an entreaty to hold Nero's memory in honour, and, when a pseudo-Nero subsequently emerged, he met with sympathy above all in the Parthian state.

Arrangements of Vespasian.

Nevertheless the Parthian was not so much concerned about the friendship of Nero as about that of the Roman

of troops to Alexandria (Tacitus, *Hist.* i. 31, 70) had reference.

[1] As the aim of the expedition both Tacitus, *Hist.* i. 6, and Suetonius, *Ner.* 19, indicate the Caspian gates, *i.e.* the pass of the Caucasus between Tiflis and Vladi-Kavkas at Darial, which, according to the legend, Alexander closed with iron gates (Plin. *H. N.* vi. 11, 30 ; Josephus, *Bell. Jud.* vii. 7, 4 ; Procopius, *Pers.* i. 10). Both from this locality and from the whole scheme of the expedition it cannot possibly have been directed against the Albani on the western shore of the Caspian Sea ; here, as well as at another passage (*Ann.* ii. 68, *ad Armenios, inde Albanos Heniochosque*), only the Alani can be meant, who in Josephus, *l. c.* and elsewhere appear just at this spot and are frequently confounded with the Caucasian Albani. No doubt the

account of Josephus is also confused. If here the Albani, with consent of the king of the Hyrcanians, invade Media and then Armenia through the Caspian gates, the writer has been thinking of the other Caspian gate eastward from Rhagae ; but this must be his mistake, since the latter pass, situated in the heart of the Parthian kingdom, cannot possibly have been the aim of the Neronian expedition, and the Alani had their seats not on the eastern shore of the Caspian but to the north of the Caucasus. On account of this expedition the best of the Roman legions, the 14th, was recalled from Britain, although it went only as far as Pannonia (Tacitus, *Hist.* ii. 11, comp. 27, 66), and a new legion, the 1st Italic, was formed by Nero (Suetonius, *Ner.* 19). One sees from this what was the scale on which the project was conceived.

state. Not merely did he refrain from any encroachment during the crises of the four-emperor-year,[1] but correctly estimating the probable result of the pending decisive struggle, he offered to Vespasian, when still in Alexandria, 40,000 mounted archers for the conflict with Vitellius, which, of course, was gratefully declined. But above all he submitted without more ado to the arrangements which the new government made for the protection of the east frontier. Vespasian had himself as governor of Judaea become acquainted with the inadequacy of the military resources statedly employed there; and, when he exchanged this governorship for the imperial power, not only was Commagene again converted, after the precedent of Tiberius, from a kingdom into a province, but the number of the standing legions in Roman Asia was raised from four to seven, to which number they had been temporarily brought up for the Parthian and again for the Jewish war. While, further, there had been hitherto in Asia only a single larger military command, that of the governor of Syria, three such posts of high command were now instituted there. Syria, to which Commagene was added, retained as hitherto four legions; the two provinces hitherto occupied only by troops of the second order, Palestine and Cappadocia, were furnished, the first with one the second with two legions.[2] Armenia remained a Roman dependent principality in possession

---

[1] In what connection he refused to Vespasian the title of emperor (Dio, lxvi. 11) is not clear; possibly immediately after his insurrection, before he had perceived that the Flavians were the stronger. His intercession for the princes of Commagene (Josephus, *Bell. Jud.* vii. 7, 3) was attended by success, and so was purely personal, by no means a protest against the conversion of the kingdom into a province.

[2] The four Syrian legions were the 3d *Gallica*, the 6th *ferrata* (both hitherto in Syria), the 4th *Scythica* (hitherto in Moesia, but having already taken part in the Parthian as in the Jewish war), and the 16th *Flavia* (new). The one legion of Palestine was the 10th *fretensis* (hitherto in Syria). The two of Cappadocia were the 12th *fulminata* (hitherto in Syria, moved by Titus to Melitene, Josephus, *Bell. Jud.* vii. 1, 3), and the 15th *Apollinaris* (hitherto in Pannonia, but having taken part, like the 4th *Scythica*, in the Parthian as in the Jewish war). The garrisons were thus changed as little as possible, only two of the legions already called earlier to Syria received fixed stations there, and one newly instituted was moved thither.—After the Jewish war under Hadrian the 6th *ferrata* was despatched from Syria to Palestine.

of the Arsacids, but under Vespasian a Roman garrison was stationed beyond the Armenian frontier in the Iberian fortress Harmozika near Tiflis,[1] and accordingly at this time Armenia also must have been militarily in the Roman power. All these measures, however little they contained even a threat of war, were pointed against the eastern neighbour. Nevertheless Vologasus was after the fall of Jerusalem the first to offer to the Roman crown-prince his congratulations on the strengthening of the Roman rule in Syria, and he accepted without remonstrance the encampment of the legions in Commagene, Cappadocia, and Lesser Armenia. Nay, he even once more incited Vespasian to that Transcaucasian expedition, and besought the sending of a Roman army against the Alani under the leadership of one of the imperial princes ; although Vespasian did not enter into this far-seeing plan, that Roman force can hardly have been sent into the region of Tiflis for any other object than for closing the pass of the Caucasus, and in so far it represented there also the interests of the Parthians. In spite of the strengthening of the military position of Rome on the Euphrates, or even perhaps in consequence of it—for to instil respect into a neighbour is a means of preserving the peace—the state of peace remained essentially undisturbed during the whole rule of the Flavians. If— as cannot be surprising, especially when we consider the constant change of the Parthian dynasts—collisions now and then occurred, and war-clouds even made their appearance, they disappeared again as quickly.[2] The emergence of a pseudo-Nero in the last years of Vespasian—he it was who gave the impulse to the Revelation

---

[1] At this time (comp. *C. I. L.* v. 6988), probably falls also the Cappadocian governorship of C. Rutilius Gallicus, of which it is said (Statius, i. 4, 78) : *hunc . . . timuit . . . Armenia et patiens Latii iam pontis Araxes*, with reference presumably to a bridge-structure executed by this Roman garrison. That Gallicus served under Corbulo, is from the silence of Tacitus not probable.

[2] That war threatened to break out under Vespasian in the year 75 on the Euphrates, while M. Ulpius Trajanus, the father of the emperor, was governor of Syria, is stated by Pliny in his panegyric on the son, c. 14, probably with strong exaggeration ; the cause is unknown.

of John—might almost have led to such a collision. The pretender, in reality a certain Terentius Maximus from Asia Minor, but strikingly resembling the poet-emperor in face, voice, and address, found not merely a conflux of adherents in the Roman region of the Euphrates, but also support among the Parthians. Among these at that time, as so often, several rulers seem to have been in conflict with each other, and one of them, Artabanus, because the emperor Titus declared against him, seems to have adopted the cause of the Roman pretender. This, however, had no consequences ; on the contrary, soon afterwards the Parthian government delivered up the pretender to the emperor Domitian.[1] The commercial intercourse, advantageous for both parties between Syria and the lower Euphrates, where just then king Vologasus called into existence the new emporium Vologasias or Vologaso-certa, not far from Ctesiphon, must have contributed its part towards promoting the state of peace.

Things came to a conflict under Trajan. In the earlier years of his government he had made no essential change in eastern affairs, apart from the conversion of the two client-states hitherto subsisting on the border of the Syrian desert—the Nabataean of Petra and the Jewish of Caesarea Paneas—into administrative districts directly Roman (A.D. 106). The relations with the ruler of the Parthian kingdom at that time, king Pacorus, were not the most friendly,[2] but it was only under his brother

The Parthian war of Trajan.

---

[1] There are coins dated, and provided with the individual names of the kings, of (V)ologasus from the years 389 and 390 = 77 - 78 ; of Pacorus from the years 389 - 394 = 77 - 82 (and again 404 - 407 = 92-95) ; of Artabanus from the year 392 = 80-1. The corresponding historical dates are lost, with the exception of the notice connecting Titus and Artabanus in Zonaras, xi. 18 (comp. Suetonius, *Ner.* 57 ; Tacitus, *Hist.* i. 2), but the coins point to an epoch of rapid changes on the throne, and, apparently, of simultaneous coinage by rival pretenders.

[2] This is proved by the detached notice from Arrian in Suidas (*s. v.* ἐπίκλημα) : ὁ δὲ Πάκορος ὁ Παρθυαίων βασιλεὺς καὶ ἄλλα τινὰ ἐπικλήματα ἐπέφερε Τραιανῷ τῷ βασιλεῖ, and by the attention which is devoted in Pliny's report to the emperor, written about the year 112 (*ad Trai.* 74), to the relations between Pacorus and the Dacian king Decebalus. The time of the reign of this Parthian king cannot be sufficiently fixed. There are no Parthian coins with the king's name from the whole period of Trajan ; the coining of silver seems to have been in abeyance during that period.

and successor Chosroes that a rupture took place, and
that again concerning Armenia. The Parthians were to
blame for it. When Trajan bestowed the vacated throne
of the Armenian king on Axidares the son of Pacorus,
he kept within the limits of his right ; but king Chosroes
described this personage as incapable of governing, and
arbitrarily installed in his stead another son of Pacorus,
Parthomasiris, as king.[1] The answer to this was the
Roman declaration of war. Trajan left the capital towards the end of the year 114,[2] to put himself at the
head of the Roman troops of the East, which were certainly once more found in the deepest degeneracy, but
were reorganised in all haste by the emperor, and reinforced besides by better legions brought up from Pannonia.[3]

[1] That Axidares (or Exedares) was
a son of Pacorus and king of Armenia
before Parthomasiris, but had been
deposed by Chosroes, is shown by
the remnants of Dio's account, lxviii.
17 ; and to this point also the two
fragments of Arrian (16 Müller),
the first, probably from an address
of a supporter of the interests of
Axidares to Trajan : 'Αξιδάρην δὲ ὅτι
ἄρχειν χρὴ 'Αρμενίας, οὔ μοι δοκεῖ εἶναί
σε ἀμφίλογον, whereupon doubtless
the complaints brought against Parthomasiris followed ; and the answer,
evidently of the emperor, that it is
not the business of Axidares, but his,
to judge as to Parthomasiris, because
he—apparently Axidares—had first
broken the treaty and suffered for it.
What fault the emperor imputes to
Axidares is not clear ; but in Dio
also Chosroes says that he has not
satisfied either the Romans or the
Parthians.

[2] The remnants of Dio's account
in Xiphilinus and Zonaras show
clearly that the Parthian expedition
falls into two campaigns, the first
(Dio, lvi. 17, 1, 18, 2, 23-25),
which is fixed at 115 A.D. by the
consulate of Pedo (the date also of
Malalas, p. 275, for the earthquake
of Antioch, 13 Dec. 164 of the Antiochene era = 115 A.D. agrees therewith), and the second (Dio, c. 26-

32, 3), which is fixed at 116 A.D. by
the conferring of the title Parthicus
(c. 28, 2), took place between April
and August of that year (see my
notice in Droysen, Hellenismus, iii. 2,
361). That at c. 23 the titles Optimus (conferred in the course of
114 A.D.) and Parthicus are mentioned out of the order of time, is
shown as well by their juxtaposition
as by the later recurrence of the
second honour. Of the fragments
most belong to the first campaign ;
c. 22, 3 and probably also 22, 1, 2
to the second. —The acclamations
of imperator do not stand in the
way. Trajan was demonstrably in
the year 113 imp. VI. (C. I. L. vi.
960) ; in the year 114 imp. VII.
(C. I. L. ix. 1558 et al.) ; in the
year 115 imp. IX. (C. I. L. ix.
5894 et al.), and imp. XI. (Fabretti,
398, 289 et al.) ; in the year 116
imp. XII. (C. I. L. viii. 621, x.
1634), and XIII. (C. I. L. iii. D.
xxvii.). Dio attests an acclamation
from the year 115 (lxviii. 19), and
one from the year 116 (lxviii. 28) ;
there is ample room for both, and
there is no reason to refer imp. VII.
precisely, as has been attempted, to
the subjugation of Armenia.

[3] The pungent description of the
Syrian army of Trajan in Fronto
(p. 206 f. Naber) agrees almost

Envoys of the Parthian king met him at Athens ; but they had nothing to offer except the information that Parthomasiris was ready to accept Armenia as a Roman fief, and were dismissed.   The war began.   In the first conflicts on the Euphrates the Romans fared worst ;[1] but when the old emperor, ready to fight and accustomed to victory, placed himself at the head of the troops in the spring of 115, the Orientals submitted to him almost without resistance.   Moreover, among the Parthians civil war once more prevailed, and a pretender, Manisarus, had appeared against Chosroes.   From Antioch the emperor marched to the Euphrates and farther northward as far as the most northerly legion-camp Satala in Lesser Armenia, whence he advanced into Armenia and took the direction of Artaxata.   On the way Parthomasiris appeared in Elegeia and took the diadem from his head, in the hope of procuring investiture through this humiliation, as Tiridates had once done.   But Trajan was resolved to make this vassal-state a province, and to shift the eastern frontier of the empire generally.   This he declared to the Parthian prince before the assembled army, and directed him with his suite to quit at once the camp and the kingdom ; thereupon a tumult took place, in which the pretender lost

literally with that of the army of Corbulo in Tacitus, *Ann.* xiii. 35. "The Roman troops generally had sadly degenerated (*ad ignaviam redactus*) through being long disused to military service ; but the most wretched of the soldiers were the Syrian, insubordinate, refractory, unpunctual at the call to arms, not to be found at their post, drunk from midday onward ; unaccustomed even to carry arms and incapable of fatigue, ridding themselves of one piece of armour after another, half naked like the light troops and the archers. Besides they were so demoralised by the defeats they had suffered that they turned their backs at the first sight of the Parthians, and the trumpets were regarded by them, as it were, as giving the signal to run away." In the contrasting description of Trajan it is said among other things : "He did not pass through the tents without closely concerning himself as to the soldiers, but showed his contempt for the Syrian luxury, and looked closely into the rough doings of the Pannonians (*sed contemnere*—so we must read—*Syrorum munditias, introspicere Pannoniorum inscitias*) ; so judged of the serviceableness (*ingenium*) of the man according to his bearing (*cultus*)." In the Oriental army of Severus also the "European" and the Syrian soldiers are distinguished (Dio, lxxv. 12).

[1] This is shown by the *mala proelia* in the passage of Fronto quoted, and by Dio's statement, lxviii. 19, that Trajan took Samosata without a struggle ; thus the 16th legion stationed there had lost it.

his life.   Armenia yielded to its fate, and became a Roman governorship.   The princes also of the Caucasian tribes, the Albani, the Iberi, farther on toward the Black Sea the Apsilae, the Colchi, the Heniochi, the Lazi, and various others, even those of the trans-Caucasian Sarmatae were confirmed in the relation of vassalage, or now subjected to it.   Trajan thereupon advanced into the territory of the Parthians and occupied Mesopotamia.   Here, too, all submitted without a blow ; Batnae, Nisibis, Singara came into the power of the Romans ; in Edessa the emperor received not merely the subjection of Abgarus, the ruler of the land, but also that of the other dynasts, and, like Armenia, Mesopotamia became a Roman province.   Trajan took up once more his winter quarters in Antioch, where a violent earthquake demanded more victims than the campaign of the summer.   In the next spring (116) Trajan, the " victor of the Parthians," as the senate now saluted him, advanced from Nisibis over the Tigris, and occupied, not without encountering resistance at the crossing and subsequently, the district of Adiabene; this became the third new Roman province, named Assyria.   The march went onward down the Tigris to Babylonia ; Seleucia and Ctesiphon fell into the hands of the Romans, and with them the golden throne of the king and his daughter ; Trajan reached even the Persian satrapy of Mesene, and the great mercantile town at the mouth of the Tigris, Charax Spasinu.   This region also seems to have been incorporated with the empire in such a way that the new province Mesopotamia embraced the whole region enclosed by the two rivers.

Revolt of
Seleucia,
and its
siege.

Full of longing, Trajan is said now to have wished for himself the youth of Alexander, in order to carry from the margin of the Persian Sea his arms into the Indian land of marvels.   But he soon learned that he needed them for nearer opponents.   The great Parthian empire had hitherto scarcely confronted in earnest his attack, and ofttimes sued in vain for peace.   But now on the way back at Babylon news reached the emperor of the revolt of Babylonia and Mesopotamia ; while he tarried at the mouth of the Tigris the whole population of these new provinces had risen against him ;[1] the citizens of Seleucia on the Tigris, of Nisibis, indeed of Edessa itself, put the Roman garrisons to death or chased them away and closed their gates.   The emperor saw himself compelled to divide his troops, and to send separate corps against the different seats of the insurrection ; one of these legions under Maximus was, with its general, surrounded and cut to pieces in Mesopotamia.   Yet the emperor mastered the insurgents, particularly through his general Lusius Quietus, already experienced in the Dacian war, a native sheikh of the Moors.   Seleucia and Edessa were besieged and burnt down.   Trajan went so far as to declare Parthia a Roman vassal-state, and invested with it at Ctesiphon a partisan of Rome, the Parthian Parthamaspates, although the Roman soldiers had not set foot on more than the western border of the great-kingdom.

Then he began his return to Syria by the route along which he had come, detained on the way by a vain attack on the Arabs in Hatra, the residence of the king of the brave tribes of the Mesopotamian desert, whose mighty works of fortification and magnificent buildings are still at the present day imposing in their ruins.   He intended to continue the war next year, and so to make the subjection of the Parthians a reality.   But the combat in the desert of Hatra, in which the sixty-year-old emperor had bravely fought with the Arab horsemen, was to be his last.   He sickened and died on the journey home (8th Aug. 117), without being able to complete his victory and to hold

Death of Trajan.

---

[1] It may be that at the same time Armenia also revolted.   But when Gutschmid (quoted by Dierauer in Büdinger's *Untersuchungen*, i. 179), makes Meherdotes and Sanatrukios, whom Malalas adduces as kings of Persia in the Trajanic war, into kings of Armenia again in revolt, this result is attained by a series of daring conjectures, which shift the names of persons and peoples as much as they transform the causal nexus of events. There are certainly found in the con- fused coil of legends of Malalas some historical facts, *e.g.* the installation of Parthamaspates (who is here son of king Chosroes of Armenia) as king of Parthia by Trajan ; and so, too, the dates of Trajan's departure from Rome in October (114), of his landing in Seleucia in December, and of his entrance into Antioch on the 7th Jan. (115) may be correct.   But, as this report stands, the historian can only decline to accept it ; he cannot rectify it.

the celebration of it in Rome ; it was in keeping with his spirit that even after death the honour of a triumph was accorded to him, and hence he is the only one of the deified Roman emperors who even as god still bears the title of victory.

Trajan's Oriental policy. Trajan had not sought war with the Parthians, but it had been forced upon him ; not he, but Chosroes had broken the agreement as to Armenia, which during the last forty years had been the basis of the state of peace in the region of the Euphrates. If it is intelligible that the Parthians did not acquiesce in it, since the continuing suzerainty of the Romans over Armenia carried in itself the stimulus to revolt, we must on the other hand acknowledge that in the way hitherto followed further steps could not be taken than were taken by Corbulo ; the unconditional renunciation of Armenia, and—which was the necessary consequence of it — the recognition of the Parthian state on a footing of full equality, lay indeed beyond the horizon of Roman policy as much as the abolition of slavery and similar ideas that could not be thought of at that time. But if permanent peace could not be attained by this alternative, there was left in the great dilemma of Roman Oriental policy only the other course—the extension of direct Roman rule to the left bank of the Euphrates. Therefore Armenia now became a Roman province, and no less Mesopotamia. This was only in keeping with the nature of the case. The conversion of Armenia from a Roman vassal-state with a Roman garrison into a Roman governorship made not much change externally ; the Parthians could only be effectively ejected from Armenia when they lost possession of the neighbouring region ; and above all, the Roman rule as well as the Roman provincial constitution found a far more favourable soil in the half-Greek Mesopotamia than in the thoroughly Oriental Armenia. Other considerations fell to be added. The Roman customs-frontier in Syria was badly constituted, and to get the international traffic from the great commercial marts of Syria towards the Euphrates and the Tigris entirely into its power was an essential gain to the Roman state, as indeed Trajan immediately set to work to institute the new customs-dues at the Euphrates and Tigris.[1]   Even in a military point of view the boundary of the Tigris was easier of defence than the previous frontier-line which ran along the Syrian desert and thence along the Euphrates.   The conversion of the region of Adiabene beyond the Tigris into a Roman province, whereby Armenia became an inland one, and the transformation of the Parthian empire itself into a Roman vassal-state were corollaries of the same idea.   It is not meant to be denied that in a policy of conquest consistency is a dangerous praise, and that Trajan after his fashion yielded in these enterprises more than was reasonable to the effort after external success, and went beyond the rational goal ;[2] but wrong is done to him when his demeanour in the East is referred to blind lust of conquest.   He did what Caesar would have done had he lived.   His policy is but the other side of that of Nero's statesmen, and the two are as opposite, as they are equally consistent and equally warranted.   Posterity has justified more the policy of conquest than that of concession.

For the moment no doubt it was otherwise.   The Oriental conquests of Trajan lit up the gloomy evening of the Roman empire like flashes of lightning in the darkness of the night ; but, like these, they brought no new morning.   His successor found himself compelled to choose between completing the unfinished work of subduing the Parthians or allowing it to drop.   The extension of the frontier could not be carried out at all without a considerable increase of the army and of the budget ; and the shifting of the centre of gravity to the East, thereby rendered inevitable, was a dubious strengthening of the empire.   Hadrian and Pius therefore returned entirely

Reaction under Hadrian and Pius.

[1] Fronto, *Princ. hist.* p. 209 Naber : *cum praesens Traianus Euphratis et Tigridis portoria equorum et camelorum trib[utaque ordinaret, Ma]cer* (?) *caesus est.* This applies to the moment when Babylonia and Mesopotamia revolted, while Trajan was tarrying at the mouth of the Tigris.

[2] Nearly with equal warrant, Julian (*Caes.* p. 328) makes the emperor say that he had not taken up arms against the Parthians before they had violated right, and Dio (lxviii. 17) reproaches him with having waged the war from ambition.

into the paths of the earlier imperial period. Hadrian allowed the Roman vassal-king of Parthia, Parthamaspates, to drop, and portioned him off in another way. He evacuated Assyria and Mesopotamia, and voluntarily gave back these provinces to their earlier ruler. He sent to him as well his captive daughter ; the permanent token of the victory won, the golden throne of Ctesiphon, even the pacific Pius refused to deliver up again to the Parthians. Hadrian as well as Pius earnestly endeavoured to live in peace and friendship with their neighbour, and at no time do the commercial relations between the Roman entrepôts on the Syrian east frontier and the mercantile towns on the Euphrates seem to have been more lively than at this epoch.

Armenia a vassal-state.

Armenia ceased likewise to be a Roman province, and returned to its former position as a Roman vassal-state and a Parthian appanage of the second son.[1] The princes of the Albani, and the Iberians on the Caucasus, and the numerous small dynasts in the south-eastern corner of the Black Sea likewise remained dependent.[2]

[1] Hadrian cannot possibly have released Armenia from the position of a Roman dependency. The notice of his biographer, c. 21 : *Armeniis regem habere permisit, cum sub Traiano legatum habuissent* points rather to the contrary, and we find at the end of Hadrian's reign a contingent of Armenians in the army of the governor of Cappadocia (Arrian. *c. Alan.* 29). Pius did not merely induce the Parthians by his representations to desist from the intended invasion of Armenia (*vita*, 9), but also in fact invested them with Armenia (coins from the years 140-144, Eckhel, vii. p. 15). The fact also that Iberia certainly stood in the relation of dependence under Pius, because otherwise the Parthians could not have brought complaints as to its king in Rome (Dio, lxix. 15), presupposes a like dependent relation for Armenia. The names of the Armenian kings of this period are not known. If the *proximae gentes*, with the rule of

which Hadrian compensated the Parthian prince nominated as Parthian king by Trajan (*vita*, c. 5), were in fact Armenians, which is not improbable, there lies in it a confirmation as well of the lasting dependence of Armenia on Rome as of the continuous rule of the Arsacids there. Even the Ἀυρήλιος Πάκορος βασιλεὺς μεγάλης Ἀρμενίας, who erected a monument in Rome to his brother Aurelius Merithates who died there (*C. I. Gr.* 6559), belongs from his name to the house of the Arsacids. But he was hardly the king of Armenia installed by Vologasus IV. and deposed by the Romans (p. 74) ; if the latter had come to Rome as a captive, we should know it, and even he would hardly have been allowed to call himself king of Great Armenia in a Roman inscription.

[2] As vassals holding from Trajan or Hadrian, Arrian (*Peripl.* c. 15) adduces the Heniochi and Machelones (comp. Dio, lxviii. 18 ; lxxi. 14); the Lazi (comp. Suidas, *s. v.* Δομετιανός),

Roman garrisons were stationed not merely on the coast in Apsarus[1] and on the Phasis, but, as can be shown, under Commodus in Armenia itself, not far from Artaxata ; in a military point of view all these states belonged to the district of the commandant of Cappadocia.[2] This supremacy, however, very indefinite in its nature, seems to have been dealt with generally, and in particular by Hadrian,[3] in such a way that it appeared more as a right of protection than as subjection proper, and at least the more powerful of these princes did, and left undone, in the main what pleased them. The common interest—which we have formerly brought out—in warding off the wild trans-Caucasian tribes became still more definitely prominent in this epoch, and evidently served as a bond in particular between Romans and Parthians. Towards the end of the reign of Hadrian the Alani, in agreement apparently with the king of Iberia, at that time Pharasmanes II., on whom it primarily devolved to bar the pass of the Caucasus against them, invaded the southern regions, and pillaged not only the territory of the Albanians and Armenians, but also the Parthian province of Media and the Roman province of Cappadocia, though matters did not come to a waging of war in common, but the gold of the ruler then reigning in Parthia, Vologasus III., and the mobilising of the Cappadocian army on the part of the Romans,[4]

over whom also Pius put a king (*vita*, 9) ; the Apsilae ; the Abasgi ; the Sanigae, these all within the imperial frontier reaching as far as Dioscurias = Sebastopolis ; beyond it, in the region of the Bosporan vassal-state, the Zichi or Zinchi (*ib.* c. 27).

[1] This is confirmed not only by Arrian, *Peripl.* c. 7, but by the officer of Hadrian's time *praepositus numerorum tendentium in Ponto Absaro* (*C. I. L.* x. 1202).

[2] Comp. p. 75 note 2. The detachment probably of 1000 men (because under a tribune) doing garrison duty in the year 185 in Valarshapat (Etshmiazin) not far from Artaxata, belonged to one of the Cappadocian legions (*C. I. L.* iii. 6052).

[3] Hadrian's efforts after the friendship of the Oriental vassal-princes are often brought into prominence, not without a hint that he was more than fairly indulgent to them (*vita*, c. 13, 17, 21). Pharasmanes of Iberia did not come to Rome on his invitation, but complied with that of Pius (*vita Hadr.* 13, 21 ; *vita Pii*, 9 ; Dio, lxix. 15, 2, which excerpt belongs to Pius).

[4] We still possess the remarkable report of the governor of Cappadocia under Hadrian, Flavius Arrianus, upon the mobilising of the Cappadocian army against the "Scythians" among his minor writings ; he was himself at the Caucasus and visited the passes there (Lydus, *de Mag.* iii. 53).

induced the barbarians to return, yet their interests coincided, and the complaint which the Parthians lodged in Rome as to Pharasmanes of Iberia, shows the concert of the two great powers.[1]

The disturbances of the *status quo* came again from the Parthian side. The suzerainty of the Romans over Armenia played a part in history similar to that of the German empire over Italy ; unsubstantial as it was, it was yet constantly felt as an encroachment, and carried within it the danger of war. Already under Hadrian the conflict was imminent ; the emperor succeeded in keeping the peace by a personal interview with the Parthian prince. Under Pius the Parthian invasion of Armenia seemed once more impending ; his earnest dissuasive was in the first instance successful. But even this most pacific of all emperors, who had it more at heart to save the life of a burgess than to kill a thousand foes, was obliged in the last period of his reign to prepare himself for the attack and to reinforce the armies of the East. Hardly had he closed his eyes (161), when the long-threatening thundercloud discharged itself. By command of Vologasus IV. the Persian general Chosroes[2] advanced into Armenia, and placed the Arsacid prince Pacorus on the throne. The governor of Cappadocia Severianus did what was his duty, and led on his part the Roman troops over the Euphrates. At Elegeia, just where a generation before the king Parthomasiris, likewise placed by the Parthians on the Armenian throne, had humbled himself in vain before Trajan, the armies encountered each other ; the Roman was not merely beaten but annihilated in a three days' conflict ; the unfortunate general put himself to death, as Varus had formerly done. The victorious Orientals were not content with the occupation of Armenia, but crossed

---

[1] This we learn from the fragments of Dio's account in Xiphilinus, Zonaras, and in the Excerpts ; Zonaras has preserved the correct reading ᾿Αλανοί instead of ᾿Αλβανοί ; that the Alani pillaged also the territory of the Albani, is shown by the setting of the exc. Ursin. lxxii.

[2] So he is named in Lucian, *Hist. conscr.* 21 ; if the same calls him (*Alex.* 27) Othryades, he is drawing here from a historian of the stamp of those whom he ridicules in that treatise, and of whom another Hellenised the same man as Oxyroes (*Hist. conscr.* c. 18).

the Euphrates and invaded Syria ; the army stationed there was also defeated, and there were fears as to the fidelity of the Syrians. The Roman government had no choice. As the troops of the East showed on this occasion their small capacity for fighting, and were besides weakened and demoralised by the defeat which they had suffered, further legions were despatched to the East from the West, even from the Rhine, and levies were ordered in Italy itself. Lucius Verus, one of the two emperors who shortly before had come to govern, went in person to the East (162) to take up the chief command, and if he, neither warlike nor yet even faithful to his duty, showed himself unequal to the task, and of his deeds in the East hardly anything else is to be told than that he married his niece there and was ridiculed for his theatrical enthusiasm even by the Antiochenes, the governors of Cappadocia and Syria—in the former case first Statius Priscus, then Martius Verus, in the latter Avidius Cassius,[1] the best generals of this epoch—managed the cause of Rome better than the wearer of the crown. Once more, before the armies met, the Romans offered peace ; willingly would Marcus have avoided the severe war. But Vologasus abruptly rejected the reasonable proposals ; and this time the pacific neighbour was also the stronger. Armenia was immediately recovered ; already, in the year 163, Priscus took the capital Artaxata, and destroyed it. Not far from it the new capital of the country, Kainepolis, in Armenia Nor-Khalakh or Valarshapat (Etshmiazin) was built by the Romans and provided with a strong garrison.[2]   In the succeeding year instead of Pacorus

[1] Syria was administered when the war broke out by L. Attidius Cornelianus (*C. I. Gr.* 4661 of the year 160 ; *vita Marci*, 8 ; *C. I. L.* iii. 129 of the year 162), after him by Julius Verus (*C. I. L.* iii. 199, probably of the year 163) and then by Avidius Cassius presumably from the year 164. The statement that the other provinces of the East were assigned to Cassius's command (Philostratus, *vit. Soph.* i. 13 ; Dio, lxxi.

3), similarly to what was done to Corbulo as legate of Cappadocia, can only relate to the time after the departure of the emperor Verus ; so long as the latter held the nominal chief command there was no room for it.

[2] A fragment probably of Dio (in Suidas *s. v.* Μάρτιος), tells that Priscus in Armenia laid out the Καινὴ πόλις and furnished it with a Roman garrison, his successor Martius Verus

Sohaemus, by descent also an Arsacid, but a Roman subject and Roman senator, was nominated as king of Great Armenia.[1]   In a legal point of view nothing was changed in Armenia ; yet the bonds which joined it to Rome were drawn tighter.

Conflicts in Syria and Mesopotamia.

The conflicts in Syria and Mesopotamia were more serious.   The line of the Euphrates was obstinately defended by the Parthians ; after a keen combat on the right bank at Sura the fortress of Nicephorium (Ragga) on the left was stormed by the Romans.   Still more vehemently was the passage at Zeugma contested; but here too victory remained with the Romans in the decisive battle at Europus (Djerabis to the south of Biredjik).   They now advanced on their part into Mesopotamia.   Edessa was besieged, Dausara not far from it stormed ; the Romans appeared before Nisibis ; the Parthian general saved himself by swimming over the Tigris.   The Romans might from Mesopotamia undertake the march to Babylon. The satraps forsook in part the banners of the defeated

silenced the national movement that had arisen there, and declared this city the first of Armenia.   This was Valarshapat (Οὐαλαρσαπάτ or Οὐαλερ- οκτίστη in Agathangelos) thenceforth the capital of Armenia.   Καινή πόλις was, as Kiepert informs me, already recognised by Stilting as translation of the Armenian Nôr-Khalakh, which second name Valarshapat constantly bears in Armenian authors of the fifth century alongside of the usual one. Moses of Chorene, following Barde- sanes, makes the town originate from a Jewish colony brought thither under king Tigranes VI., who according to him reigned 150-188 ; he refers the enclosing of it with walls and the naming of it to his son Valarsch II. 188-208.   That the town had a strong Roman garrison in 185 is shown by the inscription *C. I. L.* iii. 6052.

[1] That Sohaemus was Achaemenid and Arsacid (or professed to be) and king's son and king, as well as Roman senator and consul, before he became

king of Great Armenia, is stated by his contemporary Jamblichus (c. 10 of the extract in Photius).   Probably he belonged to the dynastic family of Hemesa (Josephus, *Arch.* xx. 8, 4, *et al.*)   If Jamblichus the Babylonian wrote " under him," this can doubt- less only be understood to the effect that he composed his romance in Artaxata.   That Sohaemus ruled over Armenia before Pacorus is nowhere stated, and is not probable, since neither Fronto's words (p. 127 Naber), *quod Sohaemo potius quam Vologaeso regnum Armeniae dedisset aut quod Pacorum regno privasset*, or those of the fragment from Dio (?) lxxi. 1 : Μάρτιος Οὐῆρος τὸν Θουκυδίδην ἐκ- πέμπει καταγαγεῖν Σόαιμον ἐς Ἀρμενίαν point to reinstatement, and the coins with *rex Armeniis datus* (Eckhel, vii. 91, comp. *vita Veri*, 7, 8) in fact exclude it.   We do not know the predecessor of Pacorus, and are not even aware whether the throne which he took possession of was vacant or occupied.

great-king; Seleucia, the great capital of the Hellenes on the Euphrates, voluntarily opened its gates to the Romans, but was afterwards burnt down by them, because the burgesses were rightly or wrongly accused of an understanding with the enemy. The Parthian capital, Ctesiphon, was also taken and destroyed; with good reason at the beginning of the year 165 the senate could salute the two rulers as the Parthian grand-victors. In the campaign of this year Cassius even penetrated into Media; but the outbreak of a pestilence, more especially in these regions, decimated the troops and compelled them to return, accelerating perhaps even the conclusion of peace. The result of the war was the cession of the western district of Mesopotamia; the princes of Edessa and of Osrhoene became vassals of Rome, and the town of Carrhae, which had for long Greek leanings, became a free town under Roman protection.[1] As regards extent, especially in presence of the complete success of the war, the increase of territory was moderate, but yet of importance, inasmuch as thereby the Romans gained a footing on the left bank of the Euphrates. We may add that the territories occupied were given back to the Parthians and the *status quo* was restored. On the whole, therefore, the policy of reserve adopted by Hadrian was now abandoned once more, and there was a return to the course of Trajan. This is the more remarkable, as the government of Marcus certainly cannot be reproached with ambition and longing after aggrandisement; what it did it did under compulsion and in modest limits.

The emperor Severus pursued the same course further and more decidedly. The year of the three emperors, 193, had led to the war between the legions of the West and those of the East, and with Pescennius Niger the latter had succumbed. The Roman vassal-princes of the East, and as well the ruler of the Parthians, Vologasus V., son of Sanatrucius, had, as was natural, recognised Niger, and even put their troops at his disposal; the latter

Parthian wars under Severus.

---

[1] This is shown by the Mesopotamian royal and urban coins. There are no accounts in our tradition as to the conditions of peace.

had at first gratefully declined, and then, when his cause took a turn to the worse, invoked their aid. The other Roman vassals, above all the prince of Armenia, cautiously kept back ; only Abgarus, the prince of Edessa, sent the desired contingent. The Parthians promised aid, and it came at least from the nearest districts, from the prince Barsemias of Hatra in the Mesopotamian desert, and from the satrap of the Adiabeni beyond the Tigris. Even after Niger's death (194) these strangers not merely remained in the Roman Mesopotamia, but even demanded the withdrawal of the Roman garrisons stationed there and the giving back of this territory.[1]

Province of Meso-potamia.

Thereupon Severus advanced into Mesopotamia and took possession of the whole extensive and important region. From Nisibis an expedition was conducted against the Arab prince of Hatra, which, however, did not succeed in taking the fortified town ; even beyond the Tigris against the satrap of Adiabene the generals of Severus accomplished nothing of importance.[2] But Mesopotamia,

---

[1] The beginning of the Ursinian excerpt of Dio, lxxv. 1, 2, is confused. Οἱ Ὀρροηνοί, it is said, καὶ οἱ Ἀδιαβηνοὶ ἀποστάντες καὶ Νίσιβιν πολιορκοῦντες καὶ ἡττηθέντες ὑπὸ Σεουήρου ἐπρεσβεύσαντο πρὸς αὐτὸν μετὰ τὸν τοῦ Νίγρου θάνατον. Osrhoene was then Roman, Adiabene Parthian ; from whom did the two districts revolt ? and whose side did the Nisibenes take ? That their opponents were defeated by Severus before the sending of the embassy is inconsistent with the course of the narrative ; for the latter makes war upon them because their envoys make unsatisfactory offers to him. Probably the supporting of Niger by subjects of the Parthians and their concert with Niger's Roman partisan are now strictly apprehended as a revolt from Severus ; the circumstance that the people afterwards maintain that they had intended rather to support Severus, is clearly indicated as a makeshift. The Nisibenes may have refused to co-operate, and therefore have been attacked by the adherents of Niger. Thus is explained what is clear from the extract given by Xiphilinus from Dio, lxxv. 2, that the left bank of the Euphrates was for Severus an enemy's land, but not Nisibis ; therefore the town need not have been Roman at that time ; on the contrary, according to all indications, it was only made Roman by Severus.

[2] As the wars against the Arabians and the Adiabenians were in fact directed against the Parthians, it was natural that the titles *Parthicus, Arabicus,* and *Parthicus Adiabenicus,* should on that account be conferred on the emperor ; they are also so found, but usually Parthicus is omitted, evidently because, as the biographer of Severus says (c. 9), *excusavit Parthicum nomen, ne Parthos lacesseret.* With this agrees the notice certainly belonging to the year 195 in Dio, lxxv. 9, 6, as to the peaceful agreement with the Parthians and the cession of a portion of Armenia to them.

i.e. the whole region between the Euphrates and Tigris
as far as the Chaboras, became a Roman province, and
was occupied with two legions newly created on account
of this extension of territory.   The principality of Edessa
continued to subsist as a Roman fief, but was now no
longer border-territory but surrounded by land directly
imperial.   The considerable and strong city of Nisibis,
thenceforth called after the name of the emperor and
organised as a Roman colony, became the capital of the new
province and seat of the governor.   After an important
portion of territory had thus been torn from the Parthian
kingdom, and armed force had been used against two
satraps dependent on it, the great-king made ready with
his troops to oppose the Romans.   Severus offered peace,
and ceded for Mesopotamia a portion of Armenia.   But
the decision of arms was thereby only postponed.   As
soon as Severus had started for the West, whither the
complication with his co-ruler in Gaul recalled him, the
Parthians broke the peace[1] and advanced into Mesopotamia ; the prince of Osrhoene was driven out, the
land was occupied, and the governor, Laetus, one of the
most excellent warriors of the time, was besieged in
Nisibis.   He was in great danger, when Severus once
more arrived in the East in the year 198, after Albinus
had succumbed.   Thereupon the fortune of war turned.
The Parthians retreated, and now Severus took the
offensive.   He advanced into Babylonia, and won
Seleucia and Ctesiphon ; the Parthian king saved himself
with a few horsemen by flight, the crown-treasure became
the spoil of the victors, the Parthian capital was abandoned
to the pillage of the Roman soldiers, and more than
100,000 captives were brought to the Roman slave
market.   The Arabians indeed in Hatra defended themselves better than the Parthian state itself ; in vain
Severus endeavoured in two severe sieges to reduce the
desert-stronghold.   But in the main the success of the
two campaigns of 198 and 199 was complete.   By the

---

[1] That Armenia also fell into their power is indicated by Herodian, v. 9, 2 ; no doubt his representation is warped and defective.

erection of the province of Mesopotamia and of the great command there, Armenia lost the intermediate position which it hitherto had; it might remain in its previous relations and apart from formal incorporation. The land retained thus its own troops, and the imperial government even paid for these subsequently a contribution from the imperial chest.[1]

The change of government in the West and in the East.

The further development of these relations as neighbours was essentially influenced by the changes which internal order underwent in the two empires. If under the dynasty of Nerva, and not less under Severus, the Parthian state, often torn asunder by civil war and contention for the crown, had been confronted by the relatively stable Roman monarchy as superior, this order of things broke down after Severus's death, and almost for a century there followed in the western empire mostly wretched and thoroughly ephemeral regents, who in presence of other countries were constantly hesitating between arrogance and weakness. While the scale of the West thus sank that of the East rose. A few years after the death of Severus (211) a revolution took place in Iran, which not merely, like so many earlier crises, overthrew the ruling regent, nor even merely called to the government another dynasty instead of the decayed Arsacids, but, unchaining the national and religious elements for a mightier upward flight, substituted for the bastard civilisation—pervaded by Hellenism—of the Parthian state the state-organisation, faith, manners, and princes of that province which had created the old Persian empire, and, since its transition to the Parthian

---

[1] When at the peace in 218 the old relation between Rome and Armenia was renewed, the king of Armenia gave himself the prospect of a renewal of the Roman annual moneys (Dio, lxxviii. 27 : τοῦ Τιριδάτου τὸ ἀργύριον ὃ κατ᾽ ἔτος παρὰ τῶν ᾽Ρωμαίων εὑρίσκετο ἐλπίσαντος λήψεσθαι). Payment of tribute proper by the Romans to the Armenians is excluded for the period of Severus and the time before Severus, and by no means agrees with the words of Dio ; the connection must be what we have indicated. In the fourth and fifth centuries the fortress of Biriparach in the Caucasus, which barred the Dariel pass, was maintained by the Persians, who played the part of masters here after the peace of 364, with a Roman contribution, and this was likewise conceived as payment of tribute (Lydus, *de Mag.* iii. 52, 53 ; Priscus, *fr.* 31, Müll.).

dynasty, preserved within it as well the tombs of Darius and Xerxes as the germs of the regeneration of the people. The re-establishment of the great-kingdom of the Persians overthrown by Alexander ensued through the emergence of the dynasty of the Sassanids. Let us cast a glance at this new shape of things before we pursue further the course of Romano-Parthian relations in the East.

It has already been stated that the Parthian dynasty, although it had wrested Iran from Hellenism, was yet regarded by the nation as, so to speak, illegitimate. Artahshatr, or in new Persian Ardashir—so the official biography of the Sassanids reports—came forward to revenge the blood of Dara murdered by Alexander, and to bring back the rule to the legitimate family and re-establish it, such as it had been at the time of his forefathers before the divisional kings. Under this legend lies a good deal of reality. The dynasty which bears the name of Sasan, the grandfather of Ardashir, was no other than the royal dynasty of the Persian province; Ardashir's father, Papak or Pabek,[1] and a long list of his ancestors had, under the supremacy of the Arsacids, swayed the sceptre in this ancestral land of the Iranian nation,[2] had resided in Istachr, not far from the old Persepolis, and marked their coins with Iranian language and Iranian writing, and with the sacred emblems of the Persian national faith, while the great-kings had their abode in the half-Greek border-land, and had their coins stamped in the Greek language and after the Greek style. The fundamental organisation of the Iranian state-system—the great-kingdom holding

The Sassanids.

---

[1] Artaxares names his father Papacus in the inscription, quoted at p. 83, note 1, king; how it is to be reconciled with this, that not merely does the native legend (in Agathias ii. 27) make Pabek a shoemaker, but also the contemporary Dio (if in reality Zonaras, xii. 15, has borrowed these words from him) names Artaxares ἐξ ἀφανῶν καὶ ἀδόξων, we do

not know. Naturally the Roman authors take the side of the weak legitimate Arsacid against the dangerous usurper.

[2] Strabo (under Tiberius) xv. 3, 24: νῦν δ'ἤδη καθ' αὑτοὺς συνεστῶτες οἱ Πέρσαι βασιλέας ἔχουσιν ὑπηκόους ἑτέροις βασιλεῦσι, πρότερον μὲν Μακεδόσι, νῦν δὲ Παρθναίοις.

superiority over the divisional kings—was under the two dynasties as little different as that of the empire of the German nation under the Saxon and the Suabian emperors. Only for this reason in that official version the time of the Arsacids is designated as that of the divisional-kings, and Ardashir as the first common head of all Iran after the last Darius, because in the old Persian empire the Persian province stood related alike to the other provinces and to the Parthians, as in the Roman state Italy stood related to the provinces, and the Persian disputed with the Parthian the legitimate title to the great-kingdom connected *de jure* with his province.[1]

Extent of the Sassanid kingdom.

What was the relation of the Sassanid kingdom to that of the Arsacids in point of extent, is a question to which tradition gives no sufficient answer. The provinces of the west collectively remained subject to the new dynasty after it sat firm in the saddle, and the claims which it set up against the Romans went, as we shall see, far beyond the pretensions of the Arsacids. But how far the rule of the Sassanids reached towards the West, and when it advanced to the Oxus which was subsequently regarded as the legitimate boundary between Iran and Turan, are matters withdrawn from our field of vision.[2]

[1] When Nöldeke says (*Tabari*, p. 449), "The subjection of the chief lands of the monarchy directly to the crown formed the chief distinction of the Sassanid kingdom from the Arsacid, which had real kings in its various provinces," the power of the great - kingdom beyond doubt is thoroughly dependent on the personality of the possessor, and under the first Sassanids must have been much stronger than under the last decayed Arsacids. But a contrast in principle is not discoverable. From Mithradates I., the proper founder of the dynasty, onward the Arsacid ruler names himself "king of kings," just as did subsequently the Sassanid, while Alexander the Great and the Seleucids never bore this title. Even under them individual vassal - kings ruled, *e.g.* in Persis (p. 81, note 2);

but the vassal-kingdom was not then the regular form of imperial administration, and the Greek rulers did not name themselves according to it, any more than the Caesars assumed the title of great - king on account of Cappadocia or Numidia. The satraps of the Arsacid state were essentially the Marzbans of the Sassanids. Perhaps rather the great imperial offices, which in the Sassanid polity correspond to the supreme administrative posts of the Diocletiano-Constantinian constitution, and probably were the model for the latter, were wanting to the Arsacid state; then certainly the two would be related to each other much as the imperial organisation of Augustus to that of Constantine. But we know too little of the Arsacid organisation to affirm this with certainty.

[2] According to the Persian records

The state-system of Iran did not undergo quite a The state of the Sassanids. fundamental transformation in consequence of the coming in of the new dynasty. The official title of the first Sassanid ruler, as it is given uniformly in three languages under the rock-relief of Nakshi-Rustam, "The Mazda-servant God Artaxares, king of kings of the Arians, of divine descent,"[1] is substantially that of the Arsacids, except that the Iranian nation, as already in the old native regal title, and the indigenous god are now expressly named. That a dynasty having its home in Persis came in lieu of one originally alien in race and only nationalised, was a work and a victory of national reaction ; but the force of circumstances placed various insurmountable barriers in the way of the consequences thence resulting. Persepolis, or, as it is now called, Istachr, becomes again nominally the capital of the empire, and there on the same rock-wall, alongside of the similar monuments of Darius, the remarkable statues and still more remarkable inscriptions just mentioned proclaim the fame of Ardashir and Shapur; but the administration could not well be conducted from this remote locality, and Ctesiphon continued still to be its centre. The new Persian government did

of the last Sassanid period preserved in the Arabic chronicle of Tabari Ardashir, after he has cut off with his own hand the head of Ardawan and has assumed the title Shahan-shah, king of kings, conquers first Hamadhan (Ecbatana) in Great Media, then Aderbijan (Atropatene), Armenia, Mosul (Adiabene) ; and further Suristan or Sawad (Babylonia). Thence he returns to Istachr unto his Persian home, and then starting afresh conquers Sagistan, Gurgan (Hyrcania), Abrashahr (Nisapur in the Parthian land), Merv (Margiane), Balkh (Bactra), and Charizm (Khiva) up to the extreme limits of Chorasan. "After he had killed many people and had sent their heads to the fire-temple of Anahedh (in Istachr), he returned from Merv to Pars and settled in Gor" (Feruzabad). How much of this is legend, we do not

know (comp. Nöldeke, *Tabari*, p. 17, 116).

[1] The title runs in Greek (*C. I. Gr.* 4675), Μάσδασνος (Mazda - servant, treated as a proper name) θεὸς 'Αρταξάρης βασιλεὺς βασιλέων 'Αριανῶν ἐκ γένους θεῶν ; with which closely agrees the title of his son Sapor I. (*ib.* 4676), only that after 'Αριανῶν there is inserted καὶ 'Αναριανῶν, and so the extension of the rule to foreign lands is brought into prominence. In the title of the Arsacids, so far as it is clear from the Greek and Persian legends of coins, θεός, βασιλεὺς βασιλέων, θεοπάτωρ (= ἐκ γένους θεῶν) recur, whereas there is no prominence given to the Arians and, significantly, to the "Mazda-servant"; by their side appear numerous other titles borrowed from the Syrian kings, such as ἐπιφάνης, δίκαιος, νικάτωρ, also the Roman αὐτοκράτωρ.

not resume the *de jure* prerogative of the Persians, as it had subsisted under the Achaemenids ; while Darius named himself "a Persian son of a Persian, an Arian from Arian stock," Ardashir named himself, as we saw, simply king of the Arians. We do not know whether Persian elements were introduced afresh into the great houses apart from the royal ; in any case several of them remained, like the Surên and the Carên ; only under the Achaemenids, not under the Sassanids these were exclusively Persian.

Church and priesthood under the Sassanids.

Even in a religious point of view no change, strictly so called, set in ; but the faith and the priests gained under the Persian great-kings an influence and a power such as they had never possessed under the Parthian. It may well be that the twofold diffusion of foreign worships in the direction of Iran—of Buddhism from the East and of the Jewish-Christian faith from the West—brought by their very hostility a regeneration to the old religion of Mazda. The founder of the new dynasty, Ardashir, was, as is credibly reported, a zealous fire-worshipper, and himself took priestly orders ; therefore, it is further said, from that time the order of the Magi became influential and arrogant, while it had hitherto by no means had such honour and such freedom, but on the contrary had not been held in much account by the rulers. "Thenceforth all the Persians honour and revere the priests ; public affairs are arranged according to their counsels and oracles ; each treaty and each law-dispute undergoes their inspection and their judgment, and nothing appears to the Persian right and legal which has not been confirmed by a priest." Accordingly we encounter an arrangement of spiritual administration which reminds us of the position of the Pope and the bishops alongside of the Emperor and the princes. Each circle is placed under a chief-Magian (Magupat, lord of Magians, in new Persian Mobedh), and these all in turn under the chiefest of the chief Magians (Mobedhan-Mobedh), the counterpart of "the king of kings," and now it is he who crowns the king. The consequences of this priestly dominion did not fail to appear : the rigid ritual, the restrictive precepts as to guilt and expiation, science resolving itself into a wild system of oracles and of magic, while belonging from the first to Parsism, in all probability only attained to their full development at this epoch.

Traces of the national reaction appear also in the use of the native language and the native customs. The largest Greek city of the Parthian empire, the ancient Seleucia, continued to subsist, but it was thenceforth called not after the name of the Greek marshal, but after that of its new master, Beh, or better, Ardashir. The Greek language hitherto at any rate always in use, although debased and no longer ruling alone, disappears on the emergence of the new dynasty at once from the coins, and only on the inscriptions of the first Sassanids is it still to be met with by the side of, and behind, the language proper of the land. The " Parthian writing," the Pahlavî, maintains its ground, but alongside of it comes a second little different and indeed, as the coins show, as properly official, probably that used hitherto in the Persian province, so that the oldest monuments of the Sassanids, like those of the Achaemenids, are trilingual, somewhat as in the German middle ages Latin, Saxon, and Franconian were employed side by side. After king Sapor I. († 272) the bilingual usage disappears, and the second mode of writing alone retains its place, inheriting the name Pahlavî. The year of the Seleucids, and the names of the months belonging to it, disappear with the change of dynasty ; in their stead come, according to old Persian custom, the years of the rulers and the native Persian names of months.[1] Even the old Persian legend is transferred to the new Persia. The still extant " history of Ardashir, son of Papak," which makes this son of a Persian shepherd arrive at the Median court, perform menial offices there, and then become the deliverer of his people, is nothing but the old tale of Cyrus changed to

[1] Frawardin, Ardhbehesht, etc. (Ideler, *Chronologie*, ii. 515). It is remarkable that essentially the same names of the months have maintained themselves in the provincial calendar of the Roman province Cappadocia (Ideler, i. 443) ; they must proceed from the time when it was a Persian satrapy.

the new names.   Another fable-book of the Indian Parsees is able to tell how king Iskander Rumi, *i.e.* " Alexander the Roman," had caused the holy books of Zarathustra to be burnt, and how they were then restored by the pious Ardaviraf when king Ardashir had mounted the throne.   Here the Romano-Hellene confronts the Persian ; the legend has, as might be expected, forgotten the illegitimate Arsacid.

Government of the Sassanids.   In other respects the state of things remained essentially the same.   In a military point of view in particular, the armies of the Sassanids were certainly not regular and trained troops, but the levy of men capable of arms, into which with the national movement a new spirit may doubtless have passed, but which afterwards, as before, was based in the main on the cavalry-service of the nobility.   The administration too remained as it was ; the able ruler took steps with inexorable sternness against the highway-robber as against the exacting official, and, compared at least with the later Arabic and the Turkish rule, the subjects of the Sassanid empire found themselves prosperous and the state-chest full.

The new Persians and the Romans.   But the alteration in the position of the new kingdom with reference to the Roman is significant.   The Arsacids never felt themselves quite on a level with the Caesars. Often as the two states encountered each other in war and peace as powers equal in weight, and decidedly as the view of two great-powers dominated the Roman East (p. 1), there remained with the Roman power a precedence similar to that which the holy Roman empire of the German nation possessed throughout centuries, very much to its hurt.   Acts of subjection, such as the Parthian kings took upon themselves in presence of Tiberius (p. 44) and of Nero (52), without being compelled to them by extreme necessity, cannot be at all conceived of on the Roman side.   It cannot be accident that a gold coin was never struck under the government of the Arsacids, and the very first Sassanid ruler practised coining in gold ; this is the most palpable sign of sovereignty unrestricted by any duties of a vassal.   To the claim of the empire of the Caesars alone to the power of coining money for universal circulation the Arsacids without exception yielded, at least in so far that they themselves refrained generally from coining, and left coinage in silver and copper to the towns or the satraps ; the Sassanids again struck gold pieces, as did king Darius. The great-kingdom of the East at length demanded its full right ; the world no longer belonged to the Romans alone. The submissiveness of the Orientals and the supremacy of the Occidentals were of the past. Accordingly, in place of the relations between Romans and Parthians, as hitherto, always reverting afresh to peace, there now came for generations embittered hostility.

Parthian war of Severus Antoninus.

After having set forth the new state organisation, with which the sinking Rome was soon to contend, we resume the thread of our narrative. Antoninus, son and successor of Severus, not a warrior and statesman like his father, but a dissolute caricature of both, must have had the design—so far as in the case of such personages we can speak of design at all—to bring the East entirely into the Roman power. It was not difficult to place the princes of Osrhoene and of Armenia, after they had been summoned to the imperial court, under arrest, and to declare their fiefs forfeited. But on the arrival of the news a revolt broke out in Armenia. The Arsacid prince Tiridates was proclaimed king, and invoked the protection of the Parthians. Thereupon Antoninus put himself at the head of a large military force, and appeared in the East in the year 216, to put down the Armenians, and in case of need also the Parthians. Tiridates himself at once gave up the cause as lost, although the division sent to Armenia subsequently encountered vehement resistance there ; and he fled to the Parthians. The Romans demanded his surrender. The Parthians were not inclined on his account to enter into a war, the more especially as just then the two sons of king Vologasus V., Vologasus VI. and Artabanus, were in bitter feud over the succession to the throne. The former yielded when the Roman demand was imperiously repeated, and delivered up Tiridates.

Thereupon the emperor desired from Artabanus, who had meanwhile obtained recognition, the hand of his daughter for the express object of thus obtaining the kingdom by marriage, and of bringing East and West under one rule. The rejection of this wild proposal[1] was the signal for war; the Romans declared it, and crossed the Tigris. The Parthians were unprepared; without encountering resistance the Romans burnt down the towns and villages in Adiabene, and ruthlessly destroyed even the old royal tombs at Arbela.[2] But Artabanus made the utmost exertions for the next campaign, and put into the field a powerful force in the spring of 217. Antoninus, who had spent the winter in Edessa, was assassinated by his officers just as he was setting out for this second campaign. His successor Macrinus, unconfirmed in the government and held in little repute, at the head, moreover, of an army defective in discipline and tone and shaken by the murder of the emperor, would gladly have rid himself of a war wantonly instigated and assuming very serious proportions. He sent the prisoners back to the Parthian king, and threw the blame of the outrages committed on his predecessor. But Artabanus was not content with this; he demanded compensation for all the devastation committed, and the evacuation of Mesopotamia. Thus matters came to a battle at Nisibis, in which the Romans had the worst. Nevertheless the Parthians, partly because their levy seemed as though it would break up, perhaps also under the influence of Roman money, granted peace (218) on comparatively favourable terms. Rome paid a considerable war compensation (50,000,000 denarii), but retained Mesopotamia. Armenia remained with Tiridates, but the latter took it as in dependency on the Romans. In Osrhoene also the old princely house was reinstated.

[1] Such is the account of the trustworthy Dio, lxxviii. 1; the version of Herodian, iv. 11, that Artabanus promised his daughter, and at the celebration of the betrothal allowed Antoninus to cut down the Parthians present, is unauthenticated

[2] If there is any truth in the mention of the Cadusians in the biography, c. 6, the Romans induced this wild tribe, not subject to the government in the south-west of the Caspian Sea, to fall at the same time upon the Parthians.

This was the last treaty of peace which the Arsacid King Ardashir.
dynasty concluded with Rome. Almost immediately afterwards, and perhaps partly in consequence of this bargain,
which certainly, as things stood, might be looked upon
by the Orientals as an abandonment by their own government of the victories achieved, the insurrection began,
which converted the state of the Parthians into a state
of the Persians. Its leader, king Ardashir or Artaxares
(A.D. 224-241) strove for several years with the adherents of the old dynasty before he attained full success ;[1]
after three great battles, in the last of which king Artabanus fell, he was master in the Parthian empire proper,
and could march into the Mesopotamian desert to subdue
the Arabs of Hatra and thence to advance against the
Roman Mesopotamia. But the brave and independent
Arabs defended themselves now against the Persians as
formerly against the Roman invasion, in their huge walls
with good success ; and Artaxares found himself led to
operate in the first instance against Media and Armenia,
where the Arsacids still maintained themselves, and the
sons of Artabanus had found a refuge. It was not till
about the year 230 that he turned against the Romans,
and not merely declared war against them, but demanded
back all the provinces which had formerly belonged to the
kingdom of his predecessors, Darius and Xerxes—in other
words, the cession of all Asia. To emphasise his threatening words, he led a mighty army over the Euphrates ;
Mesopotamia was occupied and Nisibis besieged ; the
enemy's cavalry appeared in Cappadocia and in Syria.

The Roman throne was then occupied by Severus Severus Alexander.
Alexander, a ruler in whom nothing was warlike but the

---

[1] The subsequently received chronology puts the beginning of the Sassanid dynasty in the Seleucid year
538 = 1st Oct. 226-7 A.D., or the
fourth (full) year of Severus Alexander, reigning since spring 222
(Agathias, iv. 24). According to
other data king Ardashir numbered
the year from the autumn 223-4 A.D.
as his first, and so doubtless assumed
in this the title of great-king (Nöldeke, *Tabari*, p. 410). The last
dated coin as yet known of the older
system is of the year 539. When Dio
wrote between 230 and 234, Artabanus was dead and his adherents were
overpowered, and the advance of
Artaxares into Armenia and Mesopotamia was expected.

name, and for whom in reality his mother Mamaea conducted the government. Urgent, almost humble proposals of peace on the part of the Roman government remained without effect ; nothing was left but the employment of arms. The masses of the Roman army gathered together from all the empire were divided ; the left wing took the direction of Armenia and Media, the right that of Mesene at the mouth of the Euphrates and Tigris, perhaps in the calculation that they might in the former as in the latter quarter have the support of the adherents of the Arsacids; the main army went to Mesopotamia. The troops were numerous enough, but without discipline and tone ; a Roman officer of high position at this time himself testifies that they were pampered and insubordinate, refused to fight, killed their officers, and deserted in crowds. The main force did not get beyond the Euphrates,[1] for his mother represented to the emperor that it was not his business to fight for his subjects, but theirs to fight for him. The right wing, assailed in the level country by the Persian main force and abandoned by the emperor, was cut up. Thereupon, when the emperor issued orders to the wing which had pushed forward towards Media to draw back, the latter also suffered severely in the winter retreat through Armenia. If the matter went no further than this sorry return of the great Oriental army to Antioch, if no complete disaster occurred, and even Mesopotamia remained in Roman power, this appears due, not to the merit of the Roman troops or their leaders but to the fact that the Persian levy was weary of the conflict and went home.[2] But they went not for long, the more especially

---

[1] The emperor remained probably in Palmyra ; at least a Palmyrene inscription, *C. I. Gr.* 4483, mentions the ἐπιδημία θεοῦ Ἀλεξάνδρου.

[2] The incomparably wretched accounts of this war (relatively the best is that drawn from a common source in Herodian, Zonaras, and Syncellus, p. 674) do not even decide the question who remained victor in these conflicts. While Herodian speaks of an unexampled defeat of the Romans, the Latin authorities, the Biography as well as Victor, Eutropius, and Rufius Festus, celebrate Alexander as the conqueror of Artaxerxes or Xerxes, and according to these latter the further course of things was favourable. Herodian vi. 6, 5, offers the means of adjustment. According to the Armenian accounts (Gutschmid, *Zeitschr. der deutschen morgenländ. Gesellschaft,* xxxi. 47) the Arsacids with the support of the

as soon after, upon the murder of the last offshoot of the dynasty of Severus, the several army-commanders and the government in Rome began to fight about the occupation of the Roman throne, and consequently were at one in their concern for the affairs of external foes.   Under Maximinus (235-238) the Roman Mesopotamia fell into the power of Ardashir, and the Persians once more prepared to cross the Euphrates.[1]

After the internal troubles were in some measure pacified, and Gordian III., almost still a boy, under the protection of the commandant of Rome and soon of his father-in-law Furius Timesitheus, bore undisputed sway in the whole empire, war was solemnly declared against the Persians, and in the year 242 a great Roman army advanced under the personal conduct of the emperor, or rather of his father-in-law, into Mesopotamia.   It had complete success ; Carrhae was recovered, at Resaina between Carrhae and Nisibis the army of the Persian king Shahpuhr or Sapor (reigning 241-272), who shortly before had followed his father Ardashir, was routed, and in consequence of this victory Nisibis was occupied.   All Mesopotamia was reconquered ; it was resolved to march back to the Euphrates, and thence down the stream against the enemy's capital Ctesiphon.   Unhappily Timesitheus died, and his successor, Marcus Julius Philippus, a native of Arabia from the Trachonitis, used the opportunity to set aside the young ruler.   When the army had accomplished the difficult march through the valley of the Chaboras towards the Euphrates, the soldiers in Circesium, at the confluence of the Chaboras with the Euphrates, did not find—in consequence, it is alleged, of arrangements made by Philippus—the provisions and stores which they had expected, and laid the blame of this on the emperor.

The Persian war of Gordian.

tribes of the Caucasus held their ground in Armenia down to the year 237 against Ardashir ; this diversion may be correct and may have tended to the advantage of the Romans.

[1] The best account is furnished by Syncellus, p. 683 and Zonaras, xii. 18, drawing from the same source. With this accord the individual statements of Ammianus, xxiii. 5, 7, 17, and nearly so the forged letter of Gordian to the Senate in the Biography, c. 27, from which the narrative, c. 26, is ignorantly prepared ; Antioch was in danger, but not in the hands of the Persians.

Nevertheless the march in the direction of Ctesiphon was begun, but at the very first station, near Zaitha (somewhat below Mejadîn), a number of insurgent guards killed the emperor (in the spring or summer of 244), and proclaimed their commandant, Philippus, as Augustus in his stead. The new ruler did what the soldiers or at least the guardsmen desired, and not merely gave up the intended expedition against Ctesiphon, but led the troops at once back to Italy. He purchased the permission to do so from the conquered enemy by the cession of Mesopotamia and Armenia, and so of the Euphrates frontier. But this conclusion of peace excited such indignation that the emperor did not venture to put it in execution, and allowed the garrisons to remain in the ceded provinces.[1] The fact that the Persians, at least provisionally, acquiesced in this, gives the measure of what they were then able to do. It was not the Orientals, but the Goths, the pestilence that raged for fifteen years, and the dissensions of the corps-leaders quarrelling with one another for the crown, that broke the last strength of the empire.

Palmyra. At this point, when the Roman East in its struggle with the Persian is left to its own resources, it will be appropriate to make mention of a remarkable state, which, created by and for the desert-traffic, now for a short time takes up a leading part in political history. The oasis of Palmyra, in the native language Tadmor, lies half-way between Damascus and the Euphrates. It is of importance solely as intermediate station between the Euphrates and the Mediterranean ; this significance it was late in acquiring, and early lost again, so that the flourishing time of Palmyra coincides nearly with the period which we are here describing. As to the rise of the town there is an utter absence of tradition.[2] It is mentioned first on

---

[1] So Zonaras, xii. 19, represents the course of affairs ; with this Zosimus, iii. 33, agrees, and the later course of things shows that Armenia was not quite in Persian possession. If, according to Euagrius, v. 7, at that time merely Lesser Armenia remained Roman, this may not be incorrect, in so far as the dependence of the vassal-king of Great Armenia after the peace was doubtless merely nominal.

[2] The Biblical account (1 Kings ix. 18) as to the building of the town Thamar in Idumaea by king Solomon has only been transferred to Tadmor by a misunderstanding doubtless old ;

occasion of the abode of Antonius in Syria in the year 7 1 3, when he made a vain attempt to possess himself of 41. its riches ; the documents found there—the oldest dated Palmyrene inscription is of the year 745—hardly reach 9. much further back.   It is not improbable that its flourishing was connected with the establishment of the Romans in the Syrian coast-region.   So long as the Nabataeans and the towns of Osrhoene were not directly Roman, the Romans had an interest in providing another direct communication with the Euphrates, and this thereupon led necessarily by way of Palmyra.   Palmyra was not a Roman foundation ; Antonius took as the occasion for that predatory expedition the neutrality of the merchants who were the medium of traffic between the two great states, and the Roman horsemen turned back, without having performed their work, before the chain of archers which the Palmyrenes opposed to the attack.   But already in the first imperial period the city must have been reckoned as belonging to the empire, because the tax-ordinances of Germanicus and of Corbulo issued for Syria applied also for Palmyra ; in an inscription of the year 80 we meet with a Claudian *phyle* there ; from Hadrian's time the city calls itself Hadriana Palmyra, and in the third century it even designates itself a colony.

The subjection of the Palmyrenes to the empire was, Military however, of a different nature to the ordinary one, and dependsimilar in some measure to the client-relation of the ence of dependent kingdoms.   Even in Vespasian's time Palmyra Palmyra. is called an intermediate region between the two great powers, and in every collision between the Romans and Parthians the question was asked, what policy the Palmyrenes would pursue.   We must seek the key to its distinctive position in the relations of the frontier and the arrangements made for frontier-protection.   The Syrian troops, so far as they were stationed on the Euphrates itself, had their chief position at Zeugma,

at all events the erroneous reference of it to this town among the later Jews (2 Chron. viii. 4, and the Greek translation of 1 Kings, ix. 18) form the oldest testimony for its existence (Hitzig, *Zeitschr. der deutschen morgenl. Gesellschaft*, viii. 222).

opposite to Biredjik, at the great passage of the Euphrates. Further down the stream, between the immediately Roman and the Parthian territory was interposed that of Palmyra, which reached to the Euphrates and included the next important place of crossing at Sura opposite to the Mesopotamian town Nicephorium (later Callinicon, now er-Ragga). It is more than probable that the guarding of this important border-fortress as well as the securing of the desert-road between the Euphrates and Palmyra, and also perhaps of a portion of the road from Palmyra to Damascus, was committed to the community of Palmyra, and that it was thus entitled and bound to make the military arrangements necessary for this far from slight task.[1] Subse-

[1] This is nowhere expressly stated; but all the circumstances tell in favour of it. That the Romano-Parthian frontier, before the Romans established themselves on the left bank of the Euphrates, was on the right a little below Sura, is most distinctly said by Pliny (*H. N.* v. 26, 89: *a Sura proxime est Philiscum*—comp. p. 95, note 1—*oppidum Parthorum ad Euphratem; ab eo Seleuciam dierum decem navigatio*), and there it remained till the erection of the province of Mesopotamia under Severus. The Palmyrene of Ptolemy (v. 15, 24, 25) is a district of Coele-Syria, which seems to embrace a good part of the territory to the south of Palmyra, but certainly reaches as far as the Euphrates and includes Sura; other urban centres besides Palmyra seem not to be mentioned, and there is nothing to stand in the way of our taking this large district as civic territory. So long in particular as Mesopotamia was Parthian, but subsequently also with reference to the adjoining desert, a permanent protection of the frontier could not here be dispensed with; as indeed in the fourth century, according to the tenor of the Notitia, Palmyrene was strongly occupied, the northern portion by the troops of the Dux of Syria, Palmyra itself and the southern half by those of the Dux of Phoenice. That in the earlier imperial period no Roman troops were stationed here, is vouched for by the silence of authors and the absence of inscriptions, which in Palmyra itself are numerous. If in the Tabula Peutingeriana it is remarked under Sura: *fines exercitus Syriatici et commercium barbarorum*, that is, "here end the Roman garrisons and here is the place of exchange for the traffic of the barbarians," this is only saying, what at a later time is repeated by Ammianus (xxiii. 3, 7: *Callinicum munimentum robustum et commercandi opimitate gratissimum*) and further by the emperor Honorius (*Cod. Just.* iv. 63, 4), that Callinicon was one of the few entrepôts devoted to the Romano-barbarian frontier-traffic; but it does not at all follow from this as regards the time when the Tabula originated, that these imperial troops were stationed there, since in fact the Palmyrenes in general belonged to the Syrian army and might be thought of in using the expression *exercitus Syriaticus*. The city must have furnished a force of its own in a way similar to that of the princes of Numidia and of Panticapaeum. By this means alone we come to understand as well the rejection of the troops of Antonius as the attitude of the Palmyrenes in the troubles of the third century, and not less the emergence of the *numeri Pal-*

quently doubtless the imperial troops were brought up closer to Palmyra, and one of the Syrian legions was moved to Danava between Palmyra and Damascus, and the Arabian legion to Bostra ; after Severus united Mesopotamia with the empire, even here both banks of the Euphrates were in the Roman power, and the Roman territory on the Euphrates ended no longer at Sura but at Circesium, at the confluence of the Chaboras with the Euphrates above Mejadin. Then Mesopotamia also was strongly occupied with imperial troops. But the Mesopotamian legions lay on the great road in the north near Resaina and Nisibis, and even the Syrian and Arabian troops did not supersede the need for the co-operation of the Palmyrenes. Even the protection of Circesium and of this part of the bank of the Euphrates may have been entrusted to the Palmyrenes. It was not till after the decline of Palmyra, and perhaps in compensation for it, that Circesium[1] was made by Diocletian a strong fortress, which thenceforth was here the basis of frontier-defence.

The traces of this distinctive position of Palmyra are demonstrable also in its institutions. The absence of the emperor's name on the Palmyrene coins is probably to be explained not from it, but from the fact that the community issued almost nothing but small money. But the treatment of the language speaks clearly. From the rule elsewhere followed almost without exception by the Romans—of allowing in their immediate territory only the use of the two imperial languages—Palmyra was excepted. Here that language, which in the rest of Syria and not less after the exile in Judaea was the usual medium of private intercourse, but was restricted to the latter, maintained its ground in public use, so long as the city existed at all. Essential differences cannot be shown between the Palmyrene Syriac and that of the other

Administrative independence of Palmyra.

myrenorum among the military novelties of this epoch.

[1] Ammianus, xxiii. 5, 2 : *Cercusium . . . Diocletianus exiguum ante hoc et suspectum muris turribusque circumdedit celsis, . . . ne vagarentur per Syriam Persae ita ut paucis*

ante annis cum magnis provinciarum contigerat damnis. Comp. Procopius *de aed.* ii. 6. Perhaps this place is not different from the Φάλγα or Φάλιγα of Isidorus of Charax (*mans. Parth.* 1 ; Stephanus Byz. *s. v.*) and the *Philiscum* of Pliny (p. 94, note).

regions just named ; the proper names, having not seldom an Arabic or Jewish, or even Persian form, show the striking mixture of peoples, and numerous words borrowed from Greek or Latin show the influence of the Occidentals. It becomes subsequently a rule to append to the Syrian text a Greek one, which in a decree of the Palmyrene common-council of the year 137 is placed after the Palmyrene, but afterwards usually precedes it ; but mere Greek inscriptions of native Palmyrenes are rare exceptions. Even in votive inscriptions which Palmyrenes set up to their native gods in Rome,[1] and in tombs of Palmyrene soldiers that died in Africa or Britain, the Palmyrene rendering is added. So too in Palmyra—while the Roman year was made the basis of dating as in the rest of the empire—the names of the months were not the Macedonian officially received in Roman Syria, but those which were current in it in common intercourse at least among the Jews, and were in use, moreover, among the Aramaean tribes living under Assyrian and subsequently Persian rule.[2]

Palmyrene magistrates.

The municipal organisation was moulded in the main after the pattern of the Greek municipality of the Roman empire ; the designations for magistrates and council[3] and even those of the colony are in the Palmyrene texts re-

---

[1] Of the seven dedications, hitherto found outside of Palmyra, to the Palmyrene Malach Belos the three brought to light in Rome (*C. I. L.* vi. 51, 710; *C. I. Gr.* 6015) have along with a Greek or Latin also a Palmyrene text, two African (*C. I. L.* viii. 2497, 8795 add.) and two Dacian (*Arch. epig. Mitth. aus Oesterreich*, vi. 109, 111) merely Latin. One of the latter was set up by P. Aelius Theimes a *duoviralis* of Sarmizegetusa, evidently a native of Palmyra, *diis patriis Malagbel et Bebellahamon et Benefal et Manavat.*

[2] Whence these names of the months come, is not clear ; they first appear in the Assyrian cuneiform writing, but are not of Assyrian origin. In consequence of the Assyrian rule they then remained in use within the sphere of the Syrian language. Variations are found ; the second month, the Dios of the Greek-speaking Syrians, our November, is called among the Jews Markeshvan, among the Palmyrenes Kanun (Waddington, n. 2574*b*). We may add that these names of the months, so far as they came to be applied within the Roman empire, are adapted, like the Macedonian, to the Julian calendar, so that only the designation of the month differs, the year-beginning (1 Oct.) of the Syro-Roman year finds uniformly application to the Greek as to the Aramaean appellations.

[3] *E.g.* Archon, Grammateus, Proedros, Syndikos, Dekaprotoi.

tained for the most part from the imperial languages. But in administration the district retained a greater independence than is elsewhere assigned to urban communities. Alongside of the civic officials we find, at least in the third century, the city of Palmyra with its territory under a separate "headman" of senatorial rank and Roman appointment, but chosen from the family of most repute in the place ; Septimius Hairanes, son of Odaenathus, is substantially a prince of the Palmyrenes,[1] who was doubtless not otherwise dependent on the legate of Syria than were the client-princes on the neighbouring imperial governors generally. A few years later we meet with his son,[2] Septimius Odaenathus, in the like position—indeed even raised in rank — of hereditary prince.[3]   Similarly, Palmyra formed a customs-district apart, in which the customs were leased on account, not of the state, but of the community.[4]

[1] This is shown by the inscription of Palmyra (*C. I. Gr.* 4491, 4492 = Waddington 2600 = Vogué, *Insc. sém. Palm.* 22) set up to this Hairanes in the year 251 by a soldier of the legion stationed in Arabia. His title is in Greek ὁ λαμπρότατος συνκλητικός, ἔξα[ρχος (=*princeps*) Παλμυ]ρηνῶν, in Palmyrene "illustrious senator, head of Tadmor." The epitaph (*C. I. Gr.* 4507 = Waddington 2621 = Vogué,21) of the father of Hairanes, Septimios Odaenathos, son of Hairanes, grandson of Vaballathos, great-grandson of Nassoros, gives to him also senatorial rank.

[2] Certainly the father of this Odaenathus is nowhere named ; but it is as good as certain that he was the son of the Hairanes just named, and bore the name of his grandfather. Zosimus, too, i. 39, terms him a Palmyrene distinguished from the days of his forefathers by the government (ἄνδρα Παλμυρηνὸν καὶ ἐκ προγόνων τῆς παρὰ τῶν βασιλέων ἀξιωθέντα τίμης).

[3] In the inscription Waddington 2603 = Vogué 23, which the guild of gold and silver workers of Palmyra set up in the year 257 to Odaenathus

he is called ὁ λαμπρότατος ὑπατικός, and so *vir consularis*, and in Greek δεσπότης, in Syriac *mâran.* The former designation is not a title of office, but a statement of the class in which he ranked ; so *vir consularis* stands not unfrequently after the name quite like *vir clarissimus* (*C. I. L.* x. p. 1117 and elsewhere), and ὁ λαμπρότατος ὑπατικός is found alongside of and before official titles of various kinds, *e.g.* that of the proconsul of Africa (*C. I. Gr.* 2979, where λαμπρότατος is absent), of the imperial legate of Pontus and Bithynia (*C.I.Gr.* 3747, 3748, 3771) and of Palestine (*C. I. Gr.* 4151), of the governor of Lycia and Pamphylia (*C. I. Gr.* 4272); it is only in the age after Constantine that it is in combination with the name of the province employed as an official title (*e.g.* *C.I.Gr.* 2596, 4266*e*). From this, therefore, no inference is to be drawn as to the legal position of Odaenathus. Likewise, in the Syriac designation of "lord," we may not find exactly the ruler ; it is also given to a procurator (Waddington 2606 = Vogué 25).

[4] Syria in the imperial period formed an imperial customs-district of

The importance of Palmyra depended on the caravan-traffic. The heads of the caravans (συνοδιάρχαι), which went from Palmyra to the great entrepots on the Euphrates, to Vologasias, the already mentioned Parthian foundation not far from the site of the ancient Babylon, and to Forath or Charax Spasinu, twin towns at its mouth, close on the Persian Gulf, appear in the inscriptions as the most respected city-burgesses,[1] and fill not merely

its own, and the imperial dues were levied not merely on the coast but also at the Euphrates-frontier, in particular at Zeugma. Hence it necessarily follows that farther to the south, where the Euphrates was no longer in the Roman power, similar dues were established on the Roman eastern frontier. Now a decree of the council of Palmyra of the year 137 informs us that the city and its territory formed a special customs-district, and the dues were levied for the benefit of the town upon all goods imported or exported. That this territory lay beyond the imperial dues, is probable—first, because, if there had existed an imperial customs-line enclosing the Palmyrene territory, the mention of it could not well be omitted in that detailed enactment; secondly, because a community of the empire enclosed by the imperial customs-lines would hardly have had the right of levying dues at the boundary of its territory to this extent. We shall thus have to discern in the levying of dues by the community of Palmyra the same distinctive position which must be attributed to it in a military point of view. Perhaps, on the other hand, there was an impost laid on it for the benefit of the imperial exchequer, possibly the delivering up of a quota of the produce of the dues or a heightened tribute. Arrangements similar to those for Palmyra may have existed also for Petra and Bostra ; for goods were certainly not admitted here free of dues, and according to Pliny, H. N. xii. 14, 65, imperial dues from the Arabic frankincense exported by way of Gaza seem only to have been levied at Gaza on

the coast. The indolence of Roman administration was stronger than its fiscal zeal ; it may frequently have devolved the inconvenient tolls of the land-frontier away from itself on the communities.

[1] These caravans (συνοδίαι) appear on the Palmyrene inscriptions as fixed companies, which undertake the same journeys beyond doubt at definite intervals under their foreman (συνοδιάρχης, Waddington, 2589, 2590, 2596) ; thus a statue is erected to such a one by " the merchants who went down with him to Vologasias " (οἱ σὺν αὐτῷ κατελθόντες εἰς Ὀλογεσιάδα ἔνποροι, Waddington 2599 of the year 247), or "up from Forath (comp. Pliny, H. N. vi. 28, 145) and Vologasias " (οἱ συναναβάντες μετ᾽ αὐτοῦ ἔμποροι ἀπὸ Φοράθου κὲ Ὀλογασιάδος, Waddington 2589 of the year 142), or "up from Spasinu Charax " (οἱ σὺν αὐτῷ ἀναβάντες ἀπὸ Σπασίνου Χάρακος, Waddington, 2596 of the year 193 ; similarly 2590 of the year 155). All these conductors are men of standing furnished with lists of ancestors ; their honorary monuments stand in the great colonnade beside those of queen Zenobia and her family. Specially remarkable is one of them, Septimius Vorodes, of whom there exists a series of honorary monuments of the years 262-267 (Waddington, 2606-2610) ; he, too, was a caravan-head (ἀνακομίσαντα τὰς συνοδίας ἐκ τῶν ἰδίων καὶ μαρτυρηθέντα ὑπὸ τῶν ἀρχεμπόρων, Waddington, n. 2606 a ; consequently he defrayed the costs of the journey back for the whole company, and was on account of this liberality publicly praised by the wholesale traders). But

the magistracies of their home, but in part also imperial offices ; the great traders (ἀρχέμποροι) and the guild of workers in gold and silver testify to the importance of the city for trade and manufactures, and not less is its prosperity attested by the still standing temples of the city and the long colonnades of the city halls, as well as the massy and richly decorated tombs.   The climate is little favourable to agriculture—the place lies near to the northern limit of the date palm, and does not derive its Greek name from it—but there are found in the environs the remains of great subterranean aqueducts and huge water-reservoirs artificially constructed of square blocks, with the help of which the ground, now destitute of all vegetation, must once upon a time have artificially developed a rich culture. This riches, this national idiosyncrasy not quite set aside even under Roman rule, and this administrative independence, explain in some measure the part of Palmyra about the middle of the third century in the great crisis, to the presentation of which we now return.

After the emperor Decius had fallen in the year 251 when fighting against the Goths in Europe, the government of the empire, if at that time there was still an empire and a government at all, left the East entirely to its fate. While the pirates from the Black Sea ravaged the coasts far and wide and even the interior, the Persian king Sapor again assumed the aggressive.   While his father had been content with calling himself lord of Iran, he first designated himself—as did the succeeding rulers after his example—the great-king of Iran and non-Iran (p. 83, note), and thereby laid down, as it were, the programme of his policy of conquest.   In the year 252 or 253 he occupied Armenia, or it submitted to him voluntarily, beyond doubt carried likewise away by that resuscitation of the old Persian faith and Persian habits ; the legitimate king Tiridates sought shelter with the Romans, the other members of the royal house placed themselves under the banners of the

Capture of the emperor Valerian.

---

he filled not merely the civic offices of *strategos* and *agoranomos,* he was even imperial procurator of the second class (*ducenarius*) and *argapetes* (p. 104, note 1).

Persian.[1]   After Armenia thus had become Persian, the hosts of the Orientals overran Mesopotamia, Syria, and Cappadocia ; they laid waste the level country far and wide, but the inhabitants of the larger towns, first of all the brave Edessenes, repelled the attack of enemies little equipped for besieging.   In the West, meanwhile at least, a recognised government had been set up.   The emperor Publius Licinius Valerianus, an honest and well-disposed ruler, but not resolute in character or equal to dealing with difficulties, appeared at length in the East and resorted to Antioch.   Thence he went to Cappadocia, which the Persian roving hordes evacuated.   But the plague decimated his army, and he delayed long to take up the decisive struggle in Mesopotamia.   At length he resolved to bring help to the sorely pressed Edessa, and crossed the Euphrates with his forces.   There, not far from Edessa, occurred the disaster which had nearly the same significance for the Roman East as the victory of the Goths at the mouth of the Danube and the fall of Decius—the capture of the emperor Valerianus by the Persians (end of 259 or beginning of 260).[2]   As to the more precise circumstances the accounts are conflicting.   According to one version, when he was attempting with a weak band to reach Edessa, he was surrounded and captured by the far superior Persians.   According to another, he, although defeated, reached the beleaguered town, but, as he brought no sufficient help and the provisions came to an end only the more rapidly, he dreaded the outbreak of a military insurrection, and therefore delivered himself voluntarily into the hands of the enemy.   According to a third, he, reduced to extremities, entered into negotiations with Sapor ; when

[1] According to the Greek account (Zonaras, xii. 21) king Tiridates takes refuge with the Romans, but his sons take the side of the Persians ; according to the Armenian, king Chosro is murdered by his brethren, and Chosro's son, Tiridates, fled to the Romans (Gutschmid, *Zeitschrift der deutschen morgenl. Gesellsch.* xxxi. 48). Perhaps the latter is to be preferred.

[2] The only fixed chronological basis is furnished by the Alexandrian coins, according to which Valerian was captured between 29th August 259 and 28th August 260.   That after his capture he was no longer regarded as emperor, is easily explained, seeing that the Persians compelled him in their interest to issue orders to his former subjects (continuation of Dio, *fr.* 3).

the Persian king declined to treat with envoys, he appeared personally in the enemy's camp, and was perfidiously made a prisoner.

Whichever of these narratives may come nearest to the truth, the emperor died in the captivity of the enemy,[1] and the consequence of this disaster was the forfeiture of the East to the Persians. Above all Antioch, the largest and richest city of the East, fell for the first time since it was Roman into the power of the public foe, and in good part through the fault of its own citizens. Mareades, an Antiochene of rank, whom the council had expelled for the embezzlement of public monies, brought the Persian army to his native town; whether it be a fable that the citizens were surprised in the theatre itself by the advancing foes, there is no doubt that they not merely offered no resistance, but that a great part of the lower population, partly in consideration of Mareades, partly in the hope of anarchy and pillage, saw with pleasure the entrance of the Persians. Thus the city with all its treasures became the prey of the enemy, and fearful ravages were committed in it; Mareades indeed also was —we know not why—condemned by king Sapor to perish by fire.[2] Besides numerous smaller places, the capitals of Cilicia and Cappadocia—Tarsus and Caesarea, the latter, it is stated, a town of 400,000 inhabitants— suffered the same fate. Endless trains of captives, who were led like cattle once a day to the watering, covered the desert-routes of the East. On the return home the Persians, it is alleged, in order the more rapidly to cross a ravine, filled it up with the bodies of the captives

The East without an emperor.

---

[1] The better accounts simply know the fact that Valerian died in Persian captivity. That Sapor used him as a footstool in mounting his horse (Lactantius, *de Mort. persec.* 5; Orosius, vii. 22, 4; Victor, *Ep.* 33), and finally caused him to be flayed (Lactantius, *l. c.*; Agathias, iv. 23; Cedrenus, p. 454) is a Christian invention — a requital for the persecution of the Christians ordered by Valerian.

[2] The tradition according to which Mareades (so Ammianus, xxiii. 5, 3; Mariades in Malalas, 12, p. 295; Mariadnes in contin. of Dio, *fr.* 1), or, as he is here called, Cyriades, had himself proclaimed as Augustus (*Vit. trig. tyr.* 1) is weakly attested; otherwise there might doubtless be found in it the occasion why Sapor caused him to be put to death.

whom they brought with them. It is more credible that the great "imperial dam" (Bend-i-Kaiser) at Sostra (Shuster) in Susiana, by which still at the present day the water of the Pasitigris is conveyed to the higher-lying regions, was built by these captives ; as indeed the emperor Nero's architects had helped to build the capital of Armenia, and generally in this domain the Occidentals always maintained their superiority. The Persians nowhere encountered resistance from the empire ; but Edessa still held out, and Caesarea had bravely defended itself, and had only fallen by treachery. The local resistance gradually passed beyond a mere defensive behind the walls of towns, and the breaking up of the Persian hosts, brought about by the wide extent of the conquered territory, was favourable to the bold partisan. A self-appointed Roman leader, Callistus,[1] succeeded in a happy *coup de main ;* with the vessels which he had brought together in the ports of Cilicia he sailed for Pompeiopolis—which the Persians were just besieging, while they at the same time laid waste Lycaonia,—killed several thousand men, and possessed himself of the royal harem. This induced the king, under pretext of celebrating a festival that might not be put off, to go home at once in such haste that, in order not to be detained, he purchased from the Edessenes free passage through their territory in return for all the Roman gold money which he had captured as booty. Odaenathus, prince of Palmyra, inflicted considerable losses on the bands returning home from Antioch before they crossed the Euphrates. But hardly was the most urgent danger from the Persians obviated, when two of the most noted among the army leaders of the East, left to themselves, Fulvius Macrianus, the officer who administered the chest and the depot of the army in Samosata,[2] and the

---

[1] He is called Callistus in the one tradition, doubtless traceable to Dexippus, in Syncellus, p. 716, and Zonaras, xii. 23, on the other hand, Ballista in the biographies of the emperors and in Zonaras, xii. 24.

[2] He was, according to the most trustworthy account, *procurator summarum* (ἐπὶ τῶν καθόλου λόγων βασιλέως : Dionysius in Eusebius, *H. E.* vii. 10, 5), and so finance-minister with equestrian rank ; the continu-

Callistus just mentioned, renounced allegiance to the son and co-regent and now sole ruler Gallienus—for whom, it is true, the East and the Persians were non-existent—and, themselves refusing to accept the purple, proclaimed the two sons of the former, Fulvius Macrianus and Fulvius Quietus, emperors (261). This step taken by the two distinguished generals had the effect of obtaining recognition for the two young emperors in Egypt and in all the East, with the exception of Palmyra, the prince of which took the side of Gallienus. One of them, Macrianus, went off with his father to the West, in order to install this new government also there. But soon fortune turned ; in Illyricum Macrianus lost a battle and his life, not against Gallienus, but against another pretender. Odaenathus turned against the brother who remained behind in Syria ; at Hemesa, where the armies met, the soldiers of Quietus replied to the summons to surrender that they would rather submit to anything than deliver themselves into the hands of a barbarian. Nevertheless Callistus, the general of Quietus, betrayed his master to the Palmyrene,[1] and thus ended also his short government.

Therewith Palmyra stepped into the first place in the East. Gallienus, more than sufficiently occupied by the barbarians of the West and the military insurrections everywhere breaking out there, gave to the prince of Palmyra, who alone had preserved fidelity to him in the crisis just mentioned, an exceptional position without a parallel, but under the prevailing circumstances readily intelligible ; he, as hereditary prince, or, as he was now called, king of Palmyra, became, not indeed joint ruler, but independent lieutenant of the emperor for the East.[2]

Government of Odaenathus in the East.

---

ator of Dio (*fr.* 3 Müll.) expresses this in the language of the later age by κόμης τῶν θησαυρῶν καὶ ἐφεστὼς τῇ ἀγορᾷ τοῦ σίτου.

[1] At least according to the report, which forms the basis of the imperial biographies (*vita Gallieni*, 3, and elsewhere). According to Zonaras, xii. 24, the only author who mentions

besides the end of Callistus, Odaenathus caused him to be put to death.

[2] That Odaenathus, as well as after him his son Vaballathus (apart, of course, from the time after the rupture with Aurelian), were by no means Augusti (as the *vit. Gallieni*, 12, erroneously states), is shown both by the absence of the name of Augustus

The local administration of Palmyra was conducted under him by another Palmyrene, at the same time as imperial procurator and as his deputy.[1] Therewith the whole imperial power, so far as it still subsisted at all in the East, lay in the hand of the "barbarian," and the latter with his Palmyrenes, who were strengthened by the remains of the Roman army corps and the levy of the land, re-established the sway of Rome alike rapidly and brilliantly. Asia and Syria were already evacuated by the enemy. Odaenathus crossed the Euphrates, relieved at length the brave Edessenes, and retook from the Persians the conquered towns Nisibis and Carrhae (264). Probably Armenia also was at that time brought back under

---

on the coins and by the title possible only for a subject, *v(ir) c(onsularis)* = ὑ(πατικός), which, like the father (p. 97, note 3), the son still bears. The position of governor is designated on the coins of the son by *im(perator) d(ux) R(omanorum)* = αὐτ(οκράτωρ) σ(τρατηγός) ; in agreement therewith Zonaras (xii. 23, and again xii. 24) and Syncellus (p. 716) state that Gallienus appointed Odaenathus, on account of his victory over the Persians and Ballista, as στρατηγὸς τῆς ἑῴας, or πάσης ἀνατολῆς; and the biographer of Gallienus, 10, that he *obtinuit totius Orientis imperium.* By this is meant all the Asiatic provinces and Egypt ; the added *imperator* = αὐτοκράτωρ (comp. *Trig. tyr.* 15, 6, *post reditum de Perside*—Herodes son of Odaenathus—*cum patre imperator est appellatus*) is intended beyond doubt to express the freer handling of power, different from the usual authority of the governor.—To this was added further the now formally assumed title of a king of Palmyra (*Trig. tyr.* 15, 2 : *adsumpto nomine regali*), which also the son bears, not on the Egyptian, but on the Syrian coins. The circumstance that Odaenathus is probably called *melekh malkê,* "king of kings," on an inscription set up in August 271, and so after his death and during the war of his adherents with Aurelian (Vogüé, n. 28), belongs

to the revolutionary demonstrations of this period and forms no proof for the earlier time.

[1] The numerous inscriptions of Septimius Vorodes, set up in the years 262 to 267 (Waddington, 2606-2610), and so in the lifetime of Odaenathus, all designate him as imperial procurator of the second class (*ducenarius*), but at the same time partly by the title ἀργαπέτης, which Persian word, current also among the Jews, signifies "lord of a castle," "viceroy" (Levy, *Zeitsch. der deutschen morgenl. Gesellschaft,* xviii. 90; Nöldeke, *ib.* xxiv. 107), partly as δικαιοδότης τῆς μητροκολωνίας, which, beyond doubt, is in substance at any rate, if not in language, the same office. Presumably we must understand by it that office on account of which the father of Odaenathus is called the "head of Tadmor" (p. 97, note 2); the one chief of Palmyra competent for martial law and for the administration of justice ; only that, since extended powers were given to the position of Odaenathus, this post as a subordinate office is filled by a man of equestrian rank. The conjecture of Sachau (*Zeitschr. der d. morgenl. Gesellsch.* xxxv. 738) that this Vorodes is the "Wurud" of a copper coin of the Berlin cabinet, and that both are identical with the elder son of Odaenathus, Herodes,

Roman allegiance.[1] Then he took—for the first time since Gordianus—the offensive against the Persians, and marched on Ctesiphon. In two different campaigns the capital of the Persian kingdom was invested by him, and the neighbouring region laid waste, and there was a successful battle with the Persians under its walls.[2] Even the Goths, whose predatory raids extended into the interior, retired when he set out for Cappadocia. A development of power of this sort was a blessing for the hard-pressed empire, and at the same time a serious danger. Odaenathus no doubt observed all due formalities towards his Roman lord-paramount, and sent the captured officers of the enemy and the articles of booty to Rome for the emperor, who did not disdain to triumph over them ; but in fact the East under Odaenathus was not much less independent than the West under Postumus, and we can easily understand how the officers favourably disposed towards Rome made opposition to the Palmyrene vice-emperor,[3] and on the one hand there was talk of attempts

who was killed at the same time with his father, is liable to serious difficulties. Herodes and Orodes are different names (in the Palmyrene inscription, Waddington, 2610, the two stand side by side) ; the son of a senator cannot well fill an equestrian office ; a procurator coining money with his image is not conceivable even for this exceptional state of things. Probably the coin is not Palmyrene at all. " It is," von Sallet writes to me, " probably older than Odaenathus, and belongs perhaps to an Arsacid of the second century A.D. ; it shows a head with a headdress similar to the Sassanid ; the reverse, S C in a chaplet of laurel, appears imitated from the coins of Antioch."—If subsequently, after the breach with Rome in 271, on an inscription of Palmyra (Waddington, 2611) two generals of the Palmyrenes are distinguished, ὁ μέγας στρατη-λάτης, the historically known Zabdas, and ὁ ἐνθάδε στρατηλάτης, Zabbaeos, the latter is, it may be presumed, just the Argapetes.

[1] The state of the case speaks in favour of this ; evidence is wanting. In the imperial biographies of this epoch the Armenians are wont to be adduced among the border peoples independent of Rome (*Valer.* 6 ; *Trig. tyr.* 30, 7, 18 ; *Aurel.* 11, 27, 28, 41) ; but this is one of their quite untrustworthy elements of embellishment.

[2] This more modest account (Eutropius, ix. 10 ; *vita Gallieni,* 10 ; *Trig. tyr.* 15, 4 ; Zos. i. 39, who alone attests the two expeditions) must be preferred to that which mentions the capture of the city (Syncellus, p. 716).

[3] This is shown by the accounts as to Carinus (cont. of Dio, p. 8) and as to Rufinus (p. 106, note 2). That after the death of Odaenathus Heraclianus, a general acting on Gallienus's orders against the Persians, was attacked and conquered by Zenobia (*vita Gallieni,* 13, 5), is in itself not impossible, seeing that the princes of Palmyra possessed *de iure* the chief command in all the East, and such an action,

of Odaenathus to attach himself to the Persians, which were alleged to have broken down only through Sapor's arrogance,[1] while on the other hand the assassination of Odaenathus at Hemesa in 266-7 was referred to instigation of the Roman government.[2] The real murderer was a brother's son of Odaenathus, and there are no proofs of the participation of the government. At any rate the crime made no change in the position of affairs.

Govern-
ment of
Zenobia.

The wife of the deceased, the queen Bat Zabbai, or in Greek, Zenobia, a beautiful and sagacious woman of masculine energy,[3] in virtue of the hereditary right to the principate claimed for the son of herself and Odaenathus, still in boyhood, Vaballathus or Athenodorus[4]—the elder, Herodes, had perished with his father—the position of the deceased, and in fact carried her point as well in Rome as in the East : the regnal years of the son are reckoned from the death of the father. For the son, not capable of government, the mother took part in counsel and action,[5] and she did not restrict herself to preserving the

even if it were suggested by Gallienus, might be treated as offending against this right, and this would clearly indicate the strained relation ; but the authority vouching it is so bad that little stress can be laid on it.

[1] This we learn from the characteristic narrative of Petrus, *fr.* 10, which is to be placed before *fr.* 11.

[2] The account of the continuator of Dio, *fr.* 7, that the old Odaenathus was put to death, as suspected of treason, by one (not elsewhere mentioned) Rufinus, and that the younger, when he had impeached this person at the bar of the emperor Gallienus, was dismissed on the declaration of Rufinus that the accuser deserved the same fate, cannot be correct as it stands. But Waddington's proposal to substitute Gallus for Gallienus, and to recognise in the accuser the husband of Zenobia, is not admissible, since the father of this Odaenathus was Hairanes, in whose case there existed no ground at all for such an execution, and the excerpt in its whole character undoubtedly applies

to Gallienus. Rather must the old Odaenathus have been the husband of Zenobia, and the author have erroneously assigned to Vaballathus, in whose name the charge was brought, his father's name.

[3] All the details which are current in our accounts of Zenobia originate from the imperial biographies ; and they will only be repeated by such as do not know this source.

The name Vaballathus is given, in addition to the coins and inscriptions, by Polemius Silvius, p. 243 of my edition, and the biographer of Aurelian, c. 38, while he describes as incorrect the statement that Odaenathus had left two sons, Timolaus and Herennianus. In reality these two persons emerging simply in the imperial biographies appear along with all that is connected with them as invented by the writer, to whom the thorough falsification of these biographies is to be referred. Zosimus too, i. 59, knows only of one son, who went into captivity with his mother.

[5] Whether Zenobia claimed for her-

state of possession, but on the contrary her courage or her arrogance aspired to mastery over the whole imperial domain of the Greek tongue. In the command over the East, which was committed to Odaenathus and inherited from him by his son, the supreme authority over Asia Minor and Egypt may doubtless have been included ; but *de facto* Odaenathus had in his power only Syria and Arabia, and possibly Armenia, Cilicia, and Cappadocia. Now an influential Egyptian, Timagenes, summoned the queen to occupy Egypt ; accordingly she despatched her chief general Zabdas with an army of, it is alleged, 70,000 men to the Nile. The land resisted with energy ; but the Palmyrenes defeated the Egyptian levy and possessed themselves of Egypt. A Roman admiral Probus attempted to dislodge them again, and even vanquished them, so that they set out for Syria ; but, when he attempted to bar their way at the Egyptian Babylon not far from Memphis, he was defeated by the better local knowledge of the Palmyrene general Timagenes, and he put himself to death.[1] When about the beginning of the year 270, after the death of the emperor Claudius Aurelian came in his stead, the Palmyrenes bore sway over Alexandria. In Asia Minor too they made preparations to establish themselves ; their garrisons were pushed forward as far as Ancyra in Galatia, and even in Chalcedon opposite Byzan-

---

self formal joint-rule, cannot be certainly determined. In Palmyra she names herself still after the rupture with Rome merely βασίλισση (Waddington, 2611, 2628), in the rest of the empire she may have laid claim to the title *Augusta*, Σεβαστή ; for, though there are no coins of Zenobia from the period prior to the breach with Rome, yet on the one hand the Alexandrian inscription with βασιλίσσης καὶ βασιλέως προσταξάντων (*Eph. epigr.* iv. p. 25, p. 33) cannot lay any claim to official redaction, and on the other hand the inscription of Byblos, *C. I. Gr.* 4503 b = Waddington, n. 2611, gives in fact to Zenobia the title Σεβαστή alongside of Claudius or Aurelian, while it refuses it

to Vaballathus. This is so far intelligible, as Augusta was an honorary designation, Augustus an official one, and thus that might well be conceded to the woman which was refused to the man.

[1] So Zosimus, i. 44, narrates the course of events with which Zonaras, xii. 27 and Syncellus, p. 721, in the main agree. The report in the life of Claudius, c. 11, is more displaced than properly contradictory ; the first half is only indicated by the naming of Saba ; the narrative begins with the successful attempt of Timagenes to ward off the attack of Probus (here Probatus). The view taken of this by me in Sallet (*Palmyra*, p. 44) is not tenable.

tium they had attempted to assert the rule of their queen. All this happened without the Palmyrenes renouncing the Roman government, nay probably on the footing that the control of the East committed by the Roman government to the prince of Palmyra was realised in this way, and they taxed the Roman officers, who resisted the extension of the Palmyrene rule, with rebellion against the imperial orders ; the coins struck in Alexandria name Aurelianus and Vaballathus side by side, and give the title of Augustus only to the former.   In substance, no doubt, the East here detached itself from the empire, and the latter was divided into two in the execution of an ordinance wrung from the wretched Gallienus by necessity.

Aurelian against the Palmyrenes.   The vigorous and prudent emperor, to whom the dominion now had fallen, broke at once with the Palmyrene co-ordinate government, which then could not but have and had as its consequence, that Vaballathus himself was proclaimed by his people as emperor.   Egypt was already, at the close of the year 270, brought back to the empire after hard struggles by the brave general Probus, afterwards the successor of Aurelian.[1]   It is true that the second city of the empire, Alexandria, paid for this victory almost with its existence, as will be set forth in the following section.   More difficult was the reduction of the remote Syrian oasis.   All other Oriental wars of the imperial period had chiefly been waged by imperial troops having their home in the East ; here, where the West had once more to subdue the revolted East, there fought once more, as in the time of the free republic,

---

[1] The determination of the date depends on the fact that the usurpation-coins of Vaballathus cease already in the fifth year of his Egyptian reign, *i.e.* 29th August 270-71 ; the fact that they are very rare speaks for the beginning of the year.   With this essentially agrees the circumstance that the storming of the Prucheion (which, we may add, was no part of the city, but a locality close by the city on the side of the great oasis ; Hieronymus, *vit. Hilarionis,* c. 33, 34, vol. ii. p. 32 Vall.) is put by Eusebius in his Chronicle in the first year of Claudius, by Ammianus, xxii. 16, 15, under Aurelian ; the most exact report in Eusebius, *H. Eccl.* vii. 32, is not dated.   The reconquest of Egypt by Probus stands only in his biography, c. 9 ; it may have happened as it is told, but it is possible also that in this thoroughly falsified source the history of Timagenes has been *mutatis mutandis* transferred to the emperor.

Occidentals against Orientals,[1] the soldiers of the Rhine and of the Danube with those of the Syrian desert. The mighty expedition began, apparently towards the close of the year 271 ; without encountering resistance the Roman army arrived at the frontier of Cappadocia ; here the town of Tyana, which barred the Cilician passes, gave serious opposition. After it had fallen, and Aurelian, by gentle treatment of the inhabitants, had smoothed his way to further successes, he crossed the Taurus, and, passing through Cilicia, arrived in Syria. If Zenobia, as is not to be doubted, had reckoned on active support from the side of the Persian king, she found herself deceived. The aged king Shapur did not interfere in this war, and the mistress of the Roman East continued to be left to her own military resources, of which perhaps even a portion took the side of the legitimate Augustus. At Antioch the Palmyrene chief force under the general Zabdas stopped the emperor's way ; Zenobia herself was present. A successful combat against the superior Palmyrene cavalry on the Orontes delivered into the hands of Aurelian the town, which not less than Tyana received full pardon—he justly recognised that the subjects of the empire were hardly to be blamed, when they had submitted to the Palmyrene prince appointed as commander in chief by the Roman government itself. The Palmyrenes, after having engaged in a conflict on their retreat at Daphne, the suburb of Antioch, marched off, and struck into the great route which leads from the capital of Syria to Hemesa and thence through the desert to Palmyra.

Aurelian summoned the queen to submit, pointing to the notable losses endured in the conflicts on the Orontes. These were Romans only, answered the queen ; the Orientals did not yet admit that they were conquered.

Battle at Hemesa.

---

[1] This is perhaps what the report on the battle of Hemesa, extracted by Zosimus, i. 52, wished to bring out, when it enumerates among the troops of Aurelian the Dalmatians, Moesians, Pannonians, Noricans, Raetians, Mauretanians, and the guard. When he associates with these the troops of Tyana and some divisions from Mesopotamia, Syria, Phoenice, Palestine, this applies beyond doubt to the Cappadocian gar-

At Hemesa[1] she took her stand for the decisive battle. It was long and bloody ; the Roman cavalry gave way and broke up in flight ; but the legions decided, and victory remained with the Romans. The march was more difficult than the conflict. The distance from Hemesa to Palmyra amounts in a direct line to seventy miles, and, although at that epoch of highly developed Syrian civilisation the region was not waste in the same degree as at present, the march of Aurelian still remains a considerable feat, especially as the light horsemen of the enemy swarmed round the Roman army on all sides. Aurelian, however, reached his goal, and began the siege of the strong and well-provisioned city ; more difficult than the siege itself was the bringing up of provisions for the besieging army. At length the courage of the princess sank, and she escaped from the city to seek aid from the Persians. Fortune still further helped the emperor. The pursuing Roman cavalry took her captive with her son, just when she had arrived at the Euphrates and was about to embark in the rescuing boat ; and the town, discouraged by her flight, capitulated (272). Aurelian granted here too, as in all this campaign, full pardon to the subdued burgesses. But a stern punishment was decreed over the queen and her functionaries and officers. Zenobia, after she had for years borne rule with masculine energy, did not now disdain to invoke a woman's privileges, and to throw the responsibility on her advisers, of whom not a few, including the celebrated scholar, Cassius Longinus, perished under the axe of the executioner. She herself might not be wanting from the triumphal procession of the emperor, and she did not

---

risons, which had joined after the capture of Tyana, and to some divisions of the armies of the East favourably disposed to Rome, who went over to Aurelian upon his marching into Syria.

[1] By mistake Eutropius, ix. 13, places the decisive battle *haud longe ab Antiochia :* the mistake is heightened in Rufius, c. 24 (on whom

Hieronymus, *chron. a. Abr.* 2289 depends), and in Syncellus, p. 721, by the addition *apud Immas,* ἐν Ἰμμαυς, which place, lying 33 Roman miles from Antioch on the road to Chalcis, is far away from Hemesa. The two chief accounts, in Zosimus and the biographer of Aurelian, agree in all essentials.

take the course of Cleopatra, but marched in golden chains, as a spectacle to the Roman multitude, before the chariot of the victor to the Roman capitol. But before Aurelian could celebrate his victory he had to repeat it.

A few months after the surrender the Palmyrenes once more rose, killed the small Roman garrison serving there, and proclaimed one Antiochus[1] as ruler, while they at the same time attempted to induce the governor of Mesopotamia, Marcellinus, to revolt. The news reached the emperor when he had just crossed the Hellespont. He returned at once, and stood, earlier than friend or foe had anticipated, once more before the walls of the insurgent city. The rebels had not been prepared for this ; there was this time no resistance, but also no mercy. Palmyra was destroyed, the commonwealth dissolved, the walls razed, the ornaments of the glorious temple of the sun transferred to the temple which, in memory of this victory, the emperor built to the sun-god of the East in Rome ; only the forsaken halls and walls remained, as they still stand in part at the present day. This occurred in the year 273.[2] The flourishing of Palmyra was artificial, produced by the routes assigned to traffic and the great public buildings dependent on it. Now the government withdrew its hand from the unhappy city. Traffic sought and found other paths ; as Mesopotamia was then viewed as a Roman province and soon came again to the empire,

Destruction
of Palmyra.

[1] This is the name given by Zosimus, i. 60, and Polemius Silvius, p. 243 ; the Achilleus of the biographer of Aurelian, c. 31, seems a confusion with the usurper of the time of Diocletian.—That at the same time in Egypt a partisan of Zenobia and at the same time robber-chief, by name Firmus, rose against the government, is doubtless possible, but the statement rests only on the imperial biographies, and the details added sound very suspiciously.

[2] The chronology of these events is not quite settled. The rarity of the Syrian coins of Vaballathus as Augustus shows that the rupture with Aurelian (end of 270) was soon followed by the conquest. According to the dated inscriptions of Odaenathus and Zenobia of August 271 (Waddington, 2611), the rule of the queen was at that time still intact. As an expedition of this sort, from the conditions of the climate, could not well take place otherwise than in spring, the first capture of Palmyra must have ensued in the spring of 272. The most recent (merely Palmyrene) inscription which we know from that quarter (Vogué, n. 116) is of August 272. The insurrection probably falls at this time ; the second capture and the destruction somewhere in the spring of the year 273 (in accordance with which, I. 166, note 1, is to be corrected).

and the territory of the Nabataeans as far as the port of Aelana was in Roman hands, this intermediate station might be dispensed with, and the traffic may have betaken itself instead to Bostra or Beroea (Aleppo). The short meteor-like splendour of Palmyra and its princes was immediately followed by the desolation and silence which, from that time down to the present day, enwrap the miserable desert-village and the ruins of its colonnades.

Persian war of Carus. The ephemeral kingdom of Palmyra was in its origin as in its fall closely bound up with the relations of the Romans to the non-Roman East, but not less a part of the general history of the empire. For, like the western empire of Postumus, the eastern empire of Zenobia was one of those masses into which the mighty whole seemed then about to resolve itself. If during its subsistence its leaders endeavoured earnestly to set limits to the onset of the Persians, and indeed the development of its power was dependent on that very fact, not merely did it in its collapse seek deliverance from those same Persians, but probably in consequence of the revolt of Zenobia Armenia and Mesopotamia were lost to the Romans, and after the subjugation of Palmyra the Euphrates again for a time formed the frontier. The queen, when she arrived at it, hoped to find a reception among the Persians ; and Aurelian omitted to lead the legions over it, seeing that Gaul, along with Spain and Britain, still at that time refused to recognise the government. He and his successor Probus were not able to take up this struggle. But when in the year 282, after the premature end of the latter, the troops proclaimed the commander next in rank, Marcus Aurelius Carus, as emperor, it was the first saying of the new ruler that the Persians should remember this choice, and he kept it. Immediately he advanced with the army into Armenia and re-established the earlier order there. At the frontier of the land he was met by Persian envoys, who declared themselves ready to grant all that was reasonable ;[1] but they were hardly listened

---

[1] It throws no light on the position of the Armenians, that in descrip- tions otherwise thoroughly apocryphal (*vita Valer.* 6 ; *vita Aurel.* **27, 28**)

to, and the march went on incessantly. Mesopotamia too became once more Roman, and the Parthian residential cities Seleucia and Ctesiphon were again occupied by the Romans without encountering lengthened resistance— to which the war between brothers then raging in the Persian empire contributed its part.[1] The emperor had just crossed the Tigris, and was on the point of penetrating into the heart of the enemy's country, when he met his death by violence, presumably by the hand of an assassin, and thereby the campaign also met its end. But his successor obtained in peace the cession of Armenia and Mesopotamia;[2] although Carus wore the purple little more than a year, he re-established the imperial frontier of Severus.

Some years afterwards (293) a new ruler, Narseh, son of king Shapur, ascended the throne of Ctesiphon, and declared war on the Romans in the year 296 for the

Persian war under Diocletian.

the Armenians after the catastrophe of Valerian keep to the Persians, and appear in the last crisis of the Palmyrenes as allies of Zenobia by the side of the Persians; both are obvious consequences from the general position of things. That Aurelian did not subdue Armenia any more than Mesopotamia, is supported in this case partly by the silence of the authorities, partly by the account of Synesius (*de regno*, p. 17) that the emperor Carinus (rather Carus) had in Armenia, close to the frontier of the Persian territory, summarily dismissed a Persian embassy, and that the young Persian king, alarmed by its report, had declared himself ready for any concession. I do not see how this narrative can be referred to Probus, as von Gutschmid thinks (*Zeitschr. d. deutsch. morgenl. Gesell.* xxxi. 50); on the other hand it suits very well the Persian expedition of Carus.

[1] The reconquest of Mesopotamia is reported only by the biographer, c. 8; but at the outbreak of the Persian war under Diocletian it is Roman. There is mention at the same place of internal troubles in the

Persian empire; also in a discourse held in the year 289 (*Paneg.* iii. c. 17) there is mention of the war, which is waged against the king of Persia—this was Bahram II.—by his own brother Ormies or rather Hormizd *adscitis Sacis et Ruffis* (?) *et Gellis* (comp. Nöldeke, *Tabarî,* p. 479). We have altogether only some detached notices as to this important campaign.

[2] This is stated clearly by Mamertinus (*Paneg.* ii. 7, comp. ii. 10, iii. 6) in the oration held in 289 : *Syriam velut amplexu suo tegebat Euphrates antequam Diocletiano sponte* (that is, without Diocletian needing to have recourse to arms, as is then further set forth) *se dederent regna Persarum ;* and further by another panegyrist of the year 296 (*Paneg.* v. 3) : *Partho ultra Tigrim reducto.* Turns like that in Victor, *Caes.* xxxix. 33, that Galerius *relictis finibus* had marched to Mesopotamia, or that Narseh, according to Rufius Festus, c. 25, ceded Mesopotamia in peace, cannot on the other hand be urged ; and as little, that Oriental authorities place the Roman occupation of Nisibis in 609 Sel. = 297/8 A.D. (Nöldeke, *Tabarî,*

possession of Mesopotamia and Armenia.[1] Diocletian, who then had the supreme conduct of the empire generally, and of the East in particular, entrusted the management of the war to his imperial colleague Galerius Maximianus, a rough but brave general. The beginning was unfavourable. The Persians invaded Mesopotamia and reached as far as Carrhae ; the Caesar led against them the Syrian legions over the Euphrates at Nicephorium ; between these two positions the armies encountered each other, and the far weaker Roman force gave way. It was a hard blow, and the young general had to submit to severe reproaches, but he did not despair. For the next campaign reinforcements were brought up from the whole empire, and both rulers personally took the field ; Diocletian took his position in Mesopotamia with the chief force, while Galerius, reinforced by the flower of the Illyrian troops that had in the meantime come up, met, with a force of 25,000 men, the enemy in Armenia, and inflicted on him a decisive defeat. The camp and the treasure, nay, even the harem, of the great-king fell into the hands of the warriors, and with difficulty Narseh himself escaped from capture. In order to recover the women and the children the king declared himself ready to conclude peace on any terms ; his envoy Apharban conjured the Romans to spare the Persians, saying that the two empires, the Roman and the Parthian, were, as it were, the two eyes of the world, and neither could dispense with the other. It would have lain in the power of the Romans to add one more to their Oriental provinces ; the prudent ruler contented himself with regulating the state of possession in the north-east. Mesopotamia remained, as a matter of course, in the Roman possession ; the important commercial intercourse with the neigh-

p. 50). If this were correct, the exact account as to the negotiations for peace of 297 in Petrus Patricius, *fr.* 14, could not possibly be silent as to the cession of Mesopotamia and merely make mention of the regulation of the frontier-traffic.

[1] That Narseh broke into Armenia at that time Roman, is stated by Ammianus, xxiii. 5, 11 ; for Mesopotamia the same follows from Eutropius, ix. 24. On the 1st March 296 peace was still subsisting, or at any rate the declaration of war was not yet known in the west (*Paneg.* v. 10).

bouring foreign land was placed under strict state-control and essentially directed to the strong city of Nisibis, the basis of the Roman frontier-guard in eastern Mesopotamia. The Tigris was recognised as boundary of the direct Roman rule, to such an extent, however, that the whole of southern Armenia as far as the lake Thospitis (lake of Van) and the Euphrates, and so the whole upper valley of the Tigris, should belong to the Roman empire. This region lying in front of Mesopotamia did not become a province proper, but was administered after the previous fashion as the Roman satrapy of Sophene. Some decades later the strong fortress of Amida (Diarbekir) was constructed here, thenceforth the chief stronghold of the Romans in the region of the upper Tigris. At the same time the frontier between Armenia and Media was regulated afresh, and the supremacy of Rome over that land, as over Iberia, was once more confirmed. The peace did not impose important cessions of territory on the conquered, but it established a frontier favourable to the Romans, which for a considerable time served in these much contested regions as a demarcation of the two empires.[1] The policy of Trajan thereby obtained its complete accomplishment ; at all events the centre of gravity of the Roman rule shifted itself just at this time from the West to the East.

[1] The differences in the exceptionally good accounts, particularly of Petrus Patricius, *fr.* 14, and Ammianus, xxv. 7, 9, are probably only of a formal kind. The fact that the Tigris was to be the proper boundary of the empire, as Priscus says, does not exclude, especially considering the peculiar character of its upper course, the possibility of the boundary there partially going beyond it ; on the contrary, the five districts previously named in Petrus appear to be adduced just as beyond the Tigris, and to be excepted from the following general definition. The districts adduced by Priscus here and, expressly as beyond the Tigris, by Ammianus—these are in both Arzanene, Carduene, and Zabdicene, in Priscus Sophene and Intilene ("rather Ingilene, in Armenia Angel, now Egil " ; Kiepert), in Ammianus Moxoene and Rehimene (?)—cannot possibly all have been looked on by the Romans as Persian before the peace, when at any rate Armenia was already *Romano iuri obnoxia* (Ammianus, xxiii. 5, 11); beyond doubt the more westerly of them already then formed a part of Roman Armenia, and stand here only in so far as they were, in consequence of the peace, incorporated with the empire as the satrapy of Sophene. That the question here concerned not the boundary of the cession, but that of the territory directly imperial, is shown by the conclusion, which settles the boundary between Armenia and Media.

CHAPTER X.

SYRIA AND THE LAND OF THE NABATAEANS.

Conquest
of Syria.
IT was very gradually that the Romans, after acquiring the
western half of the coasts of the Mediterranean, resolved
on possessing themselves also of the eastern half. Not the
resistance, which they here encountered in comparatively
slight measure, but a well-founded fear of the denationalising consequences of such acquisitions, led to as prolonged
an effort as possible on their part merely to preserve decisive political influence in those regions, and to the incorporation proper at least of Syria and Egypt taking place
only when the state was already almost a monarchy.
Doubtless the Roman empire became thereby geographically compact ; the Mediterranean Sea, the proper basis of
Rome after it was a great power, became on all sides a
Roman inland lake ; the navigation and commerce on its
waters and shores formed politically an unity to the advantage of all that dwelt around. But by the side of geographical compactness went national bipartition. Through
Greece and Macedonia the Roman state would never have
become binational, any more than the Greek cities of
Neapolis and Massalia had Hellenised Campania and
Provence. But, while in Europe and Africa the Greek
domain vanishes in presence of the compact mass of the
Latin, so much of the third continent as was drawn, with
the Nile-valley rightfully pertaining to it, into this cycle of
culture belonged exclusively to the Greeks, and Antioch
and Alexandria in particular were the true pillars of the
Hellenic development that attained its culmination in

Alexander—centres of Hellenic life and Hellenic culture, and great cities, as was Rome.   After having set forth in the preceding chapter the conflict between the East and West in and around Armenia and Mesopotamia, that filled the whole period of the empire, we turn to describe the relations of the Syrian regions, as they took shape at the same time.   What we mean is the territory which is separated by the mountain-chain of Pisidia, Isauria, and Western Cilicia from Asia Minor; by the eastern continuation of these mountains and the Euphrates from Armenia and Mesopotamia, by the Arabian desert from the Parthian empire and from Egypt ; only it seemed fitting to deal with the peculiar fortunes of Judaea in a special section. In accordance with the diversity of political development under the imperial government, we shall speak in the first instance of Syria proper, the northern portion of this territory, and of the Phoenician coast that stretches along under the Libanus, and then of the country lying behind Palestine—the territory of the Nabataeans.   What was to be said about Palmyra has already found its place in the preceding chapter.

After the partition of the provinces between the emperor and the senate, Syria was under imperial administration, and was in the East, like Gaul in the West, the central seat of civil and military control.   This governorship was from the beginning the most esteemed of all, and only became in course of time all the more thought of.   Its holder, like the governor of the two Germanies, wielded the command over four legions, and while the administration of the inland Gallic districts was taken away from the commanders of the Rhine-army and a certain restriction was involved in the very fact of their coordination, the governor of Syria retained the civil administration of the whole large province undiminished, and held for long alone in all Asia a command of the first rank.   Under Vespasian, indeed, he obtained in the governors of Palestine and Cappadocia two colleagues likewise commanding legions ; but, on the other hand, through the annexation of the kingdom of Commagene,

Provincial government.

and soon afterwards of the principalities in the Libanus, the field of his administration was increased. It was only in the course of the second century that a diminution of his prerogatives occurred, when Hadrian took one of the four legions from the governor of Syria and handed it over to the governor of Palestine. It was Severus who at length withdrew the first place in the Roman military hierarchy from the Syrian governor. After having subdued the province—which had wished at that time to make Niger emperor, as it had formerly done with its governor Vespasian—amidst resistance from the capital Antioch in particular, he ordained its partition into a northern and a southern half, and gave to the governor of the former, which was called Coele-Syria, two legions, to the governor of the latter, the province of Syro-Phoenicia, one.

Syrian troops.

Syria may also be compared with Gaul, in so far as this district of imperial administration was divided more sharply than most into pacified regions and border-districts needing protection. While the extensive coast of Syria and the western regions generally were not exposed to hostile attacks, and the protection on the desert frontier against the roving Bedouins devolved on the Arabian and Jewish princes, and subsequently on the troops of the province of Arabia as also on the Palmyrenes, more than on the Syrian legions, the Euphrates-frontier required, particularly before Mesopotamia became Roman, a watch against the Parthians similar to that on the Rhine against the Germans. But if the Syrian legions came to be employed on the frontier, they could not be dispensed with in western Syria as well.[1] The troops of the Rhine were

---

[1] We cannot exactly determine the standing quarters of the Syrian legions; yet what is here said is substantially assured. Under Nero the 10th legion lay at Raphaneae, north-west from Hamath (Josephus, *Bell. Jud.* vii. 1, 3); and at that same place, or at any rate nearly in this region under Tiberius the 6th (Tacitus, *Ann.* ii. 79); probably in or near Antioch the 12th under Nero (Josephus, *Bell. Jud.* ii. 18, 19). At least one legion lay on the Euphrates; for the time before the annexation of Commagene Josephus attests this (*Bell. Jud.* vii. 1, 3), and subsequently one of the Syrian legions had its headquarters in Samosata (Ptolemaeus, v. 15, 11; inscription from the time of Severus, *C. I. L.* vi. 1409; *Itin. Antonini*, p. 186). Probably the staffs of most of the Syrian legions had their seat in the western districts, and the ever-recurring complaint that encamping in the

certainly there also on account of the Gauls ; yet the
Romans might say with justifiable pride that for the great
capital of Gaul and the three Gallic provinces a direct
garrison of 1200 men sufficed.   But for the Syrian population, and especially for the capital of Roman Asia, it was
not enough to station legions on the Euphrates.   Not
merely on the edge of the desert, but also in the retreats
of the mountains there lodged daring bands of robbers,
who roamed in the neighbourhood of the rich fields and
large towns—not to the same extent as now, but constantly
even then—and, often disguised as merchants or soldiers,
pillaged the country houses and the villages.   But even
the towns themselves, above all Antioch, required like
Alexandria garrisons of their own.   Beyond doubt this
was the reason why a division into civil and military districts, like that enacted for Gaul by Augustus, was never
even so much as attempted in Syria, and why the large
self-subsistent camp-settlements, out of which *e.g.* originated
Mentz on the Rhine, Leon in Spain, Chester in England,
were altogether wanting in the Roman East.   But beyond
doubt this was also the reason why the Syrian army was
so much inferior in discipline and spirit to that of the
Western provinces ; why the stern discipline, which was
exercised in the military standing camps of the West,
never could take root in the urban cantonments of the
East.   When stationary troops have, in addition to their
more immediate destination, the task of police assigned
to them, this of itself has a demoralising effect ; and only
too often, where they are expected to keep in check turbulent civic masses, their own discipline in fact is thereby
undermined.   The Syrian wars formerly described furnish
the far from pleasant commentary on this ; none of them
found an army capable of warfare in existence, and regu-

towns disorganised the Syrian army,
applies chiefly to this arrangement. It
is doubtful whether in the better times
there existed headquarters proper of
the legions on the edge of the desert ;
at the frontier-posts there detachments
of the legions were employed, and in
particular the specially disturbed district between Damascus and Bostra
was strongly furnished with legionaries provided on the one hand by
the command of Syria, on the other
by that of Arabia after its institution
by Trajan.

larly there was need to bring up Occidental troops in order to give the turn to the struggle.

Syria in the narrower sense and its adjoining lands, the Plain Cilicia and Phoenicia, never had under the Roman emperors a history properly so called. The inhabitants of these regions belonged to the same stock as the inhabitants of Judaea and Arabia, and the ancestors of the Syrians and the Phoenicians were settled in a remote age at one spot with those of the Jews and the Arabs, and spoke one language. But while the latter clung to their peculiar character and to their language, the Syrians and the Phoenicians became Hellenised even before they came under Roman rule. This Hellenising took effect throughout in the formation of Hellenic polities. The foundation for this had indeed been laid by the native development, particularly by the old and great mercantile cities on the Phoenician coast. But above all the formation of states by Alexander and the Alexandrids, just like that of the Roman republic, had as its basis not the tribe, but the urban community ; it was not the old Macedonian hereditary principality, but the Greek polity that Alexander carried into the East ; and it was not from tribes, but from towns that he designed, and the Romans designed, to constitute their empire. The idea of the autonomous burgess-body is an elastic one, and the autonomy of Athens and Thebes was a different thing from that of the Macedonian and Syrian city, just as in the Roman circle the autonomy of free Capua had another import than that of the Latin colonies of the republic or even of the urban communities of the empire ; but the fundamental idea is everywhere that of self-administering citizenship sovereign within its own ring-wall. After the fall of the Persian empire, Syria, along with the neighbouring Mesopotamia, was, as the military bridge of connection between the West and the East, covered more than any other land with Macedonian settlements. The Macedonian names of places transferred thither to the greatest extent, and nowhere else recurring in the whole empire of Alexander, show that here the flower of the Hellenic conquerors of the East was settled, and that Syria was to become for this state the New-Macedonia ; as indeed, so long as the empire of Alexander retained a central government, this had there its seat.   Then the troubles of the last Seleucid period had helped the Syrian imperial towns to greater independence.

These arrangements the Romans found existing.   Of non-urban districts administered directly by the empire there were probably none at all in Syria according to the organisation planned by Pompeius, and, if the dependent principalities in the first epoch of the Roman rule embraced a great portion of the southern interior of the province, these were withal mostly mountainous and poorly inhabited districts of subordinate importance.   Taken as a whole, for the Romans in Syria not much was left to be done as to the increase of urban development—less than in Asia Minor.   Hence there is hardly anything to be told from the imperial period of the founding of towns in the strict sense as regards Syria.   The few colonies which were laid out here, such as Berytus under Augustus and probably also Heliopolis, had no other object than those conducted to Macedonia, namely, the settlement of veterans.

How the Greeks and the older population in Syria stood to one another, may be clearly traced by the very local names.   The majority of districts and towns here bear Greek names, in great part, as we have observed, derived from the Macedonian home, such as Pieria, Anthemusias, Arethusa, Beroea, Chalcis, Edessa, Europus, Cyrrhus, Larisa, Pella, others named after Alexander or the members of the Seleucid house, such as Alexandria, Antioch, Seleucis and Seleucia, Apamea, Laodicea, Epiphaneia.   The old native names maintain themselves doubtless side by side, as Beroea, previously in Aramaean Chalep, is also called Chalybon, Edessa or Hierapolis, previously Mabog, is called also Bambyce, Epiphaneia, previously Hamat, is also called Amathe.   But for the most part the older appellations give way before the foreign ones, and only a few districts and larger places, such as Commagene, Samosata, Hemesa, Damascus, are without newly-formed Greek names.   Eastern Cilicia has few

Continu-
ance of the
native
language
and habits
under Hel-
lenism.

Macedonian foundations to show ; but the capital Tarsus became early and completely Hellenised, and was long before the Roman time one of the centres of Hellenic culture. It was somewhat otherwise in Phoenicia ; the mercantile towns of old renown, Aradus, Byblus, Berytus, Sidon, Tyrus, did not properly lay aside the native names; but how here too the Greek gained the upper hand, is shown by the Hellenising transformation of these same names, and still more clearly by the fact that New-Aradus is known to us only under the Greek name Antaradus, and likewise the new town founded by the Tyrians, the Sidonians, and the Aradians in common on this coast only under the name Tripolis, and both have developed their modern designations Tartus and Tarabulus from the Greek. Already in the Seleucid period the coins in Syria proper bear exclusively, and those of the Phoenician towns most predominantly, Greek legends ; and from the beginning of the imperial period the sole rule of Greek is here an established fact.[1] The oasis of Palmyra alone, not merely separated by wide stretches of desert, but also preserving a certain political independence, formed, as we saw (p. 95), an exception in this respect. But in intercourse the native idioms were retained. In the mountains of the Libanus and the Anti-Libanus, where in Hemesa (Homs), Chalcis, Abila (both between Berytus and Damascus) small princely houses of native origin ruled till towards the end of the first century after Christ, the native language had probably the sole sway in the imperial period, as indeed in the mountains of the Druses so difficult of access the language of Aram has only in recent times yielded to Arabic. But two thousand years ago it was in fact the language of the people in all Syria.[2] That in the case of the double-named towns the Syrian designation predominated in common life just as did the

---

[1] There is a coin of Byblus from the time of Augustus with Greek and Phoenician legend (Imhoof-Blumer, *Monnaies grecques*, 1883, p. 443).

[2] Johannes Chrysostomus of Antioch († 407) points on several occasions (*de sanctis martyr*. Opp. ed. Paris, 1718, vol. ii. p. 651 ; *Homil.* xix. *ibid*. p. 188) to the ἑτεροφωνία, the βάρβαρος φωνή of the λαός in contrast to the language of the cultured.

Greek in literature, appears from the fact that at the present day Beroea-Chalybon is named Haleb (Aleppo), Epiphaneia-Amathe Hamat, Hierapolis-Bambyce-Mabog Membid, Tyre by its Aramaean name Sur; that the Syrian town known to us from documents and authors only as Heliopolis still bears at the present day its primitive native name Baalbec, and, in general, the modern names of places have come, not from the Greek, but from the Aramaean.

In like manner the worship shows the continued life Worship. of Syrian nationality. The Syrians of Beroea bring their votive gifts with Greek legend to Zeus Malbachos, those of Apamea to Zeus Belos, those of Berytus as Roman citizens to Jupiter Balmarcodes—all deities, in which neither Zeus nor Jupiter had real part. This Zeus Belos is no other than the Malach Belos adored at Palmyra in the Syriac language (p. 96, note 1). How vivid was, and continued to be, the hold of the native worship of the gods in Syria, is most clearly attested by the fact that the lady of Hemesa, who by her marriage-relationship with the house of Severus obtained for her grandson the imperial dignity at the beginning of the third century, not content with the boy's being called supreme Pontifex of the Roman people, urged him also to entitle himself before all Romans the chief priest of the native sun-god Elagabalus. The Romans might conquer the Syrians; but the Roman gods had in their own home yielded the field to those of Syria.

No less are the numerous Syrian proper names that have come to us mainly non-Greek, and double names are not rare; the Messiah is termed also Christus, the apostle Thomas also Didymus, the woman of Joppa raised up by Peter "the gazelle," Tabitha or Dorcas. But for literature, and presumably also for business-intercourse and the intercourse of the cultured, the Syrian idiom was as little in existence as the Celtic in the West; in these Jam- circles Greek exclusively prevailed, apart from the Latin blichus. required also in the East for the soldiers. A man of letters of the second half of the second century, whom

Sohaemus the king of Armenia formerly mentioned (p. 76) brought to his court, has inserted in a romance, which has its scene in Babylon, some points of the history of his own life that illustrate this relation. He is, he says, a Syrian, not, however, one of the immigrant Greeks, but of native lineage on the father's and mother's side, Syrian by language and habits, acquainted also with the Babylonian language and with Persian magic. But this same man, who in a certain sense declines the Hellenic character, adds that he had appropriated Hellenic culture ; and he became an esteemed teacher of youth in Syria, and a notable romance-writer of the later Greek literature.[1]

Later Syriac literature. If subsequently the Syrian idiom again became a written language and developed a literature of its own, this is to be traced not to an invigoration of national feeling, but to the immediate needs of the propagation of Christianity. That Syriac literature, which began with the translation of the writings of the Christian faith into Syriac, remained confined to the sphere of the specific culture of the Christian clergy, and hence took up only the small fragments of general Hellenic culture which the theologians of that time found conducive to, or compatible with, their ends ;[2] this authorship did not attain, and doubtless did not strive after, any higher aim than the transference of the library of the Greek monastery to the Maronite cloisters. It hardly reaches further back than to the second century of our era, and had its centre,

---

[1] The extract of Photius from the romance of Jamblichus, c. 17, which erroneously makes the author a Babylonian, is essentially corrected and supplemented by the *scholion* upon it. The private secretary of the great-king, who comes among Trajan's captives to Syria, becomes there tutor of Jamblichus, and instructs him in the " barbarian wisdom," is naturally a figure of the romance running its course in Babylon, which Jamblichus professes to have heard from this his instructor ; but characteristic of the time is the Armenian court-man-of-letters and princes' tutor (for it was doubtless as " good rhetor " that he was called by Sohaemus to Valarshapat) himself, who in virtue of his magical art not merely understands the charming of flies and the conjuring of spirits, but also predicts to Verus the victory over Vologasus, and at the same time narrates in Greek to the Greeks stories such as might stand in the *Thousand and One Nights*.

[2] Syriac literature consists almost exclusively of translations of Greek works. Among profane writings treatises of Aristotle and Plutarch stand in the first rank, then practical writings of a juristic or agronomic

not in Syria, but in Mesopotamia, particularly in Edessa,[1] where the native language had not become so entirely a dialect as in the older Roman territory.

Among the manifold bastard forms which Hellenism assumed in the course of its diffusion at once civilising and degenerating, the Syro-Hellenic is doubtless that in which the two elements are most equally balanced, but perhaps at the same time that which has most decisively influenced the collective development of the empire. The Syrians received, no doubt, the Greek urban organisation and appropriated Hellenic language and habits ; nevertheless they did not cease to feel themselves as Orientals, or rather as organs of a double civilisation. Nowhere is this perhaps more sharply expressed than in the colossal tomb-temple, which at the commencement of the imperial period Antiochus king of Commagene erected for himself on a solitary mountain-summit not far from the Euphrates. He names himself in the copious epitaph a Persian ; the priest of the sanctuary is to present to him the memorial-offering in the Persian dress, as the custom of his family demands ; but he calls the Hellenes also, like the Persians, the blessed roots of his race, and entreats the blessing of all the gods of Persis as of Macetis, that is of the Persian as well as of the Macedonian land, to rest upon his descendants. For he is the son of a native king of the family of the Achaemenids and of a Greek prince's daughter of the house of Seleucus ; and, in keeping with this, the images on the one hand of his paternal ancestors back to the first Darius, on the other hand of his maternal back to Alexander's marshal, embellished the tomb in a long double row. But the gods, whom he honours, are at the same time Persian and Greek, Zeus Oromasdes, Apollon Mithras Helios Hermes, Artagnes Herakles Ares, and the effigy of this latter, for example, bears the club of the Greek hero and at the same time the Persian tiara. This Persian

Syro-Hellenic mixed culture

Tomb of Antiochus of Commagene.

character, and books of popular entertainment, such as the romance of Alexander, the fables of Aesop, the sentences of Menander.

[1] The Syriac translation of the New Testament, the oldest text of the Syriac language known to us, probably originated in Edessa ; the στρατιῶται of the Acts of the Apostles are here called " Romans."

prince, who calls himself at the same time a friend of the
Hellenes, and as loyal subject of the emperor a friend of
the Romans, as not less that Achaemenid called by Marcus
and Lucius to the throne of Armenia, Sohaemus, are true
representatives of the native aristocracy of imperial Syria,
which bears in mind alike Persian memories and the
Romano-Hellenic present.   From such circles the Persian
worship of Mithra reached the West.   But the population, which was placed at the same time under this great
nobility Persian or calling itself Persian, and under the
government of Macedonian and later of Italian masters,
was in Syria, as in Mesopotamia and Babylonia, Aramaean;
it reminds us in various respects of the modern Roumans
in presence of the upper ranks of Saxons and Magyars.
Certainly it was the most corrupt and most corrupting
element in the conglomerate of the Romano-Hellenic
peoples.   Of the so-called Caracalla, who was born at
Lyons as son of an African father and a Syrian mother, it
was said that he united in himself the vices of three races,
Gallic frivolity, African savageness, and Syrian knavery.

Christi-
anity and
Neopla-
tonism.

This interpenetration of the East and Hellenism,
which has nowhere been carried out so completely as in
Syria, meets us predominantly in the form of the good
and noble becoming ruined in the mixture.   This, however, is not everywhere the case ; the later developments
of religion and of speculation, Christianity and Neoplaton-
ism, have proceeded from the same conjunction ; if with
the former the East penetrates into the West, the latter is
the transformation of the Occidental philosophy in the
sense and spirit of the East—a creation in the first instance
of the Egyptian Plotinus (204-270) and of his most considerable disciple the Syrian Malchus or Porphyrius (233
till after 300), and thereafter pre-eminently cultivated in
the towns of Syria.   For a discussion of these two
phenomena, so significant in the history of the world,
this is not the place ; but they may not be forgotten in
estimating the position of matters in Syria.

Antioch.

The Syrian character finds its eminent expression in
the capital of the country and, before Constantinople was

founded, of the Roman East generally—inferior as respects population only to Rome and Alexandria, and possibly also to the Babylonian Seleucia—Antioch, on which it appears requisite to dwell for a moment. The town, one of the youngest in Syria and now of small importance, did not become a great city by the natural circumstances of commerce, but was a creation of monarchic policy. The Macedonian conquerors called it into life, primarily from military considerations, as a fitting central place for a rule which embraced at once Asia Minor, the region of the Euphrates, and Egypt, and sought also to be near to the Mediterranean.[1] The like aim and the different methods of the Seleucids and the Lagids find their true expression in the similarity and the contrast of Antioch and Alexandria; as the latter was the centre for the naval power and the maritime policy of the Egyptian rulers, so Antioch was the centre for the continental Eastern monarchy of the rulers of Asia. The later Seleucids at different times undertook large new foundations here, so that the city, when it became Roman, consisted of four independent and walled-in districts, all of which again were enclosed by a common wall. Nor were immigrants from a distance wanting. When Greece proper fell under the rule of the Romans, and Antiochus the Great had vainly attempted to dislodge them thence, he granted at least to the emigrant Euboeans and Aetolians an asylum in his capital. In the capital of Syria, as in that of Egypt, a commonwealth in some measure independent and a privileged position were conceded to the Jews, and the position of the towns as centres of the Jewish Diaspora was not the weakest element in their development. Once made a residency and the seat of the supreme administration of a great empire, Antioch remained even in Roman times the

---

[1] This is said by Diodorus, xx. 47, of the forerunner of Antioch, the town of Antigonea, situated about five miles farther up the river. Antioch was for the Syria of antiquity nearly what Aleppo is for the Syria of the present day, the rendezvous of inland traffic ; only that, in the case of that foundation, as the contemporary construction of the port of Seleucia shows, the immediate connection with the Mediterranean was designed, and hence the town was laid out farther to the west.

capital of the Asiatic provinces of Rome. Here resided the emperors, when they sojourned in the East, and regularly the governor of Syria ; here was struck the imperial money for the East, and here especially, as well as in Damascus and Edessa, were found the imperial manufactories of arms. It is true that the town had lost its military importance for the Roman empire; and under the changed circumstances the bad communication with the sea was felt as a great evil, not so much on account of the distance, as because the port—the town of Seleucia, planned at the same time with Antioch—was little fitted for large traffic. The Roman emperors from the Flavians down to Constantius expended enormous sums to hew out of the masses of rocks surrounding this locality the requisite docks with their tributary canals, and to provide sufficient piers ; but the art of the engineers, which at the mouth of the Nile had succeeded in throwing up the highest mounds, contended vainly in Syria with the insurmountable difficulties of the ground. As a matter of course the largest town of Syria took an active part in the manufactures and the commerce of this province, of which we shall have to speak further on ; nevertheless it was a seat of consumers more than of producers.

Daphne.   In no city of antiquity was the enjoyment of life so much the main thing, and its duties so incidental, as in " Antioch upon Daphne," as the city was significantly called, somewhat as if we should say " Vienna upon the Prater." For Daphne [1] was a pleasure-garden, about five miles from the city, ten miles in circumference, famous for its laurel-trees, after which it was named, for its old cypresses which even the Christian emperors ordered to be spared, for its flowing and gushing waters, for its shining temple of Apollo, and its magnificent much-frequented festival of the 10th August. The whole environs of the

[1] The space between Antioch and Daphne was filled with country-houses and villas (Libanius, *pro rhetor.* ii. p. 213 Reiske), and there was also here a suburb Heraclea or else Daphne (O. Müller, *Antiq. Antioch*, p. 44 ; comp. *vita Veri*, 7); but when Tacitus, *Ann.* ii. 83, names this suburb Epidaphne, this is one of his most singular blunders. Plinius, *H. N.* v. 27, 79, says correctly : *Antiochia Epidaphnes cognominata.*

city, which lies between two wooded mountain-chains in the valley of the Orontes abounding in water, fourteen miles upward from its mouth, are even at the present day, in spite of all neglect, a blooming garden and one of the most charming spots on earth. No city in all the empire excelled it in the splendour and magnificence of its public structures. The chief street, which to the length of thirty-six stadia, nearly four and a half miles, with a covered colonnade on both sides, and a broad carriage-way in the middle, traversed the city in a straight direction along the river, was imitated in many ancient towns, but had not its match even in imperial Rome. As the water ran into every good house in Antioch,[1] so the people walked in those colonnades through the whole city at all seasons protected from rain as from the heat of the sun, and during the evening also in lighted streets, of which we have no record as to any other city of antiquity.[2]

[1] "That wherein we especially beat all," says the Antiochene Libanius, in the Panegyric on his home delivered under Constantius (i. 354 R.), after having described the springs of Daphne and the aqueducts thence to the city, "is the water-supply of our city; if in other respects any one may compete with us, all give way so soon as we come to speak of the water, its abundance and its excellence. In the public baths every stream has the proportions of a river, in the private several have the like, and the rest not much less. He who has the means of laying out a new bath does so without concern about a sufficient flow of water, and has no need to fear that, when ready, it will remain dry. Therefore every district of the city (there were eighteen of these) carefully provides for the special elegance of its bathing-establishment; these district-bathing-establishments are so much finer than the general ones, as they are smaller than these are, and the inhabitants of the district strive to surpass one another. One measures the abundance of running water by the number of the (good) dwelling-houses; for as many as are the dwel-ling-houses, so many are also the running waters, nay there are even in individual houses often several; and the majority of the workshops have also the same advantage. Therefore we have no fighting at the public wells as to who shall come first to draw—an evil, under which so many considerable towns suffer, when there is a violent crowding round the wells and outcry over the broken jars. With us the public fountains flow for ornament, since every one has water within his doors. And this water is so clear that the pail appears empty, and so pleasant that it invites us to drink."

[2] "Other lights," says the same orator, p. 363, "take the place of the sun's light, lamps which leave the Egyptian festival of illumination far behind; and with us night is distinguished from day only by the difference of the lighting; diligent hands find no difference and forge on, and he who will sings and dances, so that Hephaestos and Aphrodite here share the night between them." In the street-sport which the prince Gallus indulged in, the lamps of Antioch were very inconvenient to him (Ammianus, xiv. 1, 9).

But amidst all this luxury the Muses did not find themselves at home ; science in earnest and not less earnest
art were never truly cultivated in Syria and more especially
in Antioch.   However complete was the analogy in other
respects between Egypt and Syria as to their development,
their contrast in a literary point of view was sharp ; the
Lagids alone entered on this portion of the inheritance
of Alexander the Great.   While they fostered Hellenic
literature and promoted scientific research in an Aristotelian sense and spirit, the better Seleucids doubtless by
their political position opened up the East to the Greeks—
the mission of Megasthenes to king Chandragupta in
India on the part of Seleucus I., and the exploring of the
Caspian Sea by his contemporary the admiral Patrocles,
were epoch-making in this respect—but of immediate
interposition in literary interests on the part of the
Seleucids the history of Greek literature has nothing more
to tell than that Antiochus the Great, as he was called,
made the poet Euphorion his librarian.   Perhaps the
history of Latin literature may make a claim to serious
scientific work on the part of Berytus, the Latin island in
the sea of Oriental Hellenism.   It is perhaps no accident
that the reaction against the modernising tendency in
literature of the Julio-Claudian epoch, and the reintroduc-
tion of the language and writings of the republican time
into the school as into literature, originated with a Bery-
tian belonging to the middle class, Marcus Valerius
Probus, who in the schools that were left in his remote
home moulded himself still on the old classics, and then,
in energetic activity more as a critical author than as
strictly a teacher, laid the foundation for the classicism of
the later imperial period.   The same Berytus became
later, and remained through the whole period of the empire,
for all the East, the seat of the study of jurisprudence requisite towards an official career.   As to Hellenic literature no doubt the poetry of the epigram and the wit of
the *feuilleton* were at home in Syria ; several of the most
noted Greek minor poets, like Meleager, Philodemus of
Gadara, and Antipater of Sidon, were Syrians and unsur-

passed in sensuous charm as in refined versification ; and the father of the *feuilleton* literature was Menippus of Gadara. But these performances lie for the most part before, and some of them considerably before, the imperial period.

In the Greek literature of this epoch no province is so poorly represented as Syria; and this is hardly an accident, although, considering the universal position of Hellenism under the empire, not much stress can be laid on the home of the individual writers. On the other hand the subordinate authorship which prevailed in this epoch —such as stories of love, robbers, pirates, procurers, soothsayers, and dreams, destitute of thought or form, and fabulous travels—had probably its chief seat here. Among the colleagues of the already-mentioned Jamblichus, author of the Babylonian history, his countrymen must have been numerous ; the contact of this Greek literature with the Oriental literature of a similar kind doubtless took place through the medium of Syrians. The Greeks indeed had no need to learn lying from the Orientals ; yet the no longer plastic but fanciful story-telling of their later period has sprung from Scheherazade's horn of plenty not from the pleasantry of the Graces. It is perhaps not accidentally that the satire of this period, when it views Homer as the father of lying travels, makes him a Babylonian with the proper name of Tigranes. Apart from this entertaining reading, of which even those were somewhat ashamed who spent their time in writing or reading it, there is hardly any other prominent name to be mentioned from these regions than the contemporary of that Jamblichus, Lucian of Commagene. He, too, wrote nothing except, in imitation of Menippus, essays and fugitive pieces after a genuinely Syrian type, witty and sprightly in personal banter, but where this is at an end, incapable of saying amid his laughter the earnest truth or of even handling the plastic power of comedy.

This people valued only the day. No Greek region has so few memorial-stones to show as Syria ; the great Antioch, the third city in the empire, has—to say nothing

Minor literature.

Daily life and amusements.

of the land of hieroglyphics and obelisks—left behind fewer
inscriptions than many a small African or Arabian village.
With the exception of the rhetorician Libanius from the
time of Julian, who is more well-known than important,
this town has not given to literature a single author's
name. The Tyanitic Messiah of heathenism, or his
apostle speaking for him, was not wrong in terming the
Antiochenes an uncultivated and half-barbarous people,
and in thinking that Apollo would do well to transform
them as well as their Daphne ; for "in Antioch, while the
cypresses knew how to whisper, men knew not how to
speak." In the artistic sphere Antioch had a leading
position only as respected the theatre and sports generally.
The exhibitions which captivated the public of Antioch
were, according to the fashion of this time, less strictly
dramatic than noisy musical performances, ballets, animal
hunts, and gladiatorial games. The applauding or hissing
of this public decided the reputation of the dancer throughout the empire. The jockeys and other heroes of the
circus and theatre came pre-eminently from Syria.[1] The
ballet-dancers and the musicians, as well as the jugglers
and buffoons, whom Lucius Verus brought back from his
Oriental campaign—performed, so far as his part went,
in Antioch—to Rome, formed an epoch in the history of
Italian theatricals. The passion with which the public in
Antioch gave itself up to this pleasure is characteristically
shown by the fact, that according to tradition the gravest
disaster which befell Antioch in this period, its capture
by the Persians in 260 (p. 101), surprised the burgesses
of the city in the theatre, and from the top of the mount,
on the slope of which it was constructed, the arrows flew

---

[1] The remarkable description of the empire from the time of Constantius (Müller, *Geog. Min.* ii. p. 213 ff.), the only writing of the kind in which the state of industry meets with a certain consideration, says of Syria in this respect : "Antioch has everything that one desires in abundance, but especially its races. Laodicea, Bery- tus, Tyre, Caesarea (in Palestine) have races also. Laodicea sends abroad jockeys, Tyre and Berytus actors, Caesarea dancers (*pantomimi*), Heli- opolis on Lebanon flute-players (*chor- aulae*), Gaza musicians (*auditores*, by which ἀκροάματα is incorrectly ren- dered), Ascalon wrestlers (*athletae*), Castabala (strictly speaking in Cilicia) boxers."

into the ranks of the spectators. In Gaza, the most southerly town of Syria, where heathenism possessed a stronghold in the famous temple of Marnas, at the end of the fourth century the horses of a zealous heathen and of a zealous Christian ran at the races, and, when on that occasion " Christ beat Marnas," St. Jerome tells us, numerous heathens had themselves baptised.

All the great cities of the Roman empire doubtless vied with each other in dissoluteness of morals ; but in this the palm probably belongs to Antioch. The decorous Roman, whom the severe moral-portrait-painter of Trajan's time depicts, as he turns his back on his native place, because it had become a city of Greeks, adds that the Achaeans formed the least part of the filth ; that the Syrian Orontes had long discharged itself into the river Tiber, and flooded Rome with its language and its habits, its street-musicians, female harp-players and triangle-beaters, and the troops of its courtesans. The Romans of Augustus spoke of the Syrian female flute-player, the *ambubaia*,[1] as we speak of the Parisian *cocotte*. In the Syrian cities, it is stated even in the last age of the republic by Posidonius, an author of importance, who was himself a native of the Syrian Apamea, the citizens have become disused to hard labour ; the people there think only of feasting and carousing, and all clubs and private parties serve for this purpose ; at the royal table a garland is put on every guest, and the latter is then sprinkled with Babylonian perfume ; flute-playing and harp-playing sound through the streets ; the gymnastic institutes are converted into hot baths—by the latter is meant the institution of the so-called Thermae, which probably first emerged in Syria and subsequently became general ; they were in substance a combination of the gymnasium and the hot-bath. Four hundred years later matters went on after quite a similar fashion in Antioch. The quarrel between Julian and these townsmen arose not so much about the emperor's beard, as because in this city of taverns, which, as he expresses himself, has nothing in view but dancing

Immorality.

---

[1] From the Syrian word *abbubo*, fife.

and drinking, he regulated the prices for the hosts. The religious system of the Syrian land was also, and especially, pervaded by these dissolute and sensuous doings. The cultus of the Syrian gods was often an appanage of the Syrian brothel.[1]

Antiochene ridicule.

It would be unjust to make the Roman government responsible for this state of affairs in Syria; it had been the same under the government of the Diadochi, and was merely transmitted to the Romans. But in the history of this age the Syro-Hellenic element was an essential factor, and, although its indirect influence was of far more weight, it still in many ways made itself perceptible directly in politics. Of political partisanship proper there can be still less talk in the case of the Antiochenes of this and every age, than in the case of the burgesses of the other great cities of the empire; but in mocking and disputation they apparently excelled all others, even the Alexandrians that vied with them in this respect. They never made a revolution, but readily and earnestly supported every pretender whom the Syrian army set up, Vespasian against Vitellius, Cassius against Marcus, Niger against Severus, always ready, where they thought that they had support in reserve, to renounce allegiance to the existing government. The only talent which indisputably belonged to them—their mastery of ridicule—they exercised not merely against the actors of their stage, but no less against the rulers sojourning in the capital of the East, and the ridicule was quite the same against the actor as against the emperor; it applied to personal appearance and to individual peculiarities, just as if their sovereign appeared only to amuse them with his part. Thus there existed between the public of Antioch and their rulers—particularly those who spent a considerable time there, Hadrian, Verus, Marcus, Severus,

---

[1] The little treatise, ascribed to Lucian, as to the Syrian goddess at Hierapolis adored by all the East, furnishes a specimen of the wild and voluptuous fable-telling which was characteristic of the Syrian cultus. In this narrative—the source of Wieland's Kombabus—self-mutilation is at once celebrated and satirised in turn as an act of high morality and of pious faith.

Julian—so to speak, a perpetual warfare of sarcasm, one document of which, the reply of the last named emperor to the " beard-mockers " of Antioch, is still preserved.   While this imperial man of letters met their sarcastic sayings with satirical writings, the Antiochenes at other times had to pay more severely for their evil speaking and their other sins.   Thus Hadrian withdrew from them the right of coining silver ; Marcus withdrew the right of assembly, and closed for some time the theatre.   Severus took even from the town the primacy of Syria, and transferred it to Laodicea, which was in constant neighbourly warfare with the capital ; and, if these two ordinances were soon again withdrawn, the partition of the province, which Hadrian had already threatened, was carried into execution, as we have already said (p. 118), under Severus, and not least because the government wished to humble the turbulent great city.   This city even made a mockery of its final overthrow.   When in the year 540 the Persian king Chosroes Nushirvan appeared before the walls of Antioch he was received from its battlements not merely with showers of arrows but with the usual obscene sarcasms ; and, provoked by this, the king not merely took the town by storm, but carried also its inhabitants away to his New-Antioch in the province of Susa.

The brilliant aspect of the condition of Syria was the economic one ; in manufactures and trade Syria takes, alongside of Egypt, the first place among the provinces of the Roman empire, and even claims in a certain respect precedence over Egypt.   Agriculture throve under the permanent state of peace, and under a sagacious administration which directed its efforts particularly to the advancement of irrigation, to an extent which puts to shame modern civilisation.   No doubt various parts of Syria are still at the present day of the utmost luxuriance ; the valley of the lower Orontes, the rich garden round Tripolis with its groups of palms, groves of oranges copses of pomegranates and jasmine, the fertile coast-plain north and south of Gaza, neither the Bedouins nor the Pashas have hitherto been able to make desolate.   But

Culture of the soil.

their work is nevertheless not to be estimated lightly. Apamea in the middle of the Orontes valley, now a rocky wilderness without fields and trees, where the poor flocks on the scanty pasturages are decimated by the robbers of the mountains, is strewed far and wide with ruins, and there is documentary attestation that under Quirinius the governor of Syria, the same who is named in the Gospels, this town with its territory included numbered 117,000 free inhabitants. Beyond question the whole valley of the Orontes abounding in water—already at Hemesa it is from 30 to 40 mètres broad and one and a half to three mètres deep—was once a great seat of cultivation. But even of the districts, which are now mere deserts, and where it seems to the traveller of the present day impossible for man to live and thrive, a considerable portion was formerly a field of labour for active hands. To the east of Hemesa, where there is now not a green leaf nor a drop of water, the heavy basalt-slabs of former oil-presses are found in quantities. While at the present day olives scantily grow only in the valleys of the Lebanon abounding in springs, the olive woods must formerly have stretched far beyond the valley of the Orontes. The traveller now from Hemesa to Palmyra carries water with him on the back of camels, and all this part of the route is covered with the remains of former villas and hamlets.[1] The march of Aurelian along this route (p. 110) no army could now undertake. Of what is at present called desert a good portion is rather the laying waste of the blessed labour of better times. "All Syria," says a description of the earth from the middle of the fourth century, "over-

---

[1] The Austrian engineer, Joseph Tschernik (Petermann's *Geogr. Mittheil.* 1875, *Ergänzungsheft*, xliv. p. 3, 9) found basalt-slabs of oil-presses not merely on the desert plateau at Kala'at el-Hossn between Hemesa and the sea, but also to the number of more than twenty eastward from Hemesa at el-Ferklûs, where the basalt itself does not occur, as well as numerous walled terraces and mounds of ruins at the same place ; with terracings on the whole stretch of seventy miles between Hemesa and Palmyra. Sachau (*Reise in Syrien und Mesopotamien*, 1883, p. 23, 55) found remains of aqueducts at different places of the route from Damascus to Palmyra. The cisterns of Aradus cut in the rock, already mentioned by Strabo (xvi. 2, 13, p. 753), still perform their service at the present day (Renan, *Phénicie*, p. 40).

flows with corn, wine, and oil." But Syria was not even in antiquity an exporting land, in a strict sense, for the fruits of the earth, like Egypt and Africa, although the noble wines were sent away, *e.g.* that of Damascus to Persia, those of Laodicea, Ascalon, Gaza, to Egypt and from thence as far as Ethiopia and India, and even the Romans knew how to value the wine of Byblus, of Tyre, and of Gaza.

Of far more importance for the general position of the province were the Syrian manufactures. A series of industries, which came into account for export, were here at home, especially of linen, purple, silk, glass. The weaving of flax, practised from of old in Babylonia, was early transplanted thence to Syria ; as that description of the earth says : "Scytopolis (in Palestine), Laodicea, Byblus, Tyrus, Berytus, send out their linen into all the world," and in the tariff-law of Diocletian accordingly there are adduced as fine linen goods those of the three first-named towns alongside of those of the neighbouring Tarsus and of Egypt, and the Syrian have precedence over all. That the purple of Tyre, however many competitors with it arose, always retained the first place, is well known ; and besides the Tyrian there were in Syria numerous purple dyeworks likewise famous on the coast above and below Tyre at Sarepta, Dora, Caesarea, even in the interior, in the Palestinian Neapolis and in Lydda. The raw silk came at this epoch from China and especially by way of the Caspian Sea, and so to Syria ; it was worked up chiefly in the looms of Berytus and of Tyre, in which latter place especially was prepared the purple silk that was much in use and brought a high price. The glass manufactures of Sidon maintained their primitive fame in the imperial age, and numerous glass-vases of our museums bear the stamp of a Sidonian manufacturer. *(Manufactures.)*

To the sale of these wares, which from their nature belonged to the market of the world, fell to be added the whole mass of goods which came from the East by the Euphrates-routes to the West. It is true that the Arabian *(Commerce.)*

and Indian imports at this time turned away from this road, and took chiefly the route by way of Egypt; but not merely did the Mesopotamian traffic remain necessarily with the Syrians; the emporia also at the mouth of the Euphrates stood in regular caravan-intercourse with Palmyra (p. 98), and thus made use of the Syrian harbours. How considerable this intercourse was with the eastern neighbours is shown by nothing so clearly as by the similarity of the silver coinage in the Roman East and in the Parthian Babylonia; in the provinces of Syria and Cappadocia the Roman government coined silver, varying from the imperial currency, after the sorts and the standards of the neighbouring empire. The Syrian manufactures themselves, *e.g.* of linen and silk, were stimulated by the very import of the similar Babylonian articles of commerce, and, like these, the leather and skin goods, the ointments, the spices, the slaves of the East, came during the imperial period to a very considerable extent by way of Syria to Italy and the West in general. But this always remained characteristic of these primitive seats of commercial intercourse, that the men of Sidon and their countrymen, in this matter very different from the Egyptians, not merely sold their goods to those of other lands, but themselves conveyed them thither, and, as the ship-captains in Syria formed a prominent and respected class,[1] so Syrian merchants and Syrian factories in the imperial period were to be found nearly as much everywhere as in the remote times of which Homer tells. The Tyrians had such factories in the two great import-harbours of Italy, Ostia and Puteoli, and, as these themselves in their documents describe their establishments as the greatest and most spacious of their kind, so in the description of the earth which we have often quoted, Tyre is named the first place of the East for commerce and traffic[2]; in like manner

---

[1] In Aradus, a town very populous in Strabo's time (xvi. 2, 13, p. 753), there appears under Augustus a πρόβουλος τῶν ναυαρχησάντων (*C. I. Gr.* 4736 *h*, better in Renan, *Mission de Phénicie*, p. 31).

[2] *Totius orbis descriptio*, c. 24 : *nulla forte civitas Orientis est eius spissior in negotio.* The documents of the *statio* (*C. I. Gr.* 5853 ; *C. I. L.* x. 1601) give a lively picture of these factories. They serve in the

Strabo brings forward as a specialty at Tyre and at Aradus the unusually high houses, consisting of many stories. Berytus and Damascus, and certainly many other Syrian and Phoenician commercial towns, had similar factories in the Italian ports.[1] Accordingly we find, particularly in the later period of the empire, Syrian merchants, chiefly Apamean, settled not merely in all Italy but likewise in all the larger emporia of the West, at Salonae in Dalmatia, Apulum in Dacia, Malaca in Spain, but above all in Gaul and Germany, *e.g.* at Bordeaux, Lyons, Paris, Orleans, Treves, so that these Syrian Christians also, like the Jews, live according to their own customs and make use of their Greek in their meetings.[2]

first instance for religious ends, that is, for the worship of the Tyrian gods at a foreign place ; for this object a tax is levied at the larger station of Ostia from the Tyrian mariners and merchants, and from its produce there is granted to the lesser a yearly contribution of 1000 sesterces, which is employed for the rent of the place of meeting ; the other expenses are raised by the Tyrians in Puteoli, doubtless by voluntary contributions.

[1] For Berytus this is shown by the Puteolan inscription *C. I. L.* x. 1634 ; for Damascus it is at least suggested by that which is there set up (x. 1576) to the *Iupiter optimus maximus Damascenus.*—We may add that it is here apparent with how good reason Puteoli is called Little Delos. At Delos in the last age of its prosperity, that is, nearly in the century before the Mithradatic war, we meet with Syrian factories and Syrian worships in quite a like fashion and in still greater abundance ; we find there the guild of the Herakleistae of Tyre (τὸ κοινὸν τῶν Τυρίων Ἡρακλεϊστῶν ἐμπόρων καὶ ναυκλήρων, *C. I. Gr.* 2271) of the Poseidoniastae of Berytus (τὸ κοινὸν Βηρυτίων Ποσειδωνιαστῶν ἐμπόρων καὶ ναυκλήρων καὶ ἐγδοχέων, *Bull. de corr. Hell.* vii., p. 468), of the woshippers of Adad and Atargatis of Heliopolis (*ib.* vi. 495 f.), apart from the numerous memorial-stones of Syrian mer-

chants. Comp. Homolle *ib.* viii. p. 110 f.

[2] When Salvianus (towards 450) remonstrates with the Christians of Gaul that they are in nothing better than the heathens, he points (*de gub. Dei,* iv. 14, 69) to the worthless *negotiatorum et Syricorum omnium turbae, quae maiorem ferme civitatum universarum partem occupaverunt.* Gregory of Tours relates that king Guntchram was met at Orleans by the whole body of citizens and extolled, as in Latin, so also in Hebrew and in Syriac (viii. 1 : *hinc lingua Syrorum, hinc Latinorum, hinc . . . Judaeorum in diversis laudibus varie concrepabat*), and that after a vacancy in the episcopal see of Paris a Syrian merchant knew how to procure it for himself, and gave away to his countrymen the places belonging to it (x. 26 : *omnem scholam decessoris sui abiciens Syros de genere suo ecclesiasticae domui ministros esse statuit*). Sidonius (about 450) describes the perverse world of Ravenna (Ep. 1, 8) with the words : *fenerantur clerici, Syri psallunt ; negotiatores militant, monachi negotiantur. Usque hodie,* says Hieronymus (in Ezech. 27, vol. v. p. 513 Vall.) *permanet in Syris ingenitus negotiationis ardor, qui per totum mundum lucri cupiditate discurrunt et tantam mercandi habent vesaniam, ut occupato nunc orbe*

The state of things formerly described among the
Antiochenes and the Syrian cities generally becomes intelligible only on this basis. The world of rank there consisted
of rich manufacturers and merchants, the bulk of the population of the labourers and the mariners ;[1] and, as later the
riches acquired in the East flowed to Genoa and Venice,
so then the commercial gains of the West flowed back
to Tyre and Apamea. With the extensive field of traffic
that lay open to these traders on a great scale, and with
the on the whole moderate frontier and inland tolls, the
Syrian export trade, embracing a great part of the most
lucrative and most transportable articles, already brought
enormous capital sums into their hands; and their business
was not confined to native goods.[2] What comfort of life
once prevailed here we learn, not from the scanty remains
of the great cities that have perished, but from the more
forsaken than desolated region on the right bank of the
Orontes, from Apamea on to the point where the river

Romano (written towards the end
of the fourth century) *inter gladios et
miserorum neces quaerant divitias et
paupertatem periculis fugiant.* Other
proofs are given by Friedländer, *Sitten-
geschichte*, ii.⁵ p. 67. Without doubt we
may be allowed to add the numerous
inscriptions of the West which proceed from Syrians, even if those do
not designate themselves expressly as
merchants. Instructive as to this
point is the Coemeterium of the small
north-Italian country-town Concordia
of the fifth century ; the foreigners
buried in it are all Syrians, mostly
of Apamea (*C. I. L.* iii. p. 1060) ;
likewise all the Greek inscriptions
found in Treves belong to Syrians
(*C. I. Gr.* 9891, 9892, 9893). These
inscriptions are not merely dated in
the Syrian fashion, but show also
peculiarities of the dialectic Greek
there (*Hermes*, xix. 423).—That this
Syro-Christian Diaspora, standing in
relation to the contrast between the
Oriental and Occidental clergy, may
not be confounded with the Jewish
Diaspora, is clearly shown by the
account in Gregorius ; it evidently

stood much higher, and belonged
throughout to the better classes.

[1] This is partly so even at the
present day. The number of silk-
workers in Höms is estimated at
3000 (Tschernik, *l.c.*)

[2] One of the oldest (*i.e.* after
Severus and before Diocletian) epitaphs of this sort is the Latin-Greek
one found not far from Lyons (Wil-
manns, 2498 ; comp. Lebas - Waddington, n. 2329) of a Θαῖμος ὁ καὶ
Ἰουλιανὸς Σαάδου (in Latin *Thaemus
Iulianus Sati fil.*), a native of Atheila
(*de vico Athelani*), not far from Canatha in Syria (still called ' Atîl, not
far from Kanawât in the Hauran),
and *decurio* in Canatha, settled in
Lyons (πάτραν λείπων ἦκε τῷδ' ἐπὶ
χώρῳ), and a wholesale trader there
for Aquitanian wares ([ἐs πρ]ᾶσιν ἔχων
ἐνπόρ[ιο]ν ἀγορασμῶν [με]στὸν ἐκ Ἀκου-
ιτανίης ὧδ' ἐπὶ Λουγουδούνοιο—*nego-
tiatori Luguduni et prov. Aquitanica*).
Accordingly these Syrian merchants
must not only have dealt in Syrian
goods, but have, with their capital
and their knowledge of business, practised wholesale trading generally.

turns towards the sea. In this district of about a hundred miles in length there still stand the ruins of nearly a hundred townships, with whole streets still recognisable, the buildings with the exception of the roofs executed in massive stone-work, the dwelling-houses surrounded by colonnades, embellished with galleries and balconies, windows and portals richly and often tastefully decorated with stone arabesques, with gardens and baths laid out, with farm-offices in the ground-story, stables, wine and oil presses hewn in the rocks,[1] as also large burial chambers likewise hewn in the rock, filled with sarcophagi, and with the entrances adorned with pillars. Traces of public life are nowhere met with ; it is the country-dwellings of the merchants and of the manufacturers of Apamea and Antioch, whose assured prosperity and solid enjoyment of life are attested by these ruins. These settlements, of quite a uniform character, belong throughout to the late times of the empire, the oldest to the beginning of the fourth century, the latest to the middle of the sixth, immediately before the onslaught of Islam, under which this prosperous and flourishing life succumbed. Christian symbols and Biblical language are everywhere met with, and likewise stately churches and ecclesiastical structures. The development of culture, however, did not begin merely under Constantine, but simply grew and became consolidated in those centuries. Certainly those stone-buildings were preceded by similar villa and garden structures of a less enduring kind. The regeneration of the imperial government after the confused troubles of the third century has its expression in the upward impulse which the Syrian mercantile world then received ; but up to a certain degree this picture of it left to us may be referred also to the earlier imperial period.

The relations of the Jews in the time of the Roman empire were so peculiar and, one might say, so little *Jewish traffic.*

---

[1] Characteristic is the Latin epigram on a press-house, *C. I. L.* iii. 188, in this home of the "Apamean grape" (*vita Elagabali*, c. 21).

dependent on the province which was named in the earlier period after them, in the later rather by the revived name of the Philistaeans or Palaestinenses, that, as we have already said, it appeared more suitable to treat of them in a separate section. The little which is to be remarked as to the land of Palestine, especially the not unimportant share of its maritime and partly also of its inland towns in Syrian industry and Syrian trade, has already been mentioned in the exposition given above of these matters. The Jewish Diaspora had already, before the destruction of the temple, extended in such a way that Jerusalem, even while it still stood, was more a symbol than a home, very much as the city of Rome was for the so-called Roman burgesses of later times. The Jews of Antioch and Alexandria, and the numerous similar societies of lesser rights and minor repute took part, as a matter of course, in the commerce and intercourse of the places where they dwelt. Their Judaism comes into account in the case only perhaps so far as the feelings of mutual hatred and mutual contempt, which had become developed or rather increased since the destruction of the temple, and the repeated national-religious wars between Jews and non-Jews must have exercised their effect also in these circles. As the Syrian merchants resident abroad met together in the first instance for the worship of their native deities, the Syrian Jew in Puteoli cannot well have belonged to the Syrian merchant-guilds there ; and, if the worship of the Syrian gods found more and more an echo abroad, that which benefited the other Syrians drew one barrier the more between the Syrians believing in Moses and the Italians. If those Jews who had found a home outside of Palestine, attached themselves beyond it not to those who shared their dwelling-place but to those who shared their religion, as they could not but do, they thereby renounced the esteem and the toleration which the Alexandrians and the Antiochenes and the like met with abroad, and were taken for what they professed to be—Jews. The Palestinian Jews of the West, however, had for the most part not originated from mercantile emigration, but were captives of war or descendants of such, and in every respect homeless ; the Pariah position which the children of Abraham occupied, especially in the Roman capital—that of the mendicant Jew, whose household furniture consisted in his bundle of hay and his usurer's basket, and for whom no service was too poor and too menial—linked itself with the slave-market. Under these circumstances we can understand why the Jews during the imperial period played in the West a subordinate part alongside of the Syrians. The religious fellowship of the mercantile and proletarian immigrants told heavily on the collective body of the Jews, along with the general disparagement connected with their position. But that Diaspora, as well as this, had little to do with Palestine.

There remains still a frontier territory to be looked at, which is not often mentioned, and which yet well deserves consideration ; it is the Roman province of Arabia. It bears its name wrongly ; the emperor who erected it, Trajan, was a man of big deeds but still bigger words. The Arabian peninsula, which separates the region of the Euphrates from the valley of the Nile, lacking in rain, without rivers, on all sides surrounded by a rocky coast poor in harbours, was little fitted for agriculture or for commerce, and in old times by far the greater part of it remained the undisputed heritage of the unsettled inhabitants of the desert. In particular the Romans, who understood how to restrict their possession in Asia as in Egypt better than any other of the changing powers in the ascendant, never even attempted to subdue the Arabian peninsula. Their few enterprises against its south-eastern portion, the most rich in products, and from its relation to India the most important also for commerce, will be set forth when we discuss the business-relations of Egypt. Roman Arabia, even as a Roman client-state and especially as a Roman province, embraced only a moderate portion of the north of the peninsula, but, in addition, the land to

Province of Arabia.

the south and east of Palestine between this and the
great desert till beyond Bostra. At the same time with
this let us take into account the country belonging to
Syria between Bostra and Damascus, which is now usually
named after the Haurân mountains, according to its old
designation Trachonitis and Batanaea.

These extensive regions were only to be gained for
civilisation under special conditions. The steppe-country
proper (Hamâd) to the eastward from the region with
which we are now occupied as far as the Euphrates, was
never taken possession of by the Romans, and was incapable of cultivation ; only the roving tribes of the desert,
such as at the present day the Haneze, traverse it, to pasture their horses and camels in winter along the Euphrates,
in summer on the mountains south of Bostra, and often to
change the pasture-ground several times in the year. The
pastoral tribes settled westward of the steppe, who pursue
in particular the breeding of sheep to a great extent, stand
already at a higher degree of culture. But there is manifold room for agriculture also in these districts. The red
earth of the Haurân, decomposed lava, yields in its
primitive state much wild rye, wild barley, and wild oats,
and furnishes the finest wheat. Individual deep valleys
in the midst of the stone-deserts, such as the " seed-field,"
the Ruhbe in the Trachonitis, are the most fertile tracts in
all Syria ; without ploughing, to say nothing of manuring,
wheat yields on the average eighty and barley a hundred-
fold, and twenty-six stalks from one grain of wheat are
not uncommon. Nevertheless no fixed dwelling-place was
formed here, because in the summer months the great heat
and the want of water and pasture compel the inhabitants
to migrate to the mountain pastures of the Haurân. But
there was not wanting opportunity even for fixed settlement.
The garden-quarter around the town of Damascus,
watered by the river Baradâ in its many arms, and the
fertile even now populous districts which enclose it on the
east, north, and south, were in ancient as in modern times
the pearl of Syria. The plain round Bostra, particularly
the so-called Nukra to the west of it, is at the present day

the granary for Syria, although from the want of rain on an average every fourth harvest is lost, and the locusts often invading it from the neighbouring desert remain a scourge of the land which cannot be exterminated. Wherever the water-courses of the mountains are led into the plain, fresh life flourishes amidst them. " The fertility of this region," says one who knows it well, " is inexhaustible ; and even at the present day, where the Nomads have left neither tree nor shrub, the land, so far as the eye reaches, is like a garden." Even on the lava-surfaces of the mountainous districts the lava-streams have left not a few places (termed Kâ' in the Haurân), free for cultivation.

This natural condition has, as a rule, handed over the country to shepherds and robbers. The necessarily nomadic character of a great part of the population leads to endless feuds, particularly about places of pasture, and to constant seizures of those regions which are suited for fixed settlement ; here, still more than elsewhere, there is need for the formation of such political powers as are in a position to procure quiet and peace on a wider scale, and for these there is no right basis in the population. There is hardly a region in the wide world in which, so much as in this case, civilisation has not grown up spontaneously, but could only be called into existence by the ascendency of conquest from without. When military stations hem in the roving tribes of the desert and force those within the limit of cultivation to a peaceful pastoral life, when colonists are conducted to the regions capable of culture, and the waters of the mountains are led by human hands into the plains, then, but only then, a cheerful and plentiful life thrives in this region.

The pre-Roman period had not brought such blessings to these lands. The inhabitants of the whole territory as far as Damascus belong to the Arabian branch of the great Semitic stock ; the names of persons at least are throughout Arabic. In it, as in northern Syria, Oriental and Occidental civilisation met ; yet up to the time of the empire the two had made but little progress. The lan-

Greek influence in eastern Syria.

guage and the writing, which the Nabataeans used, were those of Syria and of the Euphrates-lands, and could only have come from thence to the natives. On the other hand the Greek settlement in Syria extended itself, in part at least, also to these regions. The great commercial town of Damascus had become Greek with the rest of Syria. The Seleucids had carried the founding of Greek towns even into the region beyond the Jordan, especially into the northern Decapolis; further to the south at least the old Rabbath Ammon had been converted by the Lagids into the city of Philadelphia. But further away and in the eastern districts bordering on the desert the Nabataean kings were not much more than nominally obedient to the Syrian or Egyptian Alexandrids, and coins or inscriptions and buildings, which might be attributed to pre-Roman Hellenism, have nowhere come to light.

Arrangements of Pompeius.

When Syria became Roman, Pompeius exerted himself to strengthen the Hellenic urban system, which he found in existence; as indeed the towns of the Decapolis

64-63.

subsequently reckoned their years from the year 690-91, in which Palestine had been added to the empire.[1] But in this region the government as well as the civilisation continued to be left to the two vassal-states, the Jewish and the Arabian.

The territory of Herod beyond the Jordan.

Of the king of the Jews, Herod and his house, we shall have to speak elsewhere; here we have to mention his activity in the extending of civilisation toward the east. His field of dominion stretched over both banks of the Jordan in all its extent, northwards as far at least as

---

[1] That the Decapolis and the reorganisation of Pompeius reached at last as far as Kanata (Kerak), north-west of Bostra, is established by the testimonies of authors and by the coins dated from the Pompeian era (Waddington on 2412, *d*). To the same town probably belong the coins with the name Γαβ(ε)ίν(ια) Κάναθα, with the name and dates of the same era (Reichardt, *Num. Zeitschrift*, 1880, p. 53); this place would accordingly belong to the numerous ones restored by Gabinius (Josephus, *Arch.* xiv. 5, 3). Waddington no doubt (on no. 2329) assigns these coins, so far as he knew them, to the second place of this name, the modern Kanawât, the proper capital of the Haurân, to the northward of Bostra; but it is far from probable that the organisation of Pompeius and Gabinius extended so far eastward. Presumably this second city was younger and named after the first, the most easterly town of the Decapolis.

Chelbon north-west from Damascus, southward as far as
the Dead Sea, while the region farther to the east between
his kingdom and the desert was assigned to the king of
the Arabians.   He and his descendants, who still bore
sway here after the annexation of the lordship of Jerusalem down to Trajan, and subsequently resided in Caesarea Paneas in the southern Lebanon, had endeavoured
energetically to tame the natives.   The oldest evidences
of a certain culture in these regions are doubtless the
cave-towns, of which there is mention in the Book of
Judges, large subterranean collective hiding-places made
habitable by air-shafts, with streets and wells, fitted to
shelter men and flocks, difficult to be found and, even
when found, difficult to be reduced.   Their mere existence
shows the oppression of the peaceful inhabitants by the
unsettled sons of the steppe.   " These districts," says
Josephus, when he describes the state of things in the
Haurân under Augustus, " were inhabited by wild tribes,
without towns and without fixed fields, who harboured with
their flocks under the earth in caves with narrow entrance
and wide intricate paths, but copiously supplied with water
and provisions were difficult to be subdued."   Several of
these cave-towns contained as many as 400 head.   A
remarkable edict of the first or second Agrippa, fragments
of which have been found at Canatha (Kanawât), summons
the inhabitants to leave off their " animal-conditions " and
to exchange their cavern-life for civilised existence.   The
non-settled Arabs live chiefly by the plundering partly of
the neighbouring peasants, partly of caravans on the march ;
the uncertainty was increased by the fact that the petty
prince Zenodorus of Abila to the north of Damascus, in the
Anti-Libanus, to whom Augustus had committed the superintendence over the Trachon, preferred to make common
cause with the robbers and secretly shared in their gains.
Just in consequence of this the emperor assigned this region
to Herod, and his remorseless energy succeeded, in some
measure, in repressing this brigandage.   The king appears
to have instituted on the east frontier a line of military
posts, fortified and put under royal commanders (ἔπαρχοι)

He would have achieved still more if the Nabataean territory had not afforded the robbers an asylum; this was
one of the causes of variance between him and his Arabian
colleague.[1]   His Hellenising tendency comes into prominence in this domain as strongly and less unpleasantly than
in his government at home.   As all the coins of Herod
and the Herodians are Greek, so in the land beyond the
Jordan, while the oldest monument with an inscription
that we know—the Temple of Baalsamin at Canatha—
bears an Aramaean dedication, the honorary bases erected
there, including one for Herod the Great,[2] are bilingual
or merely Greek; under his successors Greek rules alone.

The king-
dom
of [iv. 134.
Nabat.
By the side of the Jewish kings stood the formerly-
mentioned (iv. 140) "king of Nabat," as he called himself.
The residence of this Arabian prince was the city, known
to us only by its Greek name Petra, a rock-fastness
situated midway between the Dead Sea and the north-
east extremity of the Arabian Gulf, from of old an emporium for the traffic of India and Arabia with the region
of the Mediterranean.   These rulers possessed the northern half of the Arabian peninsula; their power extended
on the Arabian Gulf as far as Leuce Come opposite to the
Egyptian town of Berenice, in the interior at least as far
as the region of the old Thaema.[3]   To the north of the
peninsula their territory reached as far as Damascus,
which was under their protection,[4] and even beyond

---

[1] The "refugees from the tetrarchy
of Philippus," who serve in the army
of Herodes Antipas, tetrarch of Galilee, and pass over to the enemy in the
battle with Aretas the Arabian (Josephus, *Arch.* xviii. 5, 1), are beyond
doubt Arabians driven out from the
Trachonitis.

[2] Waddington, 2366 = Vogué, *Inscr. du Haouran*, n. 3.   Bilingual is
also the oldest epitaph of this region
from Suwêda, Waddington, 2320 =
Vogué, n. 1, the only one in the Haurân, which expresses the mute *iota*.
The inscriptions are so put on both
monuments that we cannot determine
which language takes precedence.

[3] At Medain Sâlih or Hijr, south-

ward from Teimâ, the ancient Thaema,
there has recently been found by the
travellers Doughty and Huber, a
series of Nabataean inscriptions, which,
in great part dated, reach from the
time of Augustus down to the death
of Vespasian.   Latin inscriptions are
wanting, and the few Greek are of
the latest period; to all appearance,
on the conversion of the Nabataean
kingdom into a Roman province, the
portion of the interior of Arabia that
belonged to the former was given up
by the Romans.

[4] The city of Damascus voluntarily
submitted under the last Seleucids
about the time of the dictatorship of
Sulla to the king of the Nabataeans

Damascus[1], and enclosed as with a girdle the whole of Palestinian Syria. The Romans, after taking possession of Judaea, came into hostile contact with them, and Marcus Scaurus led an expedition against them. At that

at the time, presumably the Aretas, with whom Scaurus fought (Josephus, *Arch.* xiii. 15). The coins with the legend βασιλέως 'Αρέτου φιλέλληνος (Eckhel, iii. 330; Luynes, *Rev. de Numism.* 1858, p. 311), were perhaps struck in Damascus, when this was dependent on the Nabataeans; the reference of the number of the year on one of them is not indeed certain, but points, it may be presumed, to the last period of the Roman republic. Probably this dependence of the city on the Nabataean kings subsisted so long as there were such kings. From the fact that the city struck coins with the heads of the Roman emperors, there follows doubtless its dependence on Rome and therewith its self-administration, but not its non-dependence on the Roman vassal-prince; such protectorates assumed shapes so various that these arrangements might well be compatible with each other. The continuance of the Nabataean rule is attested partly by the circumstance that the ethnarch of king Aretas in Damascus wished to have the Apostle Paul arrested, as the latter writes in the 2d Epistle to the Corinthians, xi. 32, partly by the recently-established fact (see following note) that the rule of the Nabataeans to the north-east of Damascus was still continuing under Trajan.—Those who start, on the other hand, from the view that, if Aretas ruled in Damascus, the city could not be Roman, have

attempted in various ways to fix the chronology of that event in the life of Paul. They have thought of the complication between Aretas and the Roman government in the last years of Tiberius; but from the course which this took it is not probable that it brought about a permanent change in the state of possession of Aretas. Melchior de Vogüé (*Mélanges d'arch. orientale*, app. p. 33) has pointed out that between Tiberius and Nero—more precisely, between the years 33 and 62 (Saulcy, *Num. de la terre sainte*, p. 36)—there are no imperial coins of Damascus, and has placed the rule of the Nabataeans there in this interval, on the assumption that the emperor Gaius showed his favour to the Arabian as to so many others of the vassal-princes, and invested him with Damascus. But such interruptions of coinage are of frequent occurrence, and require no such profound explanation. The attempt to find a chronological basis for the history of Paul's life in the sway of the Nabataean king at Damascus, and generally to define the time of Paul's abode in this city, must probably be abandoned. If we may so far trust the representation —in any case considerably shifted— of the event in Acts ix., Paul went to Damascus before his conversion, in order to continue there the persecution of the Christians in which Stephen had perished, and then, when on his conversion he took part on the con-

---

[1] The Nabataean inscription found recently near Dmêr, to the north-east of Damascus on the road to Palmyra (Sachau, *Zeitschr. der deutschen morgenl. Gesellschaft*, xxxviii. p. 535), dates from the month Ijjar of the year 410 according to the Roman (*i.e.* Seleucid) reckoning, and the 24th year of king Dabel, the last Nabataean one, and so from May 99 A.D.,

has shown that this district up to the annexation of this kingdom remained under the rule of the Nabataeans. We may add that the dominions here seem to have been, geographically, a tangled mosaic; thus the tetrarch of Galilee and the Nabataean king fought about the territory of Gamala on the lake of Gennesaret (Josephus, *Arch.* xviii. 51).

time their subjugation was not accomplished ; but it must
have ensued soon afterwards.[1]   Under Augustus their king
Obodas was just as subject to the empire[2] as Herod the
king of the Jews, and rendered, like the latter, military
service in the Roman expedition against southern Arabia.
Since that time the protection of the imperial frontier in
the south as in the east of Syria, as far up as to Damascus,
must have lain mainly in the hands of this Arabian king.
With his Jewish neighbour he was at constant feud.
Augustus, indignant that the Arabian instead of seeking
justice at the hand of his suzerain against Herod, had
encountered the latter with arms, and that Obodas's son,
Harethath, or in Greek Aretas, after the death of his
father, instead of waiting for investiture, had at once
entered upon the dominion, was on the point of deposing
the latter and of joining his territory to the Jewish ; but
the misrule of Herod in his later years withheld him from
7. this step, and so Aretas was confirmed (about 747 U.C.).
Some decades later he began again warfare at his own
hand against his son-in-law, the prince of Galilee, Herod
Antipas, on account of the divorce of his daughter in
favour of the beautiful Herodias.   He retained the upper

trary in Damascus for the Christians,
the Jews there resolved to put him to
death, in which case it must therefore
be presupposed that the officials of
Aretas, like Pilate, allowed free course
to the persecution of heretics by the
Jews. Moreover, it follows from the
trustworthy statements of the Epistle
to the Galatians, that the conversion
took place at Damascus (for the
ὑπέστρεψα shows this), and Paul went
from thence to Arabia ; further, that
he came three years after his conversion for the first time, and seventeen years after it for the second time,
to Jerusalem, in accordance with which
the apocryphal accounts of the Book
of Acts as to his Jerusalem-journeys
are to be corrected (Zeller, *Apostel-
gesch.* p. 216). But we cannot determine exactly either the time of the
death of Stephen, much less the time
intervening between this and the
flight of the converted Paul from

Damascus, or the interval between
his second journey to Jerusalem and
the composition of the Galatian letter,
or the year of that composition itself.
[1] Perhaps through Gabinius (Appian, *Syr.* 51).
[2] Strabo, xvi. 4, 21, p. 779. The
coins of these kings, however, do not
show the emperor's head. But that
in the Nabataean kingdom dates might
run by the Roman imperial years is
shown by the Nabataean inscription
of Hebrân (Vogué, *Syrie Centrale,
insc.* n. 1), dated from the seventh year
of Claudius, and so from the year 47.
Hebrân, a little to the north of Bostra,
appears to have been reckoned also at a
later time to Arabia (Lebas-Wadding-
ton, 2287) ; and Nabataean inscriptions of a public tenor are not met
with outside of the Nabataean state ;
the few of the kind from Trachonitis
are of a private nature.

hand, but the indignant suzerain Tiberius ordered the governor of Syria to proceed against him. The troops were already on the march, when Tiberius died (37) ; and his successor, Gaius, who did not wish well to Antipas, pardoned the Arabian. King Maliku or Malchus, the successor of Aretas, fought under Nero and Vespasian in the Jewish war as a Roman vassal, and transmitted his dominion to his son Dabel, the contemporary of Trajan, and the last of these rulers. More especially after the annexation of the state of Jerusalem and the reducing of the respectable dominion of Herod to the far from martial kingdom of Caesarea Paneas, the Arabian was the most considerable of the Syrian client-states, as indeed it furnished the strongest among the royal contingents to the Roman army besieging Jerusalem. This state even under Roman supremacy refrained from the use of the Greek language ; the coins struck under the rule of its kings bear, apart from Damascus, an Aramaic legend. But there appear the germs of an organised condition and of civilised government. The coinage itself probably only began after the state had come under Roman clientship. The Arabian-Indian traffic with the region of the Mediterranean moved in great part along the caravan-route watched over by the Romans, running from Leuce Come by way of Petra to Gaza.[1] The princes of the Nabataean kingdom made use, just like the community of Palmyra, of Greek official designations for their magistrates, *e.g.* of

[1] "Leuke Kome in the land of the Nabataeans," says Strabo under Tiberius, xvi. 4, 23, p. 780, "is a great place of trade, whither and whence the caravan-traders (καμηλέμποροι) go safely and easily from and to Petra with so large numbers of men and camels that they differ in nothing from encampments." The Egyptian merchant also, writing under Vespasian, in his description of the coasts of the Red Sea (c. 19), mentions "the port and the fortress (φρούριον) of Leuce Come, whence the route leads towards Petra to the king of the Nabataeans Malichas. It may be regarded as the emporium for the goods conveyed thither from Arabia in not very large vessels. Therefore there is sent thither (ἀποστέλλεται) a receiver of the import-dues of a fourth of the value, and for the sake of security a centurion (ἐκατοντάρχης) with men." As one belonging to the Roman empire here mentions officials and soldiers, these can only be Roman ; the centurion does not suit the army of the Nabataean king, and the form of tax is quite the Roman. The bringing of a client-state within the sphere of imperial taxation occurs elsewhere, *e.g.* in the regions of the Alps. The road from Petra to Gaza is mentioned by Plin. *H. N.* vi. 28, 144.

the titles of Eparch and of Strategos. If under Tiberius the good order of Syria brought about by the Romans and the security of the harvests occasioned by their military occupation are made prominent as matters of boasting, this is primarily to be referred to the arrangements made in the client-states of Jerusalem or subsequently of Caesarea Paneas and of Petra.

Institution of the province of Arabia. Under Trajan the direct rule of Rome took the place of these two client-states. In the beginning of his reign king Agrippa II. died, and his territory was united with the province of Syria. Not long after, in the year 106, the governor Aulus Cornelius Palma broke up the previous dominion of the kings of Nabat, and made the greater part of it into the Roman province of Arabia, while Damascus went to Syria, and what the Nabataean king had possessed in the interior of Arabia was abandoned by the Romans. The erection of Arabia is designated as subjugation, and the coins also which celebrate the taking possession of it attest that the Nabataeans offered resistance, as indeed generally the nature of their territory as well as their previous attitude lead us to assume a relative independence on the part of these princes. But the historical significance of these events may not be sought in warlike success ; the two annexations, which doubtless went together, were no more than acts of administration carried out perhaps by military power, and the tendency to acquire these domains for civilisation and specially for Hellenism was only heightened by the fact that the Roman government took upon itself the work. The Hellenism of the East, as summed up in Alexander, was a church militant, a thoroughly conquering power pushing its way in a political, religious, economic, and literary point of view. Here, on the edge of the desert, under the pressure of anti-Hellenic Judaism and in the hands of the spiritless and vacillating government of the Seleucids, it had hitherto achieved little. But now, pervading the Roman system, it develops a motive power, which stands related to the earlier, as the power of the Jewish and the Arabian vassal-princes to that of the Roman empire. In

this country, where everything depended and depends on
protecting the state of peace by the setting up of a superior
and standing military force, the institution of a legionary
camp in Bostra under a commander of senatorial rank
was an epoch-making event. From this centre the requisite posts were established at suitable places and provided with garrisons. For example, the stronghold of
Namara (Nemâra) deserves mention, a long day's march
beyond the boundaries of the properly habitable mountain-
land, in the midst of the stony desert, but commanding
the only spring to be found within it and the forts
attached to it in the already mentioned oasis of Ruhbe
and further on at Jebel Sês; these garrisons together
control the whole projection of the Haurân. Another series
of forts, placed under the Syrian command and primarily
under that of the legion posted at Danava (p. 95), and
laid out at uniform distances of three leagues apart,
secured the route from Damascus to Palmyra ; the best
known of them, the second in the series, was that of
Dmêr (p. 149, n. 1), a rectangle of 300 and 350 paces
respectively, provided on every side with six towers and a
portal fifteen paces in breadth, and surrounded by a ring-
wall of sixteen feet thick, once faced outwardly with beautiful blocks of hewn stone.

Never had such an aegis been extended over this land.
It was not, properly speaking, denationalised. The Arabic
names remained down to the latest time, although not
unfrequently, just as in Syria (p. 121), a Romano-Hellenic
name is appended to the local one ; thus a sheikh names
himself "Adrianos or Soaidos, son of Malechos."[1]   The
native worship also remains unaffected ; the chief deity of
the Nabataeans, Dusaris, is doubtless compared with
Dionysus, but regularly continues to be worshipped under
his local name, and down to a late period the Bostrenes
celebrate the Dusaria in honour of him.[2]   In like manner

The civilisation of east Syria under Roman rule.

---

[1] Waddington, 2196 ; Ἀδριανοῦ
τοῦ καὶ Σοαίδου Μαλέχου ἐθνάρχου
στρατηγοῦ νομάδων τὸ μνημεῖον.

[2] Epiphanius, *Haeres.* li. p. 483,
Dind., sets forth that the 25th December, the birthday of Christ, had
already been festally observed after
an analogous manner at Rome in the
festival of the Saturnalia, at Alexandria in the festival (mentioned also

in the province of Arabia temples continue to be consecrated, and offerings presented to Aumu or Helios, to
Vasaeathu, to Theandritos, to Ethaos. The tribes and
the tribal organisation no less continue : the inscriptions
mention lists of " Phylae " by the native name, and frequently Phylarchs or Ethnarchs. But alongside of traditional customs civilisation and Hellenising make progress.
If from the time before Trajan no Greek monument can
be shown in the sphere of the Nabataean state, on the
other hand no monument subsequent to Trajan's time in the
Arabic language has been found there ;[1] to all appearance
the imperial government suppressed at once upon the
annexation the written use of Arabic, although it certainly
remained the language proper of the country, as is attested
not only by the proper names but by the " interpreter of
the tax-receivers."

Agriculture and commerce.

As to the advance of agriculture we have no witnesses
to speak ; but if, on the whole eastern and southern slope
of the Haurân, from the summits of the mountains down to
the desert, the stones, with which this volcanic plain was
once strewed, are thrown into heaps or arranged in long
rows, and thus the most glorious fields are obtained, we
may recognise therein the hand of the only government
which has governed this land as it might and should be
governed. In the Ledjâ, a lava-plateau thirteen leagues
long and eight to nine broad, which is now almost unin-
habited, there grew once vines and figs between the
streams of lava ; the Roman road connecting Bostra with
Damascus ran across it ; in the Ledjâ and around it are

in the decree of Canopus) of the
Kikellia, and in other heathen worships. "This takes place in Alexandria
at the so-called Virgin's shrine (Κόριον)
. . . and if we ask people what this
mystery means, they answer and say
that to-day at this hour the Virgin has
given birth to the Eternal (τὸν αἰῶνα).
This takes place in like manner at
Petra, the capital of Arabia, in the
temple there, and in the Arabic language they sing the praise of the
Virgin, whom they call in Arabic
Chaamu, that is the maiden, and Him

born of her Dusares, that is the Only-
begotten of the Lord." The name
Chaamu is perhaps akin to the Aumu
or Aumos of the Greek inscriptions of
this region, who is compared with
Ζεὺς ἀνίκητος Ἥλιος (Waddington,
2392-2395, 2441, 2445, 2456).

[1] This is said apart from the remarkable Arabo-Greek inscription (see
below) found in Harrân, not far from
Zorava, of the year 568 A.D., set up
by the phylarch Asaraelos, son of
Talemos (Waddington, 2464). This
Christian is a precursor of Mohammed.

counted the ruins of twelve larger and thirty-nine smaller townships.   It can be shown that, at the bidding of the same governor who erected the province of Arabia, the mighty aqueduct was constructed which led the water from the mountains of the Haurân to Canatha (Kerak) in the plain, and not far from it a similar one in Arrha (Rahâ)—buildings of Trajan, which may be named by the side of the port of Ostia and the Forum of Rome.   The flourishing of commercial intercourse is attested by the very choice of the capital of the new province.   Bostra existed under the Nabataean government, and an inscription of king Malichu has been found there; but its military and commercial importance begins with the introduction of direct Roman government.   "Bostra," says Wetzstein, "has the most favourable situation of all the towns in eastern Syria; even Damascus, which owes its size to the abundance of its water and to its situation protected by the eastern Trachon, will excel Bostra only under a weak government, while the latter under a strong and wise government must elevate itself in a few decades to a fabulous prosperity.   It is the great market for the Syrian desert: the high mountains of Arabia and Peraea, and its long rows of booths of stone still in their desolation, furnish evidence of the reality of an earlier, and the possibility of a future, greatness."   The remains of the Roman road, leading thence by way of Salchat and Ezrak to the Persian Gulf, show that Bostra was, along with Petra and Palmyra, a medium of traffic from the East to the Mediterranean.   This town was probably constituted on a Hellenic basis already by Trajan; at least it is called thenceforth the "new Trajanic Bostra," and the Greek coins begin with Pius, while later the legend becomes Latin in consequence of the bestowal of colonial rights by Alexander.

Petra too had a Greek municipal constitution already under Hadrian, and several other places subsequently received municipal rights; but in this territory of the Arabians down to the latest period the tribe and the tribal village preponderated.

A peculiar civilisation was developed from the mixture of national and Greek elements in these regions during the five hundred years between Trajan and Mohammed. A fuller picture of it has been preserved to us than of other forms of the ancient world, inasmuch as the structures of Petra, in great part worked out of the rock, and the buildings in the Haurân, executed entirely of stone owing to the want of wood, comparatively little injured by the sway of the Bedouins which was here again installed with Islam in its old misrule, are still to a considerable degree extant to the present day, and throw a clear light on the artistic skill and the manner of life of those centuries. The above-mentioned temple of Baalsamin at Canatha, certainly built under Herod, shows in its original portions a complete diversity from Greek architecture and in the structural plan remarkable analogies with the temple-building of the same king in Jerusalem, while the pictorial representations shunned in the latter are by no means wanting here. A similar state of things has been observed in the monuments found at Petra. Afterwards further steps were taken. If under the Jewish and the Nabataean rulers culture freed itself but slowly from the influences of the East, a new time seems to have begun here with the transfer of the legion to Bostra. " Building," says an excellent French observer, Melchior de Vogué, " obtained thereby an impetus which was not again arrested. Everywhere rose houses, palaces, baths, temples, theatres, aqueducts, triumphal arches ; towns sprang from the ground within a few years with the regular construction and the symmetrically disposed colonnades which mark towns without a past, and which are as it were the inevitable uniform for this part of Syria during the imperial period." The eastern and southern slope of the Haurân shows nearly three hundred such desolated towns and villages, while there only five new townships now exist ; several of the former, *e.g.* Bûsân, number as many as 800 houses of one to two stories, built throughout of basalt, with well-jointed walls of square blocks without cement, with doors mostly ornamented and often provided with inscriptions,

the flat roof formed of stone-rafters, which are supported
by stone arches and made rain-proof above by a layer of
cement.   The town-wall is usually formed only by the backs
of the houses joined together, and is protected by numerous
towers.   The poor attempts at re-colonising of recent
times find the houses habitable ; there is wanting only the
diligent hand of man, or rather the strong arm that pro-
tects it.   In front of the gates lie the cisterns, often subterranean, or provided with an artificial stone roof, many of
which are still at the present day, when this deserted seat
of towns has become pasturage, kept up by the Bedouins in
order to water their flocks from them in summer.   The
style of building and the practice of art have doubtless
preserved some remains of the older Oriental type, *e.g.*
the frequent form, for a tomb, of the cube crowned with a
pyramid, perhaps also the pigeon-towers often added to
the tomb, still frequent in the present day throughout
Syria ; but, taken on the whole, the style is the usual
Greek one of the imperial period.   Only the absence of
wood has here called forth a development of the stone
arch and the cupola, which technically and artistically
lends to these buildings an original character.   In contrast to the customary repetition elsewhere usual of traditional forms there prevails here an architecture independently suiting the exigencies and the conditions, moderate
in ornamentation, thoroughly sound and rational, and not
destitute even of elegance.   The burial-places, which are
cut out in the rock-walls rising to the east and west of
Petra and in their lateral valleys, with their façades of
Doric or Corinthian pillars often placed in several tiers
one above another, and their pyramids and propylaea
reminding us of the Egyptian Thebes, are not artistically
pleasing, but imposing by their size and richness.   Only
a stirring life and a high prosperity could display such
care for its dead.   In presence of these architectural
monuments it is not surprising that the inscriptions make
mention of a theatre in the " village " (κώμη) Sakkaea
and a " theatre-shaped Odeon " in Canatha, and a local poet
of Namara in Batanaea celebrates himself as a " master

of the glorious art of proud Ausonian song."[1]   Thus at this eastern limit of the empire there was gained for Hellenic civilisation a frontier-domain which may be compared with the Romanised region of the Rhine ; the arched and domed buildings of eastern Syria well stand comparison with the castles and tombs of the nobles and of the great merchants of Belgica.

The south-Arabian immigration before Mohammed.

But the end came.   As to the Arabian tribes who immigrated to this region from the south, the historical tradition of the Romans is silent, and what the late records of the Arabs report as to that of the Ghassanids and their precursors, can hardly be fixed, at least as to chronology.[2] But the Sabaeans, after whom the place Borechath (Brêka to the north of Kanawat) is named, appear in fact to be south-Arabian emigrants ; and these were already settled here in the third century.   They and their associates may have come in peace and become settled under Roman protection, perhaps even may have carried to Syria the highly-developed and luxuriant culture of southwestern Arabia.   So long as the empire kept firmly together and each of these tribes was under its own sheikh, all obeyed the Roman lord-paramount.   But in order the better to meet the Arabians or—as they were now called —Saracens of the Persian empire united under one king,

---

[1] Αὐσονίων μούσης ὑψιυόου πρύτανις, Kaibel, *Epigr.* 440.

[2] According to the Arabian accounts the Benu Sâlih migrated from the region of Mecca (about 190 A.D., according to the conjectures of Caussin de Perceval, *Hist. des Arabes*, i. 212) to Syria, and settled there alongside of the Benu-Samaida, in whom Waddington finds anew the φυλὴ Σομαιθηνῶν of an inscription of Suwêda (n. 2308).   The Ghassanids, who (according to Caussin, about 205) migrated from Batn-Marr likewise to Syria and to the same region, were compelled by the Salihites, at the suggestion of the Romans, to pay tribute, and paid it for a time, until they (according to the same, about the year 292) overcame the Salihites, and

their leader Thalaba, son of Amos, was recognised by the Romans as phylarch.   This narrative may contain correct elements ; but our standard authority remains always the account of Procopius, *de bello Pers.* i. 17, reproduced in the text.   The phylarchs of individual provinces of Arabia (*i.e.* the province Bostra ; *Nov.* 102 c.) and of Palestine (*i.e.* province of Petra ; Procop. *de bello Pers.* i. 19), are older, but doubtless not much. Had a sheikh-in-chief of this sort been recognised by the Romans in the times before Justinian, the Roman authors and the inscriptions would doubtless show traces of it ; but there are no such traces from the period before Justinian.

Justinian, during the Persian war in the year 531, placed all the phylarchs of the Saracens subject to the Romans under Aretas son of Gabalus—Harith Abu son of Chaminos among the Arabs—and bestowed on this latter the title of king, which hitherto, it is added, had never been done. This king of all the Arabian tribes settled in Syria was still a vassal of the empire ; but, while he warded off his countrymen, he at the same time prepared the place for them. A century later, in the year 637, Arabia and Syria succumbed to Islam.

CHAPTER XI.

JUDAEA AND THE JEWS.

THE history of the Jewish land is as little the history of the Jewish people as the history of the States of the Church is that of the Catholics ; it is just as requisite to separate the two as to consider them together.

Judaea and the priestly rule under the Seleucids. The Jews in the land of the Jordan, with whom the Romans had to do, were not the people who under their judges and kings fought with Moab and Edom, and listened to the discourses of Amos and Hosea. The small community of pious exiles, driven out by foreign rule, and brought back again by a change in the hands wielding that rule, who began their new establishment by abruptly repelling the remnants of their kinsmen left behind in the old abodes and laying the foundation for the irreconcilable feud between Jews and Samaritans— the ideal of national exclusiveness and priestly control holding the mind in chains—had long before the Roman period developed under the government of the Seleucids the so-called Mosaic theocracy, a clerical corporation with the high-priest at its head, which, acquiescing in foreign rule and renouncing the formation of a state, guarded the distinctiveness of its adherents, and dominated them under the aegis of the protecting power. This retention of the national character in religious forms, while ignoring the state, was the distinctive mark of the later Judaism. Probably every idea of God is in its formation national ; but no other God has been so from the outset the God only of his people as Jahve, and no one has so remained such without distinction of time and place. Those men returning to the Holy Land, who professed to live according to the statutes of Moses and in fact lived according to the statutes of Ezra and Nehemiah,[1] had remained just as dependent on the great-kings of the East, and subsequently on the Seleucids, as they had been by the waters of Babylon. A political element no more attached to this organisation than to the Armenian or the Greek Church under its patriarchs in the Turkish empire ; no free current of political development pervades this clerical restoration ; none of the grave and serious obligations of a commonwealth standing on its own basis hampered the priests of the temple of Jerusalem in the setting up of the kingdom of Jahve upon earth.

The reaction did not fail to come. That church-without-a-state could only last so long as a secular great power served it as lord-protector or as bailiff. When the kingdom of the Seleucids fell into decay, a Jewish commonwealth was created afresh by the revolt against foreign rule, which drew its best energies precisely from the enthusiastic national faith. The high priest of Salem was called from the temple to the battlefield. The family of the Hasmonaeans restored the empire of Saul and David nearly in its old limits, and not only so, but these warlike high priests renewed also in some measure the former truly political monarchy controlling the priests. But that monarchy, at once the product of, and the contrast to, that priestly rule, was not according to the heart of the pious. The Pharisees and the Sadducees separated and began to make war on one another. It was not so much doctrines and ritual differences that here confronted each other, as, on the one hand, the persistence in a priestly government which simply clung to religious ordinances and interests, and otherwise was indifferent to the independence and the self-control of the community ; on the other hand, the monarchy aiming at political development

Kingdom of the Hasmonaeans.

---

[1] [This statement and several others of a kindred tenor in this chapter appear to rest on an unhesitating acceptance of views entertained by a recent school of Old Testament criticism, as to which it may at least be said : *Adhuc sub iudice lis est.*— TR.]

and endeavouring to procure for the Jewish people, by fighting and by treaty, its place once more in the political conflict, of which the Syrian kingdom was at that time the arena. The former tendency dominated the multitude, the latter had the preponderance in intelligence and in the upper classes ; its most considerable champion was king Iannaeus Alexander, who during his whole reign was at enmity not less with the Syrian rulers than with

iv. 133. his own Pharisees (iv. 139). Although it was properly but the other, and in fact the more natural and more potent, expression of the national revival, it yet by its greater freedom of thinking and acting came into contact with the Hellenic character, and was regarded especially by its pious opponents as foreign and unbelieving.

The Jewish Diaspora.

But the inhabitants of Palestine were only a portion, and not the most important portion, of the Jews ; the Jewish communities of Babylonia, Syria, Asia Minor, Egypt, were far superior to those of Palestine even after their regeneration by the Maccabees. The Jewish Diaspora in the imperial period was of more significance than the latter ; and it was an altogether peculiar phenomenon.

The settlements of the Jews beyond Palestine grew only in a subordinate degree out of the same impulse as those of the Phoenicians and the Hellenes. From the outset an agricultural people and dwelling far from the coast, their settlements abroad were a non-free and comparatively late formation, a creation of Alexander or of his marshals.[1] In those immense efforts at founding Greek towns continued throughout generations, such as never before and never afterwards occurred to a like extent, the Jews had a conspicuous share, however singular it was to invoke their aid in particular towards the Hellenising of

---

[1] Whether the legal position of the Jews in Alexandria is warrantably traced back by Josephus (*contra Ap.* ii. 4) to Alexander is so far doubtful, as, to the best of our knowledge, not he, but the first Ptolemy, settled Jews in masses there (Josephus, *Arch.* xii. 1. ; Appian, *Syr.* 50). The remarkable similarity of form assumed by the bodies of Jews in the different states of the Diadochi must, if it is not based on Alexander's ordinances, be traced to rivalry and imitation in the founding of towns. The fact that Palestine was now Egyptian, now Syrian, doubtless exercised an essential influence in the case of these settlements.

the East.   This was the case above all with Egypt.   The
most considerable of all the towns created by Alexander,
Alexandria on the Nile, was since the times of the first
Ptolemy, who after the occupation of Palestine transferred
thither a mass of its inhabitants, almost as much a city of
the Jews as of the Greeks, and the Jews there were to be
esteemed at least equal to those of Jerusalem in number,
wealth, intelligence, and organisation.   In the first times
of the empire there was reckoned a million of Jews to
eight millions of Egyptians, and their influence, it may be
presumed, transcended this numerical proportion.   We
have already observed that, on no smaller a scale, the Jews
in the Syrian capital of the empire had been similarly
organised and developed (p. 127).   The diffusion and the
importance of the Jews of Asia Minor are attested among
other things by the attempt which was made under
Augustus by the Ionian Greek cities, apparently after
joint concert, to compel their Jewish fellow townsmen
either to withdrawal from their faith or to full assumption
of civic burdens.   Beyond doubt there were independently
organised bodies of Jews in all the new Hellenic foundations,[1] and withal in numerous old Hellenic towns, even
in Hellas proper, *e.g.* in Corinth.   The organisation was
placed throughout on the footing that the nationality of
the Jews with the far-reaching consequences drawn from
it by themselves was preserved, and only the use of the
Greek language was required of them.   Thus amidst
this Graecising, into which the East was at that time
coaxed or forced by those in authority, the Jews of the
Greek towns became Greek-speaking Orientals.

That in the Jew-communities of the Macedonian   Greek
towns the Greek language not merely attained to dominion   language.
in the natural way of intercourse, but was a compulsory

---

[1] The community of Jews in Smyrna
is mentioned in an inscription recently
found there (Reinach, *Revue des
études juives*, 1883, p. 161) : 'Ρουφεῖνα
'Ιουδαί(α) ἀρχισυναγωγὸς κατεσκεύασεν
τὸ ἐνσόριον τοῖς ἀπελευθέροις καὶ θρέμ-
(μ)ασιν μηδένος ἀλ(λ)ου ἐξουσίαν ἔχοντος
θάψαι τινά· εἰ δέ τις τολμήσει, δώσει τῷ
ἱερωτάτῳ ταμείῳ (δηναρίους) ͵αφ, καὶ τῷ
ἔθνει τῶν 'Ιουδαίων (δηναρίους) ͵α. Ταύτης
τῆς ἐπιγραφῆς τὸ ἀντίγραφον ἀποκεῖται
εἰς τὸ ἀρχεῖον.   Simple *collegia* are, in
penal threats of this sort, not readily
put on a level with the state or the
community.

ordinance imposed upon them, seems of necessity to result
from the state of the case. In a similar way Trajan
subsequently Romanised Dacia with colonists from Asia
Minor. Without this compulsion, the external uniformity
in the foundation of towns could not have been carried
out, and this material for Hellenising generally could not
have been employed. The governments went in this
respect very far and achieved much. Already under the
second Ptolemy, and at his instigation, the sacred writings
of the Jews were translated into Greek in Egypt, and at
least at the beginning of the imperial period the knowledge of Hebrew among the Jews of Alexandria was
nearly as rare as that of the original languages of Scripture is at present in the Christian world ; there was nearly
as much discussion as to the faults of translation of the
so-called Seventy Alexandrians as on the part of pious
men among us regarding the errors of Luther's translation.
The national language of the Jews had at this epoch disappeared everywhere from the intercourse of life, and
maintained itself only in ecclesiastical use somewhat like
the Latin language in the religious domain of Catholicism.
In Judaea itself its place had been taken by the Aramaic
popular language of Syria, akin no doubt to the Hebrew ;
the Jews outside of Judaea, with whom we are concerned,
had entirely laid aside the Semitic idiom, and it was not
till long after this epoch that the reaction set in, which
scholastically brought back the knowledge and the use
of it more generally among the Jews. The literary works,
which they produced at this epoch in great number, were
in the better times of the empire all Greek. If language
alone conditioned nationality, there would be little to tell
for this period as to the Jews.

Retention
of nation-
ality.

But with this linguistic compulsion, at first perhaps
severely felt, was combined the recognition of the distinctive nationality with all its consequences. Everywhere in
the cities of the monarchy of Alexander the burgess-body
was formed of the Macedonians, that is, those really
Macedonian, or the Hellenes esteemed equal to them. By
the side of these stood, in addition to foreigners, the

natives, in Alexandria the Egyptians, in Cyrene the Libyans and generally the settlers from the East, who had indeed no other home than the new city, but were not recognised as Hellenes. To this second category the Jews belonged ; but they, and they only, were allowed to form, so to speak, a community within the community, and—while the other non-burgesses were ruled by the authorities of the burgess-body—up to a certain degree to govern themselves.[1] The "Jews," says Strabo, "have in Alexandria a national head ($\epsilon\theta\nu\acute{a}\rho\chi\eta$s) of their own, who presides over the people ($\check{\epsilon}\theta\nu$os), and decides processes and disposes of contracts and arrangements as if he ruled an independent community." This was done, because the Jews indicated a specific jurisdiction of this sort as required by their nationality or—what amounts to the same thing—their religion. Further, the general political arrangements had respect in an extensive measure to the national-religious scruples of the Jews, and accommodated them as far as possible by exemptions. The privilege of dwelling together was at least frequently added ; in Alexandria, *e.g.* two of the five divisions of the city were inhabited chiefly by Jews. This seems not to have been the Ghetto system, but rather a usage resting on the basis of settlement to begin with, and thereafter retained on both sides, whereby conflicts with neighbours were in some measure obviated.

Thus the Jews came to play a prominent part in the

[1] If the Alexandrian Jews subsequently maintained that they were legally on an equal footing with the Alexandrian Macedonians (Josephus, *contra Ap.* ii. 4; *Bell. Jud.* ii. 18, 7) this was a misrepresentation of the true state of the case. They were clients in the first instance of the Phyle of the Macedonians, probably the most eminent of all, and therefore named after Dionysos (Theophilus, *ad Autolycum*, ii. 7), and, because the Jewish quarter was a part of this Phyle, Josephus in his way makes themselves Macedonians. The legal position of the population of the Greek towns of this category is most clearly apparent from the account of Strabo (in Josephus, *Arch.* xiv. 7, 2) as to the four categories of that of Cyrene : city-burgesses, husbandmen ($\gamma\epsilon\omega\rho\gamma o\acute{\iota}$), strangers, and Jews. If we lay aside the *metoeci*, who have their legal home elsewhere, there remain as Cyrenaeans having rights in their home the burgesses of full rights, that is, the Hellenes and what were allowed to pass as such, and the two categories of those excluded from active burgess-rights—the Jews, who form a community of their own, and the subjects, the Libyans, without autonomy. This might easily be so shifted, that the two privileged categories should appear as having equal rights.

Macedonian Hellenising of the East; their pliancy and
serviceableness on the one hand, their unyielding tenacity
on the other, must have induced the very realistic statesmen
who assigned this course of action, to resolve on such
arrangements. Nevertheless the extraordinary extent
and significance of the Jewish Diaspora, as compared with
the narrowness and poorness of their home, remains at
once a fact and a problem. In dealing with it we may
not overlook the circumstance that the Palestinian Jews
furnished no more than the nucleus for the Jews of other
countries. The Judaism of the older time was anything
but exclusive; was, on the contrary, no less pervaded by
missionary zeal than were afterwards Christianity and
Islam. The Gospel makes reference to Rabbis who
traversed sea and land to make a proselyte; the admission
of half-proselytes, of whom circumcision was not expected
but to whom religious fellowship was yet accorded, is an
evidence of this converting zeal and at the same time one
of its most effective means. Motives of very various kinds
came to the help of this proselytising. The civil privileges,
which the Lagids and Seleucids conferred on the Jews,
must have induced a great number of non-Jewish Orientals and half-Hellenes to attach themselves in the new
towns to the privileged category of the non-burgesses. In
later times the decay of the traditional faith of the country
helped the Jewish *propaganda.* Numerous persons,
especially of the cultivated classes, whose sense of faith
and morality turned away with horror or derision from
what the Greeks, and still more from what the Egyptians
termed religion, sought refuge in the simpler and purer
Jewish doctrine renouncing polytheism and idolatry——a
doctrine which largely met the religious views resulting
from the development of philosophy among the cultured
and half-cultured circles. There is a remarkable Greek
moral poem, probably from the later epoch of the Roman
republic, which is drawn from the Mosaic books on such
a footing that it adopts the doctrine of monotheism and
the universal moral law, but avoids everything offensive
to the non-Jew and all direct opposition to the ruling

religion, evidently intended to gain wider acceptance for this denationalised Judaism.   Women in particular addicted themselves by preference to the Jewish faith.   When the authorities of Damascus in the year 66 resolved to put to death the captive Jews, it was agreed to keep this resolution secret, in order that the female population devoted to the Jews might not prevent its execution.   Even in the West, where the cultivated circles were otherwise averse to Jewish habits, dames of rank early formed an exception ; Poppaea Sabina, Nero's wife, sprung from a noble family, was notorious for her pious Jewish faith and her zealous protectorate of the Jews, as for other things less reputable.   Cases of formal transition to Judaism were not rare ; the royal house of Adiabene for example—king Izates and his mother Helena, as well as his brother and successor—became at the time of Tiberius and of Claudius in every respect Jews.   It certainly was the case with all those Jewish bodies, as it is expressly remarked of those of Antioch, that they consisted in great part of proselytes.

This transplanting of Judaism to the Hellenic soil with the appropriation of a foreign language, however much it took place with a retention of national individuality, was not accomplished without developing in Judaism itself a tendency running counter to its nature, and up to a certain degree denationalising it.   How powerfully the bodies of Jews living amidst the Greeks were influenced by the currents of Greek intellectual life, may be traced in the literature of the last century before, and of the first after, the birth of Christ.   It is imbued with Jewish elements ; and they are withal the clearest heads and the most gifted thinkers, who seek admission either as Hellenes into the Jewish, or as Jews into the Hellenic, system. Nicolaus of Damascus, himself a Pagan and a noted representative of the Aristotelian philosophy pleaded, as a scholar and diplomatist of king Herod, the cause of his Jewish patron and of the Jews before Agrippa as before Augustus ; and not only so, but his historical authorship shows a very earnest, and for that epoch sigificant, attempt to bring the East into the circle of Occidental research,

Hellenising tendencies in the Diaspora.

while the description still preserved of the youthful years of the emperor Augustus, who came personally into close contact with him, is a remarkable evidence of the love and honour which the Roman ruler met with in the Greek world. The dissertation on the Sublime, written in the first period of the empire by an unknown author, one of the finest aesthetic works preserved to us from antiquity, certainly proceeds, if not from a Jew, at any rate from a man who revered alike Homer and Moses.[1] Another treatise, also anonymous, upon the Universe—likewise an attempt, respectable of its kind, to blend the doctrine of Aristotle with that of the Stoa—was perhaps written also by a Jew, and dedicated certainly to the Jew of highest repute and highest station in the Neronian age, Tiberius Alexander (p. 204), chief of the staff to Corbulo and Titus. The wedding of the two worlds of intellect meets us most clearly in the Jewish-Alexandrian philosophy, the most acute and most palpable expression of a religious movement, not merely affecting but also attacking the essence of Judaism. The Hellenic intellectual development conflicted with national religions of all sorts, inasmuch as it either denied their views or else filled them with other contents, drove out the previous gods from the minds of men and put into the empty places either nothing, or the stars and abstract ideas. These attacks affected also the religion of the Jews. There was formed a Neo-Judaism of Hellenic culture, which dealt with Jehovah not quite so badly, but yet not much otherwise, than the cultivated Greeks and Romans with Zeus and Jupiter. The universal expedient of the so-called allegorical interpretation, whereby in particular the philosophers of the Stoa everywhere in courteous fashion eliminated the heathen national religions, suited equally well and equally

---

[1] Pseudo-Longinus, περὶ ὕψους, 9: "Far better than the war of the gods in Homer is the description of the gods in their perfection and genuine greatness and purity, like that of Poseidon (*Ilias*, xiii. 18 ff.). Just so writes the legislator of the Jews, no mean man (οὐχ ὁ τυχὼν ἀνήρ), after he has worthily apprehended and brought to expression the Divine power, at the very beginning of the Laws (*Genesis*, i. 3): 'God said'—what? 'Let there be light, and there was light; let the earth be, and the earth was.'"

ill for Genesis as for the gods of the Iliad ; if Moses had
meant by Abraham in a strict sense understanding, by
Sarah virtue, by Noah righteousness, if the four streams
of Paradise were the four cardinal virtues, then the most
enlightened Hellene might believe in the Law.   But this
pseudo-Judaism was also a power, and the intellectual
primacy of the Jews in Egypt was apparent above all in
the fact, that this tendency found pre-eminently its sup-
porters in Alexandria.

Notwithstanding the internal separation which had
taken place among the Jews of Palestine and had but too
often culminated directly in civil war, notwithstanding the
dispersion of a great part of the Jewish body into foreign
lands, notwithstanding the intrusion of foreign ingredients
into it and even of the destructive Hellenistic element
into its very core, the collective body of the Jews remained
united in a way, to which in the present day only the
Vatican perhaps and the Kaaba offer a certain analogy.
The holy Salem remained the banner, Zion's temple the
Palladium of the whole Jewish body, whether they obeyed
the Romans or the Parthians, whether they spoke Aramaic or Greek, whether even they believed in the old
Jahve or in the new, who was none.   The fact that the
protecting ruler conceded to the spiritual chief of the Jews
a certain secular power signified for the Jewish body just
as much, and the small extent of this power just as little,
as the so-called States of the Church in their time signified
for Roman Catholics.   Every member of a Jewish community had to pay annually to Jerusalem a *didrachmon* as
temple-tribute, which came in more regularly than the
taxes of the state ; every one was obliged at least once in
his life to sacrifice personally to Jehovah on the spot
which alone in the world was well-pleasing to Him.
Theological science remained common property ; the
Babylonian and Alexandrian Rabbins took part in it not
less than those of Jerusalem.   The feeling, cherished with
unparalleled tenacity, of belonging collectively to one nation
—a feeling which had established itself in the community
of the returning exiles and had thereafter contributed to

Fellowship
of the Jews
generally.

create that distinctive position of the Jews in the Greek world
—maintained its ground in spite of dispersion and division.

Philo.   Most worthy of remark is the continued life of Judaism
itself in circles whose inward religion was detached from
it.   The most noted and, for us, the single clearly palpable
representative of this tendency in literature, Philo, one
of the foremost and richest Jews of the time of Tiberius,
stands in fact towards the religion of his country in a
position not greatly differing from that of Cicero towards
the Roman ; but he himself believed that he was not
destroying but fulfilling it.   For him as for every other
Jew, Moses is the source of all truth, his written direction
binding law, the feeling towards him reverence and devout
belief.   This sublimated Judaism is, however, not quite
identical with the so-called faith in the gods of the Stoa.
The corporeality of God vanishes for Philo, but not His
personality, and he entirely fails in—what is the essence
of Hellenic philosophy—the transferring of the deity into
the breast of man ; it remains his view that sinful man is
dependent on a perfect being standing outside of, and above,
him.   In like manner the new Judaism submits itself to
the national ritual law far more unconditionally than the
new heathenism.   The struggle between the old and the
new faith was therefore of a different nature in the Jewish
circle than in the heathen, because the stake was a greater
one ;   reformed heathenism contended only against the
old faith, reformed Judaism would in its ultimate consequence destroy the nationality, which amidst the inundation of Hellenism necessarily disappeared with the refining
away of the native faith, and therefore shrank back from
drawing this consequence.   Hence on Greek soil and in
Greek language the form, if not the substance, of the old
faith was retained and defended with unexampled ob-
stinacy, defended even by those who in substance surrendered before Hellenism.   Philo himself, as we shall have
to tell further on, contended and suffered for the cause of
the Jews.   But on that account the Hellenistic tendency
in Judaism never exercised an overpowering influence over
the latter, never was able to take its stand against the

national Judaism, and barely availed to mitigate its fanaticism and to check its perversities and crimes.   In all essential matters, especially when confronted with oppression and persecution, the differences of Judaism disappeared; and, unimportant as was the Rabbinical state, the religious communion over which it presided was a considerable and in certain circumstances formidable power.

Such was the state of things which the Romans found confronting them when they entered on rule in the East. Conquest forces the hand of the conqueror not less than of the conquered.   The work of centuries, the Macedonian urban institutions, could not be undone either by the Arsacids or by the Caesars ; neither Seleucia on the Euphrates nor Antioch and Alexandria could be entered upon by the following governments under the benefit of the inventory.   Probably in presence of the Jewish Diaspora there the founder of the imperial government took, as in so many other things, the policy of the first Lagids as his guiding rule, and furthered rather than hampered the Judaism of the East in its distinctive position ; and this procedure thereupon became throughout the model for his successors.   We have already mentioned that the communities of Asia Minor under Augustus made the attempt to draw upon their Jewish fellow-citizens uniformly in the levy, and no longer to allow them the observance of the Sabbath ; but Agrippa decided against them and maintained the *status quo* in favour of the Jews, or rather, perhaps, now for the first time legalised the exemption of the Jews from military service and their Sabbath privilege, that had been previously conceded according to circumstances only by individual governors or communities of the Greek provinces.   Augustus further directed the governors of Asia not to apply the rigorous imperial laws respecting unions and assemblies against the Jews.   But the Roman government did not fail to see that the exempt position conceded to the Jews in the East was not compatible with the absolute obligation of those belonging to the empire to fulfil the services required by the state ; that the guaranteed distinctive position of the Jewish body carried

The Roman government and Judaism

the hatred of race and under certain circumstances civil war into the several towns; that the pious rule of the authorities at Jerusalem over all the Jews of the empire had a perilous range; and that in all this there lay a practical injury and a danger in principle for the state.

in the West

The internal dualism of the empire expresses itself in nothing more sharply than in the different treatment of the Jews in the respective domains of the Latin and Greek languages. In the West autonomous bodies of Jews were never allowed. There was toleration doubtless there for the Jewish religious usages as for the Syrian and the Egyptian, or rather somewhat less than for these; Augustus showed himself favourable to the Jewish colony in the suburb of Rome beyond the Tiber, and made supplementary allowance in his largesses for those who missed them on account of the Sabbath. But he personally avoided all contact with the Jewish worship as with the Egyptian; and, as he himself when in Egypt had gone out of the way of the sacred ox, so he thoroughly approved the conduct of his son Gaius, when he went to the East, in passing by Jerusalem. Under Tiberius in the year 19 the Jewish worship was even prohibited along with the Egyptian in Rome and in all Italy, and those who did not consent openly to renounce it and to throw the holy vessels into the fire were expelled from Italy—so far as they could not be employed as useful for military service in convict-companies, whereupon not a few became liable to court-martial on account of their religious scruples. If, as we shall see afterwards, this same emperor in the East almost anxiously evaded every conflict with the Rabbi, it is here plainly apparent that he, the ablest ruler whom the empire had, just as clearly perceived the dangers of the Jewish immigration as the unfairness and the impossibility of setting aside Judaism, where it existed.[1] Under the later rulers, as we shall see

---

[1] The Jew Philo sets down the treatment of the Jews in Italy to the account of Sejanus (*Leg.* 24; *in Flacc.* 1), that of the Jews in the East to the account of the emperor himself. But Josephus rather traces back what happened in Italy to a scandal in the capital, which had been occasioned by three Jewish pious swindlers and a lady of rank converted to

in the sequel, the attitude of disinclination towards the Jews of the West did not in the main undergo change, although they in other respects follow more the example of Augustus than that of Tiberius. They did not prevent the Jews from collecting the temple-tribute in the form of voluntary contributions and sending it to Jerusalem. They were not checked, if they preferred to bring a legal dispute before a Jewish arbiter rather than before a Roman tribunal. Of compulsory levy for service, such as Tiberius enjoined, there is no further mention afterwards in the West. But the Jews never obtained in heathen Rome or generally in the Latin West a publicly recognised distinctive position and publicly recognised separate courts. Above all in the West—apart from the capital, which in the nature of the case represented the East also, and already in Cicero's time included in it a numerous body of Jews—the Jewish communities nowhere had special extent or importance in the earlier imperial period.[1]

It was only in the East that the government yielded from the first, or rather made no attempt to change the existing state of things and to obviate the dangers thence resulting; and accordingly, as the sacred books of the Jews were first made known to the Latin world in the Latin language by means of the Christians, the great Jewish movements of the imperial period were restricted throughout to the Greek East. Here no attempt was made gradually to stop the spring of hatred towards the Jews by assigning to them a separate position in law, but just as little—apart from the caprice and perversities of individual rulers—was the hatred and persecution of the Jews fomented on the part of the government. In reality the catastrophe of Judaism did not arise from the treatment of the Jewish Diaspora in the East. It was simply the

and in the East.

Judaism; and Philo himself states that Tiberius, after the fall of Sejanus, allowed to the governors only certain modifications in the procedure against the Jews. The policy of the emperor and that of his ministers towards the Jews was essentially the same.

[1] Agrippa II., who enumerates the Jewish settlements abroad (in Philo, *Leg. ad Gaium*, 36), names no country westward of Greece, and among the strangers sojourning in Jerusalem, whom the Book of Acts, ii. 5 f., records, only Romans are named from the West.

relations, as they became fatefully developed, of the imperial government to the Jewish Rabbinical state that not merely brought about the destruction of the commonwealth of Jerusalem, but further shook and changed the position of the Jews in the empire generally. We turn to describe the events in Palestine under the Roman rule.

Judaea under the republic. The state of things in northern Syria was organised by the generals of the republic, Pompeius and his immediate successors, on such a footing, that the larger powers that were beginning to be formed there were again reduced, and the whole land was broken up into single city-domains and petty lordships. The Jews were most severely affected by this course ; not merely were they obliged to give up all the possessions which they had **iv. 136.** hitherto gained, particularly the whole coast (iv. 142), but Gabinius had even broken up the empire formerly subsisting into five independent self-administering districts, and withdrawn from the high priest Hyrcanus his secular **iv. 151.** privileges (iv. 158). Thus, as the protecting power was restored on the one hand, so was the pure theocracy on the other.

Antipater the Idumaean. This, however, was soon changed. Hyrcanus, or rather the minister governing for him, the Idumaean Antipater,[1]

[1] Antipater began his career as governor (στρατηγός) of Idumaea (Josephus, *Arch.* xiv. 1, 3), and is there called administrator of the Jewish kingdom (ὁ τῶν Ἰουδαίων ἐπιμελητής (Joseph. *Arch.* xiv. 8, 1), that is, nearly first minister. More is not implied in the narrative of Josephus coloured with flattery towards Rome as towards Herod (*Arch.* xiv. 8, 5 ; *Bell. Jud.* i. 10, 3), that Caesar had left to Antipater the option of himself determining his position of power (δυναστεία), and, when the latter left the decision with him, had appointed him administrator (ἐπίτροπος)of Judaea. This is not, as Marquardt, *Staatsalth.* v. 1, 408, would have it, the (at that time not yet existing) Roman procuratorship of the imperial period, but an office formally conferred by the Jewish ethnarch, an ἐπιτροπή, like that mentioned by Josephus, *Bell. Jud.* ii. 18, 6. In the official documents of Caesar's time the high priest and ethnarch Hyrcanus alone represents the Jews ; Caesar gave to Antipater what could be granted to the subjects of a dependent state, Roman burgessrights and personal immunity (Josephus, *Arch.* xiv. 8, 3 ; *Bell. Jud.* i. 9, 5), but he did not make him an official of Rome. That Herod, driven out of Judaea, obtained from the Romans a Roman officer's post possibly in Samaria, is credible ; but the designations στρατηγὸς τῆς Κοίλης Συρίας (Josephus, *Arch.* xiv. 9, 5, c. 11, 4), or στρατηγὸς Κοίλης Συρίας καὶ Σαμαρείας (*Bell. Jud.* i. 10, 8) are at least misleading, and with as much incorrectness the same author names Herod subsequently, for the reason that he is to serve as counsellor τοῖς ἐπιτροπεύουσι

attained once more the leading position in southern Syria
doubtless through Gabinius himself, to whom he knew
how to make himself indispensable in his Parthian and
Egyptian undertakings (iv. 345). After the pillage of the iv. 329.
temple of Jerusalem by Crassus the insurrection of the
Jews thereby occasioned was chiefly subdued by him
(iv. 355). It was for him a fortunate dispensation that iv. 339.
the Jewish government was not compelled to interfere
actively in the crisis between Caesar and Pompeius, for
whom it, like the whole East, had declared. Nevertheless,
after the brother and rival of Hyrcanus, Aristobulus as
well as his son Alexander, had on account of their taking
part for Caesar lost their lives at the hands of the Pompeians, the second son, Antigonus, would doubtless after
Caesar's victory have been installed by the latter as ruler
in Judaea. But when Caesar, coming to Egypt after the
decisive victory, found himself in a dangerous position at
Alexandria, it was chiefly Antipater who delivered him
from it (iv. 452), and this carried the day; Antigonus had iv. 430.
to give way before the more recent, but more effective,
fidelity.

Caesar's personal gratitude was not the least Caesar's
element in promoting the formal restoration of the arrange-
ments.
Jewish state. The Jewish kingdom obtained the best
position which could be granted to a client-state, complete
freedom from dues to the Romans[1] and from military

τῆς Συρίας (*Arch.* xv. 10, 3), even
Συρίας ὅλης ἐπίτροπον (*Bell. Jud.* i.
20, 4), where Marquardt's change,
Staatsalth. v. i. 408, Κοίλης destroys
the sense.

[1] In the decree of Caesar in Josephus, *Arch.* xiv. 10, 5, 6, the reading which results from Epiphanius is
the only possible one ; according to
this the land is freed from the tribute
(imposed by Pompeius ; Josephus,
Arch. xiv. 4, 4) from the second year
of the current lease onward, and it is
further ordained that the town of Joppa,
which at that time passed over from
Roman into Jewish possession, should
continue indeed to deliver the fourth
part of field-fruits at Sidon to the
Romans, but for that there should be
granted to Hyrcanus, likewise at
Sidon, as an equivalent annually 20,675
bushels of grain, besides which the
people of Joppa paid also the tenth to
Hyrcanus. The whole narrative otherwise shows that the Jewish state was
thenceforth free from payment of
tribute ; the circumstance that Herod
pays φόροι from the districts assigned
to Cleopatra which he leases from her
(*Arch.* xv. 4, 2, 4, c. 5, 3) only confirms the rule. If Appian, *B. C.* v.
75, adduces among the kings on whom
Antonius laid tribute Herod for
Idumaea and Samaria, Judaea is not
absent here without good reason ;
and even for these accessory lands the

occupation and levy,[1] whereas certainly the duties and the expenses of frontier-defence were to be undertaken by the native government. The town of Joppa, and thereby the connection with the sea, were given back, the independence of internal administration as well as the free exercise of religion was guaranteed ; the re-establishment, hitherto refused, of the fortifications of Jerusalem razed by Pompeius was allowed (707). Thus under the name of the Hasmonaean prince, a half foreigner—for the Idumaeans stood towards the Jews proper that returned from Babylon nearly as did the Samaritans—governed the Jewish state under the protection and according to the will of Rome. The Jews with national sentiments were anything but inclined towards the new government. The old families, who led in the council of Jerusalem, held in their hearts to Aristobulus, and, after his death, to his son Antigonus. In the mountains of Galilee the fanatics fought quite as much against the Romans as against their own government ; when Antipater's son Herod took captive Ezekias, the leader of this wild band, and had caused him to be put to death, the priestly council of Jerusalem compelled the weak Hyrcanus to banish Herod under the pretext of a violation of religious precepts. The latter thereupon entered the Roman army, and rendered good service to the Caesarian governor of Syria against the insurrection of the last Pompeians. But when, after the murder of Caesar, the republicans

---

tribute may have been remitted to him by Augustus. The detailed and trustworthy account as to the census enjoined by Quirinius shows with entire clearness that the land was hitherto free from Roman tribute.

[1] In the same decree it is said : καὶ ὅπως μηδεὶς μήτε ἄρχων μήτε στρατηγὸς ἢ πρεσβευτὴς ἐν τοῖς ὅροις τῶν Ἰουδαίων ἀνιστᾷ ("perhaps συνιστᾷ," Wilamowitz) συμμαχίαν καὶ στρατιώτας ἐξῇ (so Wilamowitz, for ἐξείη) ἢ τὰ χρήματα τούτων εἰσπράττεσθαι ἢ εἰς παραχειμασίαν ἢ ἄλλῳ τινὶ ὀνόματι, ἀλλ' εἶναι πανταχόθεν ἀνεπηρεάστους (comp. *Arch.* xiv. 10, 2 : παραχειμασίαν δὲ

καὶ χρήματα πράττεσθαι οὐ δοκιμάζω). This corresponds in the main to the formula of the charter, a little older, for Termessus (*C. I. L.* i. n. 204) : *nei quis magistratu prove magistratu legatus ne[ive] quis alius meilites in oppidum Thermesum . . . agrumve . . . hiemandi caussa introducito . . . nisei senatus nominatim utei Thermesum . . . in hibernacula meilites deducantur decreverit.* The marching through is accordingly allowed. In the Privilegium for Judaea the levy seems, moreover, to have been prohibited.

gained the upper hand in the East, Antipater was again the first who not merely submitted to the stronger but placed the new holders of power under obligation to him by a rapid levying of the contribution imposed by them.

Thus it happened that the leader of the republicans, when he withdrew from Syria, left Antipater in his position, and entrusted his son Herod even with a command in Syria. Then, when Antipater died, poisoned as it was said by one of his officers, Antigonus, who had found a refuge with his father-in-law, the prince Ptolemaeus of Chalcis, believed that the moment had come to set aside his weak uncle. But the sons of Antipater, Phasael and Herod, thoroughly defeated his band, and Hyrcanus agreed to grant to them the position of their father, nay, even to receive Herod in a certain measure into the reigning house by betrothing to him his niece Mariamne. Meanwhile the leaders of the republican party were beaten at Philippi. The opposition in Jerusalem hoped now to procure the overthrow of the hated Antipatrids at the hands of the victors ; but Antonius, to whom fell the office of arbiter, decidedly repelled their deputations first in Ephesus, then in Antioch, and last in Tyre ; caused, indeed, the last envoys to be put to death ; and confirmed Phasael and Herod formally as " tetrarchs "[1] of the Jews (713).

Soon the vicissitudes of world politics dragged the Jewish state once more into their vortex. The invasion of the Parthians in the following year (714) put an end in the first instance to the rule of the Antipatrids. The pretender Antigonus joined them, and possessed himself of Jerusalem and almost the whole territory. Hyrcanus

Marginal notes:
Herod.

41.
The Parthians in Judaea.
40.

---

[1] This title, which primarily denotes the collegiate tetrarchate, such as was usual among the Galatians, was then more generally employed for the rule of all together, nay, even for the rule of one, but always as in rank inferior to that of king. In this way, besides Galatia, it appears also in Syria, perhaps from the time of Pompeius, certainly from that of

Augustus. The juxtaposition of an ethnarch and two tetrarchs, as it was arranged in the year 713 for Judaea, according to Josephus (*Arch.* xiv. 13, 1 ; *Bell. Jud.* i. 12, 5), is not again met with elsewhere ; Pherores tetrarch of Peraea under his brother Herodes (*Bell. Jud.* i. 24, 5) is analogous.

Marginal note: 41.

went as a prisoner to the Parthians : Phasael, the eldest
son of Antipater, likewise a captive, put himself to death
in prison.   With great difficulty Herod concealed his
family in a rock-stronghold on the border of Judaea, and
went himself a fugitive and in search of aid first to Egypt,
and, when he no longer found Antonius there, to the two
holders of power just at that time ruling in new harmony

40.   (714) at Rome.   Readily they allowed him—as indeed
it was only in the interest of Rome—to gain back for
himself the Jewish kingdom ; he returned to Syria, so far
as the matter depended on the Romans, as recognised

Herod,
king of
Judaea.

ruler, and even equipped with the royal title.   But, just
like a pretender, he had to wrest the land not so much
from the Parthians as from the patriots.   He fought his
battles pre-eminently with the help of Samaritans and
Idumaeans and hired soldiers, and attained at length,
through the support of the Roman legions, to the possession of the long-defended capital.   The Roman execu-
tioners delivered him likewise from his rival of many
years, Antigonus ; his own made havoc among the noble
families of the council of Jerusalem.

Herod
under An-
tonius and
Cleopatra.

But the days of trouble were by no means over with
his installation.   The unfortunate expedition of Antonius
against the Parthians remained without consequences for
Herod, since the victors did not venture to advance into
Syria ; but he suffered severely under the ever increasing
claims of the Egyptian queen, who at that time more
than Antonius ruled the East ; her womanly policy,
primarily directed to the extension of her domestic power
and above all of her revenues, was far indeed from obtaining at the hands of Antonius all that she desired, but she
wrested at any rate from the king of the Jews a portion
of his most valuable possessions on the Syrian coast and
in the territory lying between Egypt and Syria, nay, even
the rich balsam plantations and palm-groves of Jericho,
and laid upon him severe financial burdens.   In order to
maintain the remnant of his rule, he was obliged either
himself to lease the new Syrian possessions of the queen
or to be guarantee for other lessees less able to pay.   After

all these troubles, and in expectation of still worse demands as little capable of being declined, the outbreak of
the war between Antonius and Caesar was hopeful for
him, and the fact that Cleopatra in her selfish perversity
released him from active participation in the war, because
he needed his troops to collect her Syrian revenues, was
a further piece of good fortune, since this facilitated his
submission to the victor.   Fortune favoured him yet further on his changing sides ; he was able to intercept a
band of faithful gladiators of Antonius, who were marching from Asia Minor through Syria towards Egypt to
lend assistance to their master.   When he, before resort- Herod
ing to Caesar at Rhodes to obtain his pardon, caused the under Au-
last male offshoot of the Maccabaean house, the eighty- gustus.
years old Hyrcanus, to whom the house of Antipater was
indebted for its position, to be at all events put to death,
he in reality exaggerated the necessary caution.   Caesar
did what policy bade him do, especially as the support
of Herod was of importance for the intended Egyptian
expedition.   He confirmed Herod, glad to be vanquished,
in his dominion, and extended it, partly by giving back
the possessions wrested from him by Cleopatra, partly by
further gifts ; the whole coast from Gaza to Strato's
Tower, the later Caesarea, the Samaritan region inserted
between Judaea and Galilee, and a number of towns to the
east of the Jordan thenceforth obeyed Herod.   On the
consolidation of the Roman monarchy the Jewish principality was withdrawn from the reach of further external
crises.

From the Roman standpoint the conduct of the new Govern-
dynasty appears correct, in a way to draw tears from the ment of
eyes of the observer.   It took part at first for Pompeius, Herod.
then for Caesar the father, then for Cassius and Brutus,
then for the triumvirs, then for Antonius, lastly for Caesar
the son ; fidelity varies, as does the watchword.   Nevertheless this conduct is not to be denied the merit of consistency and firmness.   The factions which rent the ruling
burgess-body, whether republic or monarchy, whether
Caesar or Antonius, in reality nowise concerned the depen-

dent provinces, especially those of the Greek East. The demoralisation which is combined with all revolutionary change of government—the degrading confusion between internal fidelity and external obedience—was brought in this case most glaringly to light; but the fulfilment of duty, such as the Roman commonwealth claimed from its subjects, had been satisfied by king Herod to an extent of which nobler and greater natures would certainly not have been capable. In presence of the Parthians he constantly, even in critical circumstances, held firmly to the protectors whom he had once chosen.

In its relation to the Jews.
From the standpoint of internal Jewish politics the government of Herod was the setting aside of the theocracy, and in so far a continuance of, and in fact an advance upon, the government of the Maccabees, as the separation of the political and the ecclesiastical government was carried out with the utmost precision in the contrast between the all-powerful king of foreign birth and the powerless high-priest often and arbitrarily changed. No doubt the royal position was sooner pardoned in the Jewish high-priest than in a man who was a foreigner and incapable of priestly consecration; and, if the Hasmonaeans represented outwardly the independence of Judaism, the Idumaean held his royal power over the Jews in fee from the lord-paramount. The reaction of this insoluble conflict on a deeply-impassioned nature confronts us in the whole life-career of the man, who causes much suffering, but has felt perhaps not less. At all events the energy, the constancy, the yielding to the inevitable, the military and political dexterity, where there was room for it, secure for the king of the Jews a certain place in the panorama of a remarkable epoch.

Herod's character and aims. [4.
To describe in detail the government of Herod for almost forty years—he died in the year 750—as the accounts of it preserved at great length allow us to do, is not the task of the historian of Rome. There is probably no royal house of any age in which bloody feuds raged in an equal degree between parents and children, between husbands and wives, and between brothers and sisters;

the emperor Augustus and his governors in Syria turned away with horror from the share in the work of murder which was suggested to them ; not the least revolting trait in this picture of horrors is the utter want of object in most of the executions, ordained as a rule upon groundless suspicion, and the despairing remorse of the perpetrator, which constantly followed. Vigorously and intelligently as the king took care of the interest of his country, so far as he could and might, and energetically as, not merely in Palestine but throughout the empire, he befriended the Jews with his treasures and with his no small influence— for the decision of Agrippa favourable to the Jews in the great imperial affair of Asia Minor (p. 171) they were substantially indebted to him—he found love and fidelity in Idumaea perhaps and Samaria, but not among the people of Israel ; here he was, and continued to be, not so much the man laden with the guilt of blood in many forms, as above all the foreigner. As it was one of the mainsprings of that domestic war, that his wife of the Hasmonaean family, the fair Mariamne, and their children were regarded and dreaded by him more as Jews than as his own, he himself gave expression to the feeling that he was as much drawn towards the Greeks as repelled by the Jews. It is significant that he had the sons, for whom in the first instance he destined the succession, brought up in Rome. While out of his inexhaustible riches he loaded the Greek cities of other lands with gifts and embellished them with temples, he built for the Jews no doubt also, but not in the Jewish sense. The buildings of the circus and theatre in Jerusalem itself, as well as the temples for the imperial worship in the Jewish towns, were regarded by the pious Israelite as a summons to blaspheme God. His conversion of the temple in Jerusalem into a magnificent building was done half against the will of the devout ; much as they admired the building, his introduction into it of a golden eagle was taken more amiss than all the sentences of death ordained by him, and led to a popular insurrection, to which the eagle fell a sacrifice, and thereupon doubtless the devotees as well, who tore it down.

Herod knew the land sufficiently not to let matters
come to extremities ; if it had been possible to Hellenise
it, the will to that effect would not have been wanting on
his part.   In energy the Idumaean was not inferior to the
best Hasmonaeans.   The construction of the great harbour
at Strato's Tower, or as the town entirely rebuilt by Herod
was thenceforth called, Caesarea, first gave to a coast poor
in harbours what it needed, and throughout the whole
period of the empire the town remained a chief emporium
of southern Syria.   What the government was able to
furnish in other respects—development of natural resources,
intervention in case of famine and other calamities, above
all things internal and external security—was furnished
by Herod.   The evil of brigandage was done away, and
the defence—so uncommonly difficult in these regions—
of the frontier against the roving tribes of the desert
was carried out with sternness and consistency.   Thereby
the Roman government was induced to place under him
still further regions, Ituraea, Trachonitis, Auranitis, Batanaea.   Thenceforth his dominion extended, as we have
already mentioned (p. 146), compactly over the region
beyond the Jordan as far as towards Damascus and to the
Hermon mountains ; so far as we can discern, after those
further assignments there was in the whole domain which
we have indicated no longer any free city or any rule
independent of Herod.   The defence of the frontier itself
fell more on the Arabian king than on the king of the
Jews ; but, so far as it devolved on him, the series of well-
provided frontier-forts brought about here a general peace,
such as had not hitherto been known in those regions.
We can understand how Agrippa, after inspecting the
maritime and military structures of Herod, should have
discerned in him an associate striving in a like spirit towards the great work of organising the empire, and should
have treated him in this sense.

The end of
Herod and
the parti-
tion of his
kingdom. His kingdom had no lasting existence.   Herod himself apportioned it in his testament among his three sons,
and Augustus confirmed the arrangement in the main,
only placing the important port of Gaza and the Greek

towns beyond the Jordan immediately under the governor of Syria. The northern portions of the kingdom were separated from the mainland ; the territory last acquired by Herod to the south of Damascus, Batanaea with the districts belonging to it, was obtained by Philip ; Galilee and Peraea, that is, the Transjordanic domain, so far as it was not Greek, by Herod Antipas—both as tetrarchs ; these two petty principalities continued, at first as separate, then as united under Herod " the Great's" great-grandson Agrippa II., with slight interruptions to subsist down to the time of Trajan. We have already mentioned their government when describing eastern Syria and Arabia (p. 146 f.). Here it may only be added that these Herodians continued to rule, if not with the energy, at least in the sense and spirit of the founder of the dynasty. The towns established by them—Caesarea, the ancient Paneas, in the northern territory, and Tiberias in Galilee—had a Hellenic organisation quite after the manner of Herod ; characteristic is the proscription, which the Jewish Rabbis on account of a tomb found at the laying out of Tiberias decreed over the unclean city.

The main country, Judaea, along with Samaria on the north and Idumaea on the south, was destined for Archelaus by his father's will. But this succession was not accordant with the wishes of the nation. The orthodox, that is, the Pharisees, ruled with virtual exclusiveness the mass of the people ; and, if hitherto the fear of the Lord had been in some measure kept down by the fear of the unscrupulously energetic king, the mind of the great majority of the Jews was set upon re-establishing under the protectorate of Rome the pure and godly sacerdotal government, as it had once been set up by the Persian authorities. Immediately after the death of the old king the masses in Jerusalem had congregated to demand the setting aside of the high-priest nominated by Herod and the ejection of the unbelievers from the holy city, where the Passover was just to be celebrated ; Archelaus had been under the necessity of beginning his government by charging into these masses ; a number of dead were counted,

Judaea under Archelaus.

and the observance of the festival was suspended. The Roman governor of Syria—the same Varus, whose folly soon afterwards cost the Romans Germany—on whom it primarily devolved to maintain order in the land during the interregnum, had allowed these mutinous bands in Jerusalem to send to Rome, where the occupation of the Jewish throne was just being discussed, a deputation of fifty persons to request the abolition of the monarchy; and, when Augustus gave audience to it, eight thousand Jews of the capital escorted it to the temple of Apollo. The fanatical Jews at home meanwhile continued to help themselves ; the Roman garrison, which was stationed in the temple, was assailed with violence, and pious bands of brigands filled the land ; Varus had to call out the legions and to restore quiet with the sword. It was a warning for the suzerain, a supplementary justification of king Herod's violent but effective government. But Augustus, with all the weakness which he so often showed, particularly in later years, while dismissing, no doubt, the representatives of those fanatical masses and their request, yet executed in the main the testament of Herod, and gave over the rule in Jerusalem to Archelaus shorn of the kingly title, which Augustus preferred for a time not to concede to the untried young man ; shorn, moreover, of the northern territories, and reduced also in military status by the taking away of the defence of the frontier. The circumstance that at the instigation of Augustus the taxes raised to a high pitch under Herod were lowered, could but little better the position of the tetrarch. The personal incapacity and worthlessness of Archelaus were hardly needed, in addition, to make him impossible ; a few years later (6 A.D.) Augustus saw himself compelled to depose him. Now he did at length the will of those mutineers ; the monarchy was abolished, and while on the one hand the land was taken into direct Roman administration, on the other hand, so far as an internal government was allowed by the side of this, it was given over to the senate of Jerusalem. This procedure may certainly have been determined in part by assurances given earlier by Augustus to Herod as regards

Judaea a
Roman
province.

the succession, in part by the more and more apparent, and in general doubtless justifiable, disinclination of the imperial government to larger client-states possessing some measure of independent self-movement. What took place shortly before or soon after in Galatia, in Cappadocia, in Mauretania, explains why in Palestine also the kingdom of Herod hardly survived himself. But, as the immediate government was organised in Palestine, it was even administratively a bad retrograde step as compared with the Herodian ; and above all the circumstances here were so peculiar and so difficult, that the immediate contact between the governing Romans and the governed Jews— which certainly had been obstinately striven for by the priestly party itself and ultimately obtained—redounded to the benefit neither of the one nor of the other.

Judaea thus became in the year 6 A.D. a Roman pro- Provincial vince of the second rank,[1] and, apart from the ephemeral organisa-tion.

[1] The statement of Josephus that Judaea was attached to the province of Syria and placed under its governor (*Arch.* xvii. *fin.* : τοῦ δὲ Ἀρχελάου χώρας ὑποτελοῦς προσνεμηθείσης τῇ Σύρων; xviii. 1, 1 : εἰς τὴν Ἰουδαίαν προσθήκην τῆς Συρίας γενομένην ; c. 4, 6) appears to be incorrect ; on the contrary, Judaea probably formed thenceforth a procuratorial province of itself. An exact distinction between the *de iure* and *de facto* interference of the Syrian governor may not be expected in the case of Josephus. The fact that he organised the new province and conducted the first census does not decide the question what arrangement was assigned to it. Where the Jews complain of their procurator to the governor of Syria and the latter interferes against him, the procurator is certainly dependent on the legate ; but, when L. Vitellius did this (Josephus, *Arch.* xviii. 4, 2), his power extended in quite an extraordinary way over the province (Tacitus, *Ann.* vi. 32; *Staatsrecht*, ii. 822), and in the other case the words of Tacitus, *Ann.* xii. 54 : *quia Claudius ius statuendi etiam de pro-* *curatoribus dederat,* show that the governor of Syria could not have pronounced such a judgment in virtue of his general jurisdiction. Both the *ius gladii* of these procurators (Josephus, *Bell. Jud.* ii. 8, 1 : μέχρι τοῦ κτείνειν λαβὼν παρὰ τοῦ Καίσαρος ἐξουσίαν, *Arch.* xviii. 1, 1 ; ἡγησόμενος Ἰουδαίων τῇ ἐπὶ πᾶσιν ἐξουσίᾳ) and their whole demeanour show that they did not belong to those who, placed under an imperial legate, attended only to financial affairs, but rather, like the procurators of Noricum and Raetia, formed the supreme authority for the administration of law and the command of the army. Thus the legates of Syria had there only the position which those of Pannonia had in Noricum and the upper German legate in Raetia. This corresponds also to the general development of matters ; all the larger kingdoms were on their annexation not attached to the neighbouring large governorships, whose plenitude of power it was not the tendency of this epoch to enlarge, but were made into independent governorships, mostly at first equestrian.

restoration of the kingdom of Jerusalem under Claudius in the years 41-44, thenceforth remained a Roman province. Instead of the previous native princes holding office for life and, under reservation of their being confirmed by the Roman government, hereditary, came an official of the equestrian order, nominated and liable to recall by the emperor. The port of Caesarea rebuilt by Herod after a Hellenic model became, probably at once, the seat of Roman administration. The exemption of the land from Roman garrison, as a matter of course ceased, but, as throughout in provinces of the second rank, the Roman military force consisted only of a moderate number of cavalry and infantry divisions of the inferior class ; subsequently one ala and five cohorts—about 3000 men—were stationed there. These troops were perhaps taken over from the earlier government, at least in great part formed in the country itself, mostly, however, from Samaritans and Syrian Greeks.[1] The province did not obtain a legionary garrison, and even in the territories adjoining Judaea there was stationed at the most one of the four Syrian legions. To Jerusalem there came a standing Roman commandant, who took up his abode in the royal castle, with a weak standing garrison ; only during the time of the Passover, when the whole land and countless strangers flocked to the temple, a stronger division of Roman soldiers was stationed in a colonnade belonging to the temple. That on the erection of the province the obligation of tribute towards Rome set in, follows from the very circumstance that the costs of defending the land were thereby transferred to the imperial government. After the latter had suggested a reduction of the payments at the installation of Archelaus, it is far from probable that on the annexation of the country it contemplated an immediate raising of them ; but doubtless, as in every newly-

---

[1] According to Josephus (*Arch.* xx. 8, 7, more exact than *Bell. Jud.* ii. 13, 7) the greatest part of the Roman troops in Palestine consisted of Caesareans and Sebastenes. The *ala* *Sebastenorum* fought in the Jewish war under Vespasian (Josephus, *Bell. Jud.* ii. 12, 5). Comp. *Eph. epigr.* v. 194. There are no *alae* and *cohortes Iudaeorum*.

acquired territory, steps were taken for a revision of the previous land-register.[1]

For the native authorities in Judaea as everywhere the urban communities were, as far as possible, taken as a basis. Samaria, or as the town was now called, Sebaste, the newly laid out Caesarea, and the other urban communities contained in the former kingdom of Archelaus, were self-administering, under superintendence of the Roman authority. The government also of the capital with the large territory belonging to it was organised in a similar way. Already in the pre-Roman period under the Seleucids there was formed, as we saw (p. 160), in Jerusalem a council of the elders, the Synhedrion, or as Judaised, the Sanhedrin. The presidency in it was held by the high priest, whom each ruler of the land, if he was not possibly himself high priest, appointed for the time. To the college belonged the former high priests and esteemed experts in the law. This assembly, in which the aristocratic element preponderated, acted as the supreme spiritual representative of the whole body of Jews, and, so far as this was not to be separated from it, also as the secular representative in particular of the community of Jerusalem. It is only the later Rabbinism that has by a pious fiction transformed the Synhedrion of Jerusalem into a spiritual institute of Mosaic appointment. It corresponded essentially to the council of the Greek urban constitution, but certainly bore, as respected its composition as well as its sphere of working, a more spiritual character

The native authorities.

The Synhedrion of Jerusalem.

---

[1] The revenues of Herod amounted, according to Josephus, *Arch.* xvii. 11, 4, to about 1200 talents, whereof about 100 fell to Batanaea with the adjoining lands, 200 to Galilee and Peraea, the rest to the share of Archelaus ; in this doubtless the older Hebrew talent (of about £390) is meant, not, as Hultsch (Metrol. ², p. 605) assumes, the denarial talent (of about £260), as the revenues of the same territory under Claudius are estimated in the same Josephus (*Arch.* xix. 8, 2), at 12,000,000 denarii (about £500,000). The chief item in it was formed by the land-tax, the amount of which we do not know ; in the Syrian time it amounted at least for a time to the third part of corn and the half of wine and oil (1 Maccab. x. 30) in Caesar's time for Joppa a fourth of the fruit (p. 175, note), besides which at that time the temple-tenth still existed. To this was added a number of other taxes and customs, auction - charges, salt - tax, road and bridge moneys, and the like ; it is to these that the publicans of the Gospels have reference.

than belonged to the Greek representations of the community. To this Synhedrion and its high priest, who was now nominated by the procurator as representative of the imperial suzerain, the Roman government left or committed that jurisdiction which in the Hellenic subject communities belonged to the urban authorities and the common councils. With indifferent short-sightedness it allowed to the transcendental Messianism of the Pharisees free course, and to the by no means transcendental land-consistory—acting until the Messiah should arrive—tolerably free sway in affairs of faith, of manners, and of law, where Roman interests were not directly affected thereby. This applied in particular to the administration of justice. It is true that, as far as Roman burgesses were concerned, ordinary jurisdiction in civil as in criminal affairs must have been reserved for the Roman tribunals even already before the annexation of the land. But civil jurisdiction over Jews remained even after that annexation chiefly with the local authority. Criminal justice over them was exercised by the latter probably in general concurrently with the Roman procurator ; only sentences of death could not be executed by it otherwise than after confirmation by the imperial magistrate.

The Roman provincial government.

In the main those arrangements were the inevitable consequences of the abolition of the principality, and when the Jews had obtained this request of theirs, they in fact obtained those arrangements along with it. Certainly it was the design of the government to avoid, as far as possible, harshness and abruptness in carrying them out. Publius Sulpicius Quirinius, to whom as governor of Syria the erection of the new province was entrusted, was a magistrate of repute, and quite familiar with the affairs of the East, and the several reports confirm by what they say or by their silence the fact that the difficulties of the state of things were known and taken into account. The local coining of petty moneys, as formerly practised by the kings, now took place in the name of the Roman ruler ; but on account of the Jewish abhorrence of images the head of the emperor was not even placed on the coins.

Setting foot within the interior of the temple continued to be forbidden in the case of every non-Jew under penalty of death.[1]   However averse was the attitude of Augustus personally towards the Oriental worships (p. 172), he did not disdain here any more than in Egypt to connect them in their home with the imperial government; magnificent presents of Augustus, of Livia, and of other members of the imperial house adorned the sanctuary of the Jews, and according to an endowment by the emperor the smoke of the sacrifice of a bullock and two lambs rose daily there to the "Supreme God."   The Roman soldiers were directed, when they were on service at Jerusalem, to leave the standards with the effigies of the emperor at Caesarea, and, when a governor under Tiberius omitted to do so, the government ultimately yielded to the urgent entreaties of the pious and left matters on the old footing.   Indeed, when the Roman troops were to march through Jerusalem on an expedition against the Arabians, they obtained another route for the march in consequence of the scruples entertained by the priests against the effigies on the standards. When that same governor dedicated to the emperor at the royal castle in Jerusalem shields without imagery, and the pious took offence at it, Tiberius commanded the same to be taken away, and to be hung up in the temple of Augustus at Caesarea.   The festival dress of the high priest, which was kept in Roman custody at the castle and hence had to be purified from such profanation for seven days before

---

[1] On the marble screen (δρύφακτος), which marked off the inner court of the temple, were placed for that reason tablets of warning in the Latin and Greek language (Josephus, *Bell. Jud.* v. 5, 2 ; vi. 2, 4 ; *Arch.* xv. 11, 5). One of the latter, which has recently been found (*Revue Archéologique*, xxiii. 1872, p. 220), and is now in the public museum of Constantinople, is to this effect : μηθ' ἕνα ἀλλογενῆ εἰσπορεύεσθαι ἐντὸς τοῦ περὶ τὸ ἱερὸν τρυφάκτου καὶ περιβόλου. ὃς δ'ἂν ληφθῇ, ἑαυτῷ αἴτιος ἔσται διὰ τὸ ἐξακολουθεῖν θάνατον. The iota in the dative is present, and the writing good and suitable for the early imperial period.   These tablets were hardly set up by the Jewish kings, who would scarcely have added a Latin text, and had no cause to threaten the penalty of death with this singular anonymity.   If they were set up by the Roman government, both are explained ; Titus also says (in Josephus, *Bell. Jud.* vi. 2, 4), in an appeal to the Jews: οὐχ ἡμεῖς τοὺς ὑπερβάντας ὑμῖν ἀναιρεῖν ἐπετρέψαμεν, κἂν 'Ρωμαῖός τις ᾖ ;—If the tablet really bears traces of axe-cuts, these came from the soldiers of Titus.

it was put on, was delivered up to the faithful upon their complaint ; and the commandant of the castle was directed to give himself no further concern about it.   Certainly it could not be asked of the multitude that it should feel the consequences of the incorporation less heavily, because it had itself brought them about.   Nor is it to be maintained that the annexation of the land passed off without oppression for the inhabitants, and that they had no ground to complain ; such arrangements have never been carried into effect without difficulties and disturbances of the peace.   The number, moreover, of unrighteous and violent deeds perpetrated by individual governors must not have been smaller in Judaea than elsewhere.   In the very beginning of the reign of Tiberius the Jews, like the Syrians, complained of the pressure of the taxes ; especially the prolonged administration of Pontius Pilatus is charged with all the usual official crimes by a not unfair observer. But Tiberius, as the same Jew says, had during the twenty-three years of his reign maintained the time-hallowed holy customs, and in no part set them aside or violated them.   This is the more to be recognised, seeing that the same emperor in the West interfered against the Jews more emphatically than any other (p. 172), and thus the long-suffering and caution shown by him in Judaea cannot be traced back to personal favour for Judaism.

The Jewish opposition.
In spite of all this both the opposition on principle to the Roman government and the violent efforts at self-help on the part of the faithful developed themselves even in this time of peace.   The payment of tribute was assailed, not perchance merely because it was oppressive, but as being godless. " Is it allowable," asks the Rabbi in the Gospel, " to pay the census to Caesar ?"   The ironical answer which he received did not by any means suffice for all ; there were saints, though possibly not in great number, who thought themselves polluted if they touched a coin with the emperor's image.   This was something new—an advance in the theology of opposition ; the kings Seleucus and Antiochus had also not been circumcised, and had likewise received tribute in silver pieces bearing their

image.   Such was the theory ; the practical application of
it was made, not certainly by the high council of Jerusalem, in which, under the influence of the imperial
government, the more pliant notables of the land directed
the vote, but by Judas the Galilean from Gamala on
the lake of Gennesaret, who, as Gamaliel subsequently
reminded this high council, " stood up in the days of the
census, and behind him the people rose in revolt." He
spoke out what all thought, that the so-called census was
bondage, and that it was a disgrace for the Jew to recognise another lord over him than the Lord of Zebaoth ;
but that He helped only those who helped themselves.
If not many followed his call to arms, and he ended his
life, after a few months, on the scaffold, the holy dead was
more dangerous to the unholy victors than the living man.
He and his followers were regarded by the later Jews
alongside of the Sadducees, Pharisees, and Essenes, as
the fourth " School ;" at that time they were called the
Zealots, afterwards they called themselves Sicarii, " men
of the knife."   Their teaching was simple : God alone is
Lord, death indifferent, freedom all in all.   This teaching
remained, and the children and grandchildren of Judas
became the leaders of the later insurrections.

If the Roman government had under the first two
regents, taken on the whole, skilfully and patiently sufficed
for the task of repressing, as far as possible, these ex-
plosive elements, the next change on the throne brought
matters close to the catastrophe.   The change was saluted
with rejoicing, as in the whole empire, so specially by the
Jews in Jerusalem and Alexandria ; and, after the unsoci-
able and unloved old man, the new youthful ruler Gaius
was extravagantly extolled in both quarters.   But speedily
out of trifling occasions there was developed a formidable
quarrel.   A grandson of the first Herod and of the beautiful Mariamne, named after the protector and friend of
his grandfather Herod Agrippa, about the most worthless
and abandoned of the numerous Oriental princes' sons
living in Rome, but nevertheless or on that very account
the favourite and youthful friend of the new emperor,

The em-
peror Gaius
and the
Jews.

hitherto known solely by his dissoluteness and his debts, had obtained from his protector, to whom he had been the first to convey the news of the death of Tiberius, one of the vacant Jewish petty principalities as a gift, and the title of king along with it.   This prince in the year 38, on the way to his new kingdom, came to the city of Alexandria, where he a few months previously had attempted as a runaway bill-debtor to borrow among the Jewish bankers. When he showed himself there in public in his regal dress with his splendidly equipped halberdiers, this naturally stirred up the non-Jewish inhabitants of the great city— fond as it was of ridicule and of scandal—who bore anything but good will to the Jews, to a corresponding parody ; nor did the matter stop there.   It culminated in a furious hunting-out of the Jews.   The Jewish houses which lay detached were plundered and burnt ; the Jewish ships lying in the harbour were pillaged ; the Jews that were met with in the non-Jewish quarters were maltreated and slain.   But against the purely Jewish quarters they could effect nothing by violence.   Then the leaders lighted on the idea of consecrating the synagogues, which were the object of their marked attentions, so far as these still stood, collectively as temples of the new ruler, and of setting up statues of him in all of them—in the chief synagogue a statue on a *quadriga*.   That the emperor Gaius deemed himself, as seriously as his confused mind could do so, a real and corporeal god, everybody knew— the Jews and the governor as well.   The latter, Avillius Flaccus, an able man, and, under Tiberius, an excellent administrator, but now hampered by the disfavour in which he stood with the new emperor, and expecting every moment recall and impeachment, did not disdain to use the opportunity for his rehabilitation.[1]   He not

---

[1] The special hatred of Gaius against the Jews (Philo, *Leg.* 20) was not the cause, but the consequence, of the Alexandrian Jew-hunt. Since therefore the understanding of the leaders of the Jew-hunt with the governor (Philo, *in Flacc.* 4) cannot have subsisted on the footing that the Jews imagined, because the governor could not reasonably believe that he would recommend himself to the new emperor by abandoning the Jews, the question certainly arises, why the leaders of those hostile to the Jews chose this very moment for the Jew-hunt, and above all, why the governor,

merely gave orders by edict to put no hindrance in the way of setting up the statues in the synagogues, but he entered directly into the Jew-hunting. He ordained the abolition of the Sabbath. He declared further in his edicts that these tolerated foreigners had possessed themselves unallowably of the best part of the town ; they were restricted to a single one of the five wards, and all the other Jewish houses were abandoned to the rabble, while masses of the ejected inhabitants lay without shelter on the shore. No remonstrance was even listened to ; eight and thirty members of the council of the elders, which then presided over the Jews instead of the Ethnarch,[1] were scourged in the open circus before all the people. Four hundred houses lay in ruins ; trade and commerce were suspended ; the factories stood still. There was no help left except with the emperor. Before him appeared the two Alexandrian deputations, that of the Jews led by the formerly (p. 170) mentioned Philo, a scholar of Neojudaic leanings, and of a heart more gentle than brave, but who withal faithfully took the part of his people in this distress ; that of the enemies of the Jews, led by Apion, also an Alexandrian scholar and author, the "world's clapper" [*cymbalum mundi*], as the emperor Tiberius called him, full of big words and still bigger lies,

whose excellence Philo so emphatically acknowledges, allowed it, and, at least in its further course, took personal part in it. Probably things occurred as they are narrated above : hatred and envy towards the Jews had long been fermenting in Alexandria (Josephus, *Bell. Jud.* ii. 18, 9 ; Philo, *Leg.* 18) ; the abeyance of the old stern government, and the evident disfavour in which the prefect stood with Gaius, gave room for the tumult ; the arrival of Agrippa furnished the occasion ; the adroit conversion of the synagogues into temples of Gaius stamped the Jews as enemies of the emperor, and, after this was done, Flaccus must certainly have seized on the persecution to rehabilitate himself thereby with the emperor.

[1] When Strabo was in Egypt in

the earlier Augustan period the Jews in Alexandria were under an Ethnarch (*Geogr.* xvii. 1, 13, p. 798, and in Josephus, *Arch.* xiv. 7, 2). Thereupon, when under Augustus the Ethnarchos or Genarchos, as he was called, died, a council of the elders took his place (Philo, *Leg.* 10) ; yet Augustus, as Claudius states (Josephus, *Arch.* xix. 5, 2), "did not prohibit the Jews from appointing an Ethnarch," which probably is meant to signify that the choice of a single president was only omitted for this time, not abolished once for all. Under Gaius there were evidently only elders of the Jewish body ; and also under Vespasian these are met with (Josephus, *Bell.* vii. 10, 1). An archon of the Jews in Antioch is named in Josephus, *Bell.* vii. 3, 3.

of the most assured omniscience[1] and unlimited faith in himself, conversant, if not with men, at any rate with their worthlessness, a celebrated master of discourse as of the art of misleading, ready for action, witty, unabashed, and unconditionally loyal. The result of the discussion was settled from the outset; the emperor received the deputies while he was inspecting the works designed in his gardens, but instead of giving a hearing to the suppliants, he put to them sarcastic questions, which the enemies of the Jews in defiance of all etiquette accompanied with loud laughter, and, as he was in good humour, he confined himself to expressing his regret that these otherwise good people should be so unhappily constituted as not to be able to understand his innate divine nature—as to which he was beyond doubt in earnest. Apion thus gained his case, and, wherever it pleased the adversaries of the Jews, the synagogues were changed into temples of Gaius.

The statue of the emperor in the temple of Jerusalem. But the matter was not confined to these dedications introduced by the street-youth of Alexandria. In the year 39 the governor of Syria, Publius Petronius, received orders from the emperor to march with his legions into Jerusalem, and to set up in the temple the statue of the emperor. The governor, an honourable official of the school of Tiberius, was alarmed; Jews from all the land, men and women, gray-haired and children, flocked to him, first to Ptolemais in Syria, then to Tiberias in Galilee, to entreat his mediation that the outrage might not take place; the fields throughout the country were not tilled, and the desperate multitudes declared that they would rather suffer death by the sword or famine than be willing to look on at this abomination. In reality the governor ventured to delay the execution of the orders and to make counter-representations, although he knew that his head was at stake. At the same time the king Agrippa, lately mentioned, went in person to Rome to procure from his

---

[1] Apion spoke and wrote on all and sundry matters, upon the metals and the Roman letters, on magic and concerning the Hetaerae, on the early history of Egypt and the cookery re- ceipts of Apicius; but above all he made his fortune by his discourses upon Homer, which acquired for him honorary citizenship in numerous Greek cities. He had discovered

friend the recall of the orders. The emperor in fact desisted from his desire, in consequence, it is said, of his good humour when under the influence of wine being adroitly turned to account by the Jewish prince. But at the same time he restricted the concession to the single temple of Jerusalem, and sent nevertheless to the governor on account of his disobedience a sentence of death, which indeed, accidentally delayed, was not carried into execution. Gaius now resolved to break the resistance of the Jews ; the enjoined march of the legions shows that he had this time weighed beforehand the consequences of his order. Since those occurrences the Egyptians, ready to believe in his divinity, had his full affection just as the obstinate and simple-minded Jews had his corresponding hatred ; secretive as he was and accustomed to grant favours in order afterwards to revoke them, the worst could not but appear merely postponed. He was on the point of departing for Alexandria in order there to receive in person the incense of his altars ; and the statue, which he thought of erecting to himself in Jerusalem, was—it is said—quietly in preparation, when, in January 41, the dagger of Chaerea delivered, among other things, the temple of Jehovah from the monster.

The short season of suffering left behind it no outward consequences ; with the god his altars fell. But yet the traces of it remained on both sides. The history, which is here being told, is that of an increasing hatred between Jews and non-Jews, and in it the three years' persecution of the Jews under Gaius marks a section and an advance. The hatred of Jews and the Jew-hunts were as old as the Diaspora itself ; these privileged and autonomous Oriental communities within the Hellenic could not but develop them as necessarily as the marsh generates the malaria.

Jewish dispositions.

that Homer had begun his Iliad with the unsuitable word μῆνις for the reason that the first two letters, as numerals, exhibit the number of the books of the two epics which he was to write ; he named the guest-friend in Ithaca, with whom he had made inquiries as to the draught-board of the suitors ; indeed he affirmed that he had conjured up Homer himself from the nether world to question him about his native country, and that Homer had come and had told it to him, but had bound him not to betray it to others.

But such a Jew-hunt as the Alexandrian of the year 38, instigated by defective Hellenism and directed at once by the supreme authority and by the low rabble, the older Greek and Roman history has not to show. The far way from the evil desire of the individual to the evil deed of the collective body was thus traversed, and it was shown what those so disposed had to will and to do, and were under circumstances also able to do. That this revelation was felt also on the Jewish side, is not to be doubted, although we are not in a position to adduce documentary evidence in support of it.[1] But a far deeper impression than that of the Jew-hunt at Alexandria was graven on the minds of the Jews by the statue of the god Gaius in the Holy of Holies. The thing had been done once already; a like proceeding of the king of Syria, Antiochus Epiphanes, had been followed by the rising of the Maccabees and the victorious restoration of the free

iii. 61. national state (iii. 64). That Epiphanes—the Anti-Messiah who ushers in the Messiah, as the prophet Daniel had, certainly after the event, delineated him—was thenceforth to every Jew the prototype of abomination; it was no matter of indifference, that the same conception came to be with equal warrant attached to a Roman emperor, or rather to the image of the Roman ruler in general. Since that fateful edict the Jews never ceased to dread that another emperor might issue a like command; and so far certainly with reason, as according to the organisation of the Roman polity such an enactment depended solely on the momentary pleasure of the ruler for the time.

The Apocalypse of John.

This Jewish hatred of the worship of the emperor and of imperialism itself, is depicted with glowing colours in the

[1] The writings of Philo, which bring before us this whole catastrophe with incomparable reality, nowhere strike this chord; but, apart even from the fact that this rich and aged man had in him more of the good man than of the good hater, it is obvious of itself that these consequences of the occurrences on the Jewish side were not publicly set forth. What the Jews thought and felt may not be judged of by what they found it convenient to say, particularly in their works written in Greek. If the Book of Wisdom and the third book of Maccabees are in reality directed against the Alexandrian persecution of the Jews (Hausrath, *Neutestam. Zeitgesch.* ii. 259 ff.)—which we may add is anything but certain—they are, if possible, couched in a still tamer tone than the writings of Philo.

Apocalypse of John, for which, chiefly on that account, Rome is the harlot of Babylon and the common enemy of mankind.[1]   Still less matter of indifference was the

---

[1] This is perhaps the right way of apprehending the Jewish conceptions, in which the positive facts regularly run away into generalities. In the accounts of the Anti-Messias and of the Antichrist no positive elements are found to suit the emperor Gaius ; the view that would explain the name Armillus, which the Talmud assigns to the former, by the circumstance that the emperor Gaius sometimes wore women's bracelets (*armillae*, Suetonius, *Gai.* 52), cannot be seriously maintained. In the Apocalypse of John—the classical revelation of Jewish self-esteem and of hatred towards the Romans—the picture of the Anti-Messias is associated rather with Nero, who did not cause his image to be set up in the Holy of Holies. This composition belongs, as is well known, to a time and a tendency, which still viewed Christianity as essentially a Jewish sect ; those elected and marked by the angel are all Jews, 12,000 from each of the twelve tribes, and have precedence over the "great multitude of other righteous ones," *i.e.* of proselytes (ch. vii. ; comp. ch. xii. 1). It was written, demonstrably, after Nero's fall, and when his return from the East was expected. Now it is true that a pseudo-Nero appeared immediately after the death of the real one, and was executed at the beginning of the following year (Tacitus, *Hist.* ii. 8, 9) ; but it is not of this one that John is thinking, for the very exact account makes no mention, as John does, of the Parthians in the matter, and for John there is a considerable interval between the fall of Nero and his return, the latter even still lying in the future. His Nero is the person who, under Vespasian, found adherents in the region of the Euphrates, whom king Artabanus acknowledged under Titus and prepared to reinstate in Rome by military force, and whom at length the Parthians surrendered, after prolonged negotiations, about the year 88, to Domitian. To these events the Apocalypse corresponds quite exactly.

On the other hand, in a writing of this character no inference as to the state of the siege at the time can possibly be drawn, from the circumstance that, according to xi. 1, 2, only the outer court, and not the Holy of Holies of the Temple of Jerusalem was given into the power of the heathen ; here everything in the details is imaginary, and this trait is certainly either invented at pleasure or, if the view be preferred, possibly based on orders given to the Roman soldiers, who were encamped in Jerusalem after its destruction, not to set foot in what was formerly the Holy of Holies. The foundation of the Apocalypse is indisputably the destruction of the earthly Jerusalem, and the prospect thereby for the first time opened up of its future ideal restoration ; in place of the razing of the city which had taken place there cannot possibly be put the mere expectation of its capture. If, then, it is said of the seven heads of the dragon : βασιλεῖς ἐπτά εἰσιν· οἱ πέντε ἔπεσαν, καὶ εἷς ἔστιν, ὁ ἄλλος οὔπω ἦλθεν, καὶ ὅταν ἔλθῃ ὀλίγον αὐτὸν δεῖ μεῖναι (xvii. 10), the five, presumably, are Augustus, Tiberius, Gaius, Claudius, Nero, the sixth Vespasian, the seventh undefined ; "the beast which was, and is not, and is itself the eighth, but of the seven," is, of course, Nero. The undefined seventh is incongruous, like so much in this gorgeous, but contradictory and often tangled imagery ; and it is added, not because the number seven was employed, which was easily to be got at by including Caesar, but because the writer hesitated to predicate immediately of the reigning emperor the short government of the last ruler and his overthrow by the

parallel, which naturally suggested itself, of the consequences. Mattathias of Modein had not been more than Judas the Galilean ; the insurrection of the patriots against the Syrian king was almost as hopeless as the

returning Nero. But one cannot possibly — as is done after others by Renan—by including Caesar in the reckoning, recognise in the sixth emperor, " who is," Nero, who immediately afterward is designated as he who " "was and is not," and in the seventh, who " has not yet come and will not rule long," even the aged Galba, who, according to Renan's view, was ruling at the time. It is clear that the latter does not belong at all to such a series, any more than Otho and Vitellius.

It is more important, however, to oppose the current conception, according to which the polemic is directed against the Neronian persecution of the Christians and the siege or the destruction of Jerusalem, whereas it is pointed against the Roman provincial government generally, and in particular against the worship of the emperors. If of the seven emperors Nero alone is named (by his numerical expression), this is so, not because he was the worst of the seven, but because the naming of the reigning emperor, while prophesying a speedy end of his reign in a published writing, had its risk, and some consideration towards the one " who is " beseems even a prophet. Nero's name was given up, and besides, the legend of his healing and of his return was in every one's mouth ; thereby he has become for the Apocalypse the representative of the Roman imperial rule, and the Antichrist. The crime of the monster of the sea, and of his image and instrument, the monster of the land, is not the violence to the city of Jerusalem (xi. 2)—which appears not as their misdeed, but rather as a portion of the world-judgment (in which case also consideration for the reigning emperor may have been at work)— but the divine worship, which the heathen pay to the monster of the

sea (xiii. 8 : προσκυνήσουσιν αὐτὸν πάντες οἱ κατοικοῦντες ἐπὶ τῆς γῆς), and which the monster of the land— called for that reason also the pseudo-prophet—demands and compels for that of the sea (xiii. 12 : ποιεῖ τὴν γῆν καὶ τοὺς κατοικοῦντας ἐν αὐτῇ ἵνα προσκυνήσουσιν τὸ θηρίον τὸ πρῶτον, οὗ ἐθεραπεύθη ἡ πληγὴ τοῦ θανάτου αὐτοῦ); above all, he is upbraided with the desire to make an image for the former (xiii. 14 : λέγων τοῖς κατοικοῦσιν ἐπὶ τῆς γῆς, ποιῆσαι εἰκόνα τῷ θηρίῳ ὃς ἔχει τὴν πληγὴν τῆς μαχαίρης καὶ ἔζησεν, comp. xiv. 9 ; xvi. 2 ; xix. 20). This, it is plain, is partly the imperial government beyond the sea, partly the lieutenancy on the Asiatic continent, not of this or that province or even of this or that person, but generally such representation of the emperor as the provincials of Asia and Syria knew. If trade and commerce appear associated with the use of the χάραγμα of the monster of the sea (xiii. 16, 17), there lies clearly at bottom an abhorrence of the image and legend of the imperial money— certainly transformed in a fanciful way, as in fact Satan makes the image of the emperor speak. These very governors appear afterwards (xvii.) as the ten horns, which are assigned to the monster in its copy, and are here called, quite correctly, the " ten kings, which have not the royal dignity, but have authority like kings ;" the number, which is taken over from the vision of Daniel, may not, it is true, be taken too strictly.

In the sentences of death pronounced over the righteous, John is thinking of the regular judicial procedure on account of the refusal to worship the emperor's image, such as the Letters of Pliny describe (xiii. 15 : ποιήσῃ ἵνα ὅσοι ἐὰν μὴ προσκυνήσωσιν τὴν εἰκόνα τοῦ θηρίου ἀποκτανθῶσιν, comp. vi. 9 ; xx. 4). When stress is

insurrection against the monster beyond the sea. Historical parallels in practical application are dangerous elements of opposition ; only too rapidly does the structure of long years of wise government come to be shaken.

The government of Claudius turned back on both sides into the paths of Tiberius. In Italy there was repeated, not indeed precisely the ejection of the Jews, since there could not but arise a conviction that this course was impracticable, but at any rate a prohibition of the exercise of their worship[1] in common, which, it is true, amounted nearly to the same thing and probably came as little into execution. Alongside of this edict of intolerance and in an opposite sense, by an ordinance embracing the whole empire the Jews were freed from those public

Claudius and the Jews.

laid on these sentences of death being executed with special frequency in Rome (xvii. 6 ; xvii. 24), what is thereby meant is the execution of sentences wherein men were condemned to fight as gladiators or with wild beasts, which often could not take place on the spot where they were pronounced, and, as is well known, took place chiefly in Rome itself (Modestinus, *Dig.* xlviii. 19, 31). The Neronian executions on account of alleged incendiarism do not formally belong to the class of religious processes at all, and it is only prepossession that can refer the martyrs' blood shed in Rome, of which John speaks, exclusively or pre-eminently to these events. The current conceptions as to the so-called persecutions of the Christians labour under a defective apprehension of the rule of law and the practice of law subsisting in the Roman empire ; in reality the persecution of the Christians was a standing matter as was that of robbers ; only such regulations were put into practice at times more gently or even negligently, at other times more strictly, and were doubtless on occasion specially enforced from high quarters. The "war against the saints" is only a subsequent interpolation on the part of some, for whom

John's words did not suffice (xiii. 7). The Apocalypse is a remarkable evidence of the national and religious hatred of the Jews towards the Occidental government ; but to illustrate with these colours the Neronian tale of horrors, as Renan does in particular, is to shift the place of the facts and to detract from their depth of significance. The Jewish national hatred did not wait for the conquest of Jerusalem to originate it, and it made, as might be expected, no distinction between the good and the bad Caesar ; its Anti-Messias is named Nero, doubtless, but not less Vespasian or Marcus.

[1] The circumstance that Suetonius (*Claud.* 25) names a certain Chrestus as instigator of the constant troubles in Rome, that had in the first instance called forth these measures (according to him the expulsion from Rome ; in contrast to Dio, lx. 6) has been without sufficient reason conceived as a misunderstanding of the movement called forth by Christ among Jews and proselytes. The Book of Acts xviii. 2, speaks only of the expulsion of the Jews. At any rate it is not to be doubted that, with the attitude at that time of the Christians to Judaism, they too fell under the edict.

obligations which were not compatible with their religious convictions ; whereby, as respected service in war particularly, there was doubtless conceded only what hitherto it had not been possible to compel. The exhortation, expressed at the close of this edict, to the Jews to exercise now on their part also greater moderation, and to refrain from the insulting of persons of another faith, shows that there had not been wanting transgressions also on the Jewish side. In Egypt as in Palestine the religious arrangements were, at least on the whole, re-established as they had subsisted before Gaius, although in Alexandria the Jews hardly obtained back all that they had possessed ;[1] the insurrectionary movements, which had broken out, or were on the point of breaking out, in the one case as in the other, thereupon disappeared of themselves. In Palestine Claudius even went beyond the

Agrippa. system of Tiberius and committed the whole former territory of Herod to a native prince, that same Agrippa who accidentally had come to be friendly with Claudius and useful to him in the crises of his accession. It was certainly the design of Claudius to resume the system followed at the time of Herod and to obviate the dangers of the immediate contact between the Romans and Jews. But Agrippa, leading an easy life and even as a prince in constant financial embarrassment, good-humoured, moreover, and more disposed to be on good terms with his subjects than with the distant protector, gave offence in various ways to the government, for example, by the strengthening the walls of Jerusalem, which he was forbidden to carry further ; and the towns that adhered to the Romans, Caesarea and Sebaste, as well as the troops organised in the Roman fashion, were disinclined to him. When he died early and suddenly in the year 44, it appeared hazardous to entrust the position, important in

---

[1] The Jews there at least appear later to have had only the fourth of the five wards of the city in their possession (Josephus, *Bell. Jud.* ii. 18, 8). Probably, if the 400 houses that were razed had been given back again to them in so striking a manner, the Jewish authors Josephus and Philo, who lay stress on all the imperial marks of favour shown to the Jews, would not have been silent on the subject.

a political as in a military point of view, to his only son
of seventeen years of age, and those who wielded power in
the cabinet were reluctant to let out of their hands the
lucrative procuratorships.   The Claudian government had
here, as elsewhere, lighted on the right course, but had not
the energy to carry it out irrespective of accessory considerations.   A Jewish prince with Jewish soldiers might
exercise the government in Judaea for the Romans ; the
Roman magistrate and the Roman soldiers offended probably still more frequently through ignorance of Jewish
views than through intentional action in opposition to
them, and whatever they might undertake was on their
part in the eyes of believers an offence, and the most
indifferent occurrence a religious outrage.   The demand
for mutual understanding and agreement was on both
sides just as warranted of itself as it was impossible of
execution.   But above all a conflict between the Jewish
lord of the land and his subjects was a matter of tolerable
indifference for the empire ; every conflict between the
Romans and the Jews in Jerusalem widened the gulf
which yawned between the peoples of the West and the
Hebrews living along with them ; and the danger lay,
not in the quarrels of Palestine, but in the incompatibility
of the members of the empire of different nationalities who
were now withal coupled together by fate.

Thus the ship was driving incessantly towards the
whirlpool.   In this ill-fated voyage all taking part lent
their help—the Roman government and its administrators, the Jewish authorities and the Jewish people.
The former indeed continued to show a willingness to
meet as far as possible all claims, fair and unfair, of the
Jews.   When in the year 44 the procurator again entered
Jerusalem, the nomination of the high-priest and the
administration of the temple-treasure, which were combined with the kingly office and in so far also with the
procuratorship, were taken from him and transferred to
a brother of the deceased king Agrippa, king Herod of
Chalcis, as well as, after his death in the year 48, to his
successor the younger Agrippa already mentioned.   The

Prepara-
tion for the
insurrec-
tion.

Roman chief magistrate, on the complaint of the Jews caused a Roman soldier, who, on occasion of orders to plunder a Jewish village, had torn in pieces a roll of the law, to be put to death. The whole weight of Roman imperial justice fell, according to circumstances, even upon the higher officials ; when two procurators acting alongside of one another had taken part for and against in the quarrel of the Samaritans and the Galileans, and their soldiers had fought against one another, the imperial governor of Syria, Ummidius Quadratus, was sent with extraordinary full powers to Syria to punish and to execute; as a result one of the guilty persons was sent into banishment, and a Roman military tribune named Celer was publicly beheaded in Jerusalem itself. But alongside of these examples of severity stood others of a weakness partaking of guilt ; in that same process the second at least as guilty procurator Antonius Felix escaped punishment, because he was the brother of the powerful menial Pallas and the husband of the sister of king Agrippa. Still more than with the official abuses of individual administrators must the government be chargeable with the fact that it did not strengthen the power of the officials and the number of the troops in a province so situated, and continued to recruit the garrison almost exclusively from the province. Insignificant as the province was, it was a wretched stupidity and an ill-applied parsimony to treat it after the traditional pattern ; the seasonable display of a crushing superiority of force and unrelenting sternness, a governor of higher rank, and a legionary camp, would have saved to the province and the empire great sacrifices of money, blood, and honour.

High-priestly rule. Ananias.
But not less at least was the fault of the Jews. The highpriestly rule, so far as it went—and the government was but too much inclined to allow it free scope in all internal affairs—was, even according to the Jewish accounts, at no time conducted with so much violence and worthlessness as in that from the death of Agrippa to the outbreak of the war. The best-known and most influential of these priest-rulers was Ananias son of Nebedaeus,

the "whitewashed wall," as Paul called him, when this
spiritual judge bade his attendants smite him on the
mouth, because he ventured to defend himself before the
judgment-seat. It was laid to his charge that he bribed
the governor, and that by a corresponding interpretation
of Scripture he alienated from the lower clergy the tithe-
sheaves.[1] As one of the chief instigators of the war
between the Samaritans and the Galileans, he had stood
before the Roman judge. Not because the reckless
fanatics preponderated in the ruling circles, but because
these instigators of popular tumults and organisers of trials
for heresy lacked the moral and religious authority whereby the moderate men in better times had guided the multitude, and because they misunderstood and misused the
indulgence of the Roman authorities in internal affairs,
they were unable to mediate in a peaceful sense between
the foreign rule and the nation. It was under their very
rule that the Roman authorities were assailed with the
wildest and most irrational demands, and popular movements arose of grim absurdity. Of such a nature was
that violent petition, which demanded and obtained the
blood of a Roman soldier on account of the tearing up
of a roll of the law. Another time there arose a popular
tumult, which cost the lives of many men, because a
Roman soldier had exhibited in the temple a part of his
body in unseemly nudity. Even the best of kings could
not have absolutely averted such lunacy ; but even the
most insignificant prince would not have confronted the
fanatical multitude with so little control of the helm as
these priests.

The actual result was the constant increase of the
new Maccabees. It has been customary to put the outbreak of the war in the year 66 ; with equal and perhaps
better warrant we might name for it the year 44. Since
the death of Agrippa warfare in Judaea had never ceased,
and alongside of the local feuds, which Jews fought out

The
Zealots.

---

[1] The question was, apparently,
whether the gift of the tenth sheaf
belonged to Aaron the priest (Numb.
xviii. 28), to the priest generally, or to
the high priest (Ewald, *Jüd. Gesch.*
vi.³ 635).

with Jews, there went on constantly the war of the Roman
troops against the seceders in the mountains, the Zealots,
as the Jews named them, or according to Roman designation, the Robbers.   Both names were appropriate ; here
too alongside of the fanatics the decayed or decaying
elements of society played their part—at any rate after
the victory one of the first steps of the Zealots was to burn
the bonds for debt that were kept in the temple.   Every
one of the abler procurators, onward from the first Cuspius Fadus, swept the land of them, and still the hydra
appeared afresh in greater strength.   The successor of
Fadus, Tiberius Julius Alexander, himself sprung from a
Jewish family, a nephew of the above-mentioned Alexandrian scholar Philo, caused two sons of Judas the Galilean,
Jacob and Simon, to be crucified ; this was the seed of
the new Mattathias.   In the streets of the towns the
patriots preached aloud the war, and not a few followed
to the desert ; these bands set on fire the houses of the
peaceful and rational people who refused to take part with
them.   If the soldiers seized bandits of this sort, they
carried off in turn respectable people as hostages to the
mountains ; and very often the authorities agreed to
release the former in order to liberate the latter.   At the
same time the "men of the knife" began in the capital
their dismal trade ; they murdered, doubtless also for
money—as their first victim the priest Jonathan is named,
as commissioning them in that case, the Roman procurator Felix—but, if possible, at the same time as
patriots, Roman soldiers or countrymen of their own
friendly to the Romans.   How, with such dispositions,
should wonders and signs have failed to appear, and persons
who, deceived or deceiving, roused thereby the fanaticism
of the masses ?   Under Cuspius Fadus the miracle-monger
Theudas led his faithful adherents to the Jordan, assuring
them that the waters would divide before them and swal-
low up the pursuing Roman horsemen, as in the times of
king Pharaoh.   Under Felix another worker of wonders,
named from his native country the Egyptian, promised
that the walls of Jerusalem would collapse like those of

Jericho at the trumpet blast of Joshua ; and thereupon four thousand knife-men followed him to the Mount of Olives. In the very absurdity lay the danger. The great mass of the Jewish population were small farmers, who ploughed their fields and pressed their oil in the sweat of their brow—more villagers than townsmen, of little culture and powerful faith, closely linked to the free bands in the mountains, and full of reverence for Jehovah and his priests in Jerusalem as well as full of aversion towards the unclean strangers. The war there was not a war between one power and another for the ascendency, not even properly a war of the oppressed against the oppressors for the recovery of freedom ; it was not daring statesmen,[1] but fanatical peasants that began and waged it, and paid for it with their blood. It was a further stage in the history of national hatred ; on both sides continued living together seemed impossible, and they encountered each other with the thought of mutual extirpation.

The movement, through which the tumults were changed into war, proceeded from Caesarea. In this urban community—originally Greek, and then remodelled by Herod after the pattern of the colonies of Alexander—which had

Outbreak of
the insur-
rection in
Caesarea.

---

[1] It is nothing but an empty fancy, when the statesman Josephus, in his preface to his History of the war, puts it as if the Jews of Palestine had reckoned on the one hand upon a rising of the Euphrates-lands, on the other hand, upon the troubles in Gaul and the threatening attitude of the Germans and on the crises of the year of four emperors. The Jewish war had long been in full course when Vindex appeared against Nero, and the Druids really did what is here assigned to the Rabbis ; and, however great was the importance of the Jewish Diaspora in the lands of the Euphrates, a Jewish expedition from that quarter against the Romans of the East was almost as inconceivable as from Egypt and Asia Minor. Doubtless some free-lances came from thence, as *e.g.* some young princes of the zealously Jewish royal house of Adiabene (Josephus, *Bell. Jud.* ii. 19, 2 ; vi. 6, 4), and suppliant embassies went thither from the insurgents (*ib.* vi. 6, 2) ; but even money hardly flowed to the Jews from this quarter in any considerable amount. This statement is characteristic of the author more than of the war. If it is easy to understand how the Jewish leader of insurgents and subsequent courtier of the Flavians was fond of comparing himself with the Parthians exiled at Rome, it is the less to be excused that modern historical authorship should walk in similar paths, and in endeavouring to apprehend these events as constituent parts of the history of the Roman court and city or even of the Romano-Parthian quarrels, should by this insipid introduction of so-called great policy obscure the fearful necessity of this tragic development.

developed into the first seaport of Palestine, Greeks and
Jews dwelt, equally entitled to civic privileges, without
distinction of nation and confession, the latter superior in
number and property.   But the Hellenes, after the model
of the Alexandrians, and doubtless under the immediate
impression of the occurrences of the year 38, impugned
the right of citizenship of the Jewish members of the
community by way of complaint to the supreme authority.
The minister of Nero,[1] Burrus († 62), decided in their
favour.   It was bad to make citizenship in a town formed
on Jewish soil and by a Jewish government a privilege of
the Hellenes ; but it may not be forgotten how the Jews
behaved just at that time towards the Romans, and how
naturally they suggested to the Romans the conversion of
the Roman capital and the Roman head-quarters of the
province into a purely Hellenic urban community.   The
decision led, as might be conceived, to vehement street
tumults, in which Hellenic scoffing and Jewish arrogance
seem to have almost balanced each other, particularly in
the struggle for access to the synagogue ; the Roman
authorities interfered, as a matter of course, to the disadvantage of the Jews.   These left the town, but were compelled by the governor to return, and then all of them
were slain in a street riot (6th August 66).   This the
government had at any rate not commanded, and certainly had not wished ; powers were unchained which
they themselves were no longer able to control.

Outbreak of
the insur-
rection in
Jerusalem.

If here the enemies of the Jews were the assailants,
the Jews were so in Jerusalem.   Certainly their defenders
in the narrative of these occurrences assure us that the
procurator of Palestine at the time, Gessius Florus, in
order to avoid impeachment on account of his malad-
ministration, wished to provoke an insurrection by the
excessive measure of his torture ; and there is no doubt
that the governors of that time considerably exceeded the

---

[1] Josephus (*Arch.* xx. 8, 9), makes
him indeed secretary of Nero for
Greek correspondence, although he,
where he follows Roman sources
(xx. 8, 2), designates him correctly
as prefect ; but certainly the same
person is meant.   He is called
παιδαγωγός with him as with Tacitus,
Ann. xiii. 2 : *rector imperatoriae iu-
ventae.*

usual measure of worthlessness and oppression. But, if
Florus in fact pursued such a plan, it miscarried. For
according to these very reports the prudent and the possessors of property among the Jews, and with them king
Agrippa II., familiar with the government of the temple,
and just at that time present in Jerusalem—he had meanwhile exchanged the rule of Chalcis for that of Batanaea
—lulled the masses so far, that the riotous assemblages
and the interference against them kept within the measure
that had been usual in the country for years. But the
advances made by Jewish theology were more dangerous
than the disorder of the streets and the robber patriots of
the mountains. The earlier Judaism had in a liberal
fashion opened the gates of its faith to foreigners ; it is
true that only those who belonged, in the strict sense, to
their religion were admitted to the interior of the Temple,
but as proselytes of the gate all were admitted without
ceremony into the outer courts, and even the non-Jew
was here allowed to pray on his part and offer sacrifices
to the Lord Jehovah. Thus, as we have already mentioned (p. 189), sacrifice was offered daily there for the
Roman emperor on the basis of an endowment of Augustus. These sacrifices of non-Jews were forbidden by the   Eleazar.
master of the temple at this time, Eleazar, son of the
above-mentioned high priest Ananias, a passionate young
man of rank, personally blameless and brave and, so far,
an entire contrast to his father, but more dangerous through
his virtues than the latter was through his vices. Vainly it
was pointed out to him that this was as offensive for the
Romans as dangerous for the country, and absolutely at
variance with usage ; he resolved to abide by the im-
provement of piety and the exclusion of the sovereign
of the land from worship. Believers in Judaism had for
long been divided into those who placed their trust in the
Lord of Zebaoth alone and endured the Roman rule till
it should please Him to realise the kingdom of heaven on
earth, and the more practical men, who had resolved to
establish the kingdom of heaven with their own hand and
held themselves assured of the help of the Lord of Hosts

in the pious work, or, by their watchwords, into the Pharisees and the Zealots.   The number and the repute of the
latter were constantly on the increase.   An old saying
was discovered that about this time a man would proceed
from Judaea and gain the dominion of the world ; people
believed this the more readily because it was so very
absurd, and the oracle contributed not a little to render
the masses more fanatical.

Struggle of
parties.
Victory of
the Zealots.
The moderate party perceived the danger, and resolved
to put down the fanatics by force ; it asked for troops
from the Romans in Caesarea and from king Agrippa.
From the former no support came ; Agrippa sent a
number of horsemen.   On the other hand the patriots
and the knife-men flocked into the city, among them the
wildest Manahim, also one of the sons of the oft-named
Judas of Galilee.   They were the stronger, and soon were
masters in all the city.   The handful of Roman soldiers,
which kept garrison in the castle adjoining the temple,
was quickly overpowered and put to death.   The neighbouring king's palace, with the strong towers belonging
to it, where the adherents of the moderate party, a number
of Romans under the tribune Metilius, and the soldiers of
Agrippa were stationed, offered as little resistance.   To
the latter, on their desire to capitulate, free departure was
allowed, but was refused to the Romans ; when they at
length surrendered in return for assurance of life, they
were first disarmed, and then put to death with the single
exception of the officer, who promised to undergo circumcision and so was pardoned as a Jew.   Even the leaders
of the moderates, including the father and the brother of
Eleazar, became the victims of the popular rage, which
was still more savagely indignant at the associates of the
Romans than at the Romans themselves.   Eleazar was
himself alarmed at his victory ; between the two leaders
of the fanatics, himself and Manahim, a bloody hand-
to-hand conflict took place after the victory, perhaps
on account of the broken capitulation :   Manahim
was captured and executed.   But the holy city was
free, and the Roman detachment stationed in Jerusalem

was annihilated; the new Maccabees had conquered, like
the old.

Thus, it is alleged on the same day, the 6th August
66, the non-Jews in Caesarea had massacred the Jews,
and the Jews in Jerusalem had massacred the non-Jews;
and thereby was given on both sides the signal to proceed
with this patriotic work acceptable to God. In the neighbouring Greek towns the Hellenes rid themselves of the
resident Jews after the model of Caesarea. For example,
in Damascus all the Jews were in the first instance shut
up in the gymnasium, and, on the news of a misfortune to
the Roman arms, were by way of precaution all of them
put to death. The same or something similar took place
in Ascalon, in Scytopolis, Hippos, Gadara, wherever the
Hellenes were the stronger. In the territory of king
Agrippa, inhabited mainly by Syrians, his energetic intervention saved the lives of the Jews of Caesarea Paneas
and elsewhere. In Syria Ptolemais, Tyre, and more or
less the other Greek communities followed; only the two
greatest and most civilised cities, Antioch and Apamea,
as well as Sidon, were exceptions. To this is probably
due the fact that this movement did not spread in the
direction of Asia Minor. In Egypt not merely did the
matter come to a popular riot, which claimed numerous
victims, but the Alexandrian legions themselves had to
charge the Jews.—In necessary reaction to these Jewish
" vespers " the insurrection victorious in Jerusalem immediately seized all Judaea and organised itself everywhere, with similar maltreatment of minorities, but in
other respects with rapidity and energy.

It was necessary to interfere as speedily as possible,
and to prevent the further extension of the conflagration;
on the first news the Roman governor of Syria, Gaius
Cestius Gallus, marched with his troops against the insurgents. He brought up about 20,000 Roman soldiers
and 13,000 belonging to client-states, without including
the numerous Syrian militia; took Joppa, where the whole
body of citizens was put to death; and already in September stood before, and in fact in, Jerusalem itself. But

Extension of the Jewish war.

Vain expedition of Cestius Gallus.

he could not breach the strong walls of the king's palace and of the temple, and as little made use of the opportunity several times offered to him of getting possession of the town through the moderate party. Whether the task was insoluble or whether he was not equal to it, he soon gave up the siege, and purchased even a hasty retreat by the sacrifice of his baggage and of his rearguard. Thus Judaea in the first instance, including Idumaea and Galilee, remained in, or came into, the hands of the exasperated Jews; the Samaritan district also was compelled to join. The mainly Hellenic coast towns, Anthedon and Gaza, were destroyed, Caesarea and the other Greek towns were retained with difficulty. If the rising did not go beyond the boundaries of Palestine, that was not the fault of the government, but was rather due to the national dislike of the Syro-Hellenes towards the Jews.

The Jewish war of Vespasian. The government in Rome took things in earnest, as earnest they were. Instead of the procurator an imperial legate was sent to Palestine, Titus Flavius Vespasianus, a prudent man and an experienced soldier. He obtained for the conduct of the war two legions of the West, which in consequence of the Parthian war were accidentally still in Asia, and that Syrian legion which had suffered least in the unfortunate expedition of Cestius, while the Syrian army under the new governor, Gaius Licinius Mucianus—Gallus had seasonably died—by the addition of another legion was restored to the status which it had before.[1] To

[1] It is not quite clear what were the arrangements for the forces occupying Syria after the Parthian war was ended in the year 63. At its close there were seven legions stationed in the East, the four originally Syrian, 3d Gallica, 6th Ferrata, 10th Fretensis, 12th Fulminata, and three brought up from the West, the 4th Scythica from Moesia (I. 213), the 5th Macedonica, probably from the same place (I. 219; for which probably an upper German legion was sent to Moesia I. 132), the 15th Apollinaris from Pannonia (I. 219).

Since, excepting Syria, no Asiatic province was at that time furnished with legions, and the governor of Syria certainly in times of peace had never more than four legions, the Syrian army beyond doubt had at that time been brought back, or at least ought to have been brought back, to this footing. The four legions which accordingly were to remain in Syria were, as this was most natural, the four old Syrian ones; for the 3d had in the year 70 just marched from Syria to Moesia (Suetonius, *Vesp.* 6; Tacitus, *Hist.*

these burgess-troops and their auxiliaries were added the previous garrison of Palestine, and lastly the forces of the four client-kings of the Commagenians, the Hemesenes, the Jews, and the Nabataeans, together about 50,000 men, including among them 15,000 king's soldiers.[1] In the spring of the year 67 this army was brought together at Ptolemais and advanced into Palestine. After the

ii. 74), and that the 6th, 10th, 12th belonged to the army of Cestius follows from Josephus, *Bell. Jud.* ii. 18, 9, c. 19, 7; vii. 1, 3. Then, when the Jewish war broke out, seven legions were again destined for Asia, and of these four for Syria (Tacitus, *Hist.* i. 10), three for Palestine; the three legions added were just those employed for the Parthian war, the 4th, 5th, 15th, which perhaps at that time were still in course of marching back to their old quarters. The 4th probably went at that time definitively to Syria, where it thenceforth remained; on the other hand, the Syrian army gave off the 10th to Vespasian, presumably because this had suffered least in the campaign of Cestius. In addition he received the 5th and the 15th. The 5th and the 10th legions came from Alexandria (Josephus, *Bell. Jud.* iii. 1, 3, c. 4, 2); but that they were brought up from Egypt cannot well be conceived, not merely because the 10th was one of the Syrian, but especially because the march by land from Alexandria on the Nile to Ptolemais through the middle of the insurgent territory at the beginning of the Jewish war could not have been so narrated by Josephus. Far more probably Titus went by ship from Achaia to Alexandria on the Gulf of Issus, the modern Alexandretta, and brought the two legions thence to Ptolemais. The orders to march may have reached the 15th somewhere in Asia Minor, since Vespasian, doubtless in order to take them over, went to Syria by land (Josephus, *Bell. Jud.* iii. 1, 3). To these three legions, with which Vespasian began the war, there was added

under Titus a further one of the Syrian, the 12th. Of the four legions that occupied Jerusalem the two previously Syrian remained in the East, the 10th in Judaea, the 12th in Cappadocia, while the 5th returned to Moesia, and the 15th to Pannonia (Josephus, *Bell. Jud.* vii. 1, 3 c. 5, 3).

[1] To the three legions there belonged five *alae* and eighteen cohorts, and the army of Palestine consisting of one *ala* and five cohorts. These *auxilia* numbered accordingly 3000 alarians and (since among the twenty-three cohorts ten were 1000 strong, thirteen 720, or probably rather only 420 strong; for instead of the startling ἑξακοσίους we expect rather τριακοσίους ἑξάκοντα) 16,240 (or, if 720 is retained, 19,360) cohortales. To these fell to be added 1000 horsemen from each of the four kings, and 5000 Arabian archers, with 2000 from each of the other three kings. This gives together—reckoning the legion at 6000 men—52,240 men, and so towards 60,000, as Josephus (*Bell. Jud.* iii. 4, 2) says. But as the divisions are thus all calculated at the utmost normal strength, the effective aggregate number can hardly be estimated at 50,000. These numbers of Josephus appear in the main trustworthy, just as the analogous ones for the army of Cestius (*Bell. Jud.* ii. 18, 9); whereas his figures, resting on the census, are throughout measured after the scale of the smallest village in Galilee numbering 15,000 inhabitants (*Bell. Jud.* iii. 3, 2), and are historically as useless as the figures of Falstaff. It is but seldom, *e.g.* at the siege of Jotapata, that we recognise reported numbers.

insurgents had been emphatically repulsed by the weak garrison of the town of Ascalon, they had not further attacked the cities which took part with the Romans; the hopelessness, which pervaded the whole movement, expressed itself in the renouncing at once of all offensive. When the Romans thereupon passed over to the aggressive, the insurgents nowhere confronted them in the open field, and in fact did not even make attempts to bring relief to the several places assailed. Certainly the cautious general of the Romans did not divide his troops, but kept at least the three legions together throughout. Nevertheless, as in most of the individual townships a number —often probably but small—of the fanatics exercised terror over the citizens, the resistance was obstinate, and the Roman conduct of the war neither brilliant nor rapid.

First and second campaigns.

Vespasian employed the whole first campaign (67) in bringing into his power the fortresses of the small district of Galilee and the coast as far as Ascalon; before the one little town of Jotapata the three legions lay encamped for forty-five days. During the winter of 67-8 a legion lay in Scytopolis, on the south border of Galilee, the two others in Caesarea. Meanwhile the different factions in Jerusalem fell upon one another and were in most vehement conflict; the good patriots, who were at the same time for civil order, and the still better patriots, who, partly in fanatical excitement, partly from delight in mob-riot, wished to bring about and turn to account a reign of terror, fought with each other in the streets of the city, and were only at one in accounting every attempt at reconciliation with the Romans a crime worthy of death. The Roman general, on many occasions summoned to take advantage of this disorder, adhered to the course of advancing only step by step. In the second year of the war he caused the Transjordanic territory in the first instance, particularly the important towns of Gadara and Gerasa, to be occupied, and then took up his position at Emmaus and Jericho, whence he took military possession of Idumaea in the south and Samaria in the north, so that Jerusalem in the summer of the year 68 was surrounded on all sides.

The siege was just beginning when the news of the death of Nero arrived. Thereby *de iure* the mandate conferred on the legate became extinct, and Vespasian, not less cautious in a political than in a military point of view, in fact suspended his operations until new orders as to his attitude. Before these arrived from Galba, the good season of the year was at an end. When the spring of 69 came, Galba was overthrown, and the decision was in suspense between the emperor of the praetorian guard and the emperor of the army on the Rhine. It was only after Vitellius's victory in June 69 that Vespasian resumed operations and occupied Hebron ; but very soon all the armies of the East renounced their allegiance to the former and proclaimed the previous legate of Judaea as emperor. The positions at Emmaus and Jericho were indeed maintained in front of the Jews ; but, as the German legions had denuded the Rhine to make their general emperor, so the flower of the army went from Palestine, partly with the legate of Syria, Mucianus, to Italy, partly with the new emperor and his son Titus to Syria and onward to Egypt, and it was only after the war of the succession was ended, at the close of the year 69, and the rule of Vespasian was acknowledged throughout the empire, that the latter entrusted his son with the termination of the Jewish war.

Stoppage of the war.

Thus the insurgents had entirely free sway in Jerusalem from the summer of 66 till the spring of 70. What the combination of religious and national fanaticism, the noble desire not to survive the downfall of their fatherland, the consciousness of past crimes and of inevitable punishment, the wild promiscuous tumult of all noblest and all basest passions in these four years of terror brought upon the nation, had its horrors intensified by the fact that the foreigners were only onlookers in the matter, and all the evil was inflicted directly by Jews upon Jews. The moderate patriots were soon overpowered by the zealots with the help of the levy of the

Titus against Jerusalem.

rude and fanatical inhabitants of the Idumaean villages (end of 68), and their leaders were slain. The zealots thenceforth ruled, and all the bonds of civil, religious, and moral order were dissolved. Freedom was granted to the slaves, the high priests were appointed by lot, the ritual laws were trodden under foot and scoffed at by those very fanatics whose stronghold was the temple, the captives in the prisons were put to death, and it was forbidden on pain of death to bury the slain. The different leaders fought with their separate bands against one another : John of Gischala with his band brought up from Galilee ; Simon, son of Gioras from Gerasa, the leader of a band of patriots formed in the south, and at the same time of the Idumaeans in revolt against John ; Eleazar, son of Simon, one of the champions against Cestius Gallus. The first maintained himself in the porch of the temple, the second in the city, the third in the Holy of Holies ; and there were daily combats in the streets of the city between Jews and Jews. Concord came only through the common enemy ; when the attack began, Eleazar's little band placed itself under the orders of John, and although John in the temple and Simon in the city continued to play the part of masters, they, while quarrelling among themselves, fought shoulder to shoulder against the Romans.

Task of the assailants. The task of the assailants was not an easy one. It is true that the army, which had received in place of the detachments sent to Italy a considerable contingent from the Egyptian and the Syrian troops, was quite sufficient for the investment ; and, in spite of the long interval which had been granted to the Jews to prepare for the siege, their provisions were inadequate, the more especially as a part of them had been destroyed in the street conflicts, and, as the siege began about the time of the Passover, numerous strangers who had come on that account to Jerusalem were also shut in. But though the mass of the population soon suffered distress, the combatant force took what they needed where they found it, and, well provided as they were, they carried on the struggle without reference to the multitudes that were famishing and soon dying of hunger. The young general could not make up his mind to a mere blockade ; a siege with four legions, brought to an end in this way, would yield to him personally no glory, and the new government needed a brilliant feat of arms. The town, everywhere else defended by inaccessible rocky slopes, was assailable only on the north side ; here, too, it was no easy labour to reduce the threefold rampart-wall erected without regard t) cost from the rich treasures of the temple, and further within the city to wrest the citadel, the temple, and the three vast towers of Herod from a strong, fanatically inspired, and desperate garrison. John and Simon not merely resolutely repelled the assaults, but often attacked with good success the troops working at the trenches, and destroyed or burnt the besieging machines.

But the superiority of numbers and the art of war decided for the Romans. The walls were stormed, and thereafter the citadel Antonia ; then, after long resistance, first the porticoes of the temple went on fire, and further on the 10th Ab (August) the temple itself, with all the treasures accumulated in it for six centuries. Lastly, after fighting in the streets which lasted for a month, on the 8th Elul (September) the last resistance in the town itself was broken, and the holy Salem was razed. The bloody work had lasted for five months. The sword and the arrow, and still more famine, had claimed countless victims ; the Jews killed every one so much as suspected of deserting, and forced women and children in the city to die of hunger ; the Romans just as pitilessly put to the sword the captives or crucified them. The combatants that remained, and particularly the two leaders, were drawn forth singly from the sewers, in which they had taken refuge. At the Dead Sea, just where once king David and the Maccabees in their utmost distress had found a refuge, the remnants of the insurgents still held out for years in the rock-castles Machaerus and Massada, till at length, as the last of the free Jews, Eleazar grandson of Judas the Galilean, and his adherents put to death first

Destruction of Jerusalem.

their wives and children, and then themselves. The work was done. That the emperor Vespasian, an able soldier, did not disdain on account of such an inevitable success over a small long-subject people to march as victor to the Capitol, and that the seven-armed candelabrum brought home from the Holy of Holies of the temple is still to be seen at the present day on the honorary arch which the imperial senate erected to Titus in the market of the capital,[1] gives no high conception of the warlike spirit of this time. It is true that the deep aversion, which the Occidentals cherished towards the Jewish people, made up in some measure for what was wanting in martial glory, and if the Jewish name was too vile for the emperors to assign it to themselves, like those of the Germans and the Parthians, they deemed it not beneath their dignity to prepare for the populace of the capital this triumph commemorative of the victor's pleasure in the misfortunes of others.

Breaking up of the Jewish central power. The work of the sword was followed by a change of policy. The policy pursued by the earlier Hellenistic states, and taken over from them by the Romans—which reached in reality far beyond mere tolerance towards foreign ways and foreign faith, and recognised the Jews in their collective character as a national and religious community—had become impossible. In the Jewish insurrection the dangers had been too clearly brought to light, which this formation of a national-religious union —on the one hand rigidly concentrated, on the other spreading over the whole East and having ramifications even in the West—involved. The central worship was accordingly once for all set aside. This resolution of the

---

[1] This arch was erected to Titus after his death by the imperial senate. Another, dedicated to him during his short government by the same senate in the circus (*C. I. L.* vi. 944) specifies even with express words as the ground of erecting the monument, "because he, according to the precept and direction and under the superintendence of his father, subdued the people of the Jews and destroyed the town of Hierusolyma, which up to his time had either been besieged in vain by all generals, kings, and peoples, or not assailed at all." The historic knowledge of this singular document, which ignores not merely Nebuchadnezzar and Antiochus Epiphanes, but their own Pompeius, stands on the same level with its extravagance in the praise of a very ordinary feat of arms.

government stood undoubtedly fixed, and had nothing
in common with the question, which cannot be answered
with certainty, whether the destruction of the temple took
place by design or by accident ; if, on the one hand, the
suppression of the worship required only the closing of
the temple and the magnificent structure might have
been spared, on the other hand, had the temple been
accidentally destroyed, the worship might have been
continued in a temple rebuilt.   No doubt it will always
remain probable that it was not the chance of war that
here prevailed, but the flames of the temple were rather
the programme for the altered policy of the Roman
government with reference to Judaism.[1]   More clearly
even than in the events at Jerusalem the same change is
marked in the closing—which ensued at the same time
on the order of Vespasian—of the central sanctuary of
the Egyptian Jews, the temple of Onias, not far from
Memphis, in the Heliopolitan district, which for centuries
stood alongside of that of Jerusalem, somewhat as the
translation by the Alexandrian Seventy stood side by
side with the Old Testament ; it too was divested of its
votive gifts, and the worship of God in it was forbidden.

In the further carrying out of the new order of things
the high priesthood and the Synhedrion of Jerusalem
disappeared, and thereby the Jews of the empire lost their
outward supreme head and their chief authority having
jurisdiction hitherto generally in religious questions.   The
annual tribute—previously at least tolerated—on the
part of every Jew, without distinction of dwelling-place,
to the temple did not certainly fall into abeyance, but
was with bitter parody transferred to the Capitoline

[1] The account of Josephus, that
Titus with his council of war resolved
not to destroy the temple, excites
suspicion by the manifest intention of
it, and, as the use made of Tacitus in
the chronicle of Sulpicius Severus is
completely proved by Bernays, it may
certainly well be a question whether
his quite opposite account (*Chron.* ii.
30, 6), that the council of war had
resolved to destroy the temple, does
not proceed from Tacitus, and whether
the preference is not to be given to it,
although it bears traces of Christian
revision.   This view further commends
itself through the fact that the dedication addressed to Vespasian of the
Argonautica of the poet Valerius Flaccus celebrates the victor of Solyma,
who hurls the fiery torches.

Jupiter, and his representative on earth, the Roman emperor. From the character of the Jewish institutions the suppression of the central worship involved dissolution of the community of Jerusalem. The city was not merely destroyed and burnt down, but was left lying in ruins, like Carthage and Corinth once upon a time ; its territory, public as well as private land, became imperial domain.[1] Such of the citizens of the populous town as had escaped famine or the sword came under the hammer of the slave market. Amidst the ruins of the destroyed town was pitched the camp of the legion, which, with its Spanish and Thracian auxiliaries, was thenceforth to do garrison duty in the Jewish land. The provincial troops hitherto recruited in Palestine itself were transferred elsewhere. In Emmaus, in the immediate neighbourhood of Jerusalem, a number of Roman veterans were settled, but urban rights were not conferred on this place. On the other hand, the old Sichem, the religious centre of the Samaritan community, perhaps a Greek city even from the time of Alexander the Great, was now reorganised in the forms of Hellenic polity under the name Flavia Neapolis. The capital of the land, Caesarea, hitherto a Greek urban community, obtained as " first Flavian colony " Roman organisation and Latin as the language of business. These were essays towards the Occidental municipalising of the Jewish land. Nevertheless Judaea proper, though depopulated and impoverished, remained still Jewish as before ; the light in which the government looked upon the land is shown by the thoroughly anomalous permanent military occupation, which, as Judaea was not situated on the frontier of the empire, can only have been destined to keep down the inhabitants.

The Herodians, too, did not long survive the de-

---

[1] That the emperor took this land for himself (ἰδίαν αὐτῷ τὴν χώραν φυλάττων) is stated by Josephus, *Bell. Jud.* vii. 6, 6 ; not in accord with this is his command πᾶσαν γῆν ἀποδόσθαι τῶν Ἰουδαίων (*l. c.*), in which doubtless there lurks an error or a copyist's mistake. It is in keeping with the expropriation that land was by way of grace assigned elsewhere to individual Jewish landowners (Josephus, *vit.* 16). We may add that the territory was probably employed as an endowment for the legion stationed there (*Eph. epigr.* ii. n. 696 ; Tacitus, *Ann.* xiii. 54).

struction of Jerusalem.   King Agrippa II., the ruler of The end of the Hero-dians. Caesarea Paneas and of Tiberias, had rendered faithful service to the Romans in the war against his country-men, and had even scars, honourable at least in a military sense, to show from it ; besides, his sister Berenice, a Cleopatra on a small scale, held the heart of the conqueror of Jerusalem captive with the remnant of. her much sought charms.   So he remained personally in possession of the dominion ; but after his death, some thirty years later, this last reminiscence of the Jewish state was merged in the Roman province of Syria.

No hindrances were put in the way of the Jews Further treatment of the Jews. exercising their religious customs either in Palestine or elsewhere.   Their religious instruction itself, and the assemblies in connection with it of their law-teachers and law-experts, were at least permitted in Palestine ; and there was no hindrance to these Rabbinical unions attempting to put themselves in some measure in the room of the former Synhedrion of Jerusalem, and to fix their doctrine and their laws in the groundwork of the Talmud.   Although individual partakers in the Jewish insurrection who fled to Egypt and Cyrene produced troubles there, the bodies of Jews outside of Palestine, so far as we see, were left in their previous position.   Against the Jew-hunt, which just about the time of the destruction of Jerusalem was called forth in Antioch by the circum-stance that the Jews there had been publicly charged by one of their renegade comrades in the faith with the intention of setting the town on fire, the representative of the governor of Syria interfered with energy, and did not allow what was proposed—that they should compel the Jews to sacrifice to the gods of the land and to refrain from keeping the Sabbath.   Titus himself, when he came to Antioch, most distinctly dismissed the leaders of the movement there with their request for the ejection of the Jews, or at least the cancelling of their privileges. People shrank from declaring war on the Jewish faith as such, and from driving the far-branching Diaspora to extremities ; it was enough that Judaism was in its political representation deleted from the common-wealth.

The conse-
quences of
the catas-
trophe. The alteration in the policy pursued since Alexander's time towards Judaism amounted in the main to the withdrawing from this religious society unity of leader-ship and external compactness, and to the wresting out of the hands of its leaders a power which extended not merely over the native land of the Jews, but over the bodies of Jews generally within and beyond the Roman empire, and certainly in the East was prejudicial to the unity of imperial government. The Lagids as well as the Seleucids, and not less the Roman emperors of the Julio-Claudian dynasty, had put up with this ; but the immediate rule of the Occidentals over Judaea had sharpened the contrast between the imperial power and this power of the priests to such a degree, that the catastrophe set in with inevitable necessity and brought its consequences. From a political standpoint we may censure, doubtless, the remorselessness of the conduct of the war—which, moreover, is pretty much common to this war with all similar ones in Roman history—but hardly the religious-political dissolution of the nation ordained in consequence of it. If the axe was laid at the root of institutions which had led, and could not but with a certain necessity lead, to the formation of a party like that of the zealots, there was but done what was right and necessary, however severely and unjustly in the special case the individual might be affected by it. Vespasian, who gave the decision, was a judicious and moderate ruler. The question concerned was one not of faith but of power ; the Jewish church-state, as head of the Diaspora, was not compatible with the absoluteness of the secular great-state. From the general rule of toleration the government did not even in this case depart ; it waged war not against Judaism but against the high priest and the Synhedrion.

The
Christians. Nor did the destruction of the temple wholly fail in this its aim. There were not a few Jews and still more proselytes, particularly in the Diaspora, who adhered

more to the Jewish moral law and to Jewish Monotheism
than to the strictly national form of faith ; the whole
important sect of the Christians had inwardly broken
off from Judaism and stood partly in open opposition to
the Jewish ritual. For these the fall of Jerusalem was
by no means the end of things, and within these extensive
and influential circles the government obtained in some
measure what it aimed at by breaking up the central seat
of the Jewish worship. The separation of the Christian
faith common to the Gentiles from the national Jewish,
the victory of the adherents of Paul over those of Peter,
was essentially promoted by the abolition of the Jewish
central cultus.

But among the Jews of Palestine, where the language   Palestinian
spoken was not Hebrew indeed, but Aramaic, and   Jews.
among the portion of the Diaspora which clung firmly
to Jerusalem, the breach between Judaism and the rest of
the world was deepened by the destruction of the temple.
The national-religious exclusiveness, which the government wished to obviate, was in this narrow circle rather
strengthened by the violent attempt to break it down,
and driven, in the first instance, to further desperate
struggles.

Not quite fifty years after the destruction of Jeru-   The Jewish
salem, in the year 116,[1] the Jews of the eastern Medi-   rising under
terranean rose against the imperial government. The   Trajan.
rising, although undertaken by the Diaspora, was of a
purely national character in its chief seats, Cyrene, Cyprus,
Egypt, directed to the expulsion of the Romans as of the
Hellenes, and, apparently, to the establishment of a separate Jewish state. It ramified even into Asiatic territory,
and seized Mesopotamia and Palestine itself. When the
insurgents were victorious they conducted the war with
the same exasperation as the Sicarii in Jerusalem ; they
killed those whom they seized—the historian Appian,
a native of Alexandria, narrates how he, running from

[1] Eusebius, *H. E.* iv. 2, puts the   the penultimate year of Trajan ; and
outbreak on the 18th, and so, accord-   therewith Dio, lxviii. 32, agrees.
ing to his reckoning (in the Chronicle),

them for his life, with great difficulty made his escape to Pelusium—and often they put the captives to death under excruciating torture, or compelled them—just as Titus formerly compelled the Jews captured in Jerusalem—to fall as gladiators in the arena in order to delight the eyes of the victors.   In Cyrene 220,000, in Cyprus even 240,000 men are said to have been thus put to death by them.   On the other hand, in Alexandria, which does not appear itself to have fallen into the hands of the Jews,[1] the besieged Hellenes slew whatever Jews were then in the city.   The immediate cause of the rising is not clear. The blood of the zealots, who had taken refuge at Alexandria and Cyrene, and had there sealed their loyalty to the faith by dying under the axe of the Roman executioner, may not have flowed in vain ; the Parthian war, during which the insurrection began, so far promoted it, as the troops stationed in Egypt had probably been called to the theatre of war.   To all appearance it was an outbreak of the religious exasperation of the Jews, which had been glowing in secret like a volcano since the destruction of the temple and broke out after an incalculable manner into flames, of such a kind as the East has at all times produced and produces ; if the insurgents really proclaimed a Jew as king, this rising certainly had, like that in their native country, its central seat in the great mass of the common people.   That this Jewish rising partly coincided with the formerly-mentioned (p. 68) attempt at liberation of the peoples shortly before subdued by the emperor Trajan, while the latter was in the far East at the mouth of the Euphrates, gave to it even a political significance ; if the successes of this ruler melted away under his hands at the close of his career, the Jewish insurrection, particularly in Palestine and Mesopotamia, contributed its part to that result.   In order to put down the insurrection the troops had everywhere to

---

[1] Eusebius himself (in Syncellus) says only : ᾿Αδριανὸς ᾿Ιουδαίους κατὰ ᾿Αλεξανδρέων στασιάζοντας ἐκόλασεν. The Armenian and Latin translations appear to have erroneously made out of this a restoration of Alexandria destroyed by the Jews, of which Eusebius, *H. E.* iv. 2, and Dio, lxviii. 32, know nothing.

take the field ; against the "king" of the Cyrenaean Jews, Andreas or Lukuas, and the insurgents in Egypt, Trajan sent Quintus Marcius Turbo with an army and fleet ; against the insurgents in Mesopotamia, as was already stated, Lusius Quietus—two of his most experienced generals.   The insurgents were nowhere able to offer resistance to the regular troops, although the struggle was prolonged in Africa as in Palestine to the first times of Hadrian, and similar punishments were inflicted on this Diaspora as previously on the Jews of Palestine.   That Trajan annihilated the Jews in Alexandria, as Appian says, is hardly an incorrect, although perhaps a too blunt expression for what took place ; for Cyprus it is attested that thenceforth no Jew might even set foot upon the island, and death there awaited even the shipwrecked Israelites.   If our traditional information was as copious in regard to this catastrophe as in regard to that of Jerusalem, it would probably appear as its continuation and completion, and in some sense also as its explanation ; this rising shows the relation of the Diaspora to the home-country, and the state within a state, into which Judaism had developed.

Even with this second overthrow the revolt of Judaism against the imperial power was not at an end.   We cannot say that the latter gave further provocation to it ; ordinary acts of administration, which were accepted without opposition throughout the empire, affected the Hebrews just where the full resisting power of the national faith had its seat, and thereby called forth, probably to the surprise of the governors themselves, an insurrection which was in fact a war.   If the emperor Hadrian, when his tour through the empire brought him to Palestine, resolved in the year 130 to re-erect the destroyed holy city of the Jews as a Roman colony, he certainly did not do them the honour of fearing them, and had no thought of propagating religious-political views ; but he ordained that this legionary camp should—as shortly before or soon afterwards was the case on the Rhine, on the Danube, in Africa—be connected with an urban community recruit-

The Jewish rising under Hadrian.

ing itself primarily from the veterans, which received its

Aelia Capitolina. name partly from its founder, partly from the god to whom at that time the Jews paid tribute instead of Jehovah. Similar was the state of the case as to the prohibition of circumcision ; it was issued, as will be observed at a later point, probably without any design of thereby making war on Judaism as such. As may be conceived, the Jews did not inquire as to the motives for that founding of the city and for this prohibition, but felt both as an attack on their faith and their nationality, and answered it by an insurrection which, neglected at first by the Romans, thereupon had not its match for intensity and duration in the history of the Roman imperial period. The whole body of the Jews at home and abroad was agitated by the movement and supported more or less openly the insurgents on the Jordan ;[1] even Jerusalem fell into their hands,[2] and the governor of Syria and indeed the emperor Hadrian appeared on the scene of conflict. The war was led, significantly enough, by the priest Eleazar[3] and the bandit-chief Simon, surnamed Bar-Kokheba, *i.e.* son of the stars, as the bringer of heavenly help, perhaps as Messiah. The financial power and the organisation of the insurgents are testified by the silver and copper coins struck through several years in the name of these two. After a sufficient number of troops was brought together, the experienced general Sextus Julius

---

[1] This is shown by the expressions of Dio, lxix. 13 : οἱ ἀπανταχοῦ γῆς Ἰουδαῖοι and πάσης ὡς εἰπεῖν κινουμένης ἐπὶ τούτῳ τῆς οἰκουμένης.

[2] If, according to the contemporary Appian (*Syr.* 50), Hadrian once more destroyed (κατέσκαψε) the town, this proves as well that it was preceded by an at least in some measure complete formation of the colony, as that it was captured by the insurgents. Only thereby is explained the great loss which the Romans suffered (Fronto, *de bello Parth.* p. 218 Nab. : *Hadriano imperium obtinente quantum militum a Iudaesis . . . caesum ;* Dio, lxix. 14) ; and it accords at least well with this, that the governor of Syria, Pub-

licius Marcellus, left his province to bring help to his colleague Tineius Rufus (Eusebius, *H. E.* iv. 6 ; Borghesi, *Opp.* iii. 64), in Palestine (*C. I. Gr.* 4033, 4034).

[3] That the coins with this name belong to the Hadrianic insurrection is now proved (v. Sallet, *Zeitschr. jür Numism.* v. 110) ; this is consequently the Rabbi Eleazar from Modein of the Jewish accounts (Ewald, *Gesch. Isr.* vii.[2], 418 ; Schürer, *Lehrbuch,* p. 357). That the Simon whom these coins name partly with Eleazar, partly alone, is the Bar-Kokheba of Justin Martyr and Eusebius is at least very probable.

Severus gained the upper hand, but only by a gradual and slow advance ; quite as in the war under Vespasian no. pitched battle took place, but one place after another cost time and blood, till at length after a three years' warfare[1] the last castle of the insurgents, the strong Bether, not far from Jerusalem, was stormed by the Romans. The numbers handed down to us in good accounts of 50 fortresses taken, 985 villages occupied, 580,000 that fell, are not incredible, since the war was waged with inexorable cruelty, and the male population was probably everywhere put to death.

In consequence of this rising the very name of the vanquished people was set aside ; the province was thenceforth termed, not as formerly Judaea, but by the old name of Herodotus Syria of the Philistines, or Syria Palaestina. The land remained desolate ; the new city of Hadrian continued to exist, but did not prosper. The Jews were prohibited under penalty of death from even setting foot in Jerusalem ; the garrison was doubled ; the limited territory between Egypt and Syria, to which only a small strip of the Transjordanic domain on the Dead Sea belonged, and which nowhere touched the frontier of the empire, was thenceforth furnished with two legions. In spite of all these strong measures the province remained disturbed, primarily doubtless in consequence of the bandit-habits long interwoven with the national cause. Pius issued orders to march against the Jews, and even under Severus there is mention of a war against Jews and Samaritans. But no movements on a great scale among the Jews recurred after the Hadrianic war.

Judaea after Hadrian.

It must be acknowledged that these repeated outbreaks of the animosity fermenting in the minds of the Jews against the whole of their non-Jewish fellow-citizens did not change the general policy of the government.

Position of the Jews in the second and third centuries.

---

[1] Dio (lxix. 12) calls the war protracted ($o\check{v}\tau'$ $\dot{o}\lambda\iota\gamma o\chi\rho\acute{o}\nu\iota o s$) ; Eusebius in his Chronicle puts its beginning in the sixteenth, its end in the eighteenth or nineteenth year of Hadrian ; the coins of the insurgents are dated from the first or from the second year of the deliverance of Israel. We have not trustworthy dates ; the Rabbinic tradition (Schürer, *Lehrbuch*, p. 361) is not available in this respect.

Like Vespasian, the succeeding emperors maintained, as respects the Jews in the main, the general standpoint of political and religious toleration ; and not only so, but the exceptional laws issued for the Jews were, and continued to be, chiefly directed to release them from such general civil duties as were not compatible with their habits and their faith, and they are therefore designated directly as privilegia.[1]

Since the time of Claudius, whose suppression of Jewish worship in Italy (p. 199) is at least the last measure of the sort which we know of, residence and the free exercise of religion in the whole empire appear to have been in law conceded to the Jew. It would have been no wonder if those insurrections in the African and Syrian provinces had led to the expulsion generally of the Jews settled there ; but restrictions of this sort were enacted, as we saw, only locally, *e.g.* for Cyprus. The Greek provinces always remained the chief seat of the Jews ; even in the capital in some measure bilingual, whose numerous body of Jews had a series of synagogues, these formed a portion of the Greek population of Rome. Their epitaphs in Rome are exclusively Greek ; in the Christian church at Rome developed from this Jewish body the baptismal confession was uttered in Greek down to a late period, and throughout the first three centuries the literature was exclusively Greek. But restrictive measures against the Jews appear not to have been adopted even in the Latin provinces ; through and with Hellenism the Jewish system penetrated into the West, and there too communities of Jews were found, although they were still in number and importance even now, when the blows directed against the Diaspora had severely injured the Jew-communities of the East, far inferior to the latter.

Corporative unions.   Political privileges did not follow of themselves from the toleration of worship. The Jews were not hindered

---

[1] Biography of Alexander, c. 22 : *Iudaeis privilegia reservavit, Christianos esse passus est.* Clearly the privileged position of the Jews as compared with the Christians comes here to light—a position, which certainly rests in its turn on the fact that the former represent a nation the latter do not.

in the construction of their synagogues and proseuchae any more than in the appointment of a president for the same (ἀρχισυναγωγός), as well as of a college of elders (ἄρχοντες), with a chief elder (γερουσιάρχης) at its head. Magisterial functions were not meant to be connected with these positions; but, considering the inseparableness of the Jewish church-organisation and the Jewish administration of law, the presidents probably everywhere exercised, like the bishops in the Middle Ages, a jurisdiction, although merely *de facto.* The bodies of Jews in the several towns were not recognised generally as corporations, certainly not, for example, those of Rome; yet there subsisted at many places on the ground of local privileges such corporative unions with ethnarchs or, as they were now mostly called, patriarchs at their head. Indeed, in Palestine we find at the beginning of the third century once more a president of the whole Jewish body, who, in virtue of hereditary sacerdotal right, bears sway over his fellow-believers almost like a ruler, and has power even over life and limb, and whom the government at least tolerates.[1] Beyond question this patriarch was for the Jews the old high priest, and thus, under the eyes and under the oppression of the foreign rule, the obstinate people of God had once more reconstituted themselves, and in so far overthrown Vespasian's work.

As respects the bringing of the Jews under obligations of public service, their exemption from serving in war as incompatible with their religious principles had long since been and continued to be recognised.   The special poll- **Public services.**

---

[1] In order to make good that even in bondage the Jews were able to exercise a certain self-administration, Origen (about the year 226) writes to Africanus, c. 14 : "How much even now, where the Romans rule and the Jews pay to them the tribute (τὸ δίδραχμον), has the president of the people (ὁ ἐθνάρχης) among them in his power with permission of the emperor (συγχωροῦντος Καίσαρος)? Even courts are secretly held according to the law, and even on various occasions sentence of death is pronounced. This I, who have long lived in the land of this people, have myself experienced and ascertained." The patriarch of Judaea already makes his appearance in the letter forged in the name of Hadrian in the biography of the tyrant Saturninus (c. 8), in the ordinances first in the year 392 (*C. Th.* xvi. 8, 8). Patriarchs as presidents of individual Jewish communities, for which the word from its signification is better adapted, meet us already in the ordinances of Constantine I. (*C. Th.* xvi. 8, 1, 2).

tax to which they were subject, the old temple-payment, might be regarded as a compensation for this exemption, though it had not been imposed in this sense. For other services, as *e.g.* for the undertaking of wardships and municipal offices, they were at least from the time of Severus regarded in general as capable and under obligation, but those which ran counter to their " superstition " were remitted to them ;[1] in connection with which we have to take into account that exclusion from municipal offices became more and more converted from a slight into a privilege. Even in the case of state offices in later times a similar course was probably pursued.

Forbidding of circumcision. The only serious interference of the state-power with Jewish customs concerned the ceremony of circumcision ; the measures directed against this, however, were probably not taken from a religious-political standpoint, but were connected with the forbidding of castration, and arose doubtless in part from misunderstanding of the Jewish custom. The evil habit of mutilation, becoming more and more prevalent, was first brought by Domitian within the sphere of penal offences ; when Hadrian, making the precept more stringent, placed castration under the law of murder, circumcision appears also to have been apprehended as castration,[2] which certainly could not but be felt and was felt (p. 224) by the Jews as an attack upon their existence, although this was perhaps not its intention. Soon afterwards, probably in consequence of the insurrection thereby occasioned, Pius allowed the circumcision of children of Jewish descent, while otherwise even that of the non-free Jew and of the proselyte was to involve, afterwards as before, the penalty of castration for all par-

---

[1] The jurists of the third century lay down this rule, appealing to an edict of Severus (*Dig.* xxvii. 1, 15, 6 ; l. 2, 3, 3). According to the ordinance of the year 321 (*C. Th.* xvi. 8, 3) this appears even as a right, not as a duty of the Jews, so that it depended on them to undertake or decline the office.

[2] The analogous treatment of cas-tration in the Hadrianic edict, *Dig.* xlviii. 8, 4, 2, and of circumcision in Paulus, *Sent.* v. 22, 3, 4, and Modestinus, *Dig.* xlviii. 8, 11 pr., naturally suggests this point of view. The statement that Severus *Judaeos fieri sub gravi poena vetuit* (*Vita,* 17), is doubtless nothing but the enforcement of this prohibition.

ticipating in it. This was also of political importance, in so far as thereby the formal passing over to Judaism became a penal offence ; and probably the prohibition was, not indeed issued but, retained with this in view.[1] It must have contributed its part to the abrupt demarcation of the Jews from the non-Jews.

If we look back on the fortunes of Judaism in the epoch from Augustus to Diocletian, we recognise a thorough transformation of its character and of its position. It enters upon this epoch as a national and religious power firmly concentrated round its narrow native land— a power which even confronts the imperial government in and beyond Judaea with arms in hand, and in the field of faith evolves a mighty propagandist energy. We can understand that the Roman government would not tolerate the adoration of Jehovah and the faith of Moses on another footing than that on which the cultus of Mithra and the faith of Zoroaster were tolerated. The reaction against this exclusive and self-centred Judaism came in the crushing blows directed by Vespasian and Hadrian against the Jewish land, and by Trajan against the Jews of the Diaspora, the effect of which reached far beyond the immediate destruction of the existing society and the reduction of the repute and power of the Jews as a body. In fact, the later Christianity and the later Judaism were the consequences of this reaction of the West against the East. The great propagandist movement, which carried the deeper view of religion from the East into the West, was liberated in this way, as was already said (p. 220 f.), from the narrow limits of Jewish nationality ; if it by no means gave up the attachment to Moses and the prophets, it necessarily became released at any rate from the government of the Pharisees, which had gone tò pieces. The Christian ideals of the future became universal, since there was no longer a Jerusalem upon earth. But as the enlarged and deepened faith, which with its nature changed

Altered position of the Jews in the imperial period.

---

[1] The remarkable account in Origen's treatise *against Celsus*, ii. 13 (written about 250), shows that the circumcision of the non-Jew involved *de iure* the penalty of death, although it is not clear how far this found application to Samaritans or Sicarii.

also its name, arose out of these disasters, so not less the narrowed and hardened orthodoxy, which found a rallying point, if no longer in Jerusalem, at any rate in hatred towards those who had destroyed it, and still more in hatred towards the more free and higher intellectual movement which evolved Christianity out of Judaism. The external power of the Jews was broken, and risings, such as took place in the middle of the imperial period, are not subsequently met with ; the Roman emperors were done with the state within the state, and, as the properly dangerous element—the propagandist diffusion—passed over to Christianity, the confessors of the old faith, who shut themselves off from the New Covenant, were set aside, so far as the further general development was concerned.

Altered character of Judaism.

But if the legions could destroy Jerusalem, they could not raze Judaism itself ; and what on the one side was a remedy, exercised on the other the effect of a poison. Judaism not only remained, but it became an altered thing. There is a deep gulf between the Judaism of the older time, which seeks to spread its faith, which has its temple-court filled with the Gentiles, and which has its priests offering daily sacrifices for the emperor Augustus, and the rigid Rabbinism, which knew nothing and wished to know nothing of the world beyond Abraham's bosom and the Mosaic law. Strangers the Jews always were, and had wished to be so ; but the feeling of estrangement now culminated within them as well as against them after a fearful fashion, and rudely were its hateful and pernicious consequences drawn on both sides. From the contemptuous sarcasm of Horace against the intruding Jew from the Roman Ghetto there is a wide step to the solemn enmity which Tacitus cherishes against this scum of the human race, to which everything pure is impure and everything impure pure ; in the interval lie those insurrections of the despised people, and the necessity of conquering it and of expending continuously money and men for its repression. The prohibitions of maltreating the Jew, which are constantly recurring in the imperial ordinances, show that those words of the cultured were

translated, as might be expected, by their inferiors into
deeds. The Jews, on their part, did not mend the matter.
They turned away from Hellenic literature, which was now
regarded as polluting, and even rebelled against the use
of the Greek translation of the Bible ; the ever-increasing
purification of faith turned not merely against the Greeks
and the Romans, but quite as much against the "half-
Jews" of Samaria and against the Christian heretics ; the
reverence toward the letter of the Holy Scriptures rose to
a giddy height of absurdity, and above all an—if possible—
still holier tradition established itself, in the fetters of which
all life and thought were benumbed. The gulf between that
treatise on the Sublime which ventures to place Homer's
Poseidon shaking land and sea and Jehovah, who creates
the shining sun, side by side, and the beginnings of the
Talmud which belong to this epoch, marks the contrast between the Judaism of the first and that of the
third century. The living together of Jews and non-Jews
showed itself more and more to be just as inevitable, as
under the given conditions it was intolerable ; the contrast in faith, law, and manners became sharpened, and
mutual arrogance and mutual hatred operated on both
sides with morally disorganising effect. Not merely was
their conciliation not promoted in these centuries, but
its realisation was always thrown further into the distance,
the more its necessity was apparent. This exasperation,
this arrogance, this contempt, as they became established
at that time, were indeed only the inevitable growth of a
perhaps not less inevitable sowing ; but the heritage of
these times is still at the present day a burden on mankind.

CHAPTER XII.

EGYPT.

THE two kingdoms of Egypt and Syria, which had so long striven and vied with each other in every respect, fell nearly about the same time without resistance into the power of the Romans. If these made no use of the alleged or real testament of Alexander II. († 673) and did not then annex the land, the last rulers of the Lagid house were confessedly in the position of clients of Rome ; the senate decided in disputes as to the throne, and after the Roman governor of Syria, Aulus Gabinius, had with his troops brought back the king Ptolemaeus Auletes to Egypt (699 ; comp. iv. 160), the Roman legions did not again leave the land. Like the other client-kings, the rulers of Egypt took part in the civil wars on the summons of the government recognised by them or rather imposing itself on them ; and, if it must remain undecided what part Antonius in the fanciful eastern empire of his dreams had destined for the native land of the wife whom he loved too well (p. 25), at any rate the government of Antonius in Alexandria, as well as the last struggle in the last civil war before the gates of that city, belongs as little to the special history of Egypt as the battle of Actium to that of Epirus. But doubtless this catastrophe, and the death connected with it of the last prince of the Lagid house, gave occasion for Augustus not to fill up again the vacant throne, but to take the kingdom of Egypt under his own administration. This annexation of the last portion of the coast of the Mediterranean to the

The annexation of Egypt.

81.

55. iv. 153.

sphere of direct Roman administration, and the settlement, coincident with it in point of time and of organic connection, of the new monarchy, mark—as regards the constitution and administration of the huge empire respectively—the turning-point, the end of the old and the beginning of a new epoch.

The incorporation of Egypt into the Roman empire was accomplished after an abnormal fashion, in so far as the principle—elsewhere dominating the state—of dyarchy, *i.e.* of the joint rule of the two supreme imperial powers, the princeps and the senate, found—apart from some subordinate districts—no application in Egypt alone ;[1] but, on the contrary, in this land the senate as such, as well as every individual of its members, were cut off from all participation in the government, and indeed senators and persons of senatorial rank were even prohibited from setting foot in this province.[2] We must not conceive of this position as if Egypt were connected with the rest of the empire only by a personal union ; the princeps is, according to the meaning and spirit of the Augustan organisation, an integral and permanently acting element of the Roman polity just like the senate, and his rule over Egypt is quite as much a part of the imperial rule as is the rule of the proconsul of Africa.[3] We may rather

Egypt exclusively an imperial possession.

[1] This exclusion of the joint rule of the senate as of the senators is indicated by Tacitus (*Hist.* i. 11) with the words that Augustus wished to have Egypt administered exclusively by his personal servants (*domi retinere ;* comp. *Staatsrecht,* ii. p. 963). In principle this abnormal form of government was applicable for all the provinces not administered by senators, the presidents of which were also at the outset called chiefly *praefecti* (*C. I. L.* v. p. 809, 902). But at the first division of the provinces between emperor and senate there was probably no other of these but just Egypt ; and subsequently the distinction here came into sharper prominence, in so far as all the other provinces of this category obtained no legions. For in the emergence of the equestrian commandants of the legion instead of the senatorial, as was the rule in Egypt, the exclusion of the senatorial government finds its most palpable expression.

[2] This ordinance holds only for Egypt, not for the other territories administered by non-senators. How essential it appeared to the government, we see from the constitutional and religious apparatus called into requisition to secure it (*Trig. tyr.* c. 22).

[3] The current assertion that *provincia* is only by an abuse of language put for the districts not administered by senators is not well founded. Egypt was private property of the emperor just as much or just as little as Gaul and Syria—yet Augustus himself says (*Mon. Ancyr.* 5, 24)·

illustrate the exact constitutional position by saying that the British Empire would find itself in the same plight if the ministry and Parliament should be taken into account only for the mother-land, whereas the colonies should have to obey the absolute government of the Empress of India. What motives determined the new monarch at the very outset of his sole rule to adopt this deeply influential and at no time assailed arrangement, and how it affected the general political relations, are matters belonging to the general history of the empire ; here we have to set forth how the internal relations of Egypt shaped themselves under the imperial rule.

What held true in general of all Hellenic or Hellenised territories—that the Romans, when annexing them to the empire, preserved the once existing institutions, and introduced modifications only where these seemed absolutely necessary—found application in its full compass to Egypt.

Like Syria, Egypt, when it became Roman, was a land of twofold nationality ; here too alongside of, and over, the native stood the Greek—the former the slave, the latter the master. But in law and in fact the relations of the two nations in Egypt were wholly different from those of Syria.

Greek and Egyptian towns. Syria, substantially already in the pre-Roman and entirely in the Roman epoch, came under the government of the land only after an indirect manner ; it was broken up, partly into principalities, partly into autonomous urban districts, and was administered, in the first instance, by the rulers of the land or municipal authorities. In Egypt,[1] on the other hand, there were neither native princes nor imperial cities after the Greek fashion. The two spheres of administration into which Egypt was

---

Aegyptum imperio populi Romani adieci, and assigns to the governor, since he as *eques* could not be *pro praetore*, by special law the same jurisdiction in processes as the Roman praetors had (Tacitus, *Ann.* xii. 60).

[1] As a matter of course what is here meant is the land of Egypt, not the possessions subject to the Lagids. Cyrene was similarly organised (p. 165). But the properly Egyptian government was never applied to southern Syria and to the other territories which were for a longer or a shorter time under the power of Egypt.

divided—the "land" ($\dot{\eta}$ $\chi\acute{\omega}\rho a$) of the Egyptians, with its originally thirty-six districts ($\nu o\mu o\acute{\iota}$), and the two Greek cities, Alexandria in lower and Ptolemais in upper Egypt[1]—were rigidly separated and sharply opposed to each other, and yet in a strict sense hardly different. The rural, like the urban, district was not merely marked off territorially, but the former as well as the latter was a home-district; the belonging to each was independent of dwelling-place and hereditary. The Egyptian from the Chemmitic nome belonged to it with his dependents, just as much when he had his abode in Alexandria as the Alexandrian dwelling in Chemmis belonged to the burgess-body of Alexandria. The land-district had for its centre always an urban settlement, the Chemmitic, for example, the town of Panopolis, which grew up round the temple of Chemmis or of Pan, or, as this is expressed in the Greek mode of conception, each nome had its metropolis; so far each land-district may be regarded also as a town-district. Like the cities, the nomes also became in the Christian epoch the basis of the episcopal dioceses. The land-districts were based on the arrangements for worship which dominated everything in Egypt; the centre for each one is the sanctuary of a definite deity, and usually it bears the name of this deity or of the animal sacred to the same; thus the Chemmitic district is called after the god Chemmis, or, according to Greek equivalent, Pan; other districts after the dog, the lion, the crocodile. But, on the other hand, the town-districts are not without their religious centre; the protecting god of Alexandria is Alexander, the protecting god of Ptolemais the first Ptolemy, and the priests, who are installed in the one place as in the other for this worship and that of their successors, are the Eponymi for both cities. The land-district is quite destitute of autonomy: administration, taxation, justice, are placed in the hands of the royal officials,[2] and the

---

[1] To these falls to be added Naucratis, the oldest Greek town already founded in Egypt before the Ptolemies, and further Paraetonium, which indeed in some measure lies beyond the bounds of Egypt.

[2] There was not wanting of course a certain joint action, similar to that

collegiate system, the Palladium· of the Greek as of the Roman commonwealth, was here in all stages absolutely excluded. But in the two Greek cities it was not much otherwise. There was doubtless a body of burgesses divided into phylae and demes, but no common council ;[1] the officials were doubtless different and differently named from those of the nomes, but were also throughout officials of royal nomination and likewise without collegiate arrangement. Hadrian was the first to give to an Egyptian township, Antinoopolis, laid out by him in memory of his favourite drowned in the Nile, urban rights according to the Greek fashion ; and subsequently Severus, perhaps as much out of spite to the Antiochenes as for the benefit of the Egyptians, granted to the capital of Egypt and to the town of Ptolemais, and to several other Egyptian communities, not urban magistrates indeed, but

which is exercised by the *regiones* and the *vici* of self - administering urban communities ; to this category belongs what we meet with of agoranomy and gymnasiarchy in the nomes, as also the erection of honorary memorials and the like, all of which, we may add, make their appearance only to a small extent and for the most part but late. According to the edict of Alexander (*C. I. Gr.* 4957, l. 34) the *strategoi* do not seem to have been, properly speaking, nominated by the governor, but only to have been confirmed after an examination ; we do not know who had the proposing of them.

[1] The position of matters is clearly apparent in the inscription set up at the beginning of the reign of Pius to the well-known orator Aristides by the Egyptian Greeks (*C. I. Gr.* 4679); as dedicants are named ἡ πόλις τῶν ᾿Αλεξανδρέων καὶ ῾Ερμούπολις ἡ μεγάλη καὶ ἡ βουλὴ ἡ ᾿Αντινοέων νέων ῾Ελλήνων καὶ οἱ ἐν τῷ Δέλτᾳ τῆς Αἰγύπτου καὶ οἱ τὸν Θηβαϊκὸν νομὸν οἰκοῦντες ῞Ελληνες. Thus only Antinoopolis, the city of· the "new Hellenes," has a Boule ; Alexandria appears without this, but as a Greek city in the aggregate. Moreover

there take part in this dedication the Greeks living in the Delta and those living in Thebes, but of the Egyptian towns Great - Hermopolis alone, on which probably the immediate vicinity of Antinoopolis has exercised an influence. To Ptolemais Strabo (xvii. 1, 42, p. 813) attributes a σύστημα πολιτικὸν ἐν τῷ ῾Ελληνικῷ τρόπῳ ; but in this we may hardly think of more than what belonged to the capital according to its constitution more exactly known to us—and so specially of the division of the burgesses into *phylae*. That the pre-Ptolemaic Greek city Naucratis retained in the Ptolemaic time the Boule, which it doubtless had, is possible, but cannot be decisive for the Ptolemaic arrangements.—Dio's statement (ii. 17) that Augustus left the other Egyptian towns with their existing organisation, but took the common council from the Alexandrians on account of their untrustworthiness, rests doubtless on misunderstanding, the more especially as, according to it, Alexandria appears slighted in comparison with the other Egyptian communities, which is not at all in keeping with probability.

at any rate an urban council.   Hitherto, doubtless, in
official language the Egyptian town calls itself Nomos, the
Greek Polis, but a Polis without Archontes and Bouleutae
is a meaningless name.   So was it also in the coinage.
The Egyptian nomes did not possess the right of coining;
but still less did Alexandria ever strike coins.   Egypt is,
among all the provinces of the Greek half of the empire,
the only one which knows no other than royal money.
Nor was this otherwise even in the Roman period.   The
emperors abolished the abuses that crept in under the last
Lagids ; Augustus set aside their unreal copper coinage,
and when Tiberius resumed the coinage of silver he gave
to the Egyptian silver money just as real value as to the
other provincial currency of the empire.[1]   But the character
of the coinage remained substantially the same.[2]   There
is a distinction between Nomos and Polis as between the
god Chemmis and the god Alexander; in an administrative
respect there is not any difference.   Egypt consisted of
a majority of Egyptian and of a minority of Greek
townships, all of which were destitute of autonomy, and
all were placed under the immediate and absolute
administration of the king and of the officials nominated
by him.

[1] The Egyptian coining of gold
naturally ceased with the annexation
of the land, for there was in the
Roman empire only imperial gold.
With the silver also Augustus dealt
in like manner, and as ruler of Egypt
caused simply copper to be struck,
and even this only in moderate
quantities.   At first Tiberius coined,
after 27-28 A.D., silver money for
Egyptian circulation, apparently as
token-money, as the pieces correspond
nearly in point of weight to four, in
point of silver value to one, of the
Roman denarius (Feuardent, *Numis-
matique, Égypte ancienne*, ii. p. xi.).
But as in legal currency the Alexandrian drachma was estimated as
obolus (consequently as a sixth, not
as a fourth ; comp. *Röm. Münzwesen*,
p. 43, 723) of the Roman denarius
(*Hermes*, v. p. 136), and the provincial silver always lost as compared
with the imperial silver, the Alexandrian tetradrachmon of the silver
value of a denarius has rather been
estimated at the current value of
two-thirds of a denarius.   Accordingly
down to Commodus, from whose time
the Alexandrian tetradrachmon is
essentially a copper coin, the same
has been quite as much a coin of
value as the Syrian tetradrachmon
and the Cappadocian drachma ; they
only left to the former the old name
and the old weight.

[2] That the emperor Hadrian,
among other Egyptising caprices,
gave to the nomes as well as to his
Antinoopolis for once the right of
coining, which was thereupon done
subsequently on a couple of occasions,
makes no alteration in the rule.

Absence of
a land-diet.

It was a consequence of this, that Egypt alone of all the Roman provinces had no general representation. The diet is the collective representation of the self-administering communities of the province. But in Egypt there was none such ; the nomes were simply imperial or rather royal administrative districts, and Alexandria not merely stood virtually alone, but was likewise without proper municipal organisation. The priest standing at the head of the capital of the country might doubtless call himself " chief priest of Alexandria and all Egypt " (p. 248, note), and has a certain resemblance to the Asiarch and the Bithyniarch of Asia Minor, but the deep diversity of the organisations is thereby simply concealed.

The government of the Lagids.

The rule bore accordingly in Egypt a far different character than in the rest of the domain of Greek and Roman civilisation embraced under the imperial government. In the latter the community administers throughout; the ruler of the empire is, strictly taken, only the common president of the numerous more or less autonomous bodies of burgesses, and alongside of the advantages of self-administration its disadvantages and dangers everywhere appear. In Egypt the ruler is king, the inhabitant of the land is his subject, the administration that of a domain. This administration, in principle as haughtily and absolutely conducted as it was directed to the equal welfare of all subjects without distinction of rank and of estate, was the peculiarity of the Lagid government, developed probably more from the Hellenising of the old Pharaonic rule than from the urban organisation of the universal empire, as the great Macedonian had conceived it, and as it was most completely carried out in the Syrian New-Macedonia (p. 120). The system required a king not merely leading the army in his own person, but engaged in the daily labour of administration, a developed and strictly disciplined hierarchy of officials, scrupulous justice towards high and low ; and as these rulers, not altogether without ground, ascribed to themselves the name of benefactor (εὐεργέτης), so the monarchy of the Lagids may be compared with that of Frederick, from which it was in its principles not far removed. Certainly Egypt had also experienced the reverse side, the inevitable collapse of the system in incapable hands. But the standard remained ; and the Augustan principate alongside of the rule of the senate was nothing but the intermarriage of the Lagid government with the old urban and federal development.

A further consequence of this form of government was the undoubted superiority, more especially from a financial point of view, of the Egyptian administration over that of the other provinces. We may designate the pre-Roman epoch as the struggle of the financially dominant power of Egypt with the Asiatic empire, filling, so far as space goes, the rest of the East ; under the Roman period this was continued in a certain sense in the fact that the imperial finances stood forth superior in contrast to those of the senate, especially through the exclusive possession of Egypt. If it is the aim of the state to work out the utmost possible amount from its territory, in the old world the Lagids were absolutely the masters of statecraft. In particular they were in this sphere the instructors and the models of the Caesars. How much the Romans drew out of Egypt we are not able to say with precision. In the Persian period Egypt had paid an annual tribute of 700 Babylonish talents of silver, about £200,000 ; the annual income of the Ptolemies from Egypt, or rather from their possessions generally, amounted in their most brilliant period to 14,800 Egyptian silver talents, or £2,850,000, and besides 1,500,000 artabae = 591,000 hectolitres of wheat ; at the end of their rule fully 6000 talents, or £1,250,000. The Romans drew from Egypt annually the third part of the corn necessary for the consumption of Rome, 20,000,000 Roman bushels[1] = 1,740,000

Egypt and the imperial administration.

[1] This figure is given by the so-called Epitome of Victor, c. 1, for the time of Augustus. After this payment was transferred to Constantinople there went thither under Justinian (*Ed.* xiii. c. 8) annually 8,000,000 artabae (for these are to be understood, according to c. 6, as meant), or 26⅔ millions of Roman bushels (Hultsch, *Metrol.* p. 628), to which falls further to be added the similar payment to the town of Alex-

hectolitres ; a part of it, however, was certainly derived from the domains proper, another perhaps supplied in return for compensation, while, on the other hand, the Egyptian tribute was assessed, at least for a great part, in money, so that we are not in a position even approximately to determine the Egyptian income of the Roman exchequer. But not merely by its amount was it of decisive importance for the Roman state-economy, but because it served as a pattern in the first instance for the domanial possessions of the emperors in the other provinces, and generally for the whole imperial administration, as this falls to be explained when we set it forth.

Privileged position of the Hellenes. But if the communal self-administration had no place in Egypt, and in this respect a real diversity does not exist between the two nations of which this state, just like the Syrian, was composed, there was in another respect a barrier erected between them, to which Syria offers no parallel. According to the arrangement of the Macedonian conquerors, the belonging to an Egyptian locality disqualified for all public offices and for the better military service. Where the state made gifts to its burgesses these were restricted to those of the Greek communities ;[1] on the other hand, the Egyptians only paid the poll-tax ; and even from the municipal burdens, which fell on the settlers of the individual Egyptian district, the Alexandrians settled there were exempted.[2] Although in the case of trespass the back of the Egyptian as of the Alexandrian had to suffer, the latter might boast, and did boast, that the cane struck him, and not the lash, as in the case of the former.[3] Even the

andria, introduced by Diocletian. To the shipmasters for the freight to Constantinople 8000 solidi = £5000 were annually paid from the state-chest.

[1] At least Cleopatra on a distribution of grain in Alexandria excluded the Jews (Josephus, *contra Ap.* ii. 5), and all the more, consequently, the Egyptians.

[2] The edict of Alexander (*C. I. Gr.* 4957), l. 33 ff., exempts the ἐυγενεῖς 'Αλεξανδρεῖς dwelling ἐν τῇ χώρᾳ (not ἐν τῇ πόλει) on account of their business from the λειτουργίαι χωρικαί.

[3] "There subsist," says the Alexandrian Jew Philo (*in Flacc.* 10), "as respects corporal chastisement (τῶν μαστίγων), distinctions in our city according to the rank of those to be chastised ; the Egyptians are chastised with different scourges and by others, but the Alexandrians with canes (σπάθαις ; σπάθη is the stem of

acquiring of better burgess-rights was forbidden to the Egyptians.[1] The burgess-lists of the two large Greek towns organised by and named after the two founders of the empire in lower and upper Egypt embraced in them the ruling population, and the possession of the franchise of one of these towns was in the Egypt of the Ptolemies the same as the possession of the Roman franchise was in the Roman empire. What Aristotle recommended to Alexander—to be a ruler (ἡγεμών) to the Hellenes and a master to the barbarians, to provide for the former as friends and comrades, to use the latter like animals and plants—the Ptolemies practically carried out in all its extent. The king, greater and more free than his instructor, carried in his mind the higher idea of transforming the barbarians into Hellenes, or at least of replacing the barbarian settlements by Hellenic, and to this idea his successors almost everywhere, and particularly in Syria, allowed ample scope.[2] In Egypt this was not the case. Doubtless its rulers sought to keep touch with the natives, particularly in the religious sphere, and wished not to rule as Greeks over the Egyptians, but rather as earthly gods over their subjects in common ; but with this the inequality of rights on the part of the subjects was quite compatible, just as the preference *de iure* and *de facto* of the nobility was quite as essential a part of the government of Frederick as the equality of justice towards gentle and simple.

the palm-leaf), and by the Alexandrian cane - bearers " (σπαθηφόροι, perhaps *bacillarius*). He afterwards complains bitterly that the elders of his community, if they were to be scourged at all, should not have been provided at least with decorous burgess-lashes (ταῖς ἐλευθεριωτέραις καὶ πολιτικωτέραις μάστιξιν).

[1] Josephus, *contra Ap.* ii. 4, μόνοις Αἰγυπτίοις οἱ κύριοι νῦν Ῥωμαῖοι τῆς οἰκουμένης μεταλαμβάνειν ἠστινοσοῦν πολιτείας ἀπειρήκασιν. 6, *Aegyptiis neque regum quisquam videtur ius civitatis fuisse largitus neque nunc quilibet imperatorum* (comp. *Eph. epigr.* v. p. 13). The same upbraids his adversary (ii. 3, 4) that he, a

native Egyptian, had denied his home and given himself out as an Alexandrian.—Individual exceptions are not thereby excluded.

[2] Alexandrian science, too, protested in the sense of the king against this proposition (Plutarch, *de fort. Alex.* i. 6) ; Eratosthenes designated civilisation as not peculiar to the Hellenes alone, and not to be denied to all barbarians, *e.g.* not to the Indians, the Arians, the Romans, the Carthaginians ; men were rather to be divided into " good " and " bad " (Strabo, i. *fin.* p. 66). But of this theory no practical application was made to the Egyptian race even under the Lagids.

As the Romans in the East generally continued the work of the Greeks, so the exclusion of the native Egyptians from the acquiring of Greek citizenship not merely continued to subsist, but was extended to the Roman citizenship. The Egyptian Greek, on the other hand, might acquire the latter just like any other non-burgess. Entrance to the senate, it is true, was as little allowed to him as to the Roman burgess from Gaul (p. 89), and this restriction remained much longer in force for Egypt than for Gaul ;[1] it was not till the beginning of the third century that it was disregarded in isolated cases, and it held good, as a rule, even in the fifth. In Egypt itself the positions of the upper officials, that is, of those acting for the whole province, and likewise the officers' posts, were reserved for Roman citizens in the form of the knight's horse being required as a qualification for them ; this was given by the general organisation of the empire, and similar privileges had in fact been possessed in Egypt by the Macedonians in contrast to the other Greeks. The offices of the second rank remained under the Roman rule, as previously, closed to the Egyptian Egyptians, and were filled with Greeks, primarily with the burgesses of Alexandria and Ptolemais. If in the imperial war-service for the first class Roman citizenship was required, they, at any rate in the case of the legions stationed in Egypt itself, not seldom admitted the Egyptian Greek on the footing that Roman citizenship was conferred on him upon occasion of the levy. For the category of auxiliary troops the admission of the Greeks was subject to no limitation ; but the Egyptians were little or not at all employed for this purpose, while they were employed afterwards in considerable number for the lowest class, the naval force still in the first imperial times formed of slaves. In the course of time the slighting of the native

---

[1] Admission to the equestrian positions was at least rendered difficult : *non est ex albo iudex patre Aegyptio* (*C. I. L.* iv. 1943 ; comp. *Staatsrecht*, ii. 919, note 2 ; *Eph. epigr.* v. p. 13, note 2). Yet we meet early with individual Alexandrians in equestrian offices, like Tiberius Julius Alexander (p. 246, note).

Egyptians doubtless had its rigour relaxed, and they more than once attained to Greek, and by means of it also to Roman, citizenship; but on the whole the Roman government was simply the continuation, as of the Greek rule, so also of the Greek exclusiveness. As the Macedonian government had contented itself with Alexandria and Ptolemais, so in this province alone the Romans did not found a single colony.[1]

The linguistic arrangement in Egypt remained essentially under the Romans as the Ptolemies had settled it. Apart from the military, among whom the Latin alone prevailed, the business-language for the intercourse of the upper posts was the Greek. Of the native language, which, radically different from the Semitic as from the Arian languages, is most nearly akin perhaps to that of the Berbers in North Africa, and of the native writing, the Roman rulers and their governors never made use; and, if already under the Ptolemies a Greek translation had to be appended to official documents written in Egyptian, at least the same held good for these their successors. Certainly the Egyptians were not prohibited from making use, so far as it seemed requisite according to ritual or otherwise appropriate, of the native language and of its time-hallowed written signs; in this old home, moreover, of the use of writing in ordinary intercourse the native language, alone familiar to the great public, and the usual writing must necessarily have been allowed not merely in the case of private contracts, but even as regards tax-receipts and similar documents. But this was a concession, and the ruling Hellenism strove to enlarge its domain. The effort to create for the views and traditions prevailing in the land an universally valid expression also in Greek gave an extension to the system of double names in Egypt such as we see nowhere else. All Egyptian gods whose

Native language.

---

[1] If the words of Pliny (*H. N.* v. 31, 128) are accurate, that the island of Pharos before the harbour of Alexandria was a *colonia Caesaris dictatoris* (comp. iv. 574), the dictator has here too, like Alexander, gone beyond the thought of Aristotle. But there can be no doubt as to the point, that after the annexation of Egypt there never was a Roman colony there.

names were not themselves current among the Greeks,
like that of Isis, were equalised with corresponding or else
not corresponding Greek ones ; perhaps the half of the
townships and a great number of persons bore as well
a native as a Greek appellation. Gradually Hellenism
in this case prevailed. The old sacred writing meets us
on the preserved monuments last under the emperor
Decius about the middle of the third, and its more
current degenerated form last about the middle of the fifth
century ; both disappeared from common use considerably
earlier. The neglect and the decay of the native elements
of civilisation are expressed in these facts. The language
of the land itself maintained its ground still for long
afterwards in remote places and in the lower ranks, and
only became quite extinct in the seventeenth century,
after it—the language of the Copts—had, just like the
Syriac, experienced in the later imperial period a limited
regeneration in consequence of the introduction of
Christianity and of the efforts directed to the production
of a national-Christian literature.

Abolition of
a resident
court.

In the government the first thing that strikes us is
the suppression of the court and of its residency, the
necessary consequence of the annexation of the land by
Augustus. There was left doubtless as much as could
be left. On the inscriptions written in the native
language, and so merely for Egyptians, the emperors are
termed, like the Ptolemies, kings of upper and lower
Egypt, and the elect of the Egyptian native gods, and
indeed withal—which was not the case with the
Ptolemies—great-kings.[1] Dates were reckoned in Egypt,

---

[1] The titles of Augustus run with
the Egyptian priests to the following
effect : " The beautiful boy, lovely
through worthiness to be loved, the
prince of princes, elect of Ptah and
Nun the father of the gods, king of
upper Egypt and king of lower
Egypt, lord of the two lands, Autokrator, son of the sun, lord of diadems,
Kaisar, ever living, beloved by Ptah
and Isis ;" in this case the proper
names "Autokrator, Kaisar," are

retained from the Greek. The title
of Augustus occurs first in the case
of Tiberius in an Egyptian translation
(*nti χu*), and with the retention of the
Greek Σεβαστός first under Domitian.
The title of the fair, lovely boy,
which in better times was wont to be
given only to the children proclaimed
as joint-rulers, afterwards became
stereotyped, and is found employed,
as for Caesarion and Augustus, so
also for Tiberius, Claudius, Titus,

as previously, according to the current calendar of the country and its royal year passing over to the Roman rulers ; the golden cup which every year the king threw into the swelling Nile was now thrown in by the Roman viceroy. But these things did not reach far. The Roman ruler could not carry out the part of the Egyptian king, which was incompatible with his imperial position. The new lord of the land had unpleasant experiences in his representation by a subordinate on the very first occasion of his sending a governor to Egypt ; the able officer and talented poet, who had not been able to refrain from inscribing his name also on the Pyramids, was deposed on that account and thereby ruined. It was inevitable that limits should here be set. The affairs, the transaction of which according to the system of Alexander devolved on the prince personally [1] not less than according to the arrangement of the Roman principate, might be managed by the Roman governor as by the native king ; king he might neither be nor seem.[2] That was to a certainty deeply and severely felt in the second city of the world. The mere change of dynasty would not have told so very heavily. But a court like that of the Ptolemies, regulated according to the ceremonial of the Pharaohs, king and queen in their dress as gods, the pomp of festal processions, the reception of the priesthoods and of ambassadors, the court-banquets, the great ceremonies of the coronation, of the taking the oath, of marriage, of burial, the court-offices of the bodyguards and the chief of that guard ($\dot{a}\rho\chi\iota\sigma\omega\mu\alpha\tau\sigma\phi\acute{\nu}\lambda\alpha\xi$), of the introducing chamberlain ($\epsilon\dot{\iota}\sigma\alpha\gamma\gamma\epsilon\lambda\epsilon\acute{\nu}s$), of the chief master of the table ($\dot{a}\rho\chi\epsilon\delta\acute{\epsilon}\alpha\tau\rho\sigma s$), of the chief master of the huntsmen

---

Domitian. It is more important that in deviation from the older title, as it is found, *e.g.* in Greek on the inscription of Rosetta (*C. I. Gr.* 4697), in the case of the Caesars from Augustus onward the title " prince of princes " is appended, by which beyond doubt it was intended to express their position of great-king, which the earlier kings had not.

[1] If people knew, king Seleucus was wont to say (Plutarch, *An seni,* 11), what a burden it was to write and to read so many letters, they would not take up the diadem if it lay at their feet.

[2] That he wore other insignia than the officers generally (Hirschfeld, *Verw. Gesch.* p. 271), it is hardly allowable to infer from *vita Hadr.* 4.

(ἀρχικυνηγός), the cousins and friends of the king, the wearers of decorations—all this was lost for the Alexandrians once for all with the transfer of the seat of the ruler from the Nile to the Tiber. Only the two famous Alexandrian libraries remained there, with all their belongings and staff, as a remnant of the old regal magnificence. Beyond question Egypt lost by being dispossessed of its rulers very much more than Syria ; both nations indeed were in the powerless position of having to acquiesce in what was contrived for them, and not more here than there was a rising for the lost position of a great power so much as thought of.

The officials.

The administration of the land lay, as has been already said, in the hands of the "deputy," that is, the viceroy ; for, although the new lord of the land, out of respect for his position in the empire, refrained as well for himself as for his delegates of higher station from the royal appellations in Egypt, he yet in substance conducted his rule throughout as successor of the Ptolemies, and the whole civil and military supreme power was combined in his hand and that of his representative. We have already observed that neither non-burgesses nor senators might fill this position ; it was sometimes committed to Alexandrians, if they had attained to burgess-rights, and by way of exception to equestrian rank.[1] We may add that this office stood at first before all the rest of the non-senatorial in rank and influence, and subsequently was inferior only to the commandership of the imperial guard. Besides the officers proper, in reference to whom the only departure from the general arrangement was the exclusion of the senator and the lower title, thence resulting, of the commandant of the legion (*praefectus* instead of *legatus*),

[1] Thus Tiberius Julius Alexander, an Alexandrian Jew, held this governorship in the last years of Nero (p. 204) ; certainly he belonged to a very rich family of rank, allied by marriage even with the imperial house, and he had distinguished himself in the Parthian war as chief of the staff of Corbulo—a position which he soon afterwards took up once more in the Jewish war of Titus. He must have been one of the ablest officers of this epoch. To him is dedicated the pseudo-Aristotelian treatise περὶ κόσμου (p. 168), evidently composed by another Alexandrian Jew (Bernays, *Gesammelte Abhandl.* ii. 278).

there acted alongside of and under the governor, and likewise for all Egypt, a supreme official for justice and a supreme finance-administrator, both likewise Roman citizens of equestrian rank, and apparently not borrowed from the administrative scheme of the Ptolemies, but attached and subordinated to the governor after a fashion applied also in other imperial provinces.[1]

All other officials acted only for individual districts, and were in the main taken over from the Ptolemaic arrangement. That the presidents of the three provinces of lower, middle, and upper Egypt, provided—apart from the command—with the same sphere of business as the governor, were taken in the time of Augustus from the Egyptian Greeks, and subsequently, like the superior officials proper, from the Roman knighthood, deserves to be noted as a symptom of the increasing tendency in the course of the imperial period to repress the native element in the magistracy.

Under these superior and intermediate authorities stood the local officials, the presidents of the Egyptian as of the Greek towns, along with the very numerous subalterns employed in the collecting of the revenue and

[1] Unmistakably the *iuridicus Aegypti* (*C. I. L.* x. 6976; also *missus in Aegyptum ad iurisdictionem, Bull. dell' Inst.* 1856, p. 142; *iuridicus Alexandreae, C.* vi. 1564, viii. 8925, 8934; *Dig.* i. 20, 2), and the *idiologus ad Aegyptum* (*C.* x. 4862; *procurator ducenarius Alexandriae idiulogu, Eph. ep.* v. p. 30, and *C. I. Gr.* 3751; ὁ γνώμων τοῦ ἰδίου λόγου, *C. I. Gr.* 4957, v. 44, comp. v. 39), are modelled on the assistants associated with the legates of the imperial provinces för the administration of justice (*legati iuridici*) and the finances (*procuratores provinciae; Staatsrecht* I[2], p. 223, note 5). That they were appointed for the whole land, and were subordinate to the *praefectus Aegypti*, is stated by Strabo expressly (xvii. 1, 12, p. 797), and this assumption is required by the frequent mention of Egypt in their style and title as well as by the turn in the edict *C. I. Gr.* 4957, v. 39. But their jurisdiction was not exclusive; "many processes," says Strabo, "are decided by the official administering justice" (that he assigned guardians, we learn from *Dig.* i. 20, 2), and according to the same it devolved on the Idiologus in particular to confiscate for the exchequer the *bona vacantia et caduca.* —This does not exclude the view that the Roman *iuridicus* came in place of the older court of thirty with the ἀρχιδικαστής at its head (Diodorus, i. 75), who was Egyptian, and may not be confounded with the Alexandrian ἀρχιδικαστής, had moreover perhaps been set aside already before the Roman period, and that the Idiologus originated out of the subsistence in Egypt of a claim of the king on heritages, such as did not occur to the same extent in the rest of the empire, which latter view Lumbroso (*Recherches*, p. 285) has made very probable.

the manifold imposts laid on business-dealings, and again in the individual district the presidents of the sub-districts and of the villages—positions, which were looked upon more as burdens than as honours, and were imposed by the higher officials upon persons belonging to, or settled in, the locality, to the exclusion, however, of the Alexandrians ; the most important among them, the presidency of the nome, was filled up every three years by the governor. The local authorities of the Greek towns were different as to number and title ; in Alexandria in particular four chief officials acted, the priest of Alexander,[1]

[1] The ἐξηγητής, according to Strabo, xvii. 1, 12, p. 797, the first civic official in Alexandria under the Ptolemies as under the Romans, and entitled to wear the purple, is certainly identical with the year-priest in the testament of Alexander appearing in the Alexander-romance very well instructed in such matters (iii. 33, p. 149, Müller). As the Exegetes has, along with his title, doubtless to be taken in a religious sense, the ἐπιμέλεια τῶν τῇ πόλει χρησίμων, that priest of the romance is ἐπιμελιστὴς τῆς πόλεως. The romance-writer will not have invented the payment with a talent and the hereditary character any more than the purple and the golden chaplet ; the hereditary element, in reference to which Lumbroso (*l'Egitto al tempo dei Greci e Romani*, p. 152) recalls the ἐξηγητὴς ἔναρχος of the Alexandrian inscriptions (*C. I. Gr.* 4688, 4976 c.), is presumably to be conceived to the effect that a certain circle of persons was called by hereditary right, and out of these the governor appointed the year-priest. This priest of Alexander (as well as of the following Egyptian kings, according to the stone of Canopus and that of Rosetta, *C. I. Gr.* 4697), was under the earlier Lagids the eponym for Alexandrian documents, while later as under the Romans the kings' names come in for that purpose. Not different from him probably was the "chief priest of Alexandria and all Egypt," of an inscription of the city

of Rome from Hadrian's time (*C. I. Gr.* 5900 : ἀρχιερεῖ Ἀλεξανδρείας καὶ Αἰγύπτου πάσης Λευκίῳ Ἰουλίῳ Οὐησ-τίνῳ καὶ ἐπιστάτῃ τοῦ Μουσείου καὶ ἐπὶ τῶν ἐν Ῥώμῃ βιβλιοθηκῶν Ῥωμαικῶν τε καὶ Ἑλληνικῶν καὶ ἐπὶ τῆς παιδείας Ἀδριανοῦ, ἐπιστολεῖ τοῦ αὐτοῦ αὐτοκρά-τορος) ; the proper title ἐξηγητής, was avoided out of Egypt, because it usually denoted the sexton. If the chief priesthood, as the tenor of the inscription suggests, is to be assumed as having been at that time permanent, the transition from the annual tenure to the at least titular, and not seldom also real, tenure for life repeats itself, as is well known, in the *sacerdotia* of the provinces, to which this Alexandrian one did not indeed belong, but the place of which it represented in Egypt (p. 238). That the priesthood and the presidency of the Museum are two distinct offices is shown by the inscription itself. We learn the same from the inscription of a royal chief physician of a good Lagid period, who is withal as well exegete as president of the Museum (Χρύσερμον Ἡρακλείτου Ἀλεξανδρέα τὸν συγγενῆ βασιλέως Πτολεμαίου καὶ ἐξηγητὴν καὶ ἐπὶ τῶν ἰατρῶν καὶ ἐπιστάτην τοῦ Μουσείου). But the two monuments at the same time suggest that the post of first official of Alexandria and the presidency of the Museum were frequently committed to the same man, although in the Roman time the former was conferred by the prefect, the latter by the emperor.

the town-clerk (ὑπομνηματογράφος),[1] the supreme judge (ἀρχιδικαστής), and the master of the night-watch (νυκτερινὸς στρατηγός). That they were of more consequence than the *strategoi* of the nomes, is obvious of itself, and is shown clearly by the purple dress belonging to the first Alexandrian official. We may add that they originate likewise from the Ptolemaic period, and are nominated for a time by the Roman government, like the presidents of the nomes, from the persons settled therein. Roman officials of imperial nomination are not found among these urban presidents. But the priest of the Mouseion, who is at the same time president of the Alexandrian Academy of Sciences and also disposes of the considerable pecuniary means of this institute, is nominated by the emperor ; in like manner the superintendency of the tomb of Alexander and the buildings connected with it, and some other important positions in the capital of Egypt, were filled up by the government in Rome with officials of equestrian rank.[2]

As a matter of course, Alexandrians and Egyptians were drawn into those movements of pretenders which had their origin in the East, and regularly participated in them ; in this way Vespasian, Cassius, Niger, Macrianus (p. 103), Vaballathus the son of Zenobia, Probus, were here proclaimed as rulers. But the initiative in all those cases was taken neither by the burgesses of Alexandria nor by the little esteemed Egyptian troops ; and most of those revolutions, even the unsuccessful, had for Egypt no consequences specially felt. But the movement connected with the name of Zenobia (p. 107) became almost as fateful for Alexandria and for all Egypt as for Palmyra. In town and country the Palmyrene and the Roman partisans confronted each other with arms and blazing

Insurrections.

In the Palmyrene period.

---

[1] Not to be confounded with the similar office which Philo (in *Flacc.* 16) mentions and Lucian (*Apolog.* 12) held ; this was not an urban office, but a subaltern's post in the praefecture of Egypt, in Latin *a commentariis* or *ab actis.*

[2] This is the *procurator Neaspoleos et mausolei Alexandriae* (*C. I. L.*

viii. 8934 ; Henzen, 6929). Officials of a like kind and of like rank, but whose functions are not quite clear, are the *procurator ad Mercurium Alexandreae* (*C. I. L.* x. 3847), and the *procurator Alexandreae Pelusii* (*C.* vi. 1024). The Pharos also is placed under an imperial freedman (*C.* vi. 8582)

torches in their hands. On the south frontier the barbarian Blemyes advanced, apparently in agreement with
the portion of the inhabitants of Egypt favourable to
Palmyra, and possessed themselves of a great part of
upper Egypt.[1] In Alexandria the intercourse between
the two hostile quarters was cut off; it was difficult and
dangerous even to forward letters.[2] The streets were
filled with blood and with dead bodies unburied. The
diseases thereby engendered made even more havoc than
the sword ; and, in order that none of the four steeds of
destruction might be wanting, the Nile also failed, and
famine associated itself with the other scourges. The
population melted away to such an extent that, as a contemporary says, there were formerly more gray-haired
men in Alexandria than there were afterwards citizens.

When Probus, the general sent by Claudius, at length
gained the upper hand, the Palmyrene partisans, including
the majority of the members of council, threw themselves
into the strong castle of Prucheion in the immediate
neighbourhood of the city ; and, although, when Probus
promised to spare the lives of those that should come out,
the great majority submitted, yet a considerable portion
of the citizens persevered to the uttermost in the struggle
of despair. The fortress, at length reduced by hunger
(270), was razed and lay thenceforth desolate ; but the
city lost its walls. The Blemyes still maintained them-

---

[1] The alliance of the Palmyrenes
and the Blemyes is pointed to by the
notice of the *vita Firmi*, c. 3, and
by the statement, according to Zosimus, i. 71, that Ptolemais fell away to
the Blemyes (comp. Eusebius, *Hist.
Eccl.* vii. 32). Aurelian only negotiated with these (*Vita*, 34, 41) ; it
was Probus who first drove them
again out of Egypt (Zosimus, *l.c.*;
Vita, 17).

[2] We still possess letters of this
sort, addressed by the bishop of the
city, at that time Dionysius († 265),
to the members of the church shut
off in the hostile half of the town
(Eusebius, *Hist. Eccl.* vii. 21, 22,
comp. 32). When it is therein said :

"one gets more easily from the West
to the East than from Alexandria
to Alexandria," and ἡ μεσαιτάτη τῆς
πόλεως ὁδός, consequently the street
furnished with colonnades, running
from the Lochias point right through
the town (comp. Lumbroso, *l'Egitto
al tempo dei Greci e Romani*, 1882,
p. 137) is compared with the desert
between Egypt and the promised
land, it appears almost as if Severus
Antoninus had carried out his threat
of drawing a wall across the town
and occupying it in a military fashion
(Dio, lxxvii. 23). The razing of the
walls after the overthrow of the revolt
(Ammianus, xxii. 16, 15) would then
have to be referred to this very building.

selves for years in the land; the emperor Probus first
wrested from them again Ptolemais and Coptos, and drove
them out of the country.

The state of distress, which these troubles prolonged
through a series of years, must have produced, may probably thereupon have brought to an outbreak, the only
revolution that can be shown to have arisen in Egypt.[1]
Under the government of Diocletian, we do not know why
or wherefore, as well the native Egyptians as the burgesses
of Alexandria rose in revolt against the existing government. Lucius Domitius Domitianus and Achilleus were
set up as opposition-emperors, unless possibly the two
names denote the same person; the revolt lasted from
three to four years, the towns Busiris in the Delta and
Coptos not far from Thebes were destroyed by the troops
of the government, and ultimately under the leading of
Diocletian in person in the spring of 297 the capital was
reduced after an eight months' siege. Nothing testifies
so clearly to the decline of the land, rich, but thoroughly
dependent on inward and outward peace, as the edict
issued in the year 302 by the same Diocletian, that a
portion of the Egyptian grain hitherto sent to Rome
should for the future go to the benefit of the Alexandrian
burgesses.[2] This was certainly among the measures which
aimed at the decapitalising of Rome; but the supply
would not have been directed towards the Alexandrians,
whom this emperor had truly no cause to favour, unless
they had urgently needed it.

Economically Egypt, as is well-known, is above all the
land of agriculture. It is true that the "black earth"—
that is the meaning of the native name for the country,
Chemi—is only a narrow stripe on either side of the
mighty Nile flowing from the last rapids near Syene, the

*Revolt
under Dio-
cletian.*

*Agricul-
ture.*

---

[1] The alleged Egyptian tyrants,
Aemilianus, Firmus, Saturninus, are
at least not attested as such. The
so-called description of the life of the
second is nothing else than the sadly
disfigured catastrophe of Prucheion.

[2] *Chr. Pasch.* p. 514; Procopius,
Hist. arc. 26; Gothofred. on *Cod.*

Theod. xiv. 26, 2. Stated distribu-
tions of corn had already been instituted earlier in Alexandria, but
apparently only for persons old and
decayed, and—it may be conjectured
—on account of the city, not of the
state (Eusebius, *Hist. Eccl.* vii. 21).

southern limit of Egypt proper, for 550 miles in a copious
stream, through the yellow desert extending right and
left, to the Mediterranean Sea ; only at its lower end the
" gift of the river," the Nile-delta, spreads itself out on
both sides between the manifold arms of its mouth.   The
produce of these tracts depends year by year on the Nile
and on the sixteen cubits of its flood-mark—the sixteen
children playing round their father, as the art of the
Greeks represented the river-god ; with good reason the
Arabs designate the low cubits by the name of the angels
of death, for, if the river does not reach its full height,
famine and destruction come upon the whole land of Egypt.
But in general Egypt—where the expenses of cultivation
are singularly low, wheat bears an hundred fold, and the
culture of vegetables, of the vine, of trees, particularly the
date-palm, as well as the rearing of cattle, yield good produce—is able not merely to feed a dense population, but
also to send corn in large quantity abroad.   This led to
the result that, after the installation of the foreign rule,
not much of its riches was left to the land itself.   The
Nile rose at that time nearly as in the Persian period and
as it does to-day, and the Egyptian toiled chiefly for other
lands ; and thereby in the first instance Egypt played an
important part in the history of imperial Rome.   After
the grain-cultivation in Italy itself had decayed and Rome
had become the greatest city of the world, it needed constant supplies of moderately-priced transmarine grain ;
and the principate strengthened itself above all by the
solution of the far from easy economic problem how to
make the supply of the capital financially possible and to
render it secure.   This solution depended on the possession
of Egypt, and, in as much as here the emperor bore
exclusive sway, he kept Italy with its dependencies in
check through Egypt.   When Vespasian seized the
dominion he sent his troops to Italy, but he went in
person to Egypt and possessed himself of Rome through
the corn-fleet.   Wherever a Roman ruler had, or is alleged
to have had, the idea of transferring the seat of government to the East, as is told us of Caesar, Antonius, Nero,

Geta, there the thoughts were directed, as if spontaneously, not to Antioch, although this was at that time the regular court-residence of the East, but towards the birthplace and the stronghold of the principate—to Alexandria.

For that reason, accordingly, the Roman government applied itself more zealously to the elevation of agriculture in Egypt than anywhere else. As it is dependent on the inundation of the Nile, it was possible to extend considerably the surface fitted for cultivation by systematically executed water-works, artificial canals, dykes, and reservoirs. In the good times of Egypt, the native land of the measuring-chain and of artificial building, much was done for it, but these beneficent structures fell, under the last wretched and financially oppressed governments, into sad decay. Thus the Roman occupation introduced itself worthily by Augustus subjecting the canals of the Nile to a thorough purifying and renewal by means of the troops stationed in Egypt. If at the time of the Romans taking possession a full harvest required a state of the river of fourteen cubits, and at eight cubits failure of the harvest occurred, at a later period, after the canals were put into order, twelve cubits were enough for a full harvest, and even eight cubits yielded a sufficient produce. Centuries later the emperor Probus not merely liberated Egypt from the Ethiopians but also restored the water-works on the Nile. It may be assumed, generally, that the better successors of Augustus administered in a similar sense, and that especially with the internal peace and security hardly interrupted for centuries, Egyptian agriculture stood in a permanently flourishing state under the Roman principate. What reflex effect this state of things had on the Egyptians themselves we are not able to follow out more exactly. To a great extent the revenues from Egypt rested on the possession of the imperial domains, which in Roman as in earlier times formed a considerable part of the whole area ;[1] here, especially considering the small

[1] In the town of Alexandria there appears to have been no landed property in the strict sense, but only a sort of hereditary lease (Ammianus, xxii. 11, 6 ; *Staatsrecht*, ii. 963, note 1) ; but otherwise private property in the soil prevailed also in Egypt, in the sense in which the pro-

cost of cultivation, only a moderate proportion of the produce must have been left to the small tenants who provided it, or a high money-rent must have been imposed. But even the numerous, and as a rule smaller, owners must have paid a high land-tax in corn or in money. The agricultural population, contented as it was, remained probably numerous in the imperial period ; but certainly the pressure of taxation, as well in itself as on account of the expenditure of the produce abroad, lay as a heavier burden on Egypt under the Roman foreign rule than under the by no means indulgent government of the Ptolemies.

Trades. 　Of the economy of Egypt agriculture formed but a part ; as it in this respect stood far before Syria, so it had the advantage of a high prosperity of manufactures and commerce as compared with the essentially agricultural Africa. The linen manufacture in Egypt was at least equal in age, extent, and renown to the Syrian, and maintained its ground through the whole imperial period, although the finer sorts at this epoch were especially manufactured in Syria and Phoenicia ;[1] when Aurelian

vincial law knows such a thing at all. There is often mention of domanial possession *e.g.* Strabo, xvii. 1, 51, p. 828, says that the best Egyptian dates grow on an island on which private persons might not possess any land, but it was formerly royal, now imperial, and yielded a large income. Vespasian sold a portion of the Egyptian domains and thereby exasperated the Alexandrians (Dio, lxvi. 8)—beyond doubt the great farmers who then gave the land in sub-lease to the peasants proper. Whether landed property in mortmain, especially of the priestly colleges, was in the Roman period still as extensive as formerly, may be doubted ; as also whether otherwise large estates or small properties predominated ; petty husbandry was certainly general. We possess figures neither for the domanial quota nor for that of the land-tax ; that the fifth sheaf in Orosius, i. 8, 9, is copied including the *usque ad*

nunc from Genesis, is rightly observed by Lumbroso, *Recherches*, p. 94. The domanial rent cannot have amounted to less than the half ; even for the land-tax the tenth (Lumbroso, *l. c.* p. 289, 293) may have hardly sufficed. Export of grain otherwise from Egypt needed the consent of the governor (Hirschfeld, *Annona*, p. 23), doubtless because otherwise scarcity might easily set in in the thickly-peopled land. Yet this arrangement was certainly more by way of control than of prohibition ; in the Periplus of the Egyptian corn is on several occasions (c. 7, 17, 24, 28, comp. 56) adduced among the articles of export. Even the cultivation of the fields seems to have become similarly controlled ; "the Egyptians, it is said, are fonder of cultivating rape than corn, so far as they may, on account of the rape-seed oil" (Plinius, *H. N.* xix. 5, 79).

[1] In the edict of Diocletian among

extended the contributions made from Egypt to the capital of the empire to other articles than corn, linen cloth and tow were not wanting among them. In fine glass wares, both as regards colouring and moulding, the Alexandrians held decidedly the first place, in fact, as they thought, the monopoly, in as much as certain best sorts were only to be prepared with Egyptian material. Indisputably they had such a material in the papyrus. This plant, which in antiquity was cultivated in masses on the rivers and lakes of lower Egypt, and flourished nowhere else, furnished the natives as well with nourishment as with materials for ropes, baskets, and boats, and furnished writing materials at that time for the whole writing world. What produce it must have yielded, we may gather from the measures which the Roman senate took, when once in the Roman market the papyrus became scarce and threatened to fail; and, as its laborious preparation could only take place on the spot, numberless men must have subsisted by it in Egypt. The deliveries of Alexandrian wares introduced by Aurelian in favour of the capital of the empire extended, along with linen, to glass and papyrus.[1] The intercourse with the East must have had a varied influence on Egyptian manufactures as regards supply and demand. Textures were manufactured there for export to the East, and that in the fashion required by the usage of the country; the ordinary clothes of the inhabitants of Habesh were of Egyptian manufacture; the gorgeous stuffs especially of the weaving in colours and in gold skilfully practised at Alexandria went to Arabia and India. In like manner the glass beads prepared in Egypt played the same part in the commerce of the African coast as at the present day. India procured partly glass cups, partly unwrought glass for its

---

the five fine sorts of linen the first four are Syrian or Cilician (of Tarsus) and the Egyptian linen appears not merely in the last place, but is also designated as Tarsian-Alexandrian, that is, prepared in Alexandria after the Tarsian model.

[1] It was related of a rich man in Egypt that he had lined his palace with glass instead of with marble, and that he possessed papyrus and lime enough to provide an army with them (*Vita Firmi*, 3).

own manufacture ; even at the Chinese court the glass vessels, with which the Roman strangers did homage to the emperor, are said to have excited great admiration. Egyptian merchants brought to the king of the Axomites (Habesh) as standing presents gold and silver vessels prepared after the fashion of that country, to the civilised rulers of the South-Arabian and Indian coast among other gifts also statues, probably of bronze, and musical instruments. On the other hand the materials for the manufacture of luxuries which came from the East, especially ivory and tortoise-shell, were worked up hardly perhaps in Egypt, chiefly, in all probability, at Rome. Lastly, at an epoch, which never had its match in the West for magnificent public buildings, the costly building materials supplied by the Egyptian quarries came to be employed in enormous masses outside of Egypt ; the beautiful red granite of Syene, the green breccia from the region of Kosêr, the basalt, the alabaster, after the time of Claudius the gray granite, and especially the porphyry of the mountains above Myos Hormos. The working of them was certainly effected for the most part on imperial account by penal colonists ; but the transport at least must have gone to benefit the whole country and particularly the city of Alexandria. The extent to which Egyptian traffic and Egyptian manufactures were developed is shown by an accidentally-preserved notice as to the cargo of a transport ship (ἄκατος), distinguished by its size, which under Augustus brought to Rome the obelisk now standing at the Porta del Popolo with its base ; it carried, besides 200 sailors, 1200 passengers, 400,000 Roman bushels (34,000 hectolitres) of wheat, and a cargo of linen cloth, glass, paper, and pepper. " Alexandria," says a Roman author of the third century,[1]

---

[1] That the alleged letter of Hadrian (*Vita Saturnini*, 8) is a late fabrication, is shown *e.g.* by the fact, that the emperor in this highly friendly letter addressed to his father-in-law, Servianus, complains of the injuries which the Alexandrians at his first departure had heaped on his son Verus, while on the other hand it is established that this Servianus was executed at the age of ninety in the year 136, because he had disapproved the adoption of Verus, which had taken place shortly before.

"is a town of plenty, of wealth, and of luxury, in which nobody goes idle ; this one is a glass-worker, that one a paper-maker, the third a linen-weaver ; the only god is money." This held true proportionally of the whole land.

Of the commercial intercourse of Egypt with the regions adjoining it on the south, as well as with Arabîa and India, we shall speak more fully in the sequel. The traffic with the countries of the Mediterranean comes less into prominence in the traditional account, partly, doubtless, because it belonged to the ordinary course of things, and there was not often occasion to make special mention of it. The Egyptian corn was conveyed to Italy by Alexandrian shipmasters, and in consequence of this there arose in Portus near Ostia a sanctuary modelled on the Alexandrian temple of Sarapis with a mariner's guild ;[1] but these transport-ships would hardly be concerned to any considerable extent in the sale of the wares going from Egypt to the West. This sale lay probably just as much, and perhaps more, in the hands of the Italian ship-owners and captains than of the Egyptian ; at least there was already under the Lagids a considerable Italian settlement in Alexandria,[2] and the Egyptian merchants had not the same diffusion in the West as the Syrian.[3] The ordinances of Augustus, to be mentioned afterwards, which remodelled the commercial traffic on the Arabian and Indian Seas, found no application to the navigation of

Egyptian navigation of the Mediterranean.

[1] The ναύκληροι τοῦ πορευτικοῦ Ἀλεξανδρεινοῦ στόλου, who set up the stone doubtless belonging to Portus, *C. I. Gr.* 5889, were the captains of these grain-ships. From the Serapeum of Ostia we possess a series of inscriptions (*C. I. L.* xiv. 47), according to which it was in all parts a copy of that at Alexandria ; the president is at the same time ἐπιμελητὴς παντὸς τοῦ Ἀλεξανδρείνου στόλου (*C. I. Gr.* 5973). Probably these transports were employed mainly with the carriage of grain, and this consequently took place by succession, to which also the precautions adopted by the emperor Gaius in the straits of Reggio (Josephus, *Arch.* xix. 2, 5) point.

With this well comports the fact, that the first appearance of the Alexandrian fleet in the spring was a festival for Puteoli (Seneca, *Ep.* 77, 1).

[2] This is shown by the remarkable Delian inscriptions, *Eph. epigr.* i. p. 600, 602.

[3] Already in the Delian inscriptions of the last century of the republic the Syrians predominate. The Egyptian deities had doubtless a much revered shrine there, but among the numerous priests and dedicators we meet only a single Alexandrian (Hauvette-Besnault, *Bull. de corr. Hell.* vi. 316 f.). Guilds of Alexandrian merchants are known to us at Tomi (I. 310, note) and at Perinthus (*C. I. Gr.* 2024).

the Mediterranean ; the government had no interest in favouring the Egyptian merchants more than the rest in its case. The traffic there remained, presumably, as it was.

Population. Egypt was thus not merely occupied, in its portions capable of culture, with a dense agricultural population, but also as the numerous and in part very considerable hamlets and towns enable us to recognise, a manufacturing land, and hence accordingly by far the most populous province of the Roman empire. The old Egypt is alleged to have had a population of seven millions ; under Vespasian there were counted in the official lists seven and a half millions of inhabitants liable to poll tax, to which fall to be added the Alexandrians and other Greeks exempted from poll tax, so that the population, apart from the slaves, is to be estimated at least at eight millions of persons. As the area capable of cultivation may be estimated at present at 10,500 English square miles, and for the Roman period at the most at 14,700, there dwelt at that time in Egypt on the average about 520 persons to the square mile.

When we direct our glance upon the inhabitants of Egypt, the two nations inhabiting the country—the great mass of the Egyptians and the small minority of the Alexandrians—are circles thoroughly different,[1] although the contagious power of vice and the similarity of character belonging to all vice have instituted a bad fellowship of evil between the two.

Egyptian manners. The native Egyptians cannot have been far different either in position or in character from their modern descendants. They were contented, sober, capable of labour, and active, skilful artisans and mariners, and adroit merchants, adhering to old customs and to old faith. If the Romans assure us that the Egyptians were proud

---

[1] After Juvenal has described the wild drinking bouts of the native Egyptians in honour of the local gods of the several nomes, he adds that therein the natives were in no respect inferior to the Canopus, *i.e.* the Alexandrian festival of Sarapis, notorious for its unbridled licentiousness (Strabo, xvii. 1, 17, p. 801) : *horrida sane Aegyptus, sed luxuria quantum ipse notavi, barbara famoso non cedit turba Canopo* (*Sat.* xv. 44).

of the scourge-marks received for perpetrating frauds in taxation,[1] these are views derived from the standpoint of the tax officials.   There was no want of good germs in the national culture ; with all the superiority of the Greeks in the intellectual competition of the two so utterly different races, the Egyptians in turn had the advantage of the Hellenes in various and essential things, and they felt this too.   It is, after all, only the plain reflection of their own feeling, when the Egyptian priests of the Greek conversational literature ridicule the so-called historical research of the Hellenes and its treatment of poetical fables as real tradition from primitive past times, saying that in Egypt they made no verses, but their whole ancient history was described in the temples and monuments ; although now, indeed, there were but few who knew it, since many monuments were destroyed, and tradition was made to perish through the ignorance and the indifference of later generations.   But this well-warranted complaint carried in itself hopelessness ; the venerable tree of Egyptian civilisation had long been marked for cutting down.   Hellenism penetrated with its decomposing influence even to the priesthood itself.   An Egyptian temple-scribe Chaeremon, who was called to the court of Claudius as teacher of Greek philosophy for the crown-prince, attributed in his *Egyptian History* the elements of Stoical physics to the old gods of the country, and expounded in this sense the documents written in the native character.   In the practical life of the imperial period the old Egyptian habits come into consideration almost only as regards the religious sphere.   Religion was for this people all in all.   The foreign rule in itself was willingly borne, we might say hardly felt, so long as it did not touch the sacred customs of the land and what was therewith connected.   It is true that in the internal government of the country nearly everything had such a connection—writing and language, priestly privileges and priestly arrogance, the manners of the court and the cus-

[1] Ammianus, xxii. 16, 23 : *Erubescit apud (Aegyptios), si qui non in-* *fitiando tributa plurimas in corpore vibices ostendat.*

toms of the country ; the care of the government for the
sacred ox living at the moment, the provisions made for its
burial at its decease, and for the finding out of the fitting
successor, were accounted by these priests and this
people as the test of the capacity of the ruler of the
land for the time, and as the measure of the respect
and homage due to him.   The first Persian king introduced himself in Egypt by giving back the sanctuary of
Neith in Sais to its destination—that is, to the priests ;
the first Ptolemy, when still a Macedonian governor,
brought back the images of the Egyptian gods, that had
been carried off to Asia, to their old abode, and restored
to the gods of Pe and Tep the land-gifts estranged from
them ; for the sacred temple-images brought home from
Persia in the great victorious expedition of Euergetes the
native priests convey their thanks to the king in the
famous decree of Canopus in the year 238 B.C.; the customary insertion of the living rulers male or female in the
circle of the native gods these foreigners acquiesced in for
themselves just as did the Egyptian Pharaohs.   The
Roman rulers followed their example only to a limited
extent.   As respects title they doubtless entered, as we saw
(p. 244, note) in some measure into the native cultus, but
avoided withal, even in the Egyptian setting, the customary
predicates that stood in too glaring a contrast to Occidental views.   Since these ' favourites of Ptah and of Isis '
took much the same steps in Italy against the Egyptian
worship as against the Jewish, they betrayed nothing, as
may readily be understood, of such love except in hiero-
glyphic inscriptions, and even in Egypt took no part in the
service of the native gods.   However obstinately the religion of the land was still retained under the foreign rule
among the Egyptians proper, the Pariah position in which
these found themselves alongside of the ruling Greeks and
Romans, necessarily told heavily on the cultus and the
priests ; and of the leading position, the influence, the
culture of the old Egyptian priestly order but scanty
remains were discernible under the Roman government.
On the other hand, the indigenous religion, from the out-

set disinclined to beauty of form and spiritual transfigura-
tion, served, in and out of Egypt, as a starting-point and
centre for all conceivable pious sorcery and sacred fraud
—it is enough to recall the thrice-greatest Hermes at
home in Egypt, with the literature attaching to his name
of tractates and marvel-books, as well as the corresponding widely diffused practice. But in the circles of the
natives the worst abuses were connected at this epoch with
their cultus—not merely drinking-bouts continued through
many days in honour of the individual local deities, with
the unchastity thereto appertaining, but also permanent
religious feuds between the several districts for the precedence of the ibis over the cat, or of the crocodile over
the baboon. In the year 127 A.D., on such an occasion,
the Ombites in southern Egypt were suddenly assailed by
a neighbouring community[1] at a drinking-festival, and the
victors are said to have eaten one of the slain. Soon
afterwards the community of the Hound, in defiance of the
community of the Pike, consumed a pike, and the latter in
defiance of the other consumed a hound, and thereupon a
war broke out between these two nomes, till the Romans
interfered and chastised both parties. Such incidents
were of ordinary occurrence in Egypt. Nor was there a
want otherwise of troubles in the land. The very first
viceroy of Egypt appointed by Augustus had, on account
of an increase of the taxes, to send troops to upper Egypt,
and not less, perhaps likewise in consequence of the pressure of taxation, to Heroonpolis at the upper end of the
Arabian Gulf. Once, under the emperor Marcus, a rising   Revolt
of the native Egyptians assumed even a threatening   of the
character. When in the marshes, difficult of access, on   men."
the coast to the east of Alexandria—the so-called "cattle-
pastures" (*bucolia*), which served as a place of refuge for
criminals and robbers, and formed a sort of colony of
them—some people were seized by a division of Roman
troops, the whole banditti rose to liberate them, and the

[1] This was according to Juvenal
Tentyra, which must be a mistake, if
the well known Tentyra is meant ;
but the list of the Ravennate chro-
nicler, iii. 2, names the two places
together.

population of the country joined the movement. The Roman legion from Alexandria went to oppose them, but it was defeated, and Alexandria itself had almost fallen into the hands of the insurgents. The governor of the East, Avidius Cassius, arrived doubtless with his troops, but did not venture on a conflict against the superiority of numbers, and preferred to provoke dissension in the league of the rebels ; after the one band ranged itself against the other the government easily mastered them all. This so-called revolt of the herdsmen probably bore, like such peasant wars for the most part, a religious character ; the leader Isidorus, the bravest man of Egypt, was by station a priest; and the circumstance that for the consecration of the league, after taking the oath, a captive Roman officer was sacrificed and eaten by those who swore, was as well in keeping with it as with the cannibalism of the Ombite war. An echo of these events is preserved in the stories of Egyptian robbers in the late-Greek minor literature. Much, moreover, as they may have given trouble to the Roman administration, they had not a political object, and interrupted but partially and temporarily the general tranquillity of the land.

Alexandria. By the side of the Egyptians stood the Alexandrians, somewhat as the English in India stand alongside of the natives of the country. Generally, Alexandria was regarded in the imperial period before Constantine's time as the second city of the Roman empire and the first commercial city of the world. It numbered at the end of the Lagid rule upwards of 300,000 free inhabitants, in the imperial period beyond doubt still more. The comparison of the two great capitals that grew up in rivalry on the Nile and on the Orontes yields as many points of similarity as of contrast. Both were comparatively new cities, monarchical creations out of nothing, of symmetrical plan and regular urban arrangements. Water ran into every house in Alexandria as at Antioch. In beauty of site and magnificence of buildings the city in the valley of the Orontes was as superior to its rival as the latter excelled it in the favourableness of the locality for commerce on a large scale and in the number of the population. The great public buildings of the Egyptian capital, the royal palace, the Mouseion dedicated to the Academy, above all the temple of Sarapis, were marvellous works of an earlier epoch, whose architecture was highly developed ; but the Egyptian capital, in which few of the Caesars set foot, has nothing corresponding to set off against the great number of imperial structures in the Syrian residency.

The Antiochenes and Alexandrians stood on an equal footing in insubordination and eagerness to oppose the government ; we may add also in this, that the two cities, and Alexandria more particularly, flourished precisely under and through the Roman government, and had much more reason to thank it than to play the Fronde. The attitude of the Alexandrians to their Hellenic rulers is attested by the long series of nicknames, in part still used at the present day, for which the royal Ptolemies without exception were indebted to the public of their capital. The Emperor Vespasian received from the Alexandrians for the introducing of a tax on salt fish the title of the " sardine-dealer " (Κυβιοσάκτης) ; the Syrian Severus Alexander that of the "chief Rabbin ;" but the emperors came rarely to Egypt, and the distant and foreign rulers offered no genuine butt for this ridicule. In their absence the public bestowed at least on the viceroys the same attention with persevering zeal ; even the prospect of inevitable chastisement was not able to put to silence the often witty and always saucy tongue of these townsmen.[1] Vespasian contented himself in return for that attention shown to him with raising the poll-tax about six farthings, and got for doing so the further name of the " sixfarthing-man ;" but their sayings about Severus Antoninus, the petty ape of Alexander the Great and the favourite of Mother Jocasta, were to cost them more dearly. The spiteful ruler appeared in all friendliness, and allowed the people to keep holiday for him, but then ordered his soldiers to charge into the festal multitude, so

Alexandrian Fronde.

---

[1] Seneca, *ad Helv.* 19, 6: *loquax et provincia . . . etiam periculosi sales in contumelias praefectorum ingeniosa placent.*

that for days the squares and streets of the great city ran with blood ; in fact, he enjoined the dissolution of the Academy and the transfer of the legion into the city itself—neither of which, it is true, was carried into effect.

Alexandrian tumults. But while in Antioch, as a rule, the matter did not go beyond sarcasm, the Alexandrian rabble took on the slightest pretext to stones and to cudgels. In street uproar, says an authority, himself Alexandrian, the Egyptians are before all others ; the smallest spark suffices here to kindle a tumult. On account of neglected visits, on account of the confiscation of spoiled provisions, on account of exclusion from a bathing establishment, on account of a dispute between the slave of an Alexandrian of rank and a Roman foot-soldier as to the value or non-value of their respective slippers, the legions were under the necessity of charging among the citizens of Alexandria. It here became apparent that the lower stratum of the Alexandrian population consisted in greater part of natives ; in these riots the Greeks no doubt acted as instigators, as indeed the rhetors, that is, in this case the inciting orators, are expressly mentioned ;[1] but in the further course of the matter the spite and the savageness of the Egyptian proper came into the conflict. The Syrians were cowardly, and as soldiers the Egyptians were so too ; but in a street tumult they were able to develop a courage worthy of a better cause.[2] The Antiochenes delighted in race-horses like the Alexandrians ; but among the latter no chariot race ended without stone-throwing and stabbing. Both cities were affected by the persecution of the Jews under

[1] Dio Chrysostom says in his address to the Alexandrians (*Or.* xxxii. p. 663 Reiske) : " Because now (the intelligent) keep in the background and are silent, there spring up among you endless disputes and quarrels and disorderly clamour, and bad and unbridled speeches, accusers, aspersions, trials, a rabble of orators." In the Alexandrian Jew-hunt, which Philo so drastically describes, we see these mob-orators at work.

[2] Dio Cassius, xxxix. 58 : " The Alexandrians do the utmost in all respects as to daring, and speak out everything that occurs to them. In war and its terrors their conduct is cowardly ; but in tumults, which with them are very frequent and very serious, they without scruple come to mortal blows, and for the sake of the success of the moment account their life nothing, nay, they go to their destruction as if the highest things were at stake."

the emperor Gaius ; but in Antioch an earnest word of the authorities sufficed to put an end to it, while thousands of human lives fell a sacrifice to the Alexandrian outbreak instigated by some clowns with a puppet-show. The Alexandrians, it was said, when a riot arose, gave themselves no peace till they had seen blood. The Roman officers and soldiers had a difficult position there. " Alexandria," says a reporter of the fourth century, " is entered by the governors with trembling and despair, for they fear the justice of the people ; where a governor perpetrates a wrong, there follows at once the setting of the palace on fire and stoning." The naive trust in the rectitude of this procedure marks the stand-point of the writer, who belonged to this " people." The continuation of this Lynch-system, dishonouring alike to the government and to the nation, is furnished by what is called Church-history, in the murder of the bishop Georgius, alike obnoxious to the heathen and to the orthodox, and of his associates under Julian, and that of the fair freethinker Hypatia by the pious community of Bishop Cyril under Theodosius II. These Alexandrian tumults were more malicious, more incalculable, more violent than the Antiochene, but just like these, not dangerous either for the stability of the empire or even for the individual government. Mischievous and ill-disposed lads are very inconvenient, but not more than inconvenient, in the household as in the commonwealth.

In religious matters also the two cities had an analogous position. To the worship of the land, as the native population retained it in Syria as in Egypt, the Alexandrians as well as the Antiochenes were disinclined in its original shape. But the Lagids, as well as the Seleucids, were careful of disturbing the foundations of the old religion of the country; and, merely amalgamating the older national views and sacred rites with the pliant forms of the Greek Olympus, they Hellenised these outwardly in some measure; they introduced, *e.g.* the Greek god of the lower world Pluto into the native worship, under the hitherto little mentioned name of the Egyptian god Sarapis, and then

Alexandrian worship.

gradually transferred to this the old Osiris worship.[1]
Thus the genuinely Egyptian Isis and the pseudo-Egypt-
ian Sarapis played in Alexandria nearly the same part as
Belus and Elagabalus in Syria, and made their way in a
similar manner with these, although less strongly and with
more vehement opposition, by degrees into the Occidental
worship of the imperial period. As regards the immorality
developed on occasion of these religious usages and festivals, and the unchastity approved and stimulated by
priestly blessing, neither city was in a position to upbraid
the other.

Down to a late time the old cultus retained its
firmest stronghold in the pious land of Egypt.[2] The

---

[1] The "pious Egyptians" offered
resistance, as Macrobius, *Sat.* i. 7,
14, reports, but *tyrannide Ptolemae-
orum pressi hos quoque deos* (Sarapis
and Saturnus) *in cultum recipere Alex-
andrinorum more, apud quos potis-
simum colebantur, coacti sunt.* As
they thus had to present bloody sacrifices, which was against their ritual,
they did not admit these gods, at least
into the towns ; *nullum Aegypti oppidum intra muros suos aut Saturni
aut Sarapis fanum recepit.*

[2] The often - quoted anonymous
author of a description of the empire
from the time of Constantius, a good
heathen, praises Egypt particularly on
account of its exemplary piety : "Nowhere are the mysteries of the gods so
well celebrated as there from of old
and still at present." Indeed, he
adds, some were of opinion that the
Chaldaeans—he means the Syrian
cultus—worshipped the gods better ;
but he held to what he had seen
with his own eyes—"Here there are
shrines of all sorts and magnificently
adorned temples, and there are found
numbers of sacristans and priests and
prophets and believers and excellent
theologians, and all goes on in its
order ; you find the altars everywhere
blazing with flame and the priests
with their fillets and the incense-
vessels with deliciously fragrant
spices." Nearly from the same time

(not from Hadrian), and evidently
also from a well-informed hand, proceeds another more malicious description (*vita Saturnini*, 8) : "He
who in Egypt worships Sarapis is also
a Christian, and those who call themselves Christian bishops likewise adore
Sarapis ; every grand Rabbi of the
Jews, every Samaritan, every Christian
clergyman is there at the same time
a sorcerer, a prophet, a quack (*aliptes*).
Even when the patriarch comes to
Egypt some demand that he pray to
Sarapis, others that he pray to Christ."
This diatribe is certainly connected
with the circumstance that the Christians declared the Egyptian god to be
the Joseph of the Bible, the son of
Sara, and rightfully carrying the
bushel. The position of the Egyptian
orthodox party is apprehended in a
more earnest spirit by the author,
belonging presumably to the third
century, of the Dialogue of the Gods,
preserved in a Latin translation among
the writings attributed to Appuleius,
in which the thrice-greatest Hermes
announces things future to Asklepios :
"Thou knowest withal, Asklepios,
that Egypt is a counterpart of heaven,
or, to speak more correctly, a transmigration and descent of the whole
heavenly administration and activity ;
indeed, to speak still more correctly,
our fatherland is the temple of the
whole universe. And yet a time will

restoration of the old faith, as well scientifically in the philosophy annexed to it as practically in the repelling of the attacks directed by the Christians against Polytheism, and in the revival of the heathen temple-worship and the heathen divination, had its true centre in Alexandria. Then, when the new faith conquered this stronghold also, the character of the country remained nevertheless true to itself ; Syria was the cradle of Christianity, Egypt was the cradle of monachism. Of the significance and the position of the Jewish body, in which the two cities likewise resembled each other, we have already spoken in another connection (p. 163). Immigrants called by the government into the land like the Hellenes, the Jews were doubtless inferior to these and were liable to poll-tax like the Egyptians, but accounted themselves, and were accounted, more than these. Their number amounted under Vespasian to a million, about the eighth part of the whole population of Egypt, and, like the Hellenes, they dwelt chiefly in the capital, of the five wards of which two were Jewish. In acknowledged independence, in repute, culture, and wealth, the body of Alexandrian Jews was even before the destruction of Jerusalem the first in the world ; and in consequence of this a good part of the last act of the Jewish tragedy, as has been already set forth, was played out on Egyptian soil.

Alexandria and Antioch were pre-eminently seats of wealthy merchants and manufacturers ; but in Antioch

set in, when it would appear as if Egypt had vainly with pious mind in diligent service cherished the divine, when all sacred worship of the gods will be without result and a failure. For the deity will betake itself back into heaven, Egypt will be forsaken, and the land, which was the seat of religious worships, will be deprived of the presence of divine power and left to its own resources. Then will this consecrated land, the abode of shrines and temples, be densely filled with graves and corpses. O Egypt, Egypt, of thy worships only rumours will be preserved, and even these will seem incredible to thy coming generations, only words will be preserved on the stones to tell of thy pious deeds, and Egypt will be inhabited by the Scythian or Indian or other such from the neighbouring barbarian land. New rights will be introduced, a new law, nothing holy, nothing religious, nothing worthy of heaven and of the celestials will be heard or in spirit believed. A painful separation of the gods from men sets in ; only the bad angels remain there, to mingle among mankind " (according to Bernays's translation, *Ges. Abh.* i. 330).

there was wanting the seaport and its belongings, and, however stirring matters were on the streets there, they bore no comparison with the life and doings of the Alexandrian artisans and sailors. On the other hand, for enjoyment of life, dramatic spectacles, dining, pleasures of love, Antioch had more to offer than the city in which " no one went idle." Literary amusements, linking themselves especially with the rhetorical exhibitions—such as we sketched in the description of Asia Minor—fell into the background in Egypt,[1] doubtless more amidst the pressure of the affairs of the day than through the influence of the numerous and well-paid *savants* living in Alexandria, and in great part natives of it. These men of the Museum, of whom we shall have to speak further on, did not prominently affect the character of the town as a whole, especially if they did their duty in diligent work. But the Alexandrian physicians were regarded as the best in the whole empire ; it is true that Egypt was no less the genuine home of quacks and of secret remedies, and of that strange civilised form of the "shepherd-medicine," in which pious simplicity and speculating deceit draped themselves in the mantle of science. Of the thrice-greatest Hermes we have already made mention (p. 261) ; the Alexandrian Sarapis, too, wrought more marvellous cures in antiquity than any one of his colleagues, and he infected even the practical emperor Vespasian, so that he too healed the blind and lame, but only in Alexandria.

Scholar-life in Alexandria.

Although the place which Alexandria occupies, or seems to occupy, in the intellectual and literary development of the later Greece and of Occidental culture generally cannot be fitly estimated in a description of the

---

[1] When the Romans ask from the famous rhetor Proaeresios (end of the third and beginning of the fourth century) one of his disciples for a professorial chair, he sends to them Eusebius from Alexandria ; " as respects rhetoric," it is said of the latter (Eunapius, *Proaer.* p. 92 Boiss.), " it is enough to say that he was an Egyptian ; for this people, no doubt, pursues versemaking passionately, but earnest oratory (ὁ σπουδαῖος Ἑρμῆς) is not at home among them." The remarkable resumption of Greek poetry in Egypt, to which, *e.g.* the epic of Nonnus belongs, lies beyond the bounds of our narrative.

local circumstances of Egypt, but only in the delineation of this development itself, the Alexandrian scholarship and its continuation under the Roman government are too remarkable a phenomenon not to have its general position touched on in this connection. We have already observed (p. 126) that the blending of the Oriental and the Hellenic intellectual world was accomplished pre-eminently in Egypt alongside of Syria ; and if the new faith which was to conquer the West issued from Syria, the science homogeneous with it—that philosophy which, alongside of and beyond the human mind, acknowledges and proclaims the supra-mundane God and the divine revelation—came pre-eminently from Egypt : probably already the new Pythagoreanism, certainly the philosophic Neo-Judaism—of which we have formerly spoken (p. 170)—as well as the new Platonism, whose founder, the Egyptian Plotinus, was likewise already mentioned (p. 126). Upon this interpenetration of Hellenic and Oriental elements, that was carried out especially in Alexandria, mainly depends the fact, that—as falls to be set forth more fully in surveying the state of things in Italy—the Hellenism there in the earlier imperial period bears pre-eminently an Egyptian form. As the old-new wisdoms associated with Pythagoras, Moses, Plato, penetrated from Alexandria into Italy, so Isis and her belongings played the first part in the easy, fashionable piety, which the Roman poets of the Augustan age and the Pompeian temples from that of Claudius exhibit to us. Art as practised in Egypt prevails in the Campanian frescoes of the same epoch, as in the Tiburtine villa of Hadrian. In keeping with this is the position which Alexandrian erudition occupies in the intellectual life of the imperial period. Outwardly it is based on the care of the state for intellectual interests, and would with more warrant link itself to the name of Alexander than to that of Alexandria ; it is the realisation of the thought that in a certain stage of civilisation art and science must be supported and promoted by the authority and the resources of the state, the consistent sequel of the

brilliant moment in the world's history which placed
Alexander and Aristotle side by side. It is not our
intention here to inquire how in this mighty conception
truth and error, the injuring and elevating of the intellectual
life, became mingled, nor is the scanty after-bloom
of the divine singing and of the high thinking of the
free Hellenes to be once more placed side by side with
the rank and yet also noble produce of the later
collecting, investigating, and arranging. If the institutions which sprang from this thought could not, or, what
was worse, could only apparently, renew to the Greek
nation what was irrecoverably lost, they granted to it
on the still free arena of the intellectual world the only
possible compensation, and that, too, a glorious one. For
us the local circumstances are above all to be taken into
account. Artificial gardens are in some measure independent of the soil, and it is not otherwise with these
scientific institutions ; only that they from their nature
are directed towards the courts. Material support may be
imparted to them otherwise ; but more important than
this is the favour of the highest circles, which swells their
sails, and the connections, which, meeting together in the
great centres, replenish and extend these circles of science.
In the better time of the monarchies of Alexander there
were as many such centres as there were states, and that
of the Lagid court was only the most highly-esteemed
among them. The Roman republic had brought the
others one after another into its power, and had set aside
with the courts also the scientific institutes and circles
belonging to them. The fact that the future Augustus,
when he did away with the last of these courts, allowed
the learned institutes connected with it to subsist, is a
genuine, and not the worst, indication of the changed
times. The more energetic and higher Philhellenism
of the government of the Caesars was distinguished to
its advantage from that of the republic by the fact that
it not merely allowed Greek literati to earn money in
Rome, but viewed and treated the great guardianship of
Greek science as a part of the sovereignty of Alexander.

No doubt, as in this regeneration of the empire as a whole, the building-plan was grander than the building. The royally patented and pensioned Muses, whom the Lagids had called to Alexandria, did not disdain to accept the like payments also from the Romans; and the imperial munificence was not inferior to the earlier regal. The fund for the library of Alexandria and the fund for free places for philosophers, poets, physicians, and scholars of all sorts,[1] as well as the immunities granted to these, were not diminished by Augustus, and were increased by the emperor Claudius—with the injunction, indeed, that the new Claudian academicians should have the Greek historical works of the singular founder publicly read year by year in their sittings. With the first library in the world Alexandria retained at the same time, through the whole imperial period, a certain primacy of scientific work, until Islam burnt the library and killed the ancient civilisation. It was not merely the opportunity thus offered, but at the same time the old tradition and turn of mind of these Hellenes, which preserved for the city that precedence, as indeed among the scholars the native Alexandrians are prominent in number and importance. In this epoch numerous and respectable labours of erudition, particularly philological and physical, proceeded from the circle of the *savants* "of the Museum," as they entitled themselves, like the Parisians "of the Institute"; but the literary importance, which the Alexandrian and the Pergamene court-science and court-art

---

[1] A "Homeric poet" ἐκ Μουσείου is ready to sing the praise of Memnon in four Homeric verses, without adding a word of his own (*C. I. Gr.* 4748). Hadrian makes an Alexandrian poet a member in reward for a loyal epigram (Athenaeus, xv. p. 677 *e*). Examples of rhetors from Hadrian's time may be seen in Philostratus, *Vit. Soph.* i. 22, 3 c. 25, 3. A φιλόσοφος ἀπὸ Μουσείου in Halicarnassus (*Bull. de corr. Hell.* iv. 405). At a later period, when the circus was everything, we find a noted pugilist figuring (so to say) as an honorary member of the philosophical class (inscription from Rome, *C. I. Gr.* 5914: νεωκόρος τοῦ μεγά-[λου Σαραπίδ]ος καὶ τῶν ἐν τῷ Μουσείῳ [σειτου]μένων ἀτελῶν φιλοσόφων; comp. *ib.* 4724, and Firmicus Maternus, *de errore prof. rel.* 13, 3). Οἱ ἐν Ἐφέσῳ ἀπὸ τοῦ Μουσείου ἰατροί (Wood, *Ephesus, inscriptions from tombs,* n. 7), a society of Ephesian physicians, have relation doubtless to the Museum at Alexandria, but were hardly members of it; they were rather trained in it.

had in the better epoch of Hellenism for the whole
Hellenic and Hellenising world, was never even remotely
attached to the Romano-Alexandrian. The cause lay
not in the want of talents or in other accidents, least of
all in the fact that places in the Museum were bestowed
by the emperor sometimes according to gifts and always
according to favour, and the government dealt with them
quite as with the horse of the knight and the posts of
officials of the household ; the case was not otherwise
at the older courts. Court-philosophers and court-poets
remained in Alexandria, but not the court ; it was here
very clearly apparent that the main matter was not
pensions and rewards, but the contact—quickening for
both sides—of great political and great scientific work.
The latter doubtless presented itself for the new monarchy
and brought its consequences with it ; but the place for
it was not Alexandria : this bloom of political development justly belonged to the Latins and to the Latin
capital. The Augustan poetry and Augustan science
attained, under similar circumstances, to a similar important and pleasing development with that attained by
the Hellenistic at the court of the Pergamenes and the
earlier Ptolemies. Even in the Greek circle, so far as the
Roman government operated upon it in the sense of the
Lagids, this development was linked more with Rome than
with Alexandria. It is true that the Greek libraries of
the capital were not equal to the Alexandrian, and there
was no institute in Rome comparable to the Alexandrian
Museum. But a position at the Roman libraries opened
up relations to the court. The professorship of Greek
rhetoric in the capital, instituted by Vespasian, filled up
and paid for by the government, gave to its holder,
although he was not an officer of the household in the
same sense as the imperial librarian, a similar position,
and was regarded, doubtless on that account, as the chief
professorial chair of the empire.[1] But, above all, the
office of imperial cabinet secretary in its Greek division
was the most esteemed and the most influential position

---

[1] 'Ο ἄνω θρόνος in Philostratus, *Vit. Soph.* ii. 10, 5.

to which a Greek man of letters could at all attain. Transference from the Alexandrian academy to such an office in the capital was demonstrably promotion.[1] Even apart from all which the Greek literati otherwise found in Rome alone, the court-positions and the court-offices were enough to draw the most distinguished of them thither rather than to the Egyptian " free table." The learned Alexandria of this time became a sort of "jointure" of Greek science, worthy of respect and useful, but of no pervading influence on the great movement of culture or mis-culture of the imperial period ; the places in the Museum were, as was reasonable, not seldom bestowed on scholars of note from abroad, and for the institution itself the books of the library were of more account than the burgesses of the great commercial and manufacturing city.

The military circumstances of Egypt laid down, just as in Syria, a double task for the troops there ; the protection of the south frontier and of the east coast, which indeed may not be remotely compared with that required for the line of the Euphrates, and the maintenance of internal order in the country as in the capital. The Roman garrison consisted, apart from the ships stationed at Alexandria and on the Nile, which seem chiefly to have served for the control of the customs, under Augustus of three legions, along with the not numerous auxiliary troops belonging to them, about 20,000 men. This was about half as many as he destined for all the Asiatic provinces—which was in keeping with the importance of this province for the new monarchy. But the occupy-

The Egyptian army.

---

[1] Examples are Chaeremon, the teacher of Nero, previously installed in Alexandria (Suidas, Διονύσιος᾽ Ἀλεξανδρεύς ; comp. Zeller, *Hermes*, xi. 430, and above, p. 259) ; Dionysius, son of Glaucus, at first in Alexandria, successor of Chaeremon, then from Nero down to Trajan librarian in Rome and imperial cabinet secretary (Suidas, *l.c.*) ; L. Julius Vestinus under Hadrian, who, even after the presidency of the Museum, filled the same positions as Dionysius in Rome (p. 248 note), known also as a philological author.

ing force was probably even under Augustus himself diminished about a third, and then under Domitian by about a further third. At first two legions were stationed outside of the capital ; but the main camp, and soon the only one, lay before its gates, where Caesar the younger had fought out the last battle with Antonius, in the suburb called accordingly Nicopolis. The suburb had its own amphitheatre and its own imperial popular festival, and was quite independently organised ; so that for a time the public amusements of Alexandria were thrown into the shade by those of Nicopolis. The immediate watching of the frontier fell to the auxiliaries. The same causes therefore which relaxed discipline in Syria—the police-character of their primary task and their immediate contact with the great capital—came into play also for the Egyptian troops ; to which fell to be added, that the bad custom of allowing to the soldiers with the standards a married life or at any rate a substitute for it, and of filling up the troop from their camp-children, had for long been naturalised among the Macedonian soldiers of the Ptolemies, and soon prevailed also among the Romans, at least up to a certain degree. Accordingly, the Egyptian corps, in which the Occidentals served still more rarely than in the other armies of the East, and which was recruited in great part from the citizens and the camp of Alexandria, appears to have been among all the sections of the army the least esteemed ; as indeed also the officers of this legion, as was already observed, were inferior in rank to those of the rest.

The properly military task of the Egyptian troops was closely connected with the measures for the elevation of Egyptian commerce. It will be convenient to take the two together, and to set forth in connection, in the first instance, the relations to the continental neighbours in the south, and then those to Arabia and India.

Aethiopia.   Egypt reaches on the south, as was already remarked, as far as the barrier which the last cataract, not far from Syene (Assouan), opposes to navigation. Beyond Syene begins the stock of the Kesch, as the Egyptians call them,

or, as the Greeks translated it, the dark-coloured, the
Aethiopians, probably akin to the Axomites to be afterwards mentioned, and, although perhaps sprung from the
same root as the Egyptians, at any rate confronting them
in historical development as a foreign people.   Further
to the south follow the Nahsiu of the Egyptians, that is,
the Blacks, the Nubians of the Greek, the modern Negroes.
The kings of Egypt had in better times extended their
rule far into the interior, or at least emigrant Egyptians
had established for themselves here dominions of their
own ;   the written monuments of the Pharaonic government go as far as above the third cataract to Dongola,
where Nabata (near Nûri) seems to have been the
centre of their settlements ; and considerably further up
the stream, some six days' journey to the north of Khar-
toum, near Shendy, in Sennaar, in the neighbourhood
of the long forgotten Aethiopian town Meroe, are found
groups of temples and pyramids, although destitute of
writing.   When Egypt became Roman, all this development of power was long a matter of the past ; and beyond
Syene there ruled an Aethiopian stock under queens, who
regularly bore the name or the title Candace,[1] and resided
in that once Egyptian Nabata in Dongola ; a people at
a low stage of civilisation, predominantly shepherds, in a
position to bring into the field an army of 30,000, but
equipped with shields of ox-hides, armed mostly not with
swords, but with axes or lances and iron-mounted clubs,
predatory neighbours, not a match for the Romans in
combat.   In the year 730 or 731 these invaded the 24, 23.
Roman territory—as they asserted, because the presidents
of the nearest nomes had injured them—as the Romans
thought, because the Egyptian troops were then to a
large extent occupied in Arabia, and they hoped to be
able to plunder with immunity.   In reality they over- War with
came the three cohorts who covered the frontier, and queen Candace.
dragged away the inhabitants from the nearest Egyptian

---

[1] The eunuch of Candace, who
reads in Isaiah (Acts of the Apostles,
viii. 27) is well known ;   and a
Candace reigned also in Nero's time
(Plinius, *H. N.* vi. 29, 182).

districts—Philae, Elephantine, Syene—as slaves, and the statues of the emperor, which they found there, as tokens of victory. But the governor, who just then took up the administration of the province, Gaius Petronius, speedily requited the attack ; with 10,000 infantry and 800 cavalry he not merely drove them out, but followed them along the Nile into their own land, defeated them emphatically at Pselchis (Dekkeh), and stormed their stronghold Premis (Ibrim), as well as the capital itself, which he destroyed. It is true that the queen, a brave woman, renewed the attack next year and attempted to storm Premis, where a Roman garrison had been left ; but Petronius brought seasonable relief, and so the Aethiopian queen determined to send envoys and to sue for peace. The emperor not merely granted it, but gave orders to evacuate the subject territory, and rejected the proposal of his governor to make the vanquished tributary. This event, otherwise not important, is remarkable in so far as just then the definite resolution of the Roman government became apparent, to maintain absolutely the Nile valley as far as the river was navigable, but not at all to contemplate taking possession of the wide districts on the upper Nile. Only the tract from Syene, where under Augustus the frontier-troops were stationed, as far as Hiera Sycaminos (Maharraka), the so-called Twelve-mile-land (Δωδεκάσχοινος), while never organised as a nome and never viewed as a part of Egypt, was yet regarded as belonging to the empire ; and at least under Domitian the posts were even advanced as far as Hiera Sycaminos.[1]

[1] That the imperial frontier reached to Hiera Sycaminos, is evident for the second century from Ptolemaeus, v. 5, 74, for the time of Diocletian from the Itineraries, which carry the imperial roads thus far. In the *Notitia dignitatum*, a century later, the posts again do not reach beyond Syene, Philae, Elephantine. In the tract from Philae to Hiera Sycaminos, the Dodecaschoinos of Herodotus (ii. 29) temple-tribute appears to have been raised already in early times for the Isis of Philae always common to the Egyptians and Aethiopians ; but Greek inscriptions from the Lagid period have not been found here, whereas numerous dated ones occur from the Roman period, the oldest from the time of Augustus (Pselchis, 2 A.D. ; *C. I. Gr.* n. 5086), and of Tiberius (*ib.* 26 A.D., n. 5104, 33 A.D., n. 5101), the most recent from that of Philippus (Kardassi, 248 A.D., n. 5010). These do not prove absolutely that the place where the inscription was found belonged to the empire ; but that of a land-measuring

On that footing substantially the matter remained. The Oriental expedition planned by Nero (p. 61) was certainly intended to embrace Aethiopia; but it did not go beyond the preliminary reconnoitring of the country by Roman officers as far as Meroe. The relations with the neighbours on the Egyptian southern frontier down to the middle of the third century must have been on the whole of a peaceful kind, although there were not wanting minor quarrels with that Candace and with her successors, who appear to have maintained their position for a considerable time, and subsequently perhaps with other tribes, that attained to ascendency beyond the imperial bounds.

It was not till the empire was unhinged in the period of Valerian and Gallienus, that the neighbours broke over this boundary. We have already mentioned (p. 250) that the Blemyes settled in the mountains on the south-east frontier, formerly obeying the Aethiopians, a barbarous people of revolting savageness, who even centuries later had not abandoned human sacrifices, advanced at this epoch independently against Egypt, and by an understanding with the Palmyrenes occupied a good part of upper Egypt, and held it for a series of years. The vigorous emperor Probus drove them out; but the inroads once begun did not cease,[1] and the emperor Diocletian resolved to draw

The Blemyes.

soldier of the year 33 (n. 5101), and that of a *praesidium* of the year 84 (Talmis, n. 5042 f.), as well as numerous others certainly presuppose it. Beyond the frontier indicated no similar stone has ever been found; for the remarkable inscription of the *regina* (*C. I. L.* iii. 83), found at Messaurât, to the south of Shendy (16° 25′ lat., 5 leagues to the south of the ruins of Naga), the most southern of all known Latin inscriptions, now in the Berlin Museum, has been set up, not by a Roman subject, but presumably by an envoy of an African queen, who was returning from Rome, and who spoke Latin perhaps only in order to show that he had been in Rome.

[1] The *tropaea Niliaca, sub quibus*

Aethiops et Indus intremuit, in an oration probably held in the year 296 (Paneg. v. 5), apply to such a *rencontre,* not to the Egyptian insurrection; and the oration of the year 289 speaks of attacks of the Blemyes (Paneg. iii. 17). — Procopius, *Bell. Pers.* i. 19, reports the cession of the "Twelve-mile-territory" to the Nubians. It is mentioned as standing under the dominion, not of the Nubians, but of the Blemyes by Olympiodorus, *fr.* 37, Müll. and the inscription of Silko, *C. I. Gr.* 5072. The fragment recently brought to light of a Greek heroic poem as to the victory of a late Roman emperor over the Blemyes is referred by Bücheler (*Rhein. Mus.* xxxix. 279 f.) to that of Marcianus, in the year 451 (comp. Priscus, *fr.* 27).

back the frontier. The narrow "Twelve-mile-land" demanded a strong garrison, and brought in little to the
state. The Nubians, who roamed in the Libyan desert,
and were constantly visiting in particular the great Oasis,
agreed to give up their old abodes and to settle in this
region, which was formally ceded to them ; at the same
time fixed annual payments were made to them as well
as to their eastern neighbours the Blemyes, nominally in
order to compensate them for guarding the frontier, in
reality beyond doubt to buy off their plundering expeditions, which nevertheless of course did not cease. It was
a retrograde step—the first, since Egypt became Roman.

Aethiopian commercial traffic. Of the mercantile intercourse on this frontier little is
reported from antiquity. As the cataracts of the upper
Nile closed the direct route by water, the traffic between
the interior of Africa and the Egyptians, particularly the
trade in ivory, was carried on in the Roman period more
by way of the Abyssinian ports than along the Nile ; but
it was not wanting also in this direction.[1] The Aethiopians who dwelt in numbers beside the Egyptians on
the island of Philae were evidently mostly merchants, and
the border-peace that here prevailed must have contributed
its part to the prosperity of the frontier-towns of upper
Egypt and of Egyptian trade generally.

The Egyptian east coast and general commerce. The east coast of Egypt presented to the development
of general traffic a problem difficult of solution. The
thoroughly desolate and rocky shore was incapable of
culture proper, and in ancient as in later times a desert.[2]
On the other hand the two seas, eminently important for
the development of culture in the ancient world, the
Mediterranean and the Red or Indian, approach each
other most closely at the two most northern extremities
of the latter, the Persian and the Arabian gulfs ; the
former receives into it the Euphrates, which in the middle
of its course comes near to the Mediterranean ; the latter
is only a few days' march distant from the Nile, which

---

[1] Juvenal (xi. 124) mentions the
elephant's teeth, *quos mittit porta
Syenes.*

[2] According to the mode in which

Ptolemy (iv. 5, 14, 15) treats of this
coast, it seems, just like the "Twelve-
mile-land," to have lain outside of the
division into nomes.

flows into the same sea. Hence in ancient times the commercial intercourse between the East and the West took preponderantly either the direction along the Euphrates to the Syrian and Arabian coast, or it made its way from the east coast of Egypt to the Nile. The traffic routes from the Euphrates were older than those by way of the Nile ; but the latter had the advantage of the stream being better for navigation and of the shorter land-transport ; the getting rid of the latter by preparing an artificial water-route was in the case of the Euphrates excluded, in that of Egypt found in ancient as in modern times difficult doubtless, but not impossible. Accordingly nature itself prescribed to the land of Egypt to connect the east coast with the course of the Nile and the northern coast by land or water routes ; and the beginnings of such structures go back to the time of those native rulers who first opened up Egypt to foreign countries and to traffic on a great scale. Following in the traces apparently of older structures of the great rulers of Egypt, Sethi I. and Rhamses II., king Necho, the son of Psammetichus (610- 594 B.C.) began the building of a canal, which, branching off from the Nile in the neighbourhood of Cairo, was to furnish a water-communication with the bitter lakes near Ismailia, and through these with the Red Sea, without being able, however, to complete the work. That in this he had in view not merely the control of the Arabian Gulf and the commercial traffic with the Arabians, but already brought within his horizon the Persian and the Indian seas, and the more remote East, is probable, for this reason, that the same ruler suggested the only cir-cumnavigation of Africa executed in antiquity. Beyond doubt thus thought king Darius I., the lord of Persia as well as of Egypt ; he completed the canal, but, as his memorial-stones found on the spot mention, he caused it to be filled up again, probably because his engineers feared that the water of the sea, admitted into the canal, would overflow the fields of Egypt.

The sea route to India.

The rivalry of the Lagids and the Seleucids, which dominated the policy of the post-Alexandrine period generally, was at the same time a contest between the Euphrates and the Nile. The former was in possession, the latter the pretender ; and in the better time of the Lagids the peaceful offensive was pursued with great energy. Not only was that canal undertaken by Necho and Darius, now named the "river of Ptolemaeus," opened for the first time to navigation by the second Ptolemy Philadelphus († 247 B.C.) ; but comprehensive harbour-structures were carried out at the points of the difficult east coast that were best fitted for the security of the ships

The Egyptian eastern ports.

and for the connection with the Nile. Above all, this was done at the mouth of the canal leading to the Nile, at the townships of Arsinoe, Cleopatris, Clysma, all three in the region of the present Suez. Further downward, besides several minor structures, arose the two important emporia, Myos Hormos, somewhat above the present Kosêr, and Berenice, in the land of the Trogodytes, nearly in the same latitude with Syene on the Nile as well as with the Arabian port Leuce Come, the former distant six or seven, the latter eleven days' march from the town Coptos, near which the Nile bends farthest to the eastward, and connected with this chief emporium on the Nile by roads constructed across the desert and provided with large cisterns. The goods traffic of the time of the Ptolemies probably went less through the canal than by these land routes to Coptos.

Abyssinia.

Beyond that Berenice, in the land of the Trogodytes, the Egypt proper of the Lagids did not extend. The settlements lying farther to the south, Ptolemais "for the chase" below Suâkim, and the southmost township of the Lagid kingdom, the subsequent Adulis, at that time perhaps named "Berenice the Golden" or "near Saba," Zula not far from the present Massowah, by far the best harbour on all this coast, were not more than coast-forts and had no communication by land with Egypt. These remote settlements were beyond doubt either lost or voluntarily abandoned under the later Lagids, and at the epoch when the Roman rule began, the Trogodytic Berenice was on the coast, like Syene in the interior, the limit of the empire.

In this region, never occupied or early evacuated by the Egyptians there was formed—whether at the end of the Lagid epoch or in the first age of the empire—an independent state of some extent and importance, that of the Axomites,[1] corresponding to the modern Habesh. It derives its name from the town Axômis, the modern Axum, situated in the heart of this Alpine country eight days' journey from the sea, in the modern country of Tigre ; the already-mentioned best emporium on this coast, Adulis in the bay of Massowah, served it as a port. The original population of the kingdom of Axômis, of which tolerably pure remnants still maintain themselves at the present day in individual tracts of the interior, belonged from its language, the Agau, to the same Hamitic cycle with the modern Bego, Sali, Dankali, Somali, Galla ; to the Egyptian population this linguistic circle seems related in a similar way as the Greeks to the Celts and Slaves, so that here doubtless for research an affinity may subsist, but for their historical existence rather nothing but contrast. But before our knowledge of this country so much as begins, superior Semitic immigrants belonging to the Himyaritic stocks of southern Arabia must have crossed the narrow gulf of the sea and rendered their language as well as their writing at home there. The old written language of Habesh, extinct in popular use since the seventeenth century, the Ge'ez, or as it is for the most part erroneously

---

[1] Our best information as to the kingdom of Axomis is obtained from a stone erected by one of its kings, beyond doubt in the better period of the empire, at Adulis (*C. I. Gr.* 5127 *b*), a sort of writing commemorative of the deeds of this apparent empire-founder in the style of that of Darius at Persepolis, or that of Augustus at Ancyra, and fixed on the king's throne, before which down to the sixth century criminals were executed. The skilful disquisition of Dillmann (*Abh. der Berliner Akademie*, 1877, p. 195 f.), explains as much of it as is explicable. From the Roman standpoint it is to be noted that the king does not name the Romans, but clearly has in view their imperial frontiers when he subdues the Tangaites μέχρι τῶν τῆς Αἰγύπτου ὁρίων, and constructs a road ἀπὸ τῶν τῆς ἐμῆς βασιλείας τόπων μέχρι Αἰγύπτου, and further, names as the northern limit of his Arabian expedition Leuce Come, the last Roman station on the Arabian west coast. Hence it follows further, that this inscription is more recent than the Periplus of the Red Sea written under Vespasian ; for according to this (c. 5) the king of Axomis rules ἀπὸ τῶν Μοσχοφάγων μέχρι τῆς ἄλλης Βαρβαρίας, and this is to be understood exclusively, since he names in c. 2 the τύραννοι of the Moscophages, and likewise remarks

termed, the Aethiopic,[1] is purely Semitic,[2] and the still living dialects, the Amhara and the Tigriña, are so also in the main, only disturbed by the influence of the older Agau.

Its extent and development. As to the beginnings of this commonwealth no tradition has been preserved. At the end of Nero's time, and perhaps already long before, the king of the Axomites ruled on the African coast nearly from Suâkim to the Straits of Bab el Mandeb. Some time afterwards—the epoch cannot be more precisely defined—we find him as a frontier-neighbour of the Romans on the southern border of Egypt, and on the other coast of the Arabian Gulf in warlike activity in the territory intervening between the Roman possession and that of the Sabaeans, and so coming into immediate contact towards the north with the Roman territory also in Arabia ; commanding, moreover, the African coast outside of the Gulf perhaps as far as Cape Guardafui. How far his territory of Axômis extended inland is not clear ; Aethiopia, that is, Sennaar and Dongola, at least in the earlier imperial period, hardly belonged to it ; perhaps at this time the kingdom of Nabata may have subsisted alongside of the Axomitic. Where the Axomites meet us, we find them at a comparatively advanced stage of development. Under Augustus the Egyptian commercial traffic increased not less with these African harbours than with India. The king had the command not merely of an army, but, as his very relations to Arabia presuppose, also of a fleet. A Greek merchant, who was present in Adulis, terms king

in c. 14, that beyond the Straits of Bab el Mandeb there is no "king," but only "tyrants." Thus at that time the Axomitic kingdom did not reach to the Roman frontier, but only to somewhere about Ptolemais " of the chase," just as in the other direction not to Cape Guardafui, but only as far as the Straits of Bab el Mandeb. Nor does the Periplus speak of possessions of the king of Axomis on the Arabian coast, although he on several occasions mentions the dynasts there.

[1] The name of the Aethiopians was associated in the better period with the country on the Upper Nile, especially with the kingdoms of Meroe and Nabata (p. 275), and so with the region which we now call Nubia. In later antiquity, for example by Procopius, the designation is referred to the state of Axomis, and hence in more recent times is frequently employed for Abyssinia.

[2] Hence the legend that the Axomites were Syrians settled by Alexander in Africa, and still spoke Syrian (Philostorgius, *Hist. Eccl.* iii. 6).

Zoskales, who ruled in Vespasian's time in Axômis, an
upright man and acquainted with Greek writing ; one of
his successors has set up on the spot a memorial-writing
composed in current Greek which told his deeds to the
foreigners ; he even names himself in it a son of Ares
—which title the kings of the Axomites retained down to
the fourth century—and dedicates the throne, which bears
that memorial inscription, to Zeus, to Ares, and to
Poseidon.   Already in Zoskales's time that foreigner
names Adulis a well organised emporium ; his successors
compelled the roving tribes of the Arabian coast to keep
peace by land and by sea, and restored a land communication from their capital to the Roman frontier, which,
considering the nature of this district primarily left
dependent on communication by sea, was not to be
esteemed of slight account.   Under Vespasian brass
pieces, which were divided according to need, served the
natives instead of money, and Roman coin circulated only
among the strangers settled in Adulis ; in the later
imperial period the kings themselves coined. The Axomite
ruler withal calls himself king of kings, and no trace
points to Roman clientship ; he practises coining in gold,
which the Romans did not allow, not merely in their own
territory but even within the range of their power.   There
was hardly another land in the imperial period beyond
the Romano-Hellenic bounds which had appropriated to
itself Hellenic habits with equal independence and to an
equal extent as the state of Habesh.   That in the course
of time the popular language, indigenous or rather naturalised from Arabia, gained the upper hand and dispossessed the Greek, is probably traceable partly to Arabian
influence, partly to that of Christianity and the revival
connected with it of the popular dialects, such as we found
also in Syria and Egypt ; and it does not exclude the
view that the Greek language in Axomis and Adulis in
the first and second centuries of our era had a similar
position to what it had in Syria and Egypt, so far as it is
allowable to compare small and great.

Of political relations of the Romans to the state of

Rome and the Axomites.

Axomis hardly anything is mentioned from the first three centuries of our era, to which our narrative is confined. With the rest of Egypt they took possession also of the ports of the east coast down to the remote Trogodytic Berenice, which on account of that remoteness was in the Roman period placed under a commandant of its own.[1] Of extending their territory into the inhospitable and worthless mountains along the coast there was never any thought ; nor can the sparse population, standing at the lowest stage of development, in the immediately adjoining region have ever given serious trouble to the Romans. As little did the Caesars attempt, as the early Lagids had done, to possess themselves of the emporia of the Axomitic coast.   There is express mention only of the fact that envoys of the Axomite kings negotiated with the emperor Aurelian.   But this very silence, as well as the formerly indicated independent position of the ruler,[2] leads to the inference that here the recognised frontier was permanently respected on both sides, and that a relation of good neighbourhood subsisted, which proved advantageous to the interests of peace and especially of Egyptian commerce.   That the latter, especially the important traffic in ivory, in which Adulis was the chief entrepot for the interior of Africa, was carried on predominantly from Egypt and in Egyptian vessels, cannot—considering the superior civilisation of Egypt—be subject to any doubt even as regards the Lagid period ; and in Roman times this traffic probably only increased in amount, without undergoing further change.

The west coast of Arabia.

Far more important for Egypt and the Roman empire generally than the traffic with the African south was that

---

[1] This is the *praefectus praesidiorum et montis Beronices* (*C. I. L.* ix. 3083), *praefectus montis Berenicidis* (Orelli, 3881), *praefectus Bernicidis* (*C. I. L.* x. 1129), an officer of equestrian rank, analogous to those adduced above (p. 249), as stationed in Alexandria.

[2] The letter, which the emperor Constantius in the year 356 directs to Aeizanas, the king of the Axomites at that time, is that of one ruler to another on an equal footing ; he requests his friendly and neighbourly assistance against the spread of the Athanasian heresy, and for the deposition and delivering up of an Axomitic clergyman suspected of it.   The fellowship of culture comes here into the more definite prominence, as the Christian invokes against the Christian the arm of the heathen.

which subsisted with Arabia and the coasts situated farther
to the east. The Arabian peninsula remained aloof from
the sphere of Hellenic culture. It would possibly have
been otherwise had king Alexander lived a year longer ;
death swept him away amidst the preparations for sailing
round and occupying the already-explored south coast of
Arabia, setting out from the Persian Gulf. But the voyage
which the great king had not been able to enter on was
never undertaken by any Greek after him. From the
most remote times, on the other hand, a lively intercourse
had taken place between the two coasts of the Arabian
Gulf over its moderately broad waters. In the Egyptian
accounts from the time of the Pharaohs the voyages to
the land of Punt, and the spoils thence brought home in
frankincense, ebony, emeralds, leopards' skins, play an
important part. It has been already (p. 148) mentioned
that subsequently the northern portion of the Arabian
west coast belonged to the territory of the Nabataeans,
and with this came into the power of the Romans. This
was a desolate beach ;[1] only the emporium Leuce Come,
the last town of the Nabataeans and so far also of the
Roman empire, was not merely in maritime intercourse

[1] Inland lay the primeval Teimâ, the son of Ishmael of Genesis, enumerated by the Assyrian king Tiglath-Pilesar in the eighth century before Christ among his conquests, named by the prophet Jeremiah together with Sidon, around which gather in a remarkable way Assyrian, Egyptian, Arabian relations, the further unfolding of which, after bold travellers have opened up the place, we may await from Oriental research. In Teimâ itself Euting recently found Aramaic inscriptions of the oldest epoch (Nöldeke, *Sitzungsberichte der Berliner Akademie*, 1884, p. 813 f.) From the not far distant place Medâin-Sâlih (Hijr) proceed certain coins modelled after the Attic, which in part replace the owl of Pallas by that image of a god which the Egyptians designate as Besa the lord of Punt, *i.e.* of Arabia (Erman, *Zeitschrift für Numismatik*, ix. 296 f.) We have already mentioned the Nabataean inscriptions just found there (p. 148, note 3). Not far from thence, near 'Ola (el-Ally) inscriptions have been found, which correspond in the writing and in the names of gods and kings to those of the South-Arabian Minaeans, and show that these had a considerable station here, sixty days' journey from their home, but on the frankincense-route mentioned by Eratosthenes, from Minaea to Aelana ; and alongside of these others of a cognate but not identical south-Arabian stock (D. H. Müller in the *Berichte der Wiener Akademie* of 17th December 1884). The Minaean inscriptions belong beyond doubt to the pre-Roman period. As on the annexation of the Nabataean kingdom by Trajan these districts were abandoned (p. 152), from that time another south-Arabian tribe may have ruled there.

with Berenice lying opposite, but was also the starting-point of the caravan-route leading to Petra and thence to the ports of southern Syria, and in so far, one of the centres of the traffic between the East and the West (p. 151). The adjoining regions on the south, northward and southward of the modern Mecca, corresponded in their natural character to the opposite Trogodyte country, and were, like this, neither politically nor commercially of importance, nor yet apparently united under one sceptre, but occupied by roving tribes. But at the south end of this gulf was the home of the only Arabic stock, which attained to greater importance in the pre-Islamic period. The Greeks and the Romans name these Arabs in the earlier period after the people most prominent at that time Sabaeans, in later times after another tribe usually Homerites, as, according to the new Arabic form of the latter name, now for the most part Himjarites.

The state of the Homerites. The development of this remarkable people had reached a considerable stage long before the beginning of the Roman rule over Egypt.[1] Its native seat, the Arabia Felix of the ancients, the region of Mocha and Aden, is surrounded by a narrow plain along the shore intensely hot and desolate, but the healthy and temperate interior of Yemen and Hadramaut produces on the mountain-slopes and in the valleys a luxuriant vegetation, and the numerous mountain-waters permit in many respects with careful management a garden-like cultivation. We have even at the present day an expressive testimony to the rich and peculiar civilisation of this region in the remains

---

[1] The accounts connected with the trade in frankincense in Theophrastus († 287 B.C.; *Hist. plant.* ix. 4) and more fully in Eratosthenes († 194 B.C.); in Strabo (xvi. 4, 2, p. 768) of the four great tribes of the Minaeans (Mamali Theophr.?) with the capital Carna; the Sabaeans (Saba Theophr.) with the capital Mariaba; the Cattabanes (Kitibaena Theophr.) with the capital Tamna; the Chatramotitae (Hadramyta Theophr.) with the capital Sabata, describe the very circle out of which the Homerite kingdom developed itself, and indicate its beginnings. The much sought for Minaei are now pointed out with certainty in Ma'in in the interior above Marib and Hadramaut, where hundreds of inscriptions have been found, and have yielded already no fewer than twenty-six kings' names. Mariaba is even now named Marib. The region Chatramotitis or Chatramitis is Hadramaut.

of city-walls and towers, of useful buildings, particularly aqueducts, and temples covered with inscriptions, which completely confirm the description of ancient authors as to the magnificence and luxury of this region ; the Arabian geographers have written books concerning the strongholds and castles of the numerous petty princes of Yemen. Famous are the ruins of the mighty embankment which once in the valley of Mariaba dammed up the river Dana and rendered it possible to water the fields upwards,[1] and from the bursting of which, and the migration alleged to have been thereby occasioned of the inhabitants of Yemen to the north the Arabs for long counted their years. But above all this district was one of the original seats of wholesale traffic by land and by sea, not merely because its productions, frankincense, precious stones, gum, cassia, aloes, senna, myrrh, and numerous other drugs called for export, but also because this Semitic stock was, just like that of the Phoenicians, formed by its whole character for commerce ; Strabo says, just like the more recent travellers, that the Arabs are all traders and merchants. The coining of silver is here old and peculiar ; the coins were at first modelled after Athenian dies, and

---

[1] The remarkable remains of this structure, executed with the greatest precision and skill, are described by Arnaud (*Journal Asiatique*, 7 série, tome 3, for the year 1874, p. 3 f. with plans ; comp. Ritter, *Erdkunde*, xii. 861). On the two sides of the embankment, which has now almost wholly disappeared, stand respectively two stone structures built of square blocks, of conical almost cylindrical form, between which a narrow opening is found for the water flowing out of the basin ; at least on the one side a canal lined with pebbles leads it to this outlet. It was once closed with planks placed one above another, which could be individually removed, to carry the water away as might be needed. The one of those stone cylinders bears the following inscription (according to the translation, not indeed quite certain in all its details,

of D. H. Müller, *Wiener Sitzungs-berichte*, vol. xcvii. 1880, p. 965) : "Jata'amar the glorious, son of Samah'alî the sublime, prince of Saba, caused the Balap (mountain) to be pierced (and erected) the sluice-structure named Rahab for easier irrigation." We have no secure basis for fixing the chronological place of this and numerous other royal names of the Sabaean inscriptions. The Assyrian king Sargon says in the Khorsabad inscription, after he has narrated the vanquishing of the king of Gaza, Hanno, in the year 716 B.C. : "I received the tribute of Pharaoh the king of Egypt, of Shamsiya the queen of Arabia, and of Ithamara the Sabaean ; gold, herbs of the eastern land, slaves, horses, and camels" (Müller, *l. c.* p. 988 ; Duncker, *Gesch. des Alterthums*, ii.[5] p. 327).

later after Roman coins of Augustus, but on an independent, probably Babylonian basis.[1] From the land of these Arabians the original frankincense-routes led across the desert to the marts on the Arabian gulf, Aelana and the already-mentioned Leuce Come, and the emporia of Syria, Petra and Gaza;[2] these routes of the land-traffic, which along with those of the Euphrates and the Nile, furnish the means of intercourse between East and West from the earliest times, may be conjectured to be the proper basis of the prosperity of Yemen. But the sea-traffic likewise soon became associated with them; the great mart for this was Adane, the modern Aden. From this the goods went by water, certainly in the main in Arabian ships, either to those same marts on the Arabian gulf and so to the Syrian ports, or to Berenice and Myos Hormos, and from thence to Coptos and Alexandria. We have already stated that the same Arabs likewise at a very early time possessed themselves of the opposite coast, and transplanted their language, their writing and their civilisation to Habesh. If Coptos, the Nile-emporium for the eastern traffic, had just as many Arab as Egyptian inhabitants, if even the emerald-mines above Berenice (near Jebel Zebâra) were worked by the Arabs, this shows that in the Lagid state itself they had the trade up to a certain degree in their hands; and its passive attitude in respect to the traffic on the Arabian Sea, whither at most an expedition against the pirates was once undertaken,[3] is the more readily intelligible, if a state well

[1] Sallet in the *Berliner Zeitschrift für Numismatik*, viii. 243; J. H. Mordtmann in the *Wiener Numism. Zeitschrift*, xii. 289.

[2] Pliny, *H. N.* xii. 14, 65, reckons the cost of a camel's load of frankincense by the land-route from the Arabian coast to Gaza at 688 denarii (=£30). "Along the whole tract fodder and water and shelter and various custom-dues have to be paid for; then the priests demand certain shares and the scribes of the kings; moreover the guards and the halberdiers and the body-guards and servants have their exactions; to which our imperial dues fall to be added." In the case of the water-transport these intervening expenses were not incurred.

[3] The chastising of the pirates is reported by Agatharchides in Diodorus, iii. 43, and Strabo, xvi. 4, 18, p. 777. But Ezion-Geber in Palestine, on the Elanitic gulf, ἡ νῦν Βερενίκη καλεῖται (Josephus, *Arch.* viii. 6, 4), was so called certainly not from an Egyptian princess (Droysen, *Hellenismus*, iii. 2, 349), but from the Jewess of Titus.

organised and powerful at sea ruled these waters. We
meet the Arabs of Yemen even beyond their own sea.
Adane remained down to the Roman imperial times a
mart of traffic on the one hand with India, on the other
with Egypt, and, in spite of its own unfavourable position
on the treeless shore, rose to such prosperity that the
name of "Arabia Felix" had primary reference to this
town. The dominion, which in our days the Imam of
Muscat in the south-east of the peninsula has exercised
over the islands of Socotra and Zanzibar and the African
east coast from Cape Guardafui southward, pertained in
Vespasian's time "from of old" to the princes of Arabia ;
the island of Dioscorides, that same Socotra, belonged
then to the king of Hadramaut, Azania, that is, the coast
of Somal and further southward, to one of the viceroys of
his western neighbour, the king of the Homerites. The
southernmost station on the east African coast which the
Egyptian merchants knew of, Rhapta in the region of
Zanzibar, was leased from this sheikh by the merchants of
Muza, that is nearly the modern Mocha, "and they send
thither their trading-ships, mostly manned by Arabian
captains and sailors, who are accustomed to deal and
are often connected by marriage with the natives, and are
acquainted with the localities and the languages of the
country." The cultivation of the soil and industry went
hand in hand with commerce ; in the houses of rank in
India, Arabian wine was drunk alongside of the Falernian
from Italy and the Laodicene from Syria ; and the lances
and shoemakers' awls, which the natives of the coast of
Malabar purchased from the foreign traders were manufactured at Muza. Thus this region, which moreover
sold much and bought little, became one of the richest in
the world.

How far its political development kept pace with the
economic, cannot be determined for the pre-Roman and
earlier imperial period ; only this much seems to result
both from the accounts of the Occidentals and from
the native inscriptions, that this south-west point of
Arabia was divided among several independent rulers with

territories of moderate size. There subsisted in that quarter, alongside of the more prominent Sabaeans and Homerites, the already-mentioned Chatramotitae in the Hadramaut, and northward in the interior the Minaeans, all under princes of their own.

With reference to the Arabians of Yemen the Romans pursued the very opposite policy to that adopted towards the Axomites. Augustus, for whom the non-enlargement of the empire was the starting-point of the imperial government, and who allowed almost all the plans of conquest of his father and master to drop, made an exception of the south-west coast of Arabia, and here took aggressive measures of his own free will. This was done on account of the position which this group of peoples occupied at that time in Indo-Egyptian commercial intercourse. In order to bring the province of his dominions, which was politically and financially the most important, up, in an economic aspect, to the level which his predecessors in rule had neglected to establish or had allowed to decline, he needed above all to obtain inter-communication between Arabia and India on the one hand and Europe on the other. The Nile-route for long competed successfully with the Arabian and the Euphrates routes; but Egypt played in this respect, as we saw, a subordinate part at least under the later Lagids. A trading rivalry subsisted not with the Axomites, but doubtless with the Arabians; if the Egyptian traffic was to be converted from a passive into an active, from indirect into direct, the Arabs had to be overthrown; and this it was that Augustus desired and the Roman government in some measure achieved.

25. Expedition of Gallus.

In the sixth year of his reign in Egypt (end of 729) Augustus despatched a fleet, fitted out expressly for this expedition, of 80 warships and 130 transports, and the half of the Egyptian army, a corps of 10,000 men, without reckoning the contingents of the two nearest client kings, the Nabataean Obodas and the Jew Herod, against the states of Yemen, in order either to subjugate or at

least to ruin them,[1] while at the same time the treasures
there accumulated were certainly taken into account. But
the enterprise completely miscarried, and that from the
incapacity of the leader, the governor of Egypt at the time,
Gaius Aelius Gallus.[2] Since the occupation and the
possession of the desolate coast from Leuce Come downwards to the frontier of the enemy's territory was of no
consequence at all, it was necessary that the expedition
should be directed immediately against the latter, and that
the army should be conducted from the most southern
Egyptian port at once into Arabia Felix.[3] Instead of this

[1] This (προσοικειοῦσθαι τούτους —
τοὺς Ἄραβας — ἢ καταστρέφεσθαι :
Strabo, xvi. 4, 22 p. 780; εἰ μὴ ὁ
Συλλαῖος αὐτὸν—τὸν Γάλλον—προυδί-
δου, κἂν κατεστρέψατο τὴν Εὐδαίμονα
πᾶσαν : ib. xvii. 1, 53, p. 819) was
the proper aim of the expedition,
although also the hope of spoil, just at
that time very welcome for the trea-
sury, is expressly mentioned.

[2] The account of Strabo (xvi. 4, 22
f., p. 780) as to the Arabian expedition
of his "friend" Gallus (φίλος ἡμῖν καὶ
ἑταῖρος, Strabo, ii. 5, 12, p. 118), in
whose train he travelled in Egypt, is
indeed trustworthy and honest, like all
his accounts, but evidently accepted
from this friend without any criticism.
The battle in which 10,000 of the
enemy and two Romans fell, and the
total number of the fallen in this campaign, which is seven, are self-con-
demned ; but not better is the attempt
to devolve the want of success on the
Nabataean vizier Syllaeos by means of
a "treachery," such as is familiar with
defeated generals. Certainly the latter
was so far fitted for a scapegoat, as he
some years afterwards was on the
instigation of Herod brought to trial
before Augustus, condemned and
executed (Josephus, *Arch.* xvi. 10);
but although we possess the report of
the agent who managed this matter
for Herod in Rome, there is not a
word to be found in it of this betrayal.
That Syllaeos should have had the
design of first destroying the Arabians
by means of the Romans, and then of

destroying the latter themselves, as
Strabo "thinks," is, looking to the
position of the client-states of Rome,
quite irrational. It might rather be
thought that Syllaeos was averse to
the expedition, because the commercial
traffic through the Nabataean land
might be injured by it. But to accuse
the Arabian minister of treachery because the Roman transports were not
fitted for navigating the Arabian coast,
or because the Roman army was compelled to carry water with it on camels,
to eat durra and dates instead of bread
and flesh, and butter instead of oil ;
to bring forward the deceitfulness of
the guidance as an excuse for the fact
that 180 days were employed for the
forward march over a distance overtaken on the return march in 60 days ;
and lastly, to criticise the quite correct
remark of Syllaeos that a march by
land from Arsinoe to Leuce Come was
impracticable, by saying that a caravan
route went thence to Petra, only
shows what a Roman of rank was able
to make a Greek man of letters believe.

[3] The sharpest criticism of the campaign is furnished by the detailed
account of the Egyptian merchant as
to the state of the Arabian coast from
Leuce Come (el-Haura to the north
of Janbô, the port of Medina) to the
Catacecaumene island (Jebel Taik
near Lôhaia). "Different peoples
inhabit it, who speak languages partly
somewhat different, partly wholly so.
The inhabitants of the coast live in

the fleet was got ready at the most northerly, that of Arsinoe (Suez), and the army was landed at Leuce Come, just as if it were the object to prolong as much as possible the voyage of the fleet and the march of the troops. Besides, the war-vessels were superfluous, since the Arabians possessed no war-fleet, the Roman sailors were unacquainted with the navigation on the Arabian coast, and the transports, although specially built for this expedition, were unsuited for their purpose. The pilots had difficulty in finding their way between the shallows and the rocks, and even the voyage in Roman waters from Arsinoe to Leuce Come cost many vessels and men. Here the winter was passed ; in the spring of 730 the campaign in the enemy's country began. The Arabians offered no hindrance, but Arabia undoubtedly did so. Wherever the double axes and the slings and bows came into collision with the pilum and the sword, the natives dispersed like chaff before the wind ; but the diseases, which are endemic in the country, scurvy, leprosy, palsy, decimated the soldiers worse than the most bloody battle, and all the more as the general did not know how to move rapidly forward the unwieldy mass of his army. Nevertheless the Roman army arrived in front of the walls of Mariaba, the capital of the Sabaeans first affected by the attack. But, as the inhabitants closed the gates of their powerful walls still standing,[1] and offered

pens like the ' fish-eaters ' on the opposite coast " (these pens he describes, c. 2, as isolated and built into the clefts of the rocks), "those of the interior in villages and pastoral companies ; they are ill-disposed men speaking two languages, who plunder the seafarers that drift out of their course and drag the shipwrecked into slavery. For that reason they are constantly hunted by the viceroys and chief kings of Arabia ; they are called Kanraites (or Kassanites). In general navigation on all this coast is dangerous, the shore is without harbours and inaccessible, with a troublesome surf, rocky and in general very bad. Therefore, when we sail into these waters, we keep to the middle and hasten to get to the Arabian territory at the island

Catacecaumene ; from thence onward the inhabitants are hospitable, and we meet with numerous flocks of sheep and camels." The same region between the Roman and the Homeritic frontiers, and the same state of things are in the view of the Axomite king, when he writes : πέραν δὲ τῆς ἐρυθρᾶς θαλάσσης οἰκοῦντας 'Ἀρραβίτας καὶ Κιναιδοκολπίτας (comp. Ptolemaeus vi. 7, 20), στράτευμα ναυτικὸν καὶ πεζικὸν διαπεμψάμενος καὶ ὑποτάξας αὐτῶν τοὺς βασιλέας, φόρους τῆς γῆς τελεῖν ἐκέλευσα καὶ ὁδεύεσθαι μετʼ εἰρήνης καὶ πλέεσθαι, ἀπό τε Λευκῆς κώμης ἕως τῶν Σαβαίων χώρας ἐπολέμησα.

[1] These walls, built of rubble, form a circle of a mile in diameter. They are described by Arnaud (*l.c.*, comp. p. 287, note 1).

energetic resistance, the Roman general despaired of solving the problem proposed to him ; and, after he had lain six days in front of the town, he entered on his retreat, which the Arabians hardly disturbed in earnest, and which was accomplished with comparative rapidity under the pressure of need, although with a severe loss in men.

It was a bad miscarriage ; but Augustus did not abandon the conquest of Arabia. It has already been related (p. 39) that the journey to the East, which the crown-prince Gaius entered upon in the year 753, was to terminate at Arabia ; it was this time contemplated after the subjugation of Armenia to reach, in concert with the Parthian government or in case of need after the overthrow of their armies, the mouth of the Euphrates, and from thence to take the sea-route which the admiral Nearchus had once explored for Alexander, towards Arabia Felix.[1] These hopes ended in another but not less unfortunate way, through the Parthian arrow which struck the crown-prince before the walls of Artageira. With him was buried the plan of Arabian conquest for all the future. The great peninsula remained through the whole imperial period—apart from the stripes of coast on the north and north-west—in possession of that freedom from which Islam, the executioner of Hellenism, was in its own time to issue.

But the Arabian commerce was at all events broken down partly by the measures, to be explained further on, of the Roman government for protecting the Egyptian navigation, partly by a blow struck by the Romans against the chief mart of Indo-Arabian traffic. Whether under Augustus himself, possibly among the preparations for the invasion to be carried out by Gaius, or under one of his immediate successors, a Roman fleet appeared before Adane and destroyed the place ; in Vespasian's time it

[margin note: Further enterprises against the Arabs. 1.]

[margin note: Injury to Arabian commerce.]

---

[1] That the Oriental expedition of Gaius had Arabia as its goal, is stated expressly by Pliny (particularly *H. N.* xii. 14, 55, 56 ; comp. ii. 67, 168 ; vi. 27, 141, c. 28, 160 ; xxxii. 1, 10). That it was to set out from the mouth of the Euphrates, follows from the fact that the expedition to Armenia and the negotiations with the Parthians preceded it. For that reason the Collectanea of Juba as to the impending expedition were based upon the reports of the generals of Alexander as to their exploring of Arabia.

was a village, and its prosperity was gone.　We know only the naked fact,[1] but it speaks for itself.　A counterpart to the destruction of Corinth and of Carthage by the republic, it, like these, attained its end, and secured for the Romano-Egyptian trade the supremacy in the Arabian gulf and in the Indian Sea.

Later fortunes of the Homerites.　The prosperity, however, of the blessed land of Yemen was too firmly founded to succumb to this blow ; politically it was even perhaps in this epoch only that it more

---

[1] Our only information as to this remarkable expedition has been preserved to us by the Egyptian captain, who about the year 75 has described his voyage on the coasts of the Red Sea.　He knows (c. 26) the Adane of later writers, the modern Aden, as a village on the coast (κώμη παραθαλάσσιος), which belongs to the realm of Charibael, king of the Homerites, but was earlier a flourishing town, and was so termed (εὐδαίμων δ' ἐπεκλήθη πρότερον οὖσα πόλις) because before the institution of the direct Indo-Egyptian traffic this place served as a mart : νῦν δὲ οὐ πρὸ πολλοῦ τῶν ἡμετέρων χρόνων Καῖσαρ αὐτὴν κατεστρέψατο.　The last word can here only mean "destroy," not, as more frequently, "subdue," because the conversion of the town into a village is to be accounted for.　For Καῖσαρ Schwanbeck (*Rhein. Mus. neue Folge*, vii. 353) has proposed Χαριβαήλ, C. Müller 'Ιλασάρ (on account of Strabo, xvi. 4, 21, p. 782) : neither is possible —not the latter, because this Arabian dynast ruled in a far remote district and could not possibly be presumed as well known ; not the former, because Charibael was a contemporary of the writer, and there is here reported an incident which occurred before his time.　We shall not take offence at the tradition, if we reflect what interest the Romans must have had in setting aside the Arabian mart between India and Egypt, and in bringing about direct intercourse.　That the Roman accounts are silent as to this occurrence is in keeping with their habit ; the expedition, which beyond doubt was exe-cuted by an Egyptian fleet and simply consisted in the destruction of a presumably defenceless place on the coast, would not be from a military point of view of any importance ; about great commercial dealings the annalists gave themselves no concern, and generally the incidents in Egypt came still less than those in the other imperial provinces to the knowledge of the senate and therewith of the annalists.　The naked designation Καῖσαρ, in which from the nature of the case the ruler then reigning is excluded, is probably to be explained from the circumstance that the reporting captain, while knowing doubtless the fact of the destruction by the Romans, knew not its date or author.—It is possible that to this the notice in Pliny (*H. N.* ii. 67, 168) is to be referred : *maiorem (oceani) partem et orientis victoriae magni Alexandri lustravere usque in Arabicum sinum, in quo res gerente C. Caesare Aug. f. signa navium ex Hispaniensibus naufragiis feruntur agnita.* Gaius did not reach Arabia (Plin. *H. N.* vi. 28, 160) ; but during the Armenian expedition a Roman squadron may very well have been conducted by one of his sub-commanders to this coast, in order to pave the way for the main expedition.　That silence reigns elsewhere respecting it cannot surprise us.　The Arabian expedition of Gaius had been so solemnly announced and then abandoned in so wretched a way, that loyal reporters had every reason to obliterate a fact which could not well be mentioned without also reporting the failure of the greater plan.

energetically rallied its resources. Mariaba, at the time when the arms of Gallus failed before its walls, was perhaps no more than the capital of the Sabaeans ; but already at that time the tribe of the Homerites, whose capital Sapphar lay somewhat to the south of Mariaba, also in the interior, was the strongest in Arabia Felix. A century later we find the two united under a king of the Homerites and of the Sabaeans reigning in Sapphar, whose rule extends as far as Mocha and Aden, and, as was already said, over the island of Socotra and the coast of Somal and Zanzibar ; and at least from this time we may speak of a kingdom of the Homerites. The desert northwards from Mariaba as far as the Roman frontier did not at that time belong to it, and was under no regular authority at all ;[1] the principalities of the Minaei and of the Chatramotitae continued also to be under sovereigns of their own. The eastern half of Arabia formed constantly a part of the Persian empire (p. 13), and never was under the sceptre of the rulers of Arabia Felix. Even now therefore the bounds were narrow and probably remained so ; little is known as to the further development of affairs.[2] In the middle of the fourth century the kingdom of the Homerites was united with that of the Axomites, and was governed from Axomis[3]—a subjection, however, which was subsequently broken off again. The

---

[1] The Egyptian merchant distinguishes the ἔνθεσμος βασιλεύς of the Homerites (c. 23) sharply from the τύραννοι, the tribal chiefs sometimes subordinate to him, sometimes independent (c. 14), and as sharply distinguishes these organised conditions from the lawlessness of the inhabitants of the desert (c. 2). If Strabo and Tacitus had had eyes as open for these things as that practical man had, we should have known somewhat more of antiquity.

[2] The war of Macrinus against the *Arabes eudaemones* (*vita*, 12) and their envoys sent to Aurelian (*vita*, 33), who are named along with those of the Axomites, would prove their continued independence at that time, if these statements could be depended on.

[3] The king names himself, about the year 356 (p. 284, note 2), in a document (*C. I. Gr.* 5128) βασιλεὺς 'Αξωμιτῶν καὶ 'Ομηριτῶν καὶ τοῦ 'Ραειδὰν (castle in Sapphar, the capital of the Homerites ; Dillmann, *Abh. der Berl. Akad.* 1878, p. 207) . . . καὶ Σαβα ειτῶν καὶ τοῦ Σιλεῆ (castle in Mariaba, the capital of the Sabaeans ; Dillmann, *l.c.*). With this agrees the contemporary mission of envoys *ad gentem Axumitarum et Homerita*[*rum*] (*C. Th.* xii. 12, 2). As to the later state of things comp. especially Nonnosus (*fr. hist. Gr.* iv. p. 179, Müll.) and Procopius, *Hist. Pers.* i. 20.

kingdom of the Homerites, as well as the united Axomitico-
Homeritic, stood as independent states in intercourse
and treaty with Rome during the later imperial period.

In commerce and navigation the Arabians of the
south-west of the peninsula occupied, if no longer the
place of supremacy, at any rate a prominent position
throughout the whole imperial period. After the destruction of Adane, Muza became the commercial metropolis
of this region. The representation formerly given is still
in the main appropriate for the time of Vespasian. The
place is described to us at this time as exclusively Arabian,
inhabited by shipowners and sailors, and full of stirring
mercantile life ; the Muzaites with their own ships navi-
gate the whole east coast of Africa and the west coast
of India, and not merely carry the goods of their own
country, but bring also the purple stuffs and gold embroideries prepared according to Oriental taste in the
workshops of the West, and the fine wines of Syria and
Italy, to the Orientals, and in turn to the western lands
the precious wares of the East. In frankincense and
other aromatics Muza and the emporium of the neighbouring kingdom of Hadramaut, Cane to the east of
Aden, must always have retained a sort of practical
monopoly ; these wares, used in antiquity very much
more than at present, were produced not only on the
southern coast of Arabia, but also on the African coast
from Adulis as far as the "promontory of spices," Cape
Guardafui, and from thence the merchants of Muza fetched
them and brought them into general commerce. On the
already mentioned island of Dioscorides there was a joint
trading settlement of the three great seafaring nations
of these seas, the Hellenes, that is, the Egyptians, the
Arabians, and the Indians. But of relations to Hellenism,
such as we found on the opposite coast among the
Axomites (p. 283), we meet no trace in the land of Yemen ;
if the coinage is determined by Occidental types (p. 287 f.),
these were current throughout the East. Otherwise writing and language and the exercise of art, so far as we
are able to judge, developed themselves here just as inde-

pendently as commerce and navigation ; and certainly this co-operated in producing the result that the Axomites, while they subjected to themselves the Homerites in a political point of view, subsequently reverted from the Hellenic path into the Arabic (p. 283).

In the same spirit as for the relations to southern Africa and to the Arabian states, and in a more pleasing way, provision was made in Egypt itself for the routes of commercial intercourse, in the first instance by Augustus, and beyond doubt by all its intelligent rulers. The system of roads and harbours established by the earlier Ptolemies in the footsteps of the Pharaohs had, like the whole administration, fallen into sad decay amidst the troubles of the last Lagid period. It is not expressly mentioned that Augustus put again into order the land and water routes and the ports of Egypt ; but that it was done, is none the less certain. Coptos remained through the whole imperial period the rendezvous of this traffic.[1] From a recently found document we gather that in the first imperial period the two routes leading thence to the ports of Myos Hormos and of Berenice were repaired by the Roman soldiers and provided at the fitting places with the requisite cisterns.[2] The canal which connected the Red Sea with the Nile, and so with the Mediterranean Sea, was in the Roman period only of secondary rank, employed chiefly perhaps for the conveyance of blocks of marble and porphyry from the Egyptian east coast to the Mediterranean ; but it remained navigable throughout the imperial period. The emperor Trajan renewed and probably also enlarged it—perhaps it was he who placed it in communication with the still undivided Nile near

Land-routes and harbours in Egypt.

---

[1] Aristides (*Or.* xlviii. p. 485, Dind.) names Coptos the Indian and Arabian entrepôt. In the romance of Xenophon the Ephesian (iv. 1), the Syrian robbers resort to Coptos, " for there are a number of merchants pass through, who are travelling to Aethiopia and India."

[2] Hadrian later constructed " the new Hadrian's road " which led from his town Antinoopolis near Hermopolis, probably through the desert to Myos Hormos, and from Myos Hormos along the sea to Berenice, and provided it with cisterns, stations (σταθμοί), and forts (inscription in *Revue Archéol.* N. S. xxi. year 1870, p. 314). However there is no mention of this road subsequently, and it is a question whether it continued to subsist.

Babylon (not far from Cairo), and thereby increased its water-supply—and assigned to it the name of Trajan's or the emperor's river (*Augustus amnis*), from which in later times this part of Egypt was named (*Augustamnica*).

Piracy.

Augustus exerted himself also in earnest for the suppression of piracy on the Red and Indian Seas ; the Egyptians long even after his death thanked him, that through his efforts piratical sails disappeared from the sea and gave way to trading vessels. No doubt what was done in that respect was far from enough. The facts that, while the government doubtless from time to time set naval squadrons to work in these waters, it did not station there a standing war-fleet; and that the Roman merchantmen regularly took archers on board in the Indian Sea to repel the attacks of the pirates, would be surprising, if a comparative indifference to the insecurity of the sea had not everywhere—here, as well as on the Belgian coast, and on those of the Black Sea—clung like a hereditary sin to the Roman imperial government or rather to the Roman government in general. It is true that the governments of Axomis and of Sapphar were called by their geographical position still more than the Romans at Berenice and Leuce Come to check piracy, and it may be partly due to this consideration that the Romans remained, upon the whole, on a good understanding with these weaker but indispensable neighbours.

Growth of the Egyptian active traffic to the East.

We have formerly shown that the maritime intercourse of Egypt, if not with Adulis (p. 284), at any rate with Arabia and India at the epoch which immediately preceded the Roman rule, was not carried on in the main through the medium of Egyptians. It was only through the Romans that Egypt obtained the great maritime traffic to the East. "Not twenty Egyptian ships in the year," says a contemporary of Augustus, "ventured forth under the Ptolemies from the Arabian gulf; now 120 merchantmen annually sail to India from the port of Myos Hormos alone." The commercial gain, which the Roman merchant had been obliged hitherto to share with the Persian or Arabian intermediary, flowed to him in all its extent after the opening up of direct communication with the more remote East. This result was probably brought about in the first instance by the circumstance that the Egyptian ports were, if not directly barred, at any rate practically closed, by differential custom-dues against Arabian and Indian transports ;[1] only by the hypothesis of such a navigation-act in favour of their own shipping could this sudden revolution of commercial relations be explained. But the traffic was not merely violently transformed from a passive into an active one ; it was also absolutely increased, partly in consequence of the increased inquiry in the West for the wares of the East, partly at the expense of the other routes of traffic through Arabia and Syria. For the Arabian and Indian commerce with the West the route by way of Egypt more and more proved itself the shortest and the cheapest. The frankincense, which in the olden time went in great part by the land-route through the interior of Arabia to Gaza (p. 288, note 2), came afterwards for the most part by water through Egypt. The Indian traffic received a new impulse about the time of Nero, when a skilled and courageous Egyptian captain, Hippalus, ventured, instead of making his way along the long stretch of coast, to steer from the mouth of the Arabian Gulf directly through the open sea for India ; he knew the monsoon, which thenceforth the mariners, who traversed this route after him, named the Hippalus. Thenceforth the voyage was not merely materially shortened, but was less exposed to the land and sea pirates. To what extent the secure state of peace and the increasing luxury

---

[1] This is nowhere expressly said, but it is clearly evident from the Periplus of the Egyptian. He speaks at numerous places of the intercourse of the non-Roman Africa with Arabia (c. 7, 8), and conversely of the Arabians with the non-Roman Africa (c. 17, 21, 31 ; and after him Ptolemaeus, i. 17, 6), and with Persia (c. 27, 33), and India (c. 21, 27, 49) ; as also of that of the Persians with India (c. 36), as well as of the Indian merchantmen with the non-Roman Africa (c. 14, 31, 32), and with Persia (c. 36) and Arabia (c. 32). But there is not a word indicating that these foreign merchants came to Berenice, Myos Hormos, or Leuce Come ; indeed, when he remarks with reference to the most important mart of all this circle of traffic, Muza, that these merchants sail with their own ships to the African coast outside of the Straits of Bab El Mandeb (for that is for him τὸ πέραν), and to India, Egypt cannot possibly be absent by accident.

raised the consumption of Oriental wares in the West, may be discerned in some measure from the complaints, which were in the time of Vespasian loudly expressed, regarding the enormous sums which went out of the empire for that purpose. The whole amount of the purchase-money annually paid to the Arabians and the Indians is estimated by Pliny at 100,000,000 sesterces (=£1,100,000), for Arabia alone at 55,000,000 sesterces (=£600,000), of which, it is true, a part was covered by the export of goods. The Arabians and the Indians bought doubtless the metals of the West, iron, copper, lead, tin, arsenic, the Egyptian articles mentioned formerly (p. 254), wine, purple, gold and silver plate, also precious stones, corals, saffron, balm ; but they had always far more to offer to foreign luxury than to receive for their own. Hence the Roman gold and silver money went in considerable quantities to the great Arabian and Indian emporia. In India it had already under Vespasian so naturalised itself that the people there preferred to use it. Of this Oriental traffic the greatest part went to Egypt ; and if the increase of the traffic benefited the government-chest by the increased receipts from customs, the need for building ships and making mercantile voyages of their own elevated the prosperity of private individuals.

While thus the Roman government limited its rule in Egypt to the narrow space which is marked off by the navigableness of the Nile, and, whether in pusillanimity or in wisdom, at any rate never attempted with consistent energy to conquer either Nubia or Arabia, it strove as energetically after the possession of the Arabian and the Indian wholesale traffic, and attained at least an important limitation of the competitors. As the unscrupulous pursuit of commercial interests characterised the policy of the republic, so not less did it mark that of the principate, especially in Egypt.

Romano-Indian commercial intercourse. We can only determine approximately how far the direct Roman maritime traffic went towards the East. In the first instance it took the direction of Barygaza (Barôtch on the Gulf of Cambay above Bombay), which great mart must have remained through the whole imperial period the centre of the Egyptio-Indian traffic; several places in the peninsula of Gujerat bear among the Greeks Greek designations, such as Naustathmos and Theophila. In the Flavian period, in which the monsoon-voyages had already become regular, the whole west coast of India was opened up to the Roman merchants as far down as the coast of Malabar, the home of the highly-esteemed and dear-priced pepper, for the sake of which they visited the ports of Muziris (probably Mangaluru) and Nelcynda (in Indian doubtless Nilakantha from one of the surnames of the god Shiva, probably the modern Nîlêswara); somewhat farther to the south at Kananor numerous Roman gold coins of the Julio-Claudian epoch have been found, formerly exchanged against the spices destined for the Roman kitchens. On the island Salice, the Taprobane of the older Greek navigators, the modern Ceylon, in the time of Claudius a Roman official, who had been driven thither from the Arabian coast by storms, had met with a friendly reception from the ruler of the country, and the latter, astonished, as the report says, at the uniform weight of the Roman pieces of money in spite of the diversity of the emperor's heads, had sent along with the shipwrecked man envoys to his Roman colleague. Thereby in the first instance it was only the sphere of geographical knowledge that was enlarged; it was not till later apparently that navigation was extended as far as that large and productive island, in which on several occasions Roman coins have come to light. But coins are found only by way of exception beyond Cape Comorin and Ceylon,[1] and hardly has even the coast of Coromandel and the mouth of the Ganges, to say nothing of the Further Indian peninsula and China, maintained regular commercial intercourse with the Occidentals.

---

[1] In Bâmanghati (district Singhbhum) westward from Calcutta, a great treasure of gold coins of Roman emperors (Gordian and Constantine are named), is said to have come to light (Beglar, in Cunningham's *Archae-ological Survey of India*, vol. xiii. p. 72); but such an isolated find does not prove that regular intercourse extended so far. In Further India and China Roman coins have very seldom been found.

Chinese silk was certainly already at an early period sold regularly to the West, but, as it would appear, exclusively by the land-route, and through the medium partly of the Indians of Barygaza, partly and chiefly of the Parthians ; the Silk-people or the Seres (from the Chinese name of silk Sr) of the Occidentals were the inhabitants of the Tarim-basin to the north-west of Thibet, whither the Chinese brought their silk, and the Parthian intermediaries jealously guarded the traffic thither. By sea, certainly, individual mariners reached accidentally or by way of exploration at least to the east coast of Further India and perhaps still farther ; the port of Cattigara known to the Romans at the beginning of the second century A.D. was one of the Chinese coast-towns, perhaps Hang-chow-foo at the mouth of the Yang-tse-kiang. The report of the Chinese annals that in 166 A.D. an embassy of the emperor Antun of Ta-(that is Great) Tsin (Rome) landed in Ji-nan (Tonkin), and thence by the land-route arrived at the capital Lo-yang (or Ho-nan-foo on the middle Hoang-ho) to the emperor Hwan-ti, may warrantably be referred to Rome and to Marcus Antoninus. This event, however, and what the Chinese authorities mention as to a similar appearance of the Romans in their country in the course of the third century, can hardly be understood of public missions, since as to these Roman statements would hardly have been wanting ; but possibly individual captains may have passed with the Chinese court as messengers of their government. These connections had perceptible consequences only in so far as the earlier tales regarding the procuring of silk gradually gave way to better knowledge.

CHAPTER XIII.

THE AFRICAN PROVINCES.

NORTH AFRICA, in a physical and ethnographic point of view, stands by itself like an island. Nature has isolated it on all sides, partly by the Atlantic and the Mediterranean Sea, partly by the widely-extended shore, incapable of cultivation, of the Great Syrtis below the modern Fezzan, and, in connection therewith, by the desert, likewise closed against cultivation, which shuts off the steppeland and the oases of the Sahara to the south. Ethnographically the population of this wide region forms a great family of peoples, distinguished most sharply from the Blacks of the south, but likewise strictly separated from the Egyptians, although perhaps with these there may once have subsisted a primeval fellowship. They call themselves in the Riff near Tangier Amâzigh, in the Sahara Imôshagh, and the same name meets us, referred to particular tribes, on several occasions among the Greeks and Romans, thus as Maxyes at the founding of Carthage (ii. 8), as Mazices in the Roman period at different places of the Mauretanian north coast ; the similar designation that has remained with the scattered remnants proves that this great people has once had a consciousness, and has permanently retained the impression, of the relationship of its members. To the peoples who came into contact with them this relationship was far from clear ; the diversities which prevail among their several parts are not merely at the present day glaring, after in the past thousands of years the mixture with the neighbouring peoples, particularly the Negroes in the south and the

North Africa and the Berber stock.

ii. 7.

Arabs in the north, has had its effect upon them, but certainly were as considerable even before these foreign influences as their extension in space demands. A universally valid expression for the nation as such is wanting in all other idioms ; even where the name goes beyond the designation of stock,[1] it yet does not describe the circle as a whole. That of Libyans, which the Egyptians, and after their precedent the Greeks use, belongs originally to the most easterly tribes coming into contact with Egypt, and has always remained specially pertaining to those of the eastern half. That of Nomades, of Greek origin, expresses in the first instance only the absence of settlement, and then in its Roman transformation as Numidians, has become associated with that territory which king Massinissa united under his sway. That of Mauri, of native origin, and current among the later Greeks as well as the Romans, is restricted to the western parts of the land, and continues in use for the kingdoms here formed and the Roman provinces that have proceeded from them. The tribes of the south are comprehended under the name of the Gaetulians, which, however, the stricter use of language limits to the region on the Atlantic Ocean to the south of Mauretania. We are accustomed to designate the nation by the name of Berbers, which the Arabs apply to the northern tribes.

Type.   As to their type they stand far nearer to the Indo-Germanic than to the Semitic, and form even at the present day, when since the invasion of Islam North Africa has fallen to the Semitic race, the sharpest contrast to the Arabs. It is not without warrant that various geographers of antiquity have refused to let Africa pass at all as a third continent, but have attached Egypt to Asia and the

---

[1] The designation *Afer* does not belong to this series. So far as we can follow it back in linguistic usage, it is never given to the Berber in contrast to other African stocks, but to every inhabitant of the Continent lying over against Sicily, and particularly also to the Phoenician ; if it has designated a definite people at all, this can only have been that, with which the Romans here first and chiefly came into contact (comp. Suetonius, *vita Terent.*). Reasons philological and real oppose themselves to our attempt in i. 162 to trace back the word to the name of the Hebrews ; a satisfactory etymology has not yet been found for it.   i. 154.

Berber territory to Europe. As the plants and animals of northern Africa correspond in the main to those of the opposite south-European coast, so the type of man, where it has been preserved unmixed, points altogether to the north :—the fair hair and the blue eyes of a considerable portion, the tall stature, the slender but powerfully knit form, the prevailing monogamy and respect for the position of woman, the lively and emotional temperament, the inclination to settled life, the community founded on the full equality in rights among the grown-up men, which in the usual confederation of several communities affords also the basis for the formation of a state.[1] To strictly political development and to full civilisation this nation, hemmed round by Negroes, Egyptians, Phoenicians, Romans, Arabs, at no time attained ; it must have approximated to it under the government of Massinissa. The alphabet, derived independently from the Phoenician, of which the Berbers made use under Roman rule, and which those of the Sahara still use at the present day, as well as the feeling which, as we have observed, they once had of common national relationship, may probably be referred to the great Numidian king and his descendants, whom the later generations worshipped as gods.[2] In spite of all

---

[1] A good observer, Charles Tissot, (*Géogr. de la province romaine de l'Afrique*, i. p. 403) testifies that upwards of a third of the inhabitants of Morocco have fair or brown hair, and in the colony of the inhabitants of the Riff in Tangier two-thirds. The women made the impression on him of those of Berry and of Auvergne. *Sur les hauts sommets de la chaîne atlantique, d'après les renseignements qui m'ont été fournis, la population tout entière serait remarquablement blonde. Elle aurait les yeux bleus, gris ou "verts," comme ceux des chats," pour reproduire l'expression même dont s'est servi le cheikh qui me renseignait.* The same phenomenon meets us in the mountain masses of Grand Kabylia and of the Aures, as well as on the Tunisian island Jerba and the Canary Islands. The Egyptian representations also show to us the Libu not red, like the Egyptians, but white, and with fair or brown hair.

[2] Cyprian, *Quod idola dii non sint*, c. 2 : *Mauri manifeste reges suos colunt nec ullo velamento hoc nomen obtexunt.* Tertullian, *Apolog.* 24 : *Mauretaniae (dei sunt) reguli sui.* C. I. L. viii., 8834 : *Iemsali L. Percenius L. f. Stel. Rogatus v. (s. l. a.),* found at Thubusuptu in the region of Sitifis, which place may well have belonged to the Numidian kingdom of Hiempsal. Thus the inscription also of Thubursicum (*C. I. L.* viii. n. 7* (comp. *Eph. epigr.* v. p. 651, n. 1478) must have rather been badly copied than falsified. Still, in the year 70, it was alleged that in Mauretania a pretender to the throne had ascribed to himself the name of Juba (Tacitus, *Hist.* ii. 58).

invasions they have maintained their original territory to
a considerable extent ; in Morocco now about two-thirds,
in Algiers about half of the inhabitants are reckoned of
Berber descent.

Phoenician
immigra-
tion.

The immigration, to which all the coasts of the
Mediterranean were subjected in the earliest times, made
North Africa Phoenician.   To the Phoenicians the natives
had to give up the largest and best part of the north
coast ; the Phoenicians withdrew all North Africa from
Greek civilisation.   The Great Syrtis again forms the
linguistic as well as the political line of separation ; as
on the east the Pentapolis of Cyrene belongs to the
Greek circle, so on the west the Tripolis (Tripoli) of
Great-Leptis became and remained Phoenician.   We
have formerly narrated how the Phoenicians after several
hundred years of struggle succumbed to the Romans.
Here we have to give account of the fortunes of Africa,
after the Romans had occupied the Carthaginian territory
and had made the neighbouring regions dependent on
them.

The gov-
ernment of
the Roman
republic.

The short-sightedness and narrow-mindedness—we
may here say, the perversity and brutality—of the foreign
government of the Roman republic had nowhere so full
sway as in Africa.   In southern Gaul, and still more in
Spain, the Roman government pursued at least a consolidated extension of territory, and, half involuntarily, the
rudiments of Latinising ; in the Greek East the foreign
rule was mitigated and often almost compensated by
the power of Hellenism forcing the hand even of hard
policy.   But as to this third continent the old national
hatred towards the Poeni seemed still to reach beyond
the grave of Hannibal's native city.   The Romans held
fast the territory which Carthage had possessed at its
fall, but less in order to develop it for their own benefit
than to prevent its benefiting others, not to awaken new
life there, but to watch the dead body ; it was fear and
envy, rather than ambition and covetousness, that created
the province of Africa.   Under the republic it had not
a history ; the war with Jugurtha was for Africa nothing

but a lion-hunt, and its historical significance lay in its connection with the republican party struggles. The land was, as a matter of course, turned to full account by Roman speculation ; but neither might the destroyed great city rise up afresh, nor might a neighbouring town develop into a similar prosperity ; there were here no standing camps as in Spain and Gaul ; the Roman province, with its narrow bounds, was on all sides surrounded by relatively civilised territory of the dependent king of Numidia, who had helped in the work of the destruction of Carthage, and now, as a reward for it, received not so much the spoil as the task of protecting it from the inroads of the wild hordes of the interior. That thereby a political and military importance was given to this state, such as no other client-state of Rome ever possessed, and that even on this side the Roman policy, in order merely to banish the phantom of Carthage, conjured up serious dangers, was shown by the share of Numidia in the civil wars of Rome ; never during all the internal crises of the empire before or after did a client-prince play such a part as the last king of Numidia in the war of the republicans against Caesar.

All the more necessarily the state of things in Africa became transformed by this decision of arms. In the other provinces, as a consequence of the civil wars, there was a change of rule ; in Africa there was a change of system. The African possession of the Phoenicians itself was not a proper dominion over Africa ; it may be in some measure compared with the dominion in Asia Minor of the Hellenes before Alexander. Of this dominion the Romans had then taken over but a small part, and of that part they had nipped the bud. Now Carthage arose afresh, and, as if the soil had only been waiting for the seed, soon flourished anew. The whole country lying behind—the great kingdom of Numidia—became a Roman province, and the protection of the frontier against the barbarians was undertaken by the Roman legionaries. The kingdom of Mauretania became, in the

Caesar's African policy.

first instance, a Roman dependency, and soon also a part of the Roman empire. With the dictator Caesar the civilising and Latinising of Africa took their place among the tasks of the Roman government. Here we have to set forth how the task was carried out, first as to the outward organisation, and then as to the arrangements made and results achieved for the several districts.

Extent of the Roman rule.

Territorial sovereignty over the whole of North Africa had doubtless already been claimed on the part of the Roman republic, perhaps as a portion of the Carthaginian inheritance, perhaps because " our sea " early became one of the fundamental ideas of the Roman commonwealth ; and, in so far, all its coasts were regarded by the Romans even of the developed republic as their true property. Nor had this claim of Rome ever been properly contested by the larger states of North Africa after the destruction of Carthage ; if in many places the neighbours did not submit to the dominion, they were just as little obedient to their local rulers. That the silver moneys of king Juba I. of Numidia and of king Bogud of Mauretania were coined after the Roman standard, and the Latin legend—little as it was suited to the relations of language and of intercourse then subsisting in North Africa—was never absent from them, was the direct recognition of the Roman supremacy, a consequence, it may be presumed, of the new organisation of North Africa that in the year 674 U.C. was accomplished by Pompeius. The generally insignificant resistance which the Africans, apart from Carthage, opposed to the Romans, came from the descendants of Massinissa ; after king Jugurtha, and later king Juba, were vanquished, the princes of the western country submitted without more ado to the dependence required of them. The arrangements which the emperors made were carried out quite after the same way in the territory of the dependent princes as in the immediate territory of Rome ; it was the Roman government that regulated the boundaries in all North Africa, and constituted Roman communities at its discretion in the kingdom of Mauretania no less than in the province of

80.

Numidia.   We cannot therefore speak, in the strict sense, of a Roman subjugation of North Africa.   The Romans did not conquer it like the Phoenicians or the French ; but they ruled over Numidia as over Mauretania, first as suzerains, then as successors of the native governments. It is so much the more a question, whether the notion of frontier admits of application to Africa in the usual sense. The states of Massinissa, of Bocchus, of Bogud, as also the Carthaginian, proceeded from the northern verge, and all the civilisation of North Africa is based pre-eminently on this coast ; but, so far as we can discern, they all regarded the tribes settled or roving in the south as subjects, and, if they withdrew themselves from subjection, as insurgents, so far as the distance and the desert did not by doing away with contact do away with control. Neighbouring states, with which relations of right or of treaty might have subsisted, can hardly be pointed out in the south of northern Africa, or where such a one appears, such as, in particular, the kingdom of the Garamantes, its position is not to be strictly distinguished from that of the hereditary principalities within the civilised territory.   This was the case also as regards Roman Africa ; as for the previous rulers, so also doubtless for Roman civilisation there was to be found a limit to the south, but hardly so for the Roman territorial supremacy. There is never mention of any formal extension or taking back of the frontier in Africa ; the insurrections in the Roman territory, and the inroads of the neighbouring peoples, look here all the more similar to each other, as even in the regions undoubtedly in Roman possession, still more than in Syria or Spain, many a remote and impassable district knew nothing of Roman taxation and of Roman recruiting.   For that reason it seems appropriate to connect with the view of the several provinces at the same time the slight information which has been left to us in historical tradition, or by means of preserved monuments, respecting the friendly or hostile relations of the Romans with their southern neighbours.

The former territory of Carthage and the larger part

Province of
Africa and
Numidia.

of the earlier kingdom of Numidia, united with it by the dictator Caesar, or, as they also called it, the old and the new Africa, formed until the end of the reign of Tiberius the province of that name, which extended from the boundary of Cyrene to the river Ampsaga, embracing the modern state of Tripoli as well as Tunis and the French province of Constantine (iv. 470 f.). The government, however, for this territory, which was considerable, and required an extended frontier-defence, reverted under the emperor Gaius in the main to the twofold division of the republican times, and committed the portion of the province that did not stand in need of special border-defence to the civil government, and the rest of the territory furnished with garrisons to a military commandant not further amenable to its authority. The cause of this was, that Africa in the partition of the provinces between emperor and senate was given to the latter, and, as from the state of things there a command on a larger scale could not be dispensed with, the co-ordination of the governor delegated by the senate and of the military commandant nominated by the emperor—which latter according to the subsisting hierarchy was placed under the orders of the former—could not but provoke and did provoke collisions between these officials and even between emperor and senate. To this an end was put in the year 37 by an arrangement that the coast-land from Hippo (Bonah), as far as the borders of Cyrene, should retain the old name of Africa and should remain with the proconsul, whereas the western part of the province with the capital Cirta (Constantine), as well as the interior with the great military camps to the north of the Aures, and generally all territory furnished with garrisons, should be placed under the commandant of the African legion. This commandant had senatorial rank, but belonged not to the consular, but to the praetorial class.

iv, 447.

The two
Mauretan-
ian king-
doms.

[iv. 438.

The western half of North Africa was divided at the time of the dictator Caesar (iv. 461) into the two kingdoms of Tingi (Tangier), at that time under king Bo ud and of Iol, the later Caesarea (Zershell), at that time under king Bocchus.   As both kings had as decidedly taken the side of Caesar in the struggle against the republicans as king Juba of Numidia had taken the side of the opposite party, and as they had rendered most essential services to him during the African and the Spanish wars, not merely were both left in possession of their rule, but the domain of Bocchus, and probably also that of Bogud, was enlarged by the victor.[1]   Then, when the rivalries between Antonius and Caesar the younger began, king Bogud alone in the west placed himself on the side of Antonius, and on the instigation of his brother and of his wife invaded Spain during the Perusine war (714); but his neighbour Bocchus and his own capital Tingis took part for Caesar and against him. At the conclusion of peace Antonius allowed Bogud to fall, and Caesar gave the rest of his territory to king Bocchus, but gave Roman municipal rights to the town of Tingis.   When, some years later, a rupture took place between the two rulers, the ex-king took part energetically in the struggle in the hope of regaining his kingdom on this occasion, but at the capture of the Messenian town Methone he was taken prisoner by Agrippa and executed.

40.

Already some years before (721) king Bocchus had died ; his kingdom, the whole of western Africa, was soon

33.

---

49.   [1] This is attested for the year 705 as regards both by Dio, xli. 42 (comp. Suetonius, *Caes.* 54).   In the

47.   year 707 Bogud lends assistance to the Caesarian governor of Spain (*Bell. Alex.* 59, 60), and repels an incursion of the younger Gnaeus Pompeius (*Bell. Afric.* 23).   Bocchus, in combination with P. Sittius, in the African war makes a successful diversion against Juba and conquers even the important Cirta (*Bell. Afr.* 23 ; Appian, ii. 96 ; Dio, xliii. 3). The two obtained in return from Caesar the territory of the prince Massinissa (Appian, iv. 54).   In the second Spanish war Bogud appears in the army of Caesar (Dio, xliii. 36, 38) ; the statement that the son of Bocchus had served in the Pompeian

army (Dio, *l.c.*) must be a confusion, probably with Arabio the son of Massinissa, who certainly went to the sons of Pompeius (Appian, *l.c.*). After Caesar's death Arabio possessed himself afresh of his dominion (Appian, *l.c.*), but after his death in the year 714 (Dio, xlviii. 22) the Caesarian arrangement must have again taken effect in its full extent. The bestowal on Bocchus and Sittius is probably to be understood to the effect that, in the western part of the former Numidian kingdom otherwise left to Bocchus, the colony of Cirta to be founded by Sittius was to be regarded as an independent Roman town, like Tingi subsequently in the kingdom of Mauretania.

40.

25.

Juba II.

afterwards (729) obtained by the son of the last Numidian king, Juba II., the husband of Cleopatra, the daughter of Antonius by the Egyptian queen.[1] Both had been exhibited to the Roman public in early youth as captive kings' children, Juba in the triumphal procession of Caesar the father, Cleopatra in that of the son; it was a wonderful juncture that they now were sent away from Rome as king and queen of the most esteemed vassal-state of the empire, but it was in keeping with the circumstances. Both were brought up in the imperial family; Cleopatra was treated by the legitimate wife of her father with motherly kindness like her own children; Juba had served in Caesar's army. The youth of the dependent princely houses, which was numerously represented at the imperial court and played a considerable part in the circle around the imperial princes, was generally employed in the early imperial period for the filling up of the vassal principalities, after a similar manner, according to free selection, as the first class in rank of the senate was employed for the filling up of the governorships of Syria and Germany. For almost fifty years (729—775 U.C., B.C. 25—A.D. 23) he, and after him his son Ptolemaeus, bore rule over western Africa; it is true that, like the town Tingis from his predecessor, a considerable number of the most important townships, particularly on the coast, was withdrawn from him by the bestowal of

---

[1] If, according to Dio, xl. 43, Caesar in the year 721, after the death of Bocchus, nominates no successor, but makes Mauretania a province, and then (li. 15) in the year 724, on occasion of the end of the queen of Egypt, there is mention of the marriage of her daughter with Juba and his investiture with his father's kingdom, and, lastly (liii. 26), under the year 729 there is reported Juba's investiture with a portion of Gaetulia instead of his hereditary kingdom, as well as with the kingdoms of Bocchus and Bogud; only the last account confirmed by Strabo, xvii. 3, 7, p. 828, is correct. The first is at least incorrect in its way of apprehending the matter, as Mauretania evidently was not made a province in 721, but only the investiture was held in abeyance for the time being; and the second partly anticipates, since Cleopatra, born before the triumph about 719 (*Eph. epigr.* i., p. 276), could not possibly be married in 724, and is partly mistaken, because Juba certainly never got back his paternal kingdom as such. If he had been king of Numidia before 729, and if it had been merely the extent of his kingdom that then underwent a change, he would have counted his years from the first installation and not merely from 729.

Roman municipal rights, and, apart from the capital, these kings of Mauretania were almost nothing but princes of the Berber tribes.

This government lasted up to the year 40, when it appeared fitting to the emperor Gaius, chiefly on account of the rich treasure, to call his cousin to Rome, to deliver him there to the executioner, and to take the territory into imperial administration.   Both rulers were unwarlike, the father a Greek man of letters after the fashion of this period, compiling so-called memorabilia of a historical or geographical kind, or relative to the history of art, in endless books, noteworthy by his—we might say—international literary activity, well read in Phoenician and Syrian literature, but exerting himself above all to diffuse the knowledge of Roman habits and of so-called Roman history among the Hellenes, moreover, a zealous friend of art and frequenter of the theatre ; the son a prince of the common type, passing his time in court-life and princely luxury.   Among their subjects they were held of little account, whether as regards their personality or as vassals of the Romans ; against the Gaetulians in the south king Juba had on several occasions to invoke the help of the Roman governor, and, when in Roman Africa the prince of the Numidians, Tacfarinas, revolted against the Romans, the Moors flocked in troops to his banner.   Nevertheless the end of the dynasty and the introduction of Roman provincial government into the land made a deep impression. The Moors were faithfully devoted to their royal house ; altars were still erected under the Roman rule in Africa to the kings of the race of Massinissa (p. 305).   Ptolemaeus, whatever he might be otherwise, was Massinissa's genuine descendant in the sixth generation, and the last of the old royal house.   A faithful servant of his, Aedemon, after the catastrophe called the mountain-tribes of the Atlas to arms, and it was only after a hard struggle that the governor Suetonius Paullinus—the same who afterwards fought with the Britons (I. 179)—was able to master the revolt (in the year 42).   In the organisation of the new territory the Romans reverted to the earlier division into

Erection of the provinces of Caesarea and Tingi.

an eastern and a western half, or, as they were thenceforth
called from the capitals, into the provinces of Caesarea and
of Tingi ; or rather they retained that division, for it was, as
will be afterwards shown, necessarily suggested by the
physical and political relations of the territory, and must
have continued to subsist even under the same sceptre in
one or the other form. Each of these provinces was
furnished with imperial troops of the second class, and
placed under an imperial governor not belonging to the
senate.

The state and the destinies of this great and peculiar
new seat of Latin civilisation were conditioned by the
physical constitution of North Africa. It is formed by
two great mountain-masses, of which the northern falls
steeply towards the Mediterranean, while the southern, the
Atlas, slopes off slowly in the Sahara-steppe dotted with
numerous oases towards the desert proper. A smaller
steppe, similar on the whole to the Sahara and dotted with
numerous salt-lakes, serves in the middle portion, the modern
Algeria, to separate the mountains on the north coast and
those on the southern frontier. There are in North Africa
no extensive plains capable of culture ; the coast of the
Mediterranean Sea has a level foreland only in a few districts ;
the land capable of cultivation, according to the modern
expression the Tell, consists essentially of the numerous
valleys and slopes within those two broad mountain-masses,
and so extends to its greatest width where, as in the
modern Morocco and in Tunis, no steppe intervenes between
the northern and the southern border.

Tripolis.   The region of Tripolis, politically a part of the province
of Africa, stands as respects its natural relations outside of
the territory described, and is annexed to it in peninsular
fashion. The frontier-range sloping down towards the
Mediterranean Sea touches at the bay of Tacapae (Gabes),
with its foreland of steppe and salt-lake, immediately on
the shore. To the south of Tacapae as far as the Great
Syrtis there extends along the coast the narrow Tripolitan
island of cultivation, bounded inland towards the steppe
by a chain of moderate height. Beyond it begins the

steppe-country with numerous oases. The protection of the coast against the inhabitants of the desert is here of special difficulty, because the high margin of mountains is wanting ; and traces of this are apparent in the accounts that have come to us of the military expeditions and the military positions in this region.

It was the arena of the wars with the Garamantes. Lucius Cornelius Balbus, who in his younger years had fought and administered under Caesar with the most adventurous boldness as well as with the most cruel recklessness, was selected by Augustus to reduce these inconvenient neighbours to quiet, and in his proconsulate (735) he subdued the interior as far as Cidamus (Ghadames), twelve days' journey inland from Tripolis, and Garama (Germa) in Fezzan;[1] at his triumph—he was the last commoner who celebrated such an one—a long series of towns and tribes, hitherto unknown even by name, were displayed as vanquished. This expedition is named a conquest ; and so doubtless the foreland must have been thereby brought in some measure under the Roman power. There was fighting subsequently on many occasions in this region. Soon afterwards, still under Augustus, Publius Sulpicius Quirinius made an expedition against the tribes of Marmarica, that is, of the Libyan desert above Cyrene, and at the same time against the Garamantes. That the war against Tacfarinas under Tiberius extended also over this region will be mentioned further on. After its termination the king of the Garamantes sent envoys to Rome, to procure pardon for his having taken part in it. In the year 70 an irruption of the Garamantes into the pacified territory was brought about by the circumstance that the town

The wars with the Garamantes.

---

[1] That Balbus carried on this campaign as proconsul of Africa, is shown in particular by the triumphal Fasti ; but the consul L. Cornelius of the year 732 must have been another person, since Balbus, according to Velleius ii. 51, obtained that consular governorship, *ex privato consularis*, *i.e.* without having filled a curule office. The nomination, therefore, cannot have taken place according to the usual arrangement by lot. To all appearance he fell into disgrace with Augustus for good reasons on account of his Spanish quaestorship (Drumann ii. 609), and was then, after the lapse of more than twenty years, sent, as an extraordinary measure, to Africa, on account of his undoubted aptitude for this specially difficult task.

Oea (Tripoli) called the barbarians to help the Tripolis in a quarrel, which had grown into war, with the neighbouring town Great-Leptis (Lebda), whereupon they were beaten back by the governor of Africa and pursued to their own settlements.   Under Domitian on the coast of the Great Syrtis, which had been from of old held by the Nasamones, a revolt of the natives provoked by the exorbitant taxes had to be repressed with arms by the governor of Numidia ; the territory already poor in men was utterly depopulated by this cruelly conducted war.   The emperor Severus took conspicuous care of this his native province—he was from Great-Leptis—and gave to it stronger military protection against the neighbouring barbarians.   With this we may bring into connection the fact, that in the time from Severus to Alexander the nearest oases, Cidamus (Ghadames), Gharia el Gharbia, Bonjem, were provided with detachments of the African legion, which, it is true, owing to the distance from the headquarters, could not be much more than a nucleus for the probably considerable contingents of the subject tribes here rendering services to the Romans. In fact the possession of these oases was of importance not merely for the protection of the coast, but also for the traffic, which at all times passed by way of these oases from the interior of Africa to the harbours of Tripolis.   It was not till the time of decay that the possession of these advanced posts was abandoned ; in the description of the African wars under Valentinian and Justinian we find the towns of the coast directly harassed by the natives.

The Africano-Numidian territory and army.   The basis and core of Roman Africa was the province of that name, including the Numidian, which was a branch from it.   Roman civilisation entered upon the heritage partly of the city of Carthage, partly of the kings of Numidia, and if it here attained considerable results, it may never be forgotten that it, properly speaking, merely wrote its name and inscribed its language on what was already there.   Besides the towns, which were demonstrably founded by the former or by the latter, and to which we shall still return, the former as well as the latter led the Berber tribes, inclined at any rate to agriculture, towards fixed settlements.   Even in the time of Herodotus the Libyans westward of the bay of Gabes were no longer nomads, but peacefully cultivated the soil ; and the Numidian rulers carried civilisation and agriculture still farther into the interior.   Nature, too, was here more favourable for husbandry than in the western part of North Africa ; the middle depression between the northern and the southern range is indeed here not quite absent, but the salt lakes and the steppe proper are less extensive than in the two Mauretanias.   The military arrangements were chiefly designed to plant the troops in front of the mighty Aura-sian mountain-block, the Saint Gotthard of the southern frontier-range, and to check the irruption of the non-subject tribes from the latter into the pacified territory of Africa and Numidia.   For that reason Augustus placed the stationary quarters of the legion at Theveste (Tebessa), on the high plateau between the Aures and the old province ; even to the north of it, between Ammaedara and Althiburus, Roman forts existed in the first imperial period. Of the details of the warfare we learn little ; it must have been permanent, and must have consisted in the constant repelling of the border-tribes, as well as in not less constant pillaging raids into their territory.

Only as to a single occurrence of this sort has infor- War mation in some measure accurate come to us ; namely, as against to the conflicts which derive their name from the chief leader of the Berbers, Tacfarinas.   They assumed unusual proportions ; they lasted eight years (17-24), and the garrison of the province otherwise consisting of a legion was on that account reinforced during the years 20-22 by a second despatched thither from Pannonia.   The war had its origin from the great tribe of the Musulamii on the south slope of the Aures, against whom already under Augustus Lentulus had conducted an expedition, and who now under his successor chose that Tacfarinas as their leader.   He was an African Arminius, a native Numidian, who had served in the Roman army, but had then deserted and made himself a name at the head of a band of robbers. The insurrection extended eastwards as far as the Cinithii on the Little Syrtis and the Garamantes in Fezzan, westwards over a great part of Mauretania, and became dangerous through the fact that Tacfarinas equipped a portion of his men after the Roman fashion on foot and on horseback, and gave them Roman training ; these gave steadiness to the light bands of the insurgents, and rendered possible regular combats and sieges. After long exertions, and after the senate had been on several occasions induced to disregard the legally prescribed ballot in filling up this important post of command, and to select fitting men instead of the usual generals of the type of Cicero, Quintus Iunius Blaesus in the first instance made an end of the insurrection by a combined operation, inasmuch as he sent the left flank column against the Garamantes, and with the right covered the outlets from the Aures towards Cirta, while he advanced in person with the main army into the territory of the Musulamii and permanently occupied it (year 22). But the bold partisan soon afterwards renewed the struggle, and it was only some years later that the proconsul Publius Cornelius Dolabella, after he had nipped in the bud the threatened revolt of the just chastised Musulamii by the execution of all the leaders, was able with the aid of the troops of the king of Mauretania to force a battle in his territory near Auzia (Aumale), in which Tacfarinas lost his life. With the fall of the leader, as is usual in national wars of insurrection, this movement had an end.[1]

Later conflicts.   From later times detailed accounts of a like kind are lacking ; we can only follow out in some measure the general course of the Roman work of pacification. The tribes to the south of Aures were, if not extirpated, at any rate ejected and transplanted into the northern districts ; so in particular the Musulamii themselves,[2] against whom

[1] The tribes whom Tacitus names in his account of the war, far from clear, as always, in a geographical point of view, may be in some measure determined ; and the position between the Leptitanian and the Cirtensian columns (*Ann.* iii. 74) points for the middle column to Theveste. The town of Thala (*Ann.* iii. 20) cannot possibly be sought above Ammaedara, but is probably the Thala of the Jugurthan war in the vicinity of Capsa. The last section of the war has its arena in western Mauretania about Auzia (iv. 25), and accordingly in Thubuscum (iv. 24) there lurks possibly Thubusuptu or Thubusuctu. The river Pagyda (*Ann.* iii. 20) is quite indefinable.

[2] Ptolemaeus, iv. 3, 23, puts the

an expedition was once more conducted under Claudius. The demand made by Tacfarinas to have settlements assigned to him and his people within the civilised territory, to which Tiberius, as was reasonable, only replied by redoubling his exertions to annihilate the daring claimant, was supplementarily after a certain measure fulfilled in this way, and probably contributed materially to the consolidation of the Roman government. The camps more and more enclosed the Aurasian mountain-block. The garrisons were pushed farther forward into the interior ; the headquarters themselves moved under Traian away from Theveste farther to the west ; the three considerable Roman settlements on the northern slope of the Aures, Mascula (Khenschela), at the egress of the valley of the Arab and thereby the key to the Aures mountains, a colony at least already under Marcus and Verus ; Thamugadi, a foundation of Trajan's ; and Lambaesis, after Hadrian's day the headquarters of the African army, formed together a settlement comparable to the great military camps on the Rhine and on the Danube, which, laid out on the lines of communication from the Aures to the great towns of the north and the coast Cirta (Constantine), Calama (Gelma), and Hippo regius (Bonah), secured the peace of the latter. The intervening steppe-land was, so far as it could not be gained for cultivation, at least intersected by secure routes of communication. On the west side of the Aures a strongly occupied chain of posts which followed the slope of the mountains from Lambaesis over the oases Calceus Herculis (el Kantara) and Bescera (Beskra), cut off the connection with Mauretania. Even the interior of the mountains subsequently became Roman ; the war,

---

Musulamii southward from the Aures, and it is only in accord therewith that they are called in Tacitus ii. 52, dwellers beside the steppe and neighbours of the Mauri ; later they are settled to the north and west of Theveste (*C. I. L.* viii. 270, 10667). The Nattabutes dwelt according to Ptolemaeus *l.c.* southward of the Musulamii ; subsequently we find them to the south of Calama (*C. I. L.* viii. 484). In like manner the *Chellenses Numidae*, between Lares and Althiburus (*Eph. epigr.* V. n. 639), and the *conventus (civium Romanorum et) Numidarum qui Mascululae habitant* (*ib.* n. 597), are probably Berber tribes transplanted from Numidia to the proconsular province.

which was waged under the emperor Pius in Africa, and concerning which we have not accurate information, must have brought the Aurasian mountains into the power of the Romans. At that time a military road was carried through these mountains by a legion doing garrison duty in Syria and sent beyond doubt on account of this war to Africa, and in later times we meet at that very spot traces of Roman garrisons and even of Roman towns, which reach down to Christian times ; the Aurasian range had thus at that time been occupied, and continued to be permanently occupied. The oasis Negrin, situated on its southern slope, was even already under or before Trajan furnished by the Romans with troops, and still somewhat farther southward on the extreme verge of the steppe at Bir Mohammed ben Jûnis are found the ruins of a Roman fort ; a Roman road also ran along the southern base of this range. Of the mighty slope which falls from the tableland of Theveste, the watershed between the Mediterranean and the desert, in successive stages of two to three hundred mètres down to the latter, this oasis is the last terrace ; at its base begins, in sharp contrast towards the jagged mountains piled up behind, the sand desert of Suf, with its yellow rows of dunes similar to waves, and the sandy soil moved about by the wind, a huge wilderness, without elevation of the ground, without trees, fading away without limit into the horizon. Negrin was certainly of old, as it still is in our time, the standing rendezvous and the last place of refuge of the robber chiefs as well as of the natives defying foreign rule—a position commanding far and wide the desert and its trading routes. Even to this extreme limit reached Roman occupation and even Roman settlement in Numidia.

Roman civilisation in Mauretania.

Mauretania was not a heritage like Africa and Numidia. Of its earlier condition we learn nothing ; there cannot have been considerable towns even on the coast here in earlier times, and neither Phoenician stimulus nor sovereigns after the type of Massinissa effectively promoted civilisation in this quarter. When his last descendants exchanged the Numidian crown for the Mauretanian, the capital, which changed its name Iol into Caesarea, became the residence of a cultivated and luxurious court, and a seat of seafaring and of traffic. But how much less this possession was esteemed by the government than that of the neighbouring province, is shown by the difference of the provincial organisation ; the two Mauretanian armies were together not inferior in number to the Africano-Numidian,[1] but here governors of equestrian rank and imperial soldiers of the class of *peregrini* sufficed. Caesarea remained a considerable commercial town ; but in the province the fixed settlement was restricted to the northern mountain-range, and it was only in the eastern portion that larger inland towns were to be found. Even the fertile valley of the most considerable river of this province, the Shelîf, shows weak urban development ; further to the west in the valleys of the Tafna and the Malua it almost wholly disappears, and the names of the divisions of cavalry here stationed serve partly in place of local designations. The province of Tingi (Tangier) even now embraced nothing but this town with its immediate territory and the stripe of the coast along the Atlantic Ocean as far as Sala, the modern Rebât, while in the interior Roman settlement did not even reach to Fez. No land-route connects this province with that of Caesarea ; the 220 miles from Tingi to Rusaddir (Melilla) they traversed by water, along the desolate and insubordinate coast of the Riff. Consequently for this province the communication with Baetica was nearer than that with Mauretania ; and if subsequently, when the empire was divided into larger administrative districts, the province of Tingi fell to Spain, that measure was only the outward carrying out of what in reality had long subsisted. It was for Baetica what Germany was for Gaul ; and, far from lucrative as it must have been, it was perhaps instituted and retained for the reason that its abandonment would even then have brought about an

---

[1] In the year 70 the troops of the two Mauretanias amounted together, in addition to militia levied in large numbers, to 5 alae and 19 cohortes (Tacitus, *Hist.* ii. 58), and so, if we reckon on the average every fourth as a double troop, to about 15,000 men. The regular army of Numidia was weaker rather than stronger.

invasion of Spain similar to that which Islam accomplished
after the collapse of the Roman rule.

The Gae-
tulian wars.
Beyond the limit of fixed settlement herewith indicated,
—the line of frontier tolls and of frontier posts—and in various non-civilised districts enclosed by it, the land in the two
Mauretanias during the Roman times remained doubtless
with the natives, but they came under Roman supremacy;
there would be claimed from them, as far as possible,
taxes and war-services, but the regular forms of taxation
and of levy would not be applied in their case. For
example, the tribe of Zimizes, which was settled on the
rocky coast to the west of Igilgili (Jijeli) in eastern
Mauretania, and so in the heart of the domain of the
Roman power, had assigned to it a fortress designed to
cover the town of Igilgili, to be occupied on such a footing
that the troops were not allowed to pass beyond the radius
of 500 paces round the fort.[1] They thus employed these
subject Berbers in the Roman interest, but did not organise
them in the Roman fashion, and hence did not treat them
as soldiers of the imperial army. Even beyond their own
province the irregulars from Mauretania were employed in
great numbers, particularly as horsemen in the later period,[2]
while the same did not hold of the Numidians.

How far the field of the Roman power went beyond the
Roman towns and garrisons and the end of the imperial
roads, we are not able to say. The broad steppe-land round
the salt-lakes to the west of Lambaesis, the mountain-region

[1] Inscription *C. I. L.* viii. 8369
of the year **129**: *Termini positi inter
Igilgilitanos, in quorum finibus kastel-
lum Victoriae positum est, et Zimiz(es),
ut sciant Zimizes non plus in usum se
habere ex auctoritate M. Vetti Latronis
pro(curatoris) Aug(usti) qua(m) in
circuitu a muro kast(elli) p(edes)* D.
The *Zimises* are placed by the Peu-
tingerian map alongside of Igilgili to
the westward.

[2] If the praefect of a cohort doing
garrison duty in Numidia held the
command at the same time over six
Gaetulian tribes (*nationes, C. I. L.* v.
5267), men that were natives of
Mauretania were employed as irregulars in the neighbouring province.
Irregular Mauretanian horsemen frequently occur, especially in the later
imperial period. Lusius Quietus under
Trajan, a Moor and leader of a Moorish
troop (Dio lxviii. 32), no Λίβυς ἐκ
τῆς ὑπηκόου Λιβύης, ἀλλ᾽ ἐξ ἀδόξου καὶ
ἀπῳκισμένης ἐσχατιᾶς (Themistius, *Or.*
xvi. p. 250 Dind.), was without doubt
a Gaetulian sheikh, who served with
his followers in the Roman army.
That his home was formally independent of the empire, is not affirmed in
the words of Themistius; the "subject-
territory" is that with Roman organisation, the ἐσχατιά its border inhabited
by dependent tribes.

from Tlemsen till towards Fez, including the coast of the Riff, the fine corn-country on the Atlantic Ocean southward from Sala as far as the high Atlas, the civilisation ot which in the flourishing time of the Arabs vied with the Andalusian, lastly, the Atlas range in the south of Algeria and Morocco and its southern slopes, which afforded for pastoral people abundant provision in the alternation ot mountain and steppe pastures, and developed the most luxuriant fertility in the numerous oases—all these regions remained essentially untouched by the Roman civilisation; but from this it does not follow that they were in the Roman time independent, and still less that they were not at least reckoned as belonging to the imperial domain. Tradition gives us but slight information in this respect. We have already mentioned (p. 3 1 3) that the proconsuls of Africa helped to make the Gaetulians—that is, the tribes in southern Algeria—subject to king Juba; and the latter constructed purple dyeworks at Madeira (p. 3 3 8, note). After the end of the Mauretanian dynasty and the introduction of the immediate Roman administration, Suetonius Paullinus crossed, as the first Roman general, the Atlas (p. 3 1 3), and carried his arms as far as the desert-river Ger, which still bears the same name, in the south-east of Morocco. His successor, Gnaeus Hosidius Geta, continued this enterprise, and emphatically defeated the leader of the Mauri Salabus.   Subsequently several enterprising governors of the Mauretanian provinces traversed these remote regions, and the same holds true of the Numidian, under whose command, not under the Mauretanian, was placed the frontier-range stretching southward behind the province of Caesarea ;[1] yet nothing is mentioned from later times of war-expeditions proper in the south of Mauretania or Numidia.   The Romans can scarcely have taken over the empire of the Mauretanian kings in quite the same extent as these had possessed it ; but yet the expeditions that were undertaken after the annexation of the country were

[1] To the inscriptions, which prove this (*C. I .L.* viii. p. xviii. 747), falls now to be added the remarkable dedication of the leader of an expedi- tionary column from the year 174, found in the neighbourhood of Géryville (*Eph. epigr.* v. n. 1043).

probably not without lasting consequences. At least a portion of the Gaetulians submitted, as the auxiliary troops levied there prove, even to the regular conscription during the imperial period ; and, if the native tribes in the south of the Roman provinces had given serious trouble to the Romans, the traces of it would not have been wholly wanting.[1] Probably the whole south as far as the great desert passed as imperial land,[2] and even the effective dependence extended far beyond the domain of Roman civilisation, which, it is true, does not exclude frequent levying of contributions and pillaging raids on the one side or the other.

Incursions of the Moors into Spain.

The pacified territory experienced attack, properly so called, chiefly from the inhabitants of the shore settled around and along the Riff, the Mazices, and the Baquates ; and this indeed took place, as a rule, by sea, and was directed chiefly against the Spanish coast (I. 67). Accounts of inroads of the Moors into Baetica run through the whole imperial period,[3] and show that the Romans, in consequence of the absence of energetic

[1] The *tumultus Gaetulicus* (*C. I. L.* viii. 6958) was rather an insurrection than an invasion.

[2] Ptolemy certainly takes as boundary of the province of Caesarea the line above the Shott, and does not reckon Gaetulia as belonging to it ; on the other hand he extends that of Tingis as far as the Great Atlas. Pliny v. 4, 30, numbers among the subject peoples of Africa "all Gaetulia as far as the Niger and the Ethiopian frontier," which points nearly to Timbuctoo. The latter statement will accord with the official conception of the matter.

[3] Already in Nero's time Calpurnius (*Egl.* iv. 40) terms the shore of Baetica *trucibus obnoxia Mauris.* —If under Pius the Moors were beaten off and driven back as far as and over the Atlas (*vita Pii,* 5 ; Pausanias viii. 43). the sending of troops at that time from Spain to the Tingitana (*C. I. L.* iii. 5212-5215) makes it probable that this attack of the Moors

affected Baetica, and the troops of the Tarraconensis marching against these followed them over the straits. The probably contemporary activity of the Syrian legion at the Aures (p. 320) suggests moreover that this war extended also to Numidia.—The war with the Moors under Marcus (*vita Marci,* 21, 22 ; *vita Severi,* 2), had its scene essentially in Baetica and Lusitania.—A governor of Hither Spain under Severus had to fight with the "rebels" by water and by land (*C. I. L.* ii. 4114).—Under Alexander (*vita,* 58) there was fighting in the province of Tingi, but without mention of Spain in the case.—From the time of Aurelian (*vita Saturnini,* 9) there is mention of Mauro-Spanish conflicts. We cannot exactly determine the time of a sending of troops from Numidia to Spain and against the Mazices (*C. I. L.* viii. 2786), where presumably not the Mazices of the Caesariensis but those of the Tingitana on the Riff (Ptolem. iv. 1, 10), are meant ; per-

offensive, found themselves here permanently on a defensive, which indeed did not involve a vital danger for the empire, but yet brought constant insecurity and often sore harm over rich and peaceful regions.   The civilised territories of Africa appear to have suffered less under the Moorish attacks, probably because the headquarters of Numidia, immediately on the Mauretanian frontier, and the strong garrisons on the west side of the Aures, did their duty.   But on the collapse of the imperial power in the third century the invasion here also began ; the feud of Five Peoples, as it was called, which broke out about the time of Gallienus, and on account of which twenty years later the emperor Maximianus went personally to Africa, arose from the tribes beyond the Shott on the Numido-Mauretanian frontier, and affected particularly the towns of Eastern Mauretania and of Western Numidia, such as Auzia and Mileu.[1]

Quinquegentiani.

We come to the internal organisation of the country. In respect of language, that which belonged properly to the people was treated like the Celtic in Gaul and the Iberian in Spain ; here in Africa all the more, as the earlier foreign rule had already set the example in that respect, and certainly no Roman understood this popular

Continuance of the Berber language.

haps with this is connected the fact that Gaius Vallius Maximianus, as governor of Tingitana, achieved in the province Baetica (according to Hirschfeld, *Wiener Stud.* vi. 123, under Marcus and Commodus) a victory over the Moors and relieved towns besieged by them (*C. I. L.* ii. 1120, 2015) ; these events prove at least that the conflicts with the Moors on the Riff and the associates that flocked to them from the country lying behind did not cease.   When the Baquates on the same coast besieged the pretty remote Cartenna (Tenes) in the Caesariensis (*C. I. L.* viii. 9663), they perhaps came by sea.   Where the wars with the Moors under Hadrian (*vita*, 5, 12) and Commodus (*vita*, 13) took place is not known.

[1] More information than in the scanty accounts of Victor and Eu-

tropius is supplied as to this war by the inscribed stones, *C. I. L.* viii. 2615, 8836, 9045, 9047. According to these the *Quinquegentiani* may be followed out from Gallienus to Diocletian. The beginning is made by the Baquates who, designated as *Transtagnenses*, must have dwelt beyond the Shott.   Four "kings" combine for an expedition.   The most dreaded opponent is Faraxen with his *gentiles Fraxinenses*.   Towns like Mileu in Numidia not far from Cirta and Auzia in the Caesariensis are attacked, and the citizens must in good part defend themselves against the enemy.   After the end of the war Maximian constructs great magazines in Thubusuctu not far from Saldae.   These fragmentary accounts give in some measure an insight into the relations of the time.

idiom. The Berber tribes had not merely a national language, but also a national writing (p. 305); but never, so far as we see, was use made of it in official intercourse, at least it was never put upon the coins. Even the native Berber dynasties formed no exception to this, whether because in their kingdoms the more considerable towns were more Phoenician than Libyan, or because the Phoenician civilisation prevailed so far generally. The language was written indeed also under Roman rule, in fact most of the Berber votive or sepulchral inscriptions proceed certainly from the imperial period; but their rarity proves that it attained only to limited written use in the sphere of the Roman rule. It maintained itself as a popular language above all naturally in the districts, to which the Romans came little or not at all, as in the Sahara, in the mountains of the Riff of Morocco, in the two Kabylias; but even the fertile and early cultivated island of the Tripolis, Girba (Jerba), the seat of the Carthaginian purple manufacture, still at the present day speaks Libyan. Taken on the whole, the old popular idiom in Africa defended itself better than among the Celts and the Iberians.

Continuance of the Phoenician language.

The language which prevailed in North Africa, when it became Roman, was that of the foreign rule which preceded the Roman. Leptis, probably not the Tripolitan, but that near Hadrumetum, was the only African town which marked its coins with a Greek legend, and thus conceded to this language an at least secondary position in public intercourse. The Phoenician language prevailed at that time so far as there was a civilisation in North Africa, from Great Leptis to Tingi, most thoroughly in and around Carthage, but not less in Numidia and Mauretania.[1] To this language of a highly developed

[1] Apart from the coins this is proved also by the inscriptions. According to the comparison, for which I am indebted to Herr Euting, the great mass of the old Punic inscriptions, that is, those written probably before the destruction of Carthage, falls to Carthage itself (about 2500), the rest to Hadrumetum (9), Thugga (the famous Phoenico-Berber one), Cirta (5), Iol-Caesarea (1). The new Punic occur most numerously in and around Carthage (30), and generally they are found not unfrequently in the proconsular province, also in Great Leptis (5) and on the islands of Girba

although foreign culture certain concessions were made on the change in the system of administration.   Perhaps already under Caesar, certainly under Augustus and Tiberius, as well the towns of the Roman province, such as Great Leptis and Oea, as those of the Mauretanian kingdom, like Tingi and Lix, employed in official use the Phoenician language, even those which like Tingi had become Roman burgess-communities.   Nevertheless they did not go so far in Africa as in the Greek half of the empire.   In the Greek provinces of the empire the Greek language prevailed, as in business intercourse generally, so particularly in direct intercourse with the imperial government and its officials ; the coin of the city organ- ised after the Greek fashion names also the emperor in Greek.   But in the African the coin, even if it speaks in another language, names the emperor or the imperial official always in Latin.   Even on the coins of the kings of Mauretania the name of the Greek queen stands possibly in Greek, but that of the king—also an imperial official—uniformly in Latin, even where the queen is named beside him.   That is to say, even the government did not admit the Phoenician in its intercourse with the communities and individuals in Africa, but it allowed it for internal intercourse ; it was not a third imperial language, but a language of culture recognised in its own sphere.

But this limited recognition of the Phoenician language did not long subsist.   There is no document for the public use of Phoenician from the time after Tiberius, and it hardly survived the time of the first dynasty. [1]   How and when the change set in we do not know ; probably the

(1) and Cossura (1) ; in Numidia, in and near Calama (23), and in Cirta (15) ; in Mauretania hitherto only in Portus Magnus (2).

[1] The coining in Africa ceases in the main after Tiberius, and there- after, since African inscriptions from the first century after Christ are be- fore us only in very small numbers, for a considerable period documents fail us.   The coins of Babba in the Tingitana, going from Claudius down to Galba, have exclusively Latin legends ; but the town was a colony. The Latin-Punic inscriptions of Great Leptis, *C. I. L.* viii. 7, and of Na- raggara, *C. I. L.* viii. 4636, may doubtless belong to the time after Ti- berius, but as bi-lingual tell rather for the view that, when they were set up, the Phoenician language was already degraded.

government, perhaps Tiberius or Claudius, spoke the decisive word and accomplished the linguistic and national annexation of the African Phoenicians as far as it could be done by state authority. In private intercourse the Phoenician held its ground still for a long time in Africa, longer apparently than in the motherland ; at the beginning of the third century ladies of genteel houses in Great Leptis spoke so little Latin or Greek, that there was no place for them in Roman society ; even at the end of the fourth there was a reluctance to appoint clergymen in the environs of Hippo Regius (Bona), who could not make themselves intelligible in Punic to their countrymen ; these termed themselves at that time still Canaanites, and Punic names and Punic phrases were still current. But the language was banished from the school[1] and even from written use, and had become a popular dialect ; and even this probably only in the region of the old Phoenician civilisation, particularly the old Phoenician places on the coast that stood aloof from intercourse on a large scale.[2] When the Arabs came to Africa they found as language of the country doubtless that of the Berbers, but no longer that of the Poeni ;[3] with the Carthagino-Roman civilisation the two foreign languages disappeared, while the old native one still lives in the present day. The civilised foreign dominions changed ; the Berbers remained like the palm of the oasis and the sand of the desert. The heritage of the Phoenician language fell not to

---

[1] From the expression in the epitome of Victor, that the emperor Severus was *Latinis litteris sufficienter instructus, Graecis sermonibus eruditus, Punica eloquentia promptior, quippe genitus apud Leptim,* we may not infer a Punic course of rhetoric in the Tripolis of that time ; the late and inferior author has possibly given a scholastic version of the well-known notice.

[2] On the statement of the younger Arnobius, writing about 460 (*ad Psalm.* 104, p. 481 Migne : *Cham vero secundus filius Noe a Rhinocoruris usque Gadira habens linguas sermone Punico a parte Garamantum, Latino a parte boreae, barbarico a parte meridiani, Aethiopum et Aegyptiorum ac barbaris interioribus vario sermone numero viginti duabus linguis in patriis trecentis nonaginta et quattuor*), no reliance is to be placed, still less upon the nonsense of Procopius, *de bello Vand.* ii. 10, as to the Phoenician inscription and language in Tigisis. Authorities of this sort were hardly able to distinguish Berber and Punic.

[3] In a single place on the Little Syrtis the Phoenician may still have been spoken in the eleventh century (Movers, *Phön.* ii. 2, 478).

Greek, but to Latin.   This was not involved in the
natural development.   In Caesar's time the Latin and
the Greek were alike in North Africa foreign languages, but
as the coins of Leptis already show, the latter by far more
diffused than the former ; Latin was spoken then only by
the officials, the soldiers, and the Italian merchants.   It
would have at that time been probably easier to introduce
the Hellenising of Africa than the Latinising of it.   But
it was the converse that took place.   Here the same will
prevailed, which did not allow the Hellenic germs to
spring up in Gaul, and which incorporated Greek Sicily
into the domain of Latin speech ; the same will, which
drew the boundaries between the Latin West and the
Greek East, assigned Africa to the former.

In a similar sense the internal organisation of the
country was regulated.   It was based, as in Italy on the
Latin and in the East on the Hellenic urban community,
so here on the Phoenician.   When the Roman rule in
Africa began, the Carthaginian territory at that time consisted predominantly of urban communities, for the most
part small, of which there were counted three hundred, each
administered by its sufetes ;[1] and the republic had made
no change in this respect.   Even in the kingdoms the towns
formerly Phoenician had retained their organisation under
the native rulers, and at least Calama—an inland town of
Numidia hardly of Phoenician foundation—had demonstrably the same Phoenician municipal constitution ; the
civilisation which Massinissa gave to his kingdom must
have consisted essentially in his transforming the villages

[1] More clearly than by the Latin inscriptions found in Africa, which begin too late to illustrate the state of things before the second century A.D., this is shown by the four contracts of *patronatus* from the time of Tiberius, quoted in next note, concluded by two small places of the proconsular pro-vince Apisa maius and Siagu, and two others nowhere else mentioned, probably adjacent, Themetra and Thimiligi ; according to which the statement of Strabo (xvii. 3, 15, p. 833) that at the beginning of the last war the Carthaginian territory num-bered 300 towns, appears not at all incredible.   In each of those four smaller places there were sufetes ; even where the old and new Punic inscriptions name magistrates, there are regularly two sufetes.   That these are comparatively frequent in the proconsular province, and else where can only be pointed out in Calama, serves to show how much more strongly the Phoenician urban organisation was developed in the former.

of the agricultural Berbers into towns after the Phoenician model. The same will hold good of the few older urban communities which existed in Mauretania before Augustus. So far as we see, the two annually changing sufetes of the African communities coincide in the main with the analogous presidents of the community in the Italian municipal constitution ; and that in other respects, *e.g.* in the common councils among the Carthaginians formed after a fashion altogether divergent from the Italian (ii. 16), the Phoenician urban constitution of Roman Africa has preserved national peculiarities, does not at least admit of proof.[1] But the fact itself that the contrast, if even but formal, of the Phoenician town to the Italian was retained was, like the permission of the language, a recognition of the Phoenician nationality and a certain security for its continuance even under Roman rule. That it was recognised in the first instance as the regular form of administration of the African territory, is proved by the establishment of Carthage by Caesar primarily as a Phoenician city as well under the old sufetes[2] as in a certain measure with the old inhabitants, seeing that a great, perhaps the greatest part of the new burgesses was taken from the surrounding townships, again also under the protection of the great goddess of the Punic Carthage, the queen of heaven

---

[1] The contracts of *patronatus* from the time of Caesar (*C. I. L.* viii. 10525), of Augustus (*ib.* 68 comp. 69), and Tiberius (*C. I. L.* v. 4919-4922), concluded by the *senatus populusque* of African communities (*civitates*) of peregrine rights with Romans of rank, appear to have been entered into quite after the Roman fashion by the common council, which represents and binds the community.

[2] On the coin undoubtedly struck under Caesar (Müller *Num. de l'Afr.* ii. 149) with *Kar(thago) Veneris* and *Aristo Mutumbal Ricoce suf(etes)*, the first two names are probably to be taken together as a Graeco-Phoenician double name, such as elsewhere is not rare (comp. *C. I. L.* v. 4922 : *agente Celere Imilchonis Gulalsae filio*

sufete). Since on the one hand sufetes cannot be assigned to a Roman colony, and on the other hand the conducting of such a colony to Carthage itself is well attested, Caesar himself must either have subsequently changed the form of founding the city, or the founding of the colony must have been carried into effect by the triumvirate as a posthumous ordinance of the dictator (as is hinted by Appian, *Pun.* 136). We may compare the fact that Curubis stands in the earlier time of Caesar under sufetes (*C. I. L.* viii. 10525), in the year 709 U.C. as a Caesarian colony under duoviri (*ib.* 977); yet the case is different, since this town did not, like Carthage, owe its existence to Caesar.

Astarte, who at that time marched in with her votaries anew into her old abode. It is true that in Carthage itself this organisation soon gave place to the Italian colonial constitution, and the protecting patroness Astarte became the—at least in name—Latin Caelestis. But in the rest of Africa and in Numidia the Phoenician urban organisation probably remained throughout the first century the predominant one, in so far as it pertained to all communities of recognised municipal rights and lacking Roman or Latin organisation. Abolished in the proper sense it doubtless was not, as in fact sufetes still occur under Pius ; but by degrees they everywhere make way for the duoviri, and the changed principle of government entails in this sphere also its ultimate consequences.

The transformation of Phoenician urban rights into Italian began under Caesar. The old Phoenician town of Utica, predecessor and heiress of Carthage—as some compensation for the severe injury to its interests by the restoration of the old capital of the country—obtained, as the first Italian organisation in Africa, perhaps from the dictator Caesar, Latin rights, certainly from his successor Augustus the position of a Roman *municipium.* The town of Tingi received the same rights, in gratitude for the fidelity which it had maintained during the Perusine war (p. 311). Several others soon followed ; yet the number of communities with Roman rights in Africa down to Trajan and Hadrian remained limited.[1] Thenceforth there were assigned on a great scale—although, so far as we see, throughout by individual bestowal—to communities hitherto Phoenician municipal or else colonial rights ;

Transformation of the Phoenician towns into Italian.

[1] For Africa and Numidia Pliny (*H. N.*, v. 4, 29 f.) numbers in all 516 communities, among which are 6 colonies, 15 communities of Roman burgesses, 2 Latin towns (for the *oppidum stipendiarium* must, according to the position which is given to it, have been also of Italian rights), the rest either Phoenician towns (*oppida*), among which were 30 free, or else Libyan tribes (*non civitates tantum, sed pleraeque etiam nationes iure dici possunt*). Whether these figures are to be referred to Vespasian's time or to an earlier, is not ascertained ; in any case they are not free from errors, for, besides the six colonies specially adduced, six are wanting (Assuras, Carpi, Clupea, Curubi, Hippo Diarrhytos, Neapolis), which are referable, partly with certainty partly with probability, to Caesar or Augustus.

for the latter too were subsequently as a rule conferred merely in a titular way without settlement of colonists. If the dedications and memorials of all sorts, that formerly appeared but sparingly in Africa, present themselves in abundance from the beginning of the second century, this was doubtless chiefly the consequence of the adoption of numerous townships into the imperial union of the towns with best rights.

Settlement of Italian colonists in Africa.

Besides the conversion of Phoenician towns into Italian *municipia* or colonies, not a few towns of Italian rights arose in Africa by means of the settlement of Italian colonists. For this too the dictator Caesar laid the foundation—as indeed for no province perhaps so much as for Africa were the paths prescribed by him—and the emperors of the first dynasty followed his example. We have already spoken of the founding of Carthage ; the town obtained not at once, but very soon, Italian settlers and therewith Italian organisation and full rights of Roman citizenship. Beyond doubt from the outset destined once more to be the capital of the province and laid out as a great city, it rapidly in point of fact became so. Carthage and Lugudunum were the only cities of the West which, besides the capital of the empire, had a standing garrison of imperial troops. Moreover in Africa—in part certainly already by the dictator, in part only by the first emperor—a series of small country-towns in the districts nearest to Sicily, Hippo Diarrhytus, Clupea, Curubi, Neapolis, Carpi, Maxula, Uthina, Great-Thuburbo, Assuras, were furnished with colonies, probably not merely to provide for veterans, but to promote the Latinising of this region. The two colonies which arose at that time in the former kingdom of Numidia, Cirta with its dependencies, and New-Cirta or Sicca, were the result of special obligations of Caesar towards the leader of free bands Publius Sittius from Nuceria and his Italiano-African bands (iv. 470, 574). The former, inasmuch as the territory on which it was laid out belonged at that time to a client-state (p. 311, note), obtained a peculiar and very independent organisation, and retained it in

iv. 447, 544.

part even later, although it soon became an imperial city. Both rose rapidly and became considerable centres of Roman civilisation in Africa.

The colonisation, which Augustus undertook in the kingdom of Juba and Claudius carried forward, bore another character.   In Mauretania, still at that time very primitive, there was a want both of towns and of the elements for creating them ; the settlement of soldiers of the Roman army, who had served out their time, brought civilisation here into a barbarous land.   Thus in the later province of Caesarea along the coast Igilgili, Saldae, Rusazu, Rusguniae, Gunugi, Cartenna (Tenes), and farther away from the sea Thubusuptu and Zuccabar, were settled with Augustan, and Oppidum Novum with Claudian, veterans ; as also in the province of Tingi under Augustus Zilis, Babba, Banasa, under Claudius Lix   These communities with Roman burgess-rights were not, as was already observed, under the kings of Mauretania, so long as there were such, but were attached administratively to the adjoining Roman province ; consequently there was involved in these settlements, as it were, a beginning towards the annexation of Mauretania.[1]   The pushing forward of civilisation, such as Augustus and Claudius aimed at, was not subsequently continued, or at any rate continued only to a very limited extent, although there was room enough for it in the western half of the province of Caesarea and in that of Tingi ; that the later colonies regularly proceeded from titular bestowal without settlement, has already been remarked (p. 332).

Alongside of this urban organisation we have specially to mention that of the large landed estates in this province. According to Roman arrangement it fitted itself regularly into the communal constitution ; even the extension of

And in Mauretania.

Large landed estates.

---

[1] Pliny, v. 1, 2, says indeed only of Zulil or rather Zili *regum dicioni exempta et iura in Baeticam petere iussa,* and this might be connected with the transfer of this community to Baetica as *Iulia Traducta* (Strabo, iii. 1, 8, p. 140). But probably Pliny gives this notice in the case of Zili alone, just because this is the first colony laid out beyond the imperial frontier which he names. The burgess of a Roman colony cannot possibly have had his forum of justice before the king of Mauretania.

the *latifundia* affected this relationship less injuriously than we should think, since these, as a rule, were not locally compact and were often distributed among several urban territories. But in Africa the large estates were not merely more numerous and more extensive than elsewhere, but these assumed also the compactness of urban territories; around the landlord's house there was formed a settlement, which was not inferior to the small agricultural towns of the province, and, if its president and common councillors often did not venture and still oftener were not able to subject such a fellow-burgess to the full payment of the communal burdens falling upon him, the *de facto* release of these estates from the communal bond of union became still further marked, when such a possession passed over into the hands of the emperor.[1] But this early occurred in Africa to a great extent; Nero in particular, lighted with his confiscations on the landowners, as is said, of half Africa, and what was once imperial was wont to remain so. The small lessees, to whom the domanial estate was farmed out, appear for the most part to have been brought from abroad, and these imperial *coloni* may be reckoned in a certain measure as belonging to the Italian immigration.

Organisation of the Berber communities.

We have formerly remarked (p. 306) that the Berbers formed a considerable portion of the population of Numidia and Mauretania through the whole time of the Roman rule. But as to their internal organisation hardly more can be ascertained than the emergence of the clan (*gens*)[2]

[1] Frontinus in the well-known passage, p. 53 Lachm., respecting processes between the urban communities and private persons, or, as it may be, the emperor, appears not to presuppose state-districts *de iure* independent and of a similar nature with urban territories—such as are incompatible with Roman law—but a *de facto* refractory attitude of the great landowner towards the community which makes him liable, *e.g.* for the furnishing of recruits or compulsory services, basing itself on the allegation that the piece of land made liable is not within the bounds of the community requiring the service.

[2] The technical designation *gens* comes into prominence particularly in the fixed title of the *praefectus gentis Musulamiorum, etc.*; but, as this is the lowest category of the independent commonwealth, the word is usually avoided in dedications (comp. *C. I. L.* viii. p. 1100) and *civitas* put instead, a designation, which, like the *oppidum* of Pliny foreign to the technical language (p. 331, note), includes in it all communities of non-Italian or Greek organisation. The nature of the *gens*

instead of the urban organisation under duoviri or sufetes. The societies of the natives were not, like those of North Italy, assigned as subjects to individual urban communities, but were placed like the towns immediately under the governors, doubtless also, where it seemed necessary, under a Roman officer specially placed over them (*praefectus gentis*), and further under authorities of their own[1]—the " headman " (*princeps*), who in later times bore possibly the title of king, and the " eleven first." Presumably this arrangement was monarchical in contrast to the collegiate one of the Phoenician as of the Latin community, and there stood alongside of the tribal chief a limited number of elders instead of the numerous senate of de-

is described by the paraphrase (*C. I. L.* viii. 68) alternating with *civitas Gurzensis* (*ib.* 69) : *senatus populusque civitatium stipendiariorum pago Gurzenses*, that is, the " elders and community of the clans of tributary people in the village of Gurza."

[1] When the designation *princeps* (*C. I. L.* viii. p. 1102) is not merely enunciative but an official title, it appears throughout in communities which are neither themselves urban communities nor parts of such, and with special frequency in the case of the *gentes*. We may compare the " eleven first " (comp, *Eph. epigr.* v. n. 302, 521, 533) with the *seniores* to be met with here and there. An evidence in support of both positions is given in the inscription *C. I. L.* viii. 7041 : *Florus Labaeonis f. princeps et undecimprimus gentis Saboidum*. Recently at Bu Jelîda, a little westward of the great road between Carthage and Theveste, in a valley of the Jebel Rihan, and so in a quite civilised region, there have been found the remains of a Berber village, which calls itself on a monument of the time of Pius (still unprinted) *gens Bacchuiana*, and is under " eleven elders " ; the names of gods (*Saturno Achaiaei* [?] *Aug*[*uslo*], like the names of men (*Candidus Braisamonis fil.*), are half local, half Latin. In Calama the dating after the two sufetes and the *prin-*

ceps (*C. I. L.* viii. 5306, comp. 5369) is remarkable ; it appears that this probably Libyan community was first under a chief, and then obtained sufetes without the chief being dropped. It may readily be understood that our monuments do not give much information upon the *gentes* and their organisation ; in this field doubtless little was written on stone. Even the Libyan inscriptions belong, at least as regards the majority, to towns in part or wholly inhabited by Berbers ; the bilingual inscriptions found at Tenelium (*C. I. L.* viii. p. 514), in Numidia westward from Bona in the Sheffia plain, the same place that has furnished till now most of the Berber stone inscriptions, show indeed in their Latin part Libyan names, *e.g. Chinidial Misicir* f. and *Naddhsen Cotuzanis* f., both from the clan (*tribu*) of the *Misiciri* or *Misictri* ; but one of these people, who has served in the Roman army and has acquired the Roman franchise, names himself in the Latin text *in civitate sua Tenelio flamen perpetuus*, according to which this place seems to have been organised like a town. If, therefore, success should ever attend the attempt to read and decipher the Berber inscriptions with certainty, they would hardly give us sufficient information as to the internal organisation of the Berber tribes.

curiones of the towns. The communities of natives in Roman Africa seem to have attained afterwards to Italian organisation only by way of exception ; the African towns with Italian rights, which did not originate from immigration, had doubtless for the most part Phoenician civic rights previously. Exceptions occur chiefly in the case of transplanted tribes, as indeed the considerable town Thubursicum originated from such a forced settlement of Numidians. The Berber communities possessed especially the mountains and the steppes ; they obeyed the foreigners, without either the masters or the subjects feeling any desire to come to terms with one another ; and, when other foreigners invaded the land, their position in presence of the Vandals, the Byzantines, the Arabs, the French, remained almost on the old footing.

Husbandry. In the economy of the soil the eastern half of Africa vies with Egypt. Certainly the soil is unequal, and rocks and steppes occupy not only the greater portion of the western half, but also considerable tracts in the eastern ; here too there were various inaccessible mountain-regions, which yielded but slowly or not at all to civilisation ; particularly on the rocky ridges along the coast the Roman rule left few or no traces. Even the Byzacene, the south-eastmost part of the proconsular province, is only designated as a specially productive region by an erroneous generalisation of what holds good as to individual coast districts and oases ; from Sufetula (Sbitla) westward the land is waterless and rocky ; in the fifth century A.D. Byzacene was reckoned to have about a half less per cent of land capable of culture than the other African provinces. But the northern and northwestern portion of the proconsular province, above all the valley of the largest river in north Africa, the Bagradas (Mejerda), and not less a considerable part of Numidia, yield abundant grain crops, almost like the valley of the Nile. In the favoured districts the country towns, very frequent, as their ruins show, lay so near to each other that the population here cannot have been much less dense than in the land of the Nile, and according to all traces it prosecuted especially husbandry. The mighty armed masses, with which after the defeat at Pharsalus the republicans in Africa took up the struggle against Caesar, were formed of these peasants, so that in the year of war the fields lay untilled. Since Italy used more corn than it produced, it was primarily dependent, in addition to the Italian islands, on the almost equally near Africa; and after it became subject to the Romans, its corn went thither not merely by way of commerce, but above all as tribute. Already in Cicero's time the capital of the empire doubtless subsisted for the most part on African corn; through the admission of Numidia under Caesar's dictatorship the corn thenceforth coming in as tribute increased according to the estimate about 1,200,000 Roman bushels (525,000 hectolitres) annually. After the Egyptian corn supplies were instituted under Augustus, for the third part of the corn used in Rome North Africa was reckoned upon, and Egypt for a like amount; while the desolated Sicily, Sardinia, and Baetica, along with Italy's own production, covered the rest of the need. In what measure the Italy of the imperial period was dependent for its subsistence on Africa is shown by the measures taken during the wars between Vitellius and Vespasian and between Severus and Pescennius; Vespasian thought that he had conquered Italy when he occupied Egypt and Africa; Severus sent a strong army to Africa to hinder Pescennius from occupying it.

Oil, too, and wine had already held a prominent place in the old Carthaginian husbandry, and on Little-Leptis (near Susa), for example, an annual payment of 3,000,000 pounds of oil (nearly 10,000 hectolitres) could be imposed by Caesar for the Roman baths, as indeed Susa still at the present day exports 40,000 hectolitres of oil. Accordingly the historian of the Jugurthan war terms Africa rich in corn, poor in oil and wine, and even in Vespasian's time the province gave in this respect only a moderate yield. It was only when the peace with the empire became permanent—a peace which the fruit-tree

Oil and wine.

needed even far more than the fruits of the field—that the culture of olives extended ; in the fourth century no province supplied such quantities of oil as Africa, and the African oil was predominantly employed for the baths in Rome. In quality, doubtless, it was always inferior to that of Italy and Spain, not because nature there was less favourable, but because the preparation lacked skill and care. The cultivation of the vine acquired no prominent importance in Africa for export. On the other hand the breeding of horses and of cattle flourished, especially in Numidia and Mauretania.

Manufactures and commerce. Manufactures and trade never had the same importance in the African provinces as in the East and in Egypt. The Phoenicians had transplanted the preparation of purple from their native country to these coasts, where the island of Gerba (Jerba) became the African Tyre, and was inferior only to the latter itself in quality. This manufacture flourished through the whole imperial period. Among the few deeds which king Juba II. has to show, is the arrangement for obtaining purple on the coast of the Atlantic Ocean and on the adjacent islands.[1] Woollen stuffs of inferior quality and leather goods were manufactured in Mauretania, apparently by the natives, also for export.[2] The trade in slaves was very considerable. The products of the interior of the country naturally passed by way of North Africa into general commerce, but not to such an extent as by way of Egypt. The elephant,

---

[1] That the Gaetulian purple is to be referred to Juba is stated by Pliny, *H. N.* vi. 31, 201 : *paucas (Mauretaniae insulas) constat esse ex adverso Autololum a Iuba repertas, in quibus Gaetulicam purpuram tinguere instituerat ;* by these *insulae purpurariae* (*ib.* 203) can only be meant Madeira. In fact the oldest mention of this purple is that in Horace, *Ep.* ii. 2, 181. Proofs are wanting as to the later duration of this manufacture, and, as the Roman rule did not extend to these islands, it is not probable, although from the *sagum purpurium* of the tariff of Zarai (*C. I. L.*

viii. 4508) we may infer Mauretanian manufactures of purple.

[2] The tariff of Zarai set up at the Numidian customs-frontier towards Mauretania (*C. I. L.* viii. 4508) from the year 202 gives a clear picture of the Mauretanian exports. Wine, figs, dates, sponges, are not wanting ; but slaves, cattle of all sorts, woollen stuffs (*vestis Afra*), and leather wares play the chief part. The Description of the earth also from the time of Constantius says, c. 60, that Mauretania *vestem et mancipia negotiatur.*

it is true, was the device of Mauretania in particular, and there, where it has now for long disappeared, it was still hunted down to the imperial period ; but probably only small quantities came thence into commerce.

The prosperity which subsisted in the part of Africa Prosperity. at all cultivated is clearly attested by the ruins of its numerous towns, which, in spite of the narrow bounds of their domains, everywhere exhibit baths, theatres, triumphal arches, gorgeous tombs, and generally buildings of luxury of all kinds, mostly mediocre in art, often excessive in magnificence. Not quite in the villas of the superior nobility, as in the Gallic land, but in the middle class of the farming burgesses must the economic strength of these regions have lain.[1]

The frequency of intercourse, so far as we may judge Roads. of it from our knowledge of the network of roads, must within the civilised territory have corresponded to the density of the population. During the first century the imperial roads originated, which connected the head-quarters of that time, Theveste, partly with the coast of the Lesser Syrtis—a step, having close relation to the formerly narrated pacification of the district between the Aures and the sea—partly with the great cities of the north coast, Hippo regius (Bona) and Carthage. From the second century onward we find all the larger towns and several smaller active in providing the necessary communications within their territory ; this, however, doubtless holds true of most of the imperial lands, and only comes into clearer prominence in Africa, because this opportunity was made use of more diligently here than elsewhere to do homage to the reigning emperor.

---

[1] According to an epitaph found in Mactaris in the Byzacene (*Eph. epigr.* v. n. 279), a man of free birth there, after having been actively engaged in bringing in the harvests far around in Africa, first throughout twelve years as an ordinary reaper and then for other eleven as a foreman, purchased for himself with the savings of his pay a town and a country house, and became in his turn a member of council and burgomaster. His poetical epitaph shows, if not culture, at least pretensions to it. A development of life of this sort was in the Roman imperial period doubtless not so rare as it at first may seem, but probably occurred in Africa more frequently than elsewhere.

As to the road-system of the districts, which though Roman were yet not Romanised, and as to the routes which were the medium of the important traffic through the desert, we have no general information.

Introduction of camels.

But probably a momentous revolution occurred in the desert-traffic during that time by the introduction of the camel. In older times it meets us, as is well known, only in Asia as far as Arabia, while Egypt and all Africa knew simply the horse. During the first three centuries of our era the countries effected an exchange, and, like the Arabian horse, the Libyan camel, we may say, made its appearance in history. Mention of the latter first occurs in the history of the war waged by the dictator Caesar in Africa; when here among the booty by the side of captive officers twenty-two camels of king Juba are adduced, such a possession must at that time have been of an extraordinary nature in Africa. In the fourth century the Roman generals demand from the towns of Tripolis thousands of camels for the transport of water and of provisions before they enter upon the march into the desert. This gives a glimpse of the revolution that had taken place during the interval in the circumstances of the intercourse between the north and the south of Africa; whether it originated from Egypt or from Cyrene and Tripolis we cannot tell, but it redounded to the advantage of the whole north of this continent.

Character and culture of the people.

Thus North Africa was a valuable possession for the finances of the empire. Whether the Roman nation generally gained or lost more by the assimilation of North Africa, is less ascertained. The dislike which the Italian felt from of old towards the African did not change after Carthage had become a Roman great city, and all Africa spoke Latin; if Severus Antoninus combined in himself the vices of three nations, his savage cruelty was traced to his African father, and the ship captain of the fourth century, who thought that "Africa was a fine country but the Africans were not worthy of it, for they were cunning and faithless, and there might be some good people among them, but not many," was at least not thinking of the bad Hannibal, but was speaking out the feeling of the great public at the time. So far as the influence of African elements may be recognised in the Roman literature of the imperial period, we meet with specially unpleasant leaves in a book generally far from pleasant. The new life, which bloomed for the Romans out of the ruins of the nations extirpated by them, was nowhere full and fresh and beautiful ; even the two creations of Caesar, the Celtic land and North Africa —for Latin Africa was not much less his work than Latin Gaul—remained structures of ruins. But the toga suited, at any rate, the new-Roman of the Rhone and the Garonne better than the "Seminumidians and Semigaetulians." Doubtless Carthage remained in the numbers of its population and in wealth not far behind Alexandria, and was indisputably the second city of the Latin half of the empire, next to Rome the most lively, perhaps also the most corrupt, city of the West, and the most important centre of Latin culture and literature. Augustine depicts with lively colours how many an honest youth from the province went to wreck there amid the dissolute doings of the circus, and how powerful was the impression produced on him—when, a student of seventeen years of age, he came from Madaura to Carthage —by the theatre with its love-pieces and with its tragedy. There was no lack in the African of diligence and talent ; on the contrary, perhaps more value was set upon the Latin and along with it the Greek instruction, and on its aim of general culture, in Africa than anywhere else in the empire, and the school-system was highly developed. The philosopher Appuleius under Pius, the celebrated Christian author Augustine, both descended from good burgess-families—the former from Madaura, the latter from the neighbouring smaller place Thagaste—received their first training in the schools of their native towns ; then Appuleius studied in Carthage, and finished his training in Athens and Rome ; Augustine went from Thagaste first to Madaura, then likewise to Carthage ; in this way the training of youth was completed in the better houses throughout. Juvenal advises the professor of rhetoric who would earn money to go to Gaul or, still better, to Africa, "the nurse of advocates." At a nobleman's seat in the territory of Cirta there has recently been brought to light a private bath of the later imperial period equipped with princely magnificence, the mosaic pavement of which depicts how matters went on once at the castle ; the palaces, the extensive hunting-park with the hounds and stags, the stables with the noble race-horses, occupy no doubt most of the space, but there is not wanting also the "scholar's corner" (*filosofi locus*), and beside it the noble lady sitting under the palms.

Scholas-
ticism.

But the black spot of the African literary character is just its scholasticism. It does not begin till late ; before the time of Hadrian and of Pius the Latin literary world exhibits no African name of repute, and subsequently the Africans of note were throughout, in the first instance, schoolmasters, and came as such to be authors. Under those emperors the most celebrated teachers and scholars of the capital were native Africans, the rhetor Marcus Cornelius Fronto from Cirta, instructor of the princes at the court of Pius, and the philologue Gaius Sulpicius Apollinaris from Carthage. For that reason there prevailed in these circles sometimes the foolish purism that forced back the Latin into the old-fashioned paths of Ennius and of Cato, whereby Fronto and Apollinaris made their repute, sometimes an utter oblivion of the earnest austerity innate in Latin, and a frivolity producing a worse imitation of bad Greek models, such as reaches its culmination in the—in its time much admired—"Ass-romance" of that philosopher of Madaura. The language swarmed partly with scholastic reminiscences, partly with unclassical or newly coined words and phrases. Just as in the emperor Severus, an African of good family and himself a scholar and author, his tone of speech always betrayed the African, so the style of these Africans, even those who were clever and from the first trained in Latin, like the Carthaginian Tertullian, has regularly something strange and incongruous, with its diffuseness of petty detail, its

minced sentences, its witty and fantastic conceits.   There
is a lack of both the graceful charm of the Greek and of
the dignity of the Roman.   Significantly we do not meet
in the whole field of Africano-Latin authorship a single
poet who deserves to be so much as named.

It was not till the Christian period that it became   Christian
otherwise.   In the development of Christianity Africa   literature
plays the very first part ; if it arose in Syria, it was in   in Africa.
and through Africa that it became the religion for the
world.   As the translation of the sacred books from the
Hebrew language into the Greek, and that into the popular
language of the most considerable Jewish community out
of Judaea, gave to Judaism its position in the world, so
in a similar way for the transference of Christianity from
the serving East to the ruling West the translation of its
confessional writings into the language of the West
became of decisive importance ; and this all the more,
inasmuch as these books were translated, not into the
language of the cultivated circles of the West, which early
disappeared from common life and in the imperial age
was everywhere a matter of scholastic attainment, but
into the decomposed Latin already preparing the way
for the structure of the Romance languages—the Latin
of common intercourse at that time familiar to the great
masses.   If Christianity was by the destruction of the
Jewish church-state released from its Jewish basis (p. 229),
it became the religion of the world by the fact, that in
the great world-empire it began to speak the universally
current imperial language ; and those nameless men, who
since the second century Latinised the Christian writings,
performed for this epoch just such a service, as at the
present day, in the heightened measure required by the
enlarged horizon of the nations, is carried out in the
footsteps of Luther by the Bible Societies.   And these
men were in part Italians, but above all Africans.[1]   In

[1] How far our Latin texts of the   from one and the same translation as
Bible are to be referred to several   a basis by means of manifold revision
translations originally different, or   with the aid of the originals, are
whether, as Lachmann assumed, the   questions which can scarcely be
different recensions have proceeded   definitely decided—for the present at

Africa to all appearance the knowledge of Greek, which is able to dispense with translations, was far more seldom to be met with than at least in Rome ; and, on the other hand, the Oriental element, that preponderated particularly in the early stages of Christianity, here found a readier reception than in the other Latin-speaking lands of the West. Even as regards the polemic literature called especially into existence by the new faith, since the

least—in favour of either one or the other view. But that both Italians and Africans took part in this work —whether of translation or of correction—is proved by the famous words of Augustine, *de doctr. Christ.* ii. 15, 22, *in ipsis autem interpretationibus Itala ceteris praeferatur, nam est verborum tenacior cum perspicuitate sententiae,* over which great authorities have been perplexed, but certainly without reason. Bentley's proposal, approved afresh of late (by Corssen, *Jahrb. für protestant. Theol.* vii. p. 507 f.), to change *Itala* into *illa* and *nam* into *quae,* is inadmissible alike philologically and in substance. For the twofold change is destitute of all external probability, and besides *nam* is protected by the copyist Isidorus, *Etym.* vi. 4, 2. The further objection that linguistic usage would require *Italica,* is not borne out (*e.g.* Sidonius and Iordanes as well as the inscriptions of later times, *C. I. L.* x. p. 1146, write *Italus* by turns with *Italicus*), and the designation of a single translation as the most trustworthy on the whole is quite consistent with the advice to consult as many as possible ; whereas by the change proposed an intelligent remark is converted into a meaningless commonplace. It is true that the Christian Church in Rome in the first three centuries made use throughout of the Greek language, and that we may not seek *there* for the *Itali* who took part in the Latin Bible. But that in Italy outside of Rome, especially in Upper Italy, the knowledge of Greek was not much more diffused than in Africa, is most clearly shown by the names of freedmen ; and it is just to

the non-Roman Italy that the designation used by Augustine points ; while we may perhaps also call to mind the fact that Augustine was gained for Christianity by Ambrosius in Milan. The attempt to identify the traces of the recension called by Augustine *Itala* in such remains as have survived of Bible translations before Jerome's, will at all events hardly ever be successful ; but still less will it admit of being proved that Africans only worked at the pre-Hieronymian Latin Bible texts. That they originated largely, perhaps for the most part, in Africa has certainly great probability. The contrast to the one *Itala* can only in reason have been several *Afrae;* and the vulgar Latin, in which these texts are all of them written, is in full agreement with the vulgar Latin, as it was demonstrably spoken in Africa. At the same time we must doubtless not overlook the fact that we know the vulgar Latin in general principally from African sources, and that the proof of the restriction of any individual linguistic phenomenon to Africa is as necessary as it is for the most part unadduced. There existed side by side as well vulgarisms in general use as African provincialisms (comp. *Eph. epigr.* iv. p. 520, as to the cognomina in *-osus*) ; but that forms like *glorificare, nudificare, justificare,* belong to the second category, is by no means proved from the fact that we first meet with them in Africa, since analogous documents to those which we possess, *e.g.* for Carthage in the case of Tertullian, are wanting to us as regards Capua and Milan.

Roman church at this epoch belonged to the Greek circle (p. 226), Africa took the lead in the Latin tongue. The whole Christian authorship down to the end of this period is, so far as it is Latin, African; Tertullian and Cyprian were from Carthage, Arnobius from Sicca, Lactantius, and probably in like manner Minucius Felix, were, in spite of their classic Latin, Africans, and not less the already mentioned somewhat later Augustine. In Africa the growing church found its most zealous confessors and its most gifted defenders. For the literary conflict of the faith Africa furnished by far the most and the ablest combatants, whose special characteristics, now in eloquent discussion, now in witty ridicule of fables, now in vehement indignation, found a true and mighty field for their display in the onslaught on the old gods. A mind—intoxicated first by the whirl of a dissolute life, and then by the fiery enthusiasm of faith—such as utters itself in the Confessions of Augustine, has no parallel elsewhere in antiquity.

APPENDIX: ROMAN BRITAIN

(Chapter V. Vol. I. pp. 170-194)

MOMMSEN'S sketch of Roman Britain has often been called deficient and inaccurate. As a general judgment, this is wholly unjust. The sketch has real and distinct merits. When first issued in 1885, it marked a great advance towards a right conception of its subject. It differed conspicuously, and all for the better, from the other sketches of Roman Britain which were then current and accepted, Hübner's papers since collected in his *Römische Herrschaft in Westeuropa*, Wright's *Celt, Roman, and Saxon*, Scarth's *Roman Britain*. To-day it is perhaps the best existing account of the conquest and military administration of the province, and it contains much which no one—least of all, our English archaeologists—can afford to neglect. On the other hand, it is undeniably not one of the best sections in the volume to which it belongs, and it treats some parts of its theme, notably the civil life and civilisation, very shortly. One may be pardoned for taking the occasion of its republication in English dress, to make a few additions and corrections which may interest English readers, while they fill some gaps and take note of some recent discoveries.

The accounts of the Claudian invasion and the early years of the conquest (pp. 172-9) are, in their broad outlines, beyond reasonable doubt. But details can perhaps be added or altered. The army which started in A.D. 43 in three corps (τριχῇ νεμηθέντες, Dio, 60, 20) may well have landed in the three harbours afterwards used by the Romans in Kent, Lymne, Dover, and Richborough—the last named being the principal port for passengers to and from Britain throughout the Roman period. The difficult river crossed shortly afterwards by Plautius may be the Medway near Rochester, where in after years the Roman road from the Kentish ports to London had its bridge. The subsequent course of the invading armies is not easy to trace. But it would seem that, when they had won London and Colchester, they advanced from this base-line in three separate corps to the conquest of the South and Midlands. The left wing, the Second Legion Augusta under Vespasian, overran the south as far (probably) as South Wales and Exeter (Suet. *Vesp.* 4; Tac. *Agric.* 13; *Hist.* iii. 44; tile of Legio ii. Aug. at Seaton, *Archæological Journal*, xlix. 180). The centre, the Fourteenth and Twentieth Legions, crossed the Midlands to Wroxeter and Chester (tile of Legio xx. at Whittlebury, *Vict. Hist. of Northants,* i. 215; inscriptions at Wroxeter and Chester). The right wing, the Ninth, moved up the east side of Britain to Lincoln (tile of Legio ix. at Hilly Wood, on the road towards Lincoln, *Vict. Hist. of Northants*, i. 214; inscriptions at Lincoln). These three lines of advance led direct to the positions of the fortresses where we find the legions presently posted. They agree also with the three main groups of Roman roads which radiate from London : (1) the south-west route to Silchester, and thence by branches to Winchester, Exeter, Bath, South Wales; (2) the Midland "Watling Street," by St. Albans to Wroxeter and Chester; (3) the eastern route to Colchester, Cambridge, and Castor near Peterborough, to Lincoln.[1]

In any case there can be little doubt that by A.D. 47 or 48— within four or five years of the first landing — the Roman troops had reached the basins of the Humber and the Severn, as Mommsen observes (p. 176). Thus much is plain from the fact that Ostorius, who came out in 47, had at once to deal with the Iceni of Norfolk, the Decangi of Flintshire, the Brigantes of Yorkshire, the Silures of Monmouthshire (Tac. *Ann.* xii. 31). But the difficult corruption of Tacitus (*ibid.*), *cuncta castris antonam et Sabrinam fluvios cohibere parat*, is probably to be emended (with Dr. H. Bradley, *Academy*, April and May 1883) *cuncta cis Trisantonam, i.e.* the Roman frontier at the moment was, roughly, Severn and Trent. This is preferable both to Mommsen's suggestion (given above, p. 176 note) and to mine (*Journ. Phil.* xvii. 268). The older and more violent remedy, *Avonam inter et Sabrinam*, though revived in the text of the second edition of Furneaux's *Tacitus* (1907), is pretty certainly wrong; indeed, it is not Latin.

It would seem then that, by 47 or 48, practically the whole lowlands were in the hands of the Romans. Whether Chester had already been occupied or (as seems likelier) was first garrisoned when Ostorius attacked the Decangi, must remain uncertain; it must in any case have been occupied soon (*Eph. Epigr.* vii. 903; Domaszewski, *Rhein. Mus.* xlviii. 344). Caerleon, connected by Mommsen with Tac. *Ann.* xii. 32,

---

[1] The arguments of Mr. B. W. Henderson (*English Hist. Review*, 1903, 1-23) for a different advance seem to me to be based on a misconception of some of the evidence. Thus, there is no tile of Leg. ix. at Leicester, nor any trace yet noted of Leg. ii. Aug. at Cirencester or Gloucester.

presents more difficulty, since it has yielded hardly any datable
remains earlier than about A.D. 70-80; however, no other site can
be suggested on our present evidence for the *hiberna* of the
Second Legion Augusta before 70.   Wroxeter rests its claim to
a fortress on two early inscriptions of Legio xiv. (*Vict. Hist.
Shropshire*, i. 243, 244), and this may be adequate, though
Domaszewski doubts it.   The course of Watling Street seems to
show that Wroxeter was occupied before the troops pushed on
to Chester.

Mommsen's account of the Boadicean revolt (pp. 179-181) is
famous for his denunciation of Tacitus as "the most unmilitary of
all authors."   It must be conceded that Tacitus is unmilitary—
not so much because he is condensed or discontinuous or
ignorant of geography (E. G. Hardy, *Journ. Phil.* xxxi. 123), as
because he has a literary horror of all technical detail, and
desires to give the general effect of each situation without
distracting the reader by vexatious precision and difficult *minutiae*.
But in this case his narrative (*Ann.* xii. 32 foll.) is better than
Mommsen (or indeed Domaszewski) allows.   Paullinus doubtless
marched to London, as Horsley long ago observed, because it lay
on the road (Watling Street) from Chester to Colchester; that he
hurried on in front of his main forces is implied in the *iam* at the
beginning of c. 34.

The conquest of Wales (p. 182) was completed, as Mommsen
says, in the decade A.D. 70-80.   But his statements require some
re-wording.   Roman remains are not "completely absent" in the
interior; the continuance of native resistance to Rome is very
doubtful; the existence of Celtic speech and nationality in Wales
to-day is—in large part, at least—due to a Celtic revival in the
late fourth or the fifth century, and to immigration of new Celtic
elements at that time, and cannot therefore be cited as here.
So far as present evidence goes, the district as a whole seems
during the first, second, and third centuries to have closely
resembled the similar mountainous districts of northern England,
save only that the Welsh tribes never revolted after A.D. 80,
while the Brigantes gave trouble throughout the second century.
The same system of small auxiliary *castella* was established in
Wales as in northern England.   These forts are at present almost
wholly unexplored.   But we can detect unquestionable examples
at Caerhun (Canovium, *Eph.* vii. 1099) and Carnarvon, in the
north; at Tommen-y-mur, Llanio-i-sa, and Caio, in the west; at
Caergai (*Eph.* vii. 863), Castle Collen near Llandrindod (*ibid.*
862), Caersws in the upper valley of the Severn, and the Gaer
near Brecon, in the interior; at Gelligaer (*Trans. Cardiff Nat.
Soc.* xxxv. 1903), Merthyr Tydfil, Cardiff, Abergavenny, Usk, in
the south, besides others not yet satisfactorily identified as military

sites. Several of these have yielded remains suggestive of the first century, and indeed of the Flavian period. The only one as yet properly excavated, Gelligaer, seems to have been occupied under the Flavians, and dismantled after no very long occupation, probably early in the second century. Such dismantlement suggests that the land was then growing less unquiet. But Wales never reached any higher degree of Roman civilisation than the north of England. Towns and country houses were always rare, and its population lived mostly, it would seem, in primitive villages (*Arch. Cambrensis*, 1907). Later on, in the fourth century, Celts began to come in from Ireland, much as other barbarians entered other parts of the Empire, but their dates and numbers are very little known; see my *Romanisation of Roman Britain*, pp. 27 foll. and reff. there given.

The invasion of Caledonia (p. 183) by Agricola has been illustrated by recent discoveries. As I have pointed out elsewhere, we have traces of Agricola's line of forts (Tac. *Agr.* 23) at Camelon (*Proc. Soc. Antiq. Scotland*, xxxv. fig. 10) and Bar Hill (G. Macdonald, *Roman Forts on the Bar Hill*, Glasgow, 1906). Farther north, near the junction of the Tay and Isla, at Inchtuthill, in the policies of Delvine, a large encampment of Roman type has yielded a few objects datable to the Agricolan age (*Proc. Soc. Antiq. Scot.* xxxvi. pp. 237, 242), and may give a clue to the site of Mons Graupius. Farther south, the large fort lately excavated by Mr. James Curle, at Newstead, near Melrose (*C. I. L.* vii. 1080, 1081; *Scottish Hist. Review*, 1908), was certainly occupied in the Agricolan age. To this date, too, may perhaps be assigned the siege works round the native fortress on Birrenswark in Dumfriesshire, with their leaden sling-bullets (*Proc. Soc. Antiq. Scot.* xxxiii. 198 foll.). Evidence that the Legio ii. Adiutrix was then posted at Chester, probably forming a double-legion fortress with Legio xx., was obtained in the excavations of 1890 (*Catal. of the Grosvenor Museum, Chester* (1900), pp. 7 foll. and Nos. 23-35). An inscription from Camelon with the letters MILITES L·II·Λ·DIE may have been intended to refer to this legion, but is a forgery (*Class. Review*, xix. 57). No trace of Agricolan or of Flavian remains has yet been found on the line of Hadrian's Wall, except at two points, which, strictly speaking, are near but not on the wall, Carlisle (Luguvallium), and Corbridge (Corstopitum), where the two great north roads pass on towards Caledonia. For the influence of continental frontier troubles on the British operations of Agricola see also Ritterling, *Jahreshefte des österr. arch. Instituts*, vii. 26.

The years between the recall of Agricola and the building of Hadrian's Wall (roughly A.D. 85-120) are a historical blank. Even the position of the northern frontier during these years is unknown. The Romans seem to have soon withdrawn from the line of the Clyde and Forth (Macdonald, *Bar Hill*, pp. 14, 15). Whether they also withdrew south of Cheviot is not quite clear, in the present state of the Newstead excavations.

Hadrian's Wall from Tyne to Solway (p. 186) has assumed a very different historical appearance since Mommsen wrote his paragraphs on it in 1885. Then, the theory of Hodgson and Bruce held the field—that the stone wall which is still visible, and the double rampart and ditch to the south of it (called by English antiquaries the "Vallum"), were both Hadrian's work, the wall for defence against Caledonia and the "Vallum" for defence against stray foes from the south. This view was accepted by Mommsen. But later excavation and observation have shown that the "Vallum" cannot be regarded as a military work—though it is certainly Roman and connected with the wall. Excavations have also shown that the wall itself falls into two periods. At Birdoswald (Amboglanna) there was first a wall of turf (*murus caespiticius*); later, almost but not quite on the same line, came the wall of stone and the fort of Amboglanna in its present form. Similarly at Chesters (Cilurnum) two building periods are discernible; the character of the first is obscure, but the stone wall and the fort of Cilurnum belong unquestionably to the second (*Cumberland Arch. Soc.* xiv. 187, 415, xv. 180, 347, xvi. 84; *Arch. Aeliana*, xxiii. 9). As our ancient authorities persistently mention two wall-builders, Hadrian and Severus, and as the earlier wall of turf can be assigned to no one but Hadrian, it would seem that we may assume a first fortification of the Tyne and Solway line in turf about A.D. 120, and a rebuilding in stone, on almost exactly the same *tracé*, about A.D. 208 by Severus. The "Vallum" seems to have been built in relation to one or the other—more probably the earlier—of these stone walls, and may represent a civil frontier contemporaneous with it (Mommsen, *Gesammelte Schriften*, v. 461; Pelham, *Trans. Cumberland Arch. Soc.* xiv. 175). The attempt of Dr. E. Krueger (*Bonner Jahrbücher*, cx. 1-38) to show that the "Vallum" is an earlier independent work, built by Hadrian, while the turf and stone walls are post-Hadrianic, seems to me both unproven and contradicted by recent excavations.

Mommsen's account of the Wall of Pius between Forth and Clyde and of the Roman occupation of Scotland also needs modification. Statistics of coins found in Scotland (printed in *Antonine Wall Report*, 1899, pp. 158 foll., confirmed by all later finds) show that the Romans had retired south of Cheviot by about A.D. 180, and never reoccupied the positions thus lost. The mass of inscriptions, to which Mommsen alludes, also contains nothing later than the reign of Marcus. It becomes, therefore, impossible to connect the Wall of Pius with the literary evidence relating to wall-building by Severus. That evidence must belong to the Tyne and Solway. The length which it assigns to the wall, cxxxii. miles, suits the southern line best. The numeral in any case needs emendation, but it is as easy to read lxxxii. as xxxii., and 82 Roman miles fit closer to the length of the southern line (73½ English miles) than do 32 Roman miles to the 36½ English miles of the northern wall. Our knowledge of the northern wall itself and of forts either north of it, like Ardoch, or south, like Lyne and Newstead, has been much widened by excavation, but the gain has been rather to the archaeologist than to the pure historian.

In the later history of north Britain the chief recent addition has been evidence of a serious rising about A.D. 158, which perhaps covered all the land of the Brigantes from Derbyshire to Dumfriesshire. Inscriptions found at Birrens, at Netherby between Birrens and Carlisle, at Newcastle-on-Tyne, and at Brough in north Derbyshire, mention a governor Iulius Verus as then specially active, and special reinforcements as then arriving from Germany (*Proc. Soc. Antiq. Scot.* xxxviii. 454). It is natural to connect these with the words of Pausanias (cited on p. 188, note 2), and the connection had the approval of Mommsen. For the division of the province into two by Severus see Domaszewski, *Rangordnung*, p. 173. The boundary between the two provinces is unknown ; perhaps a line from the Humber to the Mersey is not altogether improbable. Nor is there evidence to show how long the division lasted.

Of the civil life and Romanisation of Britain (pp. 191-4) I have written somewhat fully in a paper on *The Romanisation of Roman Britain*. Here I may indicate some points. Mommsen's view that the cantonal system adopted in Gaul was dropped in Britain is opposed by an inscription found at Caerwent in 1903, which records the erection of a monument by the canton of the Silures after a decree of the local senate—*ex decreto ordinis respublica civitatis Silurum* (*Athenaeum*, Sept. 26, 1903 ; *Archaeologia*, lix. 290) ; other inscriptions, if less decisive, suggest that the case of the Silures was not unique in the province. Indeed, a list of the cantonal capitals, and therefore of the cantons, seems to survive mutilated in the *Ravennas* (ed. Parthey and Pinder, pp. 425 foll.). There we meet, besides three municipalities carefully so labelled, nine or ten towns with tribal affixes—Isca Dumnoniorum, Exeter ; Venta Belgarum, Winchester ; Venta Silurum, Caerwent ; Corinium Dobunorum, Cirencester ; Calleva Atrebatum, Silchester ; Durovernum Cantiacorum, Canterbury ; Viroconium Cornoviorum, Wroxeter ; Ratae Coritanorum, Leicester ; Venta Icenorum, Caistor-by-Norwich—and perhaps Noviomagus Regentium, Chichester. Add to these Isurium Brigantum, known otherwise by this title, and Dorchester in Dorset, and there emerges a fairly complete list of just those towns which are declared by their remains to have been the chief "country towns" of Roman Britain. The reasons why so little is heard of the cantons are, I think, plain. They were smaller, poorer, and less important than those of Gaul—as, indeed, a comparison of the town-remains shows; there was, further, no British literature to mention them; and, lastly, they quickly fell before the barbarians in the fifth century.

The town-life of Roman Britain (p. 192) was somewhat more extensive than Mommsen allows. There were four *coloniae*— Colchester or *Camulodunum*, founded about A.D. 48 (Tac. *Ann.* xii. 32); Lincoln, *Lindum*, established after the transference of the Ninth Legion to York, probably in the late first century; Gloucester or *Glevum*, founded A.D. 96-98 (*C. I. L.* vi. 3346); York or *Eburacum*, planted at an unknown date, on the opposite bank of the Ouse to the legionary fortress; and one *municipium*, Verulamium, outside St. Albans, founded before A.D. 60. There were also about a dozen "country towns," already enumerated in the last paragraph. These were for the most part not large villages, but actual towns, furnished with temples, *fora*, houses, and street plans of Roman fashion, and inhabited, so far as our scanty evidence goes, by populations of which both upper and lower classes spoke and wrote Latin. At Bath, *Aquae Sulis*, were well-built baths, and a stately temple of the goddess of the waters. At London, *Londinium* (later *Augusta*), was a prosperous and wealthy trading-centre. But London was the only town of real size or splendour. The rest, like the cantons mentioned above, were small and unimportant as compared with similar towns elsewhere, and though it is not strictly true that Gloucester and Verulam have produced no inscriptions (p. 193; *Eph. Epigr.* iv. p. 195), the epigraphic yield has been scanty in every town except perhaps York.

The roads of the province (p. 192) are numerous, though fewer than our English antiquaries sometimes suppose. Those in the south, as Mommsen rightly saw, radiate from London: see p. 192 above. The northern military district is traversed by three main routes. One runs up the west coast to the Solway and Carlisle. A second runs through the east of the island, from York to Corbridge and to various points on the eastern part of Hadrian's Wall. The third, diverging from the second, crossed the Yorkshire and Westmorland hills and thus reached Carlisle. From Corbridge and Carlisle roads ran on northwards, and the eastern, if not the western, of these gave access to the Wall of Pius. The Roman roads of Wales are still imperfectly known, but there was a road from Chester to Carnarvon, another from Caerleon past Neath to Carmarthen, and a third joined the western parts of these two, while others connected the forts in the interior.

More doubt surrounds the Romanisation of the province. Vinogradoff (*Growth of the Manor*, p. 83) thinks that the Roman civilisation spread like a river with many channels which traverse a wide area, but only affect the immediate neighbourhood of their banks. I agree rather with Mommsen's conclusion (pp. 193, 194)—though the real difference between the two writers is not so very great. The towns, both municipalities and "country towns," seem to have been thoroughly Romanised. The numerous farms and country-houses (often styled "villas") are also in nearly every respect Roman, and the very scanty evidence which we possess as to the language used in them favours the idea that it was Latin. Even the villages, such as Pitt-Rivers excavated (*Excavations in Cranborne Chase*, etc., 1887-98), show little survival of native culture. It is to be noted, too, that Celtic inscriptions of Roman date, such as occur occasionally in Gaul (Rhys, *Proc. British Acad.* ii. 275 foll.), are wholly wanting in Britain. Probably, therefore, Roman civilisation came to predominate throughout the lowlands, though not in its more elaborate and splendid forms. There were, however, thinly populated areas where we can trace hardly any population of any sort, Romanised or other, as, for example, the Weald of Kent and Sussex, and a large part of the Midlands (*Vict. Hist. of Warwickshire*, i. 228), while the Cornish, Welsh, and northern hills seem never to have admitted very much Romanisation outside the forts which garrisoned parts of them. The analogies of other western provinces, of Gaul (above, vol. i. p. 101) and Africa (ii. 328), suggest that Celtic speech may have lingered on in such districts for centuries, though not as an element hostile to the Roman; it is also quite probable that Celtic private law and custom survived beside the Roman (L. Mitteis, *Reichsrecht und Volksrecht*, p. 8). But we have no distinct evidence of either fact.

The spellings Ordovici (p. 182 and map) and Cartimandus (pp. 182, 183) are Mommsen's own choice.

INDEX

ABDAGAESES, ii. 44.

Abgarus, of Edessa, ii. 46 (under Claudius), 68 (under Trajan), 78 (under Severus).

Abrinca, rivulet, i. 119 *n.*

Achaeans, diet, i. 264.

Achaemenids, dynasty, ii. 2, 3, 10; "seven houses," 6.

Achaia, province, i. 255 f. *n.*; under the emperors, 260.

Acraephia, inscription, i. 265 *n.*, 273 *n.*

Actiads, i. 296 *n.*

Actian games, i. 296 *n.*

Adane, ii. 288 f. ; destroyed, 293 f. *n.*

Adiabene, ii. 68, 78 *n.*, 88.

Adiabenicus, ii. 78 *n.*

Adminius, i. 174.

Adrianopolis, i. 307.

Adulis, ii. 280, 281, 282, 296.

Aedemon, ii. 313.

Aegium, diet of, ii. 264 *n.*

Aeizanas, ii. 284 *n.*

Aelana, ii. 288.

Aemilianus, Marcus Aemilius, i. 241.

Aemilianus, Egyptian tyrant, ii. 251.

Aethiopia and Aethiopians, ii. 275-278 ; traffic, 278.

Afer, ii. 304 *n.*

Africa, North, ii. 303 ; Berber stock, 303-305 ; Phoenician immigration, 306 ; government of republic, 306 f.; Caesar's policy, 307 f. ; extent of Roman rule, 308 f.; province of, 309 ; two Mauretanian kingdoms, 310 f. ; physical conformation, 314 ; Africano-Numidian territory, 316 f.; war against Tacfarinas and later conflicts, 317-320 ; Roman civilisation in Mauretania, 320 f.; continuance of Berber language, 325 f.; of Phoenician, 326 f.; coinage, 327 *n.*; Latin language, 329 ; Phoenician urban organisation, 329 ; transformed into Italian, 331 ;

number of towns, 331 *n.*; Italian colonists, 332 ; large landed estates, 333 f.; husbandry, 336 ; corn supplied to Rome, 337 ; oil and wine, 337 f.; manufactures and commerce, 338 f.; prosperity, 339 ; roads, 339 f. ; introduction of camels, 340 ; character and culture of people, 340 f. ; scholasticism, 342 ; Christian literature, 343-345 ; Latin Scriptures, 343 f. *n.*

Agonistic institutes, i. 289 *n.*

Agonothesia, i. 347 *n.*, 348 *n.*

Agricola, Gnaeus Julius, i. 182-184, 194.

Agrippa ; *see* Herod Agrippa.

Agrippa, M. Vipsanius, in command on the Danube, i. 22 ; transference of Ubii, 25 ; combats in Gaul, 80.

Agrippa, Marcus Fonteius, i. 218.

Agrippina (Cologne), i. 119.

Ahenobarbus, Lucius Domitius, expedition to Elbe, i. 31 ; dyke between Ems and Lower Rhine, 34.

Ahuramazda, ii. 10 f., 84.

Alamanni, war with, i. 161 f., 163 ; raids, 166 f.

Alani, ii. 62 *n.*, 64, 73, 74 *n.*

Albani, ii. 72 f.

Alexander the Great, basing his empire on towns, not on tribes, ii. 120.

Alexander II. of Egypt, testament, ii. 232.

Alexander, son of Cleopatra, ii. 24, 25, 26 ; installed king of Armenia, 33.

Alexander Severus, purchases peace in Germany, i. 162 ; murder, 162 ; ii. 91 ; character, 89 f.; war with Ardashir, 90 *n.*; nicknamed "chief Rabbi," 263.

Alexander of Abonoteichos, i. 350

Alexander, Tiberius Julius, ii. 168, 204, 242 *n.*, 246 *n.*

Alexandria, in Egypt, under the Pal-

THE END

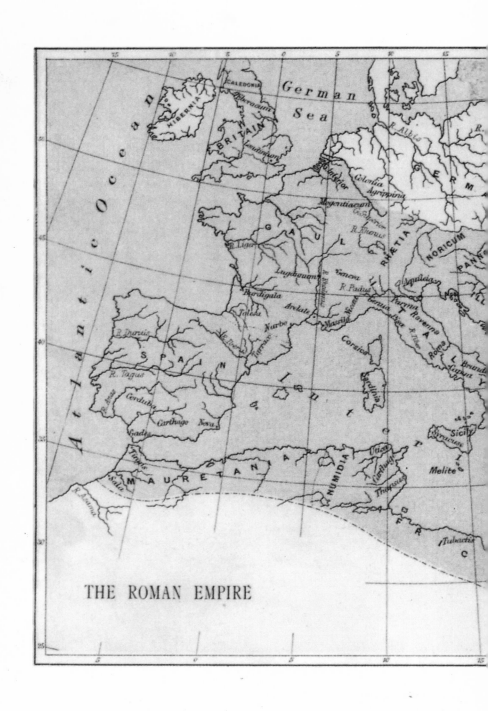

THE ROMAN EMPIRE